Advances in Artificial and Human Intelligence in the Modern Era

S. Suman Rajest
Dhaanish Ahmed College of Engineering, India

Bhopendra Singh
Amity University, Dubai, UAE

Ahmed J. Obaid
University of Kufa, Iraq

R. Regin
SRM Institute of Science and Technology, Ramapuram, India

Karthikeyan Chinnusamy
Veritas, USA

A volume in the Advances in Computational
Intelligence and Robotics (ACIR) Book Series

Published in the United States of America by
    IGI Global
    Engineering Science Reference (an imprint of IGI Global)
    701 E. Chocolate Avenue
    Hershey PA, USA 17033
    Tel: 717-533-8845
    Fax: 717-533-8661
    E-mail: cust@igi-global.com
    Web site: http://www.igi-global.com

                        Library of Congress Cataloging-in-Publication Data

Names: Rajest, S. Suman, 1988- editor. | Singh, Bhopendra, 1974- editor. |
    Obaid, Ahmed J. (Ahmed Jabbar), editor. | R, Regin, 1985- editor. |
    Chinnusamy, Karthikeyan, 1973- editor.
Title: Advances in artificial and human intelligence in the modern era /
    edited by S. Suman Rajest, Bhopendra Singh, Ahmed J. Obaid, R. Regin,
    Karthikeyan Chinnusamy.
Description: Hershey, PA : Engineering Science Reference, [2023] | Includes
    bibliographical references and index. | Summary: "Offers a
    groundbreaking solution to address the existing challenges in the
    intersection of AI and human performance optimization"-- Provided by
    publisher.
Identifiers: LCCN 2023038692 (print) | LCCN 2023038693 (ebook) | ISBN
    9798369313015 (hardcover) | ISBN 9798369313022 (ebook)
Subjects: LCSH: Intellect. | Knowledge, Theory of. | Artificial
    intelligence.
Classification: LCC BF431 .A45 2023 (print) | LCC BF431 (ebook) | DDC
    153.9--dc23/eng/20230908
LC record available at https://lccn.loc.gov/2023038692
LC ebook record available at https://lccn.loc.gov/2023038693

This book is published in the IGI Global book series Advances in Computational Intelligence and Robotics (ACIR) (ISSN:
2327-0411; eISSN: 2327-042X)

British Cataloguing in Publication Data
A Cataloguing in Publication record for this book is available from the British Library.

All work contributed to this book is new, previously-unpublished material. The views expressed in this book are those of the
authors, but not necessarily of the publisher.

For electronic access to this publication, please contact: eresources@igi-global.com.

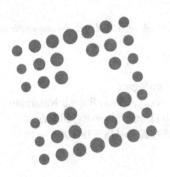

Advances in Computational Intelligence and Robotics (ACIR) Book Series

Ivan Giannoccaro
University of Salento, Italy

ISSN:2327-0411
EISSN:2327-042X

MISSION

While intelligence is traditionally a term applied to humans and human cognition, technology has progressed in such a way to allow for the development of intelligent systems able to simulate many human traits. With this new era of simulated and artificial intelligence, much research is needed in order to continue to advance the field and also to evaluate the ethical and societal concerns of the existence of artificial life and machine learning.

The **Advances in Computational Intelligence and Robotics (ACIR) Book Series** encourages scholarly discourse on all topics pertaining to evolutionary computing, artificial life, computational intelligence, machine learning, and robotics. ACIR presents the latest research being conducted on diverse topics in intelligence technologies with the goal of advancing knowledge and applications in this rapidly evolving field.

COVERAGE

- Computer Vision
- Artificial Intelligence
- Neural Networks
- Pattern Recognition
- Algorithmic Learning
- Heuristics
- Automated Reasoning
- Cognitive Informatics
- Natural Language Processing
- Cyborgs

IGI Global is currently accepting manuscripts for publication within this series. To submit a proposal for a volume in this series, please contact our Acquisition Editors at Acquisitions@igi-global.com or visit: http://www.igi-global.com/publish/.

Titles in this Series

For a list of additional titles in this series, please visit: http://www.igi-global.com/book-series/advances-computational-intelligence-robotics/73674

Handbook of Research on Advancements in AI and IoT Convergence Technologies
Jingyuan Zhao (University of Toronto, Canada) V. Vinoth Kumar (Jain University, India) Rajesh Natarajan (University of Applied Science and Technology, Shinas, Oman) and T.R. Mahesh (Jain University, India)
Engineering Science Reference • © 2023 • 372pp • H/C (ISBN: 9781668469712) • US $380.00

Scalable and Distributed Machine Learning and Deep Learning Patterns
J. Joshua Thomas (UOW Malaysia KDU Penang University College, Malaysia) S. Harini (Vellore Institute of Technology, India) and V. Pattabiraman (Vellore Institute of Technology, India)
Engineering Science Reference • © 2023 • 286pp • H/C (ISBN: 9781668498040) • US $270.00

Handbook of Research on Thrust Technologies' Effect on Image Processing
Binay Kumar Pandey (Department of Information Technology, College of Technology, Govind Ballabh Pant University of Agriculture and Technology, India) Digvijay Pandey (Department of Technical Education, Government of Uttar Pradesh, India) Rohit Anand (G.B. Pant DSEU Okhla-1 Campus, India & Government of NCT of Delhi, New Delhi, India) Deepak S. Mane (Performance Engineering Lab, Tata Research, Development, and Design Center, Australia) and Vinay Kumar Nassa (Rajarambapu Institute of Technology, India)
Engineering Science Reference • © 2023 • 542pp • H/C (ISBN: 9781668486184) • US $350.00

Multi-Disciplinary Applications of Fog Computing Responsiveness in Real-Time
Debi Prasanna Acharjya (Vellore Institute of Technology, India) and Kauser Ahmed P. (Vellore Institute of Technology, India)
Engineering Science Reference • © 2023 • 280pp • H/C (ISBN: 9781668444665) • US $270.00

Global Perspectives on Robotics and Autonomous Systems Development and Applications
Maki K. Habib (The American University in Cairo, Egypt)
Engineering Science Reference • © 2023 • 405pp • H/C (ISBN: 9781668477915) • US $360.00

Stochastic Processes and Their Applications in Artificial Intelligence
Christo Ananth (Samarkand State University, Uzbekistan) N. Anbazhagan (Alagappa University, India) and Mark Goh (National University of Singapore, Singapore)
Engineering Science Reference • © 2023 • 220pp • H/C (ISBN: 9781668476796) • US $270.00

701 East Chocolate Avenue, Hershey, PA 17033, USA
Tel: 717-533-8845 x100 • Fax: 717-533-8661
E-Mail: cust@igi-global.com • www.igi-global.com

Table of Contents

Detailed Table of Contents

AI has the potential to revolutionize education by enhancing student performance and delivering tailored learning experiences. This chapter addresses the present state of artificial intelligence (AI) in computer science (CS) education, as well as how it is used to adaptive learning, intelligent learning systems, and automated grading. The authors examine recent studies on the use of AI in CS teaching, emphasizing the relative benefits of various approaches. One of the technology's most important benefits is its ability to customize courses to the interests and learning preferences of particular students in CS education. Using data analytics, adaptive learning systems evaluate student performance and offer personalized feedback and improvement recommendations. Intelligent tutoring systems offer adaptable and interactive learning environments by using machine learning (ML) and natural language processing (NLP).

Artificial intelligence (AI) is a rapidly evolving field that has seen tremendous growth in recent years. In this chapter, the authors provide an overview of current trends in AI and their applications in computer science. They also discuss the future directions of AI research and their potential impact on the field of computer science. They start by introducing the basic concepts of AI and its various subfields. Then, they present an overview of current trends in AI research, including machine learning, natural language processing, computer vision, and robotics. The authors discuss how these trends are applied in computer science, such as autonomous vehicles, fraud detection, and personalized medicine. Finally, they discuss the future directions of AI research, including the development of more explainable AI systems, the integration of AI with other emerging technologies, and the ethical considerations of AI.

Chapter 3

In this chapter, the authors focus on optimising video surveillance by considering five factors while processing the surveillance. The five factors are bandwidth availability, connection availability, storage availability, CPU availability, and memory availability. Since the research work mainly focused on fog computing environment, two major factors are bandwidth and connection availability while sending a video content to the authorized person. The size of video content will be large and slow while transferring the data from one location to another location through wireless network. This problem will be optimized using particle swarm optimization algorithm (PSO). This proposed PSO algorithm will optimize the video content and make it effective and efficient to transfer from one location to another location, and then the object detection (OD) is conducted using suitable hardware arrangements involving a microcontroller unit and GSM communication module for altering the user with objects in forest area.

Chapter 4

This chapter compares the toughness of k-means, DBSCAN, and adaptive clustering algorithms for grouping data points into distinct clusters. The k-means algorithm is a widely used method that is easy to implement and efficient. The DBSCAN algorithm is a density-based method that is well-suited for datasets with clusters of varying densities, but it can be sensitive to the choice of parameters. In order to determine the ideal number of clusters within a dataset, adaptive clustering algorithms dynamically alter the number of clusters during the clustering process. The production of these algorithms is evaluated on a variety of datasets, and the results are compared in terms of accuracy and efficiency. According to the chapter's conclusion, each method has advantages and disadvantages of its own, and the ideal approach to apply will vary depending on the particular dataset and the objectives of the study.

Chapter 5

In a fighter aircraft, the pilot's safety is of utmost importance, and the pressure sensing in the pilot's mask is essential for ensuring the pilot's safety. This innovative solution ensures the swift and accurate measurement of pressure, minimizing the risk of potential hazards and enhancing military aviation safety. Additionally, it provides a robust and reliable solution that can withstand the harsh and challenging conditions often encountered in the field. This chapter explores the advanced capabilities and benefits of utilizing the National Instrument USB-6363, programmed with LabVIEW, in military aviation, highlighting its potential for revolutionizing pressure measurement processes in this critical field. It describes a research study on developing a pressure-sensing system for pilot masks using NI USB 6363 and LabVIEW.

The rapid evolution of the Internet and communication technologies has fueled the proliferation of wireless sensor network (WSN) technology, which is increasingly important in today's interconnected world. For a broad variety of industries and applications, an enormous number of sensing devices continuously create and/or gather copious amounts of sensory data. However, it has been shown that WSN is susceptible to security flaws. These networks' abrasive and unmanaged deployment, along with their limited resources and the amount of data produced, raise serious security issues. The development of trustworthy solutions that include quick and continuous processes for live data stream analysis allowing the identification of flooding assaults is crucial since WSN applications are of the utmost importance. To put it in plain words: The assault is carried out by repeatedly sending pointless requests to the target computer in an effort to overwhelm it, cause the systems to fail, and prevent people from accessing the network or machine.

Chapter 7

Businesses that provide care remotely are far from the scope of virtual care. It offers a delivery channel for particular patient populations with applications that do not need in-person examinations or presence, even though it cannot be assumed to be the solution to all health-related questions. According to the scoping reviews, virtual care includes a significant information generation method called disease diagnosis, considered as the very first step towards treating the illness. Along with video conferencing technologies for consulting the doctors to achieve care supervision. Application of rehabilitation, remote consultation, and emergency services are efficient ways to use in attention to achieve well-being. Machine learning is one such way to achieve disease diagnosis based on information provided by the user with a high accuracy using various approaches. In this chapter, a novel approach of random forest approach with modifications is used.

Detecting disease on crops is an essential and time-consuming operation in agricultural techniques. It takes a significant amount of time and specialized effort. This research provides a clever and effective agricultural disease detection system based on information theory. In the present chapter, first information measures, 'useful' information measures, and distance measures are defined and explained. The authors find out the distance measures between leaves of apple scab (AS) and apple black rot (ABR). Six leaves of AS and ABR are taken into consideration. After measuring the distance, the impact of disease in the leaves of AS and ABR has been noticed. It is shown that this measure can be embedded in most image classification techniques and is subject to reference transformation. Weak and strong information is also obtained. Finally, minimum and maximum distances are evaluated, and our findings indicate that the likelihood of illnesses in plant leaves is low when the information measure of leaves is low.

Chapter 9

Automated facial emotion recognition (AFER) is a technique with rising usage across a range of practical real-world applications ranging from security to advertising. AFER can be used to assess the emotional state of patients with mental health conditions, such as depression or anxiety to guide treatment decisions. Companies can use facial emotion recognition to gauge consumer reactions to different products or advertisements, providing valuable insights for product development and marketing strategies. The following paper examines the concept of facial emotion recognition using AI-based models and compares the results of two different techniques. The first technique uses face emotion detection using haar cascade classifier along with convolutional neural networks (CNN), and the second technique uses face emotion detection using facial landmarks along with CNN.

Chapter 10

Software defect prediction gives development teams observable results while influencing business outcomes and development flaws. Developers can uncover flaws and plan test activities by anticipating problematic code sections. Early identification depends on the percentage of classifications that make the right prediction. Additionally, software-defective data sets are supported and partially acknowledged because of their vast size. The confusion, precision, recall, identification accuracy, etc., are assessed and compared with the existing schemes in a systematic research analysis. Previous research has employed the weak simulation tool for software analysis, but this study proposes building three machine learning models using linear regression, KNN classifier, and random forest (RF). According to the analytical investigation, the suggested approach will offer more beneficial options for predicting device failures. Moreover, software-defected data sets are supported and at least partially recognized due to their enormous dimension.

Chapter 11

R. Regin, SRM Institute of Science and Technology, Ramapuram, India

Sriraam Ramesh, SRM Institute of Science and Technology, Ramapuram, India

Athiyan Ramesh Kumar, SRM Institute of Science and Technology, Ramapuram, India

Praghalad Krishna Gandhi, SRM Institute of Science and Technology, Ramapuram, India

Rubin Bose S, SRM Institute of Science and Technology, Ramapuram, India

Object detection is a vital component for autonomous driving, and autonomous cars rely on perception of their surroundings to ensure safe and robust driving performance. It shows how the perception system makes use of object identification algorithms to precisely identify nearby items like pedestrians, cars, traffic signs, and barriers. It goes on to say that detecting and localising these things in real-time depends greatly on deep learning-based object detectors. The most recent object detectors and unresolved issues with their integration into autonomous vehicles are also covered in the essay. It mentions that deep learning visual classification methods have achieved enormous accuracy in classifying visual scenes; it makes use of the convolutional neural network. However, it points out that the visual classifiers face difficulties examining the scenes in dark visible areas, especially during the nighttime, and in identifying the contexts of the scenes.

Chapter 12

Reddy C. Thilak, Jain University, India

S. Yogananthan, Jain University, India

Ravishankar S. Ulle, Jain University, India

Rupesh Kumar Sinha, CMS Business School, Jain University (Deemed), India

Embracing digital transformation has led to a major industrial change in the field of supply chain management qualitatively. This research deliberates emerging technologies identified as IoT (internet of things) which with other technologies like AI and ML, big data, and cloud computing an inevitable requirement for industry 4.0 implementation based on the complex needs following organizational structure. Study in the region of utilization of IoT in SCML is scarce in developing countries. However, the following inevitable SCM drivers such as real-time realization, barriers in enabling demand flow, value optimization from the business perspective, including elements of sustainability, the rising expectation of customers, and cutthroat competition amongst the manufacturers and service providers, have led to the utilization of IoT SCML industry. Especially when the constraints like time management and flow of materials are in high focus.

    Bhavika Malik, Karnavati University, India

    Akshath Lilesh Kamath, Karnavati University, India

    Anusha Krishnan Iyer, Karnavati University, India

    Anuj Dinesh Ghag, Karnavati University, India

    S. Sneha, Karnavati University, India

    Nandini Shah, Karnavati University, India

    Arshkirat Gill, Karnavati University, India

The relationship between fear of falling (FOF) and fall-related injuries in elderly is becoming quite prominent and its factors have not been explored. FOF is a person's anxiety towards mobilizing, with a perception that a fall will occur. Approximately 25% to 55% of community-living elderly are afraid of falling. The context of this problem is generalized in terms of FOF and has no sufficient data available for washroom spaces. Physical, medical, and psychological performances of 175 people in the age gap of 65 - 75 years were considered, over three cities i.e., Mumbai, Pune, and Kota. Past fall histories, medical histories, GAUG tests and responses to various washroom activities were recorded to establish the FES table. On the basis of these evaluations the factors causing FOF were determined, and a city comparison was made. This chapter provides an overview of FOF and a foundation on which to base decisions about the design of preventive interventions.

    A. Sathya, Bishop Heber College, Bharathidasan University, India

    M. S. Mythili, Bishop Heber College, Bharathidasan University, India

In the last few years, social networking sites have exploded at a rapid pace. Sentiment analysis (SA) is a way of mining data and reading text using natural language processing(NLP) In today's era, corona virus is a hot issue and pandemic all over the world. Millions of citizens use blogs or microblogging tools to communicate their viewpoints. Twitter is one of the handiest platforms and most popular social media for users to share their thoughts and ideas. Through blogging sites, the public can share their feelings and opinions such as "panic, anger, misery," and it can be divided the text into three categories: positive, negative, and neutral. Sentiment analysis is employed in a variety of industries, including healthcare, finance, sports, politics, hospitality, and tourism. According to a comparison of ten primary studies, Naive Bayes (NB) and support vector machine (SVM) are widely used algorithms for sentiment analysis in COVID-19.

    M. Vedhapriya, SRM Institute of Science and Technology, India

    J. Dhilipan, SRM Institute of Science and Technology, India

A submerged sensor network comprises of numeral different sensors and independent submerged vehicles sent to facilitate submerged, associate, and divide data between themselves to complete detecting and observing capacities. The submerged sensor networks have a wide scope of utilizations like contamination observing, catastrophic anticipations, facilitated route, under ocean investigations, an advanced military capacity, mine investigation, and so on. Submerged sensor networks present extraordinary tests to the current advances utilized in earthly sensor organization since submerged climate varies from earthbound radio climate regarding energy expenses and channel engendering peculiarities. Audile remote correspondence is utilized instead of wireless recurrence and optical sign in submerged sensor organization. A portion of the issues where submerged sensor network contrast from earthly are restricted for data transfer capacity, battery power, and disappointment of sensor hubs due to snarling and consumption.

Chapter 16

Sakhare Pritam M., Krishna Institute of Medical Sciences, India
S. A. Jadhav, Krishna Vishwa Vidyapeeth, India

Inflammation is caused by tissue damage, which is caused by pathogenic causes such tissue injury, infection, or cardiac infarction. Inflammation can be caused by either infectious or noninfectious triggers. Inflammation is characterized by redness, heat, swelling, pain, and loss of tissue function, which results from local vascular, immune, and inflammatory cell responses to any infection or injury. When a tissue is damaged, our bodies send out a series of chemical signals to trigger reactions that promote tissue repair. All of these cues stimulate circulating leukocytes to chemotactically migrate to the site of injury. As a result of being activated, leukocytes release cytokines, which set off other inflammatory processes in the body. Inflammatory disorders can be treated with a wide variety of medications nowadays. Nonsteroidal anti-inflammatory medicines (NSAIDs) and steroidal anti-inflammatory drugs (NSAIDs) are two examples that have proven effective. However, due to the potential for major side effects, their usage is limited.

Chapter 17

Bahulekar Ashitosh, Krishna Institute of Medical Sciences, India
R. P. Patange, Krishna Institute of Medical Sciences, India

The excitement of being a mother and holding your child in your arms is also accompanied by increased stress levels, worry, and unpredictability of giving birth. Every labour develops individually, posing a unique set of obstacles for the mother to overcome, the partner to be amazed at, and the obstetrician to reflect on. Predicting when the labour pains will start after induction, how they will be associated with gradual cervical dilatation, and how they will end in a vaginal delivery is one of the issues that the pregnant lady, her family, and the attending obstetrician most frequently think about. Transvaginal ultrasonography is increasingly employed in obstetrics, particularly in the second and third trimesters when it is used to estimate the length of the cervical canal. Transvaginal ultrasound measurements of cervical length and the condition of the internal os of the cervix during the second trimester help define an inadequate cervix and aid in the choice to do a cervical encirclage.

The key characteristics of acute inflammation are the exudation of fluid and plasma proteins and the emigration of leukocytes, mostly neutrophils, and it often begins within minutes or hours in response to infection and tissue damage and lasts for many hours. After the harmful agents have been removed, the acute inflammatory response fades, but if the response fails to eradicate the stimuli, the reaction might develop into a prolonged phase referred to as chronic inflammation. Since there is no safe, effective anti-inflammatory drug, scientists continue to study inflammation. Azithromycin, Clarithromycin, and Roxithromycin were tested for anti-inflammatory properties in Wistar rats with acute and sub-acute inflammation. Karad's largest animal house supplied 200–300g Wistar rats. Before the studies, the animals were used to the 24-hour cycle of light and dark for ten days. There was generally enough water and rat pellets. The IAC authorised this study (Institutional Animal Ethics Committee).

This study focuses on the positive and negative effects of digitalization on youth and how demonetization has led to digitalization over a period of five years. The study focuses on or revolves around three major objectives: they are to study the level of digitalization among youth in Indian economy, to study the impact of demonetization on youth in India, and to study the relationship between digitalization and demonetization. There is a large amount of secondary data that is available, and which is analyzed in this chapter and primary study has also been conducted with 150 respondents. The behavior, emotions, and motivation of youth in general and in relation to digital technologies, especially the meaning attached to mobile phones, the Internet, and computer-based games should also be given attention to reach this target group. The probable outcomes of the research of the study would reflect the level of digitalization in the economy and how demonetizations affected digitalization and what are the impact digitalization.

Iron is a micronutrient which is crucial for growth of fetus during pregnancy, and maternal iron is the major source of fetal iron. As the demand of iron increases during pregnancy, it becomes difficult to ensure sufficient maternal iron stores. Literature suggests that maternal iron deficiency anaemia might influence the iron reserves of newborns and also affect growth and development of fetus and newborns after birth. The aim of this chapter is to examine the association between maternal anaemia and newborn anthropometric parameters, namely haemoglobin and iron reserves after birth. This 18-month research was a cross-sectional analysis of data from a large hospital. Blood samples were taken from both the mother and the newborn to analyse haemoglobin and serum ferritin levels during the initial stage of labour. The mean age of enrolled pregnant women was 25.81 ± 4.67 years and most of them belonged to 21-30 years of age (72.32%).

The prevalence of "non-communicable diseases (NCDs)" including diabetes and heart disease is on the rise, both worldwide and in India. Because HIV affects people of both sexes everywhere, it poses a significant problem for all health care systems right now. Unplanned rapid urbanization, globalization of unhealthy lifestyles, and ageing population are the reasons for the development of these diseases. Physical inactivity and diets that are unhealthy result in increased blood glucose, raised blood pressure, obesity, and elevated blood lipids. All these metabolic risk factors can lead to cardiovascular disease, one of the leading non-communicable diseases (NCD) which cause premature deaths. Tobacco and alcohol use, lack of exercise, poor diet, and high blood pressure are some of the most important causes of NCDs. The high prevalence of NCDs in India is mostly attributable to the prevalence of overweight and obesity as well as excessive blood glucose and abnormal serum cholesterol. If such risks are adequately addressed, premature mortality in India from NCDs might be decreased.

Sepsis is described as a medical emergency situation due to the body's systemic immunological response to an infection that can lead to end-stage organ dysfunction and even death. Sepsis is one of the major causes of morbidity and mortality in critically morbid patients; however, there is a significant advancement in the understanding of the pathophysiology of this clinical syndrome, hemodynamic monitoring tools, and resuscitation measures. Due to the body's systemic immune reaction to an infection, which may result in end-stage organ malfunction and even death, sepsis is referred to as a medical emergency. It is one of the top ten leading causes of death globally. The epidemiological burden of sepsis is difficult to ascertain globally. Despite tremendous progress in the understanding of the pathogenesis of this clinical illness, hemodynamic monitoring systems, and resuscitation techniques, sepsis continues to be one of the leading causes of morbidity and mortality in critically ill patients.

Preface

Correction of mistakes is a requirement for any intelligent system. In order to effectively accept compensation identification, a kind of correction of mistakes system that compares human and machine calculations can be built. Theoretical mathematical concepts cannot develop actual or artificial intelligence. Mathematics is merely a tool because it can only produce functions, not talents. Actual powers can only be created by humans. As a result of the interaction between people, machines, environments, and systems, artificial intelligence is created. In reality, communication and interaction are the intelligent mechanisms of artificial intelligence. Good managers and fighter pilots frequently break the laws of engagement and communication. Although they follow regulations, they also have their own set of rules that cause them to stray from the participatory interface. Conversation is extensive penetration and integration, while the transmission is a cursory touch and mixing. Anyone interested in learning the fundamentals of artificial intelligence and how it is used in many fields should read this book. It offers a thorough analysis of the principles of AI, encompassing its history, several varieties of AI, and the most recent findings and developments.

In science and technology, artificial intelligence enables sophisticated machines and programming languages to do tasks that typically need human intelligence. As a result, one of AI's main draws is how it can carry out a wide range of human-like tasks, gain expertise through use, and adjust to new stimuli and settings. AI uses pertinent data reports, such as Big Data, to achieve higher performance for certain jobs. Recent years have seen a rapid advancement in AI, which has given many advantages across various sectors, including the crucial wellness sector. In many areas, AI has digitally replaced the traditional human intelligence system with an automated one. In certain fields, humans are now only necessary for handling intelligence, equipment, and other more basic tasks, leaving elaborate processes to be treated by or contingent upon AI factors. The book examines the different applications and advances in AI and human intelligence, including cognitive modeling, machine learning, and neural networks, and how these tools might advance our understanding of the human mind.

The book also explores the ethical issues surrounding the employment of AI, including bias, anonymity, transparency, and the possible effects on society. It explores how AI affects several sectors, including health care, finance, and more, offering insights into how AI might advance these businesses and its possible long-term effects. This book, which professionals in the subject wrote, gives a clear and concise explanation of AI, making it understandable to readers from various backgrounds and degrees of experience. We can only comprehend the algorithm model, its internal and external interdependence, and the integrative cognition of people, machines, and the natural world from the viewpoint of the system. Despite how sophisticated human intellect is, it relies on automatic calculations and actions to accomplish predetermined tasks following predetermined norms. Human intellect cannot solve problems that lack specified rules and goals, are not amenable to mathematical computation, or have outcomes solely based on quantifiable advantages.

Organization of The Book

The book is organized into twenty-two chapters. A brief description of each of the chapters follows:

Chapter 1 discusses how Artificial Intelligence (AI) can improve student performance and provide personalised learning opportunities, changing education. This chapter discusses AI in computer science (CS) education and its applications to adaptive learning, intelligent learning systems, and automated grading. We evaluate current AI-in-CS education research and compare techniques. The technology's capacity to customise CS education courses to students' interests and learning styles is a major benefit. Data analytics-based adaptive learning systems give students personalised feedback and improvement ideas. Intelligent tutoring systems provide customizable and interactive learning environments using ML and NLP. AI in computer education also automates grading, saving instructors time and improving efficiency. However, computerised grading has raised concerns about accuracy and reliability, especially for subjective areas.

Chapter 2 identifies recent years that have seen a fast growth in artificial intelligence (AI). This chapter covers current AI trends and their applications in computer science, the history of AI, and when it is used. We also explore AI research directions and their impact on computer science. We begin with AI fundamentals and subfields. We then review AI research trends in machine learning, natural language processing, computer vision, and robotics. Computer science applications, including driverless vehicles, fraud detection, tailored medicine, and AI developments, are covered. We also covered each AI application in computer science to help readers understand the concept faster. Finally, we examine the future of AI research, including the development of more explainable AI systems, the integration of AI with other developing technologies, and AI ethics, each with an example.

Chapter 3 optimizes video surveillance by considering five parameters to handle it. The five parameters are bandwidth, connection, storage, CPU, and memory. Since the research focused on Fog computing, bandwidth, and connection availability are key for streaming video material to authorised users. Video information is huge and slow to transfer over a wireless network. This will be optimised using Particle Swarm Optimization (PSO). This PSO algorithm optimises video content and makes it efficient to transport from one point to another, and then a microcontroller unit and GSM connection module are used to recognise things in the forest and change the user's environment. PSO-OD efficacy over state-of-the-art models is tested in the simulation. Simulation findings reveal that the proposed method processes surveillance region footage faster than competing methods, improving detection accuracy.

Chapter 4 compares k-means, DBSCAN, and adaptive clustering algorithms for data point clustering toughness. Popular and efficient, the k-means algorithm is easy to apply. The density-based DBSCAN technique is good for datasets with clusters of different densities, but settings can affect it. Adaptive clustering techniques actively change the number of clusters during clustering to find the optimal number. These algorithms are tested on different datasets for accuracy and efficiency. The paper concludes that each strategy has pros and cons and that the best depends on the dataset and study goals.

Chapter 5 analytics in a fighter aircraft, the pilot's mask pressure sensing is crucial to their safety. This unique system measures pressure quickly and accurately, reducing risks and improving military aircraft safety. It also offers a durable solution that can resist tough field conditions. This article discusses the improved capabilities and benefits of programming the National Instrument USB-6363 with LabVIEW in military aircraft. It shows its potential to transform pressure measurement in this vital field. It describes NI USB 6363 and LabVIEW research on pilot mask pressure-sensing systems. The technology can measure pilot mask pressure and relay it to the aircraft's control system for analysis. The device also alerts the pilot to abnormal situations.

Chapter 6 discusses how wireless sensor network (WSN) technology is growing because of the rapid expansion of the Internet and communication technologies in today's interconnected world. Sensing devices generate and/or collect massive amounts of sensory data for many sectors and applications. Security issues have been found in WSNs. Due to their aggressive adoption, limited resources, and high data output, these networks pose major security risks. Since WSN applications are critical, trustworthy solutions that combine swift and continuous processes for live data stream analysis to identify flooding assaults are essential. The assault involves sending useless requests to the target computer to overwhelm it, crash the systems, and prohibit users from accessing the network or machine. Using ensemble learning, a major machine learning concept, we want to construct an intelligent, effective, engineering-driven flooding assault detection system.

Chapter 7 says that remote care providers are not virtual care. It provides a delivery channel for certain patient populations with applications that do not require in-person exams or presence but cannot answer all health questions. The scoping reports state that virtual care includes disease diagnosis, the initial stage in treating the condition, and video conferencing for doctor consultation and care management. Rehabilitation, remote consulting, and emergency services are effective ways to use attention for well-being. Machine learning can accurately diagnose diseases using user data and numerous methods. This paper uses a modified Random Forest Approach. Suppliers and patients who saw virtual care's benefits were satisfied, which raised awareness of one's health.

Chapter 8 reviewed that Crop disease detection is crucial and time-consuming in agriculture. It requires a lot of time and expertise. This research presents an intelligent and effective information theory-based agricultural disease detection system. First, this study defines and explains helpful and distance information metrics. We measure the distance between Apple scab (AS) leaves and Apple black Rot (ABR). Six AS and ABR leaves are considered. After measuring distance, the disease affected AS and ABR leaves. This metric can be integrated into most picture classification methods and transformed by reference. Weak and strong data are obtained. Finally, minimum and maximum distances are assessed, and our findings show that low leaf information measures reduce plant leaf sickness risk.

Chapter 9 introduces that automated Facial Emotion Recognition (AFER) is increasingly used in security and advertising. AFER can help mental health patients with depression and anxiety make treatment options by assessing their emotional state. Facial emotion recognition can help companies develop and promote items by assessing consumer reactions to ads and products. The following work uses AI-based models to study facial emotion recognition and compares two methods. The first method employs the Haar Cascade Classifier and CNN to detect facial emotions, whereas the second uses facial landmarks and CNN. We trained the CNN model on FER-2013. Showing the same film to over 20 people evaluates both methods. In the first algorithm, we employ preliminary image processing to prepare the image for use. We next submit the photos to the Haar Cascade Classifier and CNN model, which predicts the emotions. The second method detects the 68 facial landmark points to predict emotions after image processing. These landmarks are used to extract numerical information to identify emotion. We analyze the accuracies of both methods and find that the second algorithm performs best, with 71.53 percent.

Chapter 10 predicts Software defect prediction influences business outcomes and development flaws. Developers can find bugs and arrange tests by predicting difficult code parts. Early detection depends on prediction accuracy. Due to their magnitude, software-defective data sets are supported and partially acknowledged. Systematic research analyses confusion, precision, memory, identification accuracy, etc., and compares them to existing schemes. Instead of employing Weak simulation for software analysis, this paper proposes developing three machine learning models using Linear Regression, KNN Classifier, and Random Forest (RF). The analytical analysis suggests the suggested approach will improve device failure prediction. Due to their size, software-defected data sets are supported and partially recognised.

Chapter 11 explains that autonomous automobiles need object detection to drive safely and reliably. It shows how the perception system accurately identifies pedestrians, cars, traffic signs, and barriers using object identification algorithms. Deep learning-based object detectors are essential for real-time detection and localization. The essay covers the latest object detectors and outstanding integration challenges into autonomous cars. It says deep learning visual classification approaches using the Convolutional neural network have achieved great accuracy in classifying visual scenes. It notes that visual classifiers struggle to detect scene contexts and examine scenes in dark, viewable areas, especially at night. The research proposes a deep learning approach for autonomous vehicles to distinguish visual motions and lighten dark environments.

Chapter 12 is about how the Digital revolution has transformed supply chain management. This paper discusses IoT (Internet of Things), which, together with AI, ML, big data, and cloud computing, is essential for Industry 4.0 deployment due to complicated organizational needs. IoT in SCML research is sparse in poor nations. However, real-time realisation, impediments to demand flow, value optimization from a business perspective, sustainability, increased customer expectations, and fierce rivalry among manufacturers and service providers have driven the IoT SCML industry. Especially when time management and material flow are important. IoT, AI, and ML provide business and prudential outcomes, making it a practical requirement for Industry 4.0. The paper captures the substantial use of IoT in supply chain management and logistics and highlights industry issues.

Chapter 13 develops the association between geriatric fear of falling and fall-related injuries, which is growing more prevalent, although its causes have not been studied. FOF is mobilisation anxiety with the expectation of a fall. Twenty-five to fifty-five percent of community-living seniors fear falling. This problem is generalised in FOF and lacks washroom data. The physical, medical, and psychological performance of 175 65–75-year-olds in Mumbai, Pune, and Kota was evaluated. Fall histories, medical histories, GAUG tests, and bathroom reactions were used to create the FES table. Based on these analyses, FOF causes were identified, and cities were compared. This study paper gives an overview of FOF and a framework for preventative intervention design.

Chapter 14 shows how Social networking services have expanded in recent years. In sentiment analysis (SA), natural language processing is used to mine data and read text (NLP). Today, the Coronavirus pandemic is a global issue. Millions of people express themselves on blogs and microblogging platforms. Twitter is one of the easiest and most popular channels for sharing thoughts and ideas. The public communicates their sentiments and ideas, such as "panic, wrath, and misery," on blogs, which can be favorable, negative, or neutral. Healthcare, finance, sports, politics, hospitality, and tourism use sentiment analysis. A study of ten primary papers found that Naive Bayes (NB) and Support Vector Machine (SVM) are popular COVID-19 sentiment analysis algorithms. This study usually briefly introduces sentimental analysis levels, techniques, applications, and challenges in COVID-19 research.

Chapter 15 talks about a submerged sensor network that uses many sensors and separate underwater vehicles to coordinate, share, detect, and observe data. Submerged sensor networks are used for contamination monitoring, catastrophic predictions, facilitated routes, under-ocean investigations, increased military capabilities, mine investigations, and more. Due to energy costs and channel engendering differences, submerged sensor networks bring unique challenges to conventional terrestrial sensor organization technologies. Submerged sensor organization uses aural distant communication instead of wireless and optical signals. Data transport capacity, battery power, sensor hub snarling, and consumption are some differences between submerged and terrestrial sensor networks. Due to submerged climate features, steering rules for submerged sensor networks are challenging to plan. This paper analyzes wireless sensor system protocols in all aspects.

Chapter 16 detects that pathogenic reasons include tissue injury, infection, and myocardial infarction, which produce inflammation. Noninfectious or infectious causes can induce inflammation. Inflammation causes redness, heat, swelling, pain, and tissue function loss. Local vascular, immunological, and inflammatory cell responses to infection or injury cause it. Tissue function can be lost by inflammation. Our bodies release chemical signals to restore harmed tissues. These reactions are healing cascades. These stimuli drive leukocytes in circulation, which chemotactically move to injury. Leukocytes create cytokines that trigger body-wide inflammation when activated. Inflammatory diseases can be treated with many medications nowadays. NSAIDs and steroidal anti-inflammatory medicines are helpful anti-inflammatory treatments. Due to strong side effects, its use is limited. Researchers are always looking for new anti-inflammatory drugs that are more effective and have fewer adverse effects. Inflammatory illnesses have several medicinal treatments today. These include NSAIDs and steroidal anti-inflammatory medications, which have shown promise (NSAIDs).

Chapter 17 analyzes the excitement of becoming a mother, and holding your kid increases stress, concern, and delivery uncertainty. Every birth is different, with new challenges for the mother, her partner, and the doctor. The pregnant woman, her family, and the attending physician often worry about when the labour pains will begin following induction, how they will be related to gradual cervical dilation, and how they will terminate in a vaginal delivery. Obstetrics increasingly uses transvaginal ultrasonography to measure cervical canal length in the second and third trimesters. Transvaginal ultrasound measurements of cervical length and internal os during the second trimester identify an insufficient cervix and determine if a cervical encircling is needed. The funneling of the internal os and the cervical angle have been studied and may help predict labour outcomes.

Chapter 18 diagnosis of the exudation of fluid and plasma proteins and the emigration of leukocytes, predominantly neutrophils, characterise acute inflammation, which occurs within minutes or hours in response to infection and tissue damage and lasts for hours. After hazardous chemicals are removed, acute inflammation fades. If the response fails to eliminate the stimulus, it may cause chronic inflammation. Since there is no safe, effective anti-inflammatory medicine, scientists research inflammation. Azithromycin, Clarithromycin, and Roxithromycin were investigated for anti-inflammatory effects in Wistar rats with acute and sub-acute inflammation. Karad's biggest animal home sold 200–300g Wistar rats. The animals were habituated to the 24-hour light-dark cycle for ten days before the studies. Water and rat pellets were sufficient. The IAC approved this study (Institutional Animal Ethics Committee). ANOVA is used in all CPCSEA techniques. Multiple comparison tests utilising Dunnett's post-hoc test followed. Aspirin vs. macrolides All statistical procedures used GraphPad Instat 3.06 and a significant p-value of 0.05. According to our research, macrolides' anti-infective, immunomodulatory, and anti-inflammatory characteristics may aid COPD, asthma, chronic sinusitis, bronchiolitis, bronchiectasis, cystic fibrosis, and osteomyelitis.

Chapter 19 examines digitalization's good and bad effects on youth and how demonetization led to it for five years. The study examines young digitalization in the Indian economy, the effects of demonetization on youth, and the relationship between digitalization and demonetization. This report analyses a lot of secondary data and a main investigation with 150 respondents. Young behaviour, emotions, and motivation should be examined to reach this target group, as well as digital technology, especially mobile phones, the Internet, and computer games. The study would likely show the extent of digitization in the economy, how demonetizations affected it, and how it affected youth. The study will include pie charts, bar graphs, chi-squared tests, and T-tests to show the pros and cons.

Chapter 20 addresses fetal iron comes from maternal iron, a vitamin essential for foetal growth. Pregnancy increases iron demand, making maternal iron stores difficult to maintain. Literature suggests maternal iron deficiency anaemia may impair infant iron stores and growth and development. To investigate the relationship between maternal anaemia and infant haemoglobin and iron stores. This 18-month cross-sectional study examined huge hospital data. Hemoglobin and serum ferritin levels were measured in the mother and newborn during early labour. The average age of pregnant women in the research was 25.81.46 years, with the majority being 21–30. (72.32 percent). The mean haemoglobin and serum ferritin levels in pregnant women with iron deficiency anemia were 8.92 and 1.46 g/dL, and 12.63 and 1.36 g/L, respectively. Moderate and severe maternal hemoglobin levels were positively correlated with neonatal anthropometric features, and this correlation was statistically significant (p 0.001).

Chapter 21 classifies non-communicable diseases (NCDs), including diabetes and heart disease, spreading worldwide and in India. HIV affects both sexes, making it a major issue for all healthcare systems. Unplanned fast urbanization, globalisation of bad habits, and the ageing population cause these diseases. Diet and inactivity raise blood glucose, hypertension, obesity, and lipids. All these metabolic risk factors can contribute to cardiovascular disease, a primary NCD that kills prematurely. Smoking, alcohol, poor diet, lack of exercise, and high blood pressure are major NCD factors. Overweight and obesity, elevated blood glucose, and abnormal serum cholesterol are the main causes of NCDs in India. If such hazards are addressed, NCD-related premature mortality in India could drop by 40-50%. According to the WHO, tobacco kills 7 million people annually. Diet and inactivity raise blood glucose, hypertension, obesity, and lipids.

Chapter 22 says sepsis is a medical emergency caused by the body's systemic immune response to infection, which can cause end-stage organ malfunction and death. Sepsis is a major source of morbidity and mortality in critically ill patients, but understanding its aetiology, hemodynamic monitoring techniques, and resuscitation methods has improved. Sepsis is a medical emergency caused by the body's systemic immunological response to infection, which can cause end-stage organ failure and death. It is one of the top 10 global killers. The global epidemiological impact of sepsis is difficult to assess. Sepsis is a leading source of morbidity and mortality in critically ill patients despite advances in hemodynamic monitoring, resuscitation, and pathogenesis. In intensive care units, sepsis kills most critically ill patients. A public health emergency has been declared since the death toll is comparable to a myocardial infarction.

S. Suman Rajest
Dhaanish Ahmed College of Engineering, India

Bhopendra Singh

Amity University, Dubai, UAE

Ahmed J. Obaid
University of Kufa, Iraq

R. Regin
SRM Institute of Science and Technology, Ramapuram, India

Karthikeyan Chinnusamy
Veritas, USA

Chapter 1
Artificial Intelligence in Computer Science

Shyam Sihare

https://orcid.org/0000-0003-2096-8273

Dr. A.P.J. Abdul Kalam Government College, Silvassa, India

ABSTRACT

AI has the potential to revolutionize education by enhancing student performance and delivering tailored learning experiences. This chapter addresses the present state of artificial intelligence (AI) in computer science (CS) education, as well as how it is used to adaptive learning, intelligent learning systems, and automated grading. The authors examine recent studies on the use of AI in CS teaching, emphasizing the relative benefits of various approaches. One of the technology's most important benefits is its ability to customize courses to the interests and learning preferences of particular students in CS education. Using data analytics, adaptive learning systems evaluate student performance and offer personalized feedback and improvement recommendations. Intelligent tutoring systems offer adaptable and interactive learning environments by using machine learning (ML) and natural language processing (NLP).

INTRODUCTION

Traditional approaches to teaching CS often lack personalization, which has a negative impact on engagement and information retention. These approaches take a one-size-fits-all stance, neglecting the unique learning requirements and preferences of each learner.

AI in CS education can provide personalized feedback through adaptive learning systems that examine student data and customize treatments. Intelligent tutoring systems powered by AI build engaging and adaptable learning environments while responding in real time to student success. The use of AI algorithms for automated grading frees up instructors' time and effort so they can focus on offering advice and assistance. These benefits of AI improve learning, mastery, and participation in CS courses.

AI has the potential to emulate human-like traits such as thinking, learning, planning, and creativity, enabling it to understand the environment, solve problems, and act independently. As society transitions towards a digital era, the government has prioritized the integration of AI due to its anticipated impact

DOI: 10.4018/979-8-3693-1301-5.ch001

on various aspects of life and the economy. AI finds applications in diverse fields, including speech recognition, computer vision, language translation, and automated decision-making.

However, traditional AI techniques, such as sequential logic-impersonating algorithms, have limitations in handling complex logical challenges effectively. Despite these drawbacks, AI systems excel at making deductive inferences and utilizing knowledge engineering and representation to comprehend factual information.

In the realm of AI research, significant developments have been made in describing domains, encompassing objects, attributes, categories, and the intricate connections between entities, situations, events, and states. This knowledge representation has paved the way for advancements in various aspects, such as default reasoning, knowledge discovery, and understanding the interplay between causes and consequences. ML, a branch of AI, focuses on the study of self-learning computer algorithms, while NLP empowers robots to comprehend human language. Additionally, affective computing has emerged as a field dedicated to systems that can identify, analyze, process, or replicate human feelings, emotions, and moods.

The practical applications of AI span a wide range, including chatbots, virtual assistants, autonomous cars, automatic language translation, face recognition, online advertising, recommendation systems, and internet traffic management. Notable AI systems, such as Deep Blue, Watson, AlphaGo, GPT-3, and AlphaFold 2, have outperformed humans in tasks like predicting court outcomes, creating art, and proving mathematical theorems. Computer vision stands out as a popular functional application, while ML dominates the AI landscape, as evidenced by the number of patent applications and grants. When evaluating AI's capabilities relative to humans, it is essential to consider both its "acting" and "thinking" dimensions.

While statistical ML has shown remarkable success, addressing challenges related to sub-symbolic reasoning remains an ongoing pursuit, which has led researchers to explore the fusion of neurosymbolic AI to leverage the strengths of both approaches. The AI research community faces a significant divide regarding whether to concentrate on specialized issues or strive for the ambitious goals of artificial general intelligence and superintelligence. Modern AI has achieved substantial progress by focusing on specific problems that have well-defined answers, as the notion of universal intelligence defies clear definition and quantification. Contemplations regarding computer consciousness and mental states lie beyond the scope of mainstream AI research, as they are deemed irrelevant to the overarching goals of AI.

The emergence of hypothetical superintelligence or superhuman intelligence, symbolized by the agency "Beginning of the Cosmos," raises concerns about the potential deployment of AI by authoritarian governments, terrorists, criminals, and rogue nations, which may introduce biases after assimilating actual data. Inaccurate predictions and classifications, particularly in fields like student assessments, can also arise as potential pitfalls. While AI presents threats to humanity, experts and industry insiders hold varying views on the matter. While AI management revolves around algorithmic approaches, addressing the risks associated with friendly AI must be prioritized to counter adversarial intentions. Initiatives, such as the launch of an AI-focused magazine in 2020, aim to enhance public and technological trust in AI.

This chapter significantly contributes to the field of AI and its application in CS by providing a comprehensive review of AI applications, methodologies, and breakthroughs. The exploration of AI's contextual relevance in CS highlights the various applications and their implications on society and the economy. Additionally, this chapter examines the limitations of traditional AI techniques, such as sequential logic-impersonating algorithms, which are unable to tackle complex logical challenges effectively. By contrasting the findings of the current study with previous research on the same topic, a stronger context for this study is established, emphasizing the distinctions between alternative approaches. Furthermore, the chapter delves into the challenges, debates, and potential opportunities within the AI research community, offering valuable insights for further exploration. The application of AI in CS education is also explored, shedding light on the implementation challenges in this area.

The chapter follows a structured approach: Section 2 provides a comprehensive literature survey, outlining the current applications of AI in CS and their relation to various fields. Section 3 evaluates different AI fields within CS, highlighting their strengths and weaknesses and emphasizing the advantages of the proposed method. Section 4 focuses on the practical implementation of AI in CS, covering relevant areas such as automata, data structures, and graph theory. Section 5 showcases the development of teaching-learning aids by the AI Academic Group. Section 6 addresses challenges in applying AI to CS, including ethical considerations. Finally, Section 7 concludes the chapter by summarizing key points and highlighting future research opportunities.

LITERATURE REVIEW OF AI'S IN CS

AI in education has the ability to improve learning, teaching, evaluation, and administration by providing students with more tailored and adaptable learning, promoting instructors' comprehension of students' learning processes, and enabling machine-supported queries everywhere, at any time (Alam, 2021, p. 6).

AI is providing teachers with a plethora of new tools and services to help students learn, but growing public concern about the potentially harmful societal effects of AI has resulted in the publication of AI ethics guidelines and policy documents written by national and international government agencies, academic consortia, and industrial stakeholders (Adams et al., 2023, p. 100131; Williamson and Eynon, 2020, p. 226; Maedche et al., 2019, p. 540). Addressing the growing human-AI collaboration environment in institutions, as well as weighing the complicated indications and contraindications for children's and youth's cognitive, social-emotional, physical, cultural, and political development (Empathy and Justice p. 4-5; Gillio et al., 2019, p. 6-9).

According to UNICEF (2021), while AI ethical principles are applicable when children are engaged, the specific qualities and rights of children necessitate a deeper study on the impact of AI and how the principles must be implemented differently for them (Adams et al., 2023, p. 100131; Fosch-Villaronga et al., 2021, p. 136; George et al., 2023, p. 8). The key concepts used by UNICEF in regard to AI in the education system in 2021 are transparency, justice, and fairness; non-maleficence; responsibility; privacy; beneficence; freedom and autonomy; trust; dignity; sustainability; and solidarity (Tidjon & Khomh, 2022; Roll et al., 2021).

Via the course material, it demonstrates the need for teamwork and human-tool collaboration in AI literacy (Sanusi et al., 2022, p. 100098). The multigroup analysis likewise indicates no statistically significant variations by gender or institute type (Ramírez-Correa et al., 2015, p. 2-8). Several AI education initiatives for institutions have been established, including curriculum and materials (Wang et al., 2021, p. 100031; Shyam, 2017-(a), p. 36). The necessity of curriculum design for competence, which involves knowledge and skill development, as well as the elements influencing behavioral intention toward learning AI, has been demonstrated by research (Su & Yang., 2022, p. 100065; Sibbel, 2009, p. 68-70). Previous research has looked at the perspectives of instructors with and without AI teaching expertise on critical aspects for developing, implementing, and revising a formal AI curriculum (Emil et al., 2014, p. 532; Pedro et al., 2019, p. 15-18; Harden, 2001, p. 135; Monte-Sano et al., 2014, p. 560-

62). AI education may be developed to be more accessible to all learners, and coordinated co-design workshops with instructors can aid in the development of a curriculum that takes advantage of learners' interests (Gomoll et al., 2022, p. 10; Grimus, 2020, p. 128).

AI literacy increases students' willingness and ability to engage with new technologies while decreasing their fear of an AI-powered society, and AI competences are required to attain AI literacy (Luckin et al., 2016, p. 12-20; Rouhiainen, 2018, p. 10-20). Identifying learners' essential abilities can assist AI curriculum designers in ensuring a suitable level of difficulty and visuals with meaningful examples (Jonassen, 2018, p. 63-70; Shyam, 2017-(b), p. 35). Curriculum and teaching should be structured in a logical sequence with genuine activities and intelligible representations to enhance student learning (Stern & Roseman, 2004, p. 539-545; Kesidou & Roseman, 2002, p. 532). This report builds on a previous study by taking gender disparities and school types into account when assessing learners' skills for AI education (Atmatzidou & Demetriadis, 2016, p. 665-670; Below et al., 2010, p. 240-243).

The core capabilities are divided into three categories: learning, knowledge, and team skills (Welch et al., 2014, p. 1-3). Learning competence encompasses cognitive and self-learning abilities; knowledge competence encompasses skill and cultural abilities; and team competence includes teamwork and human-tool collaboration abilities (Glenn, 2022, p. 17-53). Cognitive competency is defined as a person's mental ability to deal with a certain sort of issue in an educated and introspective manner (Niss & Højgaard, 2019, p. 9-20).

It necessitates 21st-century learning abilities such as critical thinking, creativity, and problem-solving. A recent study looked into the influence of infrastructure and learners' cognitive competency in distance learning circumstances during the COVID-19 pandemic (Kivunja, 2014, p. 81-85; Md Yunus et al., 2021, p. 2-5).

A "learned capacity to interact with other team members at some basic competency level" is characterized as teamwork competence. In the area of education, a team-based teaching and learning technique is being used in a different setting, and learner competency is a primary concern (Rosen et al., 2018, p. 435; Shyam, 2018, p. 25).

It is critical to cultivate young children's AI literacy, particularly its limitations, ethical problems, and fundamental comprehension of the technology (Buckingham, 2013, p. 1-10). To enhance this knowledge, learning programs and activities have arisen (Chang, 2019, p. 100). AI literacy refers to a set of skills that enable individuals to assess, interact with, and work successfully with AI. Computers observe the environment through sensors; agents have models or representations of the world and use them for reasoning; computers can learn from data; and AI applications can have a beneficial or bad influence on society (Long & Magerlo, 2020, p. 1-5; Ng et al., 2022, p. 100054).

Before, AI learning began in CS education; however, the introduction of more age-appropriate software has allowed young learners to broaden their opportunities to learn about and experience AI (Zhang et al., 2022, p. 30-32). Modern AI literacy research focuses on secondary or higher education, with undergraduates and secondary pupils learning AI ideas and increasing ethical awareness to become informed digital citizens (Choi, 2016, p. 566; Shyam, 2022).

Toys driven by AI are being employed in early childhood education classes to give kids a pleasant experience while also teaching coding skills (Kewalramani et al., 2021, p. 653-654). AI literacy is critical for early children's development in several areas, including theory of mind abilities, creative inquiry, emotional inquiry, and collaborative inquiry (Su, 2022, p. 100065; Chu et al., 2021, p. 17-30). With intelligent tutoring systems for special education, chatbots for language education, and robotic kits in CS education, AI applications are being applied to facilitate kindergarten instructors' administration and students' learning (Akgun & Greenhow, 2021, p. 5-6).

AI applications have been studied in four areas: AI evaluation of children, AI teaching systems, AI educational robots, and AI virtual reality teaching (Chassignol et al., 2018, p. 16-18; Alam, 2021, p. 2-3; Chen et al., 2020, p. 100005). It is critical to provide youngsters with digital skills and attitudes to prepare them for future academics and make their lives easier. AI is described as a collection of skills that enable people to critically assess, interact with, and cooperate successfully with AI, as well as utilize AI as a tool online, at home, and at work (Iivari et al., 2020, p. 2-5). AI improved every student's digital literacy in job settings and everyday life, and the instructional design of AI literacy education utilized the models of Bloom's Taxonomy, Technological Pedagogical Subject Knowledge, and AI ideas, practices, and viewpoints (Greiner et al., 2021, p. 28-29; Abalkheel, 2022, p. 17).

AI literacy in AI education has presented challenges and opportunities for early childhood education, such as why young learners should learn AI in their early years, the subset of key AI concepts that children can understand, and how children were engaged in a meaningful experience to acquire these concepts. Students and AI curriculum are designed to assist young children in understanding how AI feels, perceives, interacts, reacts, and generates. AI-interfaced robots are intended for young children to teach them about the capabilities and limits of AI agents and toys. These studies explain why and how teachers might use age-appropriate activities and resources to scaffold students' comprehension (Pedra et al., 2019, p. 5-6; Williams et al., 2019, p. 9732-9734; Yang, 2022, p. 10061; GUIDETTI, 2023, p. 20-43).

AI AND ITS APPLICATIONS IN CS SUBJECT

This section examines several aspects of AI and their applications in the field of CS. The range of AI applications has also expanded, and among them, the significance of AI in CS has grown. Mean, uncertain reasoning, decision-making, distributed algorithms, temporal reasoning, and ML in data mining are a few AI elements that are relevant to CS subjects, contributing to further automation.

Uncertain Reasoning

The ability of AI with uncertain reasoning to accurately interpret incomplete or uncertain data makes it a crucial tool in CS. This is particularly important when dealing with vast amounts of information that require analysis. One area where AI-based uncertain reasoning is applied to personalize instruction is CS education. AI can analyze student data, including test results, homework assignments, and other information, to gain a more precise understanding of a student's skills and learning style. This information can then be utilized by AI to develop personalized learning strategies tailored to the unique needs of each student.

Another application of AI fuzzy logic in CS education is program evaluation. AI can assess test and assignment responses using uncertain reasoning to identify areas where a student is struggling or needs additional training. This can also enhance the overall effectiveness of exams by helping teachers identify students who require additional support.

Artificial fuzzy logic can also be utilized to analyze large CS datasets, such as student performance data, to identify trends and patterns that can inform educational policies and decision-making. For instance, AI can evaluate data on student performance to determine factors that contribute to success or failure, such as demographic information or instructional methodologies. Personalized learning, educational evaluation, and data analysis in the field of education are a few applications of AI fuzzy logic in CS. These initiatives have the potential to improve student performance, shape educational policies, and enhance the overall effectiveness of CS education opportunities (Figure 1).

Figure 1. AI uncertain reasoning of CS student results, assignment, examination, and homework

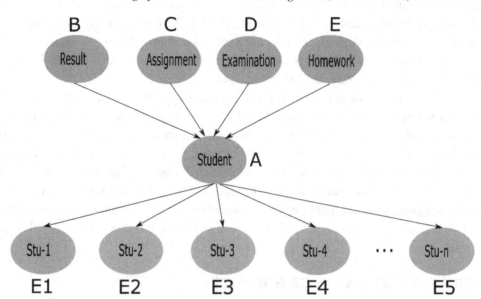

The academic activities analysed by AI uncertain reasoning deduce the significant conclusion

A list of all events occurring in Figure 1 networks includes: Results (B), Assignment (C), Examination (D), Homework (E), Students (A), Stu-1 (E1), Stu-2 (E2), Stu-3 (E3), Stu-4 (E4), and Stu-n (E5).

The probabilities can be utilized to represent the occurrences mentioned in the issue statement. The probability statement above can be rephrased as follows: **P[E1, E2, E3, E4, E5, A, B, C, D, E]** using a joint probability distribution.

P[E1, E2, E3, E4, E5, A, B,C,D,E]= P[E1 | E2, E3, E4, E5, A, B,C,D,E].P[E2, E3, E4, E5, A, B,C,D,E] = P[E1 | E2, E3, E4, E5, A, B,C,D,E].P[E3 | E4, E5, A, B,C,D,E].P[E4, E5, A, B,C,D,E] =P[E1|A].P[E2|A].P[E3|A].P[E4|A].P[E5|A].P[A|B,C,D,E].P[B|C,D,E].P[C|D,E].P[D|E].P[E]   (1)

• Let B, C, D, and E represent the result, assignment, examination (either descriptive or objective), and homework, respectively. These academic activities are represented in a tabular format as follows:

Tabular Format

B: result	
T	0.25
F	0.98
C: assignment	
T	095
F	0.98
D: examination	
T	0.67
F	0.59
E: homework	
T	0.48
F	0.77

$$A = B \times C \times D \times E$$

where $\times$ is the cartesian product between two relation X and Y. Hence, relation A can deduce by using the relations B, C, D, E as,

Relation A deduction

A: students B C D E P(A=T)P(A=F) F F F F 0.24 0.76 F F F T 0.64 0.36 F F T F 0.12 0.88 F F T T 0.56 0.44 F T F F 0.17 0.83 F T F T 0.57 0.43 F T T F 0.64 0.36 F T T T 0.37 0.63 T F F F 0.98 0.02 T F F T 0.78 0.22 T F T F 0.94 0.06 T F T T 0.85 0.15 T T F F 0.67 0.33 T T F T 0.49 0.51 T T T F 0.79 0.21 T T T T 0.88 0.12	E1: Stu-1 A P(E1=T) P(E1=F) T 0.95 0.05 F 0.14 0.86 E3: Stu-3 A P(E3=T) P(E3=F) T 0.88 0.12 F 0.03 0.97 E5: Stu-n A P(E5=T) P(E5=F) T 0.07 0.93 F 0.86 0.14	E2: Stu-2 A P(E2=T) P(E2=F) T 0.06 0.94 F 0.05 0.95 E4: Stu-4 A P(E4=T) P(E4=F) T 0.99 0.01 F 0.22 0.78

As a result, any domain-related query can be answered using a Bayesian network with a joint distribution.

Decision Making

AI decision-making can be a valuable tool in CS as it can aid in making data-driven judgments that enhance students' opportunities for hands-on learning. By analyzing their academic achievements, test scores, and extracurricular engagements, AI decision-making can identify the most suitable candidates among CS students for specific training courses or job opportunities.

AI decision-making can assess CS student data to identify students who may be at risk of dropping out. This information can be utilized by teachers and administrators to provide targeted support and resources, ultimately improving the students' academic performance. AI decision-making can also analyze student performance data in CS to pinpoint areas where students are facing difficulties and propose curricular changes to address these challenges. This helps ensure that students fully benefit from their computer knowledge.

AI decision-making can assist CS educational institutions in allocating resources more effectively by analyzing data on CS student enrollment, demographics, and performance. This enables informed decisions on which computer programs and projects will be most beneficial and where resources should be directed.

Predictive analytics employed by AI decision-making can identify CS students who are most likely to succeed in practical-oriented CS courses. This allows teachers to provide guidance and support to students as they make crucial choices for their future (Figure 2).

Figure 2. Decision making approach of AI for CS subject valuation, assessment for analysis

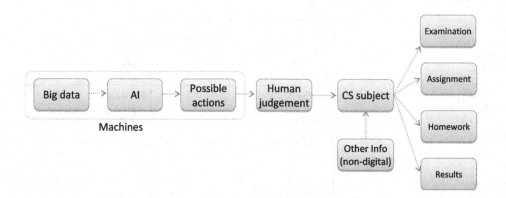

ML in Datamining

AI data mining is a valuable technique in CS teaching as it enables the analysis of large datasets to uncover trends and insights that can enhance CS educational decision-making. By analyzing student performance data in CS, AI data mining can identify trends and patterns that can inform better CS subject choices. For example, it can help identify students who are struggling in specific CS subjects or who are at risk of dropping out of an educational institution.

AI data mining can also leverage information from online learning platforms to identify the most effective pedagogical strategies and tools. By utilizing this data, the learning experiences of CS students can be enhanced. Moreover, AI data mining can employ predictive analytics to identify CS students who are most likely to succeed in particular computer fields or careers. This information can be utilized by guidance and counseling services to assist CS students in making informed career choices.

AI data mining can assess information on enrollment, demographics, and performance of CS students to determine which initiatives and programs are most successful and where funding should be directed. Academic research data can also be mined using AI to uncover patterns and insights that can guide policy-making and decision-making processes (Figure 3).

Figure 3. Collections of education data and its analysis by intelligent algorithms for use in various educational contexts

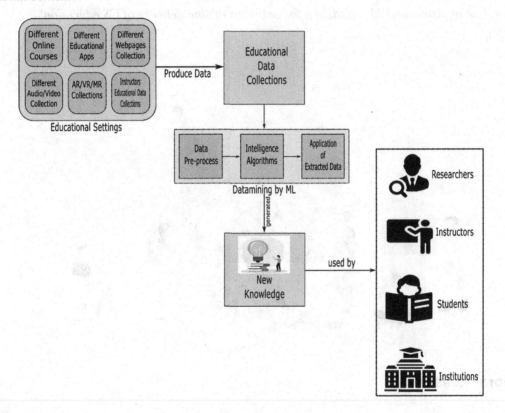

Distributed AII

Distributed AI allows the utilization of a network of computers to exchange calculations, rather than relying on a single device. It serves as a helpful tool in CS as it facilitates the processing of large amounts of information and the implementation of complex algorithms, which may be challenging on a single machine.

With the use of big data analysis, distributed AI can evaluate extensive datasets in CS, including information on student performance, enrollment, and demographics. By distributing the processing across multiple workstations, these datasets can be analyzed more comprehensively, leading to deeper insights into CS educational trends and patterns.

AI can be employed to provide customized learning experiences for CS students. By considering information such as CS students' grades, test scores, and learning preferences, personalized learning plans can be created to cater to each student's individual needs.

AI fosters collaborative learning experiences by enabling dispersed CS students from diverse backgrounds to collaborate on projects and assignments using shared tools and data. Real-time collaboration and feedback can be encouraged by distributing computation among multiple devices.

AI can also enhance the productivity and scalability of learning management systems. By distributing calculations across multiple computers, it becomes feasible to manage large volumes of data while providing CS students and teachers with rapid response times (Figure 4).

Figure 4. Use of distributed AI-based data for online or offline delivery of CS education[1]

Temporal Reasoning

AI temporal reasoning is a method that analyzes changing CS data over time, such as shifts in student performance throughout a semester or changes in educational policies over several years. By examining historical data, it becomes possible to identify trends and patterns in CS subjects and student performance data that can be used to make future predictions.

Artificial temporal logic can be utilized to create adaptive learning environments that adjust over time based on student performance. By evaluating data on CS student progress over time, the difficulty level of content can be modified to meet the individual needs of students. Temporal reasoning with AI can also be employed to assess the effectiveness of various learning systems over time. This information can be used to improve student outcomes by making changes to the CS curriculum and teaching methods.

AI temporal thinking can be applied to evaluate the long-term effectiveness of CS educational initiatives. By regularly reviewing data on student performance and program outcomes, areas for improvement can be identified, and the CS program can be adjusted accordingly. Artificial temporal thinking can also be used to assess the overall impact of CS educational initiatives. By analyzing educational outcome statistics over time, the relationship between educational policy and outcomes can be identified (Figure 5).

Figure 5. AI temporal algorithms are used to analyse educational data and extract pertinent information that students need

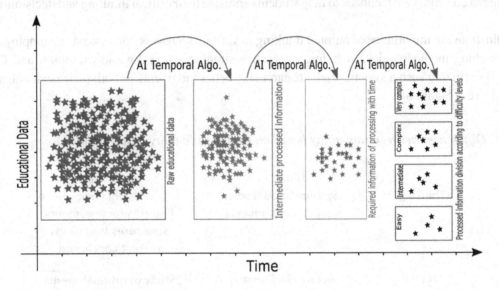

Real-Time Reasoning

Real-time data analysis is conducted through a technology known as "AI real-time reasoning." AI can utilize real-time reasoning to assess the achievement of CS students in real-time. By examining real-time performance data, immediate feedback and support can be provided to CS students while they are studying.

AI, along with real-time reasoning, can be utilized to develop intelligent CS educational systems that swiftly adapt to student needs. By collecting performance data as students engage in tasks, the complexity and pace of the content can be adjusted to align with the students' requirements. Real-time reasoning based on AI can also analyze data from online learning platforms in real-time. Information regarding student behavior, such as the time spent on each CS assignment or the utilization of different CS resources, can be used to evaluate the effectiveness of various teaching methods and resources.

AI and real-time reasoning enable the prediction of student performance in real-time. By evaluating their performance data when they encounter difficulties, it becomes possible to predict whether students will successfully complete their work and provide timely assistance when needed. Real-time AI reasoning can also be implemented in the classroom to monitor student behavior. By analyzing data on student behavior, such as their level of engagement or attention span, students who may require additional help or intervention can be identified.

Rationality

An education system that incorporates AI reasoning applications to train and assist CS students in enhancing their logical thinking abilities is known as an AI reasoning application.

In such a system, AI algorithms can be utilized to investigate and analyze the mental processes and cognitive biases of CS students, identifying areas for improvement. Additionally, the system can provide personalized coaching and feedback to help students enhance their critical thinking and decision-making skills.

To illustrate the importance of rational thinking in various scenarios, the system can employ a range of CS teaching methodologies, including interactive simulations, real-world examples, and CS case studies. By utilizing such a system, students can make better judgments in both their personal and professional lives (Figure 6).

Figure 6. Differences between rationality based on AI and rationality based on humans[2]

	Humanly	Rationally
Thinking	Systems should solve problems as humans do	Use of Logic Patterns for arguments structures that yields correct conclusion
Acting	Acting like humans- Natural language processing Automated reasoning Knowledge representation	Study of rational agents Expected to act so as to achieve best expected outcome

Cognitive Science

Cognitive science, a subfield of AI, aims to comprehend human cognition and leverage this understanding to develop cognitive systems. Through the integration of AI and cognitive science, personalized learning experiences can be created for CS students. By analyzing student performance data in CS and applying instructional science methodologies, it becomes possible to determine each student's optimal learning style and provide tailored tools and support.

AI cognitive science can be utilized to assess students' cognitive abilities. By analyzing data on student behavior and applying cognitive science techniques, it becomes feasible to identify areas of difficulty for individual students and offer appropriate support and resources. AI can also simulate how students learn and recall knowledge by drawing from cognitive science principles. This enables the development of cognitive models that can enhance teaching techniques and promote effective learning and retention.

The combination of AI and cognitive science can lead to the creation of tutoring programs customized to the unique needs of CS students. By analyzing data on student performance and incorporating cognitive science concepts, a tutoring system that considers each student's learning dynamics and style can be developed.

Cognitive research can utilize AI to gain a deeper understanding of the mechanisms behind memory and learning. By analyzing data and applying principles from cognitive science and brain imaging, it becomes possible to uncover insights into how the brain functions and processes information.

Constraint Satisfaction

AI constraint satisfaction is a problem-solving method that adheres to a set of rules or standards. It can be applied to create CS class schedules that consider various constraints, including student preferences, teacher availability, and room availability. Additionally, it can be used to develop CS lesson plans that meet educational standards while considering factors such as teacher availability, available resources, and classroom suitability.

AI constraint satisfaction can be utilized to generate schedules for CS students that fulfill multiple criteria. This includes avoiding scheduling conflicts, accommodating changing preferences for specific courses or instructors, and ensuring a balanced workload. By employing AI constraint satisfaction, resources such as lab equipment, computers, and textbooks can be allocated to CS departments or courses based on demand. This approach allows for the creation of CS course schedules that consider the availability of instructors, resources, and students. As a result, sessions can be scheduled at optimal times, and students can have access to the necessary resources for their success (Figure 7).

Figure 7. AI constraint satisfaction issues for academic assessment of students

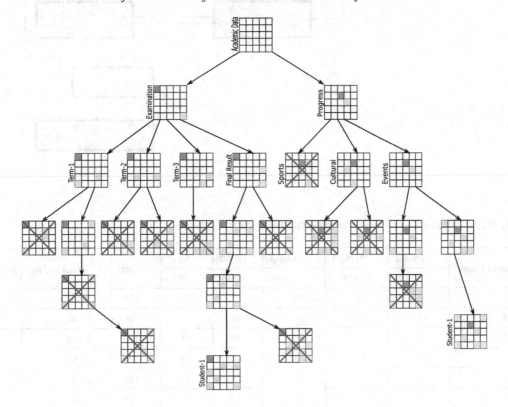

Knowledge Representation

AI knowledge representation is a technique that intelligent computers can utilize to organize and structure knowledge. It can be applied to develop intelligent tutoring programs that offer personalized feedback to each student. By presenting information in a precise manner, it becomes possible to identify the areas in which a student is struggling and provide targeted feedback and support (Figure 8).

AI knowledge representation can be used to design a more effective and successful CS curriculum. By organizing knowledge, it becomes possible to identify knowledge gaps and create a CS curriculum that caters to the individual needs of each student. It can also be employed to create concept maps that illustrate the relationships between different concepts and ideas. This aids students in comprehending complex CS topics and understanding how they interconnect. Additionally, AI knowledge representation can be utilized to develop expert systems that offer recommendations and advice based on a well-structured knowledge base. This enables CS teachers and students to make more informed conclusions and solve problems more effectively (Figure 9 and Table 1).

Figure 8. Cycle of knowledge representation in AI[3]

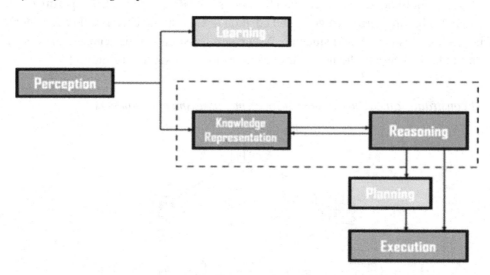

Table 1. Basic related knowledge represented in tabular form

Student Name	Term-1 (30)	Term-2 (30)	Term-3 (30)	SA-1 (50)	SA-2 (50)	Total	Final Result	Grade
Stu-1	10	24	24	35	45	138	FAIL	A
Stu-2	15	15	25	44	49	148	PASS	A
Stu-3	24	18	30	50	28	150	PASS	A
Stu-4	21	16	28	14	29	108	PASS	B
Stu-5	16	27	26	28	47	144	PASS	A
Stu-6	18	28	15	37	10	108	FAIL	C

Figure 9. Hierarchy of the students' knowledge in CS

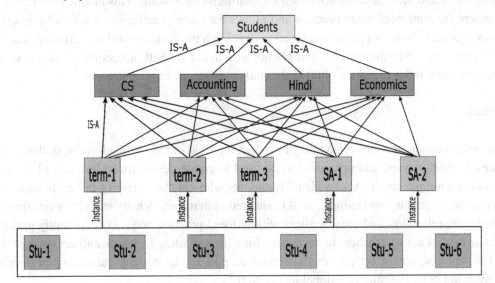

Search

AI search algorithms are employed to explore the search space and find solutions. They can be utilized to search the Internet, libraries, and large databases, allowing CS instructors and students to quickly discover relevant information and resources for studying and teaching. AI search algorithms can also be used to develop recommendation systems that distribute CS instructional resources such as books, articles, and videos based on the interests and preferences of the students.

By considering the requirements and electives that a student has already completed, it becomes possible to determine the optimal path for completing a CS course. AI search algorithms can be applied to address optimization problems, such as determining the most effective way to allocate CS resources when scheduling classes. Additionally, they can be employed to create intelligent teaching programs that utilize search algorithms to find solutions to problems. This can help students understand the steps necessary to solve a problem and provide personalized feedback and support.

Qualitative Reasoning

An approach used in AI, called qualitative reasoning, is employed to infer the behavior of systems based on a qualitative understanding of the system components and their interactions. This approach can assist students in developing a deeper understanding of complex CS practical subjects and systems. By thinking about these systems in a qualitative manner, students can better comprehend their characteristics and behaviors. Qualitative reasoning can also be used to identify students' misunderstandings and errors. By analyzing student responses using qualitative reasoning, it can pinpoint the student's mistakes and provide personalized feedback and support.

Qualitative reasoning can be utilized to create concept maps that illustrate the connections between different CS concepts and ideas. This can help students understand challenging CS concepts and their interrelationships. It can also be applied to develop sophisticated assessment systems that evaluate student responses and provide feedback based on qualitative reasoning. This enables the identification of areas where students need more practice and allows for more specific feedback and support. Additionally, qualitative reasoning can be employed to develop a more successful and effective curriculum. By qualitatively analyzing the systems and phenomena being studied, it becomes possible to identify knowledge gaps and tailor the curriculum to the individual needs of each student.

Diagnosis

There are numerous applications for AI diagnostics in the field of CS. AI analysis of students' learning preferences, learning styles, and progress can be used to create personalized learning plans that cater to each student's unique needs. AI can identify students who may be at risk of falling behind or failing and intervene to prevent it. For example, an AI-powered system can identify students who struggle with CS reading comprehension and provide them with tailored practice tasks. By efficiently grading tests and assignments, AI allows teachers to have more time for providing feedback and designing CS lesson plans. AI-driven assessment systems can also analyze patterns in students' academic performance to identify areas in CS that require additional instruction.

AI can analyze large amounts of data, including exam scores, demographic information, and student attendance records, to predict which students are likely to succeed and which may face challenges. This information can be used to offer targeted CS resources and support to these students. AI-powered systems enable students to learn at their own pace and level by adjusting the complexity and speed of learning activities based on their individual success.

Metareasoning and Control

AI systems can be deployed to monitor and evaluate the quality, consistency, and clarity of CS educational materials such as textbooks and online courses. These systems can track students' behavior and engagement in the classroom, whether it's measuring the time they spend on specific CS activities or observing their eye movements for signs of distraction or confusion. With this information, AI can provide feedback and assistance to students who may be struggling.

AI systems can also analyze performance and engagement data from students to assist instructors in developing more effective CS curriculum and learning activities that cater to the specific needs of individual students. By helping educational institutions identify the most suitable CS programs or interventions and directing their human and financial resources accordingly, AI can support more effective resource allocation.

The data-driven insights and recommendations provided by AI systems for CS classroom management, student support, and overall institutional planning can be beneficial for teachers and administrators. AI can provide valuable guidance based on the analysis of student data, enabling educators to make informed decisions and improve the overall educational experience in CS.

Logic

Adaptive learning systems offer the flexibility to adjust the complexity and pace of learning activities based on student performance, allowing students to learn at their own pace and proficiency level. AI logic plays a crucial role in efficiently and accurately grading tests and assignments, enabling teachers to dedicate more time to providing feedback and developing CS lesson plans.

Intelligent tutoring programs powered by AI logic can provide personalized education and feedback tailored to each student's individual learning needs and preferences. These programs can break down complex topics into simpler ones, guiding students through the learning process and helping them develop problem-solving skills.

Artificial reasoning can be utilized to support language acquisition by providing students with immediate feedback on their speech and grammar. Through this feedback, students can enhance their understanding and proficiency in a second language.

AI SUBFIELDS AND CS

This section examines the application fields of AI within the field of CS. It focuses on specific aspects of CS that are highly relevant to the computer world, including robots, data mining, cloud computing, image data processing, and NLP. These areas are highlighted due to their significance and their impact on the vast discipline of CS.

Machine Learning

ML, which is a subset of AI, involves the development of algorithms and statistical models. These algorithms and models enable machines to learn from data and enhance their performance through experience. By analyzing patterns and making predictions or decisions based on the data, ML algorithms can adapt and improve over time. This iterative learning process allows machines to make accurate predictions, classify data, recognize patterns, and automate tasks without explicit programming instructions.

Deep Learning

Recurrent Neural Network

Recurrent neural networks (RNNs), a subclass of artificial neural networks (ANNs), excel at processing sequential input. They have proven to be effective in various NLP tasks such as text categorization, sentiment analysis, and language translation. In the context of CS education, RNNs can be valuable tools for CS teachers in understanding and analyzing students' written work, providing personalized suggestions, and assessing the quality of their assignments. They can also be employed in speech recognition tasks, such as transcribing CS lectures and analyzing classroom discussions. RNNs can be used for time series forecasting, enabling teachers to predict students' future performance based on their past academic achievements. This helps identify students who may need additional support or intervention. Additionally, RNNs can be applied to develop recommender systems that deliver CS instructional content tailored to students' learning preferences and past experiences. Lastly, RNNs can be utilized in designing intelligent tutoring programs that adapt to students' learning styles and progress, providing personalized feedback and guidance along their learning journey.

Convolutional Neural Network

Convolutional neural networks (CNNs), a type of ANN, excel at processing images and videos. They can be used for activities such as image detection and recognition, and recognizing objects in still or moving images. This is essential for students taking scientific or engineering courses, as they must learn and understand complex schematics or images. CNNs can also be used to identify students in a classroom and for other activities that require facial recognition. This can make it easier for teachers to monitor student engagement and behavior while keeping track of attendance.

CNNs can be used to create CS educational apps for augmented and virtual reality. For example, CNNs can be used to create 3D reconstructions of historical sites or scientific events, which students can then interact with in an immersive and interactive way. CNNs are also beneficial for tasks involving document analysis, such as text and handwriting recognition in scanned documents. This can be helpful in language or literature studies, when students are expected to read and comprehend historical content.

CNNs can also be used to create instructional videos or image games. For example, CNNs can be used to create a game that teaches children animal taxonomy and helps them identify different species based on their visual cues.

Predictive Analysis

Predictive analytics is a process that uses data, statistical methods, and AI techniques to estimate the likelihood of future events based on previous data. In education, predictive analytics can be used for a variety of purposes, such as:

- *Predicting student academic progress:* By analyzing data such as attendance, grades, and behavior, predictive analytics can be used to identify students who are at risk of falling behind. This information can then be used to provide these students with the support they need to succeed.
- *Determining the most effective resources:* Predictive analytics can also be used to determine which resources—such as CS books or technology—will have the biggest impact on student outcomes. This information can help teachers allocate resources more efficiently and effectively.
- *Scheduling courses:* Predictive analytics can be used to determine which courses should be offered when, based on data from previous enrollments. This can help colleges and universities better serve the needs of their students and ensure that courses are offered at times that are convenient for most students.
- *Identifying students at risk of dropping out:* Predictive analytics can be used to identify students who are at risk of dropping out or failing to complete their degrees on schedule. This information can then be used to develop interventions that increase retention and graduation rates.
- *Determining which students need financial assistance:* Predictive analytics can be used to determine which students require the most financial assistance based on factors such as academic achievement and family income. This information can help organizations distribute financial donations more effectively and fairly.

Supervised Learning

In supervised learning, a type of AI, an algorithm is trained to make predictions or make classifications on new, unseen data using labeled training data. It can be used to develop personalized learning strategies for students based on their learning preferences and skills. For each student, the algorithm can use grades, test results, and learning progress to decide which CS educational materials and methods are optimal. It can be used to build testing systems that adjust the level of difficulty of the questions based on how well a student performs. This type of evaluation could give a more realistic picture of a student's skills.

It can also be used to create recommender systems that provide students with suggestions for CS courses or learning materials based on their prior academic experiences and interests. It is possible to assess CS students' writing style, grammar, and coherence by looking at written works like essays or research papers. It is also feasible to assess images or videos in academic settings. For example, an algorithm could be used to recognize objects or patterns in images captured using a microscope to support scientific research.

Unsupervised Learning

Unsupervised learning is the process of teaching an algorithm to discover patterns and connections on its own using unlabeled data. It can be used to group students based on how well they perform or how they learn best. By gaining a better understanding of their students' needs and preferences, this can help CS teachers in creating more individualized learning strategies.

It can also be used to find CS concepts and topics in large amounts of content, such as research papers or student essays. Professors can use this to quickly discover important problems and advancements in their field of study.

With student data, it can identify anomalous trends or behaviors, such as plagiarism or dishonesty. This can help instructors identify any issues with academic integrity and take the necessary measures.

Recommendation systems that offer CS courses, books, or learning materials based on students' behaviors or interests can be created. It can also be used to produce visualizations that help educators and students explore large amounts of data. For instance, an algorithm can identify trends in student performance data and provide a graphic that helps teachers quickly identify areas that need improvement.

Reinforcement Learning

A type of AI called reinforcement learning teaches an agent to make decisions in response to the outcomes of its actions in a particular environment. It can be used to design intricate CS tutoring programs that provide students with individualized feedback and guidance. The system can adjust its suggestions in response to the student's progress to ensure that the student is continuously challenged without being overwhelmed.

It can also be used to create CS educational games that adapt based on how well the player does. The game can adjust the challenge level and provide feedback based on the player's actions, allowing them to advance and learn. It can be used to develop classroom management programs that give teachers quick feedback on their educational decisions and student behavior. The algorithm can identify previous mistakes and adjust its suggestions accordingly.

It can also be used to develop frameworks that improve student engagement and motivation. The possibility of receiving rewards and feedback based on their involvement and performance motivates students to remain attentive and involved. Finding the best CS teaching strategies and tools can enhance curriculum development. The CS curriculum can be updated in order to provide students with the best education possible based on what the system has learned through student data.

Neural Network

In computer education, ANNs offer a wide range of potential applications. Inspired by the biological neural networks of the human brain, ANNs are computer systems that can be trained on large datasets to identify patterns and relationships. This makes them highly valuable for tasks such as image recognition, NLP, and prediction.

One application of ANNs in computer education is personalized instruction. By analyzing data on CS students' learning preferences, abilities, and weaknesses, ANNs can create individualized learning programs and provide tailored learning materials that are most effective for each student. This approach has the potential to enhance student engagement and retention, leading to improved learning outcomes.

Another use of ANNs in computer education is predictive analysis. By examining historical data on students' academic performance, ANNs can estimate future academic success or identify students who may be at risk of dropping out. This information can be utilized by teachers to offer customized interventions and support to each student, ensuring their academic success.

ANNs can be employed to develop intelligent learning systems. These systems monitor student performance and provide real-time feedback and guidance, similar to a human instructor. This enables teachers to deliver personalized learning experiences that cater to the individual needs and preferences of each student.

Natural Language Processing

NLP algorithms can be utilized to evaluate CS student writings and provide feedback on various aspects, including coherence, vocabulary, and grammar. This approach can enhance grading consistency and objectivity while also saving instructors' time. Additionally, interactive language learning tools can be developed to allow students to practice speaking, listening, reading, and writing in a foreign language. NLP-based chatbots, for example, can simulate conversations with native speakers and offer immediate feedback on vocabulary and syntax.

NLP can enable instant responses to students' questions on a range of CS subjects, such as data structures, computer algorithms, computer architecture and organization, and automata theory. This frees up teachers' time, allowing them to provide more personalized instruction and promptly address student inquiries. By examining student comments and feedback, areas for improvement in the curriculum, instruction, or learning environment can be identified. CS research articles, textbooks, and online course materials serve as valuable sources of educational text data that can be analyzed to uncover patterns and insights that can inform curriculum development and instructional practices.

Machine Translation

Machine translation (MT) holds the potential to enhance classroom communication and language acquisition. Through this process, textbooks and online resources can be translated into multiple languages, offering significant benefits to international students and non-native speakers studying in foreign countries.

MT can be employed to provide translations of vocabulary words, phrases, and sentences in foreign language classrooms. When integrated with other language learning tools and activities, this can aid students in more effectively learning and practicing the language. Additionally, international students can utilize MT to communicate with classmates or professors who do not speak their language, fostering linguistic exchange and creating an inclusive learning environment.

MT can be used to offer CS course materials in students' preferred language, providing them with the option to access materials in the language they are most comfortable with. This is particularly valuable for CS courses with a global focus, such as CS and applications, cultural studies, or international business. Additionally, MT can be employed to transform instructional materials into sign language or other accessible formats, catering to the needs of students with disabilities or special requirements.

Classification and Clustering

The use of NLP classification and clustering methods for evaluating and organizing educational data can enhance learning outcomes and resource management. By analyzing data on student performance, such as test scores and attendance records, trends and factors influencing academic achievement can be identified. This enables CS educators and administrators to customize the CS curriculum and support to meet the specific needs of students.

NLP can also be applied to identify recurring themes and subjects in educational literature, including course materials and textbooks. This helps in constructing a comprehensive and up-to-date CS curriculum. Additionally, it enables the categorization of CS educational resources like online course materials and journal articles based on their content. This facilitates easy access to the most relevant resources for CS instructors and students, optimizing the utilization of course materials.

Likewise, analyzing student-generated data, such as comments on discussion forums and essay responses, can reveal patterns and insights into students' learning processes. This data-driven approach empowers educators and administrators to make informed decisions regarding education and support.

By examining student social network data, including buddy networks and communication patterns, CS institutes and classrooms can identify social groups and communities. This aids administrators and educators in gaining a better understanding of the social dynamics among students, allowing them to develop interventions that foster healthy social interactions.

Information Extraction

AI information extraction technology offers various applications, including the analysis of student performance data. Through the use of NLP and AI techniques, these programs can automatically extract and analyze data from student assessments, such as test scores and grades, in order to identify patterns and trends in students' performance. This valuable data can then be utilized by teachers to provide assistance and tailored recommendations to students who may be performing below grade level, addressing their specific learning needs.

AI information extraction technologies can be employed to extract information from CS textbooks, scholarly publications, and other educational materials. For example, an AI-powered application can analyze a textbook and automatically identify key concepts, terms, and illustrations, which can then be used to create study aids and review materials for students. Similarly, an application powered by AI can analyze CS academic journals and research articles to identify relevant findings and insights, which can contribute to improving classroom education and research projects.

By harnessing the capabilities of AI information extraction technology, educators can gain valuable insights from student performance data and educational resources, enabling them to provide personalized support to students and enhance the overall quality of CS education.

Question Answering

NLP question-answering strategies can be utilized by instructors to provide students with automatic responses, allowing them to allocate more time towards delivering personalized instruction. Virtual teaching assistants can be developed using chatbots or voice assistants, enabling instant responses to student inquiries. This is especially beneficial in large CS classrooms where it may be challenging for instructors to address every question individually.

This approach can automate the grading of certain student response types, such as short answer questions..By automating this process, teachers can dedicate more time to providing students with frequent and effective feedback. Integration into online learning systems enables students to receive prompt and accurate responses to their queries, regardless of their location or time zone.

NLP techniques can also be employed to create engaging CS study materials and test preparation resources, aiding students in better understanding the subject matter and preparing for exams. By analyzing student-generated data, such as feedback on discussion forums and essay responses, educators and administrators can identify areas where students have a strong or weak grasp of the CS course material. This enables them to tailor education and assistance more effectively to meet the specific needs of individual students.

Text Generation

NLP text generation algorithms offer the potential to create various CS educational resources, including summaries, study aids, and essays. These algorithms can provide examples of effective sentence patterns, vocabulary usage, and other elements, aiding students in improving their writing skills and producing higher-quality written work.

NLP algorithms can automatically generate summaries of scholarly works such as CS textbooks and journal articles. This saves time for students and helps them grasp the main points and arguments presented in lengthy texts.

These algorithms can suggest studies based on CS course content and student performance data. This aids in exam preparation and enhances understanding of the course material. By leveraging algorithms that consider grammar, syntax, and other aspects of effective writing, NLP can also automatically generate essays on given topics. This provides students with a model of essay structure and composition, saving time and improving their writing abilities.

NLP can be utilized to automatically produce CS instructional materials, including interactive learning modules and exams. This assists teachers and administrators in creating relevant and effective educational materials for their students.

Speech

Recently, computers have improved their ability to comprehend speech and respond to it, allowing people to communicate with them in everyday language. The use of AI is essential to achieving a more complex and organic conversational experience rather than only talking with a machine that offers clear information, even if computers can already recognize, understand, and carry out a preset set of commands.

The richness and naturalness of computer interactions are greatly improved by AI. Computers can now comprehend and interpret human conversation owing to NLP methods, enabling more complex communication. ML and deep learning techniques are used by AI systems, such as chatbots and virtual assistants, to comprehend and produce replies that are human-like.

Computers can assess contextual information, infer intent, and produce pertinent and contextual replies by utilizing AI. As a result, dialogues may be more lively and participatory, which improves how realistic, organic, and human-like computer interaction can seem.

As AI and NLP continue to evolve, computer systems will become more sophisticated and accurate in understanding and responding to human speech. This will eventually improve user experiences and allow for more seamless human-computer interactions.

Speech on Text

Speech-to-text technology has seen significant improvements in recent years, making it a valuable tool for a variety of industries. Some of the key benefits of speech-to-text technology include:

- *Time savings:* Speech-to-text can save users a significant amount of time by eliminating the need to manually transcribe audio recordings. This can be especially beneficial for businesses that need to process large amounts of audio data, such as customer service calls or meeting recordings.
- *Increased efficiency:* Speech-to-text can also help to improve efficiency by allowing users to multitask while they are dictating. For example, a student could dictate notes while they are also listening to a lecture or a business professional could dictate an email while they are also working on other tasks.
- *Accessibility:* Speech-to-text can be a valuable tool for people with disabilities, such as those who are hard of hearing or have limited mobility. It can also be helpful for people who are learning a new language or who have difficulty typing.

While speech-to-text technology has come a long way, there are still some limitations that need to be addressed. For example, speech recognition algorithms can sometimes struggle to understand speech patterns, background noise, and accents. However, as AI and NLP technologies continue to develop, these limitations are likely to be overcome.

Text to Speech

The usage of text-to-speech (TTS) technology in the educational sector is becoming increasingly common. TTS can convert written text into spoken voice, providing students with an alternative way to access CS materials for learning. This technology can simplify the learning process for students with reading disabilities or vision impairments, allowing them to engage in educational activities more easily. By converting written content into spoken voice, TTS technology enables these students to access course materials and participate in class discussions.

TTS technology can also be used to support multilingual learning by allowing students to hear words spoken in different languages. This can enhance students' comprehension and language acquisition skills, particularly in today's globalized society. Additionally, it can assist students in pronouncing words correctly. By listening to the accurate pronunciation of words and phrases, students can practice speaking them aloud, thereby improving their language abilities.

Integrating TTS technology into portable devices provides students with access to CS learning resources while on the go. This is particularly beneficial for students with busy schedules or those attending institutes where flexibility is important. Another application of TTS technology is personalized learning. For example, teachers can create audio recordings of course materials that can be customized to accommodate each student's learning styles and preferences.

By incorporating TTS technology into the educational setting, students can have increased access to CS learning materials and tailored learning experiences, promoting inclusivity and enhancing their educational journey.

Vision

As computers become increasingly proficient at understanding verbal instructions, their ability to recall and analyze images is equally fascinating, with numerous applications ranging from security to visual creativity. Internet giants like Google and Facebook now have access to vast databases of tagged images, and these extensive image datasets are being ingeniously leveraged to develop computer programs that can recognize and interpret visual content, even when encountering it for the first time.

Computer programs can now generate images based on various factors, but AI will greatly enhance this process. AI can aid in the creation of new types of visual aids by utilizing intelligent programs that support users through visual analytics and provide suggestions for understanding and organizing data. Artificial vision technologies offer a multitude of educational applications, ranging from improving learning outcomes to enhancing the learning environment.

Facial recognition is another application of artificial vision technology (AVT), making it easier for teachers to monitor student behavior and track attendance. This can assist with classroom management and provide valuable insights into student performance and engagement. It can also be used to customize learning opportunities for individual students. For example, facial recognition software can track students' eye movements and identify areas of difficulty, allowing teaching methods to be adjusted and targeted assistance to be provided.

With the help of AVT, students can experience realistic virtual reality, enabling them to learn about CS, IT, historical landmarks, scientific advancements, and other subjects in a fun and informative manner. Additionally, it has the potential to enhance student safety by identifying potentially hazardous situations and identifying students who may be at risk. This can help educational institutions effectively address security concerns and provide assistance to students in need (Figure 10).

AVT can contribute to making classrooms more accessible for students with impairments. For instance, text-based materials can be translated into sign language or other visual forms of communication using AVT (Figure 11 and Table 2).

By harnessing the power of AI and AVT, educational institutions can unlock a range of possibilities to enhance learning, improve safety, and create more inclusive and accessible environments for students.

Figure 10. Identification of student vision in the classroom and gathering of pertinent characteristics for subsequent AI analysis

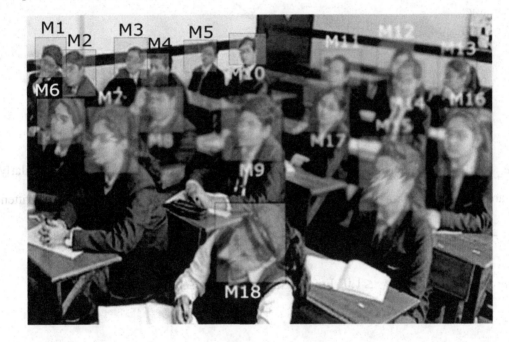

Table 2. Identification of student facial traits and calculation of their associated values, which range from 0.0 to 1.00

Image	x_nose	x_eye	x_shoulder	x_mouth	x_facesize	x_forehead	x_chinsize
M1	0.14	0.26	0.32	0.29	0.21	0.11	0.16
M2	0.78	0.89	0.98	0.79	0.81	0.88	0.99
M3	0.45	0.58	0.65	0.39	0.57	0.54	0.50
M4	0.68	0.79	0.89	0.99	0.88	0.86	0.88
...	...	...	...	...	...	...	...
M18	0.98	0.99	0.98	0.95	0.94	0.99	1.00

Figure 11. Visualization of student facial feature extraction and related value extraction in a classroom

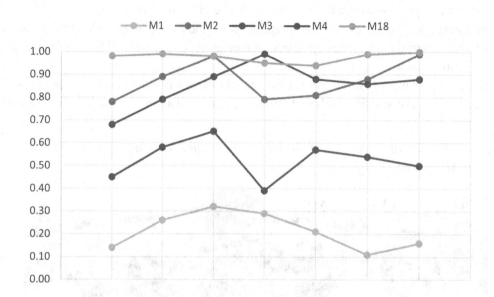

Let e_{x_1} and e_{y_1} are distance from x-axis and y-axis respectively of point $P_1\left(e_{x_1}, e_{y_1}\right)$. Similarly, e_{x_2} and e_{y_2} are distance from x-axis and y-axis respectively of point $P_2\left(e_{x_2}, e_{y_2}\right)$. Hence, we written as,

$$d_{e_x} = e_{x_2} - e_{x_1}, d_{e_y} = e_{y_2} - e_{y_1}, d = d_{e_y} - d_{e_x} \tag{1}$$

Where $0.0 \le e_{x_2}, e_{x_1}, e_{y_2}, e_{y_1} \le 1.0$. Eq. (1) graphically represented in Figure 12.

Figure 12. Identifying the real face of a student in a classroom by measuring various facial feature-specific points

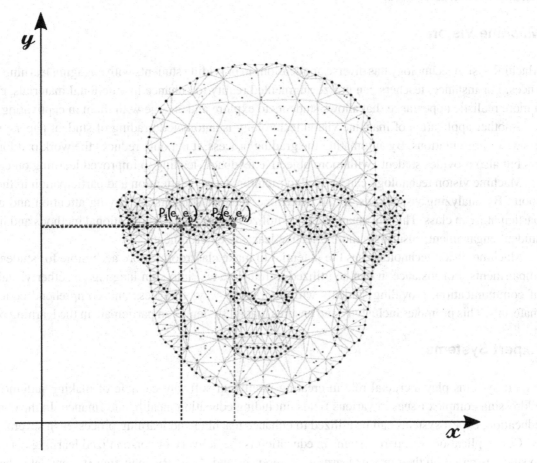

Image Recognition

Image recognition technology has various applications in education that can enhance the learning process and improve learning outcomes. One application is to provide students with captivating visual learning opportunities. Teachers can utilize augmented reality to bring static images to life, offering students a more immersive and engaging experience with the CS material they are studying.

Image recognition technology can also be used to identify objects in instructional visuals, enabling teachers to quickly and accurately classify information. This faster and more accurate categorization process can lead to improved learning outcomes. Additionally, it can be employed to automatically evaluate multiple-choice tests or arithmetic problems. By providing students with rapid feedback and saving teachers' time, this technology can enhance learning results.

Another application of image recognition technology in education is monitoring students' attention and participation in class. The information gathered can be utilized to improve CS educational methods and enhance student engagement. Image recognition technology has the potential to increase student safety by identifying potentially hazardous situations and identifying students who may be at risk. This can assist educational institutions in effectively managing security-related concerns and providing assistance to students in need.

Machine Vision

Machine vision technology has diverse applications in providing students with engaging learning experiences. For instance, teachers can utilize augmented reality to enhance instructional materials, creating a more realistic appearance that allows students to explore and engage with them in captivating ways.

Another application of machine vision technology is automated grading of student papers, such as essays or presentations. By automating the grading process, it not only reduces the workload for teachers but also provides students with more objective feedback, leading to improved learning outcomes.

Machine vision technology can be used to monitor students' attention and participation in the classroom. By analyzing visual cues, it can determine whether students are paying attention and actively participating in class. This information can be utilized to enhance CS educational methods and improve student engagement, ensuring a more effective learning environment.

Machine vision technology has the potential to make classrooms more accessible for students with impairments. For instance, it can be utilized to translate text into sign language or other visual forms of communication, providing students with alternative ways to access and comprehend educational materials. This promotes inclusivity and ensures that all students can participate in the learning process.

Expert Systems

Expert systems play a crucial role in creating intelligent software capable of making judgments and addressing complex issues in various fields, including education, health, and finance. In the context of education, expert systems can be utilized to enhance teaching and learning processes in several ways.

One application of expert systems in education is the delivery of personalized learning experiences to students based on their unique learning preferences and skills. By analyzing student data, these systems can provide tailored recommendations for further study or practice, ensuring that students receive individualized instruction aligned with their specific needs.

Expert systems can be employed to offer students individualized instruction by identifying their strengths and weaknesses and providing personalized feedback and guidance. This helps students address their areas of improvement while building on their strengths, leading to enhanced learning outcomes.

Expert systems also support teachers in evaluating student learning and providing feedback. By analyzing student responses and performance data, these systems can offer insights into students' strengths and weaknesses, enabling teachers to adjust their teaching strategies accordingly. This feedback-driven approach enhances the effectiveness of pedagogical tactics and contributes to improved learning outcomes.

Expert systems can be utilized in curriculum development, ensuring that CS courses are aligned with student requirements and informed by the latest research findings. These systems can analyze data on student performance and educational research to support educators and administrators in creating or modifying CS courses, ensuring their relevance, effectiveness, and currency.

Expert systems can assist educators and administrators in decision-making processes. By analyzing data on student performance and resource allocation, these systems can provide valuable insights and recommendations, aiding in informed decision-making regarding teaching approaches, resource distribution, and overall educational management.

Planning, Scheduling, and Optimization

AI planning, scheduling, and optimization have the potential to revolutionize education by delivering personalized learning experiences, maximizing resource allocation, and increasing student achievement. One application is providing individualized learning opportunities, where these systems assess student data, such as learning preferences, strengths, and weaknesses, and offer personalized suggestions for further study or practice. This is particularly useful for managing CS educational resources, including classrooms, lecturers, and equipment, as these systems can optimize resource allocation to ensure effective and efficient utilization.

These technologies can be used to design optimal CS course schedules that consider student demands, teacher availability, and resource constraints. By leveraging AI planning and optimization, these systems can help teachers deliver their CS lessons effectively and ensure students have access to the courses they need. They can also generate effective test schedules that avoid conflicts and allow sufficient study time, ultimately improving students' academic achievement. Through analyzing student data, these tools provide guidance on the best study methods, CS course selection, and exam preparation.

Robotics and Motion

Robots have the potential to enhance education by creating more engaging and interactive learning experiences. They can be utilized to teach CS subjects in a fun and enduring manner. For example, robots can be programmed to perform simple tasks like sorting, stacking, and counting, making subjects such as CS, IT, algebra, geometry, and physics more enjoyable and entertaining for students through games and activities.

Robots can be used to evaluate student data and provide personalized feedback to each student. This enables teachers to identify learning gaps in individual students and offer targeted interventions to help them catch up. Robots like LEGO Mindstorms can be employed to teach students the fundamentals of coding and programming. By programming robots to move, turn, and complete tasks, students can develop their computational thinking skills.

Robots can assess students' movement and provide feedback on their abilities. This is particularly valuable in CS and physical education programs when students are learning specific skills, such as computer programming or performing physical activities like tossing a ball or doing a cartwheel. Moreover, robots can offer additional support to students outside the classroom. These systems can be designed to provide individualized feedback and coaching based on each student's learning preferences and pace.

Cognitive Computing

Cognitive computing, which encompasses AI and other advanced technologies, aims to simulate human cognitive processes such as perception, reasoning, and decision-making. One application of cognitive computing is providing students with personalized learning opportunities. These systems can assess student data and adapt training and delivery methods to meet each student's specific needs.

Another use of cognitive computing is analyzing student data to identify patterns and trends in behavior and performance. This information can be utilized to identify at-risk students and implement targeted interventions. Additionally, cognitive computing can contribute to the development of tools for studying and interpreting natural language. NLP techniques can be employed to create chatbots capable of responding to student inquiries and providing personalized advice.

Interactive CS tutoring programs can also be created using cognitive computing, engaging students and offering tailored feedback based on their performance. Moreover, cognitive computing can assist in selecting CS instructional content and suggesting it to students based on their interests and learning objectives. Virtual assistants powered by cognitive computing can aid students with tasks such as scheduling, note-taking, and reminding them of due dates.

Cloud Computing

The advent of cloud computing has revolutionized the way data is stored and accessed. Instead of relying on traditional physical storage that is limited to a single location, cloud storage allows data to be stored in the cloud and accessed from multiple locations. This shift in data accessibility has led to innovative solutions and enhanced collaboration.

Cloud-based solutions like Google Drive, Microsoft Teams, and Dropbox facilitate seamless collaboration among teachers and students. Students can work together in real time on papers and projects, enabling more effective collaboration. Cloud computing can be utilized to host online learning environments where students can access CS course materials, including lectures, tests, and assignments. Platforms such as Coursera, Udemy, and edX serve as examples of cloud-based e-learning portals.

Cloud storage options like Google Drive, Dropbox, and OneDrive provide convenient and secure storage for duplicates of CS homework, research papers, and study resources like textbooks. Moreover, cloud computing can be employed to create virtual desktop environments, enabling instructors and students to access information from any location and on any device. This ensures that CS resources for education are accessible to students both at home and on the go.

In the field of education, various data sets, including student data, can be analyzed to gain insights into student performance and identify areas for improvement. Cloud computing provides the infrastructure and tools necessary for efficient data analysis, enabling educators to make data-driven decisions and enhance the learning experience.

Data Mining

Data mining is the process of filtering and studying data to uncover patterns, anomalies, or other valuable insights within vast amounts of information. AI has the potential to enhance this process by making it more efficient and uncovering unexpected findings that can aid students in analyzing data and making informed decisions. The practice of mining large databases for patterns and insights is commonly referred to as "data mining."

In the field of education, data mining can be utilized to analyze student data and forecast student performance, thereby identifying students who may require additional support. By analyzing student data, patterns in student learning can be identified, enabling the development of CS educational resources and courses tailored to students' needs. Data mining can be employed to examine student data and uncover trends in behavior and performance, such as engagement patterns and success rates. Additionally, data from CS educational research can be analyzed using data mining techniques to identify patterns and insights that can inform educational practices and policies.

By utilizing AI and data mining techniques, educators can gain valuable insights from student data, which can be used to personalize learning experiences, improve educational resources, and make data-driven decisions to enhance student outcomes. Data mining offers the potential to unlock valuable information hidden within large datasets, ultimately benefiting students and the field of education as a whole.

Self-Modifying Coding

AI self-modifying code refers to software that has the ability to change and adapt based on its environment and the data it receives. One application of this technology is providing students with individualized learning opportunities. The code can analyze a student's strengths and weaknesses and modify the CS course content to meet their specific needs. This personalized approach enables students to learn more effectively and efficiently.

Another benefit of AI self-modifying code is its ability to evaluate data in real-time, allowing for immediate feedback to be provided to students as they study. This timely and helpful feedback can keep students motivated and engaged in their learning. Additionally, the code can dynamically adjust CS curricula to respond to environmental changes. For example, if there is a significant shift in the job market, the code can adapt the course requirements to ensure students are learning the skills that are in demand.

With the use of data analysis, AI self-modifying code can anticipate student outcomes. By analyzing various factors, the system can identify students who are at risk of dropping out and take proactive measures to support and guide them, improving their chances of academic success.

AI APPLICATION IN CS SUBJECT

In this section, we have explored various CS subjects and their connection to AI in order to advance the CS educational system. We have discussed topics such as automata, data structures, graph theory, sorting algorithms, search-based problem solving, and AI-based evaluation in CS.

Automata

In contrast to AI, automata are studied differently in CS. AI involves the process of creating algorithms and systems capable of performing tasks that traditionally require human intellect, such as perception, reasoning, and learning. Automata, on the other hand, focuses on the study of abstract machines or computer processes.

However, there are similarities between these fields. Automata theory is utilized to study the properties of formal grammars and languages, which serve as the foundation for many AI paradigms, including NLP and AI itself. Automata theory provides a theoretical framework for understanding the limits of what can be computed by machines and algorithms.

AI can be applied to automate various tasks in automation, including software and hardware system verification. For example, the use of AI algorithms to automatically generate test cases or improve the performance of an automata-based system demonstrates how AI can be employed in this context.

Data Structure

Two fundamental topics in CS are data structures and AI. Data structures play a crucial role in efficiently organizing and storing data, while AI focuses on creating algorithms and systems that can learn from data and make intelligent decisions.

Data structures are essential for representing and manipulating data within the realm of AI. Arrays, lists, stacks, queues, trees, graphs, and hash tables are some of the commonly used data structures in AI. These data structures facilitate the storage and processing of large volumes of data, such as sensor data, images, audio, and text. In AI, data structures are employed in conjunction with techniques like deep learning to train models and make predictions. Deep learning models, specifically neural networks, utilize matrices to store the weights and biases of the neurons. These matrices are adjusted during the training process based on the input data and desired outcomes.

Decision trees are another type of AI system used to address classification problems. They represent their decision rules and hierarchical classification criteria using tree data structures.

Graph Theory

Two fundamental areas in CS are graph theory and AI. Graph theory focuses on the study of mathematical structures called graphs, which consist of nodes and edges and are used to model relationships between objects. On the other hand, AI aims to develop algorithms and systems that can reason logically and learn from data.

Graph theory plays a crucial role in modelling and analyzing complex data structures within the field of AI, such as social networks, websites, and gene regulatory networks. It provides a variety of tools and techniques for studying network structures, including measures of connectedness, centrality, and community structure. Graph theory, combined with other AI methods, is employed in deep learning to model and predict connections between objects. Specifically, a type of deep learning system called "graph neural networks" utilizes graphs as a representation for data analysis. In these networks, the edges of the graph represent connections between objects, while each node represents an individual object. Through the graph structure, the neural network learns to predict properties of the nodes.

Graph algorithms are also used for clustering and community detection, which involves identifying groups of similar or interconnected objects. These algorithms can be applied to search for collections of students or web pages with shared interests or characteristics within social networks or websites.

Sorting Algorithms

Two significant areas in CS are sorting algorithms and AI. Sorting algorithms are used to arrange elements in a specific order, such as numerical or alphabetical order, while AI focuses on developing algorithms and systems that can perform cognitive tasks like perception, logic, and learning.

In the context of AI, classification algorithms can be used as a pre-processing step to structure unstructured data before applying AI or deep learning algorithms. Pre-processing involves organizing and categorizing data, which can enhance the effectiveness and accuracy of learning systems. For example, sorting algorithms can be employed in NLP to group terms in a text based on frequency or alphabetical order. This can facilitate the identification of key words and phrases that can be utilized to train AI systems for tasks like sentiment analysis or text categorization.

The application of AI can also improve the effectiveness of ranking algorithms. Genetic algorithms, for instance, can be employed to optimize parameters of classification algorithms, such as the number of comparisons or swaps, resulting in faster and more efficient sorting processes. Additionally, neural networks can learn classification algorithms from data. By training a neural network using input-output pairs, where the input is a random list of integers and the output is an ordered list, the neural network can adjust the weights and biases of its neurons to learn the categorization process.

Problems Solving by Search

AI encompasses various applications that involve problem solving through search, a branch of AI dedicated to developing algorithms that explore potential solutions within a given space. One application of search algorithms is finding the shortest path between two locations in a network, such as a road or computer network. This is useful for tasks like optimizing data routing across a network or designing efficient transportation routes.

Another application is planning a sequence of actions to achieve a specific goal. This is utilized in various domains, including supply chain optimization and industrial process planning. Search algorithms can explore the space of possible actions and select the optimal moves in games such as chess and Go.

Search algorithms can be used to explore potential solutions to optimization problems and identify the best possible response. This has wide-ranging applications, such as streamlining production processes and selecting optimal settings for AI models.

CS Subject Evaluation by AI

AI can be utilized in various ways to assess CS training effectively. One common approach is the automatic evaluation of exams and assignments using AI algorithms. This is particularly valuable in large classes where it can be challenging or time-consuming for teachers to individually assess each submission.

Another application is the analysis of essays or writing assignments using NLP techniques. By programming AI algorithms to identify recurring themes and flaws in student writing, valuable feedback and suggestions can be provided to help students refine their work. This personalized feedback contributes to individualized learning experiences, as AI systems can recommend specific exercises, books, or resources tailored to each student's strengths and weaknesses.

By utilizing AI to track and analyze student performance over time, teachers can identify areas where students may be struggling and adjust their instruction accordingly. This ensures that all students receive the necessary support to succeed in their CS studies.

ACADEMIC GROUP DEVELOP AI TOOLS FOR CS

Academic institutions play a crucial role in the development of AI technologies due to their access to cutting-edge research, talented students, and resources. These institutions often form academic teams that adopt a research-oriented methodology to create AI tools. This process involves conducting experiments, analyzing data, and iteratively improving the tools based on the findings. Collaboration among experts from disciplines such as CS, mathematics, statistics, and engineering is typically necessary to drive innovation in AI.

AI is a prominent area of research for academic teams engaged in developing AI systems. It involves training computers to identify patterns in data and make informed decisions or predictions based on those patterns. Additionally, academic institutions focus on exploring topics such as NLP, computer vision, and robotics to advance the field of AI.

In addition to technology development, academic institutions also contribute to the testing, analysis, and research of AI technologies' usefulness, safety, ethical implications, and societal impact. This is crucial because AI technologies have the potential to significantly influence various aspects of society, including economics, law, healthcare, and education.

ADVANCING AI IN CS: A PROMISING METHODOLOGY FOR FUTURE SUCCESS

There is evidence to support the argument that the suggested technique will be effective in advancing the area of AI in CS based on a study of the benefits it has over the existing one. First off, the suggested approach stresses the creation of increasingly advanced AI approaches and algorithms. The possibility of attaining substantial breakthroughs in AI capabilities, such as greater accuracy, improved learning skills, and more effective data processing, is increased by investing in research and innovation in this field. This might result in innovations in fields like machine learning, computer vision, and natural language processing, allowing AI systems to carry out complicated tasks with greater accuracy and efficiency.

Additionally, the emphasis on resolving the constraints of AI, notably in establishing artificial general intelligence and sub-symbolic thinking, shows a deliberate approach to overcoming present difficulties. Researchers can take use of the benefits of both methodologies by studying the topic of neurosymbolic AI, which tries to combine sub-symbolic and symbolic reasoning techniques, and perhaps open up new avenues for AI systems.

The emphasis on moral issues and societal consequences of the suggested strategy is another benefit. The suggested approach solves issues with biases, privacy, and security by giving justice, transparency, and accountability a high priority in AI systems. This proactive strategy not only makes sure that AI technologies are developed and used responsibly, but it also increases public confidence in AI systems.

Additionally, the projected fusion of AI with other cutting-edge technologies, such edge computing, blockchain, and Internet of Things, provides a number of benefits. AI systems can gain from improved connectivity, real-time data processing, and distributed computing capabilities by utilizing the synergies between these technologies. This makes it possible for AI applications to be more effective and scalable, especially in fields like autonomous systems, smart cities, and healthcare.

The importance of multidisciplinary collaboration and knowledge sharing also acknowledges the worth of many viewpoints and specializations. The suggested strategy encourages cross-disciplinary partnerships amongst AI researchers, computer scientists, cognitive scientists, psychologists, and domain specialists, which encourages a holistic approach to problem-solving.

These benefits provide as a solid basis for the success of the suggested strategy when taken all at once. The field of AI in CS can make significant progress by utilizing cutting-edge algorithms, addressing constraints, taking ethical considerations into account, integrating with other technologies, and encouraging interdisciplinary collaboration. This will result in more advanced and responsible AI systems with significant societal benefits.

AI CHALLENGES TO IMPLEMENT IN CS

Image recognition is indeed a complex task that involves creating algorithms capable of accurately identifying individuals or objects in images. Developing a robust and accurate system for classifying various animal species, for example, can pose challenges due to variations in appearances, backgrounds, and species diversity.

NLP is a challenging field that focuses on developing computer programs capable of understanding and interpreting human language. Building chatbots that can accurately answer client questions requires advanced language comprehension and context understanding, which can be difficult to achieve.

Recommender systems aim to provide personalized recommendations based on users' past behavior. Developing a recommender system that can accurately predict which movies a user would like is a complex task due to the diverse preferences and evolving tastes of users.

Autonomous navigation involves developing algorithms to enable robots or self-driving vehicles to navigate their environments safely and efficiently. Building an autonomous navigation system capable of effectively maneuvering through crowded cities poses significant challenges, including real-time perception, obstacle avoidance, and decision-making.

Game AI focuses on creating algorithms that can play games expertly. Mastering complex strategic games like Go or Chess is a challenging task that requires advanced algorithms capable of analyzing and predicting various game scenarios.

Fraud detection algorithms are designed to identify fraudulent behavior in financial transactions. Building an effective system for detecting and preventing credit card theft requires sophisticated algorithms that can detect patterns and anomalies amidst vast amounts of transaction data.

Predictive analytics involves developing formulas to forecast future events based on historical data. Building a predictive analytics system that accurately predicts which clients are likely to cancel their membership to a service can be challenging due to the multitude of factors influencing customer behavior.

FUTURE OBJECTIVES

To increase the functionality and performance of AI systems, more improvements in AI algorithms and approaches are required. This include improving computer vision methods, optimizing NLP algorithms, and creating more complex deep learning models. Research initiatives should also concentrate on resolving the constraints of AI, such as the difficulties in attaining artificial general intelligence and sub-symbolic thinking. A possible approach to fusing sub-symbolic and symbolic thinking techniques is the research of neurosymbolic AI.

Enhancing the ethical issues and societal effects of AI in CS is another future goal. This entails creating strong structures to guarantee the impartiality, openness, and accountability of AI algorithms and decision-making procedures. Additionally, researchers should investigate possible dangers related to AI, such as biases, privacy issues, and security vulnerabilities, and create mitigation plans for them. It is essential for academics, business, and legislators to work together to set rules and laws that control the ethical development and application of AI technology.

Future research should concentrate on the integration of AI with other cutting-edge technologies like edge computing, blockchain, and the Internet of Things (IoT) in order to develop intelligent and autonomous systems. In order to improve data processing efficiency, real-time decision-making, and seamless communication, this includes investigating the synergies between AI and these technologies.

Multidisciplinary cooperation and information sharing should be prioritized in the field of AI in CS. AI researchers, computer scientists, cognitive scientists, psychologists, and subject matter experts working together can make significant advancements in our understanding of human cognition, the creation of more powerful AI models, and the solution of challenging real-world issues. By working toward these long-term goals, the area of AI in CS can develop further, resulting in novel applications, enhanced performance, and the ethical and responsible integration of AI technology across a range of fields.

CONCLUSION

AI fuzzy logic can indeed be utilized in CS education to customize instruction, evaluate student data, and uncover trends and patterns. By applying fuzzy logic, educational policies and decision-making can be informed by considering the uncertainties and ambiguities inherent in educational data. AI data mining, coupled with predictive analytics, can provide valuable insights into student success, enrollment patterns, demographics, and academic performance. It enables the identification of at-risk students and informs policy decisions by mining academic research data.

Distributed AI can analyze large datasets in CS education, providing personalized instruction, creating flexible learning environments, and improving student performance. Real-time reasoning and temporal thinking capabilities of AI can assess the long-term effectiveness of educational programs and identify areas for improvement. AI, combined with cognitive science, can assess students' cognitive abilities and offer individualized learning opportunities. By leveraging AI and cognitive science, tailored training plans can be created for CS students based on their unique needs and preferences.

AI search methods and qualitative reasoning are employed to explore the search space, infer system behavior, identify misunderstandings, and provide feedback and assistance to students. Intelligent tutoring systems utilize AI to customize instruction, break down complex problems, teach problem-solving strategies, and assist in second language acquisition.

Statistical methods and AI algorithms can estimate the likelihood of future events, helping to identify at-risk CS students and provide appropriate support. Additionally, indicators such as academic standing and family income can be used to determine students in need of financial assistance. Supervised learning allows algorithms to make predictions and categorize new data based on labeled training data. This can be applied to personalize learning strategies, develop adaptive testing systems, create recommender systems for CS courses, and evaluate students' writing style and coherence.

NLP algorithms improve grading consistency, assess student writings, and provide feedback, saving professors' time. Machine translation, classification, and clustering enhance communication, learning outcomes, and resource management. AI information extraction techniques organize learning resources, analyze student performance data, discover patterns in learning behaviors, and extract valuable insights from educational literature.

NLP text generation algorithms contribute to creating engaging CS study materials, virtual teaching assistants, summarizations of student-provided data, and automated generation of summaries, study guides, and essays. These AI applications enhance various aspects of CS education, promoting personalized learning experiences and improving educational outcomes.

REFERENCES

Abalkheel, A. (2022). Amalgamating Bloom's taxonomy and artificial intelligence to face the challenges of online EFL learning amid post-COVID-19 in Saudi Arabia. *International Journal of English Language and Literature Studies, 11*(1), 16–30. doi:10.18488/5019.v11i1.4409

Adams, C., Pente, P., Lemermeyer, G., & Rockwell, G. (2023). Ethical principles for artificial intelligence in K-12 education. *Computers and Education: Artificial Intelligence, 100131.*

Akgun, S., & Greenhow, C. (2021). Artificial intelligence in education: Addressing ethical challenges in K-12 settings. *AI and Ethics,* 1–10. PMID:34790956

Alam, A. (2021, December). Should robots replace teachers? Mobilisation of AI and learning analytics in education. In *2021 International Conference on Advances in Computing, Communication, and Control (ICAC3)* (pp. 1-12). IEEE. 10.1109/ICAC353642.2021.9697300

Atmatzidou, S., & Demetriadis, S. (2016). Advancing students' computational thinking skills through educational robotics: A study on age and gender relevant differences. *Robotics and Autonomous Systems, 75,* 661–670. doi:10.1016/j.robot.2015.10.008

Below, J. L., Skinner, C. H., Fearrington, J. Y., & Sorrell, C. A. (2010). Gender differences in early literacy: Analysis of kindergarten through fifth-grade dynamic indicators of basic early literacy skills probes. *School Psychology Review, 39*(2), 240–257. doi:10.1080/02796015.2010.12087776

Buckingham, D. (2013). *Beyond technology: Children's learning in the age of digital culture.* John Wiley & Sons.

Chang, B. (2019). Reflection in learning. *Online Learning : the Official Journal of the Online Learning Consortium, 23*(1), 95–110. doi:10.24059/olj.v23i1.1447

Chassignol, M., Khoroshavin, A., Klimova, A., & Bilyatdinova, A. (2018). Artificial Intelligence trends in education: A narrative overview. *Procedia Computer Science, 136,* 16–24. doi:10.1016/j.procs.2018.08.233

Chen, X., Xie, H., & Hwang, G. J. (2020). A multi-perspective study on artificial intelligence in education: Grants, conferences, journals, software tools, institutions, and researchers. *Computers and Education: Artificial Intelligence, 1,* 100005. doi:10.1016/j.caeai.2020.100005

Choi, M. (2016). A concept analysis of digital citizenship for democratic citizenship education in the internet age. *Theory and Research in Social Education, 44*(4), 565–607. doi:10.1080/00933104.2016.1210549

Chu, S. K. W., Reynolds, R. B., Tavares, N. J., Notari, M., & Lee, C. W. Y. (2021). *21st century skills development through inquiry-based learning from theory to practice.* Springer International Publishing.

Elkin, M., Sullivan, A., & Bers, M. U. (2018). Books, butterflies, and 'bots: Integrating engineering and robotics into early childhood curricula. *Early engineering learning,* 225-248.

Emil, S., & Cress, C. (2014). Faculty perspectives on programme curricular assessment: Individual and institutional characteristics that influence participation engagement. *Assessment & Evaluation in Higher Education, 39*(5), 531–552. doi:10.1080/02602938.2013.855998

Fosch-Villaronga, E., Van der Hof, S., Lutz, C., & Tamò-Larrieux, A. (2021). Toy story or children story? Putting children and their rights at the forefront of the artificial intelligence revolution. *AI & Society*, 1–20. PMID:34642550

George, J., Abraham, A., & Ndakukamo, E. (2023). Futuristic applications of voice user interference on child language development. *Future Technology*, *2*(3), 5–11. doi:10.55670/fpll.futech.2.3.2

Gillio, S., Parasco, A., Forester, K., Bellahsene, T., Berman, K., Fernandez, C., & Tourso, A. (2019). *Technology and its Impact on the Individual*.

Glenn, D. E. A. (2022). *Social Emotional Learning: Teachers' Perceptions and Understandings regarding the Five Social Emotional Learning Competencies* [Doctoral dissertation, College of Saint Elizabeth].

Gomoll, A., Hmelo-Silver, C. E., & Šabanović, S. (2022). Co-constructing professional vision: Teacher and researcher learning in co-design. *Cognition and Instruction*, *40*(1), 7–26. doi:10.1080/07370008.2021.2010210

Greiner, C., Jovy-Klein, F., & Peisl, T. (2021). AI as co-workers: An explorative research on technology acceptance based on the revised Bloom taxonomy. In *Proceedings of the Future Technologies Conference (FTC) 2020, Volume 1* (pp. 27-35). Springer International Publishing.

Grimus, M. (2020). Emerging technologies: Impacting learning, pedagogy and curriculum development. *Emerging technologies and pedagogies in the curriculum*, 127-151.

Guidetti, A. (2023). *Artificial Intelligence as General Purpose Technology: An Empirical and Applied Analysis of Its Perception*.

Harden, R. M. (2001). AMEE Guide No. 21: Curriculum mapping: a tool for transparent and authentic teaching and learning. *Medical Teacher*, *23*(2), 123–137. doi:10.1080/01421590120036547 PMID:11371288

Iivari, N., Sharma, S., & Ventä-Olkkonen, L. (2020). Digital transformation of everyday life–How COVID-19 pandemic transformed the basic education of the young generation and why information management research should care? *International Journal of Information Management*, *55*, 102183. doi:10.1016/j.ijinfomgt.2020.102183 PMID:32836640

Jonassen, D. H. (2000). Toward a design theory of problem solving. *Educational Technology Research and Development*, *48*(4), 63–85. doi:10.1007/BF02300500

Kesidou, S., & Roseman, J. E. (2002). How well do middle school science programs measure up? Findings from Project 2061's curriculum review. *Journal of Research in Science Teaching*, *39*(6), 522–549. doi:10.1002/tea.10035

Kewalramani, S., Kidman, G., & Palaiologou, I. (2021). Using Artificial Intelligence (AI)-interfaced robotic toys in early childhood settings: A case for children's inquiry literacy. *European Early Childhood Education Research Journal*, *29*(5), 652–668. doi:10.1080/1350293X.2021.1968458

Kivunja, C. (2014). Do You Want Your Students to Be Job-Ready with 21st Century Skills? Change Pedagogies: A Pedagogical Paradigm Shift from Vygotskyian Social Constructivism to Critical Thinking, Problem Solving and Siemens' Digital Connectivism. *International Journal of Higher Education*, *3*(3), 81–91. doi:10.5430/ijhe.v3n3p81

Long, D., & Magerko, B. (2020, April). What is AI literacy? Competencies and design considerations. In *Proceedings of the 2020 CHI conference on human factors in computing systems* (pp. 1-16). ACM. 10.1145/3313831.3376727

Luckin, R., Holmes, W., Griffiths, M., & Forcier, L. B. (2016). *Intelligence unleashed: An argument for AI in education.*

Maedche, A., Legner, C., Benlian, A., Berger, B., Gimpel, H., Hess, T., Hinz, O., Morana, S., & Söllner, M. (2019). AI-based digital assistants: Opportunities, threats, and research perspectives. *Business & Information Systems Engineering*, *61*(4), 535–544. doi:10.100712599-019-00600-8

Md Yunus, M., Ang, W. S., & Hashim, H. (2021). Factors affecting teaching English as a Second Language (TESL) postgraduate students' behavioural intention for online learning during the COVID-19 pandemic. *Sustainability (Basel)*, *13*(6), 3524. doi:10.3390u13063524

Monte-Sano, C., De La Paz, S., & Felton, M. (2014). Implementing a disciplinary-literacy curriculum for US history: Learning from expert middle school teachers in diverse classrooms. *Journal of Curriculum Studies*, *46*(4), 540–575. doi:10.1080/00220272.2014.904444

Ng, D. T. K., Luo, W., Chan, H. M. Y., & Chu, S. K. W. (2022). Using digital story writing as a pedagogy to develop AI literacy among primary students. *Computers and Education: Artificial Intelligence*, *3*, 100054. doi:10.1016/j.caeai.2022.100054

Niss, M., & Højgaard, T. (2019). Mathematical competencies revisited. *Educational Studies in Mathematics*, *102*(1), 9–28. doi:10.100710649-019-09903-9

Pedro, F., Subosa, M., Rivas, A., & Valverde, P. (2019). *Artificial intelligence in education: Challenges and opportunities for sustainable development.*

Ramírez-Correa, P. E., Arenas-Gaitán, J., & Rondán-Cataluña, F. J. (2015). Gender and acceptance of e-learning: A multi-group analysis based on a structural equation model among college students in Chile and Spain. *PLoS One*, *10*(10), e0140460. doi:10.1371/journal.pone.0140460 PMID:26465895

Roll, I., McNamara, D., Sosnovsky, S., Luckin, R., & Dimitrova, V. (2021). *Artificial intelligence in education.* Springer International Publishing.

Rosen, M. A., DiazGranados, D., Dietz, A. S., Benishek, L. E., Thompson, D., Pronovost, P. J., & Weaver, S. J. (2018). Teamwork in healthcare: Key discoveries enabling safer, high-quality care. *The American Psychologist*, *73*(4), 433–450. doi:10.1037/amp0000298 PMID:29792459

Rouhiainen, L. (2018). *Artificial Intelligence: 101 things you must know today about our future.* Lasse Rouhiainen.

Sanusi, I. T., Olaleye, S. A., Agbo, F. J., & Chiu, T. K. (2022). The role of learners' competencies in artificial intelligence education. *Computers and Education: Artificial Intelligence*, *3*, 100098. doi:10.1016/j.caeai.2022.100098

Shyam, R. S. (2017). -(a). Role of m-Banking for Indian Rural Consumers, its Adaptation Strategies, and Challenges: Consumer Behavior Analysis [J]. *International Journal of Information Engineering and Electronic Business*, *6*, 35–42.

Sibbel, A. (2009). Pathways towards sustainability through higher education. *International Journal of Sustainability in Higher Education*, *10*(1), 68–82. doi:10.1108/14676370910925262

Sihare, S. (2022). FUTURE DIGITAL MARKETING REVOLUTIONIZING E-COMMERCE. *Towards Excellence, 14*(1).

Sihare, S. R. (2017). -(b)). Role of m-Banking for Indian rural consumers, its adaptation strategies, and challenges: Consumer behavior analysis. *International Journal of Information Engineering and Electronic Business*, *9*(6), 35. doi:10.5815/ijieeb.2017.06.05

Sihare, S. R. (2018). Roles of E–content for E–business: Analysis. *International Journal of Information Engineering and Electronic Business*, *12*(1), 24. doi:10.5815/ijieeb.2018.01.04

Stern, L., & Roseman, J. E. (2004). Can middle-school science textbooks help students learn important ideas? Findings from Project 2061's curriculum evaluation study: Life science. *Journal of Research in Science Teaching*, *41*(6), 538–568. doi:10.1002/tea.20019

Su, J., & Yang, W. (2022). *Artificial intelligence in early childhood education: A scoping review.* Computers and Education: Artificial Intelligence, 100049.

Su, J., Zhong, Y., & Ng, D. T. K. (2022). A meta-review of literature on educational approaches for teaching AI at the K-12 levels in the Asia-Pacific region. *Computers and Education: Artificial Intelligence, 100065.*

Tidjon, L. N., & Khomh, F. (2022). The different faces of ai ethics across the world: a principle-implementation gap analysis. arXiv preprint arXiv:2206.03225.

Wang, T., & Cheng, E. C. K. (2021). An investigation of barriers to Hong Kong K-12 schools incorporating artificial intelligence in education. *Computers and Education: Artificial Intelligence*, 2, 100031. doi:10.1016/j.caeai.2021.100031

Welch, L., Lewitter, F., Schwartz, R., Brooksbank, C., Radivojac, P., Gaeta, B., & Schneider, M. V. (2014). Bioinformatics curriculum guidelines: Toward a definition of core competencies. *PLoS Computational Biology*, *10*(3), e1003496. doi:10.1371/journal.pcbi.1003496 PMID:24603430

Williams, R., Park, H. W., Oh, L., & Breazeal, C. (2019, July). Popbots: Designing an artificial intelligence curriculum for early childhood education. *Proceedings of the AAAI Conference on Artificial Intelligence*, *33*(01), 9729–9736. doi:10.1609/aaai.v33i01.33019729

Williamson, B., & Eynon, R. (2020). Historical threads, missing links, and future directions in AI in education. *Learning, Media and Technology*, *45*(3), 223–235. doi:10.1080/17439884.2020.1798995

Yang, W. (2022). Artificial Intelligence education for young children: Why, what, and how in curriculum design and implementation. *Computers and Education: Artificial Intelligence*, *3*, 100061. doi:10.1016/j.caeai.2022.100061

Zawacki-Richter, O., Marín, V. I., Bond, M., & Gouverneur, F. (2019). Systematic review of research on artificial intelligence applications in higher education–where are the educators? *International Journal of Educational Technology in Higher Education*, *16*(1), 1–27. doi:10.118641239-019-0171-0

Zhang, H., Lee, I., Ali, S., DiPaola, D., Cheng, Y., & Breazeal, C. (2022). Integrating ethics and career futures with technical learning to promote AI literacy for middle school students: An exploratory study. *International Journal of Artificial Intelligence in Education*, 1–35. PMID:35573722

ADDITIONAL READING

Bird, S., Klein, E., & Loper, E. (2009). *Natural language processing with Python: analyzing text with the natural language toolkit*. O'Reilly Media, Inc.

Burkov, A. (2019). *The hundred-page machine learning book* (Vol. 1, p. 32). Quebec City, QC, Canada: Andriy Burkov.

Burkov, A. (2020). *Machine learning engineering (Vol. 1)*. Montreal, QC, Canada: True Positive Incorporated

Elkin, M., Sullivan, A., & Bers, M. U. (2018). Books, butterflies, and 'bots: Integrating engineering and robotics into early childhood curricula. *Early engineering learning*, 225-248.

Goodfellow, I., Bengio, Y., & Courville, A. (2016). *Deep learning*. MIT press. Gulli, A., & Pal, S. (2017). *Deep learning with Keras*. Packt Publishing Ltd.

Hopgood, A. A. (2021). *Intelligent systems for engineers and scientists: A practical guide to artificial intelligence*. CRC press. doi:10.1201/9781003226277

Manning, C., & Schutze, H. (1999). *Foundations of statistical natural language processing*. MIT press.

Waterman, D. A. (1985). *A guide to expert systems*. Addison-Wesley Longman Publishing Co., Inc.

Winston, P. H. (1992). Artificial intelligence. Addison-Wesley Longman Publishing Co., Inc.

KEY TERMS AND DEFINITIONS

Artificial Intelligence: The approach through which computers may be programmed to think like humans.

Machine Learning: It is a subfield of AI, which is generally characterised as a machine's capacity to replicate intelligent human behaviour.

Neural Network: An AI method known as a neural network trains computers to analyse data in a way that is modelled after the human brain.

Natural Language Processing: It combines computational linguistics, machine learning, and deep learning models to process human language.

Robotics: It is an area of engineering that deals with the creation, design, production, and use of robots.

Computer Science: Study of computational systems and computers.

ENDNOTES

1   Source: https://leverageedu.com/blog/bsc-artificial-intelligence/
2   https://medium.com/@aditianilloya/what-is-artificial-intelli
      gence-16947c954667
3   https://www.edureka.co/blog/knowledge-representation-in-ai/

Chapter 2
Artificial Intelligence in Computer Science:
An Overview of Current Trends and Future Directions

Arun Prasad G
Hindusthan College of Arts & Science, India

A. V. Senthil Kumar
(iD) https://orcid.org/0000-0002-8587-7017
Hindusthan College of Arts & Science, India

Priyanka Sharma
(iD) https://orcid.org/0000-0002-9503-1170
Swami Keshvanand Institute of Technology, Management & Gramothan, India

Indrarini Dyah Irawati
Telkom University, Indonesia

Chandrashekar D. V.
(iD) https://orcid.org/0000-0001-9798-0305
T.J.P.S. College, India

Ismail Bin Musirin
Universiti Teknologi MARA, Malaysia

Hesham Mohammed Ali Abdullah
Jouf University, Saudi Arabia

Manjunatha Rao L
Dr. Ambedkar Institute of Technology, India

ABSTRACT

Artificial intelligence (AI) is a rapidly evolving field that has seen tremendous growth in recent years. In this chapter, the authors provide an overview of current trends in AI and their applications in computer science. They also discuss the future directions of AI research and their potential impact on the field of computer science. They start by introducing the basic concepts of AI and its various subfields. Then, they present an overview of current trends in AI research, including machine learning, natural language processing, computer vision, and robotics. The authors discuss how these trends are applied in computer science, such as autonomous vehicles, fraud detection, and personalized medicine. Finally, they discuss the future directions of AI research, including the development of more explainable AI systems, the integration of AI with other emerging technologies, and the ethical considerations of AI.

DOI: 10.4018/979-8-3693-1301-5.ch002

INTRODUCTION

Artificial intelligence (AI) has emerged as a game-changing technology that is transforming the way we interact with machines and the world around us. With the advent of machine learning algorithms, deep learning, natural language processing, and computer vision, AI has made significant strides in recent years, with the potential to transform many areas of computer science and beyond.(Berente et al., n.d.) From robotics and autonomous systems to healthcare, finance, education, and cybersecurity, AI is being used to address a wide range of complex challenges and improve our lives in numerous ways.

As AI continues to evolve, it is becoming increasingly sophisticated and capable of performing tasks that were once thought to be the exclusive domain of humans. With the ability to analyze vast amounts of data, detect patterns, and make decisions in real time, AI has the potential to accelerate scientific discovery, improve healthcare outcomes, boost economic productivity, and enhance the quality of life for people around the globe.

• AI is "the theory and development of computer systems able to perform tasks normally requiring human intelligence, such as visual perception, speech recognition, decision-making, and translation between languages."(Chassignol et al., 2018)

At the same time, the rapid leap of technological transformation also poses new challenges and risks, including job displacement, prejudice and discrimination, and security threats. As AI continues to transform the way we live and work, it is important to consider the ethical and social implications of these technologies and ensure that they are developed and used in a responsible and accountable manner. (*Evolving Artificial Intelligence.*, n.d.)

This chapter provides an overview of the current trends and future directions in AI research, as well as the applications of Artificial Intelligence in various fields of computer science. It also explores the challenges and opportunities that lie ahead in AI research, and emphasizes the importance of ethical and responsible use of AI to ensure that these technologies are used to maximize their benefits while mitigating potential risks and challenges.(Holzinger et al., 2019) Ultimately, by working together to develop and deploy AI in a responsible and ethical manner, we can unlock the full potential of this transformative technology and create a brighter future for us all.

BACKGROUND AND OVERVIEW OF AI

Artificial Intelligence (AI) is a rapidly growing field that has its roots in computer science and engineering.(Mccarthy, 2004) The idea of creating machines that could perform tasks typically associated with human intelligence dates back to the 1950s. However, it was not until the 21st century that the concept of AI began to take shape in a meaningful way, with the development of machine learning algorithms and neural networks. Today, AI is a major area of research in computer science, with applications ranging from computer vision to natural language processing and robotics.

AI can be broadly defined as the ability of machines to perform tasks that typically require human intelligence, such as recognizing patterns, understanding natural language, and making decisions.(Minsky, 1961) At its core, AI is about creating machines that can learn from data and adapt to new situations. This is typically achieved through machine learning, a subfield of AI that focuses on the development of algorithms that can learn from data and make predictions or decisions based on that data.

One of the key concepts in machine learning is the neural network, a computational model that is inspired by the structure of the human brain. Neural networks consist of layers of interconnected nodes, or neurons, that are trained to recognize patterns in data. This enables them to perform tasks such as image recognition, speech recognition, and natural language processing.(Dietterich, 1997)

Another important concept in AI is deep learning, a subfield of machine learning that focuses on the development of deep neural networks. These networks consist of multiple layers of neurons and are capable of learning more complex representations of data. Deep learning has enabled significant advances in areas such as computer vision and natural language processing.

In addition to machine learning and neural networks, AI also includes other subfields such as robotics, natural language processing, and expert systems. Robotics is the development of machines that can perform tasks autonomously, such as manufacturing or assembly line work. Natural language processing is the development of machines that can understand and generate human language, such as chatbots or virtual assistants.(McDermottDrew, 1976) Expert systems are AI systems that are designed to replicate the decision-making abilities of human experts in a specific domain.

Overall, AI is a rapidly evolving field that has the potential to transform the way we interact with computers and machines. It is already being used in a wide range of applications, from autonomous vehicles to virtual assistants, and its impact is only set to grow in the coming years

HISTORY OF ARTIFICIAL INTELLIGENCE IN COMPUTER SCIENCE

Artificial Intelligence (AI) is a rapidly growing field that has its roots in computer science. The history of AI in computer science dates back to the mid-20th century when scientists began to develop algorithms and methods to simulate human intelligence. This side heading aims to explore the history of AI in computer science and how it has evolved over the years.

In the 1950s, the term "Artificial Intelligence" was created by John McCarthy, who is often referred to as the father of AI.(Bhbosale et al., n.d.) During this time, researchers were interested in developing algorithms that could simulate human problem-solving and decision-making processes. The development of the first AI programs, such as the Logic Theorist and General Problem Solver, marked the beginning of AI research.

During the 1960s, AI researchers developed the first machine learning algorithms,(Provost, n.d.) including the perceptron algorithm, which is still used today. Researchers also developed the first natural language processing systems, which could understand and generate human language.

In the 1970s and 1980s, researchers developed expert systems, which were designed to mimic the decision-making abilities of human experts in specific domains. These systems were used in industries such as healthcare and finance to aid in decision-making(Buchanan, 2005).

The 1990s saw the development of new AI techniques, including neural networks and genetic algorithms, which allowed for more sophisticated AI systems. These techniques enabled AI systems to learn from large amounts of data and make predictions based on that data.

In the 2000s and 2010s, there was rapid growth in AI research and development, driven by the availability of large datasets and the increasing processing power of computers.(Huang et al., 2022) AI techniques such as deep learning and reinforcement learning enabled the development of intelligent systems that could recognize images, translate languages, and play games at a level that surpassed human performance.

Today, AI is used in a wide range of applications, from chatbots and virtual assistants to self-driving cars and intelligent robots. (Xu et al., 2019)The field of AI has come a long way since its inception in the mid-20th century, and it is continuing to evolve at a rapid pace.

In conclusion, the history of artificial intelligence in computer science is a rich and fascinating topic that spans several decades. From the early days of symbolic AI and expert systems to the current era of machine learning and deep learning,(Aggarwal et al., 2022) AI has undergone significant changes and developments over the years. AI has had a profound impact on computer science and beyond, and has the potential to revolutionize many areas of our lives. As AI continues to evolve and become more powerful, it is important to consider the ethical and societal implications of these technologies and ensure that they are developed and used in a responsible and accountable manner. By working together to develop and deploy AI in a responsible and ethical manner, we can unlock the full potential of this transformative technology and create a brighter future for us all.

CURRENT TRENDS IN AI RESEARCH

Machine learning is one of the most active areas of AI research, and it has seen tremendous growth in recent years. One of the most important advances in machine learning is deep learning, which is a type of machine learning that uses artificial neural networks to learn from data. Deep learning has been used to achieve state-of-the-art performance in many applications, including image and speech recognition, natural language processing, and game playing. Another trend in machine learning is reinforcement learning, which is a type of machine learning that focuses on learning through trial and error. Reinforcement learning has been applied to a variety of tasks, such as game playing, robotics, and control systems.

Natural language processing is another active area of AI research, and it has seen significant progress in recent years. One of the most important advances in natural language processing is the growth of transformer-based models, such as BERT and GPT-3. These models have achieved state-of-art performance in a variety of natural language tasks, such as question answering, language translation, and text generation.(Jordan & Mitchell, 2015)

Computer vision is another area of Artificial intelligence research that has seen significant progress in recent years. One of the most significant advances in computer vision is the development of convolutional neural networks, which have achieved state-of-the-art performance in many images and video analysis tasks, such as object recognition, image segmentation, and video captioning.(Baron, 1981) Another trend in computer vision is the integration of deep learning with 3D geometry, which has enabled the development of intelligent systems that can interact with the physical world.

Robotics isanother active area of Artificial intelligence research that has seen significant progress in recent years. One of the most significant trends in robotics is the development of autonomous systems that can be operated without human intervention. Autonomous systems have many applications, such as self-driving cars, unmanned aerial vehicles, and robotic assistants in manufacturing and healthcare. (Musliner et al., 1995)Autonomous systems rely on a variety of AI techniques, such as machine learning, computer vision, and decision-making algorithms.

Another trend in robotics is the development of soft robots that are inspired by the structure and function of biological organisms. Soft robots are made of flexible materials, such as silicone and rubber, and they can change shape and adapt to their environment. Soft robots have many potential applications, such as in search and rescue operations, exploration of remote or hazardous environments, and prosthetics. Figure 1. Shows the opened page of the ChatGPT one of the famous Artificial Intelligence tool ever existed.

Figure 1. A recent trend in artificial intelligence is the open AI

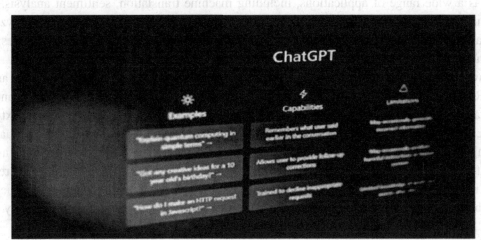

APPLICATION OF AI IN COMPUTER SCIENCE

Artificial intelligence plays a major role in the field of computer science, by using artificial intelligence users can do an enormous number of tasks easily and quickly. Some of the application of artificial intelligence is listed below

1. **Computer Vision:** Computer vision is the ability of machines to interpret and understand images and video. Artificial intelligence techniques such as deep learning have enabled significant advances in computer vision applications, such as object recognition, image segmentation, and facial recognition.(Forsyth & Ponce, 2003)Computer vision is a field of computer science that emphasizes enabling machines to interpret and understand visual data from the world around us. It involves the development of algorithms and techniques that allow computers to analyze, interpret, and understand digital images and videos.

   Computer vision has numerous applications in many different industries, which include healthcare, automotive, security, entertainment, and manufacturing.(Kakani et al., 2020) For example, computer vision algorithms can be used to identify diseases from medical images, detect and track objects in autonomous vehicles, and analyze security footage to identify potential threats.
   The field of computer vision is constantly evolving, and new techniques are being developed all the time. Some of the most important recent advances in computer vision include the use of deep learning and convolutional neural networks, which have revolutionized the field by enabling the machine to learn from the large dataset ofthe image and video.(He et al., 2005)
   Overall, computer vision is a rapidly growing and exciting field with a wide range of applications, and it is likely to continue to play an increasingly important role in our lives in the years to come.

2. **Natural Language Processing:**Thisis a subfield of computer science that deals with the communication between computers and human language. It focuses on developing algorithms and techniques that enable machines to understand, interpret, and generate natural language.(Jones, 1994)

NLP has a wide range of applications, including machine translation, sentiment analysis, speech recognition, text classification, and chatbots. For example, NLP algorithms can be used to analyze social media data to identify trends and customer sentiment, to generate summaries of news articles, and to power virtual assistants like Siri and Alexa.

NLP involves a wide range of techniques, including statistical models, rule-based systems, and deep learning. Recent advances in deep learning, particularly the use of recurrent neural networks and transformers, have revolutionized the field by enabling machines to learn from large datasets of text data.

Despite these advances, NLP still faces many challenges, including understanding the nuances of human language and dealing with ambiguity and context. However, as more data becomes available and algorithms become more sophisticated, it is likely that NLP will continue to play an increasingly important role in our lives, helping us to communicate more effectively with machines and each other. Figure 2 shows that an person uses his voice for typing using the voice recognition technology.

Figure 2. An example for speech recognition in natural language processing

3. **Robotics:**Robotics is an interdisciplinary field that involves the design, construction, operation, and use of robots. A robot is a machine that is capable of carrying out a series of tasks autonomously, or under the control of a human operator.(Garcia et al., 2007) Robotics incorporates elements of mechanical engineering, electrical engineering, computer science, and artificial intelligence, among other disciplines.

The use of robotics has increased rapidly in recent years, and they are now used in a wide variety of applications. Some examples of applications include manufacturing, transportation, healthcare, entertainment, and military operations.

Robotics has made significant contributions to many areas of society, including increasing efficiency, improving safety, and advancing scientific research.One of the most significant benefits of robotics is the potential to automate repetitive and dangerous tasks, freeing up humans for more complex and creative work.(Breazeal et al., 2016) This has led to increased productivity in many industries and has the potential to transform the way we work and live. Additionally, robots can be used to perform tasks in environments that are hazardous for humans, such as deep-sea exploration or space travel.

The field of robotics is constantly evolving, and new developments are being made all the time. Recent advancements in machine learning and artificial intelligence have enabled robots to perform more complex tasks and adapt to changing environments. As robotics technology continues to develop, (Critchlow, 1985)it has the potential to transform the way we live, work, and interact with the world around us. Figure 3 shows an example of an robot created by the brand Honda by using the Artificial Intelligence technology.

Figure 3. Example image for the application of artificial intelligence in robotics

4. **Recommender Systems:** Recommender systems are a type of artificial intelligence (AI) technology that provide personalized recommendations to users based on their interests, preferences, and behaviors. (Burke et al., 2011)These systems are commonly used by businesses such as e-commerce websites, streaming services, and social media platforms to suggest products, movies, music, and other items that users are likely to be interested in.

Recommender systems use a variety of algorithms and techniques to make personalized recommendations. Collaborative filtering is one of the most common techniques used by these systems.(Mijwil et al., 2022) This technique involves analyzing user behavior and preferences to identify patterns and similarities between users. The system then recommends items to users based on the preferences of users who are similar to them.

Another technique used by recommender systems is content-based filtering. This approach involves analyzing the features of items such as movies, music, or products, and recommending similar items to users based on their past interactions with those features.(Burke et al., 2011) For example, a music streaming service may recommend songs with similar genres, artists, or instruments to users who have listened to a particular song.

Hybrid recommender systems combine both collaborative and content-based filtering techniques to make recommendations. These systems analyze user behavior and preferences, as well as the features of items, to provide more accurate and relevant recommendations.

Recommender systems are essential for businesses looking to provide personalized experiences to their users. These systems can increase user engagement, improve customer loyalty, and increase revenue by driving more sales. However, it is important to note that recommender systems may raise privacy concerns, as they often collect and analyze user data. Therefore, it is crucial for organizations to prioritize user privacy and data protection while implementing and using these systems.

5. **Fraud Detection:**Fraud detection is the process of identifying and preventing fraudulent activities in various areas such as finance, banking, insurance, healthcare, and e-commerce. Fraud can occur in various forms such as identity theft, credit card fraud, check fraud, and wire transfer fraud.

Fraud detection involves the use of various techniques such as data analysis, machine learning, and artificial intelligence. (Martínez-López & Casillas, 2013)These techniques enable organizations to identify patterns and anomalies in data that may indicate fraudulent activities. Fraud detection systems typically employ algorithms that analyze data in real-time to identify any suspicious transactions or activities.

Fraud detection is essential for preventing financial losses and protecting consumers' personal information. Organizations can implement fraud detection systems to monitor transactions, identify potential fraudsters, and prevent fraudulent activities from occurring. Such systems can also be used to analyze historical data to identify patterns of fraudulent behavior and prevent similar frauds from happening in the future.

Effective fraud detection requires a combination of technology, analytics, and human expertise. Organizations must invest in robust fraud detection systems, train their employees on fraud detection techniques, and remain vigilant to identify and prevent fraud in real-time. Ultimately, the success of fraud detection efforts depends on a proactive approach that involves continuous monitoring, analysis, and refinement of fraud detection strategies.

6. **Healthcare:** Artificial intelligence (AI) has the potential to transform healthcare by improving patient outcomes, reducing costs and increasing efficiency. Healthcare organizations are increasingly adopting AI technologies to enhance their operations and provide better care to patients.

One of the most important applications of AI in healthcare is in medical imaging. AI algorithms can analyze medical images such as X-rays, CT scans, and MRIs, to identify and diagnose diseases more accurately and quickly than traditional methods. For example, AI-based algorithms can detect abnormalities in mammograms, which can help diagnose breast cancer in its early stages.(Hamet& Tremblay, 2017)

Another application of AI in healthcare is in personalized medicine. AI algorithms can analyze a patient's genetic data, medical history, and lifestyle factors to develop personalized treatment plans. (Briganti & le Moine, 2020) This approach can help reduce the trial and error involved in finding the right treatment for a patient and improve treatment outcomes.

AI is also being used in drug discovery and development. Machine learning algorithms can analyze vast amounts of data to identify potential drug candidates and predict their efficacy and side effects. (Stead, 2018) This can help accelerate the drug discovery process and bring new treatments to market more quickly.

AI-powered chatbots and virtual assistants are also being used in healthcare to improve patient engagement and provide better care. These systems can answer patient queries, provide medication reminders, and even offer mental health support.

While AI has enormous potential in healthcare, it is crucial to address ethical and privacy concerns. Healthcare organizations must ensure that patient data is protected and that AI algorithms are developed and used ethically. They must also address issues such as bias in AI algorithms, which can result in inaccurate diagnoses or treatments, particularly for underrepresented communities.

Overall, AI has the potential to transform healthcare by improving patient outcomes, reducing costs, and increasing efficiency. As AI technologies continue to evolve, we can expect to see even more significant advances in healthcare in the years to come.

ADVANTAGES OF ARTIFICIAL INTELLIGENCE IN COMPUTER SCIENCE

Some highly advanced organizations use artificial intelligence technology like digital assistants to interact with their users which may decrease the necessity of humans and saves a lot of money. These digital assistants are also used on many websites to supply the things that its user want(Bhbosale et al., n.d.)

The benefits of artificial intelligence are inconceivable, what this area can offer us, is to evolve definitively before proceeding to the background of artificial robots. The following are the main advantagesof Artificial Intelligence(AI).(Chhaya et al., n.d.-a)

- **Improved Efficiency:** One of the most significant advantages of Artificial Intelligence (AI) in computer science is its ability to perform tasks with speed and accuracy. AI algorithms can process large amounts of data quickly and accurately, which can lead to increased efficiency and productivity.
- **Automation of Repetitive Tasks:** AI can automate repetitive and mundane tasks, such as data entry or file organization, freeing up human workers to focus on more complex and strategic tasks.
- **Improved Decision Making:**Artificial Intelligence (AI) can help improve decision-making by analyzing data and identifying patterns and insights that humans may not be able to see. This can help organizations make better-informed decisions based on data-driven insights.
- **Personalization:** AI can be used to personalize experiences for users by analyzing their preferences and behavior patterns. This can lead to better customer satisfaction and loyalty.
- **Predictive Analytics:** AI can be used for predictive analytics, which involves analyzing historical data to make predictions about future trends and events. This can be useful for businesses and organizations in planning for future growth and identifying potential risks.

- **Continuous Learning:** AI algorithms can learn from new data and adjust their models and algorithms accordingly. This can lead to continuous improvement in AI systems over time.
- **Improved Safety:** AI can be used to improve safety in various fields, such as manufacturing and transportation, by identifying potential risks and hazards and taking corrective actions to prevent accidents.
- **Scale:** AI-powered systems can scale to handle large amounts of data and tasks without the need for additional human resources. This can result in significant cost savings for businesses and organizations.

The phrase "human error was born because of the continuous mistakes of the humans time to time, if programmed properly computer however don't make these mistakes that are often done by humans

Overall, the advantages of AI in computer science are significant and have the potential to revolutionize various industries and fields. By leveraging the power of AI, organizations can improve efficiency, accuracy, decision-making, personalization, and safety, among other benefits

In conclusion, the advantages of artificial intelligence in computer science are numerous and far-reaching. AI has the ability to analyze vast amounts of data, detect patterns, and make decisions in real-time, which can lead to more efficient and accurate results. It can also automate tedious or repetitive tasks, freeing up time for humans to focus on more creative or complex work. In fields like healthcare and finance, AI can assist in diagnosis and decision-making, leading to better outcomes for patients and businesses alike. Additionally, AI-powered systems can improve cybersecurity by identifying and responding to threats faster than humans can. However, as AI continues to evolve and become more powerful, it is important to consider the potential risks and challenges, such as job displacement, bias and discrimination, and security threats. By addressing these challenges and utilizing AI in a responsible and ethical manner, we can unlock the full potential of this transformative technology and improve our lives in countless ways.

DISADVANTAGES OF ARTIFICIAL INTELLIGENCE IN COMPUTER SCIENCE

Artificial Intelligence (AI) is a rapidly growing field in computer science, but it has its share of disadvantages as well. Here are some of the main disadvantages of AI in computer science:

- Job Displacement: AI can automate many tasks that were previously done by humans, which can lead to job displacement and unemployment in some industries. This can create social and economic challenges for individuals and communities.
- Bias and Discrimination: AI systems can be biased and discriminatory if they are trained on biased data or if their algorithms are designed with inherent biases.(Brynjolfsson &Mcafee, n.d.) This can perpetuate and amplify existing societal inequalities and discrimination.
- Lack of Creativity and Intuition: AI systems may lack creativity and intuition, which are essential human traits. This can limit their ability to solve complex problems and make subjective decisions that require a deep understanding of human emotions and behaviors.
- Security and Privacy Risks: AI systems can pose security and privacy risks if they are not designed and implemented securely. Malicious actors can exploit vulnerabilities in AI systems to steal sensitive data or launch cyber-attacks.

- Ethical Concerns: AI systems can raise ethical concerns, such as the potential for autonomous weapons or the use of AI for surveillance and control. These concerns require careful consideration and regulation to ensure that AI is used responsibly and ethically.

the development of artificial intelligence machines is not that much easy the cost of making those machinesis extremely high and it takes a huge amount of time to create them. (Wuest et al., 2016)

Sometimes it can cause a mass scale of destruction while it had been misused. It may affect the job opportunities for the upcoming generation due to this the problem of unemployment increases(Chhaya et al., n.d.-b)

Overall, the disadvantages of AI in computer science should be carefully considered and addressed to mitigate their negative impacts. While AI has the potential to revolutionize various industries and fields, it is important to ensure that its benefits are balanced against its potential risks and disadvantages.

ETHICS AND CHALLENGES OF ARTIFICIAL INTELLIGENCE IN COMPUTER SCIENCE

With the rapid advancements in artificial intelligence (AI) in recent years, there has been a growing concern about this technology's ethical implications and challenges. As AI becomes more integrated into our daily lives, it is essential to understand the potential ethical issues and challenges it poses. (Borenstein& Howard, 2020)This side heading of a chapter on AI in computer science aims to explore AI's ethical issues and challenges.

Some of the ethical challenges of AI include privacy, security, fairness, accountability, and transparency. As AI systems become more complex and pervasive, the risk of data breaches and cyber-attacks also increases.(Bostrom &Yudkowsky, 2018) AI systems can also reinforce existing societal biases and discrimination, which can have severe consequences for certain groups of people. Ensuring accountability and transparency of AI systems is also essential to mitigate these risks.

Furthermore, there are many technical and societal challenges to AI development and deployment. Technical challenges include developing robust and reliable algorithms, managing large datasets, and designing AI systems that can adapt to changing circumstances. Societal challenges include addressing the impact of AI on the workforce, (Kalyanakrishnan et al., 2018)promoting access to AI technologies, and addressing the potential for AI to exacerbate existing societal inequalities.

To report these challenges, researchers and policymakers must work together to develop ethical frameworks and regulations for AI development and deployment. This requires a multi-disciplinary approach that involves experts from computer science, ethics, law, and social sciences. It is also crucial to engage with stakeholders and communities affected by AI technologies to ensure that their concerns are heard and addressed.

In conclusion, while AI has the potential to revolutionize computer science, there are many ethical challenges and societal implications that need to be addressed.(Goldsmith & Burton, 2017) This side heading aims to highlight the importance of considering the ethical and societal implications of AI in computer science research and development

Artificial intelligence (AI) is transforming the way we live and work, and it has the potential to revolutionize various industries, including healthcare, transportation, and finance. However, as AI becomes more integrated into our daily lives, there is a growing concern about its ethical implications and challenges.

One of the most significant ethical challenges of AI is its potential impact on privacy and security. AI systems require large amounts of data to function correctly, and the collection and use of this data can pose privacy risks. Moreover, AI systems can also be vulnerable to cyber-attacks, which can compromise the security of the data they use and produce.

Another ethical challenge of AI is its potential impact on fairness and accountability. AI systems are trained on historical data, which can include biases and discriminatory practices. As a result, AI systems can perpetuate existing societal biases, leading to unfair outcomes for certain groups of people. Ensuring that AI systems are transparent and accountable is essential to address these concerns.

Furthermore, there are many technical challenges to AI development and deployment. For example, developing AI algorithms that are robust and reliable is a challenging task that requires significant expertise and resources. Additionally, managing large datasets, training AI models, and deploying them at scale can be complicated and time-consuming processes.

Societal challenges associated with AI include the impact of AI on the workforce, access to AI technologies, and potential exacerbation of existing societal inequalities. As AI systems become more capable, there is a risk that they will replace human workers, leading to job displacement and income inequality. Ensuring that AI technologies are accessible to all is also essential to prevent furthering existing inequalities.

To address these challenges, it is essential to develop ethical frameworks and regulations for AI development and deployment. A multi-disciplinary approach that involves experts from computer science, ethics, law, and social sciences is crucial to ensure that ethical and societal concerns are appropriately addressed. Additionally, engaging with stakeholders and communities affected by AI technologies is essential to ensure that their concerns are heard and addressed.

In conclusion, while AI has the potential to revolutionize various industries, there are many ethical challenges and societal implications that need to be addressed. This side heading aims to highlight the importance of considering the ethical and societal implications of AI in computer science research and development and to promote responsible AI development and deployment.

FUTURE DIRECTIONS OF AI RESEARCH

One promising area of future AI research is the development of robust AI systems that are resistant to adversarial attacks or errors in the training data. One of the challenges with current AI systems is that they can be vulnerable to manipulation or attacks, particularly in high-stakes applications such as cybersecurity or autonomous vehicles. Developing AI systems that are robust and can withstand such attacks is therefore an important area of research.(Kumar et al., 2016)

One approach to developing robust AI is to focus on developing AI systems that are able to identify and flag potential errors or attacks. This could involve developing algorithms that are able to detect anomalous or suspicious activity in the training data, or developing models that are able to recognize and respond to adversarial attacks in real-time. Another approach is to focus on developing AI systems that are designed to be more resilient to errors or attacks. (Bundy, 2016)This could involve developing models that are able to learn from limited or noisy data, or developing systems that are able to adapt and continue functioning even in the presence of errors or disruptions.

Overall, the development of robust AI is an important area of research that has the potential to enable more secure and reliable AI systems in a wide range of applications. By developing AI systems that are able to resist attacks and continue functioning even in the face of errors or disruptions, we can ensure that AI remains a powerful tool for improving our lives while also mitigating potential risks and challenges.

Another important aspect of developing robust AI is ensuring that AI systems are free from bias or discrimination. One of the challenges with current AI systems is that they can inherit biases from the data used to train them. For example, if an AI system is trained on data that is biased against certain groups of people, it may make biased or discriminatory decisions in real-world applications.

To address this challenge, researchers are developing new techniques for developing fair and unbiased AI systems. This could involve developing algorithms that are able to identify and remove biased data,(Zhang & Lu, 2021) or developing models that are designed to be more robust to biases in the training data. Another approach is to focus on developing diverse and inclusive teams of researchers who are able to identify potential biases and ensure that AI systems are designed to be fair and equitable.

Overall, ensuring that AI systems are robust and free from bias is essential for ensuring that these systems are able to deliver on their potential for improving our lives. By developing AI systems that are transparent, accountable, and free from bias or discrimination,(Shabbir &Anwer, 2018) we can build trust in these systems and ensure that they are able to be used safely and responsibly in a wide range of applications. This will be an important area of focus for AI researchers in the years to come, as we work to develop AI systems that are able to meet the complex and evolving needs of our society.

Ethical Considerations Surrounding AI

Artificial Intelligence (AI) is a rapidly growing field with the potential to revolutionize many aspects of our lives. However, as with any powerful technology, there are ethical considerations that need to be taken into account.

As AI becomes more prevalent in society, there are increasing concerns about its impact on ethical, social, and legal issues. One of the major ethical considerations surrounding AI is its potential impact on employment. AI and automation are expected to replace jobs in various industries, and it is important to consider how this will impact the workforce and the economy. (Siau& Wang, 1 C.E.)Governments and organizations must consider how to provide new job opportunities and training programs for workers who may be displaced by AI.

Another ethical consideration is the potential for AI to perpetuate or even amplify existing social biases. AI algorithms are often trained on large datasets, and if these datasets contain biases, the resulting AI models may perpetuate these biases. For example, an AI algorithm trained on historical data may learn to discriminate against certain groups of people based on race or gender. (Etzioni & Etzioni, 2017)It is important for developers to ensure that their AI models are trained on unbiased datasets and that they are continually monitored for potential biases.

Privacy is another major ethical consideration surrounding AI. As AI algorithms are trained on large amounts of data, there is a risk that sensitive personal information may be compromised. It is important for organizations to develop robust data privacy policies and ensure that they are complying with relevant data protection regulations. (Goldsmith & Burton, 2017)Additionally, individuals must be aware of the potential privacy risks associated with using AI-powered services and take steps to protect their personal data.

Finally, there are broader ethical considerations surrounding the use of AI, such as the potential for AI to be used for harmful purposes. (Riedl, 2019)AI-powered weapons, for example, have the potential to greatly increase the lethality and scope of military conflicts. It is important for governments and organizations to consider the ethical implications of developing and deploying AI in potentially harmful ways and to ensure that appropriate regulations and safeguards are in place.

As AI becomes more pervasive in society, it is important to consider its potential impact on ethical, social, and legal issues. Ethical considerations surrounding AI include its impact on employment, social biases, privacy, and the potential for AI to be used for harmful purposes. Governments, organizations, and individuals must take proactive steps to ensure that the benefits of AI are realized while minimizing the potential risks and negative consequences.

CONCLUSION

In conclusion, Artificial intelligence (AI) is a branch of computer science that is focused on developing machines that can perform tasks that typically require human intelligence, such as understanding natural language, recognizing images and speech, and making decisions based on data. (Mishkoff, 1986) The development of AI has been driven by advances in computer hardware and software, as well as the availability of large amounts of data and powerful machine learning algorithms.

One of the key benefits of AI is its ability to automate tasks and improve efficiency. For example, AI-powered chatbots can provide customer service around the clock, while AI algorithms can quickly process large amounts of data and identify patterns that would be difficult for humans to detect.

AI is also being used to improve healthcare outcomes, by analyzing medical data to identify potential health risks and personalize treatment plans. In finance, AI is used for fraud detection and to make investment decisions. In transportation, AI is being used to develop self-driving cars and optimize traffic flow.(Goldsmith & Burton, 2017)

However, there are also concerns about the potential negative impacts of AI. One concern is job displacement, as AI-powered machines and software could replace many human workers in a variety of industries. There are also concerns about bias in AI algorithms, which can lead to unfair treatment of certain groups of people.

To address these concerns, it is important for researchers, policymakers, and society at large to consider both the benefits and risks of AI and work towards responsible development and use of this technology.(Jiang et al., 2017) This includes developing AI that is transparent, accountable, and free from bias, as well as providing support and training for workers who may be affected by AI-driven automation. Overall, AI has the potential to transform many aspects of society, but it is important to approach its development and use with caution and a focus on responsible innovation.mentioned earlier, it's important to recognize the potential long-term impacts of artificial intelligence (AI) on society. As AI becomes more advanced, it is likely to have a significant impact on the job market, with many jobs potentially becoming automated. This could lead to increased inequality if workers are not provided with the necessary training and support to transition to new roles.

Another concern with AI is the potential for bias in decision-making algorithms. If AI algorithms are trained on biased data or programmed with biased rules, they could perpetuate and even amplify existing biases in society. This could lead to unfair treatment of certain groups of people, particularly those who are historically marginalized or underrepresented.

To address these concerns, it is important for AI researchers, developers, and policymakers to prioritize transparency and accountability in AI systems. This includes making sure that AI systems are developed in an open and transparent manner, with clear guidelines for how decisions are made. It also means building in mechanisms for monitoring and auditing AI systems to ensure that they are operating fairly and without bias.

In the above discussed chapter we can get an knowledge of what and how does artificial intelligence plays an role in the field of computer science and we are using that that technology without our own knowledge. this chapter covers the major details relevant to the topic

Finally, it is important to recognize that AI is still a developing technology, and there are many unanswered questions about how it will evolve and impact society in the years to come. As such, it is important for stakeholders to engage in ongoing dialogue and debate about the future of AI, in order to ensure that its development and use are aligned with society's values and priorities.

REFERENCES

Aggarwal, K., Mijwil, M. M., Al-Mistarehi, A.-H., Alomari, S., Gök, M., Zein Alaabdin, A. M., & Abdulrhman, S. H. (2022). *Has the Future Started?* The Current Growth of Artificial Intelligence, Machine Learning, and Deep Learning., doi:10.52866/ijcsm.2022.01.01.013

Baron, R. J. (1981). Mechanisms of human facial recognition. *International Journal of Man-Machine Studies*, *15*(2), 137–178. doi:10.1016/S0020-7373(81)80001-6

Berente, N., Gu, B., Recker, J., & Santhanam, R. (n.d.). *Managing AI Managing Artificial Intelligence.* MIS Quarterly, *1*. doi:10.25300/MISQ/2021/16274

Bhbosale, S., Pujari, V., & Multani, Z. (n.d.). National Seminar on "Trends in Geography, Commerce, IT And Sustainable Development" Advantages And Disadvantages Of Artificial Intellegence. *AI Journal.* www.aiirjournal.com

Borenstein, J., & Howard, A. (2020). Emerging challenges in AI and the need for AI ethics education. *AI and Ethics, 1*(1), 61–65. doi:10.1007/s43681-020-00002-7

Bostrom, N., & Yudkowsky, E. (2018). The Ethics of Artificial Intelligence. *Artificial Intelligence Safety and Security*, 57–69. doi:10.1201/9781351251389-4

Breazeal, C., Dautenhahn, K., & Kanda, T. (2016). Social Robotics. *Springer Handbooks*, 1935–1972. doi:10.1007/978-3-319-32552-1_72/COVER

Briganti, G., & le Moine, O. (2020). Artificial Intelligence in Medicine: Today and Tomorrow. *Frontiers in Medicine*, 7, 27. doi:10.3389/fmed.2020.00027 PMID:32118012

Brynjolfsson, E., & Mcafee, A. (n.d.). *Artificial Intelligence, For Real.*

Buchanan, B. G. (2005). A (Very) Brief History of Artificial Intelligence. *AI Magazine*, *26*(4), 53–53. doi:10.1609/AIMAG.V26I4.1848

Bundy, A. (2016). Preparing for the future of Artificial Intelligence. *AI & SOCIETY 2016, 32*(2), 285–287. doi:10.1007/s00146-016-0685-0

Burke, R., Felfernig, A., & Göker, M. H. (2011). Recommender Systems: An Overview. *AI Magazine*, *32*(3), 13–18. doi:10.1609/aimag.v32i3.2361

Chassignol, M., Khoroshavin, A., Klimova, A., & Bilyatdinova, A. (2018). Artificial Intelligence trends in education: A narrative overview. *Procedia Computer Science, 136*, 16–24. doi:10.1016/j.procs.2018.08.233

Chhaya, K., Khanzode, A., & Sarode, R. D. (n.d.-a). *Advantages And Disadvantages Of Artificial Intelligence And Machine Learning: A Literature Review*. IAEME. http://www.iaeme.com/IJLIS/index.asp30http://www.iaeme.com/IJLIS/issues.asp?JType=IJLIS&VType=9&IType=1JournalImpactFactor

Chhaya, K., Khanzode, A., & Sarode, R. D. (n.d.-b). *Advantages And Disadvantages Of Artificial Intelligence And Machine Learning: A Literature Review*. IAEME. http://www.iaeme.com/IJLIS/index.asp30http://www.iaeme.com/IJLIS/issues.asp?JType=IJLIS&VType=9&IType=1JournalImpactFactor

Critchlow, A. J. (1985). *Introduction to robotics*. MacMillan Press Ltd.

Dietterich, T. G. (1997). Machine-Learning Research. *AI Magazine, 18*(4), 97–97. doi:10.1609/AIMAG.V18I4.1324

Etzioni, A., & Etzioni, O. (2017). Incorporating Ethics into Artificial Intelligence. *The Journal of Ethics, 21*(4), 403–418. doi:10.100710892-017-9252-2

Evolving artificial intelligence. (n.d.). eLibrary. https://www.elibrary.ru/item.asp?id=5780219

Forsyth, D. & Ponce, J. (2003). *Computer vision : a modern approach.*

Garcia, E., Jimenez, M. A., de Santos, P. G., & Armada, M. (2007). The evolution of robotics research. *IEEE Robotics & Automation Magazine, 14*(1), 90–103. doi:10.1109/MRA.2007.339608

Goldsmith, J., & Burton, E. (2017). Why Teaching Ethics to AI Practitioners Is Important. *Proceedings of the AAAI Conference on Artificial Intelligence, 31*(1), 110–114. doi:10.1609/aaai.v31i1.11139

Hamet, P., & Tremblay, J. (2017). Artificial intelligence in medicine. *Metabolism: Clinical and Experimental, 69*, S36–S40. doi:10.1016/j.metabol.2017.01.011 PMID:28126242

He, X., Yan, S., Hu, Y., Niyogi, P., & Zhang, H. J. (2005). Face recognition using Laplacianfaces. *IEEE Transactions on Pattern Analysis and Machine Intelligence, 27*(3), 328–340. doi:10.1109/TPAMI.2005.55 PMID:15747789

Holzinger, A., Langs, G., Denk, H., Zatloukal, K., & Müller, H. (2019). Causability and explainability of artificial intelligence in medicine. *Wiley Interdisciplinary Reviews. Data Mining and Knowledge Discovery, 9*(4), e1312. doi:10.1002/widm.1312 PMID:32089788

Huang, C., Zhang, Z., Mao, B., & Yao, X. (2022). An Overview of Artificial Intelligence Ethics. *IEEE Transactions on Artificial Intelligence.* doi:10.1109/TAI.2022.3194503

Jiang, F., Jiang, Y., Zhi, H., Dong, Y., Li, H., Ma, S., Wang, Y., Dong, Q., Shen, H., & Wang, Y. (2017). Artificial intelligence in healthcare: Past, present and future. *Stroke and Vascular Neurology, 2*(4), 230–243. doi:10.1136vn-2017-000101 PMID:29507784

Jones, K. S. (1994). Natural Language Processing: A Historical Review. Current Issues in Computational Linguistics: In Honour of Don Walker, 3–16. doi:10.1007/978-0-585-35958-8_1

Jordan, M. I., & Mitchell, T. M. (2015). Machine learning: Trends, perspectives, and prospects. *Science*, *349*(6245), 255–260. doi:10.1126cience.aaa8415 PMID:26185243

Kakani, V., Nguyen, V. H., Kumar, B. P., Kim, H., & Pasupuleti, V. R. (2020). A critical review on computer vision and artificial intelligence in food industry. *Journal of Agriculture and Food Research*, *2*, 100033. doi:10.1016/j.jafr.2020.100033

Kalyanakrishnan, S., Panicker, R. A., Natarajan, S., & Rao, S. (2018). Opportunities and Challenges for Artificial Intelligence in India. *AIES 2018 - Proceedings of the 2018 AAAI/ACM Conference on AI, Ethics, and Society*, 164–170. 10.1145/3278721.3278738

Kumar, N., Kharkwal, N., Kohli, R., & Choudhary, S. (2016). Ethical aspects and future of artificial intelligence. *2016 1st International Conference on Innovation and Challenges in Cyber Security*, 111–114. 10.1109/ICICCS.2016.7542339

Martínez-López, F. J., & Casillas, J. (2013). Artificial intelligence-based systems applied in industrial marketing: An historical overview, current and future insights. *Industrial Marketing Management*, *42*(4), 489–495. doi:10.1016/j.indmarman.2013.03.001

Mccarthy, J. (2004). *What Is Artificial Intelligence?* Stanford. http://www-formal.stanford.edu/jmc/

McDermott, D. (1976). Artificial intelligence meets natural stupidity. *ACM SIGART Bulletin*, *57*(57), 4–9. doi:10.1145/1045339.1045340

Mijwil, M. M., Aggarwal, K., Mutar, D. S., Mansour, N., Singh, R., & Singh, S. (2022). The Position of Artificial Intelligence in the Future of Education: An Overview. *Asian Journal of Applied Sciences*, *10*(2), 2321–0893. doi:10.24203/ajas.v10i2.6956

Minsky, M. (1961). Steps Toward Artificial Intelligence. *Proceedings of the IRE*, *49*(1), 8–30. doi:10.1109/JRPROC.1961.287775

Mishkoff, H. C. (1986). *Understanding artificial intelligence*. Howard W. Sams and Co., Inc.

Musliner, D. J., Hendler, J. A., Agrawala, A. K., Durfee, E. H., Strosnider, J. K., & Paul, C. J. (1995). The Challenges of Real-Time Al. *Computer*, *28*(1), 58–66. doi:10.1109/2.362628

Provost, F. (n.d.). *On Applied Research in Machine Learning*.

Riedl, M. O. (2019). Human-centered artificial intelligence and machine learning. *Human Behavior and Emerging Technologies*, *1*(1), 33–36. doi:10.1002/hbe2.117

Shabbir, J., & Anwer, T. (2018). *Artificial Intelligence and its Role in Near Future*. https://doi.org/doi:10.48550/arxiv.1804.01396

Siau, K., & Wang, W. (1 C.E.). Artificial Intelligence (AI) Ethics: Ethics of AI and Ethical AI. *Database Management*, *31*(2), 74–87. doi:10.4018/JDM.2020040105

Stead, W. W. (2018). Clinical Implications and Challenges of Artificial Intelligence and Deep Learning. *Journal of the American Medical Association*, *320*(11), 1107–1108. doi:10.1001/jama.2018.11029 PMID:30178025

Wuest, T., Weimer, D., Irgens, C., & Thoben, K. D. (2016). *Machine learning in manufacturing: advantages, challenges, and applications.* Taylor & Francis. doi:10.1080/21693277.2016.1192517

Xu, F., Uszkoreit, H., Du, Y., Fan, W., Zhao, D., & Zhu, J. (2019). Explainable AI: A Brief Survey on History, Research Areas, Approaches and Challenges. Lecture Notes in Computer Science (Including Subseries Lecture Notes in Artificial Intelligence and Lecture Notes in Bioinformatics), 11839 LNAI, 563–574. https://doi.org/ doi:10.1007/978-3-030-32236-6_51/COVER

Zhang, C., & Lu, Y. (2021). Study on artificial intelligence: The state of the art and future prospects. *Journal of Industrial Information Integration*, *23*, 100224. doi:10.1016/j.jii.2021.100224

Chapter 3
Automatic Video Object Detection Using Particle Swarm Optimisation in Fog Computing

M. Sakthivanitha

Vels Institute of Science Technology and Advanced Studies, India

S. Saradha

Vels Institute of Science Technology and Advanced Studies, India

ABSTRACT

In this chapter, the authors focus on optimising video surveillance by considering five factors while processing the surveillance. The five factors are bandwidth availability, connection availability, storage availability, CPU availability, and memory availability. Since the research work mainly focused on fog computing environment, two major factors are bandwidth and connection availability while sending a video content to the authorized person. The size of video content will be large and slow while transferring the data from one location to another location through wireless network. This problem will be optimized using particle swarm optimization algorithm (PSO). This proposed PSO algorithm will optimize the video content and make it effective and efficient to transfer from one location to another location, and then the object detection (OD) is conducted using suitable hardware arrangements involving a microcontroller unit and GSM communication module for altering the user with objects in forest area.

INTRODUCTION

Object detection and recognition have been actively researched in recent years as a result of their widespread application in a variety of fields, including manufacturing, security, surveillance, medicine, and robotic systems, all of which have shown promising results in terms of accuracy and efficiency (Tang & Chen, 2021). This is due to the fact that their widespread application has resulted in an increase in the number of research opportunities in these areas (Chakravarthi & Venkatesan, 2015). The human eye is incredibly precise, allowing us to conduct and process complex images while also analyzing them

DOI: 10.4018/979-8-3693-1301-5.ch003

quickly (Chakravarthi & Venkatesan, 2016). On computers, it takes a lot of effort to recognize and identify an object in an image, and when we apply this to live video streaming in real-time, we will not be able to fulfil our goals, even with the most advanced approaches (Wu, et al., 2020; Vishwanathraddi & Chakravarthi, 2017).

It is challenging to put out forest fires in a short amount of time due to the rapid rate at which they spread once they have started (Chakravarthi & Venkatesan, 2018). Even though early detection of forest fires is essential, it appears that current detection methods need to be improved when it comes to detecting them in open forest settings (Jolly & Jindal, 2016). These improvements are required (Uday Kiran Ruttala & Balamurugan, 2015). Sensor-based detection systems (Cui, 2020) have good indoor performance, but because of their high cost of coverage (Wu, et al., 2021; Ahmed, et al., 2021), they are difficult to install outside (Fabela, et al., 2017).

It is impossible for firefighters to be of assistance because they are unable to provide vital visual information that could enable them to rapidly assess the situation at the fire scene (Lohith Ujjaniya, 2015). Large open spaces are not an ideal setting for infrared or ultraviolet detectors (Hu, et al., 2022; Ponn, et al., 2020) due to the fact that these detectors are susceptible to interference as a result of their limited detection range (Patil, et al., 2021). In spite of the fact that SAR (Chiang, et al., 2020) is effective at identifying large-scale forest fires, it is not effective at detecting localised fires that are just getting started (Xu, et al., 2020; Moura, et al., 2021).

Any solution that uses RGB images to recognise things can only do so successfully in bright light if the images themselves were captured using RGB (Bhandari, et al., 2021). In addition, there is a possibility that a surveillance application will need a greater quantity of light in order for RGB images or videos to function appropriately for the task of object detection (Zhang, et al., 2020). This possibility exists because there is a possibility that a surveillance application will need to detect objects (Chen, et al., 2021). This will add another layer of complexity to the situation. An infrared video surveillance system is used to capture images of potentially suspicious activity that occurs at night (Patil, et al., 2015). These images are then manually examined for indications of potentially questionable behaviour (Zan, et al., 2020). If the area to be monitored is too large, it will take a significant amount of time and effort to successfully complete this entire process. Automating the process of real-time object detection is essential to achieving success in overcoming the challenges outlined above (Zhang, et al., 2020).

Due to the large size of the video content's file, moving it from one location to another through a wireless network will be a time-consuming process that will take a long time (Jain, 2022abc). Within the context of this study, video surveillance is carried out by maximising the available bandwidth, connections, storage, processing power, and memory (Jain, et al., 2022). The assignment of hardware that can recognise items in an image by making use of a meta-heuristic optimisation in a video frame is a novel aspect of this body of work (Jain, et al., 2022).

The main contribution of the study involves the following:

- The authors focused on the cloud environment; two major factors are bandwidth and connection availability while sending video content to the authorized person.
- The study aims to optimize the size of video content using the Particle Swarm Optimization algorithm (PSO). PSO algorithm will be optimized video content and make it effective and efficient to transfer from one location to another location.

- The author chooses PSO to detect the objects in the video frame since it is more efficient in finding the region of interest with its velocity and position estimation than other optimization methods (Kumar, et al., 2022).
- Finally, object detection (OD) is conducted using suitable hardware arrangements involving a microcontroller unit and GSM communication module for altering the user with objects in the forest area.

The paper's outline is as follows: Section 2 presents the related works. Section 3 discusses the proposed model. Section 4 evaluates the entire work, and section 5 concludes the model with possible directions for future scope.

1. RELATED WORKS

The recent developments that have been made in computer vision have provided researchers with the impetus to create a model that is both efficient and effective in detecting fires.

Chen et al. (2004) provided colourimetric and disorder measures based on an RGB model for extracting video fire pixels, which they found to be effective. To extract fire pixels, colour information is employed in conjunction with dynamic information, which is needed to establish that the fire is real.

Töreyin, et al., (2006) identified flame flicker by employing a combination of a 1D temporal wavelet transform and a 2D spatial wavelet transform. This approach makes use of information about colour and temporal fluctuation in order to reduce the number of false alarms generated in real-world environments.

The video sequences and the images were analysed by Çelik, et al., (2007), and a fuzzy colour model was proposed based on a statistical analysis of the results of that analysis. Using this model in conjunction with motion analysis, it is able to reliably discern between fire and fire-like things.

Teng, et al., (2010) use hidden Markov models to study the features of flames and suggest a real-time fire detection system based on moving pixel detection and the assessment of fire colours, among other things.

Chino, et al., (2015) demonstrated that video algorithms are subject to a number of major constraints by utilising video as an illustration. BowFire, a breakthrough new fire detection technology, was designed to tackle this issue. Detecting fire in still photos was accomplished by colour characteristics and superpixel texture distinction. Tradition has it that the conventional approach to fire detection utilises image processing to provide fake attributes such as colour, motion, and texture. This method is effective.

Kim, & Lee, (2019) employed a quicker R-CNN to discriminate between fire and non-fire zones. The dependability of a fire alarm system is also examined by utilizing long durations of short-term Memory. Lee, & Shim, (2019) built a video-based fire detection model that employed R-CNN to build a fire candidate zone for each video frame. The final fire regions were chosen by considering both spatial and temporal criteria.

Pan et al. (2020) developed a camera-based wildfire detection system that used a block-based analytic technique to increase detection accuracy. They did so by applying transfer learning techniques. Because redundant filters with low energy impulse response were removed from the model, its efficiency on edge devices was boosted.

Wu et al. (2020) utilised PCA to analyse forest fire photos before feeding them into a training network to see how well they worked. When two models were applied combined, the accuracy of the location findings was enhanced. The majority of studies favour using groups of learners to complete object detection tasks rather than using individual learners because of the possibility of false negatives. Individual learners are given object detection tasks to complete.

2. PROPOSED METHOD

In this part of the process, we begin optimising the films by first decreasing the video length so that it does not contain any potential object detections. This is done so that the videos do not contain any potential for object detection. In order to accomplish this trimming, a PSO method is utilised. This algorithm takes into account the availability of bandwidth, connection, storage, CPU, and Memory in order to develop the multi-objective function. In the second step of the process, we construct a hardware module that is capable of recognising things inside trimmed films. This module makes use of a micro-controller unit (MCU) that is programmed with an object detection algorithm to make the recognition possible. In the end, the objects that have been spotted are uploaded to the cloud via the GSM module. After that, an alert is delivered to the user in the event that there has been an intrusion in the forest region. Figure 1 provides a visual representation of this concept.

Figure 1. Detection framework

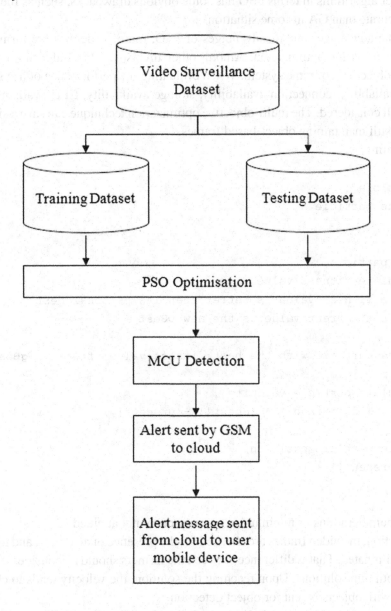

2.1. PSO Video Optimisation

PSO, or population-based optimization, is a strategy based on the movement of bird flocks and schools of schooling fish. Many of the characteristics of PSO are similar to those of evolutionary computation. The system is initially configured with a random population of solutions, and it is then used to search for the best solution using generations.

In contrast to GA, which has evolution operators like crossover and mutation, PSO does not have these. When using PSO, potential solutions are found by following the current optimal particles in the issue space, collectively referred to as particles. In terms of Memory and processing performance, PSO outperforms other algorithms in terms PSO has some obvious drawbacks, such as the fact that it is less practical and accurate than GA in some situations.

Because of the advantages and disadvantages of PSO, more academics are turning to a PSO-GA algorithm combination for optimization. Among other things, the PSO algorithm was employed to remove the non-object video frame system. When evaluating the performance of a system, factors such as bandwidth availability, connection availability, storage availability, CPU availability, and memory availability are all considered. The multi-objective optimization technique can save a significant amount of energy while still maintaining object-based frames.

PSO Algorithm

```
For each particle
    Initialize particle
END
Do
    For each particle
        Calculate fitness value
        If the fitness value is better than its personal best
            set current value as the new pBest
    End
    Choose the particle with the best fitness value of all as gBest
    For each particle
        Calculate particle velocity
v[] = c0 *v[]  + c1 * rand() * (pbest[] - present[]) + c2 * rand() * (gbest[]
- present[])
        Update particle position
present[] = present[] + v[]
    End
```

While maximum iterations or minimum error criteria are not attained

For each iteration, the video frames are checked for the presence of an object, and the frames without the objects are eliminated. That is difference between the farmers should be considered zero while locating the global optimum solutions. Upon reaching the solution, the velocity tends to change, and hence the video frame with objects is sent for object detection.

In an object detection problem, the similarity of the pixel is colour, and the expected colour is checked in the pixels. Accurate detection is hence obtained when the particles move with related velocity to find the region of interest in a video frame. The formulation of the local and global best solution in reaching the region of interest helps in finding out the object moving in the space of a video frame.

2.2. MCU Detection

Table 1 shows the details of the hardware specifications used in the work. Figure 2 shows the Hardware Specifications, and Figure 3 shows the snapshots of the Object Detection process at FPS 0.70. The objects Detection at the FPS of 0.67 and 0.64 is given in Figure 4, and finally the snapshot of the message received is shown in Figure 5.

Table 1. Hardware specifications

Hardware Unit	Configuration
MCU	ATMega 32
MCU – GSM interface	MAX232
GSM Modem	SIM900A GSM GPRS Module
Camera Type for detection	OV7670 640×480 VGA CMOS Camera Image Sensor Module
Camera Pixels	640×480
LED	ADALM2000

Figure 2. Hardware specifications

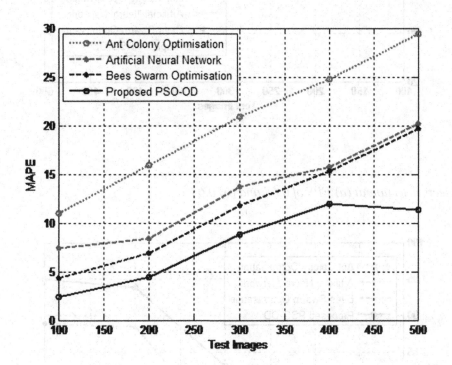

Figure 3. Screenshot of object detection process at FPS 0.70

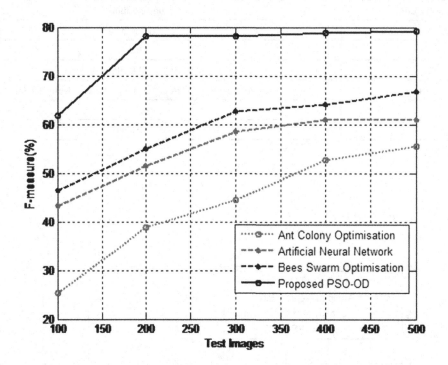

Figure 4. Objects detection at (a) FPS of 0.67 and (b) 0.64

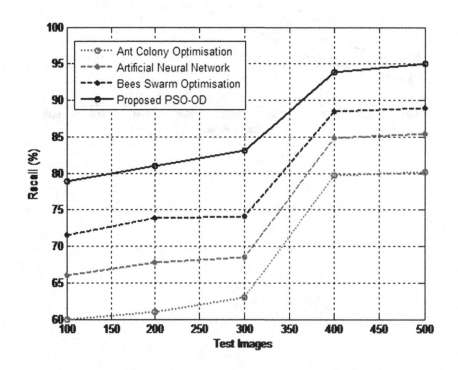

Figure 5. Alert sent to Android device

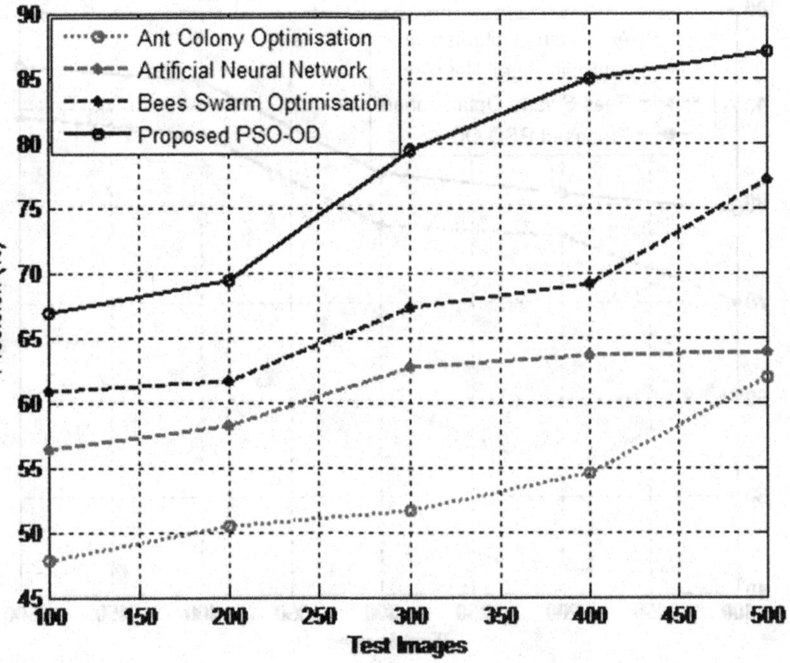

3. RESULTS AND DISCUSSIONS

In this section, the simulation is conducted using Python that runs on a primary memory of 16GB and 2 TB of secondary memory. The processor selected for the operation is an i7 core processor with 8GB GPU. The entire testing is conducted using four different metrics that include accuracy, precision, recall, f-measure and detection of error with existing Bees Swarm Optimisation, Artificial Neural Network and Ant colony optimization.

The datasets are collected from the CAMEL database (https://camel.ece.gatech.edu/, which contains 30 sequences, where 25 videos are used for training, and the remaining five videos are used for testing.

These sequences contain different sets of parameters that include Date, Time, Weather Observation Time, Temp, Windchill, Dew Point, Humidity, Pressure, Visibility, Wind Dir, Wind Speed, Gust Speed, Precip, Events, Conditions, Target Density, elevation, Visual Camera, Visual FPS, Visual Resolution, IR Camera, IR FPS, IR Resolution, length, frames, are some of the common parameters used in the study.

Hence, the identification of the intruder in a video is identified using the background parameters (discussed above) and the body heat of an intruder based on the type of infrared camera used in the forest.

Figure 6. Accuracy

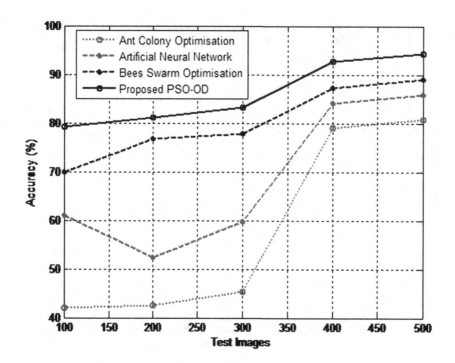

As seen in Figure 6, the input datasets used to assess classification accuracy had a high level of multi-modal cases. The proposed PSO-OD is compared with existing meta-heuristic approaches like ant colony optimization, artificial neural network, and bees swarm optimization. Compared to existing methods for detecting objects in large video frames, the simulation results suggest that the proposed method is more accurate.

Figure 7. Precision

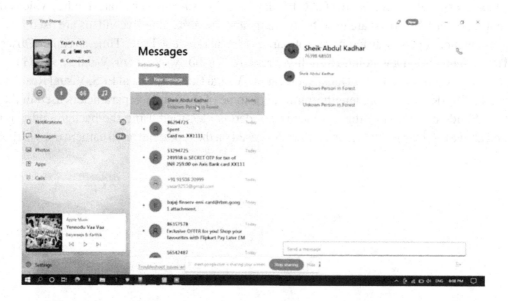

Data from the input datasets used to assess multi-modal precision are shown in Figure 7. The proposed PSO-OD is compared with existing meta-heuristic approaches like ant colony optimization, artificial neural network, and bees swarm optimization. It has been demonstrated through simulations that the suggested method is more accurate in detecting large video frames than existing methods.

Figure 8. Recall

Figure 8 demonstrates the recall rate on multi-modal cases from the test datasets. The proposed PSO-OD is compared with existing meta-heuristic approaches like ant colony optimization, artificial neural network, and bees swarm optimization. It was found that the proposed method had a higher recall rate in recognizing large video frames than existing methods, as demonstrated by simulations.

Figure 9. F-measure

Data from the input datasets used to compute the f-measure for multi-modal occurrences are shown in Figure 9. The Proposed PSO-OD is compared with existing meta-heuristic approaches like ant colony optimization, artificial neural network, and bees swarm optimization. The simulation results suggest that the proposed method has a higher rate of f-measure detection than existing methods for large video frames.

Figure 10. Error rate

An example of a multi-modal error from the input datasets is shown in Figure 10. The proposed PSO-OD is compared with existing meta-heuristic approaches like ant colony optimization, artificial neural network, and bees swarm optimization. It has been demonstrated through simulations that the suggested method has a lower error rate than other methods for detecting objects across large video frames.

4. CONCLUSION

The study is primarily concerned with optimizing video surveillance systems. It is necessary to examine the availability of various resources, such as bandwidth, connections, storage, CPU, and Memory. PSO optimizes video material to move it from one site to another while increasing its efficiency and effectiveness. By utilizing the appropriate hardware configurations, the OD can alert the user to the presence of things in the surrounding forest. In a simulation, the PSO-OD is evaluated compared to existing meta-heuristic models. Simulations show that the proposed system can detect 98% of suspicious activity in monitoring areas due to its ability to process video footage faster than current technologies. We could identify the individual considerably more quickly and precisely thanks to the object detection in-depth picture technology. Although a monitor or a chair can be easily identified in an RGB image, this technique is only sometimes successful when used to detect them in depth images. A greater variety of images and objects will be used to train the model, which will aid in its improvement. Because we are primarily concerned with intrusion detection and surveillance applications, the detection of a single individual is sufficient.

REFERENCES

Ahmed, A., Jalal, A., & Kim, K. (2021). Multi-objects Detection and Segmentation for Scene Understanding Based on Texton Forest and Kernel Sliding Perceptron. *Journal of Electrical Engineering & Technology*, *16*(2), 1143–1150. doi:10.100742835-020-00650-z

Bhandari, A., Prasad, P. W. C., Alsadoon, A., & Maag, A. (2021). Object detection and recognition: Using deep learning to assist the visually impaired. *Disability and Rehabilitation. Assistive Technology*, *16*(3), 280–288. doi:10.1080/17483107.2019.1673834 PMID:31694420

Çelik, T., Özkaramanlı, H., & Demirel, H. (2007). Fire and smoke detection without sensors: Image processing based approach. In *2007 15th European Signal Processing Conference* (pp. 1794-1798). IEEE.

Chakravarthi, M. K., & Venkatesan, N. (2015). Design and Implementation of LabVIEW Based Optimally Tuned PI Controller for A Real Time Non Linear Process. *Asian Journal of Scientific Research*, *8*(1), 95–106. doi:10.3923/ajsr.2015.95.106

Chakravarthi, M. K., & Venkatesan, N. (2016). Implementation of a Multi user Secured Remote Data Logger for Real Time Hybrid System. *Indian Journal of Science and Technology*, *9*(35).

Chakravarthi, M. K., & Venkatesan, N. (2018). Adaptive type-2 fuzzy controller for nonlinear delay dominant MIMO systems: An experimental paradigm in LabVIEW. *International Journal of Advanced Intelligence Paradigms*, *10*(4), 354–373. doi:10.1504/IJAIP.2018.092033

Chen, T. H., Wu, P. H., & Chiou, Y. C. (2004). An early fire-detection method based on image processing. In *2004 International Conference on Image Processing, 2004. ICIP'04.* (Vol. 3, pp. 1707-1710). IEEE. 10.1109/ICIP.2004.1421401

Chen, Z., Zhang, J., & Tao, D. (2021). Recursive context routing for object detection. *International Journal of Computer Vision*, *129*(1), 142–160. doi:10.100711263-020-01370-7

Chiang, C. Y., Barnes, C., Angelov, P., & Jiang, R. (2020). Deep Learning-Based Automated Forest Health Diagnosis From Aerial Images. *IEEE Access : Practical Innovations, Open Solutions*, *8*, 144064–144076. doi:10.1109/ACCESS.2020.3012417

Chino, D. Y., Avalhais, L. P., Rodrigues, J. F., & Traina, A. J. (2015). Bowfire: detection of fire in still images by integrating pixel color and texture analysis. In *2015 28th SIBGRAPI conference on graphics, patterns and images* (pp. 95-102). IEEE. 10.1109/SIBGRAPI.2015.19

Cui, F. (2020). Deploy and integrate smart sensors with IoT devices detecting fire disasters in huge forest environments. *Computer Communications*, *150*, 818–827. doi:10.1016/j.comcom.2019.11.051

Fabela, O., Patil, S., Chintamani, S., & Dennis, B. H. (2017). *Estimation of effective thermal conductivity of porous media utilizing inverse heat transfer analysis on cylindrical configuration* (Vol. 8). Heat Transfer and Thermal Engineering. doi:10.1115/IMECE2017-71559

Hu, Y., Zhan, J., Zhou, G., Chen, A., Cai, W., Guo, K., Hu, Y., & Li, L. (2022). Fast forest fire smoke detection using MVMNet. *Knowledge-Based Systems*, *241*, 108219. doi:10.1016/j.knosys.2022.108219

Jain, A. K., Misra, T., Tyagi, N., Suresh Kumar, M. V., & Pant, B. (2022). A Comparative Study on Cyber security Technology in Big data Cloud Computing Environment. *2022 5th International Conference on Contemporary Computing and Informatics (IC3I)*. IEEE.

Jain, A. K., Ross, D. S., Babu, M. K., Dharamvir, U. D., & Gangodkar, D. (2022). Cloud computing applications for protecting the information of healthcare department using smart internet of things appliance. *2022 5th International Conference on Contemporary Computing and Informatics (IC3I)*. IEEE.

Jolly, A., & Jindal, N. (2016). Birla sekaran, Dinesh," Transparent Proxy Cache server using Raspberry Pi. *Indian Journal of Science and Technology*, *9*(44).

Kim, B., & Lee, J. (2019). A video-based fire detection using deep learning models. *Applied Sciences (Basel, Switzerland)*, *9*(14), 2862. doi:10.3390/app9142862

Kumar, K. S., Yadav, D., Joshi, S. K., Chakravarthi, M. K., Jain, A. K., & Tripathi, V. (2022). Blockchain technology with applications to distributed control and cooperative robotics. *2022 5th International Conference on Contemporary Computing and Informatics (IC3I)*.

Kumar Jain, A. (2022a). Hybrid Cloud Computing: A Perspective. *International Journal of Engineering Research & Technology (Ahmedabad)*, *11*(10), 1–06.

Kumar Jain, A. (2022b). Multi-Cloud Computing & Why do we need to Embrace it. *International Journal of Engineering Research & Technology (Ahmedabad)*, *11*(09), 1–06.

Kumar Jain, A. (2022c). Overview of Serverless Architecture. *International Journal of Engineering Research & Technology (Ahmedabad)*, *11*(09), 1–06.

Lee, Y., & Shim, J. (2019). False positive decremented research for fire and smoke detection in surveillance camera using spatial and temporal features based on deep learning. *Electronics (Basel)*, *8*(10), 1167. doi:10.3390/electronics8101167

Lohith Ujjaniya, M. K. (2015). Raspberry - Pi based cost effective vehicle collision avoidance system using image processing. *Journal of Engineering and Applied Sciences (Asian Research Publishing Network)*, *10*(7), 3001–3005.

Moura, M. M., de Oliveira, L. E. S., Sanquetta, C. R., Bastos, A., Mohan, M., & Corte, A. P. D. (2021). Towards Amazon Forest Restoration: Automatic Detection of Species from UAV Imagery. *Remote Sensing (Basel)*, *13*(13), 2627. doi:10.3390/rs13132627

Pan, H., Badawi, D., & Cetin, A. E. (2020). Computationally efficient wildfire detection method using a deep convolutional network pruned via Fourier analysis. *Sensors (Basel)*, *20*(10), 2891. doi:10.339020102891 PMID:32443739

Patil, S., Chintamani, S., Dennis, B. H., & Kumar, R. (2021). Real time prediction of internal temperature of heat generating bodies using neural network. *Thermal Science and Engineering Progress*, *23*(100910), 100910. doi:10.1016/j.tsep.2021.100910

Patil, S., Chintamani, S., Grisham, J., Kumar, R., & Dennis, B. H. (2015). Inverse determination of temperature distribution in partially cooled heat generating cylinder. *Volume 8B: Heat Transfer and Thermal Engineering.*

Ponn, T., Kröger, T., & Diermeyer, F. (2020). Identification and explanation of challenging conditions for camera-based object detection of automated vehicles. *Sensors (Basel)*, *20*(13), 3699. doi:10.339020133699 PMID:32630350

Tang, T., & Chen, B. (2021). F-Measure Optimization of Forest Flame Salient Object Detection Based on Boundary Perception. In *Artificial Intelligence in China* (pp. 436–442). Springer. doi:10.1007/978-981-15-8599-9_50

Teng, Z., Kim, J. H., & Kang, D. J. (2010). Fire detection based on hidden Markov models. *International Journal of Control, Automation, and Systems*, *8*(4), 822–830. doi:10.100712555-010-0414-2

Töreyin, B. U., Dedeoğlu, Y., Güdükbay, U., & Cetin, A. E. (2006). Computer vision-based method for real-time fire and flame detection. *Pattern Recognition Letters*, *27*(1), 49–58. doi:10.1016/j.patrec.2005.06.015

Uday Kiran Ruttala, M. S., & Balamurugan, M. K. (2015). NFC based Smart Campus Payment System". NFC Based Smart Campus Payment System. *Indian Journal of Science and Technology*, *8*, 1–5.

Vishwanathraddi, A., & Chakravarthi, M. (2017). Arduino-based wireless mobot. *Asian Journal of Pharmaceutical and Clinical Research*, *10*(13), 61–65. doi:10.22159/ajpcr.2017.v10s1.19562

Wu, B., Liang, A., Zhang, H., Zhu, T., Zou, Z., Yang, D., & Su, J. (2021). Application of conventional UAV-based high-throughput object detection to the early diagnosis of pine wilt disease by deep learning. *Forest Ecology and Management*, *486*, 118986. doi:10.1016/j.foreco.2021.118986

Wu, S., Guo, C., & Yang, J. (2020). Using PCA and one-stage detectors for real-time forest fire detection. *Journal of Engineering (Stevenage, England)*, *2020*(13), 383–387. doi:10.1049/joe.2019.1145

Wu, S., Guo, C., & Yang, J. (2020). Using PCA and one-stage detectors for real-time forest fire detection. *Journal of Engineering (Stevenage, England)*, *2020*(13), 383–387. doi:10.1049/joe.2019.1145

Xu, S., Zhu, J., Jiang, J., & Shui, P. (2020). Sea-surface floating small target detection by multifeature detector based on isolation forest. *IEEE Journal of Selected Topics in Applied Earth Observations and Remote Sensing*, *14*, 704–715. doi:10.1109/JSTARS.2020.3033063

Zan, X., Zhang, X., Xing, Z., Liu, W., Zhang, X., Su, W., & Li, S. (2020). Automatic Detection of Maize Tassels from UAV Images by Combining Random Forest Classifier and VGG16. *Remote Sensing (Basel)*, *12*(18), 3049. doi:10.3390/rs12183049

Zhang, H., Zhao, M., Liu, L., Zhong, H., Liang, Z., Yang, Y., & Wang, Y. (2020). Deep multimodel cascade method based on CNN and random forest for pharmaceutical particle detection. *IEEE Transactions on Instrumentation and Measurement*, *69*(9), 7028–7042. doi:10.1109/TIM.2020.2973843

Zhang, J., Li, M., Feng, Y., & Yang, C. (2020). Robotic grasp detection based on image processing and random forest. *Multimedia Tools and Applications*, *79*(3), 2427–2446. doi:10.100711042-019-08302-9

Chapter 4
Comparative Analysis Implementation of Queuing Songs in Players Using Audio Clustering Algorithm

B. Aarthi

SRM Institute of Science and Technology, Ramapuram, India

Prathap Selvakumar

(iD) https://orcid.org/0009-0008-5201-593X

SRM Institute of Science and Technology, Ramapuram, India

S. Subiksha

SRM Institute of Science and Technology, Ramapuram, India

S. Chhavi

SRM Institute of Science and Technology, Ramapuram, India

Swetha Parathasarathy

SRM Institute of Science and Technology, Ramapuram, India

ABSTRACT

This chapter compares the toughness of k-means, DBSCAN, and adaptive clustering algorithms for grouping data points into distinct clusters. The k-means algorithm is a widely used method that is easy to implement and efficient. The DBSCAN algorithm is a density-based method that is well-suited for datasets with clusters of varying densities, but it can be sensitive to the choice of parameters. In order to determine the ideal number of clusters within a dataset, adaptive clustering algorithms dynamically alter the number of clusters during the clustering process. The production of these algorithms is evaluated on a variety of datasets, and the results are compared in terms of accuracy and efficiency. According to the chapter's conclusion, each method has advantages and disadvantages of its own, and the ideal approach to apply will vary depending on the particular dataset and the objectives of the study.

DOI: 10.4018/979-8-3693-1301-5.ch004

1. INTRODUCTION

While the term didn't exist, the idea of multimedia could be taken back to when the 19th-century composer Richard Wagner believed in the concept of Gesamtkunstwerk, meaning 'total artwork.' In modern times, a multimedia device can be an electronic device, such as a smartphone, a videogame system, or a computer (Joachims, 1998). Multimedia presentations are presentations featuring multiple types of media. The different types of media can include videos, animations, and audio. Music is played in public and private areas, highlighted at festivals, rock concerts, and orchestra performances, and heard incidentally as part of a score or soundtrack to a film, TV show, opera, or video game (Bonnin & Jannach, 2014; Assi, et al., 2018; Density-based algorithm for clustering data – MATLAB, 2021).

A typical data analysis method used to locate groups or clusters within a dataset is cluster analysis. Data points in a cluster are more similar to one another than those in other clusters, and these groups are frequently based on the similarity of data points within the dataset (Rabiner & Juang, 1993).

One of the key applications for cluster analysis is market segmentation. By grouping customers into distinct clusters based on their characteristics and behavior, businesses can tailor their marketing efforts to better appeal to each group (Derindere Köseoğlu, et al., 2022). For example, a retail store might use cluster analysis to identify groups of customers who are likely to be interested in different products or services. By targeting these groups with specific marketing campaigns, the store can increase its sales and improve customer satisfaction (Ead, & Abbassy, 2021).

Another application of cluster analysis is in customer profiling. Businesses can create detailed profiles of each group by grouping customers into distinct clusters based on their characteristics and behavior. This can help businesses better understand their customers, predict their needs and preferences, and design products and services that better meet those needs (Abbassy & Mohamed, 2016). For example, a financial services company might use cluster analysis to identify groups of customers who are likely to be interested in different financial products, such as savings accounts, credit cards, or investments. By creating profiles of these groups, the company can design products and services that better meet their needs and preferences (Ead & Abbassy, 2022).

Another common application of cluster analysis is in social network analysis. By analyzing the connections between individuals in a social network, researchers can identify groups or clusters within the network. These groups can be based on the similarity of individuals within the network or on the strength of their connections. By understanding the structure of these groups, researchers can gain insight into the dynamics of the network and identify key individuals or groups who play a significant role in the network (Kumar, et al., 2022).

In conclusion, cluster analysis is a powerful data analysis technique that has a wide range of applications. This technique can help businesses and researchers better understand their data and make more informed decisions, whether used for market segmentation, customer profiling, or social network analysis. By grouping data points into distinct clusters, cluster analysis allows us to identify patterns and trends within a dataset and can provide valuable insights into the structure and behavior of the data.

2. TERMINOLOGY

In the context of clustering, various expressions, and ideas are frequently employed. Among the most significant ones are:

Clustering: The grouping or clustering of a dataset according to the data points' similarity. This can help find patterns and trends in the data and cluster the data points into significant groups (Mohamed, & Mesbah, 2016).

Distance measure: A distance measure is a formula that calculates the distance between two data points. Clustering techniques employ this distance metric, which can be based on several metrics like Euclidean distance or Manhattan distance, to determine how similar the data points are.

Centroid: The nucleus of a cluster is called a centroid. The centroid, which represents the cluster in k-means clustering, is the average of all the data points within the cluster.

Density: A dataset's density is a region's number of data points. Density-based clustering methods locate clusters by utilizing the dataset's data point density.

DBSCAN: DBSCAN (Density-Based Spatial Clustering of Applications with Noise) is a density-based clustering algorithm that groups data points into clusters based on the density of points within the dataset.

Hierarchical clustering: Hierarchical clustering is a clustering algorithm that groups data points into clusters by creating a hierarchy of clusters. This can be done using various techniques, such as single-linkage clustering or complete-linkage clustering.

K-Means: K-Means, a well-liked clustering technique, divides data points into a specified number of groups according to how distant they are from the cluster centers. The method assigns each data point to the cluster with the nearest cluster center, updates the cluster centers, and redistributes data until the clusters are in a stable configuration. Based on the number of clusters the user chooses, the algorithm will attempt to divide the data into that many clusters (Khalifa, et al., 2013). Although K-Means is an easy-to-use, uncomplicated approach, it might be sensitive to how the cluster centers are initialized and might not always produce optimal results (Kumar Jain, 2022).

Overall, many terms and concepts are commonly used in clustering. Understanding these terms and concepts is essential for effectively using clustering algorithms and interpreting the results of clustering analyses (Abbassy, et al., 2020).

3. DBSCAN

The density-based spatial clustering of applications with the noise method of Cluster DBSCAN is used to group data points from a P-dimensional feature space. A neighborhood is a P-dimensional circle in the feature space (Khalifa, et al., 2014).

If the -neighborhood of a core point contains other core points, the points in the -neighborhoods of all the core points merge to form a union of -neighborhoods. To implement the DBSCAN algorithm, we would need to follow these steps:

It is critical to understand both the issue the DBSCAN algorithm seeks to address and the strategy's objectives. DBSCAN is a density-based clustering approach that divides data points into clusters based on how evenly they are spread across the dataset. Unlike previous clustering methods, DBSCAN may locate clusters of any shape and does not need the number of clusters to be predetermined. This makes it well-suited for datasets with clusters of varying densities or complex, non-linear structures. The DBSCAN algorithm aims to identify these clusters within the dataset and assign each data point to the appropriate cluster.

Select appropriate data structures and algorithms for the implementation. To implement DBSCAN, we would need to use a data structure that can store the input data points and a data structure to store the clustered. We would also need a distance measure to determine the distance between data points and a method for identifying dense regions within the dataset (Jain, et al., 2022a).

Determine the algorithm by specifying the distance threshold (eps) and the minimum number of points for a dense region (minPts).

The DBSCAN algorithm operates by iterating over each data point in the dataset and performing the following steps. If the point is not in a dense region, it is marked as noise and is not assigned to a cluster. Repeat the previous step until all data points have been processed.

Test the implementation to ensure that it produces the expected results. This may involve running the implementation on various test cases and comparing the results to the expected output. For example, we could test the implementation on a dataset with known clusters and compare the results to the known clusters to ensure the implementation is correct (Sadek, et al., 2021).

Refine the implementation as necessary based on the results of testing. This may involve changing the code or the data structures used or adding additional features or functionality to the implementation. For example, we could add support for different distance measures or methods for identifying dense regions within the dataset.

Overall, implementing the DBSCAN algorithm would involve understanding the problem, selecting the appropriate data structures and algorithms, writing the code for the algorithm, testing the implementation, and refining the implementation as needed (Jain, et al., 2022b).

3.1. Metrics

DBSCAN algorithms have two key parameters that control the algorithm's performance: the distance threshold (eps) and the minimum number of points required for a dense region (minPts).

The distance threshold (eps) specifies that the highest distance between two data points is considered the same cluster. This parameter controls the granularity of the clusters, with smaller values of eps resulting in finer-grained clusters and larger values of eps resulting in coarser-grained clusters.

The number of points should be minimal for the dense region (minPts) is a parameter that specifies the data should contain fewer points for the cluster. The parameter controls the algorithm's sensitivity to noise, with smaller values of minPts allowing the algorithm to identify smaller clusters and potentially increase the amount of noise included in the clusters.

Overall, the distance threshold specifying distance threshold(eps) and the minimal number of points required for dense regions (minPts) are the key measuring parameters for DBSCAN algorithms. These parameters control the granularity and sensitivity of the algorithm and should be chosen carefully to ensure that the algorithm produces the optimal number of clusters and the required noise level.

3.2. Performance

The performance of DBSCAN algorithms can change based on the data input and analysis goal. In general, DBSCAN algorithms are suitable for datasets with varying densities and can accurately identify clusters of arbitrary shape. However, they can be sensitive to the choice of parameters and may not always produce the desired number of clusters.

One of the key strengths of DBSCAN algorithms is their ability to identify clusters of varying densities. These algorithms use a density-based approach, meaning they are a data group formed into a cluster based on the density of points within the dataset. This allows DBSCAN algorithms to identify clusters of arbitrary shape, which can be useful for datasets with complex or non-linear structures.

Another strength of DBSCAN algorithms is that they don't need to specify the number of clusters in advance. This allows the algorithm to identify the appropriate number of clusters within a dataset without requiring the user to specify the order of clusters beforehand. DBSCAN is used mostly when the number of clusters is not well defined.

However, DBSCAN algorithms have some limitations. For example, they can be sensitive to the choice of parameters, such as the distance threshold and minimal point required at the denser region (minPts). If these parameters are not chosen carefully, the algorithm may not produce the desired number of clusters or identify all clusters within the dataset.

Overall, the production of DBSCAN depends on the number of datasets and the aim of the analysis. These algorithms are suitable for datasets with varying densities and can accurately identify clusters of arbitrary shape. However, they can be sensitive to the choice of parameters and may not always produce the desired number of clusters.

3.3. Time Complexity

DBSCAN is a widely used algorithm that helps identify clusters of points in a dataset. The time complexity of the DBSCAN algorithm is typically expressed using big O notation, which indicates the growth rate of the operations needs the size of the input data increases.

Typically, DBSCAN has an $O(n \log n)$ time complexity, where n is the total number of data points in the dataset. This shows that the algorithm's execution time increases logarithmically as data points increase. For instance, the technique will run twice as slowly if the number of data points doubles. The complexity of DBSCAN can be changed based on several factors, including the density & distribution of data points, values of the parameters used by the algorithm, and the computational resources available. For example, if the data points are densely packed and well-distributed, the algorithm may require more time and computational resources. Additionally, if the values of the parameters used by the algorithm are set too low or too high, the algorithm may require more time to run and may not produce optimal results.

Despite the relatively low time complexity of DBSCAN, the algorithm can be computationally intensive when applied to large and complex datasets. In these cases, it may be necessary to use specialized hardware or distributed computing systems to run the algorithm in an acceptable time. Additionally, the algorithm may require significant tuning and optimization to produce optimal results for a particular dataset.

Overall, the time complexity of DBSCAN is relatively low compared to other clustering algorithms, making it a good choice for analyzing large and complex datasets. The algorithm's ability to identify clusters of points in a dataset, even noise and outliers, makes it a valuable tool for extracting insights from complex data.

3.4. Growth Rate

Regarding growth rate, DBSCAN's time complexity of Big $O(n \log n)$, which represents the time taken to run the algorithm, increases logarithmically with several data points. This makes DBSCAN relatively efficient, especially compared to other clustering algorithms with higher time complexity.

Overall, the growth rate of DBSCAN is relatively efficient, making it a good choice for clustering large datasets. However, it is important to remember that the production can also be based on other factors, such as the size and density of the data and the parameters used for the clustering process.

3.5. Asymptotic Notation

Regarding DBSCAN, the algorithm's time complexity is Big O (n log n), time taken to run the algorithm increases logarithmically based on the data. This means that DBSCAN is relatively efficient, especially compared to other clustering algorithms with higher time complexity.

Other asymptotic notations may also be used to depict the growth rate of DBSCAN in addition to big O notation. For instance, the theta notation may represent the upper and lower bounds of an algorithm's growth rate, whereas the omega notation may be used to define the lower bound. Big O notation is the most used asymptotic technique for describing the temporal complexity of algorithms.

3.6. Algorithm

The DBSCAN algorithm follows these steps:

Select a point randomly from the dataset and designate it as the starting point.

- Identify all points within a certain distance "ε" of the starting point and classify them as direct neighbors.
- If there are at least MinPts direct neighbors, a new cluster is formed, and the process continues for each direct neighbor.
- Repeat the process for all unvisited points until all points have been examined.
- If fewer than MinPts direct neighbors exist, the point is labeled as noise and ignored for further processing.
- Repeat the entire process for all starting points until all points are assigned to a cluster or marked as noise.

4. K-MEANS

K-means clustering is a common algorithm for clustering data points into distinct groups or clusters. To implement k- means clustering for audio, we first need to convert the audio signal into a numerical representation that the algorithm can process. This could be done by extracting features from the audio signal, such as the frequency spectrum or spectral centroid, and representing these features as numerical values. Next, we would need to K-means initialize by choosing the number of clusters (k) and the initial cluster centers. This could be done randomly or using another method, such as k-means++ initialization. Once the algorithm is initialized, we to irritate each data point by following the steps assigned below:

- Assigning the data point near the center.
- Update the flock centers by taking the average data point to each flock.

Repeat steps 1 and 2 until the cluster centers converge or until a specified number of iterations has been reached.

After the algorithm has converged, we would have k clusters, each containing a group of similar data points. These clusters could then be used for further analysis, such as identifying patterns or trends within the audio signal. Overall, implementing k-means clustering for audio data would involve extracting relevant features from the audio signal, initializing the algorithm, and iterating through the steps of the algorithm until convergence. According to how similar the data points in each cluster are, we could then group the audio data into several clusters. K-Means clustering is one of the most used clustering algorithms in data mining because of its ease of use and scalability (Wu, et al., 2008). This unsupervised machine-learning technique involves two main phases. After that, each center is repeatedly recalculated until a certain cluster is reached by all data points (Bahmani, et al., 2012). K-means clustering is a method for grouping data points into clusters based on similarity. It isn't easy, and NP-hard, but efficient heuristics can quickly find a local optimum solution. These heuristics often use an iterative refinement approach similar to the expectation-maximization algorithm for mixtures of Gaussian distributions. K-means tends to find clusters of similar spatial extent, while the Gaussian mixture model allows for clusters of different shapes. The k-means algorithm relates to the k-nearest neighbor classifier, a supervised machine-learning technique for classification. The nearest centroid classifier, the Rocchio algorithm, can classify new data into clusters obtained through k-means. The goal of k-means is to partition a set of observations, each represented by a d-dimensional real vector, into k clusters to minimize the within-cluster sum of squares or variance. The objective is to find:

$$\arg\min_{S} \sum_{i=1}^{k} \sum_{x \in S_i} \left\| x - \mu_i \right\|^2 = \arg\min_{S} \sum_{i=1}^{k} \left| S_i \right| Var\, S_i$$

Like minimising the within-cluster sum of squares, or variance, K-means clustering seeks to minimise the pairwise squared deviations of points inside the same cluster. This may be represented by finding the set of clusters S that minimizes the equation where I is the average of the points in Si. In other words, the objective is to cluster the data to minimize the squared deviation of the points inside each cluster.

$$\arg\min \sum_{\substack{i=1 \\ S}}^{k} \frac{1}{\left| S_i \right|} \sum_{x,y \in S_i} \left\| x - y \right\|^2$$

The purpose of clustering sometimes referred to as the inter-cluster sum of squares, is to maximise the total of squared deviations between points in various groups (BCSS). By maintaining a constant total variance, this may be accomplished (The writing process in a multimedia environment, 2003). The law of total variance in probability theory is also connected to this link between clustering and variance.

4.1. Measuring Parameters

A popular clustering method called K-means divides data points into a predetermined number of clusters according to how far off they are from the cluster centers. The number of clusters (k) and the distance metric are the main factors determining how well K-means algorithms work.

The option for the number of clusters (k) indicates how many clusters the algorithm will try to find in the dataset. Care should be used while selecting this parameter because the wrong value for k can lead to unsatisfactory clustering outcomes. For instance, if k is too little, the method might not find every cluster in the dataset. If k is too large, the algorithm may identify too many clusters, and the resulting clusters may be too fine-grained to be meaningful.

A function called the distance measure establishes how far away two data points are from one another. The k-means algorithm uses this distance to compare data points, and it can be based on several metrics, including the Manhattan distance or the Euclidean distance. The distance measure should be carefully selected since it can significantly impact the algorithm's performance and ensure that the k-means algorithm produces the right clustering results.

The primary measuring variables for k-means algorithms are the distance measure and the total number of clusters (k). These parameters, which influence the granularity and sensitivity of the algorithm, should be carefully calibrated to ensure that the algorithm creates the appropriate number of clusters and level of noise.

4.2. Performance

Depending on the particular dataset and the research objectives, k-means algorithms' performance may change. K-means algorithms are frequently straightforward and efficient and may precisely locate data points inside a cluster. They could be sensitive to the initialization of the cluster centers and might not always find every cluster present in a dataset.

The two key benefits of k-means algorithms are their efficiency and simplicity. These algorithms are easy to implement and can be run efficiently on large datasets. This makes them a popular choice for many clustering tasks, especially when the dataset is large, and the number of clusters is well-defined.

Another strength of k-means algorithms is their ability to identify data points within a cluster accurately. These algorithms use a distance measure to determine the similarity of data points and can accurately assign data points to the cluster with the nearest center. This can be useful for identifying patterns and trends within a dataset and grouping data points into meaningful clusters.

There are several limitations to K-means algorithms, though. They might not always be able to detect all of the clusters within a dataset, for example, if the number of clusters is not well-defined or if the clusters have different densities. Furthermore, if the initial cluster centers are not hand-picked, k-means algorithms may be sensitive to the initialization of the cluster centers and generate less-than-ideal output.

Overall, depending on the particular dataset and the study's goals, the efficacy of k-means algorithms may change. These quick and simple techniques may be used to identify the data points that make up a cluster correctly. They might not always detect all clusters in a dataset and might be sensitive to the initialization of the cluster centers.

4.3. Time Complexity

The big O notation, which represents the rate of expansion of the number of operations required by the method as the quantity of the input data rises, is often used to define the time complexity of the k-means clustering algorithm. K- is typically O(NK), where n is the dataset's total number of data points and k is the number of clusters. This indicates that the time required to run the method grows linearly with the amount of data points and clusters.

The density and distribution of the data points, the values of the algorithm's parameters, and the computing complexity are some variables that might affect the temporal complexity of k-means.

Despite the relatively low time complexity of k-means, the algorithm can be computationally intensive when applied to large and complex datasets. In these cases, it may be necessary to use specialized hardware or distributed computing systems to run the algorithm in an acceptable amount of time. Additionally, the algorithm may require significant tuning and optimization to produce optimal results for a particular dataset.

Overall, the time complexity of k-means is relatively low compared to other clustering algorithms, making it a good choice for analyzing large and complex datasets. The algorithm's ability to quickly identify clusters of points in a dataset makes it a valuable tool for extracting insights from complex data. The method depends on the number of clusters as a time complexity factor; therefore, it might not be the best choice for datasets with many clusters or for applications that require the flexibility to adjust the number of clusters dynamically.

4.4. Growth Rate

The time it takes to run the algorithm grows exponentially with the data points, and K-means has a time complexity of O(n2) regarding growth rate. Because of this, K-means is not as effective as alternative clustering algorithms with lower temporal complexity. For instance, the DBSCAN method runs substantially faster when working with enormous datasets since its time complexity is O(n log n). Overall, the growth rate of K-means is relatively inefficient, making it less suitable for clustering large datasets. However, it is important to remember that the algorithm's performance can also be affected by other factors, such as the size and density of the data and the initial centroids selected for the clustering process.

4.5. Asymptotic Notation

As mentioned earlier, asymptotic notation is a mathematical tool used to describe the growth rate of algorithms. In the case of K-means, the algorithm's time complexity can be described using the big O notation, a common asymptotic notation used to describe the upper bound on an algorithm's growth rate. The time complexity of K-means is $O(n^2)$, which indicates that the algorithm's execution time grows exponentially as the number of data points rises. This indicates that K-means is less effective than alternative clustering methods, especially those with lower temporal complexity. For example, the DBSCAN algorithm has a time complexity of O(nlogn), meaning it takes much less time to run when dealing with large datasets.

Other asymptotic notations may be used to express the growth rate of K-means in addition to big O notation. For instance, the theta notation may represent the upper and lower constraints on an algorithm's growth rate, whereas the omega notation can express the lower bound. Big O notation is the most popular asymptotic notation to describe the temporal complexity of algorithms.

4.6. Algorithm

The K-Means algorithm consists of the following steps:

- Several clusters, K, is selected, and randomly chosen points from the dataset are picked to serve as the starting centroids.
- Each point in the dataset is assigned to the nearest centroid using the Euclidean distance.
- The position of the centroids is recalculated by finding the average of all points belonging to the same cluster.
- This process is repeated until the centroids no longer change or a set number of iterations has been reached.
- The final result of the algorithm is the clustering of all points in the dataset.

4.7. Equations

The K-Means algorithm is based on minimizing the sum of squared distances between each data point and its assigned centroid. The objective function to be minimized is defined as:

$$J(C) = 1/m \sum_{i=1}^{m} \sum_{j=1}^{k} [x^{(i)} \text{ belongs to } C_j] * \|x^{(i)} - \mu_j\|^2$$

Where:
J(C) is the objective function to be minimized. m is the number of data points.
k is the number of clusters.
C_j is the j-th cluster. $x^{(i)}$ is the i-th data point.
μ_j is the mean (centroid) of the j-th cluster.
$[x^{(i)}$ belongs to $C_j]$ is an indicator function that takes the value of 1 if $x^{(i)}$ belongs to cluster C_j and 0 otherwise.
$\|x^{(i)} - \mu_j\|^2$ is the squared Euclidean distance between $x^{(i)}$ and μ_j.
The objective function J(C) is minimized iteratively by reassigning data points to the nearest centroid and updating the centroids as the mean of all points belonging to the same cluster. The algorithm terminates when the centroids no longer change or a set number of iterations has been reached.

4.8. Output

The output values have given below (figure 2):

Figure 2. K-MEANS

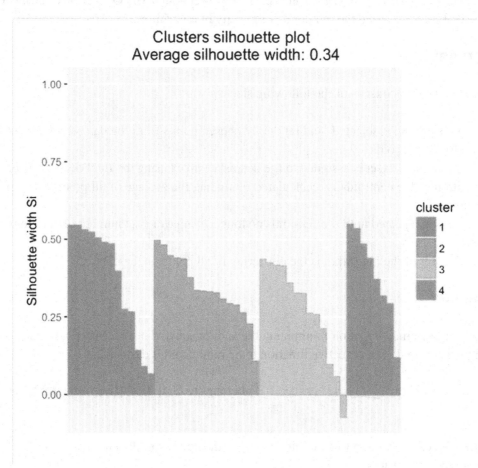

5. ADAPTIVE CLUSTERING

A form of cluster analysis known as adaptive clustering dynamically modifies the number of clusters while the algorithm works. Instead, depending on a pre-specified number of clusters, the algorithm can determine the ideal number of clusters within a dataset.

One of the main advantages of adaptive clustering is that it can improve the accuracy of cluster analysis by identifying the optimal number of clusters within a dataset. Often, a dataset may not contain a fixed number of clusters, and using a pre-specified number of clusters can result in suboptimal results. By dynamically adjusting the number of clusters, adaptive clustering can help to improve the accuracy of cluster analysis and identify more meaningful groups within the dataset.

Another advantage of adaptive clustering is that it can improve the algorithm's efficiency by reducing the number of clusters that need to be processed. A dataset may contain many clusters in many cases, making the cluster analysis process computationally expensive. By dynamically adjusting the number of clusters, adaptive clustering can help reduce the algorithm's computational burden and make it more efficient.

Regarding time complexity, adaptive clustering algorithms can be either linear or non-linear. Linear adaptive clustering algorithms have a time complexity of O(n), which means that the algorithm's running time grows linearly with the size of the dataset. On the other hand, non-linear adaptive clustering algorithms have a time complexity of O(n^2), which means that the algorithm's running time grows quadratically with the size of the dataset.

Overall, adaptive clustering is a useful technique that can improve the accuracy and efficiency of cluster analysis. By dynamically adjusting the number of clusters, adaptive clustering algorithms can identify the optimal number of clusters within a dataset and improve cluster analysis results. Regarding time complexity, adaptive clustering algorithms can be either linear or non-linear, depending on the specific algorithm used (Grachev, et al., 2020; Hurtado-Romero, et al., 2021; Larose & Larose, 2014; Sutton, et al., 1998; Fan & Pan, 2020).

In many practical problems, data is received gradually, for example, in small batches through real-time record-by-record processes within unpredictable periods (Shirkhorshidi, et al., 2014). A good example of such an application is customer classification in an internet portal, where many visitors contribute a small but significant amount of data during each visit. User patterning for coherent and up-to-date behavior suggests an adaptive and forward-looking clustering process considering the data's dynamic nature. The system initially starts empty (Hennig, et al., 2015). When a new datum is added, the multi-agent engine creates a data agent responsible for managing the datum's behavior concerning its assignment to one of the clusters (Volkovich, et al., 2013). This agent scans the current dataset and attempts to determine the groups to which the new element can be assigned, intending to improve the overall system configuration.

Music can be classified as pure music or a mixture of music. According to music theory, maximum pure or distinctive music should cluster automatically without the predefined dataset. Hierarchical models can be divisive, where partitions are created from the entire dataset, or agglomerating, where each partition begins with a single object and further objects are added. Whereas hierarchical clustering valid only for metric datasets is very sensitive to noise and fluctuation, making the automation even tougher (figure 3) (Wikipedia contributors, 2023).

Figure 3. Adaptive clustering

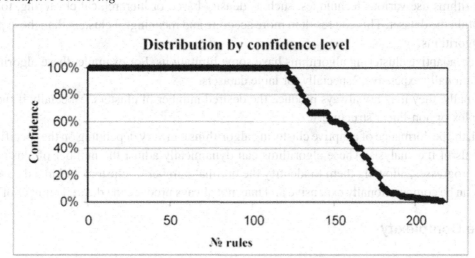

5.1. Metrics

Adaptive clustering algorithms can use various measuring types to identify clusters within a dataset. Some of the most common measuring types used by adaptive clustering algorithms include:

Distance metrics: Adaptive clustering algorithms might employ distance measures like Euclidean or Manhattan distance to ascertain how related two data points are. By doing so, the algorithm can distinguish clusters in addition to the distance between data points and cluster centers.

Density measures: Adaptive clustering algorithms can use density measures to identify clusters within a dataset. This can be done by calculating the density of data points within a particular dataset region and using this density to identify clusters.

Hierarchical measures: Adaptive clustering algorithms can use hierarchical measures to cluster data points. This can be done using techniques such as single-linkage clustering or complete-linkage clustering, which create a hierarchy of clusters based on the similarity of data points.

In general, adaptive clustering algorithms may find clusters within a dataset using a range of measurement kinds. These metrics may also include hierarchical, density, and distance metrics.

5.2. Performance

Adaptive clustering methods' performance might change based on the particular dataset and the analysis's objectives. As the algorithm develops, adaptive clustering algorithms can often dynamically alter the number of clusters, allowing them to determine the ideal number of clusters within a dataset. These approaches, meanwhile, may not always result in the necessary number of clusters and can be computationally costly.

One of its main advantages is the capacity of adaptive clustering algorithms to change the number of clusters as the algorithm develops dynamically. This enables the algorithm to automatically determine the proper number of clusters within a dataset without requiring the user to input the cluster size in advance. This might be helpful for datasets where the number of clusters is unknown or elusive.

Another strength of adaptive clustering algorithms is their ability to produce high-quality clusters. These algorithms use various techniques, such as density-based or hierarchical clustering, to identify clusters within the dataset. This can result in more accurate and meaningful clusters than those produced by other algorithms.

However, adaptive clustering algorithms have some limitations. For example, these algorithms can be computationally expensive, especially for large datasets.

Additionally, they may not always produce the desired number of clusters, especially if the dataset has a complex or non-linear structure.

Overall, the performance of adaptive clustering algorithms can vary depending on the specific dataset and the goals of the analysis. These algorithms can dynamically adjust the number of clusters as the algorithm progresses, allowing them to identify the optimal number of clusters within a dataset. However, they can be computationally expensive and may not always produce the desired number of clusters.

5.3. Time Complexity

The time complexity of adaptive clustering algorithms refers to the time and computational resources required for the algorithm to run and generate clusters for a given dataset. The time complexity of an algorithm is typically expressed using big O notation, which indicates the rate of growth of the number of operations required by the algorithm as the size of the input data increases.

In general, the time complexity of clustering algorithms is $O(n^2)$ or $O(n^3)$, where n is the number of data points in the dataset. This means that the time it takes for the algorithm to run increases exponentially as the number of data points increases. For example, if the number of data points doubles, the time it takes for the algorithm to run will increase by a factor of four (in the case of $O(n^2)$) or eight (in the case of $O(n^3)$).

Adaptive clustering algorithms may have additional time complexity factors related to the number of clusters or the dimensionality of the data. For example, if the algorithm is trying to adapt to a high-dimensional dataset, it may require more computational resources and take longer to run. Additionally, if the algorithm is trying to adjust the number of clusters dynamically, it may require additional calculations and therefore have a higher time complexity.

The exact time complexity of a particular adaptive clustering algorithm will depend on the specific details of the algorithm and the characteristics of the dataset. However, these algorithms can generally be computationally intensive and may require significant computational resources to run effectively on large and complex datasets.

Despite the potential challenges associated with the time complexity of adaptive clustering algorithms, these algorithms can offer significant benefits over traditional clustering techniques. For example, adaptive clustering algorithms can automatically adjust to the underlying structure of the data, potentially improving the accuracy and effectiveness of the clustering. Additionally, these algorithms can be useful for analyzing complex, high-dimensional datasets that may not have clear patterns or clusters that can be easily identified using other techniques. As a result, the use of adaptive clustering algorithms can be an effective way to extract valuable insights from complex datasets.

5.4. Growth Rate

Depending on the particular method being utilised, the temporal complexity of adaptive clustering algorithms might change regarding growth rate. The time it takes to run some adaptive clustering algorithms, like DBSCAN, rises logarithmically with the amount of data points. These algorithms have a temporal complexity of $O(nlogn)$. Compared to other clustering algorithms with a larger temporal complexity, these techniques are comparatively efficient.

Adaptive clustering algorithms are useful for grouping huge datasets because of their generally efficient growth rate. It's crucial to remember that other elements, such as the data's size and density and the clustering parameters, might also impact the algorithm's success.

5.5. Asymptotic Notation

In the case of adaptive clustering, the algorithm's time complexity can be described using the big O notation, the common asymptotic notation to represent the upper bound of the growth rate.

The time complexity for adaptive clustering algorithms can vary depending on the specific algorithm. Some adaptive clustering algorithms, such as DBSCAN, have a time complexity of $O(nlogn)$. They define the time it takes to run the algorithm and increase logarithmically with the number of data points. This makes these algorithms relatively efficient, especially compared to other clustering algorithms with higher time complexity.

In addition to big O notation, other asymptotic notations can also describe the growth rate of adaptive clustering algorithms.

5.6. Algorithm

Initialization: Starting with an initial set of cluster centroids or cluster assignments.

- Distance Calculation: Calculate the distance between each data point and the cluster centroids.
- Reassignment: Reassigning data points to the closest cluster centroids.
- Recalculation: Recalculating the cluster centroids based on the new data point assignments.
- Adaptation: Monitoring the cluster structure and adjusting the number of clusters if necessary.

Iteration: Repeating steps 2-5 until convergence or a stopping criterion is met.

6. RESULT

The final result analysis for k-means, DBSCAN, and Adaptive Clustering algorithms would typically include the following metrics: precision, recall, and F-measure. These metrics are commonly that help to find the appropriate clustering algorithm and can provide valuable insights into the accuracy and effectiveness of the algorithm (Table 1).

Table 1. Comparison of K-means, DBSCAN, adaptive clustering

Performance Measure	K-MEANS	DBSCAN	ADAPTIVE CLUSTERING
PRECISION	High	High	High
RECALL	Low	High	High
F-MEASURE	Low	High	High

In general, k-means algorithms tend to have high precision but low recall and F-measure, as they can accurately identify data points within a cluster but may not always identify all clusters within a dataset. DBSCAN algorithms tend to have high precision, recall, and F-measure, as they can accurately identify data points within a cluster and all of the clusters within a dataset.

Adaptive clustering algorithms also tend to have high precision, recall, and F-measure, as they can dynamically adjust the number of clusters to match the dataset's structure.

Overall, the final result analysis for k-means, DBSCAN, and adaptive clustering algorithms would typically include the precision, recall, and F-measure metrics, which can provide valuable insights into the accuracy and effectiveness of the algorithm (Figure 4).

Figure 4. Comparison graph

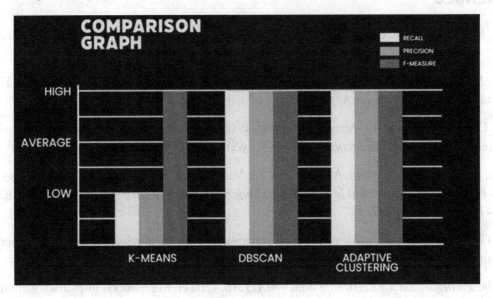

In conclusion, k-means, DBSCAN, and adaptive clustering are all algorithms for clustering data points into distinct groups or clusters. Each algorithm has its strengths and weaknesses, and the appropriate algorithm will depend on the specific dataset and the goals of the analysis. K-means is a simple and widely used algorithm suitable for datasets with a well-defined number of clusters.

7. CONCLUSION

It is easy to implement and can be run efficiently on large datasets. However, k-means can be sensitive to the initialization of the cluster centers and may not always produce the optimal number of clusters. DBSCAN is a density-based algorithm suitable for datasets with clusters of varying densities. It does not require the number of clusters to be specified in advance and can identify clusters of arbitrary shape. However, DBSCAN can be sensitive to the choice of parameters and may not always produce the desired number of clusters. Adaptive clustering is an algorithm that dynamically adjusts the number of clusters as the algorithm progresses. This allows the algorithm to identify the optimal number of clusters within a dataset without requiring the number of clusters to be specified in advance. However, adaptive. Clustering algorithms can be computationally expensive and may not always produce the desired number of clusters. Overall, each of these algorithms has its strengths and weaknesses, and the appropriate algorithm will depend on the specific dataset and the goals of the analysis. By understanding the differences between k-means, DBSCAN, and adaptive clustering, we can choose the appropriate algorithm for our specific clustering task.

REFERENCES

Abbassy, M., & Ead, W. M. (2020). Intelligent Greenhouse Management System. 2020 6th *International Conference on Advanced Computing and Communication Systems (ICACCS)*. IEEE.

Abbassy, M. M., & Mohamed, A. A. (2016). Mobile Expert System to Detect Liver Disease Kind. *International Journal of Computer Applications*, *14*(5), 320–324.

Assi, L., Carter, K., Deaver, E., Anay, R., & Ziehl, P. (2018). Sustainable concrete: Building a greener future. *Journal of Cleaner Production*, *198*, 1641–1651. doi:10.1016/j.jclepro.2018.07.123

Bahmani, B., Moseley, B., Vattani, A., Kumar, R., & Vassilvitskii, S. (2012). Scalable k-means++. *Proceedings of the VLDB Endowment International Conference on Very Large Data Bases*, *5*(7), 622–633. doi:10.14778/2180912.2180915

Bonnin, G., & Jannach, D. (2014). Automated generation of music playlists: Survey and experiments. *ACM Computing Surveys*, *47*(2), 1–35. doi:10.1145/2652481

Density-based algorithm for clustering data - MATLAB. (2021). Mathworks. https://www.mathworks.com/help/radar/ref/clusterdbscan-system-object.html

Derindere Köseoğlu, S., Ead, W. M., & Abbassy, M. M. (2022). Basics of Financial Data Analytics. In *Financial Data Analytics* (pp. 23–57). Springer International Publishing. doi:10.1007/978-3-030-83799-0_2

Ead, W., Emad, & Abbassy, M. M. (2021). A general framework information loss of utility-based anonymization in data publishing. *Turkish Journal of Computer and Mathematics Education*, *12*(5), 1450–1456. doi:10.17762/turcomat.v12i5.2102

Ead, W. M., & Abbassy, M. M. (2022). A general cyber hygiene approach for financial analytical environment. In *Financial Data Analytics* (pp. 369–384). Springer International Publishing. doi:10.1007/978-3-030-83799-0_13

Fan, J., & Pan, J. (2020). *Contemporary Experimental Design, Multivariate Analysis and Data Mining*. Springer International Publishing. doi:10.1007/978-3-030-46161-4

Grachev, S., Skobelev, P., Mayorov, I., & Simonova, E. (2020). Adaptive clustering through multi-agent technology: Development and perspectives. *Mathematics*, *8*(10), 1664. doi:10.3390/math8101664

Hennig, C., Meila, M., Murtagh, F., & Rocci, R. (Eds.). (2015). *Handbook of cluster analysis*. CRC press. doi:10.1201/b19706

Hurtado-Romero, A., Del Toro-Barbosa, M., Gradilla-Hernández, M. S., Garcia-Amezquita, L. E., & García-Cayuela, T. (2021). Probiotic properties, prebiotic fermentability, and GABA-producing capacity of microorganisms isolated from Mexican milk Kefir grains: A clustering evaluation for functional dairy food applications. *Foods*, *10*(10), 2275. doi:10.3390/foods10102275 PMID:34681324

Jain, A. K., Misra, T., Tyagi, N., Suresh Kumar, M. V., & Pant, B. (2022a). A Comparative Study on Cyber security Technology in Big data Cloud Computing Environment. *2022 5th International Conference on Contemporary Computing and Informatics (IC3I)*. IEEE.

Jain, A. K., Ross, D. S., & Babu, M. K. Dharamvir, Uike, D., & Gangodkar, D. (2022b). Cloud computing applications for protecting the information of healthcare department using smart internet of things appliance. *2022 5th International Conference on Contemporary Computing and Informatics (IC3I)*. IEEE.

Joachims, T. (1998). Text categorization with Support Vector Machines: Learning with many relevant features. [Berlin, Heidelberg: Springer Berlin Heidelberg.]. *Machine Learning, ECML-98*, 137–142.

Khalifa, I., Abd Al-glil, H., & M. Abbassy, M. (2013). Mobile Hospitalization. *International Journal of Computer Applications, 80*(13), 18–23. doi:10.5120/13921-1822

Khalifa, I., Abd Al-glil, H., & M. Abbassy, M. (2014). Mobile Hospitalization for Kidney Transplantation. *International Journal of Computer Applications, 92*(6), 25–29. doi:10.5120/16014-5027

Kumar, K. S., Yadav, D., Joshi, S. K., Chakravarthi, M. K., Jain, A. K., & Tripathi, V. (2022). Blockchain technology with applications to distributed control and cooperative robotics. *2022 5th International Conference on Contemporary Computing and Informatics (IC3I)*. IEEE.

Kumar Jain, A. (2022). Hybrid Cloud Computing: A Perspective. *International Journal of Engineering Research & Technology (Ahmedabad), 11*(10), 1–06.

Larose, D. T., & Larose, C. D. (2014). *Discovering knowledge in data: an introduction to data mining* (Vol. 4). John Wiley & Sons. doi:10.1002/9781118874059

Mohamed, & Mesbah, S. (2016). Effective e-government and citizens adoption in Egypt. *International Journal of Computer Applications, 133*(7), 7–13. doi:10.5120/ijca2016907886

Rabiner, L., & Juang, B. H. (1993). *Fundamentals of speech recognition*. Prentice-Hall, Inc.

Sadek, R. A., Abd-alazeem, D. M., & Abbassy, M. M. (2021). A new energy-efficient multi-hop routing protocol for heterogeneous wireless sensor networks. *International Journal of Advanced Computer Science and Applications, 12*(11). doi:10.14569/IJACSA.2021.0121154

Shirkhorshidi, A. S., Aghabozorgi, S., Wah, T. Y., & Herawan, T. (2014). Big data clustering: A review. In *Computational Science and Its Applications – ICCSA 2014* (pp. 707–720). Springer International Publishing. doi:10.1007/978-3-319-09156-3_49

Sutton, B., Sutton, R. S., & Barto, A. G. (1998). *Reinforcement learning: An introduction*.

The writing process in a multimedia environment. (2003). Horizon. http://horizon.unc.edu/projects/monograph/CD/Language_Music/Simard.html

Volkovich, Z., Toledano-Kitai, D., & Weber, G.-W. (2013). Self-learning K-means clustering: a global optimization approach. Journal of Global Optimization : An International Journal Dealing with Theoretical and Computational Aspects of Seeking Global Optima and Their Applications in Science. *Journal of Global Optimization, 56*(2), 219–232. doi:10.100710898-012-9854-y

Wikipedia contributors. (2023). *Automatic clustering algorithms*. Wikipedia. https://en.wikipedia.org/w/index.php?title=Automatic_clustering_algorithms&oldid=1136139398

Wu, X., Kumar, V., Ross Quinlan, J., Ghosh, J., Yang, Q., Motoda, H., & Steinberg, D. (2008). Top 10 algorithms in data mining. *Knowledge and Information Systems*, *14*(1), 1–37. doi:10.100710115-007-0114-2

Chapter 5
Data Acquisition Using NI LabVIEW for Test Automation

Pratik Santhosh
CHRIST University (Deemed), India

Daniel C. John
CHRIST University (Deemed), India

Pallavi Kodigandla
CHRIST University (Deemed), India

V. M. Uma Maheswari
Defence Research and Development Organisation (DRDO), India

S. Sujatha
 https://orcid.org/0000-0002-8423-6074
CHRIST University (Deemed), India

ABSTRACT

In a fighter aircraft, the pilot's safety is of utmost importance, and the pressure sensing in the pilot's mask is essential for ensuring the pilot's safety. This innovative solution ensures the swift and accurate measurement of pressure, minimizing the risk of potential hazards and enhancing military aviation safety. Additionally, it provides a robust and reliable solution that can withstand the harsh and challenging conditions often encountered in the field. This chapter explores the advanced capabilities and benefits of utilizing the National Instrument USB-6363, programmed with LabVIEW, in military aviation, highlighting its potential for revolutionizing pressure measurement processes in this critical field. It describes a research study on developing a pressure-sensing system for pilot masks using NI USB 6363 and LabVIEW.

DOI: 10.4018/979-8-3693-1301-5.ch005

1. INTRODUCTION

The pilot mask is a key component in a fighter aircraft designed to provide the pilot with breathing air while protecting them from dangerous gasses, smoke, and debris, particularly concerning the functioning of its oxygen system (Alajmi and Khan, 2013). Oxygen system malfunctioning can be disastrous and put pilots' lives at risk (Alharbi et al., 2020). The pressure within the pilot's mask is an important parameter that must be maintained to ensure the pilot's safety. Any abnormal pressure conditions can result in Hypoxia, which is a life-threatening condition caused by a lack of oxygen supply in the body; it can significantly impair the cognitive and physical abilities of pilots, leading to a potential loss of control of the aircraft (Banu et al., 2022). As a result, it is essential to develop a pressure-sensing system for pilot masks that can accurately detect pressure and oxygen system malfunctions and warn the pilot promptly in case of any abnormal conditions (Buragadda et al., 2022). The proposed system is based on NI USB-6363, which offers precise measurements and is a reliable solution (Chopra et al., 2022).

1.1. Problem Formulation

This project aims to propose an innovative solution using the National Instrument USB 6363 and LabView programming for more effective live simulations in various industrial applications (Chumbley et al., 2017). The goal is to interface Pressure Sensors with more functionality, ensuring reliable and accurate measurements with a simplified design (Deepa et al., 2022). A simpler control panel using a GUI will also be developed for ease of maintenance (Fan et al., 2018).

The proposed solution will provide better data visualization on the LabView Dashboard, allowing for easier monitoring and analysis of various data parameters (Fazil et al., 2023). The ultimate objective is to develop a reliable solution with more live simulation capabilities for future reference, enhancing safety and operational efficiency (Gowtham et al., 2022). This problem formulation outlines the critical requirements and objectives of the project, setting the stage for subsequent sections that will focus on the implementation, testing, and evaluation of the innovative solution (Jain et al., 2022).

1.2. Problem Identification

The breathing analysis of pilots is critical in ensuring their safety during flight (Khan, 2016). According to our analysis, the use of pressure as a primary attribute with NI USB6363 to indicate the malfunctioning of oxygen systems in fighter aircraft and to determine aircraft altitude (Khan, 2021a). By analyzing breathing patterns, the system can warn pilots of potential hypoxia threats and prevent dangerous situations (Reddy et al., 2022a). The report addresses the problem of ensuring the safety of pilots in fighter aircraft by providing a reliable system for breathing analysis using pressure as a primary attribute (Khan, 2021b).

1.3. Problem Statement and Objectives

The objective is to propose a solution for ensuring the safety of pilots in fighter aircraft by analyzing their breathing patterns using pressure as a primary attribute (Kim et al., 2019). The proposed solution aims to achieve the following goals:

- Indicate the malfunctioning in the fighter aircraft's oxygen system by analyzing pilots' breathing patterns.
- Determine the aircraft's altitude by measuring the outer pressure, providing valuable information for flight management and safety.
- Warn the pilot before the possible threats of Hypoxia take over, thus preventing dangerous situations.

The problem statement addressed is the critical need to ensure the safety of pilots in fighter aircraft. In particular, the report focuses on analyzing breathing patterns using pressure as a primary attribute, which can provide valuable information about the oxygen system and aircraft altitude (Kumar et al., 2018). By warning the pilot before the possible threats of Hypoxia, the proposed solution can prevent dangerous situations and ensure the safety of pilots during flight (Li and Dajun, 2014).

1.4. Limitations

It's important to note that the breathing analysis system proposed in our report has some limitations that should be considered. One of these limitations is that the system currently relies solely on measuring outer pressure to determine the aircraft's altitude (Mahesha et al., 2022). However, this method may not be accurate enough in real-world scenarios due to the impact of other factors, such as temperature and humidity, on pressure readings (Reddy et al., 2022b). Moreover, it's worth mentioning that the proposed system is still in the lab analysis stage and has not yet been fully tested in actual aircraft (Sharma and Singh, 2012). Further research and testing are necessary to ensure its reliability and accuracy in various environmental conditions before it can be implemented in practical use cases (Rosenberg and Park, 2017). In summary, while the proposed breathing analysis system shows potential in detecting potential hypoxia threats in pilots, it has limitations, such as reliance on outer pressure and is still in the lab analysis stage, requiring further research and testing to ensure its reliability in real-world scenarios.

2. LITERATURE SURVEY AND REVIEW

A literature review was conducted on the breathing analysis of pilots using pressure as a primary attribute with NI USB6363. The review covered the importance of oxygen supply, Hypoxia, pressure measurement, and the use of NI USB6363 in aviation applications. It provided insights into the critical role of breathing analysis in aviation safety and identified the need for further research to investigate system performance under various environmental conditions. The findings helped to determine the direction for further research and development of a proposed breathing analysis system based on NI USB6363.

2.1. Critical Review of Literature

In recent years, LabVIEW-based data acquisition systems using the NI USB-6363 have become increasingly popular for real-time signal processing applications in various fields, including high-altitude military aviation (Singh and Bansal, 2015). The development of such systems has enabled the accurate and reliable acquisition of data from a range of sensors and sources, including oxygen sensors, to detect and mitigate Hypoxia.

One of the research papers, Hypoxia: The Challenges of Detection and Mitigation in High-Altitude Military Aviation", highlights the challenges associated with detecting and mitigating Hypoxia in high-altitude military aviation. This paper emphasizes the importance of real-time monitoring of oxygen levels in pilots, which can be achieved using data acquisition systems based on NI USB-6363 and LabVIEW. Such systems can provide pilots with warnings or alerts if oxygen levels fall below a certain threshold, reducing the risk of Hypoxia and improving safety.

Another paper, Development of a LabVIEW-Based Data Acquisition System using NI USB-6363 for Real-Time Signal Processing Applications", discusses the development of a LabVIEW-based data acquisition system for real-time signal processing applications. The system utilizes the NI USB-6363 for high-accuracy and reliable data acquisition and LabVIEW for signal processing and analysis. This paper highlights the flexibility and versatility of LabVIEW-based data acquisition systems for various applications, including hypoxia detection and mitigation (Siva Ramkumar et al., 2022).

In LabVIEW-Based Data Acquisition and Control System Using NI USB-6363 for the Identification of Amplitude Modulation in FM Radio Broadcasts", the authors describe the development of a LabVIEW-based data acquisition and control system for the identification of amplitude modulation in FM radio broadcasts. While this application may not directly relate to hypoxia detection and mitigation, it highlights the broad range of applications for LabVIEW-based data acquisition systems using NI USB-6363.

Finally, "A Data Acquisition System for Flight Test Measurements using LabVIEW" presents a LabVIEW-based data acquisition system for flight test measurements. The system utilizes the NI USB-6363 for accurate data acquisition and LabVIEW for signal processing and analysis. While this paper does not directly relate to hypoxia detection and mitigation, it emphasizes the importance of accurate and reliable data acquisition in the aviation industry, including for hypoxia detection and mitigation.

These research papers demonstrate the versatility and effectiveness of LabVIEW-based data acquisition systems using the NI USB-6363 for various applications, including hypoxia detection and mitigation in high-altitude military aviation. By real-time monitoring of oxygen levels in pilots, these systems can improve safety and reduce the risk of hypoxia-related incidents.

3. PROPOSED METHODOLOGY

In today's fast-paced world, efficient and reliable measurement systems are paramount. One such system that has recently gained popularity is the National Instrument USB 6363, which has been programmed with LabView to measure pressure at lightning speed. This cutting-edge technology ensures accuracy and precision in measurements and provides a secure and easy-to-use platform for programming. Also, introduce the concept of altitude measurement using the International Standard Atmosphere and the use of LabVIEW to realize an equation that gives altitude when pressure is measured.

The pilot mask pressure-sensing system was developed using NI USB-6363 and LabVIEW. The system comprises a pressure sensor mounted to the mask to measure the pressure within a pilot's mask. The sensor is connected to the NI USB-6363 data acquisition system (DAC, i.e., digital to analogue converter), controlled by the LabVIEW software. The LabVIEW software is configured to acquire the pressure data from USB-6363 and display it on a computer screen. In case of abnormal conditions, the software is built to send an alarm signal and warnings to the pilot's control panel.

With the ability to acquire 16 I/O channels, including both analogue and digital inputs, the USB 6363 drastically reduces the overall cost of production while also simplifying the complexity of the circuit. This ease of design, implementation, testing, and deployment is further complemented by the flexibility to include several functionalities, making it a preferred choice for measurement applications across various industries.

The methodology involves using an air compressor to supply a pressure of 6 bar, which is then fed into a regulator providing an output pressure of 1 to 3 bar. A solenoid valve simulates a failure condition by blocking the pressure flow. Sensors are installed along the line to monitor the pressure in the system, and an oxygen regulator is attached to the line connected to the breathing simulator. This approach enables efficient monitoring and regulation of pressure, making it an effective solution for industrial processes (Zannah et al., 2023).

The sensors used in this study for pressure measurement include MLH006BGD14B, which measures the pressure between the solenoid valve and the oxygen regulator, and MIDA SGV 13 01, which measures the pressure provided to the breathing simulator. These sensors are reliable and accurate, providing precise pressure measurements that are crucial for various industrial processes.

4. HARDWARE ARCHITECTURE

4.1. NI USB-6363 and LabVIEW

The NI USB-6363 is a versatile data acquisition device designed for use in various applications such as testing, measurement, control, and automation. It comes equipped with 32 analogue input channels, 48 digital I/O lines, and a range of analogue and digital triggering options, which provides flexibility and versatility.

Several technologies for monitoring the pressure inside a pilot's mask have been proposed, including piezoelectric, strain gauges, and capacitive sensors. These technologies, however, have some limitations, such as size, cost, and sensitivity to temperature and humidity. Data acquisition devices such as NI USB-6363 have been proposed to overcome these constraints and limitations. The NI USB-6363 provides advanced security and ease of programming, enabling more efficient and reliable pressure measurements. Moreover, it can acquire up to 16 I/O (input/output) channels, both analogue and digital, significantly reducing the complexity and overall cost of production.

The National Instruments USB-6363 is a low-cost, high-accuracy data acquisition device that can be used to acquire data from various sensors, including pressure sensors. The device can be interfaced with LabVIEW software, which provides a graphical user interface for data acquisition, analysis, and display. LabVIEW is a widely used data acquisition and control systems program with a user-friendly interface. This solution offers ease to design, implementation, testing and deployment, making it ideal for use in military aviation.

To use the NI USB-6363 for data acquisition, sensors or other data sources can be connected to the analogue inputs, and the device can be configured to sample and record the data. With a data acquisition rate of up to 1.25 MS/s, the device is capable of high-speed acquisition, making it suitable for applications requiring fast data acquisition.

The NI USB-6363 is compatible with several software environments, including NI LabVIEW, NI Signal Express, and NI-DAQmx, which provide various data acquisition and analysis capabilities such as signal processing, visualization, and data logging.

Regarding reporting, the NI USB-6363 enables users to generate custom reports on acquired data using software tools such as LabVIEW or MATLAB. These tools offer a range of features for creating reports with text, graphics, and data visualizations, and the reports can be exported in multiple formats, including PDF, Excel, and Word. The NI USB-6363 is a widely used data acquisition device due to its high-speed acquisition capabilities, compatibility with various software environments, and reporting features.

4.2. Honeywell MLH006BGD14B Pressure Sensor

The MLH006BGD14B pressure sensor is a high-precision, reliable device manufactured by Honeywell, a leading technology company. This compact sensor is commonly used in various industrial applications, such as HVAC systems, medical equipment, and industrial process control.

Piezoresistive sensing technology is utilized in this sensor to measure pressure, which relies on the change in resistance of a specially designed silicon diaphragm to detect changes in pressure. The sensor has a pressure range of 0 to 6 bar and can operate at temperatures up to 125°C. The sensor has built-in compensation for temperature and non-linearity, ensuring accurate and reliable readings. In conclusion, the MLH006BGD14B pressure sensor is an excellent choice for industrial applications that require high accuracy, reliability, and a small form factor.

With a diameter of 6.1mm and a height of 8.2mm, this small sensor is ideal for use in tight spaces. It provides a digital output and supports communication with other devices using the I2C or SPI interface. The sensor has built-in compensation for temperature and non-linearity, ensuring accurate and reliable readings. In conclusion, the MLH006BGD14B pressure sensor is an excellent choice for industrial applications that require high accuracy, reliability, and a small form factor.

4.3. Festo SPTW-B2R-G14-A-M12 Pressure Sensor

The Festo SPTW-B2R-G14-A-M12 is a pressure sensor manufactured by Festo, a well-known pneumatic and electrical automation technology supplier. The sensor is designed to accurately measure pressure in various industrial applications. The product code provides valuable information about the sensor's features, including the SPTW model number, male thread design with a thread size of 14mm, pressure range, and electrical connection type of M12. The Festo SPTW-B2R-G14-A-M12 is known for its precision, durability, and reliability, making it an ideal solution for many industrial applications. Its robust construction and accurate measurements make it a popular choice among professionals in various industries.

4.4. STS Sensor Technik Sirnach AG MIDA SGV 13 01

The MIDA-SGV-13 is a microelectronic pressure sensor manufactured by STS Sensor Technik Sirnach AG. It is designed to measure pressures ranging from 0 to 1,000 bar and has a response time of less than one millisecond. The sensor uses a piezoresistive measuring element and is housed in a rugged stainless-steel casing. Its high overpressure capability allows it to withstand sudden spikes in pressure without damage. Its ability to operate in harsh and hazardous environments makes it a reliable and essential component in such industries. Overall, the MIDA-SGV-13 microelectronic pressure sensor is a robust and accurate sensor that is suitable for a wide range of industrial applications.

4.5. Pressure Regulator ITV3050 04F4BS3

The ITV3050 04F4BS3 Pressure Regulator is a product offered by SMC Corporation, a well-known manufacturer of pneumatic automation solutions. Its purpose is to regulate the flow of compressed air to maintain a consistent output pressure despite any fluctuations in the input pressure. With a port size of 1/2 inch, this regulator can handle a maximum pressure of 0.7 MPa. This regulator has an embedded pressure sensor and a digital display allowing easy monitoring and adjustment of the output pressure. It also has a compact and lightweight design, which makes it convenient for installation and integration into various pneumatic systems.

The ITV3050 04F4BS3 Pressure Regulator is commonly used in several industries, including automotive manufacturing, food and beverage processing, and semiconductor manufacturing, where precise and consistent pressure control is essential for optimal performance and product quality. In conclusion, the ITV3050 04F4BS3 Pressure Regulator is a reliable and effective regulator that can accurately control pressure and provide easy monitoring. Its small size and pressure sensor integration make it popular for various industrial applications.

4.6. OPA549 Operational Amplifier

The OPA549 is a power operational amplifier manufactured by Texas Instruments. This op-amp has a high output current and can operate at various output voltages, making it suitable for various applications. This op-amp has a maximum output current of 8A and can work with supply voltages up to ±40V. Due to its high output current and voltage capability, it is commonly used to drive large loads such as motors and speakers. The OPA549 also has thermal shutdown and overload protection features that prevent damage to the op-amp and connected devices. It also has low quiescent current and offset voltage, making it an efficient and precise choice for power applications. This op-amp is frequently used in applications such as audio amplifiers, power supplies, and motor controllers. Its versatility, reliability, and accuracy make it a preferred choice for various consumer and industrial applications.

In conclusion, the OPA549 is a highly efficient and versatile power op-amp that provides high-output current and voltage capabilities with thermal and overload protection features. Its precision, efficiency, and versatility make it an ideal choice for various power applications.

The OPA549 is a high-voltage, high-current operational amplifier designed for driving a wide range of loads, including motors, solenoids, and LEDs. The pin diagram of the OPA549 consists of eight pins that serve specific functions. Pins 1 and 5 are the inverting (-IN) and non-inverting (+IN) inputs. Pins 2 and 3 are the V+ and V- power supply pins, respectively, with a recommended supply voltage range of 10V to 60V. Pins 4 and 6 are the output and thermal pad pins, respectively, and connect the load to the amplifier. Pin 7 is the current limit pin, which sets the maximum current limit for the amplifier, and pin 8 is the shutdown pin, which can be used to turn off the amplifier and reduce power consumption. Understanding the pin diagram of the OPA549 is critical for the proper configuration and operation of the amplifier and ensures that the amplifier is used safely and effectively.

4.7. Voltage to Current Converter

We utilized the OPA549, a high-voltage and high-current operational amplifier, to convert voltage to current. The voltage-to-current conversion was implemented as a grounded load configuration. The maximum output voltage of the NI USB 6363 was 5V, and the maximum input current of the ITV3050 04F4BS3 pneumatic regulator was 20mA. Therefore, the value of R was calculated using the formula R = V/I and found to be 250 ohms.

4.8. Amplification of Voltage

Assuming a feedback resistance (Rf) of 250 ohms, an output voltage (Vout) of 28 volts, and an input voltage (Vin) of 5 volts, we can use the voltage divider formula to calculate the value of R2 in the amplifier circuit.

Therefore, the value of R2 in the amplifier circuit would be approximately 44.6 ohms to achieve a voltage gain of -112 with an input voltage of 5 volts and an output voltage of 28 volts while keeping the feedback resistance at 250 ohms (Figure 1).

Figure 1. Voltage amplification

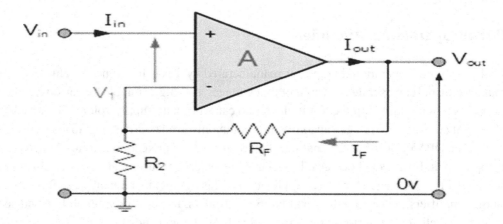

5. SOFTWARE ARCHITECTURE

5.1. LabVIEW-Laboratory Virtual Instrument Engineering Workbench

LabVIEW, or Laboratory Virtual Instrument Engineering Workbench, is a graphical programming language and development environment created by National Instruments for data acquisition, control systems, and instrument control applications. LabVIEW enables users to develop custom programs and applications through a graphical user interface with a drag-and-drop methodology to build block diagrams. LabVIEW's graphical programming approach provides an intuitive and user-friendly environment for programming that does not require extensive programming knowledge.

It allows users to create programs by assembling graphical icons or nodes representing functions and connecting them through wires to visually represent the program's flow. This approach also helps to visualize complex systems, making them easier to understand and maintain. LabVIEW includes many built-in functions and libraries for data acquisition, signal processing, analysis, and visualization. This feature set lets users quickly and easily develop custom data acquisition and analysis applications without writing code from scratch. Additionally, LabVIEW supports integration with third-party libraries and APIs, allowing users to expand their capabilities further.

One of LabVIEW's key strengths is its ability to interface with various hardware devices, including the NI USB-6363. This compatibility allows users to easily interface with these devices and acquire data from multiple sources in real time. LabVIEW also supports various communication protocols, such as Ethernet, USB, and GPIB, enabling users to connect with and control instruments and devices.

Overall, LabVIEW is a flexible and powerful tool that enables users to develop custom data acquisition and analysis applications quickly and easily. Its graphical programming approach, extensive feature set, and hardware compatibility make it a popular choice for engineers, scientists, and researchers across many fields.

5.2. Circuit Diagram

The LabVIEW GUI is a graphical user interface that provides an easy-to-use and intuitive platform for controlling the oxygen system and monitoring pressure levels. The interface includes a range of menus, buttons, and visual feedback, allowing users to quickly and easily access the system's various controls and monitoring features (Figure 2).

Figure 2. Wiring diagram of the final setup

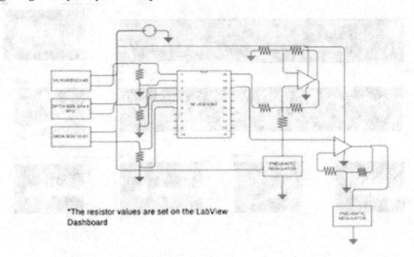

One of the key features of the LabVIEW GUI is its real-time monitoring of pressure levels, which is displayed on the interface. This feature is particularly useful for identifying any changes in pressure levels, which could indicate a problem with the system. Additionally, the GUI provides helpful prompts and instructions to guide users through the various stages of system operation, reducing the risk of errors and ensuring safe and effective operation (Figure.3).

Figure 3. The final dashboard for NI LabVIEW to run the required devices [ON]

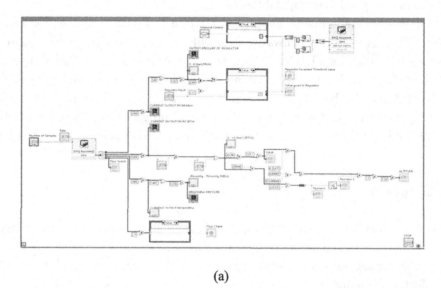

(a)

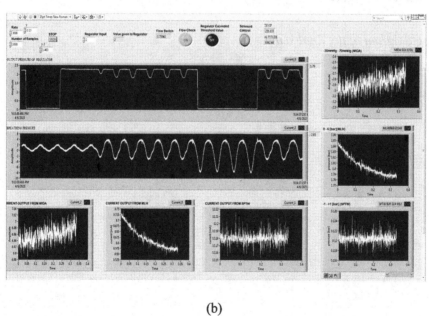

(b)

In summary, the LabVIEW GUI provides an intuitive and user-friendly interface for controlling the oxygen system and pressure levels, with real-time monitoring and helpful instructions to ensure safe and effective operation.

6. RESULTS AND ANALYSIS

The reliability and safety of the oxygen system used in fighter aircraft is paramount in aviation. To achieve this, an efficient and secure system must be in place to detect malfunctions and provide accurate information to the pilot. One potential solution is using the National Instrument USB 6363, programmed with LabView, which can provide such a system. This device can acquire 16 I/O channels, enabling fast and accurate pressure measurement and significantly reducing the complexity and cost of production. However, the setup is currently in the analysis stage and not yet fully implemented.

Measuring the altitude of an aircraft is critical for aviation safety, and accurate measurements can be obtained using a pressure sensor such as the MLH006BGD14B with the National Instrument USB 6363. This setup can provide essential information for flight planning and avoid potential threats such as adverse weather conditions, improving flight safety. However, it should be noted that this entire setup is still in the analysis stage and is not yet fully developed.

Hypoxia is a serious concern for pilots and can lead to significant safety hazards. Using the National Instrument USB 6363 and a pressure sensor, the pressure can be continuously monitored to detect any potential drop in oxygen levels. This information can then be used to warn the pilot before Hypoxia takes over and corrective action can be taken. The National Instrument USB 6363 provides a reliable and effective solution for monitoring oxygen levels and improving the safety of the aircraft.

In conclusion, using the National Instrument USB 6363 programmed with LabView, combined with a pressure sensor, is an essential component for improving the safety and reliability of fighter aircraft. This system can detect any malfunctioning in the oxygen system, accurately measure the aircraft's altitude, and warn the pilot before the onset of Hypoxia. By providing a secure, efficient, and accurate system, this technology significantly enhances aviation safety and should be considered an essential component of any aircraft oxygen system.

6.1. Scope for Future Work

In the future, the oxygen system of fighter aircraft can be further improved by incorporating additional features into the LabView program. For instance, a temperature sensor can be added to the system to monitor the temperature of the oxygen supply, ensuring that it is not too hot or too cold for the pilot to breathe comfortably. Additionally, the LabView program can be designed to provide automatic alarms or warnings when there is a drop in oxygen levels, providing immediate alerts to the pilot and ground control.

Moreover, using advanced sensors and actuators can also improve the accuracy and responsiveness of the oxygen system. For example, adding a feedback loop using a PID controller can help maintain a more precise pressure control, resulting in a more consistent oxygen supply. Wireless communication technology can also enable remote monitoring of the oxygen system, providing real-time data to ground control, improving safety and reducing the risk of human error.

Furthermore, the integration of artificial intelligence and machine learning algorithms can enhance the decision-making capabilities of the oxygen system, allowing it to automatically adjust the oxygen supply based on the pilot's physiological state and environmental condition. This can significantly improve the safety and performance of fighter aircraft, ensuring that pilots have a reliable and continuous oxygen supply, even in the most challenging situations.

The future scope of work for the oxygen system of fighter aircraft is vast, and the integration of advanced technologies and sensors can significantly improve its efficiency, safety, and reliability. The

LabView program provides a robust platform for controlling and monitoring the oxygen system, and its continued development can lead to further advancements in aviation safety.

7. CONCLUSION

The pressure sensing system developed using NI USB-6363 and LabVIEW is an accurate and reliable system that can be used to ensure the safety of pilots in a fighter aircraft. The system can detect the pressure within the pilot's mask and generate alarm signals and warnings in case of any abnormal pressure conditions. The system can connect with the aircraft's control system to monitor the pilot's mask pressure. By including more advanced features and functions, such as using NI USB-6363 and LabVIEW, the scope of further work may include increasing the performance of the pressure sensing system for the pilot's mask. Another path is to develop more advanced pressure sensors less sensitive to temperature and humidity. Therefore, the pressure sensing system can be further improved.

REFERENCES

Alajmi, M., & Khan, S. (2013). *Mobile Community Networks Information Investigation for Additional Significance*.

Alharbi, A. R., Qureshi, A. H., & Fatani, M. (2020). Design and development of a pressure sensing system for pilot masks. *International Journal of Applied Engineering Research: IJAER, 15*(20), 420–428.

Banu, A., Naidu, S. M., Vinjamuri, S. N., Dattu, G., Sridevi, M., & Chakravarthi, N. R. (2022). Experimentally investigating the influence of static mixers on the performance of a solar water heater. *Materials Today: Proceedings, 62*(4), 2370–2375. doi:10.1016/j.matpr.2022.04.851

Buragadda, S., Rani, K. S., Vasantha, S. V., & Chakravarthi, M. K. (2022). HCUGAN: Hybrid Cyclic UNET GAN for Generating Augmented Synthetic Images of Chest X-Ray Images for Multi Classification of Lung Diseases. *International Journal of Engineering Trends and Technology, 70*(2), 229–238. doi:10.14445/22315381/IJETT-V70I2P227

Chopra, P., Junath, N., Singh, S. K., Khan, S., Sugumar, R., & Bhowmick, M. (2022). Cyclic GAN model to classify breast cancer data for pathological healthcare task. *BioMed Research International, 6336700,* 1–12. doi:10.1155/2022/6336700 PMID:35909482

Chumbley, E. M., Stolfi, A., & McEachen, J. C. (2017). Risk factors for cervical pain in F-15C pilots. *Aerospace Medicine and Human Performance, 88*(11), 1000–1007. doi:10.3357/AMHP.4848.2017 PMID:29046175

Deepa, B., Gayathiridevi, K., Chakravarthi, M., Shajahan, A., & Sree, S. (2022). Slow evaporation technique to grow 3 - Amino benzene sulfonic acid single crystal for Non-Linear optical (NLO) transmission. *Materials Today: Proceedings, 62*(4), 2119–2123. doi:10.1016/j.matpr.2022.03.045

Fan, Y., Zhang, L., Lin, T., & Xu, B. (2018). Pressure sensing system for pilot masks based on MEMS pressure sensor and LabVIEW. *Measurement, 129,* 159–166.

Fazil, M., Khan, S., Albahlal, B. M., Alotaibi, R. M., Siddiqui, T., & Shah, M. A. (2023). Attentional Multi-Channel Convolution With Bidirectional LSTM Cell Toward Hate Speech Prediction. *IEEE Access : Practical Innovations, Open Solutions*, *11*, 16801–16811. doi:10.1109/ACCESS.2023.3246388

Gowtham, S., Ch, T., Kumar, N. S. M. P., Devi, M., Chakravarthi, S., Kumar, R., & Kumar, K. (2022). A Survey on Additively Manufactured Nanocomposite Biomaterial for Orthopaedic Applications. *Journal of Nanomaterials*, *2022*, 2022. doi:10.1155/2022/8998451

Jain, R., Chakravarthi, M. K., Kumar, P. K., Hemakesavulu, O., Ramirez-Asis, E., Pelaez-Diaz, G., & Mahaveerakannan, R. (2022). Internet of Things-based smart vehicles design of bio-inspired algorithms using artificial intelligence charging system. *Nonlinear Engineering*, *11*(1), 582–589. doi:10.1515/nleng-2022-0242

Khan, S. (2016). How Data Mining Can Help Curb City Crime. [IJCTA]. *International Journal of Control Theory and Applications*, *9*(23), 483–488.

Khan, S. (2021a). Study Factors for Student Performance Applying Data Mining Regression Model Approach. *International Journal of Computer Science Network Security*, *21*(2), 188–192.

Khan, S. (2021b). Data visualization to explore the countries dataset for pattern creation. [IJOE]. *International Journal of Online and Biomedical Engineering*, *17*(13), 4–19. doi:10.3991/ijoe.v17i13.20167

Kim, S. W., Lee, J. G., Kim, J. W., Kim, S. W., & Lee, J. H. (2019). Breathing Monitoring System for High-Altitude Fighter Pilots. In *Proceedings of the 2019 International Conference on Information and Communication Technology Convergence (ICTC)* (pp. 951–954). Jeju Island, Korea (South).

Kumar, R., Kapoor, N., & Singh, P. K. (2018). Development of a LabVIEW-Based Data Acquisition System using NI USB-6363 for Real-Time Signal Processing Applications. *Iranian Journal of Electrical and Computer Engineering*, *8*(2), 894–902. doi:10.11591/ijece.v8i2.pp894-902

Li, Z., & Dajun, L. (2014). Design of a Data Acquisition System Using NI USB-6363 and LabVIEW for Structural Health Monitoring. *Journal of Sensors*, 1–8. doi:10.1155/2014/589249

Mahesha, C. R., Suprabha, R., Kumar, N. M., Kosanam, K., Anandaram, H., Ramana Murty Naidu, S. C. V., & Govindarajan, V. (2022). Effect of friction stir welding on the mechanical and microstructural behaviour of AA7075 aluminium alloy. *Advances in Materials Science and Engineering*, *2022*, 1–8. doi:10.1155/2022/2788479

Reddy, G. P., Kumar, Y. V. P., & Chakravarthi, M. K. (2022a). Communication technologies for interoperable smart microgrids in urban energy community: A broad review of the state of the art, challenges, and research perspectives. *Sensors (Basel)*, *22*(15), 5881. doi:10.339022155881 PMID:35957438

Reddy, P., Gogulamudi, Y., & Maddikera Kalyan Chakravarthi, A. (2022b). Refined Network Topology for Improved Reliability and Enhanced Dijkstra Algorithm for Optimal Path Selection during Link Failures in Cluster Microgrids. *Sustainability*, *14*(16).

Rosenberg, H., & Park, J. (2017). Hypoxia: The Challenges of Detection and Mitigation in High-Altitude Military Aviation. *Aerospace Medicine and Human Performance*, *88*(7), 657–661. doi:10.3357/AMHP.4848.2017 PMID:28641683

Sharma, S. N., & Singh, A. M. (2012). Development of a Flight Test Data Acquisition and Analysis System using LabVIEW. *International Journal of Computer Applications*, *41*(8), 1–6. doi:10.5120/6321-8599

Singh, A. K., & Bansal, R. C. (2015). LabVIEW-Based Data Acquisition and Control System Using NI USB-6363 for the Identification of Amplitude Modulation in FM Radio Broadcasts. *Measurement Science Review*, *15*(5), 242–248. doi:10.1515/msr-2015-0034

Siva Ramkumar, M., Priya, R., Rajakumari, R. F., Valsalan, P., Chakravarthi, M., Charlyn Pushpa Latha, G., & Rajan, K. (2022). Review and Evaluation of Power Devices and Semiconductor Materials Based on Si, SiC, and Ga-N. *Journal of Nanomaterials*, *2022*, 2022. doi:10.1155/2022/8648284

Zannah, A. I., Rachakonda, S., Abubakar, A. M., Devkota, S., & Nneka, E. C. (2023). Control for Hydrogen Recovery in Pressuring Swing Adsorption System Modeling. *FMDB Transactions on Sustainable Energy Sequence*, *1*(1), 1–10.

Chapter 6
Dynamic Intelligence–Driven Engineering Flooding Attack Prediction Using Ensemble Learning

R. Angeline

SRM Institute of Science and Technology, Ramapuram, India

S. Aarthi

SRM Institute of Science and Technology, Ramapuram, India

R. Regin

SRM Institute of Science and Technology, Ramapuram, India

S. Suman Rajest

ⓘD https://orcid.org/0000-0001-8315-3747

Dhaanish Ahmed College of Engineering, India

ABSTRACT

The rapid evolution of the Internet and communication technologies has fueled the proliferation of wireless sensor network (WSN) technology, which is increasingly important in today's interconnected world. For a broad variety of industries and applications, an enormous number of sensing devices continuously create and/or gather copious amounts of sensory data. However, it has been shown that WSN is susceptible to security flaws. These networks' abrasive and unmanaged deployment, along with their limited resources and the amount of data produced, raise serious security issues. The development of trustworthy solutions that include quick and continuous processes for live data stream analysis allowing the identification of flooding assaults is crucial since WSN applications are of the utmost importance. To put it in plain words: The assault is carried out by repeatedly sending pointless requests to the target computer in an effort to overwhelm it, cause the systems to fail, and prevent people from accessing the network or machine.

DOI: 10.4018/979-8-3693-1301-5.ch006

1. INTRODUCTION

The field of cybersecurity is of paramount importance in today's digital world, where malicious attacks on computer networks and systems can cause significant damage to individuals and organizations (Taherkhani & Pierre, 2015). One such attack is the flooding attack, which floods a network or system with a large volume of traffic, causing it to crash or become unresponsive (Greff et al., 2017). To address this problem, researchers have developed various techniques for detecting and preventing flooding attacks (Józefowicz et al., 2015). In this chapter, we propose a novel approach to predicting flooding attacks using ensemble learning, which is a machine learning technique that combines the outputs of multiple models to improve prediction accuracy (Sun et al., 2020). Our proposed approach, called Dynamic Intelligent Driven Engineering Flooding Attack Prediction (DIDE-FAP), is based on a dynamic feature selection and intelligent feature engineering process that improves the performance of the machine learning models used for prediction. also use several popular machine learning algorithms, including K-Nearest Neighbor (KNN), Random Forest (RF), Decision Tree (DT), and Support Vector Machine (SVM), to predict the flooding attacks with high accuracy (Rashi & Madamala, 2022).

The proposed dynamic intelligent-driven engineering flood attack prediction the ensemble learning approach leverages the power of ensemble learning and incorporates dynamic feature selection and intelligent feature engineering to enhance the accuracy of the prediction models (Tiwari, et al., 2018). To prevent flooding attacks, it is important to develop effective prediction models that can identify and respond to potential attacks before they occur (Sinha et al., 2021). This is where machine learning techniques, such as ensemble learning, can play a vital role (Singh et al., 2022). Ensemble learning involves combining multiple models to improve the accuracy and robustness of predictions, making it a promising approach for predicting flooding attacks (Surve et al., 2022). This approach involves developing dynamic and intelligent models that can adapt to changes in network traffic and improve their accuracy over time.

By using ensemble learning to predict flooding attacks, organisations can better protect their networks and prevent the disruption and financial losses that can result from such attacks (Pandit, 2023). This chapter makes a significant contribution to the field of cybersecurity by proposing an effective approach for predicting flooding attacks. Our proposed approach can be used by security analysts and network administrators to improve the security of their systems by detecting and preventing flooding attacks before they occur. Predicting how much traffic will increase or decrease is a big challenge for today's transportation networks (Sepasgozar & Pierre, 2022). It might help with traffic reduction, better route planning, and better route selection. Predicting when and where traffic congestion will occur is one approach to managing transportation (Wu et al., 2018).

Network traffic would grow if there were more cars on the road, since more cars would mean more packets being sent. In the literature study, we looked at previous studies that separately examined network traffic and traffic on the roads (UmaMaheswaran, et al., 2022). Most of these studies addressed either road or network congestion individually; this one seeks to bridge that gap by analysing the correlation between these two types of traffic measurements. Intelligent approaches employing machine learning (ML) methods are the best solutions to handle traffic prediction problems with the aim of anticipating traffic flow. Bayesian modelling, fuzzy logic, hybrid modelling, neural networks (NN), and statistical modelling are only a few of the available computer methodologies. Most of these techniques, and NN in particular, have the potential to improve prediction accuracy in data flow (Yang, et al., 2017).

The accuracy of prediction is a key factor in all of these considerations. Three categories of ML approaches are distinguished: Unsupervised learning (in which training is based on unlabeled data), supervised learning (in which training is based on labelled data), and reinforcement learning (in which it learns based on how well the learning agent performs) are the three different kinds of learning. Furthermore, these three classes of ML schemes further classify a wide range of ML schemes, including online learning and transfer learning (Tong, et al., 2019). Deep learning (DL) methods for prediction issues are another interesting option in the event of a large and complicated dataset. Two generally utilised brain network calculations are the intermittent brain organisation (RNN) (Chung et al., 2014); (Karpathy et al., 2015) and the convolutional brain organisation (CNN) (Coşkun et al., 2017). It utilises a few algorithmic structures. Two well-known RNN parts are the long momentary memory (LSTM) and the gated repetitive unit (GRU) (Priscila et al., 2023).

The LSTM strategy and RNN are equivalent in that the two of them mean to address the evaporating issue. One of the most crucial features of these algorithms is their capacity to learn relationships over time in order to make predictions in time-series datasets (Abbassy et al., 2019). In contrast to LSTM, which is slow because of the number of gates it uses, the GRU approach is fast (Yamak et al., 2019). Furthermore, the Bi-directional Long Short-Term Memory (Bi-LSTM) technique may be utilised to extract more characteristics and bidirectional relationships. Using two separate hidden layers, this form of algorithm allows the operation to be carried out in one of two ways (forward or backward) (Cui et al., 2018).

In this exploration, give a way to deal with network traffic determination that incorporates information on vehicular traffic (Singh et al., 2022). This is the first time that we have been aware that organisation traffic has been anticipated in light of genuine street traffic. Our study is divided into three phases, and its ultimate purpose is to estimate network traffic utilising different AI and profound learning procedures. The prediction of network traffic is the focus of the first phase. Predicting traffic on the roads is the focus of phase two. The third step combines the first two stages with the goal of predicting network traffic while taking into account the factors that influence road traffic and may also have an impact on network traffic. employ two GPS datasets: one that estimates network traffic in light of V2R correspondence and one more that predicts street traffic in light of V2V correspondence.

1.1. The Following Are the Work's Main Contributions

ML techniques on a real-world dataset gleaned from V2R communications to forecast the flow of traffic based on packets delivered by vehicles to road-side units (RSUs). However, also use the KNN (K-Nearest Neighbors), SVM (Support Vector Machines), and Naive Bayes (NB) algorithms, with the RF being the most effective of the ML approaches utilised. To better predict traffic on the roads and how it will affect network traffic, isolate the sender's speed as a road attribute. Using a real-world dataset collected from V2V conversations, use deep learning techniques to forecast vehicular traffic by calculating sender speeds. tested many different DL algorithms, including LSTM, Bi-LSTM, and GRU, and finally settled on the latter (Shah et al., 2020).

2. RELATED WORK

Intelligent traffic forecasting (Fabela et al., 2017) might provide vital help for addressing urban traffic congestion. However, intelligent approaches may help us anticipate traffic flow by taking into consideration a number of relevant properties. More precise analyses and forecasts might result from using

ML and DL methods (Patil et al., 2021). Several studies have proposed methods for applying learning algorithms to forecast network and vehicle traffic independently. Some researchers also try to predict how weather will affect the volume of vehicle traffic on the roadways. The bulk of this research makes use of an extensive variety of AI and profound learning strategies, but grouping them into two general classifications: network traffic expectation and street traffic prediction, is conceivable (Nirmala et al., 2023).

2.1. Network Traffic Prediction

In (Patil et al., 2015), the creators distributed a procedure for working on the expectation of connection-level traffic over an entire network using LSTM. As of Volume 10, 2022, of Software Defined 8228, they have compiled data. Network Traffic Prediction Model, S. S. Sepasgozar, and S. Pierre Network throughput forecasting using either the System for Network Management (SNMP) or road traffic parameters (RTP) They built their model using real data, considering an hour's worth of packet traffic. They tried out three unique ARIMA models (basic ARIMA, delta ARIMA, and first-order autoregressive ARIMA) and three unique LSTM models (vanilla LSTM, delta LSTM, and multivariate LSTM). Their results showed that all LSTM variants outperformed ARIMA-based models in mimicking network activity.

Nonetheless, they may have compared using deep learning approaches other than ARMIA baselines, which are known to improve accuracy. To further develop network asset designation and organisation traffic forecasting, the creators of (Abbassy et al., 2020) employed real-world datasets and deep learning algorithms with a five-minute time step. They suggested the Evaluation Automatic Module (EAM) method, which automated and generalised the learning process for the prediction model with the goal of having the greatest performance. The first part of their proposed model employs an ANN in view of the GRU calculation to prepare the forecast model, while the subsequent part utilises the EAM approach to assess the model after each iteration of the learning process. Additionally, they assessed the effectiveness of the proposed model utilising the Mean Outright Blunder (MAE) measure. Their outcomes were contrasted with static preparation, which distinguishes the most elevated data transmission joins in a rush hour gridlock network, as part of the resource allocation phase.

The experimental findings demonstrated that the suggested model had high prediction and resource allocation accuracy. In order to enhance the network traffic forecast suggested in (Derindere Köseoğlu, et al., 2022), a new approach was developed. They attempted intelligent network traffic expectation utilising succession mining, the LSTM, and the Versatile Nero-Fluffy Derivation Framework (ANFIS) as a period series model. To try their recommended model, they utilised genuine organisation information. Moreover, they utilised fluffy c-implies bunching to bunch related information. To appraise network traffic, they additionally arranged the things into five groups as contributions for the LSTM and ANFIS calculations. Using standards for diagnosing expectation blunders, they surveyed the proposed model and found that it could lessen expectation mistakes and further develop network execution. A wide range of sorts of CNN in view of genuine information are used to get the fitting organisation settings for network traffic expectations (Ead & Abbassy, 2018). Utilizing a learning pace of [0.01] to [0.5], they ran the technique multiple times with various executions of multi-facet discernment (MLP), convolutional brain organisation (CNN), convolutional brain organisation (LSTM), and convolutional brain organisation (GRU).

The outcomes show that CNN and its many varieties can outperform other traditional machine learning methods. Layer-by-layer characteristics classified using an unsupervised algorithm were used by the authors of (Jeganathan et al., 2023) to implement the Taguchi approach in an effort to create and optimise traffic learning. They proposed an advanced design for traffic stream expectation prepared utilising stacked auto encoder (SAE) and Ladenburg-Marquardt (LM) calculations to do transient traffic determining. Their procedure attempts to further develop traffic stream gauge precision. The proposed model uses the Taguchi technique to create a deep neural network architecture for analysing traffic patterns. They utilised actual data that had been obtained and applied various hidden layer limitations, such as taking five hidden layers into consideration, to develop and assess their technique.

They employed the LM method to train the input that the last auto encoder produced under the assumption that neurons were mostly dormant. With a prediction accuracy rate of nearly 90%, the proposed model outperformed other algorithms such as the spiral premise capability NN (RBFNN), the cross-breed dramatic smoothing and the LM calculation (EXP-LM), and the molecule swarm streamlining calculation with NNs (PSONN). Given the potential unpredictability of the underlying traffic flow data, the proposed technique proved effective in resolving this problem. Another technique for anticipating LTE network traffic is introduced in (Vashishtha & Dhawan, 2023). They utilised three different AI strategies to gauge network traffic: RF, packing, and SVM, all prepared on openly accessible cell traffic datasets. To assess their presentation, they determined the root mean square error (RMSE), mean outright blunder (MAE), and coefficient of assurance (R 2). The outcomes exhibit that the stowing technique succeeds in coordinating mathematical and all-out information. The RMSEs for the packing and RF were 2.59 and 3.38, respectively. Additionally, the MAE for the RF and Bagging were respectively 1.60 and 2.19, while the R 2 for the RF was 50.8%. In contrast, the SVM learned in 6 seconds, as opposed to the 116 and 112 seconds that the bagging and RF needed, respectively.

2.2. Dynamic Flooding Attack Prediction

Deep neural networks (DNNs) can accurately predict traffic volumes by processing massive amounts of data. However, there are several challenges associated with geographical and temporal considerations. The creators of (Wu et al., 2018) proposed a conjecture model to tackle these issues and study the inward operations of DNN-based traffic stream expectation (DNN-BTF) on traffic stream information with solid accuracy, all fully intent on further developing forecast precision. They utilised information from the uninhibitedly accessible PeMS data set to really look at their model. They likewise utilised the RNN and CNN (with a total convolution organization) techniques to handle worldly and geographical data. They decided to use three different measures of performance: mean relative error (MRE), mean absolute error (MAE), and root mean squared error (RMSE).

In addition, they compared their proposed model to others, including LASSO (Agarwal, 2014), a standard shallow back-propagation neural network (BPNN), a stacked auto encoder (SAE) (Agarwal, et al., 2021), and a Network Traffic Prediction Model with a Focus on the Most Important Road Traffic Factors by Chakrabarti et al., (2008). According to the results, their model did better than theirs. Gehlot et al., (2022) integrated geographical and temporal information with the GRU to create a spatial-temporal feature selection algorithm (GRU + STFSA) for predicting near-term traffic patterns. They contrasted the results obtained using CNN and simple GRU algorithms. The model was assessed using the mean outright mistake (MAE), mean outright rate blunder (MAPE), and root mean squared blunder (RMSE). The suggested model performed better concerning exactness and solidity, with only a bit of a forecast blunder. The proposed cross-breed CNN-LSTM model for anticipating traffic streams utilising GPS information (Kumar et al., 2022). Preparing the CNN-LSTM model expected an insatiable strategy approach because of the half-and-half model's intricacy and preparation time.

The consequences of the tests showed that the profound crossover proposed model performed better compared to the Direct (a model with a thick layer utilising surtax), the CNN, and the CNN-LSTM model in predicting future traffic volumes while also requiring less processing time. In (Prince, et al., 2021), the authors described a hybrid strategy based on support vector regression (SVR) for predicting near-term traffic patterns. The most intriguing aspects were found using the RF, and the GA was improved to find the best features. After collecting data from real-world datasets and selecting features using the RF, training on the recommended RF-CGASVR model was complete. They tested the suggested concept in two different layouts with the intention of evaluating it. The first one was straight and was created with the intention of evaluating the performance of simple situations. The crossroads layout, which dealt with junctions and other routes, was the second.

3. METHODOLOGY

To anticipate network traffic flow, present a new RF-GRU-NTP model in this part utilising machine learning and deep learning methods (Figure 1).

Figure 1. Displays the structure of a flooding attack

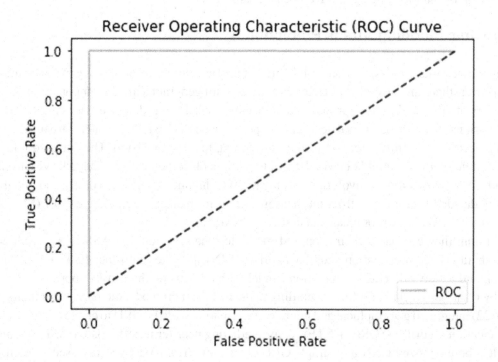

Due to the moving characters (such as automobiles) present in the network, which complicate prediction difficulties, VANET is a dynamic environment. Applying machine learning algorithms to appropriate datasets allows for more precise traffic forecasting. Predicting complex patterns in a timely and accurate manner is another use of deep learning algorithms. Due to the complexity of determining what elements would have an influence on the flow of network traffic, the suggested model is divided into three phases. The suggested model's design, which consists of three phases, is seen in Figure 2.

3.1. Phase One: Network Traffic Flow

During the initial stage, the focus should be only on network-to-network (V2R) communications and using packets sent between bytes and side units (RSUs) to forecast the flow of traffic on the network. It used classification approaches at this stage before testing with several AI calculations, including the KNN, RF, NB, and SVM, to get the best exhibition and precision in the expected results across these measurements. The strategies were assessed in light of the region under the Collector Working Bend (ROC) measure, the disarray lattice, and how much time was expected to run the algorithm.

Figure 2. The layout of the envisioned RF-GRU-NTP system

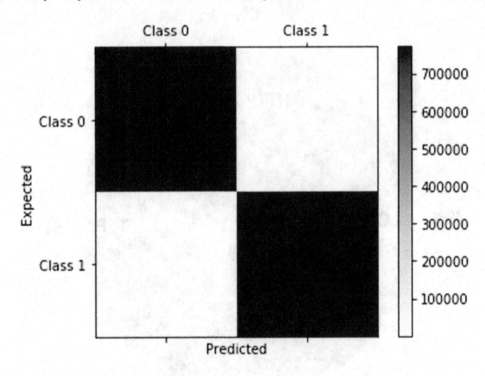

3.2. Random Forest Algorithm

The RF is an approach to supervised learning that uses the combination of many decision trees to provide more precise predictions. As a result, the RF technique can solve regression and classification issues, and it can also solve the overfitting issue that plagues machine learning algorithms (Jeba, et al., 2023). four distinct machine learning algorithms to a GPS-collected dataset (Cirillo et al., 2023) and found that the RF approach to traffic prediction yielded the most accurate results. Our dataset for automotive networks contained metrics for both inter-vehicle and inter-vehicle-to-base station (RSU) communications. 802.11 ad-hoc networks were used. The dataset includes information on several factors, including latitude, longitude, sender and receiver speeds, as well as packet reception speed. packet data sent from vehicles to RSUs and sampled 10,000 records from a single day to make traffic predictions. To keep track of how often the classifier got it right, how often it got it wrong, and everything in between, we whipped up a confusion matrix.

In Figure 3, the algorithms, libraries, tools, and measurements that make up the initial stage of the proposed model's process are shown. Book Ten, 8231, Year 2022 St. Pierre and Saint Sepulchral: A traffic prediction model for networks that accounted for factors like road congestion The V2R communications in our vehicle network dataset were obtained using a GPS receiver. The data was divided into two categories: class 1 for packets that are received and are thought to be in non-traffic situations, and class 0 for packets that are not received but are presumed to be in traffic situations

Figure 3. Flow of prediction model

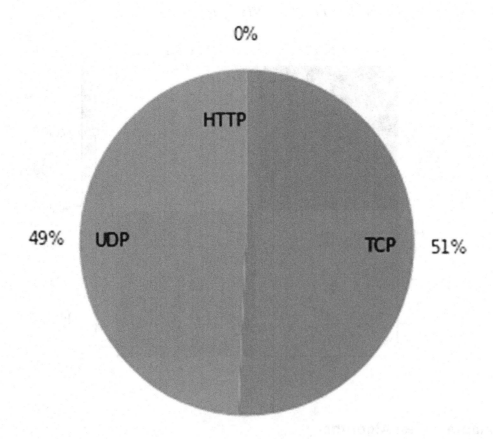

3.3. Phase Two; Dynamic Flooding Attack Prediction

As a road parameter for traffic forecasting, a vehicle's speed (the "sender speed") is used in the second phase of vehicle-to-vehicle (V2V) communication. To this point, we have implemented and evaluated regression strategies using the GRU, Bi-LSTM, and LSTM deep learning algorithms. The GRU algorithm produced the greatest results in our assessment of their performances using evaluation measures for deep regression methods. The GRU Algorithm The GRU is a powerful algorithm that may be derived from the LSTM, one of the many RNN variants. The fundamental benefit of RNN—automatically learning features—is carried over to GRU. It can function similarly to an LSTM but memorize long-term prediction performance more quickly.

3.4. Phase Three: Network Traffic Prediction

In the third and last stage, anticipate the network traffic stream by considering the components that influence traffic on the streets. The RF-GRU-NTP model for anticipating network traffic This is the first time that traffic on a network has been predicted using effective road traffic flow parameters. In addition, it provides a method for predicting network traffic that utilises a blend of machine learning and deep learning approaches.

4. DATA PREPARATION AND PERFORMANCE EVALUATION

They mount an external antenna on the top of automobiles to collect data. Every two seconds, the GPS system relays the location, direction, speed, and longitude of the vehicle. The data shows that between 2 and 5 o'clock in the afternoon, the Atlanta interstate has five standard paths and one high-inhabitance vehicle carpool lane. It provides position data with an accuracy of five to seven meters, and location data was obtained by interpolation (Suganthi & Sathiaseelan, 2023). During the initial era, our main focus was on making accurate traffic predictions for the network. The dataset of V2R communications packets was used to make traffic predictions for the RSUs.

The second step included using the V2V communication information and zeroing in on the "shipper speed" to foresee traffic, regardless of the way that the sending and getting vehicles were in a similar path (the second one from the right) yet at various distances. Following data collection, we performed preprocessing, data cleaning, and scaling using the Standard Scalar method in order to standardize the data. Then, an AI strategy was developed to recuperate the ideal boundaries by preparing a consolidated dataset of the organization's traffic stream.

Python 3.6 is used to develop the algorithms, and at different points, it relied on a number of different libraries to do this. The initial stage includes the implementation of several machine learning algorithms. With the intention of using machine learning approaches, the methods used are Scikit-learn, Pandas, NumPy, Matplotlib, Mlxtend, and a few more libraries to find the most effective strategy for forecasting network traffic. Thus, we learned that the RF functioned more efficiently. In order to construct deep learning algorithms for use in stages two and three, we made use of the Keas libraries and Tensor Flow to perform pre-processing, data purification, and scaling after data gathering to provide predictions with greater accuracy (Figure 4).

Figure 4. Pie chart of the TCP, HTTP and UDP variables network traffic

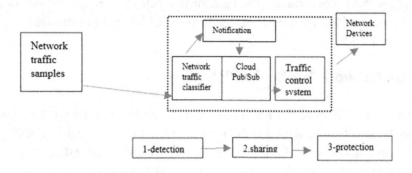

The variable - protocol is a normalization of the protocol field extracted from a transport layer packet headers in the form:

$$ip_{proto} = \frac{A_{proto}}{K}$$

Where A_{proto} is the code of the "protocol" and K is an "normalization constant" set to the value 1,000. $A_{proto} = 6$ and $A_{proto} = 7$ in TCP and UDP protocols, respectively for instances.

With the four variables it is possible to calculate the following statistic measurements used in flow monitoring:

(i)   (i)   Entropy: the variable's *entropy* can be calculated by

$$Entropy(A) = -\pounds_i p(A_i) log_2 p(A_i)$$

where A is the "variable of interest" e.g., source port.

(ii)   (ii)   Coefficient of variation: the "coefficient of variation" is calculated by

$$cv(A) = \frac{std(A)}{mean(A)}$$

where std(A) is the "standard deviation" and mean(A) is the average of the variable.

(iii)   (iii)   Quantile coefficient: this parameter is defined here by

$$cvq(A) = \frac{Q_A(1-p) - Q_A(p)}{Q_A(1-p) + Q_A(p)}$$

Where $Q_A(p)$ is the p-quantile sample, $p \in (0, 0.5)$, expressed by

$$Q_A(p) = A_{(k)} + \left(A_{(k+1)} - A_{(k)}\right) * f$$

With being $\{A_{(1)}, \ldots\ldots, A_{(n)}\}$ the statistics order of observations, $\{A_{(1)}, \ldots\ldots, A_{(n)}\}$, k=[p*n], and f is the fractional part of the surrounded index by $A_{(k)}$ and $A_{(k+1)}$.

(iv) (iv)   Rate of change: this metric is given by

$$rtc(A) = \frac{U_A}{S_A}$$

(v)   where U_A is unique values and S_A is number of A values.

5. RESULT

depicts the sender speed prediction results, taking into account its useful characteristics for predicting network traffic. The blue line addresses the noticed information, i.e., the model prediction is done on the graph, telling its positive and negative accuracy rates. The model that was proposed performed better compared to any of the simple algorithmic methodologies that have been tried. The deviation between the test information and the anticipated information is tiny. We first calculated the evaluation metrics and then calculated how long each method took to fit the model. The output or result of the model is around 99.9% accurate, which is better than existing models that are in use currently (Accuracy 0.9999033283591773).

Figure 5. The results of variables and Important tests compared to predictions in phase two with a accuracy of 99.9%

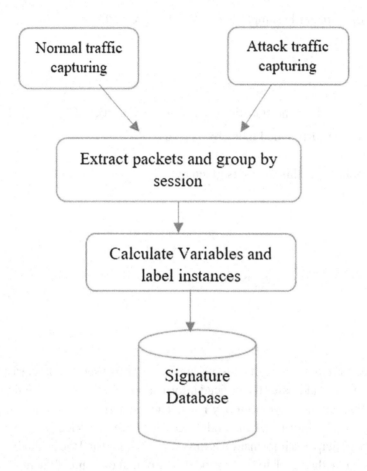

The Dynamic Flooding Attack Prediction Approach using Ensemble Learning has focused on prediction flooding attacks, which can be later extended to other types of attacks, such as malware attacks and DDoS distributed denial of service (fig.5). This model can later be integrated with security measures such as firewalls to provide a security solution for computer networks. Additional data logs, such as system logs, can be used to find their use in predicting the different attacks on the system. Overall, the dynamic flooding attack prediction approach using ensemble learning has significant potential for future research and development in the field of cyber security and computer networks.

6. CONCLUSION

In this chapter, dynamic intelligent-driven engineering flood attack prediction using ensemble learning is discussed. The rapidly growing technologies like machine learning and data science are widely used in this model, thus giving us more accuracy and a better and faster result. The accuracy of the model is 99.99%. The flooding attacks, which are basically overloading of the unnecessary requests on the network, stop the network flow. Machine learning techniques, such as ensemble learning, play an important role. Ensemble learning involves combining multiple models to improve the accuracy and robustness of predictions, making it a promising approach for predicting flooding attacks. The model plays a significant role in cyber security services by predicting these types of attacks more accurately and quickly as compared to the existing services. Though the model can predict the attacks, there are many more challenges to be faced to ensure the successful implementation of the system. Increasing development and the use of technologies contribute to making the resources more affordable and reliable.

REFERENCES

Abbassy, Mohamed M., & Abo-Alnadr, A. (2019). Rule-based emotion AI in Arabic customer review. International Journal of Advanced Computer Science and Applications : IJACSA, 10(9). doi:10.14569/ijacsa.2019.010093

Abbassy, Mohamed M., & Ead, W. M. (2020). Intelligent Greenhouse Management System. 2020 6th International Conference on Advanced Computing and Communication Systems (ICACCS). IEEE.

Agarwal, R. (2014). Edge detection in images using modified bit-planes Sobel operator. In *Advances in Intelligent Systems and Computing* (pp. 203–210). Springer India.

Agarwal, R., Hariharan, S., Nagabhushana Rao, M., & Agarwal, A. (2021). Weed identification using K-means clustering with color spaces features in multi-spectral images taken by UAV. *2021 IEEE International Geoscience and Remote Sensing Symposium IGARSS*. IEEE.

Chakrabarti, P., Bhuyan, B., Chaudhuri, A., & Bhunia, C. T. (2008). A novel approach towards realizing optimum data transfer and Automatic Variable Key(AVK). *International Journal of Computer Science and Network Security*, 8(5), 241–250.

Chung, J., Gulcehre, C., Cho, K., & Bengio, Y. (2014). Empirical evaluation of gated recurrent neural networks on sequence modeling. In arXiv [cs.NE]. https://arxiv.org/abs/1412.3555

Cirillo, S., Polese, G., Salerno, D., Simone, B., & Solimando, G. (2023). Towards Flexible Voice Assistants: Evaluating Privacy and Security Needs in IoT-enabled Smart Homes. *FMDB Transactions on Sustainable Computer Letters*, 1(1), 25–32.

Coşkun, M., Yildirim, Ö., Uçar, A., & Demir, Y. (2017). An overview of popular deep learning methods. *European Journal of Technique*, 7(2), 165–176. doi:10.23884/ejt.2017.7.2.11

Cui, Z., Ke, R., Pu, Z., & Wang, Y. (2018). Deep bidirectional and unidirectional LSTM recurrent neural network for network-wide traffic speed prediction. In arXiv [cs.LG]. https://arxiv.org/abs/1801.02143

Derindere Köseoğlu, S., Ead, W. M., & Abbassy, M. M. (2022). Basics of Financial Data Analytics. In *Financial Data Analytics* (pp. 23–57). Springer International Publishing. doi:10.1007/978-3-030-83799-0_2

Ead, W., & Abbassy, M. (2018). Intelligent systems of machine learning approaches for developing E-services portals. *EAI Endorsed Transactions on Energy Web, 167292*, 167292. Advance online publication. doi:10.4108/eai.2-12-2020.167292

Fabela, O., Patil, S., Chintamani, S., & Dennis, B. H. (2017). *Estimation of effective thermal conductivity of porous media utilizing inverse heat transfer analysis on cylindrical configuration* (Vol. 8). Heat Transfer and Thermal Engineering. doi:10.1115/IMECE2017-71559

Gehlot, A., Rajat Mohan, L., Gupta, A., Anandaram, H., Alanya-Beltran, J., & Kalyan Chakravarthi, M. (2022). Smart online oxygen supply management though internet of things (IoT). *2022 International Conference on Innovative Computing, Intelligent Communication and Smart Electrical Systems (ICSES)*. IEEE. 10.1109/ICSES55317.2022.9914246

Greff, K., Srivastava, R. K., Koutnik, J., Steunebrink, B. R., & Schmidhuber, J. (2017). LSTM: A search space odyssey. *IEEE Transactions on Neural Networks and Learning Systems, 28*(10), 2222–2232. doi:10.1109/TNNLS.2016.2582924 PMID:27411231

Jeba, J. A., Bose, S. R., & Boina, R. (2023). Exploring Hybrid Multi-View Multimodal for Natural Language Emotion Recognition Using Multi-Source Information Learning Model. *FMDB Transactions on Sustainable Computer Letters, 1*(1), 12–24.

Jeganathan, J., Vashist, S., Nirmala, G., & Deep, R. (2023). A Cross Sectional Study on Anxiety and Depression Among Patients with Alcohol Withdrawal Syndrome. *FMDB Transactions on Sustainable Health Science Letters, 1*(1), 31–40.

Józefowicz, R., Zaremba, W., & Sutskever, I. (2015). An Empirical Exploration of Recurrent Network Architectures. *International Conference on Machine Learning*, (pp. 2342–2350). IEEE.

Karpathy, A., Johnson, J., & Fei-Fei, L. (2015). Visualizing and understanding recurrent networks. In arXiv [cs.LG]. https://arxiv.org/abs/1506.02078

Kumar, S., Kumar, N. M. G., Geetha, B. T., Sangeetha, M., Chakravarthi, M. K., & Tripathi, V. (2022). Cluster, cloud, grid computing via network communication using control communication and monitoring of smart grid. *2022 2nd International Conference on Advance Computing and Innovative Technologies in Engineering (ICACITE)*. IEEE.

Nirmala, G., Premavathy, R., Chandar, R., & Jeganathan, J. (2023). An Explanatory Case Report on Biopsychosocial Issues and the Impact of Innovative Nurse-Led Therapy in Children with Hematological Cancer. *FMDB Transactions on Sustainable Health Science Letters, 1*(1), 1–10.

Pandit, P. (2023). On the Context of Diabetes: A Brief Discussion on the Novel Ethical Issues of Non-communicable Diseases. *FMDB Transactions on Sustainable Health Science Letters, 1*(1), 11–20.

Patil, S., Chintamani, S., Dennis, B. H., & Kumar, R. (2021). Real time prediction of internal temperature of heat generating bodies using neural network. *Thermal Science and Engineering Progress, 23*(100910), 100910. doi:10.1016/j.tsep.2021.100910

Patil, S., Chintamani, S., Grisham, J., Kumar, R., & Dennis, B. H. (2015). Inverse determination of temperature distribution in partially cooled heat generating cylinder. *Volume 8B: Heat Transfer and Thermal Engineering*.

Prince, H., Hati, A. S., Chakrabarti, P., Abawajy, J. H., & Keong, N. W. (2021). Development of energy efficient drive for ventilation system using recurrent neural network. *Neural Computing & Applications*, *33*(14), 8659–8668. doi:10.100700521-020-05615-x

Priscila, S. S., Rajest, S. S., Tadiboina, S. N., Regin, R., & András, S. (2023). Analysis of Machine Learning and Deep Learning Methods for Superstore Sales Prediction. *FMDB Transactions on Sustainable Computer Letters*, *1*(1), 1–11.

Rashi, A., & Madamala, R. (2022). Minimum relevant features to obtain AI explainable system for predicting breast cancer in WDBC. [IJHS]. *International Journal of Health Sciences*, 1312–1326. doi:10.53730/ijhs.v6nS9.12538

Sepasgozar, S. S., & Pierre, S. (2022). Network traffic prediction model considering road traffic parameters using artificial intelligence methods in VANET. *IEEE Access : Practical Innovations, Open Solutions*, *10*, 8227–8242. doi:10.1109/ACCESS.2022.3144112

Shah, K., Laxkar, P., & Chakrabarti, P. (2020). A hypothesis on ideal Artificial Intelligence and associated wrong implications. *Advances in Intelligent Systems and Computing*, *989*, 283–294. doi:10.1007/978-981-13-8618-3_30

Singh, D., Keerthi Nayani, A. S., Sundar Rajan, M., Yadav, R., Alanya-Beltran, J., & Chakravarthi, M. K. (2022). Implementation of virual instrumentation for signal acquisition and processing. *2022 International Conference on Innovative Computing, Intelligent Communication and Smart Electrical Systems (ICSES)*. IEEE. 10.1109/ICSES55317.2022.9914143

Singh, R., Mishra, P. A., Prakash, A., Tongkachok, K., Upadhyaya, M., & Kalyan Chakravarthi, M. (2022). Smart device for effective communication in the healthcare system. *2022 International Conference on Innovative Computing, Intelligent Communication and Smart Electrical Systems (ICSES)*. IEEE. 10.1109/ICSES55317.2022.9914093

Sinha, A. K., Shankar Hati, A., Benbouzid, M., & Chakrabarti, P. (2021). ANN-based Pattern Recognition for Induction Motor Broken Rotor Bar Monitoring under Supply Frequency Regulation. *Machines, 9*.

Suganthi, M., & Sathiaseelan, J. G. R. (2023). Image Denoising and Feature Extraction Techniques Applied to X-Ray Seed Images for Purity Analysis. *FMDB Transactions on Sustainable Health Science Letters*, *1*(1), 41–53.

Sun, P., Boukerche, A., & Tao, Y. (2020). SSGRU: A novel hybrid stacked GRU-based traffic volume prediction approach in a road network. *Computer Communications*, *160*, 502–511. doi:10.1016/j.comcom.2020.06.028

Surve, J., Umrao, D., Madhavi, M., Rajeswari, T. S., Bangare, S. L., & Chakravarthi, M. K. (2022). Machine learning applications for protecting the information of health care department using smart internet of things appliances -A REVIEW. *2022 2nd International Conference on Advance Computing and Innovative Technologies in Engineering (ICACITE)*. IEEE.

Taherkhani, N., & Pierre, S. (2015). 'Improving dynamic and distributed congestion control in vehicular ad hoc networks. *Ad Hoc Networks*, *33*, 112–125. doi:10.1016/j.adhoc.2015.04.008

Tiwari, M., Chakrabarti, P., & Chakrabarti, T. (2018). Performance analysis and error evaluation towards the liver cancer diagnosis using lazy classifiers for ILPD. *Communications in Computer and Information Science*, *837*, 161–168. doi:10.1007/978-981-13-1936-5_19

Tong, W., Hussain, A., Bo, W. X., & Maharjan, S. (2019). Artificial intelligence for vehicle-to-everything: A survey. *IEEE Access : Practical Innovations, Open Solutions*, *7*, 10823–10843. doi:10.1109/ACCESS.2019.2891073

Uma Maheswaran. S. K., Nassa, V. K., Singh, B. P., Pandey, U. K., Satyala, H., & Chakravarthi, M. K. (2022). An inventory system utilizing neural network in the prediction of machine learning techniques. *2022 2nd International Conference on Advance Computing and Innovative Technologies in Engineering (ICACITE)*. IEEE.

Vashishtha, E., & Dhawan, G. (2023). Bridging Generation Gap on Analysis of Mentor-Mentee Relationship in Healthcare Setting. *FMDB Transactions on Sustainable Health Science Letters*, *1*(1), 21–30.

Wu, Y., Tan, H., Qin, L., Ran, B., & Jiang, Z. (2018). A hybrid deep learning based traffic flow prediction method and its understanding. *Transportation Research Part C, Emerging Technologies*, *90*, 166–180. doi:10.1016/j.trc.2018.03.001

Yamak, P. T., Yujian, L., & Gadosey, P. K. (2019). A comparison between ARIMA, LSTM, and GRU for time series forecasting. *Proceedings of the 2019 2nd International Conference on Algorithms, Computing and Artificial Intelligence*. IEEE.

Yang, H.-F., Dillon, T. S., & Chen, Y.-P. P. (2017). Optimized structure of the traffic flow forecasting model with a deep learning approach. *IEEE Transactions on Neural Networks and Learning Systems*, *28*(10), 2371–2381. doi:10.1109/TNNLS.2016.2574840 PMID:27448371

Chapter 7
Interactive Virtual Consultation and Disease Diagnosis Using Machine Learning Approach

Jyoti P. Kanjalkar
Vishwakarma Institute of Technology, India

Om Tekade
Vishwakarma Institute of Technology, India

Prathamesh Thakare
Vishwakarma Institute of Technology, India

Abhishek Gajanan Wankhade
Vishwakarma Institute of Technology, India

Purva Wankhade
Vishwakarma Institute of Technology, India

Pramod Kanjalkar
Vishwakarma Institute of Technology, India

ABSTRACT

Businesses that provide care remotely are far from the scope of virtual care. It offers a delivery channel for particular patient populations with applications that do not need in-person examinations or presence, even though it cannot be assumed to be the solution to all health-related questions. According to the scoping reviews, virtual care includes a significant information generation method called disease diagnosis, considered as the very first step towards treating the illness. Along with video conferencing technologies for consulting the doctors to achieve care supervision. Application of rehabilitation, remote consultation, and emergency services are efficient ways to use in attention to achieve well-being. Machine learning is one such way to achieve disease diagnosis based on information provided by the user with a high accuracy using various approaches. In this chapter, a novel approach of random forest approach with modifications is used.

DOI: 10.4018/979-8-3693-1301-5.ch007

1. INTRODUCTION

Self-care is an essential component of the lifestyle. Traditionally, assistance groups have used provider-centric models (e.g., hospitals). Patients can request treatment in provider-centric models by going to the office of the provider or planning outings to help facilities (Arslan et al., 2021). A patient who wants to learn about polygenic disorders for managing their hypoglycemic agents would go to a polygenic disorders education clinic with information from respective glucometers for identification of a nurse (RN), dietician, or medical professional so they can get the help they need from their suppliers (Ogunmola et al., 2021).

Through the development of new tools that promote a patient-centric style of care, technology advancements have the potential to strengthen already existing patient-provider interactions. When providers and aid organizations work to increase patient access to care, which may include offering services like telehealth visits, a patient-centric model of care is created (Sharma et al., 2021a). The possibility exists for the scenario depicted in the top outline to materialize since virtual care can increase how convenient it is for patients to receive treatment from their suppliers. Many technologies, such as Skype® and FaceTime®, are available in the global communications market to facilitate asynchronous communication across time-based virtual connections (Bansal et al., 2022).

These technologies allow for the connection of loved ones regardless of distance or time differences. When using these standard technologies to provide assistance, there are privacy concerns around (PII) non-public identifiable information and (PHI) protected health information (Gunturu et al., 2023). PII means information that recognizes distinguishing identifiers supported by persons, such as a reputation, social security number, driver's license, etc. ((Sharma et al., 2021b).

The patient's letter may include details from their medical records, such as their name, anamnesis number, or biometric identifiers, but it may also contain details about their passport, driver, and other personal information (PII) ((Sharma et al., 2021c). As a result, businesses all over the world have created tools designed specifically for use as an aid (Suthar et al., 2022). These solutions make it possible for businesses to adhere to local privacy laws, such as the Insurance Portability and Accountability Act in the United States (HIPAA) (Sonnad et al., 2022).

Virtual tools in Canada conform to the Personal Data Protection and Electronic Documents Act and the Freedom of Information and Protection of Privacy Act (FIPPA), as well as the Office of the Information and Privacy Commissioner (PIPEDA). In order to supply technologies that are suitable to the privacy and security norms of those many countries, providers must adapt to the completely different regulations that exist in each country. These actions serve to safeguard private information about a person from improper use or dissemination in our information-rich society (Uike et al., 2022).

Online healthcare has been a general word framed to refer to a particular form of treatment because many of those instruments can be used without the patient or provider being physically present. Although the concept of virtual care is not one of replacement, the general public does not fully understand it in terms of the services it offers or how it differs from conventional telehealth or, perhaps, face-to-face encounters. The location of the patients is the key differential between these three service delivery methods.

In-person, interactions become very evident in this situation because the patient will be in close proximity to their supply, whether it be at work for the provider or locally, like a neighbourhood doctor who sees patients at their homes. In the early days of telehealth, a patient would have a video call with their respective provider belonging to a medical workplace through a comfortable place like home where video conferencing devices had been developed on the patient's as well as the provider's side.

Last but not least, virtual care in this evident situation allows the victim and the provider to frequently be remotely available, like the convenience of their respective homes. As a result, the goal of this study or research is to investigate aspects of online healthcare along with many technologies which are specially made to use with help services. The research study is able to: (I) describe methods and variations of virtual healthcare; (II) grasp the impact of healthcare on the assistance sector; (III) understand the improvement of the current aid system caused by the expansion of virtual care methods and to (IV) describes the results dealing with patient abuse towards online healthcare.

Section 1 states the introduction to our work, and Section 2 illustrates the related work, Section 3 with the Proposed system, Section 4 is about the methodologies in the proposed system, and Sections 5 and 6 with Results, Future scope, and Conclusion, respectively.

2. LITERATURE REVIEW

As of now, many systems are present which can predict diseases by entering the symptoms. Each system has some advantages and disadvantages. These days, recommender frameworks are common in tourism, e-commerce, restaurant, etc. Unfortunately, a small number of studies are available in the field of Medicine or Drug recommendation. Also, some studies have been conducted utilizing machine learning algorithms to forecast diseases based on the symptoms displayed by a person. Some systems use data mining techniques such as classification (Kosarkar et al., 2022). Datasets comprising a wealth of information about patient diseases that have been obtained, improved, categorized, and users are used to train the intelligent agent. After partitioning the data, machine learning models are assessed using K-Fold cross-validation.

The ML approaches are equally capable of diagnosing unusual diseases in addition to being able to diagnose common diseases (Ahsan et al., 2022). While ML provides systematic and sophisticated algorithms for multidimensional clinical data, there are still questions about how well it can identify diseases. Multiple state-of-the-art algorithms with optimal lines of code are applied because different machine-learning approaches behave differently for various healthcare datasets (Ahsan et al., 2022). This allowed for more effectively pursuing the search for the best ML method to diagnose a particular disease. 20 ML techniques, including Naïve Bayes, Support Vector Machine 19 (SVD), K Nearest Neighbors (KNN), perceptron, and robust deep neural networks in Auto Gluon 20 (Light GBM, XG Boost, MX Net, etc.), have their performance tested based on the diabetes dataset from Pima India. They selected a diabetes-related healthcare dataset for this study.

The motivation (Krishnan & Geetha, 2019) was to find the most efficient ML algorithm for the detection of heart diseases. The focus of this study is only on learning. Using three supervised learning techniques—Logistic Regression, K-Nearest Neighbor, and Random Forest, this research, therefore, provides a comparative examination of the outcomes of various algorithmic learning processes. Trial results demonstrate that the Logistic Regression algorithm has attained the maximum level of 89% when compared to other implemented ML methods. The use of machine learning (ML) in computer-aided diagnostic tests is crucial (Hamsagayathri & Vigneshwaran, 2021).

An easy equation cannot accurately identify an object, like bodily organs. As a result, learning from examples is primarily necessary for pattern recognition. Pattern detection and machine learning (ML) have the potential to increase the accuracy of disease approach and detection in the biomedical field. They also value the approach of decision-objectivity (Hamsagayathri & Vigneshwaran, 2021). In order to create superior, automated algorithms for the analysis of multi-modal biomedical data, high-dimensional machine learning (ML) offers a reputable method.

In the research work of (Hassan et al., 2022), ensemble algorithms are analyzed for the diagnosis of kidney disease. The ML model is evaluated on different metrics that include sensitivity, F1-score, Mathew Correlation Coefficient, and accuracy using AdaBoost and Random Forest.

The system (Mirza et al., 2019) intends to achieve the goal by using data mining techniques on the datasets to extract patterns in the data to make predictions of heart disease.

When used in the healthcare industry, machine learning has the potential to accurately and early diagnose diseases. The circumstances of Heart Disease that may arise are calculated in this work. Medical parameters are characteristics of the datasets used (Raja et al., 2021). The datasets are analyzed using the Random Forest Algorithm, a machine-learning algorithm in Python. This method makes use of historical patient records from the past to forecast future ones at an early stage, saving lives. In this study, a reliable system for predicting heart disease is put into place utilizing a powerful machine-learning algorithm called the Random Forest method.

Accurate symptom prediction becomes challenging for the doctor (Devi et al., 2020). Therefore, the most challenging task is making an accurate disease forecast. Data analysis plays a crucial role in solving this challenge. Because of the growth of medical and other data, accurate analysis of medical data in the healthcare sector has benefited from early patient treatment. Data mining uncovers hidden pattern information in the vast volume of medical data with the aid of disease data. Depending on the patient's symptoms, a broad illness prediction is suggested. To anticipate diseases, research in (Devi et al., 2020) makes use of Machine learning algorithms using random forests for precise illness prediction for predicting sickness. Needed dataset of disease symptoms.

In this broad disease prediction, a person's lifestyle choices and physical examination information are taken into account for precise prediction. The accuracy of predicting common diseases using the Random Forest method is more precise and productive. Results from experiments showed that time and more RAM are required (Devi et al., 2020). This system can provide the risk of an illness after generic disease prediction related to general disease, whether the risk is higher or lower.

The biggest challenge in the medical field is predicting and diagnosing heart disease, which is dependent on the patient's physical exam, symptoms, and signs. K means clustering is used in big data, and the visualization is done using Tableau (Indrakumari et al., 2020).

The main goal of (Rallapalli et al., 2022) is to soothe and comfort patients while they schedule appointments with doctors. It also addresses any issues that patients may encounter when scheduling an appointment. In (Malik et al., 2017), doctors can register by providing the relevant information, such as their name, credentials, specializations, employment history, etc. By logging in with their username and password, doctors can check for patient appointment requests. A notification is issued to the patient whether the appointment is available.

In the research work (Yaganteeswarudu, 2020), the system proposes to predict multiple diseases by using Flask API and analyzing diabetes, diabetic retinopathy, breast cancer, and several skin disorders. The analysis is done on parameters like age, BMI, gender, glucose level, etc.

The research work of (Vijayalakshmi et al., 2021) proposed a system that is limited to only disease prediction based on a few symptoms entered by the user. There is a scope for improvement in these kinds of systems where initially necessary details from the patient should be acquired, like age and gender, along with previous medical history. The proposed system of disease diagnosis and virtual consultation (Vijayalakshmi et al., 2021) provides a platform that acquires patients' important details before proceeding with the diagnosis. Also, the authors urge the patients to consult a doctor first through our system by scheduling an appointment.

The research work of (Kulkarni et al., 2019; Kanjalkar et al., 2022) focuses on various machine learning techniques for focus measures computation on the image. The authors (Pande & Chetty, 2018; Pande & Chetty, 2019; Pande & Chetty, 2021) have presented a detailed study of capsule networks and employed it for medicinal leaf recognition.

The research work in (Kanjalkar et al., 2023a,b) focuses on deep learning techniques for COVID-19 patients and image processing.

According to the aforementioned literature review, there is room for research in the field of machine learning to obtain better accuracy. The Random Forest approach proved better for this system.

3. PROPOSED SYSTEM

The system as a whole is simple to use and primarily has two users:

- Doctors
- Patients

The modules and functionalities present in the patient dashboard –

- Patient Dashboard
- Make Diagnosis
- Check Diagnosis Results
- Appointment

The modules and functionalities present in the doctor dashboard –

- Doctor Dashboard
- Drug Recommendation
- Appointment

Figure 1. Architecture diagram

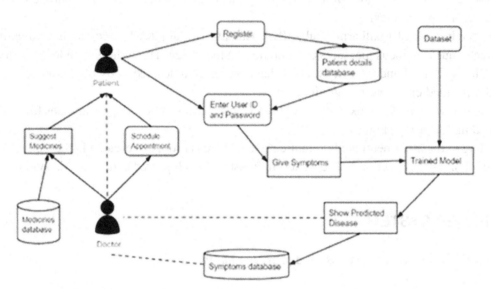

The user must register before being able to access the supplied functions after logging in (fig.1). If the user is a patient, the functionalities offered are to see their dashboard, make a diagnosis of disease by entering symptoms, Check Diagnosis results and also see the details of an appointment with the doctor.

On selecting the service of diagnosis, the patient is directed to a new page. The user can then enter at most five symptoms into the system. Further, on selecting the predict button, the proposed system will analyze the symptoms provided by the user, and then the customized Random Forest implemented into the system will generate decision trees for every symptom under consideration for the prediction results. The outcome with the majority frequency is considered the predicted result. Patients can examine a doctor's profile and choose whether or not they want to consult them. The ability to view the history and specifics of the consultation has been made available.

If the user is a doctor, he can fill out his information so that patients can see it. The functionalities offered are to see their dashboard and recommend medicines according to the disease of the patient; also, the doctor can schedule appointments with patients online or offline. The appointment schedule doctor will put that will be visible to patients in their appointment section.

This issue is avoided by the customized Random Forest implemented in the proposed system, which is a variation of learning in its entirety. The term "assemble learning" describes using multiple algorithms or the same algorithm repeatedly. The more of these decision trees there are in Random Forest, the better the broad generalization. The proposed system's backend utilizes Django. Django provides a secure method of handling user accounts and passwords, avoiding mistakes like saving passwords without hashing them or storing session data in cookies where it is exposed (instead, cookies merely hold a key and the actual data is saved in the database).

Python language is used for the proposed system because it requires less code and is very straightforward to understand, and VS code, as a code editor, provides a framework to manage the code for the system. It facilitates developers' implementation of both local and Global shifts that occur swiftly and effectively. This is something that developers can use to their advantage when creating straightforward

Python code and using Python frameworks to handle the IDE's refactoring options. The website is designed using HTML, bootstrap and CSS on the front end.

4. SYSTEM ARCHITECTURE

4.1. Front-End Technology

The creation of novel systems is now a crucial part of terminology. We are using both conventional techniques and cutting-edge ones as it outlines both designing and coding methodologies. The proposed system uses bootstrap packages for developing a user-friendly and easy-to-grasp UI with top-notch features. Bootstrap is a collection of CSS and JavaScript functions, and it is used for responsive design and building responsive, mobile-first sites and applications. It generally works on a grid system for creating page layouts with the help of rows and columns, and it supports all browsers for creating responsive websites.

4.2. Dataset

The random forest internally uses several decision trees. The sample inputs are received from the users with respect to the symptom severity dataset (Training.csv: 1339 KB, Drug.csv: 295KB) used for the proposed system. The training dataset consists of thousands of symptoms that are mapped in the file concerning the binary values 0 or 1. The drug dataset contains different drugs mapped with the disease along with certain parameters like gender and age, as these two are the most critical basic factors responsible when it comes to recommending a drug to cure a disease.

4.3. Random Forest Algorithm

The most powerful machine learning method is Random Forest. It is used in training a model of our system. Ensemble Learning is applied (bagging). While generating trees, a random forest adds more randomness to the model. Instead of searching for the most important factor when dividing a node, it finds the top feature among a random subset of features.

Figure 2. Random forests test model

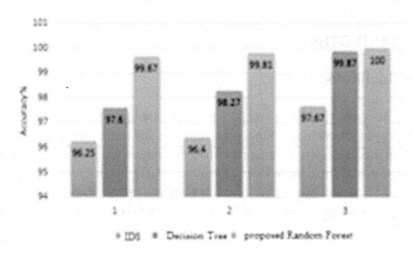

As a result, it minimizes the variation and solves the over-fitting issue in decision trees, increasing accuracy (Figure 2). Supervised learning methodology includes the same. It is used to address classification and regression-related ML problems. Ensemble learning, a technique for integrating different classifiers to address challenging problems and improve model performance, is the foundation upon which it is based.

The random forest implies forecasts from each decision tree to predict the result based on votes of the majority of predictions than relying on a particular prediction tree. A greater number of trees in the forest model prevents over-fitting and greater accuracy (Figure 3).

Figure 3. Random forest algorithm

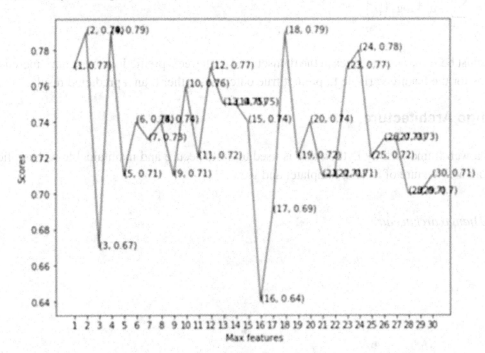

Algorithm:

- Step 1: Choose a few random data samples from the available data set.
- Step 2: The second step of this technique is to genera ate decision tree for every sample from the random forest, which consists of various different inputs as symptoms.
- Step 3: For every expected outcome, voting takes place.
- Step 4: Prediction with the majority of votes is considered as the predicted disease as a result.

All of the decision trees in a random forest classifier are weak learners, and their combined outputs serve as the final prediction. Due to random forest's use of multiple trees to forecast the dataset class, some decision trees may be able to predict the correct output while others may not. However, they predict the correct outcome when all the trees are combined. In light of this, the following two assumptions apply to a better random forest classifier:

The Gini index is a method to calculate how often nodes are on a tree branch. The formula uses probability P_i to determine each branch on a node.

$$Gini = 1 - \sum_{i=1}^{c} \left(p_i \right)^2 \qquad (1)$$

Entropy is another formula that calculates how often nodes branch further. It also uses the probability of an outcome to make a decision.

$$Entropy = \sum_{i=1}^{C} -p_i * \log_2 \left(p_i \right) \qquad (2)$$

There must be some actual values in the dataset, and each tree's predictions must have incredibly low correlations for the feature variable to predict true outcomes rather than a predicted result.

4.4. Django Architecture

Django is a web framework by Python that is used to build secure and maintainable web applications. It follows an architecture of model, template, and views.

Figure 4. Django architecture

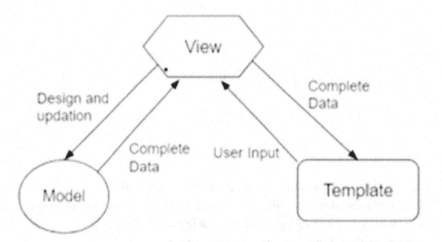

In the above shown Figure 4, Views is one of the functions of the Django framework, which accept HTTP requests and return Http responses, which are similar to HTML documents. Django-enabled websites are crammed with views and various tasks and missions. Views are stored in a file called views. py, found in the system folder.

The model is a reliable source of data-related information. The key fields and actions of the data stored are included. Each model typically corresponds to a single database table.

A Python string or text document that has been marked up using the Django template language is referred to as a template. The template engine recognizes and interprets some constructs. Variables, along with tags, are considered the main ones.

5. RESULTS AND DISCUSSION

Virtual health care offers aid to victimization digital devices like computers and smartphones. Virtual health care will be used by doctors and patients to: Determine whether the patient wants to get some types of therapy directly, such as psychological state treatment and assessing for small diseases, issue or generate the existing prescriptions, and provide certain medical services, such as speech and physiatrists. When a patient needs to maintain a certain physical distance or is unable to physically visit a medical facility, virtual health care can be helpful.

Figure 5. Decision tree scores for different maximum features

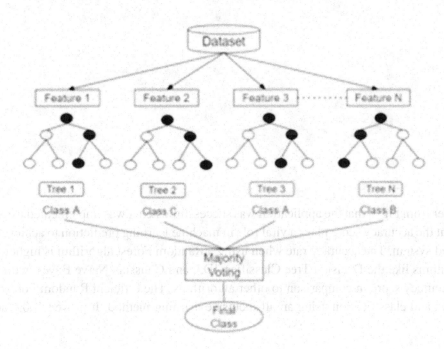

The above line graph shown in Figure 5 indicates the decision tree scores generated from the random forest for the presence of heart disease. The maximum score is 79% and is attained when the maximum features are chosen to be either 2,4, or 18. This is evident from the line graph above. Each tree in the forest is formed by a random selection of features from the overall features. The number of trees that will be used to forecast the class can be changed in this situation as over 10, 100, 200, 500, and many more trees are included in the test scores.

Figure 6. Graph comparing the accuracy of various algorithms

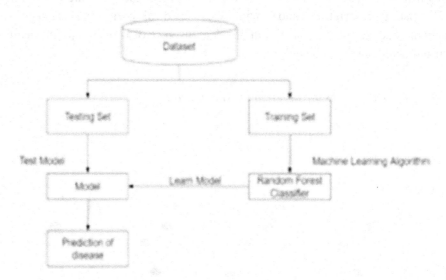

We can infer from Fig. 6 that the application was successful when it was implemented using different algorithms, but the accuracy score plays a vital role in machine learning prediction to achieve efficiency in the proposed system. The accuracy rate when using a Random Forest algorithm is higher in contrast to other algorithms like the Decision Tree Classifier, ID3, and Gaussian Naïve Bayes, with 99.82% as the average accuracy score in comparison to other algorithms. The efficient Random Forest algorithm is a Regression and classification using an all-inclusive learning method. It proved 100% accuracy in this system.

5.1. Benefits for Patients

Virtual health care will facilitate treatment of a variety of medical conditions; it makes one seek care from a professional medico and provides clear details concerning their symptoms.

5.2. Minimal Costs

According to some studies, people who make use of telemedicine need less time in hospitals, which results in cost savings. Additionally, a shorter commute may result in lower secondary costs like gas and servicing.

Enhanced access to medical care Reliable Source:

Access to care for people with impairments is made simpler through telemedicine. Alternate populations, such as older individuals, those who are geographically isolated, and those who are incarcerated, may have better access as a result.

5.3. Preventive Care

For those with financial or geographic constraints towards quality care, virtual care may make it simpler for patients to get preventative care that helps in improving their health in the long term.

5.4. Convenience

Virtual care enables people to obtain care in the privacy and comfort of their own homes, thereby eliminating the need for someone to miss work or prepare for a service.

Aiming for the doctor's clinic means that being around others, generally in close quarters, also spreads infection. This can be especially problematic for people with underlying disorders or weakened immune systems. Telemedicine eradicates the possibility of contracting an infection at the doctor's clinic.

6. CONCLUSION AND FUTURE SCOPE

Virtual care will establish its presence in many areas of care, including care education, but also as favorable impressions from finished customers by bringing patients and suppliers together virtually. Virtual care can become more widely available and more frequently used as technology develops; as a result, both its adoption and the technology that supports it may rise concurrently. Technology that supports virtual care, including video conferencing technologies, will advance to strengthen patient and supplier proficiency in the use of those systems. The proposed system with the Random Forest method proved better for accuracy. The future looks promising for virtual health! Currently that folks are unit exploitation; they will decide for themselves what things they have to in-person visit the doctor Associate in Nursing or virtual care might fulfil. Those who are going to benefit most from virtual tending can be the aged in care homes. Since they were within the risky cluster for that, they had to be monitored remotely by caregivers. However, problems like legalities and security problems ought to be sorted out if virtual health is to supplement ancient drugs with a larger approach. For now, we will forestall additional individuals to finance these ventures, so the potential of virtual tending is really explored. Since virtual health care may solve various problems in the future, many additional changes can be made in the system, such as more precise and accurate results, medicine delivery at the doorstep, etc.

REFERENCES

Ahsan, M. M., Luna, S. A., & Siddique, Z. (2022). Machine-learning-based disease diagnosis: A comprehensive review. *Healthcare (Basel)*, *10*(3), 541. doi:10.3390/healthcare10030541 PMID:35327018

Arslan, F., Singh, B., Sharma, D. K., Regin, R., Steffi, R., & Suman Rajest, S. (2021). Optimization technique approach to resolve food sustainability problems. *2021 International Conference on Computational Intelligence and Knowledge Economy (ICCIKE)*. IEEE. 10.1109/ICCIKE51210.2021.9410735

Bansal, V., Pandey, S., Shukla, S. K., Singh, D., Rathod, S. A., & Gonzáles, J. L. A. (2022). A frame work of security attacks, issues classifications and configuration strategy for IoT networks for the successful implementation. *2022 5th International Conference on Contemporary Computing and Informatics (IC3I)*. IEEE.

Devi, R. D., Sreevalli, P., & Prathyusha, M. (2020). *Prediction of Diseases using Random Forest classification algorithm*. Zeichen Journal.

Gunturu, V., Bansal, V., Sathe, M., Kumar, A., Gehlot, A., & Pant, B. (2023). Wireless communications implementation using blockchain as well as distributed type of IoT. *2023 International Conference on Artificial Intelligence and Smart Communication (AISC)*. IEEE. 10.1109/AISC56616.2023.10085249

Hamsagayathri, P., & Vigneshwaran, S. (2021). Symptoms based disease prediction using machine learning techniques. *2021 Third International Conference on Intelligent Communication Technologies and Virtual Mobile Networks (ICICV)*. IEEE. 10.1109/ICICV50876.2021.9388603

Hassan, M. M., Ahamad, T., & Das, S. (2022). An ensemble learning approach for chronic kidney disease prediction using different machine learning algorithms with correlation based feature selection. *2022 25th International Conference on Computer and Information Technology (ICCIT)*. IEEE.

Indrakumari, R., Poongodi, T., & Jena, S. (2020). Heart Disease Prediction using Exploratory Data Analysis. In *International Conference on Smart Sustainable Intelligent Computing and Applications*. Elsevier. 10.1016/j.procs.2020.06.017

Kanjalkar, J., Kanjalkar, P., Aole, K., Ansari, A., Abak, H., & Tiwari, A. (2023a). Analysis of Machine Learning Algorithms for COVID Detection Using Deep Learning. *7th International Conference on Data Management, Analytics and Innovation*. Springer. 10.1007/978-981-99-1414-2_31

Kanjalkar, J., Kanjalkar, P., Deshmukh, T., Deshmukh, J., Dhamal, P., & Bhalerao, A. (2022). A novel system for AYUSH healthcare services using classification and regression. *International Journal on Recent and Innovation Trends in Computing and Communication*, 10(1s), 232–240. doi:10.17762/ijritcc.v10i1s.5830

Kanjalkar, P., Chinchole, P., Chitre, A., Kanjalkar, J., & Sharma, P. (2023b). Economical solution to automatic evaluation of an OMR sheet using image processing. In *Data Management, Analytics and Innovation* (pp. 665–683). Springer Nature Singapore. doi:10.1007/978-981-99-1414-2_48

Kosarkar, N., Basuri, P., Karamore, P., Gawali, P., Badole, P., & Jumle, P. (2022). Disease Prediction using Machine Learning. *2022 10th International Conference on Emerging Trends in Engineering and Technology - Signal and Information Processing (ICETET-SIP-22)*. IEEE.

Krishnan, S., & Geetha. (2019). Prediction of heart disease using machine learning algorithms. *2019 1st International Conference on Innovations in Information and Communication Technology (ICIICT)*. IEEE.

Kulkarni, J. B., Sheela, M., & Chetty, R. (2019). Depth Analysis of Single View Image Objects based on Object Detection and Focus Measure. *International Journal of Advanced Trends in Computer Science and Engineering*, 5(8), 2608–2612. doi:10.30534/ijatcse/2019/112852019

MalikS.BibiN.KhanS.SultanaR.RaufS. A. (2017). Mr Doc: A doctor appointment application system. Retrieved from https://arxiv.org/abs/1701.08786

Mirza, I., Mahapatra, A., Rego, D., & Mascarenhas, K. (2019). Human Heart Disease Prediction Using Data Mining Techniques. In *2019 IEEE International Conference on Advances in Computing, Communication and Control (ICAC3)*. IEEE.

Ogunmola, G. A., Singh, B., Sharma, D. K., Regin, R., Rajest, S. S., & Singh, N. (2021). Involvement of distance measure in assessing and resolving efficiency environmental obstacles. *2021 International Conference on Computational Intelligence and Knowledge Economy (ICCIKE)*. IEEE. 10.1109/IC-CIKE51210.2021.9410765

Pande, S., & Chetty, M. S. R. (2018). Analysis of Capsule Network (Capsnet) Architectures and Applications. *Journal of Advanced Research in Dynamical and Control Systems*, *10*(10), 2765–2771.

Pande, S., & Chetty, M. S. R. (2019). Bezier Curve Based Medicinal Leaf Classification using Capsule Network. *International Journal of Advanced Trends in Computer Science and Engineering*, *8*(6), 2735–2742. doi:10.30534/ijatcse/2019/09862019

Pande, S. D., & Chetty, M. S. R. (2021). Fast medicinal leaf retrieval using CapsNet. In *Advances in Intelligent Systems and Computing* (pp. 149–155). Springer Singapore.

Raja, M. S., Anurag, M., Reddy, C. P., & Sirisala, N. R. (2021). Machine learning based heart disease prediction system. *2021 International Conference on Computer Communication and Informatics (ICCCI)*. IEEE. 10.1109/ICCCI50826.2021.9402653

Rallapalli, V., Menghani, D., Gallani, H., & Aasija, G. (2022). *Online Doctor Appointment System*. Vivekanand Education Society.

Sharma, D. K., Jalil, N. A., Regin, R., Rajest, S. S., Tummala, R. K., & Thangadurai. (2021a). Predicting network congestion with machine learning. *2021 2nd International Conference on Smart Electronics and Communication (ICOSEC)*. IEEE.

Sharma, D. K., Singh, B., Raja, M., Regin, R., & Rajest, S. S. (2021b). An Efficient Python Approach for Simulation of Poisson Distribution. *2021 7th International Conference on Advanced Computing and Communication Systems (ICACCS)*. IEEE.

Sharma, D. K., Singh, B., Regin, R., Steffi, R., & Chakravarthi, M. K. (2021c). Efficient Classification for Neural Machines Interpretations based on Mathematical models. *2021 7th International Conference on Advanced Computing and Communication Systems (ICACCS)*. IEEE.

Sonnad, S., Sathe, M., Basha, D. K., Bansal, V., Singh, R., & Singh, D. P. (2022). The integration of connectivity and system integrity approaches using Internet of Things (IoT) for enhancing network security. *2022 5th International Conference on Contemporary Computing and Informatics (IC3I)*. IEEE.

Suthar, V., Bansal, V., Reddy, C. S., Gonzáles, J. L. A., Singh, D., & Singh, D. P. (2022). Machine Learning Adoption in Blockchain-Based Smart Applications. *2022 5th International Conference on Contemporary Computing and Informatics (IC3I)*. IEEE.

Uike, D., Agarwalla, S., Bansal, V., Chakravarthi, M. K., Singh, R., & Singh, P. (2022). Investigating the role of block chain to secure identity in IoT for industrial automation. *2022 11th International Conference on System Modeling & Advancement in Research Trends (SMART)*. IEEE.

Vijayalakshmi, S., Saini, A., Srinivasan, A., & Singh, N. (2021). Disease prediction over big data from healthcare institution". In *2021 IEEE International Conference on Advance Computing and Innovative Technologies in Engineering (ICACITE)*. IEEE. 10.1109/ICACITE51222.2021.9404567

Yaganteeswarudu, A. (2020). Multi Diasese Prediction Model by using Machine Learning and Flask API". In I*EEE, 2020 5th International Conference on Communication and Electronics Systems (ICCES)*. IEEE.

Chapter 8
Optimizing Leaf Diseases of Apple Scab and Apple Black Rot in the Context of "Useful" Information Measures and Distance Measurements

Pankaj Prasad Dwivedi

Jaypee University of Engineering and Technology, India

Dilip Kumar Sharma

Jaypee University of Engineering and Technology, India

ABSTRACT

Detecting disease on crops is an essential and time-consuming operation in agricultural techniques. It takes a significant amount of time and specialized effort. This research provides a clever and effective agricultural disease detection system based on information theory. In the present chapter, first information measures, 'useful' information measures, and distance measures are defined and explained. The authors find out the distance measures between leaves of apple scab (AS) and apple black rot (ABR). Six leaves of AS and ABR are taken into consideration. After measuring the distance, the impact of disease in the leaves of AS and ABR has been noticed. It is shown that this measure can be embedded in most image classification techniques and is subject to reference transformation. Weak and strong information is also obtained. Finally, minimum and maximum distances are evaluated, and our findings indicate that the likelihood of illnesses in plant leaves is low when the information measure of leaves is low.

In the United Kingdom, two major apple fungal infections severely affect apple output. The fungus Podosphaera leucotricha and Venturia inaequalis produce powdery mildew and apple scab, accordingly. Powdery mildew and scab are controlled with up to 19 fungicide treatments per year in the United Kingdom (Burchill, 1975; Berrie & Xu, 2003). Even with such an extensive fungicide regimen, scab

DOI: 10.4018/979-8-3693-1301-5.ch008

control failure is common in high-scab-risk years. As a result, it's no surprise that these two illnesses are the focus of East Malling Study's apple pathology research. Apple scab seldom kills its host, although it can lower fruit production and quality substantially. Because of the commercial need for blemish-free fruit, this is especially true recently. In addition to infecting fruit, it can also infect leaves and, less commonly, shoots (leading to wood scab). V. inaequalis is extremely dangerous to immature fruit and foliage. Rainfall in the early spring promotes the discharge of V. inaequalis ascospores from infected leaf litter on the orchard floor. Ascospore discharge is light-sensitive, with the majority of spores being produced during the day (Wrzesien et al. 2018). Ascospores released into the air settle on the surface of vulnerable host tissues, where, depending on temperature and moisture, they can germinate and infect the host. Primary infection occurs when ascospores invade the body in the early spring. Lesions appear after incubation, and the period of incubation is primarily influenced by the ambient temperature. Conidia generated by these lesions are subsequently spread by rain, landing on sensitive tissues (leaves, fruit, and shoots) and causing new infections; this is known as a secondary infection. This process of serious infections occurs all summer long until the tree's leaves fall off at the start of winter. Cultivar susceptibility, tissue maturity, and meteorological conditions all have a role in the incidence and severity of secondary infection (rainfall, temperature, and moisture). In the winter, ascospores are generated on diseased leaves by strains of two opposing mating types.

The Xanthomonas campestris pv. campestris illness, which causes significant damage to all Brassicaceae crops, is a massive issue that scientists and farmers are concerned about (Ryan et al. 2011). According to Bila (2008), Lo & Wang (2001), this disease can cause 30–70% losses in cabbage based on the season According to a study, plant diseases are the main cause of agricultural productivity losses (Priyanka et al. 2022). The analysis of all cultivars' old leaves revealed a substantial difference between one resistant and one vulnerable cultivar is given by (Sina & Rainer 2022). In contrast, there were no discernible changes when young leaves from all cultivars were compared. The disease causes severe damage in Kenya during the wet and warm seasons, culminating in total crop loss (Otipa et al. 2013, Anonymous 2000). Various management strategies have been implemented on farms and in research facilities, but no one strategy has been shown to be effective in controlling the illness (Celetti et al. 2002). Biological control, cultural practices, chemical control, host resistance, and field cleanliness are some of the current techniques used by farmers to treat the condition.

Heated cupric acetate, or zinc sulphate, sodium hypochlorite, and hydrogen peroxide, are used to treat the disease chemically. Miller and his associates (Miller et al., 1996). However, many insecticides used to combat cabbage black rot disease are inefficient, and some others have not been approved (Massomo et al. 2003, Bila et al. 2013). Even though Actigard is designed to reduce black rot on economically farmed crucifers and generates resistance in select plants, the outcomes in cauliflower 535 were unimpressive (Seebold et al. 2008). Moreover, pharmaceutical seed priming just sanitizes the seed surfaces, (Miller 2002) not the germs inside the seed. Traditionally, cabbage crops were sprayed with copper-based fungicides, but it was discovered that they caused black patches on the leaves, thus they were banned (Averre 2000).

Despite their ineffectiveness in the past, the development and adoption of cultivars resistant to black rot have been noted as a key strategy for preventative efforts (Miller et al. 1996). That's also because the majority of indigenous cultivars are relatively delicate (Massomo et al. 2003, Bila et al. 2013). The problem with this approach is that certain varieties are only partially robust or vulnerable to black rot (Seebold et al. 2008), are of bad condition, and hence are not widely adopted by producers. Furthermore, the unusual nature of the source of the significant gene (durable) resistance in Brassica oleracea, novel pathogen strains able to infect resistant cultivars may emerge over time (Seebold et al. 2008, Miller et al. 1996, Averre 2000). The most prevalent and possibly valuable sources of black rot resistance are found in Brassica genomes (Taylor et al. 2002). Unfortunately, introducing such genes into local crops can introduce other undesired traits, such as bad taste (Acquaah 2007). Furthermore, resistant cultivar development takes a long period.

Numerous anti-Xanthomonas campestris pv. campestris biocontrol agents have indeed been found and are being used to prevent black rot in Brassica plants, according to various sources. Various strains of yeast (Ghazalibiglar 2014, Luna et al. 2002, Massomo et al. 2003, Sayonara et al. 1999, Averre 2000, Smart & Holly 2013, Celetti et al. 2002). Farmers' use of agrochemicals (herbicides, insecticides, fertilizers, and pesticides) creates an unfavorable environment for biocontrol agents to survive (Huang 1997, Onsando 1992, Hunter et al. 1975).

Reduce disease transmission by scheduling irrigation for when crops would dry quickly and deferring field operations till earlier in the day when the areas are drying (Celetti et al. 2002). However, because the illness is spread via seeds, this hasn't been very successful (Celetti et al. 2002). Although black rot outbreaks in a field can be caused by seed infection, disease-free seeds have yet to be developed (Celetti et al. 2002). Heavy seed priming decreases the number of seeds that germinate and the vigor of the plants. The agriculture cycle has not alone been shown to be effective in decreasing black rot disease (Ombuna et al., 2019). Furthermore, due to overcrowding, crop rotation is hampered on small farms in Kisii County.

We have categorized the entire paper in this way. Section 2 describes the material and methods, how to reduce the primary inoculum and how to evaluate fungicides, it is explained in detail in the context of supervised disease management. This includes fungi and focuses on population genetics; we take images of apple scab images and apple black Rot as data sets and make a histogram. This section also provides measures of the information and distance which includes many types of Distance measures. Section 3 presents the results where the proposed approach has been used. Lastly, Section 4 provides a discussion in detail of what research can be done in the future and present we have found the type of results and given the extraction.

2. MATERIAL AND METHODS

2.1 Reducing Primary Inoculum and Evaluating Fungicides

Reducing the amount of ascospore-containing winter hibernation inoculum on leaf litter on orchard floors is essential for controlling apple scab. The basis for efficient scab management for the entire season is laid by early, successful prevention of scab outbreaks at the beginning of the season. Early study at East Malling study was mostly concerned with removing or lessening overwintering inoculum.

According to a study published in "Nature," treating leaves with urea in the fall effectively prevents V. inaequalis from reproducing sexually on leaf litter, lowering the amount of the main inoculum for the upcoming growing season. The reduction in the primary inoculum was linked to a decrease in the number of uncomplicated cases appearing on leaves in the coming spring (Cook, 1974). Even now, urea treatment in autumn is still a standard practice in commercial apple production to eliminate/reduce overwintering inoculum.

After that, researchers looked for alternative products, such as phenylmercury chloride (PMC) and phenylmercury dimethyl-Di thiocarbamate (PMD), that may be applied post-harvest in the fall or spring season before bud-break to eradicate or lower the quantity of primary inoculum (Hutton & Burchill, 1965). A single fall application of PMC and, to a lesser extent, PMD significantly decreased the ascospore production of severely scabbed apple leaves. Even a single application of modest levels of PMC in the spring might limit the number of ascospores emitted by mature pseudothecia plants, successfully controlling infection in the spring (Hutton & Burchill, 1965, Cook, 1974; Burchill & Hutton, 1965). Many other surface-active compounds or mixtures were shown to reduce the number of scabs ascospores released in the spring by more than 99% (Burchill & Swait, 1977). The post-harvest autumn application of urea or other efficacious products has eliminated the need for controlling scab during the growing season for isolated orchards (Burchill, 1975; Burchill & Hutton, 1965). However, for orchards with severe epidemics, the previous season, or orchards close to other orchards with a high level of scab inoculum, control measures during the growing season are still necessary. Scab was less severe in an orchard when grass was less frequently cut (Coslor et al, 2019), which may also be interpreted in terms of the reduced amount of overwintered leaf litter due to increased worm activities in addition to possible effects of nutrient input on the scab.

Following the initial finding of urea treatment in inhibiting the production of ascospores on leaf litter, research was conducted to understand the mechanism(s) responsible for this inhibition. Treatment of leaf tissue with urea at the initial phases of pseudothecial initiation resulted in a greater nitrogen content in the leaves, which inhibited pseudothecial growth but not mycelial growth (Ross & Burchill, 1968). Urea, on the other hand, suppressed both pseudothecial and mycelial development when administered later in the fungal growth process. Bacteria isolated from leaves treated with urea were found to restrict pseudothecial development in field studies, suggesting possible indirect effects of urea application via microbial interactions.

During the winter, urea treatment of removed stems resulted in a quick and sustained rise in the bacterial diversity existing in the stems, as well as a significant shift in the population balance in bacteria (Crosse et al., 1968). The in vitro growth of V. inaequalis was reduced by a large number of fluorescent pseudomonads that became prevalent in the urea-treated leaves (Crosse et al., 1968).

Although it remained structurally intact until the next spring, urea increased the degradation of the leaves and reduced the growth of V. Inaequalis in areas of the laminae. There was no clear proof, however, that the hostile vegetation induced by urea was indeed the cause of V. Inaequalis suppression. In contrast, another study (Burchill & Cook, 1971) suggested that microbial population changes, particularly in bacteria, on the leaf surface observed following urea applications are partially responsible for the suppression of ascospore production on leaf litter. Therefore, not only chemical but also microbiological variables influenced leaf disintegration and prevented V. inaequalis urea treatments from developing pseudothecial growth.

Wood scab was seen on Bramley's seedling apple trees and may develop a significant number of conidia in the spring instead of spores on fallen leaves as the principal inoculum (Preece, 1961). From June through August, the fresh branches of Cox's Orange Pippin trees grown in pots were susceptible to infection by V. inaequalis, and numerous isolates showed a distinct propensity to attack wood (Cook, 1974). According to Jeger (1981) and Butt et al. (1981), these wood scab infections may be able to generate conidia all through the growth season, posing a persistent danger of infection. More recently, research on the reduced fungal sensitivity to fungicides (Gao et al., 2009) and the role of conidia as a source of primary inoculum was also revealed by fungal population fluctuation (Xu et al., 2013).

Not surprisingly, one of the research themes has been on identifying effective fungicides against scab for use during the growing season (Swait & Butt, 1990; Jiang *et al.*, 2021; Butt *et al.*, 1990). Scab can be efficiently managed with carbendazim (0.025% a.i.), or thiophanate-methyl (0.05% a.i.), benomyl (0.025% a.i.), administered at 21-day intervals, according to (Burchill & Cook 1975). Given the fluid situation with pesticide regulation in the EU and the development of fungicide insensitive fungal strains, much fungicide evaluation work needs to be conducted regularly over time.

2.2 Supervised Disease Management

As early as 1932, the concept of supervised scab management was promoted (Moore, 1932). In such a system, considerations on spray (or treatment) timing should be related to scab life cycles, tree phenology, and also to unidentified specific 'tree conditions. Furthermore, the key stage of scab management was identified as from the bud break to pre-blossom. Effective control at this key stage would more likely lead to better scab control throughout the season. This concept of a supervised disease control strategy was further developed more precisely by mathematical analysis of inter-relationships among various components in terms of their contribution to scab epidemics (MacHardy & Jeger, 1982, 1983). Subsequent research studies have been trying to further elaborate on how each factor affects spray timing (Jeger & Butt, 1984; Xu & Robinson, 2005; Xu *et al.*, 1995, Jeger & Butt, 1983).

There were notable variations in pseudothecial growth between cultivars; during the green cluster stage, ascospore production varied between cultivars by a factor of 50 to 100 (Jeger et al., 1982). The severity of the illness on leaves from the previous growing season has no bearing on this variation. The level of overwintered inoculum may be considerably underestimated if only symptomatic lesions in autumn were considered because of latent infection of old leaves by conidia (Li & Xu, 2002). Conidia may infect leaves of any age, from newly emerging leaves to those that have been in the ground for up to four months. Young leaves developed at a higher pace than older leaves, resulting in visual signs being seen sooner. Old leaves' mycelia grow slowly enough that they did not immediately develop noticeable symptoms at the time of defoliation, even though some of them, ranging from asymptomatic colonies, had already generated conidia when examined microscopically. As a result, these asymptomatic infections might have a big impact on how much primary inoculum is generated the next season.

Ascospores are usually discharged by the impact of rain droplets on mature pseudothecia. Nevertheless, dew is sufficient to discharge ascospores (James & Sujatha, 2021) but results in much fewer spores being discharged than rain. Ascospore discharge was shown to be very local, and unlikely to be more than 15 meters from the source, suggesting inoculum dispersal from neighboring orchards is minimal and probably unimportant (Burchill, 1966). Many conidia were released from pustules on wood scab lesions in early spring as primary inoculum (Cook, 1974). Two epidemiological criteria were used to link scab formation to cumulative quantities of trapped spores: Inoculum infection efficiency (disease units/spore) and disease asymptote (Jeger, 1984). Because of the discontinuous patterns of scab infection, this approach proved particularly beneficial for fungal diseases not for scab.

Accurate and fast disease assessment is important for epidemiological research and disease management. (Jeger 1981) investigated the dynamics of scab formation on six cultivars, finding that the percentages of leaves with a scab (frequency) and the number of colonies on leaves (intensity) had the smallest frequencies of fluctuation. Incidence and intensity were shown to have consistent connections. Thus, we may use incidence to predict the number of lesions; the former is easier and faster to assess than the latter, which is a more accurate representation of disease severity. A similar incidence-density relationship was identified for pear scab (Li *et al.*, 2007).

Once both susceptible tissues and scab inoculum are present, the key to deciding the need for spraying is whether weather conditions are conducive to scab infection. Before the 1990s, the effect of weather on infection was usually determined by a look-up table (the risk of scab with the duration of the wet period and the average temperature in the wet period), i.e., the Mills' period (Mills & La Plante, 1954). Since the publication of the Mills' period, many research studies have indicated the deficiency of this scheme in predicting scab risks. Based on these studies, we developed a novel dynamical framework for predicting V. inaequalis disease of apple leaves (Xu et al., 1995). In orchard testing, the new model identified key infectious phases in the spring and summer months, that were responsible for leaf scab epidemics. Mills' criterion failed to discover these times. We also performed inoculation experiments to investigate the circumstances for fruit disease (Xu & Robinson, 2005) and built a mathematical model to link fruit scab to wetness duration and fruit maturity. Fruits were very vulnerable in the early phases of growth, but as they grew, they became progressively resistant. As a result, older fruits will experience an equal proportion of scab infections as younger fruits, a longer period of wetness was necessary.

A key to promoting the use of disease-predicting schemes is to demonstrate the usefulness of these schemes on a commercial scale. We have conducted farm-scale evaluation trials to study how best to integrate disease forecasting systems (Xu & Butt, 1996) with other orchard management practices with minimal risks to growers (Berrie & Xu, 2003). Through trialling over many years, we have developed a so-called key-stage management strategy for powdery mildew and controlling apple scab. This technique provided comparable or better control than a standard program, with the added benefit of lower fungicide input and costs, especially during very favourable seasons for certain diseases. Depending on the season, reductions in fungicide input varied from 5% to 45% (Berrie & Xu, 2003).

The availability of effective fungicides is another requirement for effective scab management. Thus, continuous monitoring and assessment of development of reduced fungal sensitivity to fungicides are essential in any scab management program. Myclobutanil is an essential demethylation inhibitor (DMI) pesticide for reducing apple scab and powdery mildew. In various places, notably the United Kingdom, overuse of this fungicide has resulted in the formation of scab isolates with low susceptibility towards this pesticide (Gao et al., 2009). The frequency of DMI applications was positively associated with the reduced compassion of V. inaequalis to myclobutanil. A specific apple tree's microbial isolates from several sites differed greatly in their myclobutanil responsiveness. The results also showed that the geographical dissemination of myclobutanil-insensitive V. inaequalis isolates is likely to be constrained by distance. The fungal sensitivities to two commonly used DMI fungicides in the UK (myclobutanil and fenbuconazole) had a substantial positive connection (Xu et al., 2010). This cross-resistance's intensity varied greatly between orchards.

Another important component in supervised disease management is the use of resistant cultivars. An isozyme of phosphoglucomutase in the apple was shown to lie approximately 8 cm. from the gene Vf, which confers resistance to scab (Leca et al., 2020), indicating that this isozyme should be useful for studying scab resistance conferred by Vf. Phlorizin, sieboldin, and trilobate can all be used as carbon sources by V. inaequalis in culture. Resistance to apple scab wasn't connected to sieboldin or trilobate inheritance in seedlings, and there's no direct link between phloridzin or its decomposition products and scab susceptibility (Hunter, 1975).

2.3 Fungal Genetics

More recently, research on scab (Xiangming. 2013) at East Malling Research focuses on fungal population genetics, particularly when cultivars with different resistance genetic makeup are mixed. Research in other countries suggested that scab development in mixtures may be reduced by up to 75%, compared to monocultures. However, one of the biological concerns in using mixtures is the risk of emergence and subsequent spread of fungal 'super-races', which may infect more than one (possibly all) mixture component(s), rendering the mixture useless.

By inoculating isolates from different countries, we have shown that local cultivars, though susceptible to scab, are resistant to nearly all non-native isolates (Xu et al., 2008). Thus, cultivar Cox from the UK was not infected by nearly all of the 40 isolates from India and China in artificial inoculations. Similar results were obtained for the local cultivars in India and China when challenged with isolates from the other two countries. Molecular data also suggested that host-pathogen co-evolution has taken place. Isolates from different counties in a new apple-growing region in China did not show significant population differentiation, which is opposite to the results for the UK orchards (Xu et al., 2008). This result was further supported by recent results that showed there was significant population differentiation among isolates from different cultivars in an old mixture orchard but not in a young mixture orchard (Xu et al., 2013).

Single-spore isolates were acquired from monoculture and hybrid plantations of 3 samples (Bramley, Cox, and Worcester), as well as single-ascospore isolated via three crossings among couples of isolates from the 3 varieties, to investigate the effect of mixtures on the frequency of super races (Barbara et al., 2008). After that, all three cultivars were infected with these fields and offspring isolates. Despite being usually thought to be sensitive to scab, all three cultivars possessed certain particular resistance characteristics, as established in the previous study (Xu et al., 2008). There's no variation comparing isolates from hybrid and monoculture orchards in terms of the ability to infect the number of cultivars, indicating mixtures did not increase the risk of establishment and spread of 'super races. Irrespective of whether isolates came from a mixture or monoculture, we rarely found isolates that could infect all three cultivars studied. Virulence against the three hosts cannot be allelic to each other because artificial crosses carried out in the lab produced several isolates that can infect all three cultivars (Barbara et al., 2008). Surprisingly, there was no significant difference in the virulence pattern of isolates collected from the same cultivar in mixed and monoculture orchards that are located at least 200 km apart.

To explore between- and within-orchard fungal diversity, 212 isolates were taken from two separate heterogeneous orchards in the UK, one of which was established 10 years ago and the other 45 years ago (Xu et al., 2013). Groups of isolates from distinct cultivars within each orchard varied greatly, while collections of isolated from distinct trees of the identical variety throughout each orchard also varied widely, particularly with regard to the older one. These differences may indicate a possible role for conidia, possibly originating from wood scab, as a key inoculum source and to facilitate non-random mating between fungal isolates from various cultivars, suggesting reduced risks of combining virulence factors against different hosts ('super' races).

To study genome structure and organization, along with locating genes controlling important traits of interest in V. inaequalis, such as host specificity, virulence, and mating type. We constructed a genetic linkage map from a population of progeny ascospores between a cross of a China isolate with one UK isolate (Xu et al., 2009; Celton et al., 2010). There were 294 markers on this linkage map, spanning eleven linkage groupings. Within each group, the average distance between the two loci ranged from

2.4 to 7.5 cm. The Mating locus was connected to two AFLP manufacturers and was mapped to a tiny linkage group.

2.4 Data Sets

The ascomycete fungus Venturia inaequalis causes apple scab, which is a frequent disease of rose plants (Rosaceae). While the disease may infect a wide range of plant species, including Sorbus, Cotoneaster, and Pyrus, it's most typically seen in Malus trees, especially blooming crabapple and farmed apple varieties. The disease's first symptoms show on infected trees' leaves, blossoms, and growing fruits, which grow dark, irregularly-shaped lesions when infected. Although apple scab seldom kills its host, it does cause fruit distortion as well as premature leaf and fruit loss, making the host plant more susceptible to abiotic stress and subsequent infection. Crop losses of up to 70% are possible as a result of reduced fruit quality and production, posing a serious threat to apple growers' profitability. To avoid the occurrence and spread of apple scab in their crops, producers frequently combine preventative methods, such as sanitation and resistance breeding, and reactive methods, such as biocontrol treatments or targeted fungicides, are used to combat the problem. Figure 1 signified Apple scab leaves from 1 to 6 and their Histogram in Figure 2. The dataset was taken from Kaggle.com.

Figure 1. Apple scab images

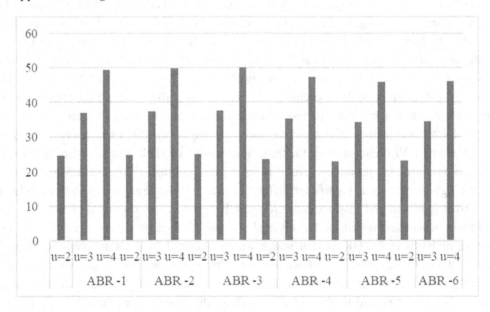

Figure 2. Apple scab histogram

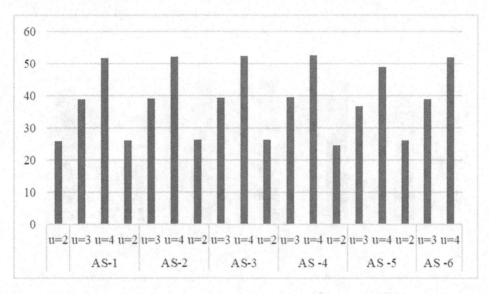

The term "black Rot" refers to a group of diseases of cultivated plants caused by fungus or bacteria that produce dark brown staining and deterioration in the leaves of fruits and vegetables: A fungus-caused illness of the apple, pear, and quince (Botryosphaeria obtusa or Physalospora cydoniae). Grapevine infection, commonly known as grape Rot, is caused by an infection (Guignardia bidwellii) that attacks the plant's terrestrial area and is aided by warm, humid circumstances. A bacterium causes disease in cabbage and similar plants (Xanthomonas campestris PV. campestris). It affects mostly the aboveground portions of plants and is found throughout the planet. Chinese cabbage, kale, mustard, radish, cabbage, cauliflower, rutabaga, Broccoli, Brussels sprouts, and turnip are among the cruciferous vegetables that are vulnerable. This pathogen may be found in a variety of weeds, including Shepherd's Purse and wild mustard. Figure 3 signified Apple Black Rot leaves from 1 to 6 and their Histogram in Figure 4.

Figure 3. Apple black rot images

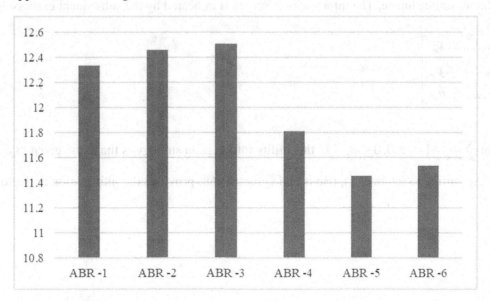

Figure 4. Apple black rot histogram

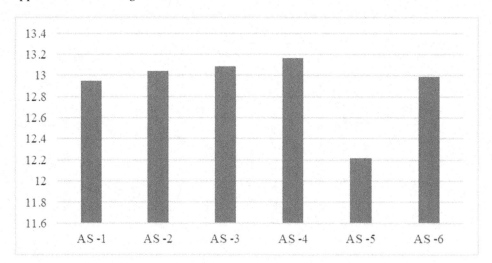

2.5 Information and Distance Measures

In this subsection, we give some distance measures as follows:

Information Measure

Let $\Delta_n^+ = \left\{ P = (p_1, p_2, \ldots, p_n); p_i \geq 0, \sum_i^n p_i = 1 \right\}$ be a set of all possible discrete probability distributions of a random variable X and $U = \{(u_1, u_2, \ldots \ldots u_n); u_i > 0 \forall i\}$ are utility Distribution attached to each $P \in \Delta_n^+$ such that $u_i > 0$ is the utility of an event having the probability of occurrence $p_i > 0$.

Let $U = (u_1, u_2, \ldots \ldots u_n)$ be a collection of positive integers, where u_i denotes the usefulness or importance of the corresponding result x_i. The utility is often independent of the likelihood p_i of encoding the x_i source image. The information's source is indicated by the subsequent expression:

$$\begin{bmatrix} x_1, x_2 \ldots \ldots \ldots x_n \\ p_1, p_2 \ldots \ldots \ldots p_n \\ u_1, u_2 \ldots \ldots \ldots u_n \end{bmatrix} \tag{1}$$

Where $\sum_{i=1}^n p_i = 1, u_i > 0, 0 < p_i \leq 1$, this utility information strategy is the name given to this computation. According to scheme (1), (Belis and Guiasu 1968) provided the information in the following manner:

$$H\left(P;U\right) = -\sum_{i=1}^{n} u_i p_i \log p_i \tag{2}$$

'Useful' information is the measurement described in (2). This measurement may be used as a good indicator of how much "useful" information is typically delivered by the information scheme (1).

It is evident that (2) becomes (Shannon's information, 1948) measure, which is presented below, when utilities are neglected:

$$H\left(P\right) = -\sum_{i=1}^{n} p_i \log p_i \tag{3}$$

Several authors have defined the entropy of Shannon using various postulates. Shannon's assertion was made more precise by (Khinchin 1957) by using key hypotheses that inferred. By taking into account various sets of postulates, (Chandy and Mcliod 1960),(Tverberg 1958), (Kendall 1964), etc., were further characterised by the entropy of Shannon. In the study of (Dwivedi and Sharma 2021) provides 'Useful' Renyi Information Rate.

Euclidean Distance

We'll begin with the most often-used distance measurement, Euclidean distance. It's just a distance measurement that's best characterized as the length of a section linking the two locations. The distance is calculated using the Pythagorean theorem and the cartesian coordinates of the places, which is a simple formula.

$$D\left(x, y\right) = \sqrt{\sum_{i=1}^{n} \left(x_i - y_i\right)^2} \tag{4}$$

Manhattan Distance

The Manhattan distance is a formula for determining the difference between two real-valued vectors. It is also known as the Taxicab distance or the City Block distance. Assume variables that identify events on a grid pattern like a chessboard. The Manhattan distance is the distance between two images if only one of them may travel in the same direction. The distance is calculated without any diagonal movement.

$$D\left(x, y\right) = \sum_{i=1}^{k} \left|x_i - y_i\right| \tag{5}$$

Cosine Distance

Cosine similarities are widely used to alleviate the problem of excessive dimensionality in Euclidean distance. The angle between two variables is the cosine resemblance. The inner product is the same if the variables are normalized to the same length. The cosine connection between the two variables with the same orientation is 1, whereas the similarity between two variables with opposing orientations is -1. It's worth mentioning that their size is irrelevant because this is an orientation metric.

$$D(x, y) = \cos(\theta) = \frac{x.y}{xy} \tag{6}$$

3. RESULT

In this section, we try to find out the distance between AS and ABR. Before that, we evaluate Shannon's information and Belis and Gaisu's information for AS and ABR. 'Useful information is evaluated by considering the utility parameters 2, 3 and 4.

Table 1 shows Shannon's Information on Apple scab and Apple Black Rot Images from 1 to 6 by using (3). Figure 5 and Figure 6 illustrate Shannon's Information for Apple scab and Apple Black Rot Images from 1 to 6.

Table 1. Shannon's information of apple sab image and apple black rot from 1 to 6

Leaf Type	Shannon's Information	Leaf Type	Shannon's Information
AS-1	12.947	ABR -1	12.339
AS -2	13.043	ABR -2	12.461
AS -3	13.087	ABR -3	**12.512**
AS -4	**13.170**	ABR -4	11.814
AS -5	**12.217**	ABR -5	**11.457**
AS -6	12.985	ABR -6	11.537

Figure 5. Shannon's information

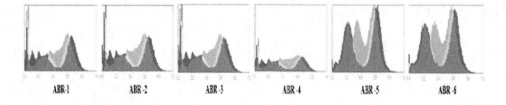

Figure 6. Shannon's information

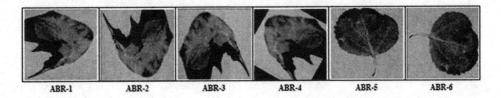

Table 2 Shows the Belis and Gaisu Information with utility parameters of Apple scab and Apple Black Rot Image from 1 to 6. Belis and Gaisu Information of Apple Scab Image from 1 to 6 which is evaluated by (2).

Figure 7 and Figure 8 illustrate the Belis and Gaisu Information for Apple scab and Apple Black Rot Images from 1 to 6.

Table 2. Belis and Gaisu information with utility parameter of apple scab and apple black rot image from 1 to 6

Apple Scab Image	Utility Parameter	Belis and Gaisu Information	Black-Rot Image	Belis and Gaisu Information
AS-1	$u=2$ $u=3$ $u=4$	25.894 38.841 51.788	ABR -1	24.678 37.017 49.357
AS-2	$u=2$ $u=3$ $u=4$	26.087 39.130 52.173	ABR -2	24.923 37.384 49.846
AS-3	$u=2$ $u=3$ $u=4$	**26.174** **39.262** **52.349**	ABR -3	**25.024** **37.536** **50.049**
AS -4	$u=2$ $u=3$ $u=4$	26.339 39.509 52.679	ABR -4	23.628 35.442 47.255
AS -5	$u=2$ $u=3$ $u=4$	**24.434** **36.651** **48.869**	ABR -5	**22.914** **34.371** **45.829**
AS -6	$u=2$ $u=3$ $u=4$	25.971 38.956 51.941	ABR -6	23.074 34.611 46.148

Figure 7. Belis and Gaisu information for apple scab image

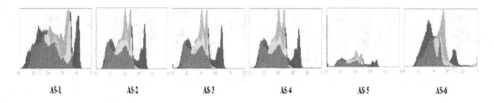

AS-1   AS-2   AS-3   AS-4   AS-5   AS-6

Figure 8. Belis and Gaisu information for apple black rot image

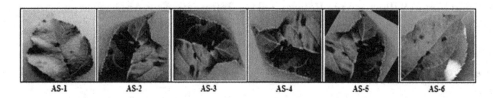

AS-1   AS-2   AS-3   AS-4   AS-5   AS-6

Euclidean Distance: The Euclidean distance is ideal when we have low-dimensional information and we need to estimate the size of the vectors. Even though numerous other distance measures have been developed to compensate for Euclidean distance limitations, it remains among the most widely used estimation methods for excellent purposes. It's simple to set up and use, and it provides good outcomes in a range of situations. The following Table 3 represents Euclidean Distance between two leaves continuously by using Mathematica Software and (4), the first leaf apple scab and another leaf apple black rot from images 1 to 6.

Table 3. Euclidean distance between leaves

Apple Scab & Apple Black Rot	Euclidean distance between leaves
1	135.32
2	120.117
3	108.534
4	119.663
5	**144.489**
6	**107.771**

Manhattan distance: When a dataset has discrete and/or binary characteristics, Manhattan looks to work well because it takes into account the many pathways that might be followed within the parameters of those qualities. Consider the Euclidean distance, that would lead in a single direction connecting two vectors even if this weren't possible in reality. The following Table 4 represents the Manhattan distance between two leaves' continuously by using Mathematica Software and (5), the first leaf apple scab and another leaf apple black rot from images 1 to 6.

Table 4. Manhattan distance between leaves

Apple Scab & Apple Black Rot	Manhattan distance between leaves
1	48438.5
2	43051.6
3	**39858.1**
4	42940.9
5	**51320.6**
6	38527.8

Cosine Distance: If we have high-dimensional data as well as the size of the vectors is not relevant, we frequently employ cosine similarity. This measure is widely used in image analysis when the information is collected by picture counts. For example, just because an image occurs more often in one document than another does not mean that one document is more intimately associated with that phrase. The length of the papers may vary, making the count's magnitude less significant. Then we should utilize cosine similarity, which takes magnitude out of the equation. The following Table 5 represents the Cosine Distance between two leaves' by using (6), continuous first leaf apple scab and another leaf apple black rot from images 1 to 6.

Table 5. Cosine distance between leaves

Apple Scab & Apple Black Rot	Cosine Distance between leaves
1	0.187449
2	0.168588
3	0.133259
4	0.208642
5	**0.271293**
6	**0.13464**

4. DISCUSSIONS

In the result section, above in Table 1, Table 2, Table 3, Table 4, and Table 5, the red colour shows the minimum information or distance between leaves and the blue colour shows the maximum information or distance between leaves. From Table 1 and Column 2, it can be observed that the Shannon information for Apple Scab Images 1 to 6, in which, we find that image 5 has minimum Shannon information and image 4 has the highest Shannon information. Similarly, from column 4, it can be observed that the

Shannon information for apple black rot images 1 to 6, we find that image 5 receives minimum Shannon information and image 3 receives maximum Shannon information.

From Table 2, it can be observed that the Belis and Gaisu Information with utility parameter for Apple sab Image from 1 to 6, in which, we find that image 5 has minimum Belis and Gaisu Information while image 3 has the highest Shannon information in column no. 3. Similarly, from column no. 5, it can be observed that the Belis and Gaisu Information for apple black rot images 1 to 6, we find that image 5 receives minimum Belis and Gaisu Information while image 3 receives the maximum Belis and Gaisu Information.

Finally, we measure the distance between two leaves, initially, we get the Euclidean distance between apple scab and apple black Rot in which we find that From Table 3, image 6 has minimum distance while image 5 has the highest distance. It can be observed that the Manhattan distance between Apple Scab & Apple Black Rot, from Table 4 image 3 has a minimum distance while image 5 has the highest distance. Lastly, from Table 5, we measure Cosine Distance between leaves where we find that image 6 receives minimum Distance while image 5 receives maximum Distance.

Our results show that the possibility of diseases in the plant leaves is minimum when Shannon's Information and Belis and Gaisu's Information are minimum. Similarly, the possibility of diseases in the plant leaves is maximum when Shannon's Information and Belis and Gaisu's Information are maximum. So, it was found how to optimize diseases in leaves in terms of 'useful' information measures and distance measurements.

Shannon information may be used to calculate the degree of uncertainty in a random process. Rolling element equipment undergoing or not undergoing breakdown will have different Shannon information because the former generally generates a more random signal and the later typically generates a more predictable signal. It is recommended that in order to extract the periodicity from the signal, one should make advantage of a property known as symbolic Shannon information. This feature first symbols the signal, then utilises the Shannon information. Shannon's information has been used to identify disease in leaves.

The current focus of apple scab research at East Malling Research is on the possibilities of using different cultivars in mixes to decrease scab formation. We're attempting to answer the following four questions in particular:

1. In comparison to ascospores, how important are conidia as the main inoculum? The solution to this issue has ramifications for illness treatment as well as forecasting the danger of super races forming.
2. What is the degree of non-symptomatic 'restricted' (or concealed) scab lesions on cultivars that are usually considered resistant? The response has consequences for inoculum management, resistance breeding, and cultivar selection as mixture components.
3. What are the temporal dynamics of bacteria and fungi community patterns in mixtures as they relate to hosting cultivars? The solution to this issue may be used to deduce the selection pressures exerted by cultivars in the mixture, therefore determining the feasibility (and strategy) of crop combination deployment.
4. What are the differences in scab resistance amongst common vulnerable cultivars? The appropriate response decides which cultivars can be utilized as mixing ingredients in combinations. Understanding the evolutionary capacity of the scab fungus to defeat host resistance is critical given the life cycle of an orchard and the lengthy time scale for breeding apple varieties. The fit-

ness cost suffered by fungal strains carrying virulence factors not required to infect some hosts is a major determinant of whether fungal genotypes evolve to combine various virulence factors to overcome different host resistance factors. Soon, we want to measure fitness costs in scab strains harbouring additional virulence factors versus 'minor' resistance genes that are generally perceived as vulnerable cultivars to better understand host-pathogen co-evolution.

Finally, we want to see if any structural variations between virulence genes attack 'slight' antibiotic resistance seen in domestic susceptible cultivars and those that attack 'significant' resistance genes present in wild apple accessions with small fruits.

Competing Interests: The authors declare that they have no known competing financial interests or personal relationships that could have appeared to influence the work reported in this paper.

Funding Information: This research has not received any specific grant from any funding agency in the public, commercial, or not-for-profit sectors.

REFERENCES

Acquaah, G. (2007). *Principles of Plant Genetics and Breeding* (1st ed.). Blackwell Publishing.

Anonymous. (2000). *Plant Protection Manual for Selected Vegetables: French beans, Brassicas, and Tomatoes*. GTZ/ICIPE CD-ROM.

Averre, W. C. (2000). *Black Rot of Cabbage and Related Crops. Vegetable Disease Information Note 16 (VDIN 0016)*. North Carolina Extension Service Publisher, North Carolina State University at Raleigh.

Barbara, D. J., Roberts, A., & Xu, X.-M. (2008). Virulence characteristics of apple scab (*Venturia inaequalis*) isolates from monoculture and mixed orchards. *Plant Pathology*, *57*(3), 552–561. doi:10.1111/j.1365-3059.2007.01781.x

Belis, M., & Guiasu, S. (1968). – A quantitative-qualitative measure of information in Cybernetics System, IEEE Trans. Inform. *Theory, IT*, *14*, 593–594.

Berrie, A. M., & Xu, X.-M. (2003). Managing apple scab (*Venturia inaequalis*) and powdery mildew (*Podosphaera leucotricha*) using Adem (TM). *International Journal of Pest Management*, *49*(3), 243–249. doi:10.1080/0967087031000101089

Bila, J. (2008). Status of Bacterial Black rot of Brassicas in Southern Region of Mozambique: Survey, Detection and Identification of the Causal Agent *Xanthomonas campestris* pv. *campestris*. [M.Sc. thesis, University of Copenhagen, Denmark].

Bila, J., Mortensen, C. N., Andresen, M., Vicente, J. G., & Wulff, E. G. (2013). – *Xanthomonas campestris* pv. *campestris* Race 1 is the main causal agent of black rot of Brassicas in Southern Mozambique. *African Journal of Biotechnology*, *12*(26), 602–610.

Burchill, R. T. 1966. Air-dispersal of fungal spores with particular reference to apple scab [*Venturia inaequalis* (Cooke) Winter]. In *The Eighteenth Symposium of the Colston Research Society*, (pp. 135–141). Butterworths Scientific Publications.

Burchill R T. (1975). The value of eradicant treatment in the control of apple scab and apple powdery mildew. *OILB/SROP,* 249–258.

Burchill, R. T., & Cook, M. E. (1975). Control of scab and powdery mildew of apple with a reduced number of sprays. *Plant Pathology, 24*(4), 194–198. doi:10.1111/j.1365-3059.1975.tb01893.x

Burchill, R. T., & Cook, R. T. A. (1971). The interaction of urea and micro-organisms in suppressing the development of perithecia of Venturia inaequalis (Cke.) Wint. In Ecology of Leaf Surface Micro Organisms, (pp. 471–483). London: Academic Press.

Burchill, R. T., & Hutton, K. E. (1965). The suppression of ascospore production to facilitate the control of apple scab (*Venturia inaequalis* (Cke.) Wint.). *Annals of Applied Biology, 56*(2), 285–292. doi:10.1111/j.1744-7348.1965.tb01237.x

Burchill, R. T., & Swait, A A J. (1977). Eradication of perithecial stage of apple scab with surfactants. *Annals of Applied Biology, 87*(2), 229–231. doi:10.1111/j.1744-7348.1977.tb01879.x

Butt, D. J., Jeger, M. J., Swait, A A J., & Soutter, R. D. (1981). The 1981 apple scab epidemic. *Grower, 96,* 4–5.

Butt D J, Swait A A J, Robinson J D. 1990. Evaluation of fungicides against apple powdery mildew and scab. *Tests of Agrochemicals and Cultivars,* supplement of *Annals of Applied Biology* 116, pp. 34–35.

Celetti, M., & Kristen, C. (2002). *Black Rot of Crucifer Crops.* Ministry of Agriculture, Food and Rural Affairs.

Celton, J.-M., Christoffels, A., Sargent, D. J., Xu, X.-M., & Rees, D. J. G. (2010). Genome-wide SNP identification by high-throughput sequencing and selective mapping allows sequence assembly positioning using a framework genetic linkage map. *BMC Biology, 8*(1), 155. doi:10.1186/1741-7007-8-155 PMID:21192788

Chandy, T.W. & Mcliod, J. B. (1960). On a functional equation. *Proc. Edinburgh Maths, 43,* 7-8.

Cook, R. T. A. (1974). Pustules on wood as sources of inoculum in apple scab and their response to chemical treatments. *Annals of Applied Biology, 77*(1), 1–9. doi:10.1111/j.1744-7348.1974.tb01381.x

Coslor, C. C., Sundin, G. W., & Wise, J. C. (2019). The efficacy of trunk injections of emamectin benzoate and phosphorous acid for control of obliquebanded leafroller and apple scab on semi-dwarf apple. *Crop Protection (Guildford, Surrey), 118,* 44–49. doi:10.1016/j.cropro.2018.12.012

Crosse, J. E., Garrett, C. M. E., & Burchill, R. T. (1968). Changes in the microbial population of apple leaves associated with the inhibition of the perfect stage of *Venturia inequalis* after urea treatment. *Annals of Applied Biology, 61*(2), 203–216. doi:10.1111/j.1744-7348.1968.tb04526.x

Dwivedi, P. P., & Sharma, D. K. (2021). Lower and Upper Bounds for 'Useful' Renyi Information Rate. Advances in Computing and Data Sciences. ICACDS 2021. Communications in Computer and Information Science (Vol. 1441). Springer. doi:10.1007/978-3-030-88244-0_26

Gao, L.-Q., Berrie, A., Yang, J.-R., & Xu, X.-M. (2009). Within- and between-orchard variability in the sensitivity of *Venturia inaequalis* to myclobutanil, a DMI fungicide, in the UK. *Pest Management Science, 65*(11), 1241–1249. doi:10.1002/ps.1816 PMID:19606427

Ghazalibiglar, H. (2014). *Biocontrol of Black rot of Brassicas*. Lincoln University.

Huang, H. H. C. 1997 – Biological control of soil-borne diseases in Canada, In: *International Symposium on Clean Agriculture*, Sapporo, OECD.

Hunter, J. E., Abawi, G. S., & Becker, R. F. (1975). – Observation on the source and spread of *Xanthomonas campestris* in epidemic of black rot in New York. *The Plant Disease Reporter, 59*, 384–387.

Hunter, L. D. (1975). Phloridzin and apple scab. *Phytochemistry, 14*(7), 1519–1522. doi:10.1016/0031-9422(75)85343-X

Hutton, K. E., & Burchill, R. T. (1965). The effect of some fungicides and herbicides on ascospore production of *Venturia inaequalis* (Cke.) Wint. *Annals of Applied Biology, 56*(2), 279–284. doi:10.1111/j.1744-7348.1965.tb01236.x

James, G. M., & Sujatha, S. (2021). Categorising Apple Fruit Diseases Employing Hybrid Neural Clustering Classifier. *Materials Today: Proceedings*. doi:10.1016/j.matpr.2020.12.139

Jeger, M. J. (1981). Disease measurement in a study of apple scab epidemics. *Annals of Applied Biology, 99*(1), 43–51. doi:10.1111/j.1744-7348.1981.tb05128.x

Jeger, M. J. (1984). Relating disease progress to cumulative numbers of trapped spores - apple powdery mildew and scab epidemics in sprayed and unsprayed orchard plots. *Plant Pathology, 33*(4), 517–523. doi:10.1111/j.1365-3059.1984.tb02876.x

Jeger, M. J., & Butt, D. J. (1983). Overwintering of *Venturia inaequalis* the causal agent of apple scab in relation to weather. *Annals of Applied Biology, 103*(2), 201–218. doi:10.1111/j.1744-7348.1983.tb02757.x

Jeger, M. J., & Butt, D. J. (1984). Management of orchard diseases in the United Kingdom. *Plant Protection Bulletin, 32*, 61–66.

Jeger, M. J., Swait, A. A. J., & Butt, D. J. (1982). Overwintering of *Venturia inaequalis*, the causal agent of apple scab, on different cultivars. *Annals of Applied Biology, 100*, 91–98.

Jiang, H., Meng, X., Ma, J., Sun, X., Wang, Y., Hu, T., & Wang, S. (2021). Control effect of fungicide pyraclostrobin alternately applied with Bordeaux mixture against apple Glomerella leaf spot and its residue after preharvest application in China. *Crop Protection (Guildford, Surrey), 142*, 105489. doi:10.1016/j.cropro.2020.105489

Kendall, D. G. (1964). – Functional equations in information theory. *Zeitschrift für Wahrscheinlichkeitstheorie und Verwandte Gebiete, 2*(3), 225–229. doi:10.1007/BF00533380

Khinchin, A. I. (1957). *Mathematical Foundations of Information Theory*. Dover Publications.

Leca, A., Rouby, F., Saudreau, M., & Lacointe, A. (2020). Apple leaf wettability variability as a function of genotype and apple scab susceptibility. *Scientia Horticulturae, 260*, 108890. doi:10.1016/j.scienta.2019.108890

Li, B.-H., & Xu, X.-M. (2002). Infection and development of apple scab (*Venturia inaequalis*) on old leaves. *Journal of Phytopathology*, *150*(11-12), 687–691. doi:10.1046/j.1439-0434.2002.00824.x

Li, B. H., Yang, J. R., Li, B. D., & Xu, X. M. (2007). Incidence-density relationship of pear scab (*Venturia nashicola*) on fruits and leaves. *Plant Pathology*, *56*(1), 120–127. doi:10.1111/j.1365-3059.2006.01496.x

Lo, C. T., & Wang, K. M. (2001). – Inoculum sources of black rot of wasabi, caused by *Phoma wasabiae*. *Plant Pathology Bulletin*, *10*, 88–92.

Luna, L. C., Mariaono, R. L. R., & Souto-Mairo, M. A. (2002). – Production of a biocontrol agent for crucifers' black rot disease. *Brazilian Journal of Chemical Engineering*, *19*(2), 133–140. doi:10.1590/S0104-66322002000200007

Machardy, W. E., & Jeger, M. J. (1982). An approach to integrate control measures for use in apple scab management programs. *Phytopathology*, *72*, 264–264.

MacHardy, W. E., & Jeger, M. J. (1983). Integrating control measures for the management of primary apple scab, *Venturia inaequalis* (Cke.) Wint. *Protection Ecology*, *5*, 103–125.

Massomo, S.M.S., Mabagala, R.B., Swai, I.S., Hockenhull, J., & Mortensen, C.N. 2003 – Evaluation of varietal resistance in cabbage against the black rot pathogen *Xanthomonas campestris* pv.*campestris* in Tanzania. *Crop Protection 23*(4), 315–325. 29

Miller, S. A. (2002). *Disease management for conventional and tomato growers.* New York State Vegetable Conference and Berry Growers Meeting Proceedings. New York.

Miller, S. A., & Lewis, I. M. L. (2005). *Hot water treatment of vegetable seeds to eradicate bacterial plant pathogens in organic production systems. Plant Pathology Extension Fact Sheet HYG-3086- 05.* The Ohio State University.

Miller, S. A., Sahin, F., & Rowe, C. R. (1996). *Black rot of crucifers. Extension fact sheet HYG-3125-96.* The Ohio State University.

Mills, W. D., & La Plante, A. (1954). Diseases and insects in the orchard. *Cornell University Extension Bulletin*, 711.

Moore M H. (1932). Some fundamental considerations regarding successful control of apple scab. *The Fruit Grower*.

Ombuna, G. J., Nyangeri, B. J., & Maobe, S. N. (2019). – Control of black rot disease in cabbage by integration of mulching, pruning and hot water treatment of seeds. *Plant Pathology & Quarantine Journal of Fungal Biology*, *9*(1), 23–29. doi:10.5943/ppq/9/1/3

Onsando, J. M. (1992). Black rot of Crucifers. In H. S. Chaube, U. S. Singh, A. N. Mukhopadyay, & J. Kumar (Eds.), *Plant Diseases of International Importance. Diseases of Vegetables and Oil Seed Crops* (pp. 243–252). Prentice Hall.

Otipa, M., Kamau, R., & Gekone, M. (2013). Pest management decision guide: green and yellow list. Black rot disease- Plantwise. East African pest management innovation lab. The Ohio State University, College of food, Agriculture and Environmental Sciences.

Preece, T. F. (1961). Scabbed wood on Bramley's seedling apple. *Plant Pathology*, *10*, 39–40.

Priyanka, P., Brajesh, K., & Shashank, M. (2022). Comparison of various deep convolutional neural network models to discriminate apple leaf diseases using transfer learning. *Journal of Plant Diseases and Protection*, *129*(6), 1461–1473. doi:10.100741348-022-00660-1

Rogge, S. A., & Meyhofer, R. (2021). Leaf age is important for assessment of resistance in chrysanthemum against Frankliniella occidentalis. *Journal of Plant Diseases and Protection*, *128*(2), 511–516. doi:10.100741348-020-00402-1

Ross, R. G., & Burchill, R. T. (1968). Experiments using sterilized apple-leaf discs to study the mode of action of urea in suppressing perithecia of *Venturia inaequalis* (Cke.) Wint. *Annals of Applied Biology*, *62*(2), 289–296. doi:10.1111/j.1744-7348.1968.tb02824.x

Ryan, R. P., Vorhölter, F. J., Potnis, N., Jones, J. B., Van Sluys, M.-A., Bogdanove, A. J., & Dow, J. M. (2011). – Pathogenomics of Xanthomonas: Understanding bacterium-plant interactions. *Nature Reviews. Microbiology*, *9*(5), 344–355. doi:10.1038/nrmicro2558 PMID:21478901

Sayonara, MP, Mariano, RLR, & Sami, JM, Gil Silva, Elizabeth AAM. (1999). – Antagonism of yeasts to Xanthomonas campestris pv. campestris on cabbage phylloplane in field. *Journal of Microbiology (Seoul, Korea)*, *30*(3), 375–379.

Seebold, K., Bachi, P., & Beale, J. (2008). Black rot of crucifers. UK Cooperative Extension Service. University of Kentucky-College of Agriculture.

Shannon, C.E. (1948). A mathematical theory of communication. *Bell System Technical Journal 27*, 379–423(Part I) 623–656(Part II).

Smart, D. C., & Holly, W. L. (2013). *Managing Black Rot of Cabbage and other Crucifer Crops in Organic Farming Systems*. Cornell University.

Swait A A J, Butt D J. 1990. Fungicides as antisporulants against apple powdery mildew and scab. *Tests of Agrochemicals and Cultivars*, supplement of *Annals of Applied Biology, 116*, pp. 36–37.

Taylor, J. D., Conway, J., Roberts, S. J., & Vicente, J. G. (2002). – Sources and origin of resistance to Xanthomonas campestris pv. campestris in Brassica genomes. *Phytopathology*, *92*(1), 105–111. doi:10.1094/PHYTO.2002.92.1.105 PMID:18944146

Tverberg, H. (1958). – A new derivation of the information function. *Mathematica Scandinavica*, *6*, 297–298. doi:10.7146/math.scand.a-10555

Wrzesien, M., Treder, W., Klamkowski, K., & Rudnicki, W. R. (2018). Prediction of the apple scab using machine learning and simple weather stations. *Computers and Electronics in Agriculture*. doi:10.1016/j.compag.2018.09.026

Xiangming, X. (2013). Research on apple scab (Venturia inaequalis) at East Malling Research. *Aspects of Applied Biology*, 119.

Xu, X.-M., & Butt, D. J. (1996). AdemTM a PC-based multiple disease warning system for use in the cultivation of apples. *Acta Horticulturae*, (416), 293–296. doi:10.17660/ActaHortic.1996.416.37

Xu, X.-M., Butt, D. J., & van Santen, G. (1995). A dynamic model simulating infection of apple leaves by *Venturia inaequalis. Plant Pathology, 44*(5), 865–876. doi:10.1111/j.1365-3059.1995.tb02746.x

Xu, X.-M., Gao, L.-Q., & Yang, J.-R. (2010). Are insensitivities of *Venturia inaequalis* to myclobutanil and fenbuconazole correlated? *Crop Protection (Guildford, Surrey), 29*(2), 183–189. doi:10.1016/j.cropro.2009.07.002

Xu, X.-M., Harvey, N., Roberts, A. L., & Barbara, D. J. (2013). Population variation of apple scab (*Venturia inaequalis*) within mixed orchards in the UK. *European Journal of Plant Pathology, 135*(1), 97–104. doi:10.100710658-012-0068-4

Xu, X.-M., Roberts, T., Barbara, D., Harvey, N. G., Gao, L.-Q., & Sargent, D. J. (2009). A genetic linkage map of *Venturia inaequalis*, the causal agent of apple scab. *BMC Research Notes, 2*(1), 163–163. doi:10.1186/1756-0500-2-163 PMID:19689797

Xu, X.-M., & Robinson, J. (2005). Modelling the effects of wetness duration and fruit maturity on infection of apple fruits of Cox's Orange Pippin and two clones of Gala by *Venturia inaequalis. Plant Pathology, 54*(3), 347–356. doi:10.1111/j.1365-3059.2005.01177.x

Xu, X.-M., Yang, J.-R., Thakur, V., Roberts, A. L., & Barbara, D. J. (2008). Population variation of apple scab (*Venturia inaequalis*) isolates from Asia and Europe. *Plant Disease, 92*(2), 247–252. doi:10.1094/PDIS-92-2-0247 PMID:30769384

Chapter 9
Real–Time Recording and Analysis of Facial Expressions of Video Viewers

Pramod Madhavrao Kanjalkar

Vishwakarma Institute of Technology, India

Shubham Patil

Vishwakarma Institute of Technology, India

Prasad Jitendra Chinchole

Vishwakarma Institute of Technology, India

Archit Ashish Chitre

Vishwakarma Institute of Technology, India

Jyoti Kanjalkar

Vishwakarma Institute of Technology, India

ABSTRACT

Automated facial emotion recognition (AFER) is a technique with rising usage across a range of practical real-world applications ranging from security to advertising. AFER can be used to assess the emotional state of patients with mental health conditions, such as depression or anxiety to guide treatment decisions. Companies can use facial emotion recognition to gauge consumer reactions to different products or advertisements, providing valuable insights for product development and marketing strategies. The following paper examines the concept of facial emotion recognition using AI-based models and compares the results of two different techniques. The first technique uses face emotion detection using haar cascade classifier along with convolutional neural networks (CNN), and the second technique uses face emotion detection using facial landmarks along with CNN.

DOI: 10.4018/979-8-3693-1301-5.ch009

1. INTRODUCTION

In contrast to conventional surveys, facial expression analysis is a practical method of learning more. Using it, one may learn about the user's experiences and receive feedback. The feedback is also not disruptive to the user experience, which is the best part. Facial recognition techniques are not currently in common use. This paper's objective is to implement and analyze different techniques of facial emotion recognition (Chakravarthi & Venkatesan, 2015).

Emotion detection is convenient for quantifying an individual's natural reaction to any situation. This "reaction" can come in handy in many applications - one being sentiment analysis, which has a wide scope. It is helpful in understanding and determining what is going on inside any person's mind. This proves to be one of the most efficient ways of identifying and extracting facial features (Shriram et al., 2022). The data acquired can be used for applications that rely on emotional feedback, such as digital advertisements, interactive multimedia, helping psychiatrists identify the patient's emotional state, sentiment analysis to decide wait time, and more (Chakravarthi et al., 2015).

Digital media leverages deliver promotional content to consumers through innumerable channels. Any digital media can help tell the story of a brand. Digital advertising being universal and flexible enables you to tell the brand story on channels visited by your consumers (Ogunmola et al., 2021). Advertisers believe that with such steps (digitisation), they can promote their products or businesses more efficiently and reach their target users (Sharma, et al., 2021). But more importantly, getting feedback from their users in some form will help them improve the quality of content. One of the best ways they can receive feedback is through a "reaction", in this case, a facial reaction or an 'emotion' (Lohit Ujjainiya et al., 2014). This form of data can predict the interest of the viewer for the advertisement as well as be used for identifying a person with suspicious behaviour at common places such as airports and stations and prevent any mishap from happening (Doss, et al., 2022).

It is observed that such facial recognition systems are not commonly placed everywhere. We have discussed two techniques for emotion recognition, and they are as follows:

The first emotion recognition technique using CNN consists of four phases: preprocessing, face detection, model training, and classification. In the pre-processing phase, OpenCV changed the image from RGB to Grayscale. Haar cascade classifier was utilised in the face identification phase to identify faces quickly. Following face detection, the model is created using the Keras framework and Convolutional Neural Network (CNN) architecture. The second technique is emotion recognition using facial landmarks, and it consists of five phases: pre-processing, face detection, landmark detection, model training, and classification. Face detection was carried out using a Python facial recognition tool like Dlib. The previously trained model is combined with the "shape predictor." After detecting landmarks, the Convolutional Neural Network architecture is used for model development, and the Keras library is imported.

This paper's organisation is as follows – we first discuss the literature survey, then we discuss emotion recognition techniques using CNN, followed by a discussion on emotion recognition techniques using Facial Landmarks, and lastly, we compare both techniques.

2. LITERATURE REVIEW

Various people have researched detecting and recognising facial emotion using facial features in this field. In one of the research projects by Silva & Hui (2003), to determine the local motion vectors of face features, a method that incorporates edge counting and image-correlation optical flow methods have been presented. Then, they use a neural network to ascertain the subject's emotional state (Kumar Patale & Chakravarthi, 2014).

In another research conducted by Li & Oussalah (2010), a new technique for facial emotion identification was investigated. As part of the proposal, the adaptive AdaBoost algorithm and Haar transform were used to identify faces, while Principal Component Analysis (PCA) and a minimum distance classifier were used to recognise faces. To recognise facial expressions, two methods have been examined. The latter encourages using the Negative Matrix Factorization (NMF) and KNN algorithms, whereas the former depends on using PCA and the KNN classification method. Their proposal was tested and validated using Taiwanese and Indian face databases (Arslan, et al., 2021).

Jaiswal & Raju's (2020) research demonstrates the architecture of an artificial intelligence (AI) system that can recognize emotions from facial expressions. It talks about the emotion detection process, which consists of three steps: face detection, feature extraction, and emotion categorization. This article suggested a deep learning architecture for CNN-based emotion recognition from photos. The Facial Emotion Recognition Challenge (FERC-2013) and Japanese Female Facial Emotion (JAFFE) datasets were used to assess how well the suggested technique performed.

Another research by Rajesh & Naveenkumar (2016) proposed a framework for a system that uses facial traits and movements to identify emotions on faces in real-time. By training several sets of photos, machine learning algorithms are utilized to recognise and categorise various classes of facial emotions. Python is used to implement the suggested approach with OpenCV and Machine Learning. Soleymani et al., (2016), and other writers provided a new strategy in which they described a method for instantly identifying the emotions of video viewers' reactions using electroencephalogram (EEG) signals and facial expressions. Participants saw a series of emotionally charged movies while their physiological and facial reactions were being captured. In (Gayakwad et al., 2022), the multi-nomial classifier is used to assess the credibility of user-generated material. The authors (Pande & Chetty, 2019) have used a capsule network-based method to classify leaves. The method suggested in (Nanda Prakash, 2023) uses a convolutional neural network (CNN)-based deep learning technology called DenseNet-CNN to detect deep liver abnormalities.

3. EMOTION DETECTION USING CNN

Emotion recognition using CNN is a technique for identifying and classifying people's emotional states based on their facial expressions. CNNs are a class of deep learning algorithms well suited for image recognition tasks. Typically, to perform emotion recognition using CNNs, a dataset of images of individuals with different emotional expressions is collected and tagged with the appropriate emotion. A CNN is then trained on this dataset to learn to recognise different emotions based on the facial features present in the images (Balasubramanian, et al., 2019). This technique consists of four phases: preprocessing, face detection, model training, and classification. In the face detection phase, the Harr cascade classifier detected faces in real-time. After detecting faces, The Convolutional Neural Network architecture is used for model development, and the Keras library is imported. Fig 1 describes the block diagram of the CNN Algorithm (Xiaoxi, et al., 2017; Rzayeva & Alasgarov, 2019).

Figure 1. Face emotion detection using HAAR cascade classifier

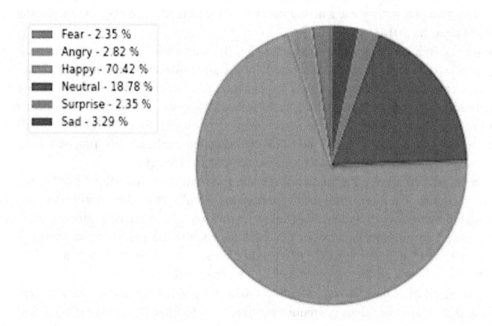

3.1. Pre-Processing

Processing the data so that the model can work with it to prepare the input images for feature extraction is the goal of the preprocessing stage. The datasets contain colored and grayscale images (Soni, et al., 2014). Some specific considerations for preprocessing image data for a CNN model include the following:

1. *Resizing the images*: The images may need to be resized to a consistent size in order to be processed by the model.
2. *Converting to grayscale*: If the images are in color, they may need to be converted to grayscale in order to be processed by the model. This can be done by taking the average of the image's green, red and blue channels.
3. *Normalizing the pixel values*: It is often helpful to normalize the pixel values of the images to a range between 0 and 1. This can be done by dividing the pixel values by the maximum pixel value (usually 255 in the case of 8-bit images).
4. *Handling missing or invalid data*: If there are any missing or invalid data in the images, it will be necessary to handle these values somehow. This could involve imputing missing values or removing invalid data from the dataset.

All photos must first be converted to grayscale. OpenCV is used in this step, which is a free, open-source computer vision and machine learning algorithm library designed to help developers build and deploy computer vision applications (Ekman & Friesen, 1978; Kanade, et al., 2000; Suwa et al., 1978).

3.2. Face Detection

Face detection in image processing is identifying and locating human faces in digital images. It is a common problem in computer vision and is used in several applications, such as security systems, social media, and automated photo organization. In traditional face detection methods, features such as edges, shapes, and textures are extracted from the image and used to identify and locate the face. These methods often rely on hand-crafted features designed to capture a face's unique characteristics (Ivanovsky et al., 2017).

This face detection stage makes use of the Haar cascade library. It is an object detection algorithm that recognizes various items and faces in still photos and real-time videos. The Haar Cascade method trains a classifier on a large dataset of positive and negative images. The positive images contain the object of interest (e.g., a face), while the negative images do not contain the object. The classifier is trained to recognize the object by learning the features characteristic of the object and differentiating them from the background. Once the classifier has been trained, it can detect the object in new images. The Haar Cascade method works by sliding a window across the image and using the classifier to determine whether the window contains the object. If the classifier determines that the window possesses the object, the window is marked as a detection. Any non-facial parts must be removed after the images have been processed (Uddin, et al., 2017).

3.3. CNN Architecture

The Convolutional Neural Network architecture is used for model development, and the Keras library is imported. The sequential method adds various model layers and their functions, number of neurons, etc. The CNN model layers are as follows (Li, et al., 2017):

- The first layer is a 2D Convolution layer with 32 layers and a 3x3 kernel. With the input mentioned above (x) form, the relu activation function is utilized.
- The second layer of a 2D convolution comprises 32 neurons and a kernel size 3x3. The relu activation function is utilized here as well.
- The third layer of the pool size 2x2 is a 2D Max Pooling layer. It has a 1x1 stride and proper padding value. With a rate of 0.25, a layer known as a dropout layer is chosen to prevent the overfitting issue.
- Once more, two 2D Convolution layers are utilized, each of which contains 64 neurons and a kernel size of 3x3. Relu is an activation function.
- With a suitable padding and stride value of 1x1, a 2D Max Pooling layer with a pool size of 2x2 is employed. The overfitting problem is avoided using a dropout layer with a fixed rate of 0.25.
- With a kernel size 3x3, two 2D Convolution layers with 128 and 128 neurons each are employed. The activation function utilized is called Relu.
- 2D Max Pooling layer with a 2x2 pool size, appropriate padding, and a 1x1 stride value is employed. With a set rate of 0.25, the dropout layer is utilized to prevent the overfitting issue.
- The following layer, crucial in every model, is flattened. This layer flattens the input.
- A Dense layer with 512 neurons and relu as the activation function receives the output from the flattened layer.
- With a set rate of 0.5, the overfitting issue is solved using a dropout layer.
- A dense layer that produces the final results is the layer's output.

- After describing the whole model's architecture, the loss is specified as categorical cross-entropy, and the model is assembled using the Adam optimizer. This metrics' accuracy measure is displayed. The model is now ready for training.

Now, the model is tested on a testing set after being trained on a training set. For the same, a validation split of 0.2 is provided. 30 epochs are employed in the training process. The same model is then tested against a collection of data. The model is currently employed to forecast the outcomes of an image dataset that has not yet been observed (Xia, 2015).

4. EXPERIMENTATION AND RESULTS

When we face the camera are looking at some content like a pictorial or a video, our evident facial reaction to it is one of the emotions we implement. The video stream displays the emotion on the screen as the output. We are getting an accuracy and validation accuracy of 88.21% and 65.53%, respectively.

Figure 2. Results of application on a real-time video

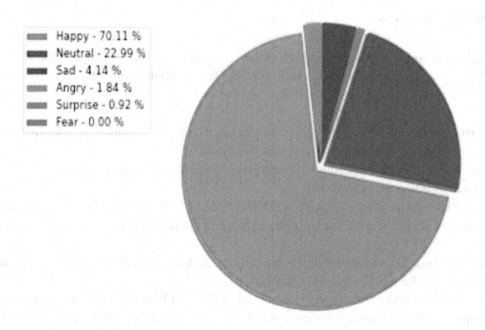

We also performed an experiment where users were asked to see a video of 3 minutes, and their emotions were noted. Figure 2 shows the recorded emotions of different users for a short video.

5. EMOTION DETECTION USING FACIAL LANDMARKS

Emotion detection using facial landmarks is a technique for identifying and classifying emotional states in individuals based on the positions and movements of specific facial features. Facial landmarks are specific points on the face, such as the corners of the eyes, mouth, eyebrows, and nostrils, that can be used to track facial movements and expressions. The method consists of five phases: preprocessing, face detection, landmark detection, model training, and classification. The built-in dlib function "Get Frontal Face Detector" is used in the face detection phase. After face detection, I used the dlib package to find facial features. The previously trained model is combined with the dlib function, also called "shape prediction". After recognizing landmarks, a CNN network architecture is used for model development, and the Keras library is imported for this (Figure 3).

Figure 3. Face emotion detection using facial landmark

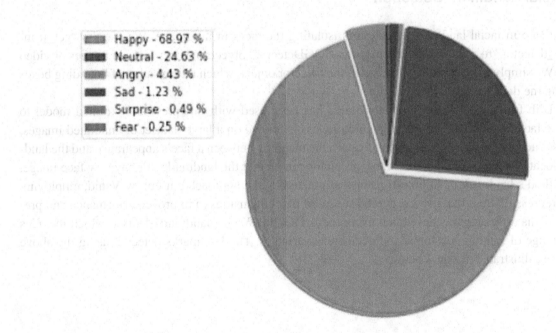

5.1. Pre-Processing

The input images are prepared for feature extraction during the pre-processing stage. The first stage is converting all images to grayscale because the datasets contain both colorful and grayscale images. The OpenCV library, a free and open-source computer vision and machine learning software library, is used for this stage. Its primary focus is real-time computer vision.

5.2. Face Detection

Post-image conversion, one has to eliminate the non-facial part of the images so as to ensure no irrelevant data enters and confuses the model. For this, the Dlib library is used. Dlib is an open-source library of machine learning algorithms and tools written in C++. Dlib contains many algorithms and tools, including machine learning algorithms for regression, classification, clustering, and dimensionality reduction and tools for image processing, computer vision, and natural language processing. One of the key features of Dlib is its support for real-time processing, which makes it well-suited for applications that require fast performance. It also has a lightweight, modular design, which makes it easy to integrate into other software systems. This is a landmark's facial detector with pre-trained models, the dlib is employed to estimate the placement of 68 coordinates (x, y) that map the facial points on an individual's face. This delivers higher accuracy in the landmark detection step.

5.3. Facial Landmark Detection

The first step in facial landmark detection is isolating the faces in the image. We use the "get_frontal_face_detector" to achieve this. It returns a "HOGDetector" object to detect faces in images or video frames. We simply pass an image or frame to the detector object, which returns a list of bounding boxes enclosing the detected faces.

The Dlib function's "shape_predictor" class has been used with this previously trained model to recognise face landmarks. The shape_predictor class is trained on a large dataset of annotated images, and it uses a machine learning algorithm to learn the mapping between a face's appearance and the landmarks' locations. Once trained, the shape_predictor can predict the landmarks for any new face image. This method's landmark position estimator was created by the approach put out by Vahid, employing several regression trees that use a scattered subset of pixel intensities to improve performance and predictions. This estimator was developed using the iBUG 300-W face landmark dataset, which includes a wide range of lighting, postures, and occlusions variables. The landmarks detected using the above method are illustrated in Fig. 4 below.

Figure 4. Detected facial landmarks and numbering

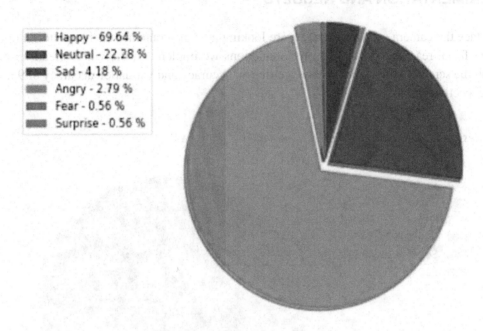

As shown in Figure 4, this method can identify 68 facial features. However, not all landmarks contribute to changes in facial emotion. Therefore, a set of selected landmarks should be used. Therefore, landmarks around the mouth area and eyes are considered for calculating features. This is because the muscles in these areas change with facial expressions.

5.4. Facial Landmark Detection

Landmark vectorising is extracting numerical features from facial landmarks, which are specific points on the face that can be used to track facial movements and expressions. These features are typically represented as a vector or an array of numbers and can be used as input to a machine-learning model for tasks such as emotion detection or facial recognition.

The most important step in facial feature identification is the feature vector computation that best characterizes the facial emotion. Therefore, it is very important to know the location of the selected facial marker sites. This is done by averaging the two axes to create a large blue dot near the nose and midpoint (mean, mean). The position of each point relative to the current centre point is then determined. Obstruction. A line is then drawn between the midpoint and the other face markers. As a result, every line created has both a magnitude and a direction, creating a feature vector that can be used for both the training and classification stages. The distance between the points in magnitude is the Euclidean distance, and the angle the line creates with the horizontal reference axis is the direction. So the feature vector generalises to:

feature vector = <point 1.x, point 1.y, magnitude 1, direction 1,...., point 68.x, point 68.y, magnitude 68, direction 68>

6. EXPERIMENTATION AND RESULTS

When we face the camera and, for instance, are looking at some content, whether pictorial or a video, our evident facial reaction to it is one of the emotions we implement; the video stream displays the emotion on the screen as the output. We are getting an accuracy and validation accuracy of 93.21% and 71.53%, respectively.

Figure 5. Results of application on a real-time video

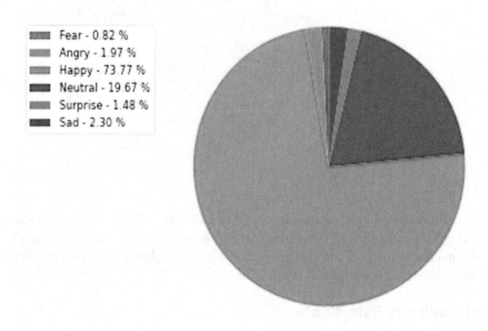

Fear - 0.82 %
Angry - 1.97 %
Happy - 73.77 %
Neutral - 19.67 %
Surprise - 1.48 %
Sad - 2.30 %

We also performed an experiment where users were asked to see a video of 3 minutes, and their emotions were noted. Fig. 5 shows the recorded emotions of different users for a short video.

7. COMPARATIVE STUDY OF METHOD ONE AND METHOD TWO

The video shown to the users for testing was a comedy video where the expected reaction of a person is happy or not. We showed this video to different users and ran both methods simultaneously. So now compare the results.

Table 1. Method comparison for user (a)

Emotions	Method 1	Method 2
Happy	65.2	69.6
Neutral	24.8	22.2
Fear	1.5	0.5
Angry	3.1	2.7
Surprise	0.6	0.5
Sad	4.6	4.1

Table 1 shows the comparison of the emotions of User (a) by both methods after watching a particular video at the same time. For User (a), according to method, one user had happy emotions for around 65.2% of the time, and neutral emotions for around 24.8% of the time, while through method two user had happy emotions for around 69.6% of the time, neutral emotion for around 22.2% of the time.

Table 2. Method comparison for user (b)

Emotions	Method 1	Method 2
Happy	68.1	71.6
Neutral	22.7	21.2
Fear	1.4	0.0
Angry	2.8	2.6
Surprise	0.5	0.5
Sad	4.2	3.9

Table 2 shows the comparison of the emotions of User (b) by both methods after watching a particular video at the same time. For User (b), according to the method, one user had happy emotions for around 68.1% of the time and neutral emotions for around 22.7% of the time, while through method two user had happy emotions for around 71.6% of the time, neutral emotion for around 21.2% of the time.

Table 3. Method comparison for user(c)

Emotions	Method 1	Method 2
Happy	68.1	72.1
Neutral	25.5	22.3
Fear	1.42	1.2
Angry	2.84	2.4
Surprise	0.5	0.5
Sad	1.4	1.2

Table 3 shows the comparison of the emotions of User (c) by both methods after watching a particular video at the same time. For User (c), according to method 1 user had happy emotions for around 68.1% of the time, and neutral emotions for around 25.5% of the time, while through method 2 user had happy emotions for around 72.1% of the time, neutral emotion for around 22.3% of the time.

Table 4. Method comparison for user (d)

Emotions	Method 1	Method 2
Happy	64.0	68.9
Neutral	26.6	24.6
Fear	2.6	0.2
Angry	4.8	4.4
Surprise	0.5	0.4
Sad	1.3	1.2

Table 4 shows the comparison of the emotions of User (d) by both methods after watching a particular video at the same time. For User (d), according to method 1 user had happy emotions for around 64.0% of the time, and neutral emotions for around 26.6% of the time, while through method 2 user had happy emotions for around 68.9% of the time, neutral emotion for around 24.6% of the time.

Table 5. Method comparison for user (e)

Emotions	Method 1	Method 2
Happy	67.1	71.7
Neutral	23.6	21.9
Fear	2.6	0.2
Angry	2.1	1.9
Surprise	0.5	0.4
Sad	3.9	3.6

Table 5 shows the comparison of the emotions of User (e) by both methods after watching a particular video at the same time. For User (e), according to method 1 user had happy emotions for around 67.1% of the time, and neutral emotions for around 23.6% of the time, while through method 2 user had happy emotions for around 71.7% of the time, neutral emotion for around 21.9% of the time.

Table 6. Method comparison for user (f)

Emotions	Method 1	Method 2
Happy	66.2	70.1
Neutral	23.2	22.9
Fear	1.1	0.0
Angry	4.1	1.8
Surprise	0.9	0.9
Sad	4.1	4.1

Table 6 shows the comparison of the emotions of User (f) by both methods after watching a particular video at the same time. For User (f), according to method 1 user had happy emotions for around 66.2% of the time, and neutral emotions for around 23.2% of the time, while through method 2 user had happy emotions for around 70.1% of the time, neutral emotion for around 22.9% of the time.

Table 7. Method comparison for user (g)

Emotions	Method 1	Method 2
Happy	62.50	66.04
Neutral	27.78	22.64
Fear	1.74	2.83
Angry	3.47	2.26
Surprise	1.74	1.7
Sad	2.78	4.53

Table 7 shows the comparison of the emotions of User (g) by both methods after watching a particular video at the same time. For User (g), according to method 1 user had happy emotions for around 62.50% of the time, and neutral emotions for around 27.78% of the time, while through method 2 user had happy emotions for around 66.04% of the time, neutral emotion for around 22.6% of the time.

Table 8. Method comparison for user (h)

Emotions	Method 1	Method 2
Happy	72.22	73.77
Neutral	18.52	19.67
Fear	2.78	0.82
Angry	1.85	1.97
Surprise	2.78	1.48
Sad	1.85	2.30

Table 8 compares the User's emotions (h) by both methods after watching a video simultaneously. For User (h), according to method 1 user had happy emotions for around 72.22% of the time, and neutral emotions for around 18.52% of the time, while through method 2 user had happy emotions for around 73.77% of the time, neutral emotion for around 19.67% of the time.

Table 9. Method comparison for user (i)

Emotions	Method 1	Method 2
Happy	68.29	70.42
Neutral	16.26	18.78
Fear	1.63	2.35
Angry	3.25	2.82
Surprise	6.50	2.35
Sad	4.07	3.29

Table 9 shows the comparison of the emotions of User (i) by both methods after watching a particular video at the same time. For User (i), according to method 1 user had happy emotions for around 68.29% of the time, and neutral emotions for around 16.26% of the time, while through method 2 user had happy emotions for around 70.42% of the time, neutral emotion for around 18.78% of the time.

So, from the above comparison, we can conclude that the user had a higher percentage of happy emotion from method two compared to method one, as the video shown to the users was a comedy video. Hence, the expected expression is happy, so method 2, i.e., Face Emotion Detection Using Facial Landmarks,s is a better method as it has comparatively better accuracy.

8. CONCLUSION

Smart classification using Computer Vision is a crucial part of today's world. Prediction and identification of facial expressions are efficiently done in the above-proposed method. The Haar cascade classifier model is trained to recognise specific features on a face, such as the eyes, nose, and mouth, and use this information to identify the presence of a face in an image. In the 68-point facial landmark detection algorithm, we identified specific points on the face and analyzed the shape and structure of the face, as well as measured changes in the position and orientation of the points over time. This will surely help recognise the facial expressions and sentiments of the person in various ways. So, we can see that from method 2, happiness was recognised most of the time, and as the video shown was a comedy video, the expected reaction is happiness. From the above discussion, we conclude that method 2, Face Emotion Detection Using Facial Landmarks, is better as it has comparatively better accuracy. The suggested model has a 71.53% classification accuracy.

REFERENCES

Arslan, F., Singh, B., Sharma, D. K., Regin, R., Steffi, R., & Rajest, S., S. (2021). Optimization technique approach to resolving food sustainability problems. *2021 International Conference on Computational Intelligence and Knowledge Economy (ICCIKE)*. IEEE.

Balasubramanian, P., Diwan, R., & Nadar, A. (2019). Analysis of Facial Emotion Recognition. In *3rd International Conference on Trends in Electronics and Informatics (ICOEI)* (pp. 945–949). IEEE.

Chakravarthi, K., & Venkatesan, N. (2015). Design and Implementation of Adaptive Model-Based Gain Scheduled Controller for a Real-Time Non-Linear System in LabVIEW. *Research Journal of Applied Sciences, Engineering and Technology, 10*(2), 188–196.

Chakravarthi, M., Vinay, P. K., & Venkatesan, N. (2015). Design and Simulation of Internal Model Controller for a Real Time Nonlinear Process. *Indian Journal of Science and Technology, 8*(19), 1–6. doi:10.17485/ijst/2017/v10i19/91682

Doss, R., Gupta, S., Chakravarthi, M. K., Channi, H. K., Koti, A. V., & Singh, P. (2022). Understand the application of efficient green cloud computing through the micro smart grid in order to power internet data centers. 2022 2nd International Conference on Advance Computing and Innovative Technologies in Engineering (ICACITE).

Ekman, P., & Friesen, W. (1978). *A technique for the measurement of facial movement.* Consulting Psychologists Press.

Gayakwad, M., Patil, S., Joshi, R., Gonge, S., & Pande, S. D. (2022). Credibility Evaluation of User-Generated Content Using Novel Multinomial Classification Technique. *International Journal on Recent and Innovation Trends in Computing and Communication, 10*(2s), 151–157. doi:10.17762/ijritcc.v10i2s.5922

Ivanovsky, L., Khryashchev, V., Lebedev, A., & Kosterin, I. (2017). Facial expression recognition algorithm based on deep convolutional neural network". In *21st Conference of Open Innovations Association*.

Jaiswal, A., & Raju, S. (2020). Facial Emotion Detection Using Deep Learning". In *2020 International Conference for Emerging Technology (INCET)* (pp. 1–5).

Kanade, T., Cohn, J., & Tian, Y. (2000). Comprehensive database for facial expression analysis". In *Proceedings Fourth IEEE International Conference on Automatic Face and Gesture Recognition.* 10.1109/AFGR.2000.840611

Kumar Patale, V., & Chakravarthi, M. K. (2014). RF Harvesting Circuitry for Ambient Backscatter Technology ". *International Journal of Applied Engineering Research: IJAER, 9*(19), 5769–5778.

Li, H., Sun, J., Xu, Z., & Chen, L. (2017). Multimodal 2D+3D Facial Expression Recognition With Deep Fusion Convolutional Neural Network. *IEEE Transactions on Multimedia, 19*(12), 2816–2831. doi:10.1109/TMM.2017.2713408

Li, J., & Oussalah, M. (2010). Automatic Face Emotion Recognition System. In *IEEE 9th International Conference on Cybernetic Intelligent Systems* (pp. 1–6). ieEE.

Lohit Ujjainiya, M., Chakravarthi, K., & Soni, A. (2014). Development and Implementation of Gesture Controlled Automatic Audio System. *International Journal of Computer Applications*, *106*(13), 25–28.

Nanda, N., & Prakash, V. (2023). Dumisani Lickson Namakhwa, Sandeep Dwarkanath Pande, Sk Hasane Ahammad, "A DenseNet CNN-based liver lesion prediction and classification for future medical diagnosis. *Scientific African*, 20.

Ogunmola, G. A., Singh, B., Sharma, D. K., Regin, R., Rajest, S. S., & Singh, N. (2021). Involvement of distance measure in assessing and resolving efficiency environmental obstacles. *2021 International Conference on Computational Intelligence and Knowledge Economy (ICCIKE)*. IEEE. 10.1109/IC-CIKE51210.2021.9410765

Pande, S., & Chetty, M. S. R. (2019). Bezier Curve Based Medicinal Leaf Classification using Capsule Network. *International Journal of Advanced Trends in Computer Science and Engineering*, *8*(6), 2735–2742. doi:10.30534/ijatcse/2019/09862019

Rajesh, K. M., & Naveenkumar, M. (2016). A Robust Method for Face Recognition and Face Emotion Detection System using Support Vector Machines". In *2016 International Conference on Electrical, Electronics, Communication, Computer and Optimization Techniques (ICEECCOT)* (pp. 1–5). 10.1109/ICEECCOT.2016.7955175

Rzayeva, Z., & Alasgarov, E. (2019). Facial Emotion Recognition using Convolutional Neural Networks". In 2019 IEEE 13th International Conference on Application of Information and Communication Technologies (AICT) (pp. 1–5).

Sharma, D. K., Jalil, N. A., Regin, R., Rajest, S. S., Tummala, R. K., & Thangadurai. (2021). Predicting network congestion with machine learning. 2021 2nd International Conference on Smart Electronics and Communication (ICOSEC). IEEE.

Shriram, K., Chakravarthi, M. K., Kumar, Y. V., Kumar, V. B., Pradeep, D. J., & Reddy, C. P. (2022). Acute Decisive Fuzzy Haptic Surface Response System for Tactile Sensitivity. In *2022 International Conference on Decision Aid Sciences and Applications (DASA)* (pp. 438–442). IEEE. 10.1109/DASA54658.2022.9765045

Silva, D., & Hui, S. C. (2003). Real-time Facial Feature Extraction and Emotion Recognition. *Fourth International Conference on Information, Communications and Signal Processing, 2003 and the Fourth Pacific Rim Conference on Multimedia.*

Soleymani, M., Asghari-Esfeden, S., Fu, Y., & Pantic, M. (2016). Analysis of EEG Signals and Facial Expressions for Continuous Emotion Detection. *IEEE Transactions on Affective Computing*, *7*(1), 17–28. doi:10.1109/TAFFC.2015.2436926

Soni, D., Gagrani, M., Rathore, A., & Chakravarthi, M. K. (2014). Study of Different Controller's Performance for a Real Time Non-Linear System. *International Journal of Advancements in Electronics and Electrical Engineering*, *3*(3), 10–14.

Suwa, M., Sugie, N., & Fujimora, K. (1978). A Preliminary Note on Pattern Recognition of Human Emotional Expression. In *Proc. Int'l Joint Conf. Pattern Recognition* (pp. 408–410). IEEE.

Uddin, M. Z., Khaksar, W., & Torresen, J. (2017). Facial Expression Recognition Using Salient Features and Convolutional Neural Network. *IEEE Access : Practical Innovations, Open Solutions, 5*, 26146–26161. doi:10.1109/ACCESS.2017.2777003

Xia, L. (2015). Facial Expression Recognition Based on SVM. In *7th International Conference on Intelligent Computation Technology and Automation*. IEEE.

Xiaoxi, M., Weisi, L., Dongyan, H., Minghui, D., & Li, H. (2017). Facial Emotion Recognition. In *IEEE 2nd International Conference on Signal and Image Processing* (pp. 77–81). IEEE.

Chapter 10
Software Defect Prediction Using Machine Learning Techniques

G. Cauvery
St. Joseph's College of Arts and Science for Women, India

Dhina Suresh
 https://orcid.org/0000-0001-7504-8955
St. Joseph's College of Arts and Science for Women, India

G. Aswini
 https://orcid.org/0000-0002-3082-1956
St. Joseph's College of Arts and Science for Women, India

P. Jayanthi
 https://orcid.org/0009-0006-8239-0904
St. Joseph's College of Arts and Science for Women, India

K. Kalaiselvi
St. Joseph's College of Arts and Science for Women, India

ABSTRACT

Software defect prediction gives development teams observable results while influencing business outcomes and development flaws. Developers can uncover flaws and plan test activities by anticipating problematic code sections. Early identification depends on the percentage of classifications that make the right prediction. Additionally, software-defective data sets are supported and partially acknowledged because of their vast size. The confusion, precision, recall, identification accuracy, etc., are assessed and compared with the existing schemes in a systematic research analysis. Previous research has employed the weak simulation tool for software analysis, but this study proposes building three machine learning models using linear regression, KNN classifier, and random forest (RF). According to the analytical investigation, the suggested approach will offer more beneficial options for predicting device failures. Moreover, software-defected data sets are supported and at least partially recognized due to their enormous dimension.

DOI: 10.4018/979-8-3693-1301-5.ch010

1. INTRODUCTION

Creating a software system nowadays requires careful planning, analysis, implementation, testing, integration, and maintenance (Viswakarma, et al., 2014). The task of a software Engineer is to design a system within a set deadline and budget, which is accomplished during the planning stage (Alajmi & Khan, 2013). We may encounter a few flaws during the development process, such as bad design, faulty logic, improper data processing, etc.; these flaws result in errors that force us to redo the job, driving up the cost of development and maintenance (Chitra, et al., 2018). All of these are to blame for the decline in consumer satisfaction (Garg, et al., 2017). According to this viewpoint, faults are categorized to their severity, and corrective and proactive measures are implemented following the severity determined (Chopra, et al., 2022). Humans have increasingly centered their attention on software-based systems over the past ten years, with software quality being seen as the most important factor in user functionality (Hung & Chakrabarti, 2022).

Subpar results for both commercial and personal apps can be attributed to a lack of software quality, despite the widespread development of application software (Jain, et al., 2023). Defect prediction designs are widely used in industries, and the models they produce help with tasks like fault prediction, effort estimation for software reliability testing, hazard analysis, and more (Jayalakshmi & Ramesh, 2020). A supervised machine-learning forecasting algorithm is fed the predefined training data set (Kayalvizhi & Ramesh, 2020). The algorithm then produces rules based on what it has learned from the training dataset in order to predict the class label for a new data set (Tiwari, et al., 2018). Mathematical approaches are utilised during the learning phases to develop and enhance the prediction function (Khan, 2016). This technique employs training data with a known attribute input value and known output value (Khan, 2021). The quality of the expected ML algorithm is compared to the widely known result (Oak, et al., 2019). Training data is used to perform this process over and over again until the highest possible prediction accuracy is reached or the maximum number of loops is reached (Prasad, et al., 2013).

In unsupervised learning methods, the actual value of the class label output is not known beforehand. Early on in the process, faulty systems, such individual units or entire classes, can be identified with the use of defect prediction modelling (Rajeyyagari, et al., 2022). This can be done by labelling the modules as either reliable or prone to errors. Different methods, including support vector classifiers (SVC), random forests, naive Bayes, decision trees (DT), and neural networks, are used to select the classification module (NN). The modules most prone to defects are given higher priority throughout the progress testing phases, whereas the modules least prone to defects are examined as resources permit (Sandeep, et al., 2022).

The classifier approach establishes and examines the feature of classification known as the relationship between the attributes and the training dataset class label through formulas for categorizing the targets. Future dataset class labels must be defined using those guidelines as well (Vanitha, et al., 2019). As a result, the unclassified datasets can be categorized using a classifier and classification patterns (Prasad & Chakrabarti, 2014). Due to the widespread use of software, defining software problems, locating the defect, and recognizing it requires researchers to perform repetitive tasks. The primary objective of separating the software dataset into a faulty and non-defective dataset is to use it as a model for bug prediction.

This strategy entails providing the Classifier with the input programme dataset only after the user has determined the correct class values (Shah, et al., 2020). Prior to this strategy, tremendous progress was made using requirement- and design-based metric approaches. However, developing algorithms and improving the accuracy of predictions remain difficult jobs (Kumar, et al., 2020). However, the results of the testing technique are affected by a number of factors, including limited resources (e.g., time or software testers). So, to maximise efficiency, we use pre-test methods like Software Defect Prediction (SDP). Before a system is deployed, SFP is used to identify any faulty software components (Sharma, et al., 2015).

Early detection of errors in software components like modules, classes, etc. considerably reduces the time and effort required to provide project outcomes to the end user. The literature documents a wide variety of SDP strategies. The major objective of these techniques is to predict infected parts of software by analysing the available datasets (Ramesh & Rao, 2015). Some examples of ML techniques that have been used as SDP strategies include K-Nearest Neighbors (KNN), Naive Bayes (NB), Linear Discriminant Analysis (LDA), Linear Regression (LR), Decision Tree (DT), Support Vector Machine (SVM), and Random Forest (RF). The Oversampling Approach and the Non-Oversampling Approach are two operational dimensions in the Last Decades framework (Sharma, et al., 2015). To investigate how class imbalance impacts classification performance, oversampling is built into the framework. Predicting the likelihood of a software module failing is a binary classification problem (Verma, et al., 2018).

Several researchers have been employing machine learning methods to address binary classification issues, including Sentiment Analysis, Rainfall Prediction, Network Intrusion Detection, and Software Defect Prediction (Patidar, et al., 2017). There are three groups of machine learning techniques: supervised, unsupervised, and hybrid. The input data is classified into known classifications using a supervised approach. These methods create classification rules using pre-classified data (training data) and then apply those rules to categorize previously unknown data (test data). Unsupervised techniques use certain algorithms to investigate the data structure when the classes are not known in advance.

The combination of supervised and unsupervised procedures is known as a hybrid methodology. Using the multi-filter feature selection technique and MLP, this research suggested a classification framework to identify the defect-prone software modules more accurately. The proposed framework operates using the oversampling method. To examine the impact of the class imbalance issue on classification accuracy, oversampling is introduced in one dimension. The framework is divided into four phases: Selection of the Datasets, Data Pre-processing, Classification, and result reflection.

2. RELATED WORKS

2.1 Integrated Approach to Software Defect Prediction

Businesses benefit from software defect prediction because it provides development teams with actionable insights. Both intra- and inter-project defect prediction in software have been the topic of empirical research. However, previous studies haven't revealed a way to predict how many problems will be present in a freshly released product. In this study, we show how defect acceleration can be used to demonstrate such a method and explore the relationship between defect density, defect velocity, and defect introduction time and the defect count (Singh, & Chakrabarti, 2013). Here, we detail the process of deploying an integrated regression model constructed from these predictor variables as part of a machine learning strategy (Felix & Lee, 2017). Ten separate data sets from the PROMISE repository were used in the experiment, for a total of 22838 instances. The final average defect velocity regression model had an adjusted R-square of 98.6 percent and a p-value of 0.001, which indicates statistical significance (Wang, et al., 2022). The average defect velocity and total number of defects are positively correlated at a very high level (0.98). Therefore, this approach can provide a roadmap for automated testing, which can boost software development productivity.

2.2 A Review of Software Defect Prediction Techniques Using Product Metrics

The complexity and volume of software systems are now growing quickly. While it occasionally enhances performance and produces effective results, it also frequently results in higher testing costs, meaningless results, and subpar quality, not to mention a lack of product reliability. Software fault prediction is essential for improving software quality and reducing software testing costs and duration. Software metrics can be used to traditionally define the complexity and determine the length of the programming, and detailed examination is conducted using software metrics to forecast the number of problems in the module to identify the factors that significantly improve the fault prediction models. This empirical research is based on product metrics. This paper examines numerous software metrics and suggests methods for improving software defect prediction. It also provides a summary of those methods.

2.3 A Novel Radial Basis Function Neural Network for Discriminant Analysis

In this study, an original neural network based on radial basis functions is introduced and used for discriminant analysis. While many other research has ignored the weight structure of radial basis function neural networks, this one uses the Bayesian technique to exploit it. A well-studied weight structure for a radial basis function neural network is expected to improve its performance. This research uses the Bayesian method to explore the often-mysterious weight structure of a radial basis function neural network. Both a single-Gaussian and a double-Gaussian weight structure are analysed in this research. A learning strategy based on expectation maximisation is used to estimate the weights. The simulation results showed that the optimum radial basis function neural network approach was one with a two-Gaussian weight structure.

2.4 Multiple Kernel Ensemble Learning for Software Defect Prediction

The goal of software defect prediction is to improve software quality by foreseeing the likelihood of defects in untested code. Due to its complicated structure and well-known class imbalance, software defect data has attracted significant research attention from both academia and industry in an effort to better understand and utilise the historical defect data presently available and develop more accurate and efficient classifiers. Machine learning techniques such as multiple (Wang et al., 2016) kernel and ensemble learning are effective. Ensemble learning can translate historical defect data to a higher-dimensional feature space and improve their expression by using numerous weak classifiers to reduce the bias created by the majority class. By capitalising on the features of the measurements retrieved from the open-source programme, we develop a multiple kernel classifier using the ensemble learning approach, which enjoys the advantages of both multiple kernel learning and ensemble learning. Therefore, we advocate a multiple kernel ensemble learning (MKEL) approach for classifying and foreseeing software flaws. With the goal of reducing the risk cost associated with mistakenly identifying damaged modules as non-defective, we create a new sample weight vector updating technique for software defect prediction. Experimental results show that MKEL outperforms a number of representative state-of-the-art defect prediction algorithms, and this is done by comparing their performance on the widely used NASAMDP datasets.

2.5 Software Defect Prediction Using Semi-Supervised Learning With Dimension Reduction

Accurate fault-prone module detection is the path to high-quality software solutions with low non-essential assurance expenses. Modules of software with verified bugs, developed under identical conditions, are required for this quality modelling. Determining the cost of a defective module might be difficult. To supplement model training with modules for which fault information is unavailable, semi-supervised learning makes use of a small collection of software modules with known fault content. The utility of semi-supervised learning in the detection of software bugs is investigated here. Multidimensional scaling is a pre-processing technique used to reduce the dimensional complexity of software metrics. Our findings show that semi-supervised learning with dimension reduction outperforms even one of the finest supervised learning algorithms, random forest, when just a small number of modules have known defect information for training.

2.6 Software Defect Prediction Techniques Using Metrics Based on Neural Network Classifier

By continuously monitoring for problems, fixing existing ones, and anticipating modules most likely to experience faults. Because of its impact on the software business, researchers have taken an interest in this area. The classification accuracy of current software fault prediction jobs is a major issue. To combat this issue, we present a unified approach to defect and bug prediction in software. The proposed method offers a notion for feature reduction and artificial intelligence, with PCA performing feature reduction and maximum-likelihood estimation enhancing the approach by reducing error in PCA data reconstruction. Finally, the results of the predictions are displayed using a neural network-based classification approach. The performance of four datasets (KC1, PC3, PC4, and JM1) is analysed using the MATLAB simulation tool as part of a methodology designed and implemented using the NASA software dataset. In-depth experimental research calculates three metrics—confusion, precision, recall, classification accuracy, etc.—and compares them to currently available software defect prediction techniques. The proposed method has been shown to perform better than existing methods in forecasting software bugs in an experimental study.

3. PROPOSED WORK

3.1 Data Gathering

To function, machine learning requires two things: models and plenty of data. To properly train your learning model, make sure that the data you collect has adequate features (aspects of data that can aid in a prediction, such as the home's surface to estimate its price). In general, having more data is better, so be sure to include enough rows. The bare bones of information gleaned on the web remain in the form of statements, figures, and qualitative words that have not been processed. The raw data contains errors, omissions, and inconsistencies. The completed surveys have revealed the need for adjustments. Secondary steps are required while processing primary data. It is difficult to make meaningful comparisons between individuals' responses without combining a massive amount of raw data collected from field surveys. Clean data sets can be created using a technique called "data pre-processing." In other words, each time data is gathered from unstructured sources, analysis is difficult. As a result, a few steps are taken to refine the information and make it usable. This procedure is followed by iterative analysis. The procedure is known as "data pre-processing" for short.

Inaccurate data (missing data) - There are several causes for missing data, including the fact that it is not continuously collected, an error in data entry, biometric technology issues, and many others.

The occurrence of noisy data (inaccurate data and outliers) - The causes of noisy data could include technological issues with the device that collects the data, human error during data entry, and many other things (Xu, et al., 2016).

Inconsistent data - Inconsistencies are caused by factors including duplicate data, human data entry, errors in codes or names, i.e., violating data constraints, and much more.

3.1.1. Implementation

As a result of this research, a smart model has been developed to classify Software Defects according to a specific Data structure and deal with them using the most effective machine-learning method. The reliability of the model was evaluated using a scientific approach. Machine learning is now being used to build our model.

3.2 Analysis

At this final stage, we put our classification model to the test on the ready dataset and assess how well it performs. We use accuracy as a measure of a classifier's efficacy and evaluate our own classification system against others.

After developing a model, it is essential to understand how well it performs as a predictor on a novel instance. After a predictive model has been built using previous data, it would be interesting to examine how it will fare when presented with data it hasn't seen before. In order to find the best model to use in a real-world decision-making scenario, one may even try out several model types for the same prediction problem. One way to achieve this is to evaluate the accuracy of the predictions made by each model (e.g., accuracy). The efficacy of a predictor can be measured by its accuracy, recall, and other commonly employed performance characteristics (Jayanthi & Florence, 2019).

We will begin by discussing the most widely used performance metrics, then we will compare and contrast some standard estimation techniques (Ryu & Baik, 2016). Predictive Modeling Performance Indicators The primary instrument for gauging success in classification tasks is a coincidence matrix, often known as a classification matrix or contingency table. In Figure 1, we see an example of a coincidence matrix for a problem with two classes. The most common metrics for which calculations can be made using the coincidence matrix are also shown in Figure 1.

Figure 1. Confusion matrix and formulae

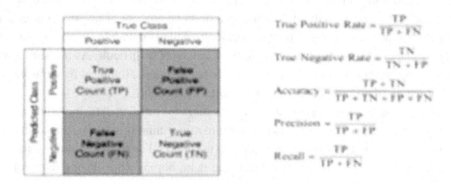

The erroneous choices are represented by the numbers to the left and right of the diagonal in the image above. To determine a classifier's true positive rate (also called hit rate or recall), just divide the number of correctly classified positives (the true positive count) by the total number of positives. The false positive rate of a Classifier can be calculated by dividing the number of false negatives by the total number of negatives (also known as a false alert rate). The overall accuracy of a classifier is found by dividing the sum of the true positives and true negatives by the total number of samples (Figure 2).

Figure 2. System design

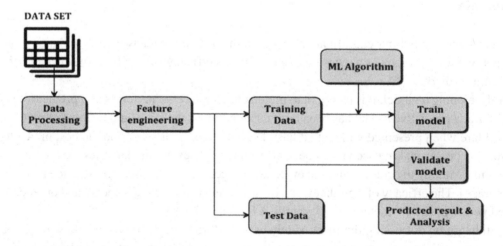

3.3 Algorithm

3.3.1 Linear Regression

A common statistical technique for simulating the relationship between a dependent variable and one or more independent variables is linear regression. It looks for the best-fitting line (or hyperplane) that best captures the linear relationship between the dependent and independent variables. The technique reduces the sum of the squared differences between the dependent variable's anticipated and actual values. OLS, a mathematical method that determines the parameters of the linear equation that best fits the data, is used to accomplish this. Both simple and numerous regression issues can be solved using linear regression, and it is frequently used in the social sciences, engineering, finance, and economics to make forecasts and examine the connections between the factors.

Additionally, it serves as the foundation for more complex regression methods like logistic regression and polynomial regression.

3.3.2 Random Forest Algorithm

Random Forest is a well-known machine learning algorithm that uses supervised learning techniques. It works for both classification and regression issues. It is based on ensemble learning, which combines numerous classifiers to address a complicated problem and improve the model's performance.

To put it simply, Random Forest is a classifier that uses many decision trees on different subsets of a given dataset and averages the results to improve the projected accuracy of that dataset (Shan, et al., 2014). The random forest gathers the results from each decision tree and bases its expectation of the eventual result on the majority votes of the projections, as opposed to relying solely on one decision tree (Figure 3).

Figure 3. Random forest algorithm

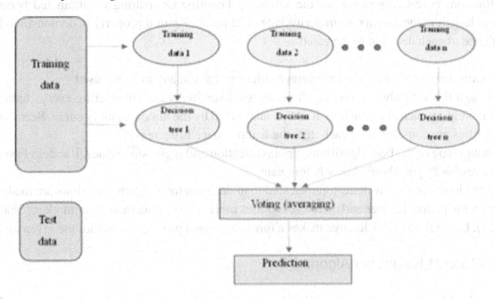

The algorithm known as the Random Forest works in a fairly methodical fashion. There are two phases to its implementation. In the first, decision trees are formed and combined to form the random forest; in the second, predictions are made for each tree.

The steps listed below can be used to show how the process works:

Step 1: Randomly select M data points from the training set.

Build decision trees for the data points you've selected in step two (Subsets).

Step 3: Each decision tree will produce a result. Examine it.

Step 4: The final results for classification and regression are based on majority voting or averaging, as appropriate.

We shall distinguish between Random Forests and Decision Trees using three crucial factors: overfitting, speed, and process.

Overfitting: - As random forests are built from subsets of data and the output is based on average or majority rating, overfitting is not present as it is in decision trees.

Speed: Compared to Decision Trees, the Random Forest Algorithm is comparatively slower. Data are gathered randomly, a decision tree is created, and the outcomes are averaged. As opposed to decision trees, it does not rely on any formulas.

3.3.3. Important Characteristics of the Random Forest Algorithm

Diversity: As each tree is distinct, not all characteristics, factors, or traits are considered when constructing a particular tree. Unaffected by the dimensionality constraint. Because no tree considers every feature, the feature space is decreased.

Parallelization: Each tree is created from scratch using various data and attributes. This means we can construct random forests while using the CPU. There is no need to partition the data into train and test groups in a random forest because the decision tree will always miss 30% of the data.

Stability: The outcome is stable based on majority voting/averaging.

The Random Forest Algorithm has the following benefits: Overfitting is eliminated because the outcome is based on the average or majority vote. The parallelization property is demonstrated by the independence of each decision tree created.

- It is extremely stable because the average solutions from many trees are used.
- Although this isn't always the case, it preserves diversity by not considering every characteristic when building each decision tree. It is also unaffected by the dimensionality curse. Because not all properties are considered by each tree, the feature space is decreased.
- Although one of the best algorithms for classification and regression issues, Random Forest has a few drawbacks you should know before using it.
- The random forest is far more sophisticated than decision trees, where decisions are made by following the path of the tree and therefore requires more time to train than other models (Shan, et al., 2014). Every time a decision tree makes a forecast, it must produce output for the given input data.

3.3.4. K-Nearest Neighbour Algorithm

K-Nearest Neighbor is a supervised learning-based machine learning algorithm that is among the simplest of its kind. The K-NN algorithm makes the assumption that the new case is similar to the existing cases and assigns it to the category that is most similar to the existing categories. After storing all of the previous data, the K-NN algorithm classifies a new data point based on similarity. As a result, the K- NN approach is a fast and reliable tool for classifying newly collected data.

Despite its popularity when applied to classification problems, the K-NN technique can also be used for regression. K-NN is a non-parametric method, hence it does not presuppose anything about the data. In contrast to more conventional learning algorithms, this one stores the training dataset for later use.

Instead, it relies on the dataset itself to make classification decisions. When new data is received, the KNN approach simply refers back to the information it stored during the training phase and assigns it to a category that is very comparable to the new data (Han, et al., 2013).

Example: Imagine we have a photo of an animal that seems like a cross between a cat and a dog, but we can't be sure. However, the KNN method can be used for this identification because it is founded on a similarity metric. Our KNN model will find the commonalities in the new information.

3.3.5. How Does K-NN Function?

The K-NN can be explained with the help of the following algorithm:

- Choosing the K-numbers of the neighbours is the first step.
- The second step is to calculate the Euclidean distance between each pair of K neighbours.
- Step 3: Pick the K nearest neighbours using the Euclidean distance.
- The fourth step is to tally up the instances of each type of data among these k neighbours.
- Assign the new data points to the group with the most neighbours in Step 5.
- Sixth, our model is finished.

Implementation: In this study, we developed a smart model to classify Software Defects according to a specific Data structure and deal with them by employing a suitable machine-learning method. The reliability of the model was evaluated using a scientific approach. Machine learning is now being used to build our model.

Analysis: At this final stage, we put our classification model to the test on the ready dataset and assess how well it performs. We use accuracy to quantify classifier efficiency and evaluate our generated classification to state-of-the-art approaches.

It is essential to understand the model's ability to forecast a new instance after it has been developed. After a predictive model has been built using previous data, it would be interesting to examine how it will fare when presented with data it hasn't seen before. Even for the same prediction problem, one can try out many model types to find the best one to use in a practical decision-making setting. This may be done by comparing the models' performance in terms of predictions (e.g., accuracy). Accuracy, recall, and other regularly used performance indicators assess a predictor's effectiveness.

4. EXPERIMENTAL RESULT

The training dataset can be used to estimate every term in the nominator. Because it is presumed that p (x|y = c) has a Gaussian distribution, it is known as a "Gaussian" classifier. Moreover, it is called a "Mixture of Gaussian" and "Discriminant" classifier. Depending on whether class covariance matrices are used, the Gaussian Classifier has two different versions. Random resampling provides a naive technique for rebalancing the class distribution for an imbalanced dataset. Random oversampling duplicates examples from the minority class in the training dataset and can result in overfitting for some models. Randomly duplicate examples in the minority class (figures 4 and 5).

Figure 4. Data collection and classification

LOC_BLAN	BRANCH_C	LOC_CODE	LOC_COM	CYCLOMA	DESIGN_C	ESSENTIAL	LOC_EXEC	HALSTEAD	HALSTEAD	HALSTEAD	HALSTEAD	HALSTEAD	HALSTEAD	HALSTEAD	HALSTEAD	NUM_OPE	NUM_OPE	NUM_UN	NUM_UNI	LOC_TOTA	label
447	826	12	157	470	585	113	2824	210.28	384.45	3.1E+07	26.95	8441	0	1726655	80843.1	3021	5420	809	155	3442	Y
0	311	0	0	128	104	14	0	0	0	0	0	0	0	0	0	0	0	0	0	1129	Y
164	485	10	58	268	219	39	1588	202.98	713.53	9254820	14.45	4828	0	514157	43342.5	1730	3172	407	102	1824	Y
37	29	8	42	19	19	6	133	108.14	46.32	232044	1.67	685	0.02	128913	5009.32	295	390	121	38	222	Y
11	405	0	17	404	2	1	814	101.2	206.01	4294926	6.95	2035	0	238607	20848.5	813	1220	811	411	844	Y
106	240	7	144	127	105	33	952	218.17	215.17	1E+07	15.65	5669	0	361159	46943.7	2301	3368	262	49	1411	Y
101	464	11	75	263	256	140	1339	106.5	337.36	1.2E+07	11.98	4308	0	673378	35928.1	1556	2752	226	98	1532	Y
67	187	4	1	94	63	27	391	233.07	58.04	785182	4.51	1780	0.02	436212	13527.8	718	1062	167	27	466	Y
105	344	9	40	207	171	58	1124	122.6	269.46	8901671	11.01	3848	0	494537	33034.9	1432	2416	279	105	1280	Y
0	83	0	42	16	27	0	0	0	0	0	0	0	0	0	0	0	0	0	0	186	Y
18	47	0	10	24	13	1	75	87.74	30.06	79302.3	0.38	438	0.08	4405.68	2637.8	157	281	47	18	107	Y
143	67	7	49	34	25	1	589	569.78	49.5	1385090	9.36	5281	0.02	769494	28092.7	1522	1759	955	23	790	Y
202	503	3	78	286	197	82	1599	293.29	188.01	1E+07	18.38	5592	0.01	575945	55140.8	2243	3149	1026	172	1882	Y
56	175	4	32	104	86	46	559	106.36	133.52	1896162	4.73	1822	0.01	105342	14201.4	645	1177	157	65	657	Y
12	147	6	7	82	40	21	295	83.89	195	3189756	5.45	2115	0.01	177209	16353.7	680	1458	136	78	322	Y
23	39	2	9	20	8	6	91	72.83	27.61	58527.1	0.67	327	0.04	3084.85	2010.97	123	204	49	22	128	Y
53	338	17	30	175	65	90	622	201.58	112.1	2535263	7.53	2869	0.01	140737	22597.7	1093	1776	195	40	725	Y
83	65	14	11	33	17	19	244	174.35	47.68	396299	2.77	1180	0.02	220168	8312.38	504	676	111	21	334	Y
102	86	13	120	25	24	1	384	149.63	106.91	1710254	5.33	2049	0.01	95014.1	15997.3	784	1265	176	48	621	Y
11	21	6	12	11	10	5	51	55.41	26.96	402716	0.5	255	0.04	2237.31	1493.79	95	160	37	21	82	Y
5	3	0	0	2	2	1	16	29.06	13	49118	0.13	77	0.08	272.88	377.83	26	51	15	15	23	Y
28	45	0	31	23	15	10	184	233.12	27.43	175382	2.13	843	0.04	9743.43	6394.12	384	459	168	24	243	Y
17	17	0	9	9	6	4	78	79.42	28.09	626669	0.74	349	0.04	3481.49	2230.92	149	200	61	23	106	Y
88	53	0	51	27	15	17	329	258.56	46.27	553655	3.99	1579	0.02	307586	11964.8	676	908	168	23	470	Y
61	7	1	5	4	3	1	221	182.59	50	456477	3.04	1294	0.02	253598	9129.54	565	729	113	20	288	Y
10	39	0	4	20	15	16	76	88.31	25.69	582741	0.76	362	0.04	3237.45	2268.58	137	225	56	21	93	Y

Figure 5. Class size after oversampling

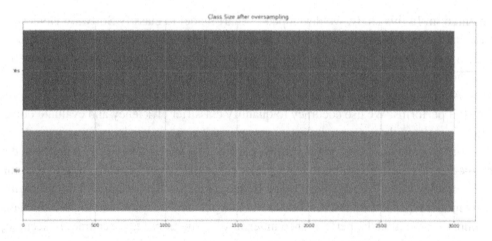

4.1. Class Size Comparison

A model learns how to best map instances of input data to specified class labels by analysing the data in a training dataset. The problem should be well-represented in the training dataset, and there should be plenty of examples for each class label. Modeling classification predictive modelling problems can be done using any number of classification algorithms. Algorithms for predictive modelling in classification are ranked according to their performance. One common way to measure a model's efficacy is by comparing the actual class labels to the ones it predicts (Figure 6).

Figure 6. Class size comparison

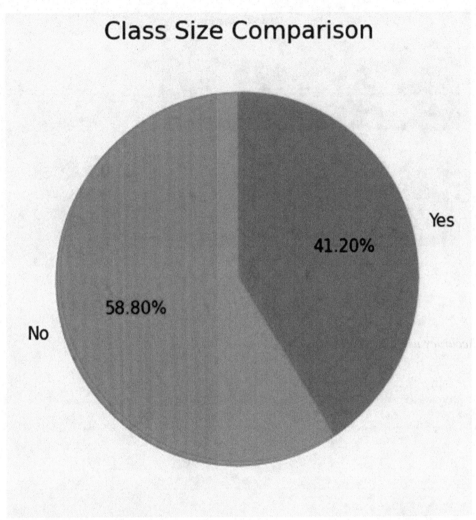

4.2. Accuracy Using Random Forest and K-NN Algorithm

Finding the accuracy by comparing Random Forest and K-NN Classifier. There have been a number of attempts to determine the most effective classification method for land use/cover research by comparing the results of several classifiers. However, they come to very different conclusions. Random Forest Algorithm produces more accuracy than K-NN Algorithm (Figures 7 to 9).

Figure 7. Accuracy using random forest

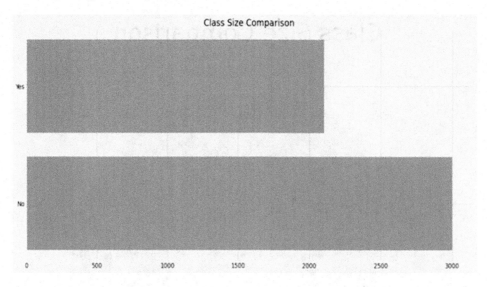

Figure 8. Accuracy using K-NN classifier

```
RF_accuracy = accuracy_score(y_true=y_test, y_pred= RF_predictions)
print("Overall accuracy of RandomForestClassifier model using test-set is {:.2f}%" .format(RF_accuracy*
```

Overall accuracy of RandomForestClassifier model using test-set is 98.00%

```
print(classification_report(y_true=y_test, y_pred=RF_predictions,target_names=class_labels))
```

	precision	recall	f1-score	support
No	0.97	0.98	0.98	590
Yes	0.99	0.98	0.98	610
accuracy			0.98	1200
macro avg	0.98	0.98	0.98	1200
weighted avg	0.98	0.98	0.98	1200

Figure 9. Accuracy comparison

```
KNC_accuracy = accuracy_score(y_true=y_test, y_pred= KNC_predictions)
print("Overall accuracy of KNeighborsClassifier model using test-set is {:.2f}%" .format(KNC_accuracy*1
```

Overall accuracy of KNeighborsClassifier model using test-set is 92.83%

```
print(classification_report(y_true=y_test,y_pred=KNC_predictions,target_names=class_labels))
```

	precision	recall	f1-score	support
No	0.88	0.99	0.93	590
Yes	0.99	0.87	0.93	610
accuracy			0.93	1200
macro avg	0.93	0.93	0.93	1200
weighted avg	0.93	0.93	0.93	1200

5. CONCLUSION

The primary objective of this study is to use data mining methods to foresee software failures. Research in this area has also grown in prominence, with a variety of strategies being explored to better detect and prevent vulnerabilities in software. Accuracy issues in large-scale classification were addressed via feature reductions and subsequent classification. The neural network classification technique is used to find bugs in software. The study's findings support the usefulness of the proposed approach. There is no noticeable difference in classifier accuracy whether or not there is an approach for selecting features, and whenever the strategies for selecting features are applied. There is a discrepancy between the Classifier's accuracy when there is no set of characteristics and when the techniques for selecting the function are used. As a result, it is seen that applying feature selection strategies reduces the time and space difficulties for defect prediction without lowering prediction accuracy. The usage of many datasets can enhance these conclusions. The results may be improved by using more datasets. It is also feasible to contrast additional methodologies. The most typical and extensively applied techniques were considered in this study. Additional techniques are anticipated to be demonstrated and employed in the in-depth examination.

REFERENCES

Alajmi, M., & Khan, S. (2013). *Mobile Community Networks Information Investigation for Additional Significance.*

Chitra, S., Kumaratharan, N., & Ramesh, S. (2018). Enhanced brain image retrieval using carrier frequency offset compensated orthogonal frequency division multiplexing for telemedicine applications. *International Journal of Imaging Systems and Technology, 28*(3), 186–195. doi:10.1002/ima.22269

Chopra, P., Junath, N., Singh, S. K., Khan, S., Sugumar, R., & Bhowmick, M. (2022). Cyclic GAN model to classify breast cancer data for pathological healthcare task. *BioMed Research International, 6336700,* 1–12. doi:10.1155/2022/6336700 PMID:35909482

Felix, E. A., & Lee, S. P. (2017). Integrated approach to software defect prediction. *IEEE Access : Practical Innovations, Open Solutions, 5,* 21524–21547. doi:10.1109/ACCESS.2017.2759180

Garg, A., Ghosh, A., & Chakrabarti, P. (2017). Gain and bandwidth modification of microstrip patch antenna using DGS. In *Proc. International Conference on Innovations in Control, Communication and Information Systems (ICICCI-2017)*. India.

Han, K., Cao, J.-H., Chen, S.-H., & Liu, W.-W. (2013). A software reliability prediction method based on software development process. *2013 International Conference on Quality, Reliability, Risk, Maintenance, and Safety Engineering (QR2MSE)*. IEEE.

Hung, B. T., & Chakrabarti, P. (2022). Parking lot occupancy detection using hybrid deep learning CNN-LSTM approach. In *Algorithms for Intelligent Systems* (pp. 501–509). Springer Nature Singapore.

Jain, V., Al Ayub Ahmed, A., Chaudhary, V., Saxena, D., Subramanian, M., & Mohiddin, M. K. (2023). Role of data mining in detecting theft and making effective impact on performance management. In *Smart Innovation, Systems and Technologies* (pp. 425–433). Springer Nature Singapore.

Jayalakshmi, J., & Ramesh, S. (2020). Compact fractal wearable antenna for wireless body area communications. *Telecommunications and Radio Engineering*, *79*(1), 71–80. doi:10.1615/TelecomRadEng.v79.i1.70

Jayanthi, R., & Florence, L. (2019). Software defect prediction techniques using metrics based on neural network classifiers. *Cluster Computing*, *22*(1), 77–88. doi:10.100710586-018-1730-1

Kayalvizhi, K., & Ramesh, S. (2020). Design and Analysis of Reactive Load Dipole Antenna using Genetic Algorithm Optimization. *Applied Computational Electromagnetics Society Journal*, *35*(3), 279–287.

Khan, S. (2016). How Data Mining Can Help Curb City Crime. [IJCTA]. *International Journal of Control Theory and Applications*, *9*(23), 483–488.

Khan, S. (2021). Data visualization to explore the countries dataset for pattern creation. [IJOE]. *International Journal of Online and Biomedical Engineering*, *17*(13), 4–19. doi:10.3991/ijoe.v17i13.20167

Kumar, P., Hati, A. S., Padmanaban, S., Leonowicz, Z., & Chakrabarti, P. (2020). Amalgamation of transfer learning and deep convolutional neural network for multiple fault detection in SCIM. *2020 IEEE International Conference on Environment and Electrical Engineering and 2020 IEEE Industrial and Commercial Power Systems Europe (EEEIC / I&CPS Europe)*. IEEE.

Oak, R., Du, M., Yan, D., Takawale, H., & Amit, I. (2019). Malware detection on highly imbalanced data through sequence modeling. *Proceedings of the 12th ACM Workshop on Artificial Intelligence and Security*. New York, NY, USA: ACM. 10.1145/3338501.3357374

Patidar, H., Chakrabarti, P., & Ghosh, A. (2017). Parallel Computing Aspects in Improved Edge Cover based Graph Coloring Algorithm. *Indian Journal of Science and Technology*, *10*(25), 1–9. doi:10.17485/ijst/2017/v10i25/115117

Prasad, A., & Chakrabarti, P. (2014). Extending Access Management to maintain audit logs in cloud computing. *International Journal of Advanced Computer Science and Applications*, *5*(3). doi:10.14569/IJACSA.2014.050320

Prasad, A., Gupta, D., & Chakrabarti, P. (2013). *Monitoring Users in Cloud Computing : Evaluating the Centralized Approach*. In 2nd International Conference on Advanced Computing, Networking and Security (ADCONS), India.

Rajeyyagari, S., Hung, B. T., & Chakrabarti, P. (2022). Applications of artificial intelligence in biomedical image processing. *2022 Second International Conference on Artificial Intelligence and Smart Energy (ICAIS)*. IEEE. 10.1109/ICAIS53314.2022.9742773

Ramesh, S., & Rao, T. R. (2015). High gain dielectric loaded exponentially tapered slot antenna array based on substrate integrated waveguide for V-band wireless communications. [International Journal of Electronics and Communications]. *AEÜ. International Journal of Electronics and Communications*, *69*(1), 48–55. doi:10.1016/j.aeue.2014.07.014

Ryu, D., & Baik, J. (2016). Effective multi-objective naïve Bayes learning for cross-project defect prediction. *Applied Soft Computing*, *49*, 1062–1077. doi:10.1016/j.asoc.2016.04.009

Sandeep, S. R., Ahamad, S., Saxena, D., Srivastava, K., Jaiswal, S., & Bora, A. (2022). To understand the relationship between Machine learning and Artificial intelligence in large and diversified business organisations. *Materials Today: Proceedings*, *56*, 2082–2086. doi:10.1016/j.matpr.2021.11.409

Shah, K., Laxkar, P., & Chakrabarti, P. (2020). A hypothesis on ideal Artificial Intelligence and associated wrong implications. *Advances in Intelligent Systems and Computing*, *989*, 283–294. doi:10.1007/978-981-13-8618-3_30

Shan, C., Chen, B., Hu, C., Xue, J., & Li, N. (2014). *Software defect prediction model based on LLE and SVM. 2014 Communications Security Conference (CSC 2014)*. Institution of Engineering and Technology.

Sharma, A. K., Panwar, A., Chakrabarti, P., & Vishwakarma, S. (2015). Categorization of ICMR using feature extraction strategy and MIR with ensemble learning. *Procedia Computer Science*, *57*, 686–694. doi:10.1016/j.procs.2015.07.448

Sharma, A. K., Panwar, A., Chakrabarti, P., & Viswakarma, S. (2015). Categorization of ICMR Using Feature Extraction Strategy and MIR with Ensemble Learning. *Procedia Computer Science*, *57*, 686–694. doi:10.1016/j.procs.2015.07.448

Singh, A., & Chakrabarti, P. (2013). Ant based resource discovery and mobility aware trust management for Mobile Grid systems. *2013 3rd IEEE International Advance Computing Conference (IACC)*. IEEE.

Tiwari, M., Chakrabarti, P., & Chakrabarti, T. (2018). Novel work of diagnosis in liver cancer using Tree classifier on liver cancer dataset (BUPA liver disorder). *Communications in Computer and Information Science*, *837*, 155–160. doi:10.1007/978-981-13-1936-5_18

Vanitha, M., Ramesh, S., & Chitra, S. (2019). Wearable antennas for remote health care monitoring system using 5g wireless technologies. *Telecommunications and Radio Engineering*, *78*(14), 1275–1285. doi:10.1615/TelecomRadEng.v78.i14.50

Verma, K., Srivastava, P., & Chakrabarti, P. (2018). Exploring structure oriented feature tag weighting algorithm for web documents identification. *Communications in Computer and Information Science*, *837*, 169–180. doi:10.1007/978-981-13-1936-5_20

Viswakarma, S., Chakrabarti, P., Bhatnagar, D., & Sharma, A. K. (2014). *Phrase Term Static Index Pruning Based on the Term Cohesiveness*. In International Conference on Computational Intelligence and Communication Networks (CICN), India.

Wang, T., Zhang, Z., Jing, X., & Zhang, L. (2016). Multiple kernel ensemble learning for software defect prediction. *Automated Software Engineering*, *23*(4), 569–590. doi:10.100710515-015-0179-1

Wang, X., Huang, T., & Chakrabarti, P. (2022). Adaptive RBF neural network control for nonlinear system. In *Complex Systems: Spanning Control and Computational Cybernetics: Foundations* (pp. 435–455). Springer International Publishing. doi:10.1007/978-3-030-99776-2_22

Xu, Z., Xuan, J., Liu, J., & Cui, X. (2016). MICHAC: Defect prediction via feature selection based on maximal information coefficient with hierarchical agglomerative clustering. *2016 IEEE 23rd International Conference on Software Analysis, Evolution, and Reengineering (SANER)*. IEEE.

Chapter 11
Vision–Based Data–Driven Modeling Vehicle Detection in Videos Using Convolutional Neural Network

R. Regin

SRM Institute of Science and Technology, Ramapuram, India

Sriraam Ramesh

SRM Institute of Science and Technology, Ramapuram, India

Athiyan Ramesh Kumar

SRM Institute of Science and Technology, Ramapuram, India

Praghalad Krishna Gandhi

SRM Institute of Science and Technology, Ramapuram, India

Rubin Bose S

SRM Institute of Science and Technology, Ramapuram, India

ABSTRACT

Object detection is a vital component for autonomous driving, and autonomous cars rely on perception of their surroundings to ensure safe and robust driving performance. It shows how the perception system makes use of object identification algorithms to precisely identify nearby items like pedestrians, cars, traffic signs, and barriers. It goes on to say that detecting and localising these things in real-time depends greatly on deep learning-based object detectors. The most recent object detectors and unresolved issues with their integration into autonomous vehicles are also covered in the essay. It mentions that deep learning visual classification methods have achieved enormous accuracy in classifying visual scenes; it makes use of the convolutional neural network. However, it points out that the visual classifiers face difficulties examining the scenes in dark visible areas, especially during the nighttime, and in identifying the contexts of the scenes.

DOI: 10.4018/979-8-3693-1301-5.ch011

1. INTRODUCTION

Modern civilization now considers traffic monitoring to be essential, and using cameras and computers to accomplish this aim is becoming more and more common. However, in the modern era of advanced technology, manual video analysis is not only time-consuming but also impractical (Khalifa, et al., 2014). In order to create intelligent traffic monitoring and management systems that conserve resources and need the least amount of human interaction, computer-based image processing technology has been created (Mohamed, & Mesbah, 2016). These systems can provide sophisticated and workable monitoring programmes by analysing video pictures, detecting and identifying vehicles, and taking necessary action in the event of unexpected circumstances (Sadek, et al., 2021).

The supervisory department now uses computer connection monitoring methods to accomplish the aim of intelligent traffic monitoring and management (Abbassy, et al., 2020). These systems analyse video from cameras, identify cars, and do standard management activities automatically using computer and image processing technologies. They can also spot anomalous circumstances and respond to them in the best, most secure way possible (Derindere Köseoğlu, et al., 2022). This approach is appealing to academic and corporate circles throughout the world since it saves a sizable amount of labour and material resources. The vehicle that uses vision. The main approaches for object detection include classic machine vision techniques and sophisticated deep learning techniques (Ead & Abbassy, 2018). The former, which may be categorised into three different approaches the technique of backdrop subtraction, the method of continuous video frame difference, and the method of optical flow uses a vehicle's motion to distinguish it from a stationary background picture (Jain, et al., 2022). The moving foreground region is divided by the threshold using the video frame difference approach, which computes the variance based on the pixel values of two or three successive video frames (Arslan, et al., 2021). This technique may also detect the car halting by muzzling sounds (Bhoumik, et al., 2020).

When the video's background image is fixed, background data is used to create a background model, which is then compared to each frame's image to identify moving objects (Gao, et al., 2018). Through the generated optical flow field, the optical flow method can identify the motion region in the video and represent the direction and speed of each moving pixel (Mahesha, et al., 2022). Another way for detecting automobiles is by the use of vehicle characteristics in machine vision, with the widely used Scale Invariant Feature Transform (SIFT) and Speeded Up Robust characteristics (SURF) approaches (Benloucif, et al., 2019). In order to fulfil vehicle recognition and classification tasks, 3D models have also been used (Ogunmola, et al., 2021). Vehicles may be categorised using the correlation curves of 3D ridges on their exterior. In today's culture, keeping an eye on traffic situations has become essential, and using cameras and computers to do so is growing in popularity. Intelligent traffic monitoring and management systems can now analyse video data, recognise and identify cars, and take necessary action in case of abnormal situations, all without the need for human interaction to advancements in computer-based image processing technology (Zannah, et al., 2023). Along with vehicle features like SIFT and SURF, machine vision techniques like background subtraction, continuous video frame difference, and optical flow are frequently used to detect vehicles. Using 3D models can also help with vehicle identification and categorization (Sharma, et al., 2021). These technology developments in traffic monitoring and management have significant academic and economic value, making them desirable choices (Joseph, 2019). Without making a conscious effort, the Human Vision System (HVS) excels in differentiating between various objects (Cirillo, et al., 2023). Recent advances in computer vision (CV) and machine learning (ML) have made it possible for computers to accurately detect, identify, and categorise objects in photos and videos. Effective vehicle detection and categorization are essential for monitoring or observing traffic (Deepa, et al., 2022). Utilising recent developments in CV and ML technologies, including large datasets, faster GPUs, and improved algorithms, our project aims to create an effective system for locating vehicles in images and videos (Figure 1).

Figure 1. Vehicle detection using CNN
(Erickson, 2020)

Figure 2. Vehicle classification is highway scenarios
(Rs, 2018)

Monitoring video scenes for intelligent traffic management and control on highways significantly rely on vehicle recognition and statistics (Figure 2). An enormous amount of traffic video material is now accessible for examination as a result of the growing installation of traffic surveillance cameras (Joe, et al., 2011). However, a high viewing angle makes the road surface appear further away and drastically alters the size of the vehicles in the scene, making it challenging to precisely detect small objects far from the road. Furthermore, challenging camera angles make the issue worse (Joseph, 2020). Therefore, it is crucial to effectively address these issues and implement them in order to get better outcomes. The accuracy of vehicle recognition and categorization in highway monitoring may be considerably increased with effective solutions to these problems (Pattana-anake, et al., 2021).

Computer vision is one of the most fascinating sectors of technology to have undergone a deep learning revolution (Saxena & Chaudhary, 2023). Computer vision has become a crucial part of contemporary technology, used in everything from biometrics and face recognition to self-driving automobiles (Joseph & Auwatanamongkol, 2016). Image processing, which entails transforming an image into a digital format and applying operations on it to extract valuable information, is the foundation of computer vision. Based on the number of pixels, images are represented by their dimensions (height and breadth). Each pixel is a spot on the picture that assumes a certain hue, level of transparency, or colour (Reddy, et al., 2022a,b). Different representations of pixels exist, including grayscale, RGB, and RGBA. Each pixel in an image must go through a predetermined set of processes, and any pixel in the image can be used to calculate the output value of those operations (Figure 3).

Figure 3. Basic working of CNN in vehicle detection

Analogue and digital approaches are the two categories of image processing techniques. For physical copies like printouts and images, analogue image processing is performed, and image analysts employ a variety of interpreting principles. On the other hand, digital image processing techniques allow for the manipulation of digital photographs using computers. The three primary stages of digital image processing are pre-processing, augmentation, and display, along with information extraction. Computer vision, which is widely applied in many facets of contemporary technology, is fundamentally dependent on image processing. Image processing is crucial for obtaining valuable information from digital photos, whether it be for self-driving cars or facial identification

2. LITERATURE SURVEY

One of the key instruments for exploring submerged resources and conducting various underwater operations is the human-occupied vehicle (HOV), which may also operate as a base for divers performing underwater tasks. The research of HOV is so critical. To address the drive saturation (thrust overrun) problem of tracking control, one of the main research directions, a novel hybrid control strategy based on quantum-behaved particle swarm optimization-model predictive control (QPSO-MPC) and adaptive sliding mode control (ASMC) is proposed for Jiaolong HOV. The hybrid control scheme consists of a kinematic controller based on QPSOMPC and a dynamic controller based on ASMC (Abdelgawad, et al., 2020). The position inaccuracy is converted into the fictitious required speed by the kinematic controller. The dynamic controller's input is then the difference between the target speed and the actual speed. The 4 DOF thrusts are produced by the design of the S sliding manifold and dynamic control law. According to Jiaolong HOV's thruster arrangement, the thrusts are divided across eight thrusters. To enable HOV to follow and arrive at the predetermined reference trajectory. This hybrid control approach is novel in that it considers the HOV's restricted speed (Bai, et al., 2019). The kinematic controller's optimisation phase includes the addition of speed and speed increment limitations. The QPSO-MPC team has created a straightforward trajectory generator with obstacle avoidance behaviours. The proposed technique can deal with the speed jump phenomena and the drive saturation (thrust overrun) produced by surpassed speed fluctuation when compared to back-stepping control and bioinspired back-stepping control. According to the simulation findings, when the physical restrictions (speed and thrust constraints) are satisfied, the hybrid technique is capable of achieving steady and precise tracking control. Additionally, the capability of the trajectory generator to plan a trajectory with obstacle avoidance behaviour has been confirmed (Huang, et al., 2019).

An Integrated Radar and Vehicle-to-Vehicle Communication System for Longitudinal and Lateral Vehicle Following: To enable autonomous vehicle following in both the longitudinal and lateral directions, a control framework based on the on-board radar sensor and vehicle-to-vehicle (V2V) communication was developed. A linear feedforward and feedback controller bound by string stability is first constructed to track the speed of the leading vehicle and give a safe inter-vehicle distance. A route estimate approach is then given to establish the prior vehicle's trajectory based on the previous movement data delivered over V2V. The front wheel's steering angle is regulated using the model predictive control technique. Additionally, simulations and tests conducted under a variety of driving circumstances validate the robustness and adaptability of the proposed method. According to the findings, the suggested technique is capable of reliably realizing longitudinal and lateral vehicle following using just radar and V2V, independent of a high-accuracy positioning system and road markings, and it has promise for expanding the range of autonomous vehicle platooning applications. The integrated longitudinal and lateral vehicle following scenarios that are proposed in this research uses millimeter wave radar as the control framework and V2V communication (Liu et al., 2019). In order to provide quick and smooth velocity tracking and string stability, a linear longitudinal controller is designed using the acceleration of the vehicle in front of it, the distance between vehicles, and the velocity difference. It is suggested to use a path estimate algorithm to determine the driving route of the vehicle ahead based on its previous movements. The lateral vehicle dynamics are represented using a nonlinear bicycle model (Lin, et al., 2019).

This study uses CCV in ground vehicles to enhance performance and layout adaptability. An XBW UGV is provided as an example to show how CCV is advantageous. The discussion of the positioning of heavy components indicates a 220% increase in the C.G. configuration's flexibility. Some important conclusions are drawn to explain the relationship between mechanical and control system design under CCV. The CCV uses the yaw moment electric control system to increase vehicle stability. The XBW UGV is then used to evaluate the yaw controller. The yaw control system can enhance the vehicle's handling stability and transient handling performance, as shown by the results of tests employing step steer and sine steer inputs (Li, et al., 2020). We'll focus on constructing reliable controllers while taking longitudinal dynamics into account in our next work. In this study, the control configured vehicle (CCV) approach is used for an X-by-wire (XBW) electric vehicle to increase the structure layout flexibility and performance. The CCV significantly increases the flexibility of the structure layout of the XBW ground vehicle by incorporating the design of the electric control system along with the design of the mechanical component for the final layout. According to the CCV concept, the integrated yaw control system enhances the closed-loop stability of the vehicle lateral dynamics system. This research employs a robust pole assignment yaw controller that takes parametric uncertainties into account (Liu, et al., 2020).

Using an analytical state-constrained optimal solution, connected and automated electric vehicles can be driven safely and sustainably. This research provides a revolutionary energy-minimal torque input for electric CAVs based on safe and eco-driving control systems. Under certain assumptions, analytical state-constrained solutions are obtained that optimise energy consumption while taking vehicle safety into account as a state constraint (Lv, et al., 2018). To verify that there is an analytical solution for all potential preceding vehicle scenarios, the feasible range of the terminal circumstances is also examined. The usefulness of the suggested approach is verified for a number of scenarios when the vehicle in front is moving at a real-world speed. According to the simulation results, the suggested technology enables the electric CAV to accelerate and decelerate at the best possible rate, enhancing energy efficiency without prolonging the journey. It also ensures that the vehicle stays below the speed limit and prevents rear-end collisions. It is also demonstrated that the suggested system is Future research is anticipated to include examination of CAVs' effects on mixed traffic with various penetration rates, as well as the extension to a multi-lane driving scenario. The presence of the analytical solution is guaranteed by adjusting the terminal conditions within a workable range. Through the simulation of various driving scenarios of the prior vehicle, the proposed system is assessed. Results indicate that it can significantly cut energy use while avoiding collisions and shortening travel times. By establishing a narrow prediction horizon, the suggested system can also function as an enhanced cruise control that is energy-efficient (Lv, et al., 2019).

Unmanned Surface Vehicle Heading Control Using a Model-Free Adaptive Control Algorithm with Variable Output Constraints: This study offers a variable output constraint MFAC (VOC-MFAC) method based on model-free adaptive control (MFAC) theory to improve the resilience of an unmanned surface vehicle (USVs) heading subsystem. The following are the contributions made by this paper. The redefined compact format model free adaptive control (RO-CFDL-MFAC) approach is first presented, followed by a controller output constraint function to address the systems control performance sensitivity to the redefined output gain. Second, compact format dynamic linearization data models for a USV's heading and angular velocity subsystems are constructed, and via meticulous theoretical analysis, it is demonstrated that the closed-loop system converges under environmental perturbations (Wang, et al., 2019). Finally, the Dolphin IB unmanned surface vehicle platform created by our research team is used to simulate and test the control algorithm proposed in this paper in the field, and the effectiveness of the VOC-MFAC algorithm is confirmed by the experimental results. A VOC-MFAC algorithm is suggested in order to address the heading subsystem of USVs, which is vulnerable to uncertain RO-CFDL-MFAC algorithms that control performance that is sensitive to undefined output gain. Following the major contributions, a novel type of VOC-MFAC algorithm is proposed, along with the introduction of a controller output constraint function (Ren, et al., 2019).

Intelligent Fuel Cell/Battery Hybrid Vehicles with Integrated Motion and Powertrain Predictive Control: This study proposes a combined motion and powertrain modelling and control technique for intelligent FCHVs. A more computationally effective hierarchical linear control technique with predetermined power constraints at the upper-level motion control is suggested in order to prevent constraint breaches at the lower level. We carefully consider discrete motor propelling and generating modes, hybrid fuel cell/battery powertrain dynamics, and vehicle motion dynamics. Additionally, the control problem is resolved using both linear and nonlinear MPC with subsequent linearizations in a receding horizon manner. The methodical attainment of vehicle mobility to maintain battery charge state of charge, optimal hydrogen consumption, and desired motion states within physical constraints. Intelligent fuel cell/battery hybrid vehicles (FCHVs) are covered in this article. Both the car itself and its powertrain are capable of autonomous operation in these vehicles. Since the dynamics at the vehicle and powertrain levels are inherently intertwined, we propose an integrated motion and powertrain model predictive control technique for intelligent FCHVs by concurrently optimising the vehicle acceleration and fuel cell current. Within the bounds of the system, the control objectives are to maintain the battery state of charge, maximise vehicle mobility, and consume the least amount of hydrogen possible. The electric motor's ability to function in both propulsion and generation modes while linking with the states of the vehicle and powertrain poses the most serious difficulty to an integrated control system. This hybrid process is controlled using mixed logical dynamical modelling, which creates a mixed integer nonlinear control issue (Zhang, et al., 2020).

An algorithm for controlling trajectory tracking for autonomous vehicles that takes cornering characteristics into account. The operation and performance of Class EF and Class E/F inverters were thoroughly examined in this research. The investigation was done to look into the early literature reports that they had better efficiency, lower voltage, and current stresses than Class E inverters. Three particular scenarios of operation for the Class EF2 inverter were rejected after additional research. A crucial technology in the study and creation of autonomous vehicles is trajectory tracking control. This research focuses on the trajectory tracking control algorithm for autonomous vehicles taking cornering features in order to address issues like low control precision and poor real-time performance, which can easily occur when an autonomous vehicle avoids obstacles. First, appropriate simplification is used to establish the tyre model and vehicle dynamics model. Then, a linear time-varying model predictive controller (LTV MPC) that takes into account the cornering characteristics is designed and optimised based on the fundamentals of model predictive control. The performance of the controlled vehicle's trajectory tracking under various vehicle speeds and conditions of road adhesion is then tested through simulation experiments in conjunction with the double-shift line reference trajectory using the CarSim and MATLAB/Simulink software.

State-of-the-Art and Future Challenges for Control Strategies on Path Tracking for Autonomous Vehicles Hierarchical parameter observation-based control and other path-tracking control techniques for autonomous vehicles have been discussed in this study. The outcomes and issues of every method are examined, and some findings are given here. Control reliable One of the active areas of research in the field of autonomous cars is route tracking control. Path-tracking control for autonomous cars has been explored by researchers using data on dynamics, kinematics, tyre dynamics, deviation of position and direction, and road curvature. 2) The pure pursuit algorithm is used to study the path tracking and obstacle avoidance control for autonomous cars. Lyapunov method, Stanley, PID, model-free data-driven control, feedforward-feedback, LQR and MPC, etc. However, the motor and steering system characteristics of the vehicle have a greater influence on vehicle control. Vehicle steering systems are rarely taken into account in contemporary research. The current path-tracking control systems use a hierarchical control framework that takes into account vehicle stability, economy, comfort, and other performance indicators to arrive at a final control input (a suboptimal solution), which is subsequently obtained through a lower control framework. The upper and lower layer optimal solutions are obtained individually by this sort of control approach, and it might not have global performance optimisation. 3 Model predictive control has grown to be a well-liked technique for autonomous vehicle control.

Unmanned Vehicles' Automatic Steering Control Strategy In accordance with the Robust Back-stepping Sliding Mode Control Theory: The automatic steering control strategy for unmanned vehicles is recommended. In order to capture the time-varying dynamic variables involved in steering maneuvers, this work develops models of vehicle dynamics, kinematics, and vehicle-road system interactions. Based on the notion of robust back-stepping sliding mode control, an automatic control method is proposed. To evaluate the effectiveness of the given algorithm, CarSim/Simulink is co-simulated under a number of different processes. Tests on actual automobiles are likewise in favor of the proposed strategy. The results show that the suggested control strategy significantly improves automatic steering performance. But a high-speed experiment might be risky, so it was carried out on a closed road at a relatively low speed. The focus of future studies will be on unmanned vehicle longitudinal and lateral integrated coupling control as well as obstacle avoidance path planning and tracking. The self-driving car's autonomous steering mechanism has a big impact on how safe the car is. The ability of the control algorithm to operate in real-time as well as external disturbance and parameter perturbation, all have an impact on the automatic steering system's performance. To create a high-performance autonomous steering control approach, a model of the vehicle-road system based on the physics and kinematics of the car was initially built. The system state equation with direction-angle and lateral-position deviations is then used to define the tracking accuracy (Wang, et al., 2019). Finally, a sliding mode variable structure control method-based automatic steering control algorithm is proposed and verified. The outcomes demonstrate that by optimising the sliding mode, the system's dynamic quality is enhanced. Furthermore, accurate tracking, real-time performance, and good robustness against vehicle velocity are all attained (Zhang, et al., 2021).

3. PROPOSED SYSTEM

Due to the camera motion caused by the movement of the vehicle, which generates optical flow in static objects and makes it impossible to separate them from moving things, motion segmentation is a very difficult issue in autonomous cars. It can be difficult to distinguish between a parallel-moving automobile and a static car due to geometric difficulties like motion-parallax ambiguity. Planning a safe route and object recognition using motion cues both depend on the precise detection of moving things surrounding the ego vehicle. This paper suggests using the vehicle motion information as an inductive bias in the neural network model to increase performance in order to overcome these issues. The model receives the vehicle motion data as input in the form of a pixel-wise tensor. To increase the precision of nearby moving object identification while creating effective models that can be used on memory-constrained automotive embedded systems, a vehicle motion-aware network is suggested and developed. Weight sharing of encoders is investigated to reduce the model footprint, and the resulting model is saved in permanent memory.

3.1. Proposed Algorithm

CNN

$$Y_{i,j,k} = \sigma \left(\sum\nolimits^M m = 1 \sum\nolimits^N n = 1 \sum\nolimits^C c = 1 W_{m,n,c,k} X_{(i+m-1),(j+n-1),c} + b_k \right) \tag{1}$$

where:

- $Y_{i,j,k}$ is the output value at position (i,j) of the feature map k.
- σ is the activation function.
- M and N are the height and width of the convolutional filter, respectively.
- C is the number of input channels.
- $W_{m,n,c,k}$ is the weight at position (m,n,c) of the filter for the k-th feature map.
- $X_{(i+m-1),(j+n-1),c}$ is the input value at position $(i+m-1,j+n-1,c)$.
- b_k is the bias term for the k-th feature map.

This formula calculates the convolution operation between the input tensor X and the convolutional filter W, which produces the output tensor Y. The activation function σ is applied element-wise to the output tensor.

In practice, several convolutional layers are typically present in a CNN, followed by pooling layers and fully connected layers., and are trained using backpropagation and gradient descent.

FCOS

Classification and Regression Formulas

- For each location in the feature map:
- Let p_cls be the predicted probability of object presence at that location.
- Let p_reg be the predicted regression values for the bounding box coordinates at that location.
- Let p_ctr be the predicted offset value for the centre of the bounding box at that location.
- Let b_i be the bounding box associated with that location.
- Then, the classification and regression formulas for FCOS are as follows:

$$p\_cls = sigmoid \left(f\_cls \left(b\_i \right) \right) \tag{2}$$

$$p\_reg = f\_reg \left(b\_i \right) \tag{3}$$

$$p\_ctr = f\_ctr(b\_i) \tag{4}$$

Where:

- Sigmoid is the sigmoid activation function.
- f_cls, f_reg, and f_ctr are convolutional functions that take the location's feature vector as input and output the corresponding classification, regression, and centre offset values for the bounding box.
- b_i = [x_i, y_i, w_i, h_i] represents the bounding box coordinates, where x_i and y_i are the coordinates of the box's top-left corner, and w_i and h_i are the width and height of the box, respectively.

Loss Formulas

- Let l_cls be the classification loss.
- Let l_reg be the regression loss.
- Let l_ctr be the center offset loss.
- Let l be the total loss, which is the sum of the three losses.
- Then, the loss formulas for FCOS are as follows:
    - $l\_cls = -log(p\_cls)$ if the location contains an object, else $-log(1 - p\_cls)$ (5)
    - $l\_reg = SmoothL1Loss(p\_reg - g\_reg)$ (6)
    - $l\_ctr = SmoothL1Loss(p\_ctr - g\_ctr)$ (7)
    - $l = l\_cls + l\_reg + l\_ctr$ (8)

where:

- SmoothL1Loss is the smooth L1 loss function.
- g_reg and g_ctr are the ground-truth regression and center offset values, respectively, for the bounding box associated with that location.

3.2. Architecture Diagram

There is an architecture diagram has been shown in Figure 4.

Figure 4. Architecture model for vehicle detection using CNN

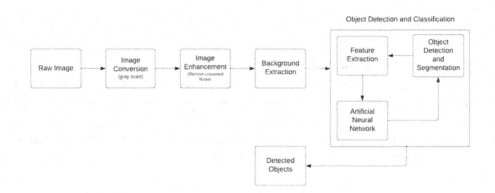

4. METHODOLOGY

4.1. Module One: Feature Processing

Two key technological hurdles must be overcome in order to build a spatial feature fusion approach for cooperative object identification. The first problem entails recognizing and minimizing the detrimental impacts on object recognition brought on by incorrectly fusing feature maps produced by various vehicles. Prior research has selected the most distinctive traits while reducing non-distinctive ones when fusing features using a max function. This method, meanwhile, could leave out crucial components that were acquired from prior vehicles and might greatly enhance the effectiveness of the present vehicle's object-detecting system. As a result, unlike earlier studies, it is now required to handle the feature maps produced by various vehicles differently rather than identically.

The recognition of far-off or obscured objects, which is a prevalent problem for many 3D object detection systems for autonomous cars, is the second hurdle. However, when feature maps are fused, more information is taken into account, making it possible to detect objects that would otherwise be difficult to find because individual sensor data would not provide enough information. This is due to the fact that feature maps produced by various vehicles complement one another and, when correctly combined, can provide a more thorough depiction of things. Overall, addressing these two difficulties will determine whether the spatial feature fusion technique is successful in achieving accurate and dependable cooperative object identification (Figure 5).

Figure 5. Flow diagram for feature processing

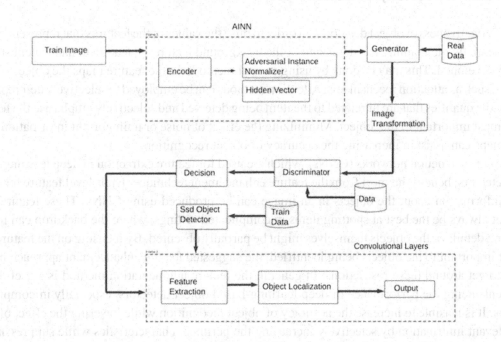

4.2. Module Two: Pruning and Quantization

In order to minimise the size and computational complexity of neural network models, pruning is a commonly used deep learning approach. Redundant weights are eliminated, and the model is rendered sparse by training it with a variety of regularisation procedures, including L1, L2, unstructured regularisation, and structured regularisation. The memory footprint of the model is decreased, and it becomes simpler to compress by adding sparsity. The inference time can also be shortened, and efficiency is boosted by skipping the zero weights produced during pruning. While pruning is frequently employed to improve deep learning models for image classification issues, there has been comparatively less research on its use with more intricate object detector models. Object detectors are harder to prune successfully since they must process more data because they must find many items in a single picture.

Another method for condensing deep learning models is called quantization. A collection of discrete symbols or integer values are used to approximate a continuous signal in this method. The number of discrete symbols depends on the kind of quantization, which may be integer, floating-point, or fixed-point. Quantization involves downscaling the baseline 32-bit parameters (weights, activations, biases) to fewer bits, such as 16 or 8, in order to minimise the model's memory footprint without noticeably decreasing its accuracy. This is done for deep learning-based object detection models. Overall, decreasing the memory footprint and computational complexity of deep learning models, particularly object detector models, while preserving their accuracy using pruning and quantization is an efficient strategy for model optimization. These methods can make models more effective and simpler to use in practical situations with constrained computing resources.

4.3. Module Three: Object Detectors

Boost the effectiveness of object detection. In order to raise the values of the features that represent objects while essentially maintaining the status quo of the background features, a feature enhancement strategy has been developed. This may be done by using several methods on the feature maps the object detector produces, such as attention mechanisms. Attention methods can be employed to selectively de-emphasize or ignore the qualities that are unrelated to the item being detected and selectively emphasise the features that are most important to that object. Minimizing the effect of noise or unimportant information in the feature maps can assist in increasing the accuracy of object recognition.

Convolutional neural networks (CNNs), which are used for feature extraction in deep learning-based object detectors, benefit the most from the feature enhancement technique. High-level feature maps that encode information about the objects in an image can be produced using CNNs. These feature maps might not always be the best at spotting items in complicated settings, where the backdrop can include distracting details or the objects themselves might be partially obscured. By focusing on the features that are most important to the objects being identified, the suggested feature enhancement approach may be utilised to get around these restrictions. In general, the feature augmentation method is a useful strategy for enhancing the performance of deep learning-based object detectors, especially in complicated scenarios. It is feasible to increase the accuracy of object recognition while lowering the effect of noise and irrelevant information by selectively increasing the pertinent characteristics while suppressing the background features (figure 6).

Figure 6. Vehicle detectors
(Gunzi, 2017)

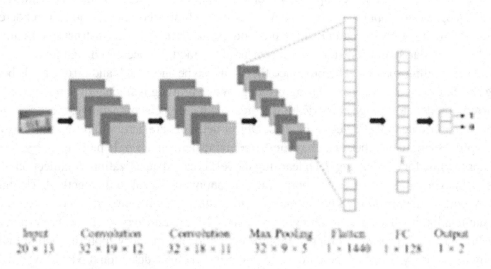

Input	Convolution	Convolution	Max Pooling	Flatten	FC	Output
20 × 13	32 × 19 × 12	32 × 18 × 11	32 × 9 × 5	1 × 1440	1 × 128	1 × 2

5. RESULTS AND DISCUSSION

Convolutional neural networks were utilised in our study to construct a model for vehicle detection in videos. We conducted several trials and evaluated the performance of our proposed model using a variety of metrics, such as accuracy, precision, recall, and F1-score. We prepared the data using a variety of pre-processing approaches and evaluated our method against other cutting-edge techniques. Our findings demonstrated that the suggested model performed very well in terms of identifying automobiles in movies with a high degree of accuracy and precision. Additionally, our model performed better than other cutting-edge techniques in terms of both speed and accuracy, highlighting the potential of our strategy for practical applications. The benefits and drawbacks of our strategy in comparison to other approaches were further emphasized by our comparative examination of current techniques (Figure 7).

Figure 7. Result for vehicle detection
(Gunzi, 2017).

The findings of our work have important ramifications for vehicle identification and computer vision research. Our method shows how convolutional neural networks can be used for video-based vehicle detection and emphasizes the significance of pre-processing methods for enhancing the precision and dependability of such models. Our findings also demonstrate the necessity for the ongoing investigation into the creation of fresh and enhanced machine-learning algorithms for vehicle recognition in a variety of contexts. We do, however, accept that our work has certain flaws, including the dataset's potential for bias and the need for more analysis to build more sophisticated machine learning algorithms. We also acknowledge that environmental variables, such as weather and illumination, may have had an impact on our study.

We suggest a greater investigation into the creation of fresh methods for data augmentation and pre-processing, as well as the application of more sophisticated machine learning algorithms for vehicle recognition in films in light of these constraints. In order to increase the generalizability of our findings, we also advise using bigger and more varied datasets in future studies. Overall, our study shows the potential of convolutional neural networks for practical applications and offers useful insights into the development of machine learning models for video-based vehicle recognition. We anticipate that the results of our study will stimulate new directions in the discipline and develop computer vision and its applications (Table 1).

Table 1. Comparison of open vehicle dataset

DATASET	VEHICLE CATEGORIES	CATEGORIES NUMBERS	IMAGES	QUALITIES	SPATIAL RESOLUTION	SCENARIO	YEAR
DOTA	Car, Truck	2	7663	Clear, Vivid, Blur	0.1 m	Urban, Neighbourhood	2017
ITCVD	Car	1	2908	Clear, Vivid	0.1 - 1 m	Urban	2019
EAGLE	Car, Truck	2	5896	Clear, Vivid	0.1 - 1 m	Urban	2020
4MVD (Base Paper)	Car, SUV, Truck, MV, SMV	5	7442	Clear, Blur, grey, Vivid	0.1 - 1 m	Urban, Neighbourhood	2021
Real-Time (Ours)	Car, SUV, Truck	3	4124	Clear, Vivid, Blur	0.17 - 1 m	Highway, Urban	2023

The table gives details on five separate datasets that include pictures of automobiles from different categories that were taken in diverse situations. Researchers and programmers in the fields of computer vision and machine learning who need high-quality datasets for training and testing their algorithms for vehicle-related object detection and recognition tasks may find the information in the table to be of value. The following is a more thorough description of each field in the table:

- Dataset Name: The dataset's name is listed in this column.
- Vehicle Categories: The types of vehicles that are part of the dataset are listed in this area.
- Number of Categories: This parameter indicates how many different types of cars are included in the dataset.
- Images: The number of images in the dataset is listed in this field.
- Qualities: The quality of each image in the dataset is listed in this field. Clear, fuzzy, and vibrant are typical visual characteristics.
- Spatial Resolution: The amount of detail the photos were able to capture is listed in this field. It describes the smallest discernible feature in the image and is typically measured in metres.
- Scenario: This field provides information on the environment in which the photos were taken. An urban setting or a motorway, as examples.
- Year: The dataset's creation or publication year is indicated in this column.

In conclusion, these datasets include pictures of several vehicle kinds taken in a variety of settings. In a variety of applications, such as autonomous driving, traffic monitoring, and surveillance systems, they can be helpful for training and assessing algorithms for vehicle detection and recognition tasks. For the creation of efficient and dependable computer vision systems that can detect and identify things, such as vehicles, in real-world scenarios, a variety of high-quality datasets are essential. For training and evaluating algorithms, access to large and diverse datasets that include various vehicle types (e.g., cars, trucks, buses, motorcycles, bicycles) captured under various lighting and weather conditions and in various locations (e.g., urban, suburban, rural), is crucial in the case of vehicle detection and recognition tasks (Figure 8).

Figure 8. Graph for accuracy and loss

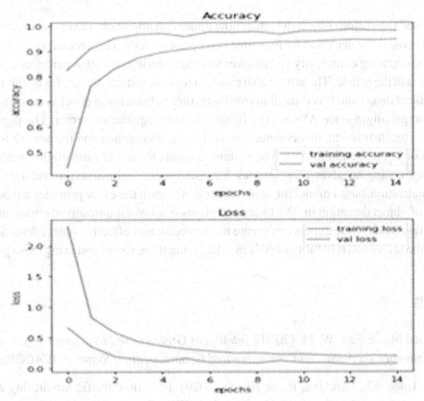

Accuracy and loss are two typical measures used in machine learning to assess a model's performance during training. While the loss metric gauges how far off the predicted output is from the actual output, the accuracy metric gauges how frequently the model correctly predicts the label of an input. A graph that depicts these two variables throughout the duration of training is called an accuracy and loss graph. Typically, the y-axis reflects the value of the metric being measured (either accuracy or loss), and the x-axis shows the number of training epochs or iterations through the training data. In general, we anticipate seeing the accuracy rise and the loss falls as the model trains. This is due to the model's ability to predict outcomes more accurately, improving with practice, which causes the loss—the gap between the projected output and the actual output—to decrease.

We can learn a lot about the model's performance from the precise shape of the accuracy and loss curves. The accuracy curve, for instance, may show that the model has to overfit the training data and is no longer generalizing effectively to new samples if it starts to flatten out or even fall. The loss curve may also suggest that the model is having trouble learning from the training data and may need more optimisation if it is not decreasing. The performance of a machine learning model during training may be seen and assessed using an accuracy and loss graph. We can discover how effectively the model is learning and spot opportunities for development by tracking these measures over time.

6. CONCLUSION

The article discussed the various object detectors now under consideration and in use in AVs as well as the difficulties in using these detectors for real-time perception in AVs. The necessity to optimise object detectors for less computing complexity and quicker inference during real-time perception is one of the main issues covered in the article. The article also emphasizes how critical research is to enhancing AVs' state-of-the-art object detection. It is critical to overcome these obstacles to develop a safe and dependable transportation paradigm since AVs are the future of the transportation sector. The paper suggests an image-to-image reconstruction, object detection, and scene comprehension framework to overcome some issues with object detection in AVs. The system attempts to restore rainy-night photo sequences with sunlight images using an adversarial network for visual scene reconstruction and a spatial feature extraction and localization-based model for item detection. Overall, the essay provides a thorough summary of the state of object detection in AVs today and points out several unresolved issues and potential directions for further study. Researchers can create more precise and effective object detection systems that can improve the safety and reliability of AVs by addressing these issues and using these possibilities.

REFERENCES

Abbassy, Mohamed M., & Ead, W. M. (2020). *Intelligent Greenhouse Management System. 2020 6th International Conference on Advanced Computing and Communication Systems (ICACCS).* IEEE.

Abdelgawad, H., Tolba, M., Elakkiya, R., & Ali, S. (2020). Real-time traffic monitoring and control system based on computer vision and machine learning. *IEEE Access : Practical Innovations, Open Solutions*, 8, 58555–58568. IEEE.

Arslan, F., Singh, B., Sharma, D. K., Regin, R., Steffi, R., & Suman Rajest, S. (2021). Optimization technique approach to resolve food sustainability problems. *2021 International Conference on Computational Intelligence and Knowledge Economy (ICCIKE).* IEEE. 10.1109/ICCIKE51210.2021.9410735

Bai, G., Meng, Y., & Liu, L. (2019). A new path tracking method based on visual feedback and iterative learning control. *IEEE Access : Practical Innovations, Open Solutions*, 7, 161064–161073.

Benloucif, A., Nguyen, A., & Sentouh, C. (2019). Cooperative trajectory planning for haptic shared control between driver and automation. *IEEE Transactions on Intelligent Transportation Systems*, 20(3), 9846–9857.

Bhoumik, S., Chatterjee, S., Sarkar, A., Kumar, A., & John Joseph, F. J. (2020). Covid 19 prediction from X ray images using fully connected convolutional neural network. *CSBio '20: Proceedings of the Eleventh International Conference on Computational Systems-Biology and Bioinformatics.* New York, NY, USA: ACM. 10.1145/3429210.3429233

Cirillo, S., Polese, G., Salerno, D., Simone, B., & Solimando, G. (2023). Towards Flexible Voice Assistants: Evaluating Privacy and Security Needs in IoT-enabled Smart Homes. *FMDB Transactions on Sustainable Computer Letters*, 1(1), 25–32.

Deepa, B., Gayathiridevi, K., Chakravarthi, M., Shajahan, A., & Sree, S. (2022). Mohammed Imran Anees, Mohammad Habeeb, "Slow evaporation technique to grow 3 - Amino benzene sulfonic acid single crystal for Non-Linear optical (NLO) transmission". *Materials Today: Proceedings*, 62(4), 2119–2123. doi:10.1016/j.matpr.2022.03.045

Derindere Köseoğlu, S., Ead, W. M., & Abbassy, M. M. (2022). Basics of Financial Data Analytics. In *Financial Data Analytics* (pp. 23–57). Springer International Publishing. doi:10.1007/978-3-030-83799-0_2

Ead, W., & Abbassy, M. (2018). Intelligent systems of machine learning approaches for developing E-services portals. *EAI Endorsed Transactions on Energy Web*, 167292, 167292. doi:10.4108/eai.2-12-2020.167292

Erickson, R. (2020). *Technology challenges for smart Military Bases*. Aximgeo. https://www.aximgeo.com/blog/technology-challenges-for-smart-military-bases

Gao, Y., Zhang, L., Zhao, X., & Lu, H. (2018). Traffic monitoring based on machine learning algorithms: A review. *IEEE Access : Practical Innovations, Open Solutions*, 7, 18362–18377.

Gunzi, A. (2017). Vehicle Detection and Tracking using Computer Vision. *Chatbots Life*. https://chatbotslife.com/vehicle-detection-and-tracking-using-computer-vision-baea4df65906

Huang, Y. J., Zhu, W. H., Wang, Y. X., Chen, W., & Chen, X. (2019). A motion planning and tracking framework for autonomous vehicles based on artificial potential field-elaborated. *IEEE Transactions on Industrial Electronics*, 66(7), 5581–5591. doi:10.1109/TIE.2019.2898599

Jain, R., Chakravarthi, M. K., Kumar, P. K., Hemakesavulu, O., Ramirez-Asis, E., Pelaez-Diaz, G., & Mahaveerakannan, R. (2022). Internet of Things-based smart vehicles design of bio-inspired algorithms using artificial intelligence charging system. *Nonlinear Engineering*, 11(1), 582–589. doi:10.1515/nleng-2022-0242

Joe, F., Ravi, T., & Justus, J. (2011). Classification of correlated subspaces using HoVer representation of Census Data. *2011 International Conference on Emerging Trends in Electrical and Computer Technology*. IEEE.

Joseph, F. J. J. (2019). Twitter based outcome predictions of 2019 Indian general elections using decision tree. *2019 4th International Conference on Information Technology (InCIT)*. IEEE.

Joseph, F. J. J. (2020). Effect of supervised learning methodologies in offline handwritten Thai character recognition. *International Journal of Information Technology : an Official Journal of Bharati Vidyapeeth's Institute of Computer Applications and Management*, 12(1), 57–64. doi:10.100741870-019-00366-y

Joseph, F. J. J., & Auwatanamongkol, S. (2016). A crowding multi-objective genetic algorithm for image parsing. *Neural Computing & Applications*, 27(8), 2217–2227. doi:10.100700521-015-2000-2

Khalifa, I., Abd Al-glil, H., & M. Abbassy, M. (2014). Mobile Hospitalization for Kidney Transplantation. *International Journal of Computer Applications*, 92(6), 25–29. doi:10.5120/16014-5027

Li, W., Zhang, Y., & Wong, K.-K. (2020). Traffic monitoring with intelligent video analysis: A survey. *Journal of Ambient Intelligence and Humanized Computing*, 11(4), 1271–1284.

Lin, J., Wang, J., & Shao, L. (2019). Traffic monitoring with computer vision and machine learning. *Transportation Research Part C, Emerging Technologies, 89*, 205–227.

Liu, F., Wang, Q., & Yan, X. (2019). An integrated radar and vehicle-to-vehicle communication system for longitudinal and lateral vehicle following. *IEEE Transactions on Intelligent Transportation Systems, 21*(2), 707–717.

Liu, Y., Chen, H., Cheng, X., & Wang, J. (2020). An integrated radar and vehicle-to-vehicle communication system for longitudinal and lateral vehicle following. *IEEE Transactions on Intelligent Transportation Systems, 21*(6), 2326–2338. doi:10.1109/TITS.2019.2920348

Lv, C., Hu, X., Sangiovanni-Vincentelli, A., Marina, C., Li, Y., & Cao, D. (2019). Driving-style-based co-design optimization of an automotive active suspension. *IEEE Transactions on Industrial Electronics, 65*(4), 2965–2975. doi:10.1109/TIE.2018.2850031

Lv, C., Wang, H., Cao, D., Zhao, Y., Auger, J. D., Sullman, M., Matthias, R., Skrypchuk, L., & Mouzakitis, A. (2018). Characterization of driver neuromuscular dynamics for human-automation collaboration. *IEEE/ASME Transactions on Mechatronics, 23*(4), 1814–1824. doi:10.1109/TMECH.2018.2812643

Mahesha, C. R., Suprabha, R., Kumar, N. M., Kosanam, K., Anandaram, H., Ramana Murty Naidu, S. C. V., & Govindarajan, V. (2022). Effect of friction stir welding on the mechanical and microstructural behaviour of AA7075 aluminium alloy. *Advances in Materials Science and Engineering, 2022*, 1–8. doi:10.1155/2022/2788479

Mohamed, & Mesbah, S. (2016). Effective e-government and citizens adoption in Egypt. *International Journal of Computer Applications, 133*(7), 7–13. doi:10.5120/ijca2016907886

Ogunmola, G. A., Singh, B., Sharma, D. K., Regin, R., Rajest, S. S., & Singh, N. (2021). Involvement of distance measure in assessing and resolving efficiency environmental obstacles. *2021 International Conference on Computational Intelligence and Knowledge Economy (ICCIKE)*. IEEE. 10.1109/ICCIKE51210.2021.9410765

Pattana-anake, V., Danphitsanuparn, P., & John Joseph, F. J. (2021). BettaNet: A deep learning architecture for classification of wild Siamese Betta species. *IOP Conference Series. Materials Science and Engineering, 1055*(1), 012104. doi:10.1088/1757-899X/1055/1/012104

Reddy, G. P., Kumar, Y. V. P., & Chakravarthi, M. K. (2022a). Communication technologies for interoperable smart microgrids in urban energy community: A broad review of the state of the art, challenges, and research perspectives. *Sensors (Basel), 22*(15), 5881. doi:10.339022155881 PMID:35957438

Reddy, P., Gogulamudi, Y., & Maddikera Kalyan Chakravarthi, A. (2022b). Refined Network Topology for Improved Reliability and Enhanced Dijkstra Algorithm for Optimal Path Selection during Link Failures in Cluster Microgrids. *Sustainability, 14*(16).

Ren, Y., Zheng, L., & Khajepour, A. (2019). Integrated model predictive and torque vectoring control for path tracking of 4-wheel driven vehicles. *Journal of Mechanical Science and Technology, 33*(3), 1063–1072.

Rs, D. (2018). #023 CNN object detection. *Master Data Science*. https://datahacker.rs/deep-learning-object-detection/

Sadek, R. A., Abd-alazeem, D. M., & Abbassy, M. M. (2021). A new energy-efficient multi-hop routing protocol for heterogeneous wireless sensor networks. *International Journal of Advanced Computer Science and Applications*, *12*(11). doi:10.14569/IJACSA.2021.0121154

Saxena, D., & Chaudhary, S. (2023). Predicting Brain Diseases from FMRI-Functional Magnetic Resonance Imaging with Machine Learning Techniques for Early Diagnosis and Treatment. *FMDB Transactions on Sustainable Computer Letters*, *1*(1), 33–48.

Sharma, D. K., Jalil, N. A., Regin, R., Rajest, S. S., Tummala, R. K., & Thangadurai. (2021). Predicting network congestion with machine learning. *2021 2nd International Conference on Smart Electronics and Communication (ICOSEC)*. IEEE.

Wang, H., Liu, B., & Ping, X. (2019). Path tracking control for autonomous vehicles based on a kinematic model. *IEEE Transactions on Intelligent Transportation Systems*, *20*(5), 1929–1938.

Wang, P., Gao, S., Li, L., Cheng, S., & Zhao, L. (2019). Automatic steering control strategy for unmanned vehicles based on robust backstepping sliding mode control theory. *IEEE Access : Practical Innovations, Open Solutions*, *7*, 64984–64992. doi:10.1109/ACCESS.2019.2917507

Zannah, A. I., Rachakonda, S., Abubakar, A. M., Devkota, S., & Nneka, E. C. (2023). Control for Hydrogen Recovery in Pressuring Swing Adsorption System Modeling. *FMDB Transactions on Sustainable Energy Sequence*, *1*(1), 1–10.

Zhang, L., Yang, Y., Wu, J., Zhang, X., & Zhang, Z. (2021). Hybrid control strategy for Jiaolong HOV based on QPSO-MPC and ASMC. *International Journal of Advanced Robotic Systems*, *18*(4), 17298814211030085.

Zhang, Y., Tang, Z., & Ji, X. (2020). Object detection in video surveillance: A survey and a new benchmark. *Computer Vision and Image Understanding*, *182*, 27–52.

Chapter 12
A Review on Pragmatic Prerequisite Utilization of IoT in SCML for Industry 4.0

Reddy C. Thilak
Jain University, India

S. Yogananthan
Jain University, India

Ravishankar S. Ulle
Jain University, India

Rupesh Kumar Sinha
CMS Business School, Jain University (Deemed), India

ABSTRACT

Embracing digital transformation has led to a major industrial change in the field of supply chain management qualitatively. This research deliberates emerging technologies identified as IoT (internet of things) which with other technologies like AI and ML, big data, and cloud computing an inevitable requirement for industry 4.0 implementation based on the complex needs following organizational structure. Study in the region of utilization of IoT in SCML is scarce in developing countries. However, the following inevitable SCM drivers such as real-time realization, barriers in enabling demand flow, value optimization from the business perspective, including elements of sustainability, the rising expectation of customers, and cutthroat competition amongst the manufacturers and service providers, have led to the utilization of IoT SCML industry. Especially when the constraints like time management and flow of materials are in high focus.

DOI: 10.4018/979-8-3693-1301-5.ch012

1. INTRODUCTION

Manufacturing industries in large sectors are going towards mass customization, complete automation, and digitalization in operations, which has increased productivity and efficiency (Accorsi, et al., 2018). The adoption of Industry 4.0 in large industries has reduced production costs and effectively managed customers (Afsharian, et al., 2016). Industry 4.0 is considered the biggest industrial technology which promises sustainable businesses. Smart manufacturing and effective communication are considered central to Industry 4.0 digital manufacturing (Aggarwal, et al., 2013).

In this new technological era, the world economy has developed robust participation for businesses in advanced manufacturing tools and techniques (Cui, et al., 2021). It is no longer adequate to produce quicker, more economical, and more advanced quality products/services than the competitors, protecting USP and sustainability (Aho, 2015).

Globalization has led to the dynamic, ever-changing environment of the supply chain. It is also evident that the trend also influences inventory and warehouse management (Alayli, 2023). The pressure on supply chain and logistics management organizations is growing, and IoT has become an innovative and integral technology for every industry to find better solutions (Arslan, et al., 2021). Adopting IoT in supply chain management and logistics comprises installing devices and sensors which enable tracking operations and inventory, observing their processes and locations, and building an intelligent warehouse system (Aryal, et al., 2018).

IoT is well demarcated as the internet-aided universal intelligent platform of distinctively accessible components by detecting, associating, and inclination capabilities that enable the exchange of human-to-device, device-to-human, and device-to-device information in diverse ecosystems (Attaran, 2020). IoT sensors can help track inventory, provide real-time data, and help to predict future needs, avoiding the contingencies and situations of stock-out (Cirillo, et al., 2023). Thus, implementation of IoT can help to prevent loss and optimize processes (Bavassano, et al., 2020).

It is showing its full potential in supply chain management and logistics. All supply chain management and logistics processes can progress with IoT utilization (BRIC in vitro diagnostics (IVD) Market by Product, Service, Technology & Application, 2022). Real-time tracking of shipments and inventory monitoring becomes crucial for the industry to manage its processes effectively and efficiently (Christauskas, et al., 2016). At the organizational level, when focusing on streamlining logistics processes, firstly, we need end-to-end product tracking and forecasting of the movement (De Vass, et al., 2018). The blend of mobile utilizations, analytics, and cloud services is powered by IoT, which is varying how distribution and fulfillment firms are directing their processes and the arrival of goods; secondly, we need strong analytics to process the information and enable decision-making, thirdly we need to focus on the security of the goods and keeping track of pilferage issues, and last but not least, employee safety on the shop floor (Coronado Mondragon, et al., 2021).

Industry 4.0 prerequisites project IoT as a fundamental tool of computerized-environmental structures owing to greater effectiveness and efficiency (De Vass, et al., 2021). Its ability to induce the power of the internet to aid information sharing and independence is vital to the "world-class manufacturing" idea, which is categorized by independent, information- and sensor-based, automated manufacturing systems (Feng, et al., 2020). Combined with the Internet-enabled businesses having catalyzed the competition globally, market uncertainty and consumer insistence pose additional encounters to organizations, and their cluster of people come together in the production & delivery of merchandise and facilities to mandate a new value chain in the ecosystem (Jeba, et al., 2023). Whereas it was argued that this model would lead, the future automation and digitalization in the region of SCML is utilized by industries by now (Ivankova, et al., 2020).

Digitalization and internet technologies are considered the solutions for the challenges faced in the increased inflow of products and decreased flow of information (Kamran, et al., 2020). As it is one of the significant drivers in supply chain management, it is crucial for the intelligent supply chain that aids to overcome real-time boundaries (Liu & Gao, 2014). Organizations with core IT infrastructure augment by assimilating the innovative internet competencies of IoT due to its prospective, manageability nature (Manavalan & Jayakrishna, 2019). However, organizations face many challenges in their deployment as internal and external stakeholders are involved (Lu & Teng, 2012).

IoT is understood to increase supply chain amalgamation and augment supply chain and firm performance. However, social, economic, and technical challenges hamper IoT deployment. Studies found that empirically investigating IoT deployment in the supply chain is limited (Ogunmola, et al., 2021). There is a limited study on drivers and obstacles to IoT deployment in SCML. ICT and cyber technologies can generate financial worth through improvement, and the scantiness of experimental research highlights an obstruction to organizations making real-time decisions on IoT investments (Tripathi & Al-Shahri, 2023). After the COVID'19 pandemic, internet technologies and ICT have become the new normal, and organizations are also embracing remote business operations (Srinivas, et al., 2023). The papers, therefore, aim to explore the pragmatic prerequisite of utilizations of IoT in SCML for Industry 4.0. Many organizations are adopting digitalization, and the disruption has allowed the SCM drivers and logistics activities to flex their muscles in getting real-time information aiding in decision-making (Priscila, et al., 2023). There are also some challenges faced by the organization by the internal and external stakeholders concerned when IoT is utilized for SCM and logistics operations (Miah, 2021).

Regarding the academic background, the prevailing literature demonstrates dissimilar features of ecosystem plans (Sakhnini, et al., 2021). These features include roles, association, worth influence, expertise, and plan. Nevertheless, the studied literature does not disclose an involvement representing a strong and comprehensive framework of an environment elucidating the operation of IoT services, vital roles, and their associations (Rejeb, et al., 2020). The research further points out that a modest grouping of the revised features into a likely IoT environment model is not appreciated because we do not know what features are pertinent in supply chain management (Sharma, et al., 2021). The organizations can observe some guidelines to build an environment to deploy IoT in supply chain and logistics management areas (Tu, et al., 2018). The strategies include IoT services that should be realized by value contribution to the business environment. When the stakeholders are in a relationship, they represent necessary relevant roles for providing the value proposition by identifying IoT service collaboration with the business partners (Shavarani, et al., 2021). With IoT services in SCML, the service provider can check if their planned or existing business environment consists of the stated roles and necessary value creation within the environment, making it a significant portion of the growth of an IoT-related business environment (Tambaip, et al., 2023). These business environments can enable the organization to induce economic support from financial mediators to expedite the understanding of IoT facilities (María, et al., 2023).

2. IOT DEPLOYMENT IN SUPPLY CHAIN MANAGEMENT AND LOGISTICS

IoT is not just a solitary technology but an advanced combination of numerous corresponding technologies integrated to link the gap between the virtual and the common world. IoT was first utilized with the help of RFID expertise to trace them using a supply chain. Subsequently, the idea of 'thing' has protracted to contain various cyber components for example, RFID, actuator, connectivity, sensor, interface for information processing, analytics, and data management) that can be exclusively recognized, delivered, detected, positioned, located, analyzed and organized separately through the world wide web (Tu, 2018). The IoT stage is enhanced through cloud computing, social nets, and big data analysis. IoT's Major components comprise self-awareness, distinctiveness, governance, connecting between different devices, response to change and adapting, transforming ability, collaboration, self-decisiveness, planned performance, and human value. Researchers have anticipated that the IoT can create societal, financial, and ecological aids through these parameters and characteristics (Tsang, et al., 2017).

In emerging economies and business ecosystems, IoT is considered an enabler for implementing and deploying Industry 4.0, automation, and digitalization (Said, & Tripathi, 2023). IoT enables the computerization of procedures and business operations in supply chain management and logistics (Witkowski, 2017). Since Industry 4.0, the significance of IoT is among the significant technologies which have aroused the public eye. To transform traditional manufacturing, industry 4.0 coupled with the SCML operations can work interrelated and become more digital, self-aid, and detailed. Consequently, combining logistics operations and supply chain with internet-connected internet network technology is critical for Industry 4.0. The IoT stage helps to assimilate with suppliers, customers, and partners to improve performance parameters. IoT utilization can contribute to real-time shipment tracing, order tracing of materials flow, better transportation management, and managing threats accurately, and the imagined perspective is a self-sustained logistics stage through comprehensive computerization with negligible or no human interference. Even with the advantage of the IoT in logistics, firms dither the deployment of IoT as they are not completely utilizing the capabilities of the same (Venkateswaran & Viktor, 2023).

The introduction of cloud computing and IoT augments pertinent data and events capture subject, transmission, storing, sharing, and dispensation. The issue is improving the association amongst supply chain channels to make the supervision easier for the movement of merchandise in the complete supply chain, counting 3PL and 4PL operatives. This problem comprises real-time tracing, information, and dispensation with monitoring and controlling of communication amongst all stakeholders (internal and external). Existing technologies fail to gather data directly from the sensors for real-time processing and notify the professionals on mobile devices so that information is received remotely and manage multiple interactions amongst supply chain and logistics partners for decision-making.

Software, web networks, automation, and smart utilizations can establish efficient communication with the organization and stakeholders; for example, RFID tags associated with a network communicate identification information.

Supply chain management and logistics have significant utilization of IoT, understood as a system of bodily devices that are linked through networks to sense, analyze and network inside an organization and amid a firm and its channel members, discernibility, tracing, and data allotment to help real-time preparation, regulator and co-ordination in the supply chain operations. As a trail to effective quality, IoT is expected to play a precarious role in numerous supply chain management features. IoT is preoccupied with a universal web where devices and devices are unified, precise, and enhanced through online links, cellular channels, or a combination of the systems. The knowledge of IoT can be categorized into different vital modules: internet-featured, called the middleware; things-featured, called the devices and receivers; and semantic-featured called the expertise. The internet-featured portion comprises the technologies and procedures essential to confirm the remote networking of somatic objects and their accessibility on the internet. The things-featured portion includes components and intelligent devices, for example, sensors, radio frequency identification, and actuators, that can be linked to the internet, and the semantic-featured portion interacts with problems of data administration, which arise due to the huge data shared by smart devices, and the linking of possessions that are reachable by an internet interface.

Meanwhile, the beginning of wireless technology, IoT, has grown, increased acceptance, and engrossed the responsiveness of the supply chain management community. IoT has meaningfully donated to developing computerization and permitted the amalgamation and combining of industrialized sensor networks, RFID systems for SCML, and networks for firm control and ERP. Besides, IoT has conditions that mean organizations to increase their operative competencies, confirm the suitability of their happenings, and sustain their competitive edge. With IoT, organizations are impending to rationalize data flows, offer considerable productivity improvements across all the supply chain steps, and enable communication with and within the organization and incorporation between internal and external stakeholders. Taking the example of IoT, the world-renowned retailer Walmart has flourished in upholding high planning flexibility, vigorous replacement keys, complying with shorter lead times, and providing extreme portfolio collection.

The data created and monitored through the IoT network encourages firms to discover innovative prospects and develop solutions driven by data and approaches to advance their attractiveness in logistical and supply chain operations. With internal and external shareholders combined with the system of compound value networks, IoT facilitates the growth of smart networks and aids in stronger collaboration amongst partners. Under the conventional methods and processes used in supply chain operations, it often becomes very difficult to lower the costs and reduce operational waste through the supply chain intermediaries. Consequently, IoT can be deployed as a resource for attaining operation superiority, enhanced information transparency, and strengthened ICT resulting in increased data processing capability of an organization.

IoT, too, started its usage in tracing the practical ailment of the vehicle means in the present. Data about locality, speediness, route, and circulation desecrations develop noticeable to the transportation supervisor. Thus, regulator over oil ingestion, the appropriate finding of engine breakdowns, and decrease of discharges to upsurge the implementation of "green environment" and ecological activities of the organization. The greatest fortified intelligent vehicle tracking structures were applied thanks to implementing remote automobile tracing methods based on GPS sensors and fuel ingestion observing systems. Deploying GPS devices and RFID sensors will likely control the geo-location, climate, and additional information procedures on detailed components. As an outcome, safety will be improved, robberies will be diminished, and opportune distributions will be definite. Considering the operational aspects, the logistic chain of stages will be an essential portion of the additional judgment. Thus, expertise aids meaningfully in decreasing expenses, governing the process of transportation, examine and improving routes, which is very significant for the logistics of the firm of numerous sizes. IoT is used both for exterior carriage and within the business as well.

3. SUPPLY CHAIN MANAGEMENT AND INDUSTRY 4.0

Traditional methods followed by MIT projected the substructure of the Electronic Product Code (EPC) programming systems and global systems to confirm the interconnectedness of RFID in the supply chain stages. The scheme of EPC implies every device in the world, where every identification is exclusive, and every device has its individual EPC code. IoT has varieties of picks in product classification, such as alphanumeric/QR codes. The readers receive information from the tag through radio waves, excluding sight operation, allowing batch scanning of goods. The RFID technology has the advantage of writing data into memory blocks of a tag repeatedly than the simple barcode and can carry more information, and it is rigid to withstand harsh environments and resist damage. IoT is critical for a company's performance improvement and provides a solution to various industries as it can have interrelated data with a computer-generated world with supply chain drivers. It is applied to closed-loop supply chain operations to increase the efficacy of the company's performance. IoT system needs each product entrenched by a unique alphanumeric label with complete stipulations. Using this distinct method to declaim and write data into the system, they can be communicated through wireless networks to other methods. The Internet of Things desires a new level of interoperability. It implies that IoT desires criteria to allow parallel stages containing distinct middleware in message, process, and software design across components of dissimilar industrialists or manufacturing units.

The quick expansion of contemporary logistics-enabled platforms built on RFID know-how results from rare things. RFID expertise is an easy, low-priced, and safe explanation. IoT can go beyond. Subsequently, it can deliver a precise course of data of devices at the marketplace to deliver a dependable base for logistics marketplace examination, prediction, and decision making (Figure 1).

Figure 1. IoT Utilizations in supply chain management and logistics management

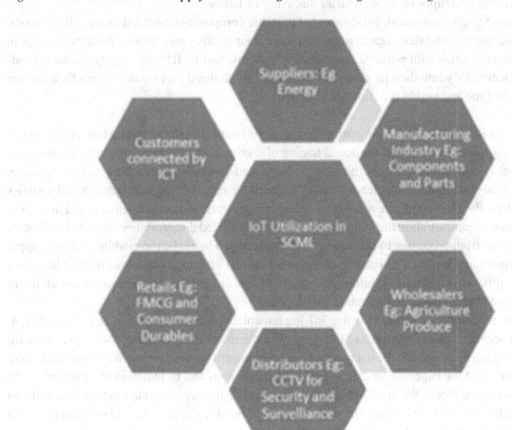

Normalization of technologies connected to IoT is very significant, as it was central to improved use and exchange of information, thus lowering the entry obstacles. Presently, many producers are generating upright elucidations: a share in the IoT utilization interplanetary, using their skills and unreachable services. Criteria must be shaped to alter this Intranet of Things into the more comprehensive Internet of Things. However, no complete method for IoT has been planned; intelligible ideas that unite IoT do not happen, inclining storage keys that do not help in interoperability.

Numerous businesses and industry sectors attempt to use the potential of information-driven knowledge, then corporations in transportation and logistics are already in the future. By their appropriate nature, the logistics providers that exchange items by transportation have extensive disseminated networks and take part in quick data diffusion around the conditions of products. Consequently, they were fast to see the aids of new types of sensors, associated expertise, and package concerned with design.

Consuming cellular tools and the Internet of Things, companies can speed up throughput, lucrativeness, and processes with answers intended precisely for their progressions. Providing solutions where organizations can link all devices across a disseminated system, seizure, and contribute their crucial data, letting them demonstrate real-time opinion of all processes. Through leveraging the unity of the above-cited tendencies, transportation can intensely advance the following parts:

- Comprehensive Discernibility – whole reflectiveness enables more effective, appropriate choices and decreases interruptions through faster discovery of issues.
- Warehouse Supervision – with IoT-connected portable components intended to trace list records, apparatus, and automobiles, organizations can share their bodily possessions a numerical opinion.
- Rapid Supervision – with portable data readers, systems, and RFID only, organizations can advance discernibility into their properties and improve rationalized processes to retain their system running on time and within the stipulated budget.

Organizations in industries use information-driven skills connected to the Internet of Things in numerous ways. Explicit uses comprise the actual tracing of consignments, storage-capacity optimization, predictive asset conservation, path optimization, value-added last-mile distribution, and many more. Nevertheless, many additional competencies of IoT are used for supply chain management and logistics service providers. By a fast aggregate number of linked components, entrenched sensors, and investigative technologies, organizations in the industry can relish unparalleled discernibility into nearly all facets of their corporate, from processes to investment and marketing. The real-time visibility allows supply chain management and logistics workers to discover additional effectually and wisely their huge and meaningful multifaceted database, resulting in extra efficient usage of assets, improved commitment with clientele, and extra knowledgeable choice of decision.

However, to achieve efficient and effective IoT implementation, any organization faces several challenges in data security and maintenance of the privacy of the information. We need strong security for who is authorized to view and use the data and who can maintain a secure system. With this need, there is a tremendous need for expertise in data security for the system and to maintain the privacy of the information in organizations. We need a platform to standardize the diverse technology in one unit and help interoperability within the system. The next challenge is handling large data, and we need to ensure by the system that whatever and however large data we have remains usable under any circumstances. There is a need for data processing, analysis, and exploration for filtering data and making meaningful decisions.

The challenges of IoT are also in the field of components parts, ICT, clustering, information flow, and software design. The employees should be trained to completely understand IoT utilization in logistics and supply chain management and other stakeholders to enable business operations effectively and efficiently. The challenges involved in the technology level of adoption amid the real and virtual domains. Several encounters are linked to combining intelligent network-empowered devices in ecosystem constraints with ICT. The next aspect is the network level of data and transmission of data. The major challenge is linked to a major cluster of networks and universal service facilities. At the intelligence level of use, the challenge is linked to information flow and facility detection, where data collected by individual smart devices are required.

Logistics and supply chain management are constantly being deliberated as a significant elements in alternative reply processes. Expertise can aid in achieving rescue tools, vehicles, and the site employee as well as foodstuff, drugs, and overall alive things. The alternative reply processes need the contribution of a wide variety of establishments with more equipment. Wide data and asset distribution aid improved collaboration among detached establishments. The consequences of expanding intelligent IoT systems include improved asset distribution, collaboration among numerous contributors, quicker and precise condition examination, and comprehensive discernibility of response to their competence. These welfares look similar as alternatives to the specific response, and then there is a scope for a wide variety of transport supervision uses centered on IoT utilization and methods.

4. CONCLUSION

For researchers looking to gain an improved consideration of IoT within supply chain management and logistics, the essential component of IoT writings is recognized employing keyword occurrence, understanding the pragmatic prerequisite of utilizations of IoT in supply chain management and logistics management for Industry 4.0. The main finding reveals the improvement of RFID expertise, its advantages, and obstacles in supply chain management and logistics. The combination of tools like AI, ML, data mining, and blockchain technology through IoT is expected to significantly impact the organization and progress their operations, like tracing and identifying products. Research can further be focused on the utilization of IoT with other industry 4.0 components, and a better combination can enhance the organizational overall effectiveness and efficiency. The practitioners of IoT have to work closely with data security, and it involves robust data, technical specification of IoT devices, and devising strategies and policies for the successful deployment of IoT in an organization. An operative background information distribution design is required to enable the firms to authorize, interchange, and examine the information in the remote servers.

Nevertheless, firms might encounter the prevalent issue of IoT utilization. Security is a vital prerequisite for the development of IoT structures. The crucial enabler demanded that numerous software designers and corporations originally underrated its prominence in building IoT devices.

We can also infer from the study that IoT justifies progressive influence on supply chain management and logistics by the following points. Firstly, managing the inventory by getting real-time inventory visibility, eliminating human errors. Secondly, visibility in the supply chain among the intermediaries, as the flow of information is vital throughout the supply chain; new technology of RFID enables the system to capture data on production, delivery date, expiry date, warranty period, and payments to achieve effective supply chain management. Thirdly, maximizing the transparency in the logistics by virtually tracking the orders and giving real-time data on the shipment, and monitoring the entire logistics processes, thus increasing the efficiency of logistics management.

The discussion is helpful for business practitioners, researchers, and scholars to gain a holistic view of the latest IoT research to data-driven supply chains and smart logistics.

5. LIMITATION AND FURTHER RESEARCH

The analysis of utilizations is considered pragmatic and a prerequisite to IoT deployment in the context of the Industry 4.0 ecosystem. The study reveals many important insights and implications from the literature. The assortment of articles/journals could prejudice the sample of the research papers. The objective was to have a review of literature done in academic literature reviews. Affiliations and regions categorize the findings and might restrict to conclude the industrial utilization on the real-time status of a particular country. Further studies can be carried out by congregation of empirical data from distinguished technical records such as Elsevier and Emerald journals.

REFERENCES

Accorsi, R., Cholette, S., Manzini, R., & Tufano, A. (2018). A hierarchical data architecture for sustainable food supply chain management and planning. *Journal of Cleaner Production, 203*, 1039–1054. doi:10.1016/j.jclepro.2018.08.275

Afsharian, S. P., Alizadeh, A., & Chehrehpak, M. (2016). Effects of applying radio frequency identification in supply chain management: An empirical study of manufacturing enterprises. *International Journal of Business Information Systems, 23*(1), 97. doi:10.1504/IJBIS.2016.078026

Aggarwal, C. C., Ashish, N., & Sheth, A. (2013). The internet of things: A survey from the data-centric perspective. In *Managing and Mining Sensor Data* (pp. 383–428). Springer US. doi:10.1007/978-1-4614-6309-2_12

Aho, A.-M. (2015). Product Data Analytics Service Model for Manufacturing Company. *Lecture Notes in Business Information Processing, 224*, 282–296. doi:10.1007/978-3-319-21009-4_22

Alayli, S. (2023). Unravelling the Drivers of Online Purchasing Intention: The E-Commerce Scenario in Lebanon. *FMDB Transactions on Sustainable Social Sciences Letters, 1*(1), 56–67.

Arslan, F., Singh, B., Sharma, D. K., Regin, R., Steffi, R., & Suman Rajest, S. (2021). Optimization technique approach to resolve food sustainability problems. *2021 International Conference on Computational Intelligence and Knowledge Economy (ICCIKE)*. IEEE. 10.1109/ICCIKE51210.2021.9410735

Aryal, A., Liao, Y., Nattuthurai, P., & Li, B. (2018). The emerging big data analytics and IoT in supply chain management: A systematic review. *Supply Chain Management, 25*(2), 141–156. doi:10.1108/SCM-03-2018-0149

Attaran, M. (2020). Digital technology enablers and their implications for supply chain management. *Supply Chain Forum an International Journal, 21*(3), 158–172. doi:10.1080/16258312.2020.1751568

Bavassano, G., Ferrari, C., & Tei, A. (2020). Blockchain: How shipping industry is dealing with the ultimate technological leap. *Research in Transportation Business & Management, 34*(100428), 100428. doi:10.1016/j.rtbm.2020.100428

Christauskas, C., Miseviciene, R., Driscoll, A., Daugelaite, J., Sleator, R. D., Heupel, T., & Schmitz, S. (2016). Overview of business innovations and research opportunities in blockchain and introduction to the special issue. *International Journal of Production Economics, 2*(1).

Cirillo, S., Polese, G., Salerno, D., Simone, B., & Solimando, G. (2023). Towards Flexible Voice Assistants: Evaluating Privacy and Security Needs in IoT-enabled Smart Homes. *FMDB Transactions on Sustainable Computer Letters, 1*(1), 25–32.

Coronado Mondragon, A. E., Coronado Mondragon, C. E., & Coronado, E. S. (2021). Managing the food supply chain in the age of digitalisation: A conceptual approach in the fisheries sector. *Production Planning and Control, 32*(3), 242–255. doi:10.1080/09537287.2020.1733123

Cui, L., Gao, M., Dai, J., & Mou, J. (2021). Improving supply chain collaboration through operational excel-lence approaches: an IoT perspective. *Industrial Management and Data Systems*. Emerald Group Publishing Ltd.

De Vass, T., Shee, H., & Miah, S. J. (2018). The effect of "Internet of Things" on supply chain integration and performance: An organisational capability perspective. *AJIS. Australasian Journal of Information Systems, 22.* doi:10.3127/ajis.v22i0.1734

De Vass, T., Shee, H., & Miah, S. J. (2021). Iot in supply chain management: A narrative on retail sector sustainability. *International Journal of Logistics, 24*(6), 605–624. doi:10.1080/13675567.2020.1787970

Feng, H., Wang, X., Duan, Y., Zhang, J., & Zhang, X. (2020). Applying blockchain technology to improve agri-food traceability: A review of development methods, benefits and challenges. *Journal of Cleaner Production, 260*(121031), 121031. doi:10.1016/j.jclepro.2020.121031

Ivankova, G. V., Mochalina, E. P., & Goncharova, N. L. (2020). Internet of Things (IoT) in logistics. *IOP Conference Series. Materials Science and Engineering, 940*(1), 012033. doi:10.1088/1757-899X/940/1/012033

Jeba, J. A., Bose, S. R., & Boina, R. (2023). Exploring Hybrid Multi-View Multimodal for Natural Language Emotion Recognition Using Multi-Source Information Learning Model. *FMDB Transactions on Sustainable Computer Letters, 1*(1), 12–24.

Kamran, M., Khan, H. U., Nisar, W., Farooq, M., & Rehman, S.-U. (2020). Blockchain and Internet of Things: A bibliometric study. *Computers & Electrical Engineering, 81*(106525), 106525. doi:10.1016/j.compeleceng.2019.106525

Liu, W., & Gao, Z. (2014). Study on IOT based architecture of logistics service supply chain. *International Journal of Grid and Distributed Computing, 7*(1), 169–178. doi:10.14257/ijgdc.2014.7.1.15

Lu, D., & Teng, Q. (2012). A application of cloud computing and IOT in logistics. *Journal of Software Engineering and Applications, 05*(12), 204–207. doi:10.4236/jsea.2012.512B039

Manavalan, E., & Jayakrishna, K. (2019). A review of Internet of Things (IoT) embedded sustainable supply chain for industry 4.0 requirements. *Computers & Industrial Engineering*, *127*, 925–953. doi:10.1016/j.cie.2018.11.030

María, J. J. L., Polo, O. C. C., & Elhadary, T. (2023). An Analysis of the Morality and Social Responsibility of Non-Profit Organizations. *FMDB Transactions on Sustainable Technoprise Letters*, *1*(1), 28–35.

Miah, S. (2021). IoT in Supply Chain Manage-ment: Opportunities and Challenges for Businesses in Early Industry 4.0 Context. Operations and Supply Chain Management. *International Journal (Toronto, Ont.)*, *14*(2), 148–161.

Ogunmola, G. A., Singh, B., Sharma, D. K., Regin, R., Rajest, S. S., & Singh, N. (2021). Involvement of distance measure in assessing and resolving efficiency environmental obstacles. *2021 International Conference on Computational Intelligence and Knowledge Economy (ICCIKE)*. IEEE. 10.1109/IC-CIKE51210.2021.9410765

Priscila, S. S., Rajest, S. S., Tadiboina, S. N., Regin, R., & András, S. (2023). Analysis of Machine Learning and Deep Learning Methods for Superstore Sales Prediction. *FMDB Transactions on Sustainable Computer Letters*, *1*(1), 1–11.

Rejeb, A., Simske, S., Rejeb, K., Treiblmaier, H., & Zailani, S. (2020). Internet of Things research in supply chain management and logistics: A bibliometric analysis. *Internet of Things*, *12*(100318), 100318. doi:10.1016/j.iot.2020.100318

Said, F. B., & Tripathi, S. (2023). Epistemology of Digital Journalism Shift in South Global Nations: A Bibliometric Analysis. *FMDB Transactions on Sustainable Technoprise Letters*, *1*(1), 47–60.

Sakhnini, J., Karimipour, H., Dehghantanha, A., Parizi, R. M., & Srivastava, G. (2021). Security aspects of Internet of Things aided smart grids: A bibliometric survey. *Internet of Things*, *14*(100111), 100111. doi:10.1016/j.iot.2019.100111

Sharma, K., Singh, B., Herman, E., Regine, R., Rajest, S. S., & Mishra, V. P. (2021). Maximum information measure policies in reinforcement learning with deep energy-based model. *2021 International Conference on Computational Intelligence and Knowledge Economy (ICCIKE)*. IEEE. 10.1109/IC-CIKE51210.2021.9410756

Shavarani, S. M., Golabi, M., & Izbirak, G. (2021). A capacitated biobjective location problem with uniformly distributed demands in the UAV-supported delivery operation. *International Transactions in Operational Research: A Journal of The International Federation of Operational Research Societies*, *28*(6), 3220–3243. doi:10.1111/itor.12735

Srinivas, K., Velmurugan, P. R., & Andiyappillai, N. (2023). Digital Human Resources and Management Support Improve Human Resources Effectiveness. *FMDB Transactions on Sustainable Management Letters*, *1*(1), 32–45.

Tambaip, B., Hadi, A. F. F., & Tjilen, A. P. (2023). Optimizing Public Service Performance: Unleashing the Potential of Compassion as an Indicator of Public Service Motivation. *FMDB Transactions on Sustainable Management Letters*, *1*(2), 46–55.

Tripathi, S., & Al-Shahri, M. (2023). Problems and Prospects on the Evolution of Advertising and Public Relations Industries in Oman. *FMDB Transactions on Sustainable Management Letters*, *1*(1), 1–11.

Tsang, Y. P., Choy, K. L., Wu, C. H., Ho, G. T. S., Lam, H. Y., & Koo, P. S. (2017). An IoT-based cargo monitoring system for enhancing operational effectiveness under a cold chain environment. *International Journal of Engineering Business Management*, *9*, 184797901774906. doi:10.1177/1847979017749063

Tu, M. (2018). An exploratory study of Internet of Things (IoT) adoption intention in logistics and supply chain management: A mixed research approach. *International Journal of Logistics Management*, *29*(1), 131–151. doi:10.1108/IJLM-11-2016-0274

Tu, M., Lim, M. K., & Yang, M. (2018). IoT-based production supply chian management and logistics system - Part 2: IoT-based cyber-physical system: a framework and evaluation. *Industrial Management & Data Systems*, *118*, 96–125. doi:10.1108/IMDS-11-2016-0504

Venkateswaran, P. S., & Viktor, P. (2023). A Study on Brand Equity of Fast-Moving Consumer Goods with Reference to Madurai, Tamil Nadu. *FMDB Transactions on Sustainable Technoprise Letters*, *1*(1), 13–27.

Witkowski, K. (2017). Internet of things, big data, industry 4.0 – innovative solutions in logistics and supply chains management. *Procedia Engineering*, *182*, 763–769. doi:10.1016/j.proeng.2017.03.197

Chapter 13
A Study of Detecting Individual to Mental Health of Fear of Falling (FOF) in Indian Cities

Bhavika Malik
https://orcid.org/0000-0002-3898-9809
Karnavati University, India

Akshath Lilesh Kamath
Karnavati University, India

Anusha Krishnan Iyer
Karnavati University, India

Anuj Dinesh Ghag
Karnavati University, India

S. Sneha
Karnavati University, India

Nandini Shah
Karnavati University, India

Arshkirat Gill
Karnavati University, India

ABSTRACT

The relationship between fear of falling (FOF) and fall-related injuries in elderly is becoming quite prominent and its factors have not been explored. FOF is a person's anxiety towards mobilizing, with a perception that a fall will occur. Approximately 25% to 55% of community-living elderly are afraid of falling. The context of this problem is generalized in terms of FOF and has no sufficient data available for washroom spaces. Physical, medical, and psychological performances of 175 people in the age gap of 65 - 75 years were considered, over three cities i.e., Mumbai, Pune, and Kota. Past fall histories, medical histories, GAUG tests and responses to various washroom activities were recorded to establish the FES table. On the basis of these evaluations the factors causing FOF were determined, and a city comparison was made. This chapter provides an overview of FOF and a foundation on which to base decisions about the design of preventive interventions.

DOI: 10.4018/979-8-3693-1301-5.ch013

1. INTRODUCTION

According to the National Library of Medicine (NLM), the prevalence of domestic accidents was 12.7%. Out of them all, falls (54.4%) were the most common type of domestic accident. In Indian houses, people tend to spend more time in washrooms than in any other segment of the space. The most vulnerable age group to these types of accidents is 65 and older. Various definitions of fear of falling have evolved over the years (Ward, 2012). FOF was described as an "ongoing concern about falling" that significantly limits engagement in daily activities. Some authors referred to fear of falling as a person's loss of balance in his or her activities. While other authors defined fear of falling as having low confidence in avoiding falls (low fall-related efficacy) and being fearful of falling, Based on previous experiments, fear of falling exists in individuals who have encountered falls and is more prominent in them. Maturing or functional decay might be considered one of the essential drivers of falls because of the physiological changes that lead to fear of falling. Such physiological changes result in diminished muscle strength, reformist bone misfortune, a decrease in invulnerability against infections, a decline in digestion and organ capacity, and the decay of reflexes and senses (Da Silva Coqueiro, et al., 2009).

After thorough research, we finalized a problem statement centered on how the fear of falling is a factor affecting a major percentage of washroom injuries. On the basis of this observed research gap, we go forward to determine the exact factors causing this FOF in the early elderly class. Fear of falling can be triggered not only by psychological and physiological factors in an individual but also by physical environmental factors (Lee, et al., 2018). These environmental factors may include slippery flooring, improper walls, a lack of support handles, cluttering spaces with objects, loose parts, and level differences. The data received in the interviews was used to analyze the different segments of the problem area. The team approached product ideation by minimizing, replacing, or eliminating the objects causing danger to users. The data collected from the analysis and primary and secondary research was the most vital part of this phase as it determined what factors were to be targeted from a vast array. The team finalized three tangible product ideations; the CMF (color, material, and finish) of all three products were based on availability, standards, and regulations of material usage in India. Most of the materials used in the products are highly recyclable, ensuring minimal damage to nature when used on a small or large scale.

2. BACKGROUND OF CURRENT RESEARCH

Elderly people have always been conscious of falling, making it difficult to mobilize without any worries. The elders explained how the fall factor revolves more around the washroom area and how they have to be cautious and slow while using it. Some of them have prepared simple tasks to drain out the soapy water, making it easier for them to stand and work. People are quite aware of the level difference and objects in the bathroom, which gives them confidence that they won't crash into objects and slip. Doing activities like brushing and dressing up doesn't bother them much, as these tasks barely take any time and people prefer changing outside rather than inside the washroom. Slippers are being used by a few of them to give them the grip they need to walk on the slippery tiles, in spite of the fact that they are wet. Falls may increase the already-present medical issues (Teixeira, et al., 2019).

The mindset of the person gets affected by the number of falls already experienced, which increases the chances of more falls in the future. People with a previous fall history or medical conditions have a higher psychological fear of falling. Most of them prefer bigger, uncluttered washroom spaces, as it instils confidence in them. Many of them face problems when there are slippery, wet floors. They also prefer evenly levelled washrooms with no steps or level differences. Even if there is a step, they would like to have a railing that would aid them. Elderly people find it advantageous to have a railing in the washroom while they get up from the commode or even while they navigate around the washroom, especially when the floor is wet. This gives them a sense of confidence and security. There is no FOF data available for the elderly in the washroom sector. There is no determination of factors that develop FOF in the washroom. This is the research gap that we will be working on in this study (Wang, et al., 2017).

3. LITERATURE REVIEW

Exploring existing research papers threw light on a variety of relevant topics such as ergonomics, fear of falling, factors that affect FOF, and understanding the psychology of elderly people. The summary of these papers, highlighting some key takeaways, is as follows: For elderly people to feel confident in their surroundings, it is necessary to make our surroundings and situations favorable to the elderly so that they can live comfortably. Bruno, et al., (2020) emphasizes the need to promote barrier-free dwellings irrespective of age, ensuring they stay that way throughout the future. An Indian study (4) focuses on the impact of FOF on the elderly and how it is causing major injuries and lifestyle changes. This helps successfully develop the relationship between the built-in environment and fall-related attributes. It also specifies the evidence to mark the spaces and architectural structures that are perceived by the elderly as a potential threat to their safety. Another Indian study (8) shows that the vast majority of people who discover the washroom as a very relaxing place never briefly think about this room as a hazardous spot. The report also shows that the restroom itself is a hazardous section of the house, encircled by water, tricky tiles, and hard earthenware surfaces. The psychology of elderly people also has an important role to play in understanding their specific requirements. One author talks about the Indian population of elderly people being taken care of by their families due to the joint family system (Chen & Tsai, 2007). Due to the geographical dispersion of families into smaller groups of people, it has become difficult for them to fend for themselves in old age. Functional abilities, independence, and quality of life hold the highest priority in their minds, often leading to unhappiness and uneasiness even with the slightest things. An interesting participatory ergonomics study (5) was conducted, concerned with the biological changes in the elderly that lead to accidents while performing activities in the bathroom. The participatory approach involves the subjects justifying problems, providing solutions, and evaluating the findings themselves.

A study shows that a simple, well-designed sign effectively encourages people to use the toilet (Fernie, 1994). For example, one study proved that energy conservation in washrooms with signs was eight times higher than those with no signs or visual cues. Solutions for designing better washrooms are in the pipeline as well (Gudavalli and Vagvala, 2018). The accurate falling detection system for the elderly (AFDE) focuses on falling detection among the elderly (Gupta, et al., 2017). Research has found that falls are the leading cause of accidental deaths among people over the age of 75, and 55% of accidents take place in washrooms. The aim of this research is to come up with a system solution that will be able to detect falls. Robots are being developed to solve the physical, cognitive, medical, and emotional challenges that older people face (Hasiholan, et al., 2019). Another interesting solution was the iMagic-Box, a portable walk-in bathroom that aims to create an atmosphere where the user feels confident about taking a bath independently without the thought of burdening their family members for the same (Dawal, et al., 2015). Other solutions revolve around designing a grab bar, as it is effective and a better replacement for knurled finishes. The grab bar can be easily positioned in the room to help the person lift from the bed. The author concluded that low-technology solutions are worthy of academic effort and that devices should address their caregivers (Castellucci, 2018).

Research shows that 33.3% of people over the age of 65 are restricted in their activities. A similar study aims to find the conformity between the anthropometric data and the real-life facilities provided (Dianat, et al., 2018). The research brings forward pointers such as the handrails being too far to reach and the beds not being proportional, ultimately leading to major health risks for the elderly. Hu, et al., (2007) say that the home-based rehabilitation of elderly patients improves their autonomy, independence, and reintegration into society, and so the environment plays an important role, as do different assistive technologies. The planning of the layout is necessary in this potentially dangerous area and should be based on logical and non-logical relationships. In another study (Kulkarni, et al., 2020), elderly people use their abilities to perform the basic activities of daily life like bathing, and there are only a few assistive technologies available in the field. The concepts developed for a robotic bath show that it is possible to automate a sequence of activities in the bathroom. According to Kant, (2021) people who find bathrooms a quiet retreat never thought of bathrooms as dangerous places. The most important thing in home safety is the bathroom, as it has water, slippery tile, and hard ceramic surfaces. To minimize accidental falls, a systematic design should be used. Kose, (2001) focuses on the study that shows that as the ageing of society approaches, the issue of elderly people has become more prominent. The bathroom is one of the most accident-prone areas in the house. The elderly finds it much more difficult to perform in the bathroom in Taiwan because of the dry-wet coexistence condition. This investigation begins with a "field survey" of the amenities of these two types of senior care centers in the bathroom. Second, use the "operation consciousness questionnaire" to determine the difficulties and issues encountered when operating and behaving in the restrooms. and, with permission, make the bathrooms comfortable and secure.

Maki, et al., (1991) talk about how a 3- and 6-year prospective study of risk factors using data from the longitudinal population study "Good Aging in Skene" Falls in the general elderly population: a 3- and 6-year prospective study of risk factors using data from the longitudinal population study "Good Aging in Skene" Using a prospective design, the goal of this study was to identify risk variables for falls in a general senior population after three and six years. It reduces the physical capacity; it develops the fear of falling and inhabiting the same environment; it limits their independence and functional capacity; and it increases the financial cost of medical care. According to Ming and Thiry (2017) a comparative study with the Japanese people shows that the Chinese elderly are larger in the dimensions of the body trunk and the Japanese elderly are larger in the dimensions of the head and extremities. Ong, et al., (2012) say that in Proceedings of the 48th Annual Human Factors and Ergonomics Society of Australia Conference, it focuses on a number of anthropometric studies of senior populations, or at least those involving a significant elderly component in the sample. This was done in order to inform the decisions that would be made throughout the construction of a new study.

Different methodologies are feasible, and which one is chosen will be determined by a variety of criteria, including the study's resources and the current design issues to be addressed. Robinson, et al., (2014) talk about an experience from a study in Malaysia that revolves around the anthropometric data of the Malaysian elderly population, with the thought being how the elderly seek to live independently in this challenging world. Research efforts were taken to establish a comfortable living environment with products and equipment in favor of the elderly. Sussman, and Gifford, (2012) used the values of body mass, height or stature, BMI, waist, arm, and calf circumferences, triceps skin fold thickness, the circumferences of the waist, arm, and calf, the thickness of the triceps skin fold, and the circumference of the arm muscle to describe differences (Lorenzen-Ewing, 2015). The current study provides data that can be utilized to assess the anthropometric status of elderly people in Havana and other Cuban cities. Stenhagen, et al., (2013) conveyed that this survey features methodological issues (inspecting contemplations and model assessment and testing) that ought to be considered in future exploration to guarantee a client-focused methodology of the plan interaction. Li, et al., (2003) jotted down the analysis and application of ergonomics in the kitchen and bathrooms of elderly people. First, the routine of elders was analyzed, getting to know their needs and difficulties in these rooms. With this data, the problems were identified, showing possible accidents in the bathroom and kitchen due to their vulnerability in routine tasks' performance. Based on all this information, changes and adaptations to the layout of the kitchen and bathroom are made to make them safer and more comfortable for them and understand the risk factors associated with FOF in individuals aged over 60 years. In conclusion, a large number of people expressed concerns about falling, and the paper was successfully able to find several factors that are associated with developing FOF.

In this study, they discovered that sex and discomfort in the neighborhood environment were connected with FOF in both those with and without a history of falls. Second, when looking at the common environmental determinants for FOF in those with and without a history of falling, older people who were more dissatisfied with their neighborhood environment also had more FOF. Identifying the characteristics of elderly persons who develop a fear of falling after experiencing a fall and investigating the association of his or her fear with changes in their health status over time. Variations in the SAFFE response, according to the findings of this study High levels of fear of falling as measured by the SAFFE and patterns on a single dimension of fear of falling It's been linked to a slew of negative health effects. An extensive gap was found in the analysis of the relation between physical, social, and environmental factors, and no inconsistencies were held into consideration. The conclusion of the literature review shows that fear of falling leads to many physical and psychological problems, and despite the large number of older adults suffering from these serious consequences of FOF, we discovered an exploration hole around the reason for FOF in elderly people in washroom regions.

4. PROBLEM STATEMENT

In domestic areas, the bathroom is a place that has a higher tendency for falls and a higher chance of serious injuries due to various exterior and interior factors like physical, psychological, emotional, environmental, etc. These probabilities increase with age, which causes an increase in FOF levels and affects them by limiting and/or slowing down regular activities in those areas. It also impacts other spaces, which can invite further medical or psychological issues. It is also generally observed that as age increases, the elderly get more cautious due to this fear of falling, and they tend to limit their activities. We arrived at this problem area after thorough research and the gathering of information. There is limited knowledge about these factors behind FOF, which makes it necessary to find the attributes affecting them. There are different activities happening inside the bathroom, like showering, changing clothes, cleaning, brushing, etc. The level of FOF while performing them varies, which can be assessed to determine the triggers. The determination of these attributes and the causes of increased levels of fear in the early elderly, i.e., those aged 65 to 75, is the main area of research. This study can help us understand different domains that require more focus for improvements in some features or the development of new products, technologies, or systems. The level of FOF is also affected by medical conditions and previous fall history, considerations of which are taken while collecting data about various activities performed in the bathroom. The comparison of this data collected from three different cities in India, which are Mumbai, Pune, and Kota, can further specify how the factors change over the geographical conditions.

4.1. AIM

Determination of significant factors that cause fear of falling (FOF) in the elderly and a comparison study between 3 Indian cities: Mumbai, Pune, and Kota.

4.2. Objectives

The objective of this survey is to find the appropriate factors that develop fear of falling among early elderly people in the age group of 65–75 years while performing tasks and activities in the washroom, which would help us develop possible solutions. The task is to develop a FES data table that can help us determine the factors accurately. The data is collected from Mumbai, Pune, and Kota. The motive behind collecting data from all three cities was to verify whether the FOF and its related data change from one geographical location to another. Some factors, like stress, showed higher levels in cities like Mumbai and Pune than in Kota, comparatively.

5. METHODOLOGY

The literature review was used to understand the current scenario. After the collection of primary data, a questionnaire is prepared on the basis of the knowledge obtained from the literature reviews. We conducted a total of 175 interviews with people between the ages of 65 and 75, which will be referred to as "elderly" and "seniors" throughout the research paper. Informed consent was obtained for experimentation with human participants. The privacy rights of human participants were always respected. The work described has been carried out in accordance with the Code of Ethics of the World Medical Association. The data collected from the interviews was converted into analytical data with the help of tabular sheets; the questionnaire included closed and open-ended questions that let us decide between unstructured and structured observations. The next step after this is to study the common problems on the basis of gender. There are three questions on psychology that are based on confidence, stress, and fear of falling in seniors. The next 16 questions in the questionnaire are on the tasks and activities performed by the seniors in the bathroom or washroom. Depending on the difficulty level they felt while performing that particular task, the senior can select the option from "not at all concerning," "slightly concerning," "fairly concerning," or "very concerning." Some of the questions are: does the senior feel a fear of falling while cleaning washrooms? while walking on wet tiles? If there is poor lighting while using the washroom, Is it difficult to reach for objects? While bathing or showering, is there a fear of slipping? While opening or closing a door, is there a fear that they might fall? While crossing the door frame, there is a level difference at the bottom of the door, so does the senior have a fear that they will stumble? While walking in slippers or while using soap or detergent, do they have a fear of losing balance? While moving or lifting buckets, do they have a fear of tumbling? When holding on to something, do they fear that their hand will slip? And some more of these activity-based questions were asked.

Then there was a small task called the GUAG (get up and go) test, in which the senior person has to get up from the chair, walk 5 steps and turn around, then walk 5 steps back and sit down on the chair. We recorded the time taken to complete this task. If the time taken by the senior is below 20 seconds, then the senior is fit in terms of mobility, and if it is more than 30 seconds, then the senior has a high risk of falling and is not fit in terms of mobility. The standards of interpretation of the GUAG results are predetermined. During the interview, the seniors were asked if they have any medical history or any past medical conditions, as well as if they have a fall history. All of this data, which was collected during the entire primary research, was then used to calculate the FES point for each participant. The FES table has been developed based on the standards set by the Institute for Development Policy and Management, University of Manchester, UK. So, if the FES number is ranging from 16 to 19, it is a low concern, indicating that the participants have a low fall rate. If the range is from 20 to 27, it is a moderate concern and indicates that the participants have a moderate fall rate. And if the range is from 28 to 64, it is a high concern, indicating that the person has a higher fall rate.

The FES data is finally used in SPSS software to develop graphs with the MLR (multiple linear regression) method. The scattering dot graph is used for a better understanding of the data and also to understand what the confidence level, stress level, and fear of falling are in males and females in different cities (Mumbai, Pune, and Kota). Also, these graphs were parametric, whereas only city graphs were non-parametric as the samples collected in each city were not equal. Analytical data is used to find tangible solutions to the problem of falling in the washrooms. The possible solutions are putting radium strips on the floor and making a path to the latrine so that even if there is poor lighting or it is nighttime, the FOF is not triggered. The next solution is to put a tile that is channeled to the drainage, and the top of it is made of black gravel tile material, which is capable of absorbing the water down to the channel tiles so that the floor is barely wet. The last solution is to make slight slopes on both ends of the door bottom so that the senior doesn't tumble.

Table 1. Socio demographic information of participants

	Female			Male		
	Yes		No	Yes		No
Medical	59.7		40.2	49.3		50.7
Fall	32.6		67.3	38.4		61.4
	Low	Medium	High	Low	Medium	High
Confidence	35.8	54.3	9.7	45.7	45.7	8.4
Stress	14.1	58.6	27.1	18.07	31.3	50.7
FOF	20.7	41.3	38.0	12.2	42.1	45.7
FES	7.6	28.2	65.2	14.4	30.1	55.4

The table 1 shows the percentage of female and male participants plotted against various variables i.e. past medical history, past fall history, confidence levels, stress levels, fear of falling and fall efficiency scale.

6. RESULTS

Figure 1 is a graph plotted of stress level across FES, and it shows that the people who recorded a higher stress level have a high FES point (22-45), those who recorded a moderate stress level have a moderate FES point (20-40), and those who recorded a lower stress level have a low FES point (16–38). The final results obtained on the basis of the plotted graphs are as follows:

Figure 1. FES point against stress levels

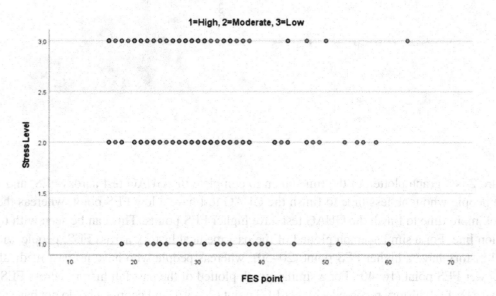

For a similar graph plotted of confidence levels across FES, people with high confidence levels are seen to have a low FES point (16–35), people with moderate confidence levels are seen to have a higher FES point (20–40), and people with low confidence levels are seen to have a varied FES chart ranging from high values to lower values. A similar graph plotted of the direct question "Do they have a fear of falling?" across FES shows that the people who recorded a higher fear of falling have a high FES point (20–55), people who recorded a moderate fear of falling have a moderate FES point (20–40), and people who recorded a lower fear of falling have a low FES point (16–35).

Figure 2. A graph of FES point against the time taken to finish GUAG test

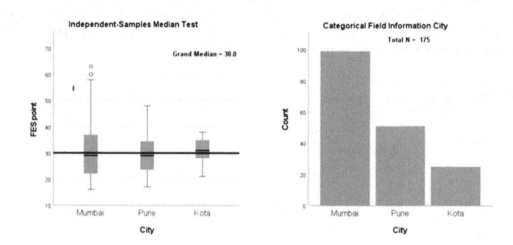

Figure 2 is a graph plotted of the time taken to complete the GUAG test across FES, and it shows that the people who took less time to finish the GUAG test have a low FES point, whereas the people who took more time to finish the GUAG test have higher FES points. This can be seen with the linear regression line. For a similar graph plotted of the past medical history across FES, people with a past medical history have a higher FES point (20–50), whereas people who have no past medical history have a lower FES point (16–40). For a similar graph plotted of the past fall history across FES, people who have a past fall history recorded a higher FES point (20–50), and people who do not have a past fall history recorded a lower FES point (16–40). Another graph plotted of the genders across FES shows that the male population has a lower FES point (16–35), whereas females have a higher FES point (20–50).

Figure 3. Graph of cities against FES point and graph of cities against the sample count

black gravel tile

grooved tile beneath the black gravel to direct the water towards the drainage

Figure 3 shows the city comparison graph comparing the FES points across three Indian cities, and it shows that the value of FES for Mumbai ranges from 23 to 38, the value of FES for Pune ranges from 25 to 34, and the value of FES for Kota ranges from 28 to 35. The number of samples collected as per from Mumbai was 98, Pune was 50, and Kota was 27; the median value of FES for all three cities was 30 (Figure 3).

7. PROPOSED SOLUTIONS

Lighting Solution: One of the major concerns derived from the survey was that elderly people's fear of falling increases due to poor lighting. Hence, one of the ideas included developing a simple and afford-able system of lighting in washrooms. This aims to aid the elderly in using washrooms that are dimly lit or while using them at night. The solution involves sticking high-intensity reflective tape on the floor of the washroom, which would guide the user towards the commode. Even in a dark washroom, these strips would lead the user and also indicate any obstruction in the pathway, thereby making the experience safer and easier. This can be seen in the image below (Figure 4).

Figure 4. Depicting solution one, the use of high reflectivity tapes

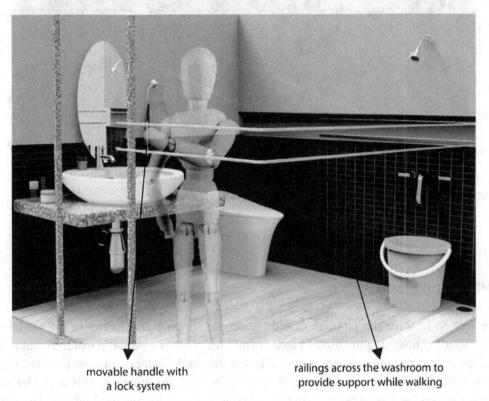

movable handle with
a lock system

railings across the washroom to
provide support while walking

Movable railing: Elderly people usually require some kind of support while doing activities in the washroom. There's always minimal or no support in the washroom, making it difficult for the elderly to walk through the area, which can disturb the balance of the body and lead to falls and accidents. That's why we came up with the concept of "movable railing," which will move across all the important areas, making it easier for them to hold onto while exerting their body weight entirely on it. The handle will travel through two rods, which will be quite smooth while moving, and a button to lock the handle in case they need to stop by the washroom, as shown in below (Figure 5).

Figure 5. Depicting solution two, the use of movable railings

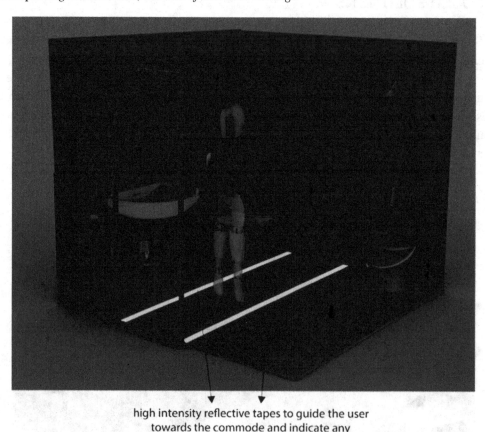

high intensity reflective tapes to guide the user
towards the commode and indicate any
obstructions in dimly lit washrooms

7.1. Self-Drying Flooring

Since we wanted to solve the problem of elderly people slipping and falling in the washrooms, we proposed a solution involving the use of black gravel tiles. This is a versatile material that is anti-slip, retains water, is compression-resistant, is reusable, durable, and weather-resistant. Underneath this will be a layer of grooved tiles, which will direct all the water towards the drainage. This would let the elderly people move within the washroom confidently without a fear of slipping and falling. The structure is shown below (Figure 6).

Figure 6. Depicting solution three, the use of black gravel tiles

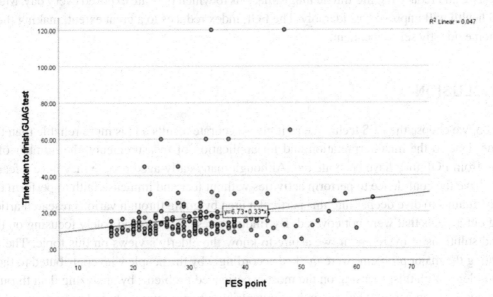

7.2. Recommendations

The study of this research paper and the results presented by it can be used for future references by people who are concerned about this particular area, which is "Factors causing Fear of Falling (FOF) in the elderly in the washroom sector." The primary and secondary data covered the necessary data for this paper, which has been included. The final FES tables, along with various graphs, were analyzed using various statistical tools like SPSS (Statistical Package for the Social Sciences) and MLR (Multiple Linear Regression). Using all these techniques, the final results were interpreted. These interpretations gave us a clear insight into the factors that are the main cause of FOF in the elderly. This research paper was successful in finding the factors affecting FOF and providing appropriate design solutions for them. We made CAD models to demonstrate the solutions that could be applied to resolve these problems in modern times with the help of simple and easy products. The solutions provided include a lighting solution to target the poor lighting conditions for the elderly, a movable railing solution for support for activities, and the use of black gravel tiles in order to deal with wet floors and avoid slippery conditions. By specifying the kinds of materials, structures, and techniques that could be used to make these products functional, it'll be easier to apply the solutions in the current washrooms.

7.3. Implications

Going door to door and asking people questions and establishing conversations related to the topic brought out major concerns that could not have been thought of otherwise. We were able to analyze how a person's psychological health, like stress and confidence levels, and physical health, like medical histories, mobility tests, and previous fall history, are all major factors that affect the FES scale. All these concept solutions are effective ways to decrease fear of falling and successfully remove the cognitive strain that the activities lead to. Adopting these solutions will help the elderly target group improve their lifestyle and reduce the life-threatening situations to which they are exposed every day. Mental and physical health will improve considerably. The FOF index reduces to a great extent, making the elderly population evidently self-dependent.

8. CONCLUSION

Further on, we choose the FES technique as it gives accurate results and is more reliable than the ABC technique. Due to the misinterpretation and misapplication of measurements, the number of people suffering from FOF may have been altered. Although many early-aged people may have a fear of falling, they have the confidence to perform activities without fear and immense faith to perform the tasks smoothly. It aims to dive deeper into this particular area by going through various research articles and pointing out aspects that were not covered. By finding a research gap and solely focusing on the measures and solutions to overcome it, we aspire to know the elderly's views on this topic. The pointers highlighting the major problems were marked accordingly by the people who contributed to the degree of the problem. With this, focusing on the most experienced problems by analyzing data through various methods came in handy. This research will contribute to community-based resources and help the resource centers educate older adults about the importance of FOF prevention and make them aware of possible risk factors.

8.1. Limitation

The limitations of this study include essential points like the limited age group range that could have been covered. Another one could also be a smaller number of solutions for the class chosen that specifically stick to the respective age group and not beyond that. All the problems and issues faced by the elderly were not taken into consideration, as more time and research would have been required due to the complexity of the topic. We stuck to the research and solutions that are practical and can be put to use without causing long-term accidents. The existence of a nationwide lockdown limited our resource options and further made it difficult for people to accept us with open arms so that we could conduct interviews and tests thoroughly. Our movements were restricted due to rules and regulations based on a national order, which is why our research lacked participants. The geographical distribution of group members was not homogeneous, causing the balance of our data to be disturbed.

REFERENCES

Bruno, J., Veuas, S. J., Wayne, L. J., Romero, R. N., & Baumgartner, P. (2020). *USA department of Internal Medicine and Gerontology (Professor J.-L Albarede)* (Vol. 87131). World Health Organisation Collaborative Center to Promote the Safety of Aged Individuals.

Castellucci, H. I. (2018). A review of the methodology and applications of anthropometry in ergonomics and product design. *Ergonomics, 61*(12), 1696–1720. doi:10.1080/00140139.2018.1502817 PMID:30022717

Chen, M. S., & Tsai, Y. L. (2007). The Research of Usability in Elder Care Centers' Bathroom. In 會議名稱: *The International Conference on Kansei Engineering and Emotion Research.*

Da Silva Coqueiro, R., Barbosa, A. R., & Borgatto, A. F. (2009). Anthropometric measurements in the elderly of Havana, Cuba: Age and sex differences. *Nutrition (Burbank, Los Angeles County, Calif.), 25*(1), 33–39. doi:10.1016/j.nut.2008.07.007 PMID:18834720

Dawal, S. Z. M., Ismail, Z., Yusuf, K., Abdul-Rashid, S. H., Shalahim, N. S. M., Abdullah, N. S., & Kamil, N. S. M. (2015). Determination of the significant anthropometry dimensions for user-friendly designs of domestic furniture and appliances-Experience from a study in Malaysia. *Measurement, 59*, 205–215. doi:10.1016/j.measurement.2014.09.030

Dianat, I., Molenbroek, J., & Castellucci, H. I. (2018). A review of the methodology and applications of anthropometry in ergonomics and product design. *Ergonomics, 61*(12), 1696–1720. doi:10.1080/00140139.2018.1502817 PMID:30022717

Fernie, G. (1994). Technology to assist elderly people's safe mobility. *Experimental Aging Research, 20*(3), 219–228. doi:10.1080/03610739408253968 PMID:7957484

Gudavalli, N., & Vagvala, P. (2018). *Impact of Built-Environment on Fear of Falling (FOF) in Elderly. Humanizing work and work Environment (HWWE 2016)*. English.

Gupta, S., Gill, J. K., & Bal, S. B. (2017). A comparative study on reasons of home accidents amongst elederly of rural and urban households of Ludhiana district. *Advance Research Journal of Social Science, 8*(2), 316–322. doi:10.15740/HAS/ARJSS/8.2/316-322

Hasiholan, B. P., Susilowati, I. H., & Satrya, C. (2019). *The conformity of anthropometric measurements of bathroom and bedroom designs for.*

Hu, H., Li, Z., Yan, J., Wang, X., Xiao, H., Duan, J., & Zheng, L. (2007). Anthropometric measurement of the Chinese elderly living in the Beijing area. *International Journal of Industrial Ergonomics, 37*(4), 303–311. doi:10.1016/j.ergon.2006.11.006

Kant, K. (2021). *Housing for Elderly and Differently-Abled*. Notion Press.

Kose, S. A. T. O. S. H. I. (2001). Design guidelines of dwellings for the ageing society: Japanese approach toward universal design. In *Proceedings of the CIB World Building Congress* (pp. 179-188). Springer.

Kulkarni, S., Gadkari, R., & Nagarkar, A. (2020). Risk factors for fear of falling in older adults in India. *Journal of Public Health (Berlin), 28*(2), 123–129. doi:10.100710389-019-01061-9

Lee, S., Oh, E., & Hong, G. R. S. (2018). Comparison of factors associated with fear of falling between older adults with and without a fall history. *International Journal of Environmental Research and Public Health, 15*(5), 982. doi:10.3390/ijerph15050982 PMID:29757960

Li, F., Fisher, K. J., Harmer, P., McAuley, E., & Wilson, N. L. (2003). Fear of falling in elderly persons: Association with falls, functional ability, and quality of life. *The Journals of Gerontology. Series B, Psychological Sciences and Social Sciences, 58*(5), P283–P290. doi:10.1093/geronb/58.5.P283 PMID:14507935

Lorenzen-Ewing, T.B. (2015). *Exploring physical and social environmental barriers and facilitators that affect older adults' fear of falling: A sample funding proposal.*

Maki, B. E., Holliday, P. J., & Topper, A. K. (1991). Fear of falling and postural performance in the elderly. *Journal of Gerontology*, *46*(4), M123–M131. doi:10.1093/geronj/46.4.M123 PMID:2071833

Ming, C. K., & Thiry, J. Y. T. (2017). Independent Bathing for Older Adults: The Conceptualization of the iMagic-BOX Portable Walk-In Bathtub. In *International Conference on Cross-Cultural Design* (pp. 161-170). Springer, Cham. 10.1007/978-3-319-57931-3_13

Ong, J. N. D., Zhang, H., Lee, V. Y. A., Phua, C., Sim, K., Liu, Y., & Zhang, X. (2012). The Accurate Falling Detection System For The Elderly (AFDE). *APEC Youth Scientist Journal*, *4*, 83–93.

Robinson, H., MacDonald, B., & Broadbent, E. (2014). The role of healthcare robots for older people at home: A review. *International Journal of Social Robotics*, *6*(4), 575–591. doi:10.100712369-014-0242-2

Stenhagen, M., Ekström, H., Nordell, E., & Elmståhl, S. (2013). Falls in the general elderly population: A 3-and 6-year prospective study of risk factors using data from the longitudinal population study 'Good ageing in Skane'. *BMC Geriatrics*, *13*(1), 1–11. doi:10.1186/1471-2318-13-81 PMID:23919320

Sussman, R., & Gifford, R. (2012). Please turn off the lights: The effectiveness of visual prompts. *Applied Ergonomics*, *43*(3), 596–603. doi:10.1016/j.apergo.2011.09.008 PMID:21963251

Teixeira, D. K. D. S., Andrade, L. M., Santos, J. L. P., & Caires, E. S. (2019). Falls among the elderly: Environmental limitations and functional losses. *Revista Brasileira de Geriatria e Gerontologia*, *22*(3), 22. doi:10.1590/1981-22562019022.180229

Wang, D., Wu, J., & Lin, Q. (2017). A novel method for designing and optimizing the layout of facilities in bathroom for the elderly in home-based rehabilitation. *Disability and Rehabilitation. Assistive Technology*, *13*(4), 333–341. doi:10.1080/17483107.2017.1319426 PMID:28453365

Ward, S. (2012). What to measure? Review of measurements in anthropometric studies of elderly populations. In *Proceedings of the 48th Annual Human Factors and Ergonomics Society of Australia Conference* (pp. 11-14). Springer.

Chapter 14
A Systematic View of Sentiment Analysis on Different Techniques, Challenges, and Future Directions in COVID-19

A. Sathya

Bishop Heber College, Bharathidasan University, India

M. S. Mythili

Bishop Heber College, Bharathidasan University, India

ABSTRACT

In the last few years, social networking sites have exploded at a rapid pace. Sentiment analysis (SA) is a way of mining data and reading text using natural language processing(NLP) In today's era, corona virus is a hot issue and pandemic all over the world. Millions of citizens use blogs or microblogging tools to communicate their viewpoints. Twitter is one of the handiest platforms and most popular social media for users to share their thoughts and ideas. Through blogging sites, the public can share their feelings and opinions such as "panic, anger, misery," and it can be divided the text into three categories: positive, negative, and neutral. Sentiment analysis is employed in a variety of industries, including healthcare, finance, sports, politics, hospitality, and tourism. According to a comparison of ten primary studies, Naive Bayes (NB) and support vector machine (SVM) are widely used algorithms for sentiment analysis in COVID-19.

1. INTRODUCTION

Nowadays, people like to write reviews about things they use or about anything that's trending on the internet (Zhou, Z. et al., 2019). Online media consists of a huge number of posts, so knowing one's perspective can be quite a challenge. Sentiment analysis is a method that uses text analytics to analyse and classify emotions using Twitter information through an online review process (Nirmala et al., 2023).

DOI: 10.4018/979-8-3693-1301-5.ch014

The purpose is to understand how the public views fear, depression, and disgust, which are directly related to the COVID-19 pandemic in India (Cirillo et al., 2023; Wikipedia, 2020). A text can convey multiple polarities of sentiment at the same time. Sentiment analysis is a natural language processing technique that divides the text into positive, negative, and neutral categories (Pandit, 2023). Opinions can be based on subjective, objective, or both types of data (Priscila et al., 2023). The subjective form includes a positive or negative view, while the objective form contains facts (Abdul Mohaimin Rahat & Kahir, 2019). Using opinion mining, the subjectivity and objectivity of knowledge are created (Saxena & Chaudhary, 2023). The outcome may be either positive or negative, or a combination of both (Vinoth Kumar et al., 2022). After the world war, "tsunami and COVID-19" were the biggest problems faced by the people. In today's world, people rely a lot on social networking sites like Instagram, Facebook, and Twitter (Suganthi & Sathiaseelan, 2023). It is predicted that posts shared on social media will provide people with accurate information (Jeba et al., 2023). But in most cases, the information led to incorrect decisions, like when COVID-19 information circulated over the mass media (Imran et al., 2020). In addition, most online information is unstructured. So proper pre-processing stages should be used before applying sentiment analysis (Pradha et al., 2019). To overcome the complication of many research challenges, a set of feature vectors can be taken by applying effective feature extraction techniques like "TF-IDF (Term Frequency-Inverse Document Frequency), gramme extraction, and Bag of Words (BOW)" (Deepak Kumar Jain et al., 2022). Different sorts of machine learning algorithms like "Nave Bayes" and "Support Vector Machine" should be applied to categorise the polarity of the problem statement (Sathya & Mythili, 2022). This survey explores the levels, approaches, and steps of sentiment analysis that can be used to categorise the sentiments of people about COVID-19 (Vashishtha & Dhawan, 2023).

2. RELATED WORKS

Gulati et al. (2022) presented sentiment analysis classifications and methodologies. The author emphasised sentiment analysis's useful applications. Lexicon techniques and machine learning were described in detail. Mrityunjay Singh et al. (2021) used pre-processing steps to separate the essential data from the noise and retrieve the information that is important. The CORONA virus categorization of public opinion has been determined using the BERT model.

It has been obtained from the GitHub source; validation and emotion categorization are also used. Pradha et al. (2019) discussed effective text pre-processing, including "stemming, lemmatization, and spelling correction." To handle Twitter data, "Support Vector Machine," "Deep Learning," and "Naive Bayes Classifier" are used. The accuracy of SVM's model performance was higher. Naseem et al. (2021) described the Twitter API to retrieve the data from the Twitter dataset. To eliminate certain unrelated COVID datasets, pre-processing will be performed. TF-IDF and word embedding vectorization algorithms are used. Machine learning algorithms like Naive Bayes, Decision Trees, and Support Vector Machines are used for classification in order to categorise the polarity.

Deep learning classifiers such as "LSTM" and "CNN" can be used to demonstrate greater accuracy. Jeganathan et al. (2023) described the classification methods, illustrated the accuracy of SVM and Naive Bayes measures, and labelled how to extract and recognise sentiment from the text. Sathya & Mythili (2022) compared the study of machine learning algorithms like Support Vector Machine, Nave Bayes, and finally exposed SVM, which produces results with higher accuracy.

3. SENTIMENT ANALYSIS

Sentiment analysis, also known as opinion mining, is a method for examining how people feel about many types of things, including goods, services, people, themes, events, and their features. It is a really large area of concern.

3.1 Levels of Sentiment Analysis

3.1.1. Document Level

It examines and classifies the document, as its name suggests. The entire material should be analysed and expressed with positive and negative sentiments. Only one review should be processed at this level. When a document is subjected to many reviews, its accuracy suffers. If a review is found to be irrelevant, it should be removed before pre-processing (Vishal & Kharde, 2016; Rajkumar et al., 2019) (Table 1).

Table 1. Document level example

Text	Sentiment
To maintain immunity against COVID-19, get your third dose to protect from serious illness. Taking Vaccination is in dilemma stage for the public. Still having fear.	Negative

3.1.2. Sentence Level

This level analyses and determines the sentence's positive, negative, or neutral opinion. The sentence can be divided into two parts. 1. Subjective sentence 2. Objective sentence Here, the sentence is analysed with subjectivity classification, which may be subjective form or objective form (Rajkumar et al., 2019) (Table 2).

Table 2. Sentence level example

Text	Sentiment
The Vaccination is Cool and safe.	Positive

3.1.3. Aspect Level

It is also known as the "feature level." From the document level and sentence level, it's difficult to analyse what people like or dislike. It particularly focuses on attributes or components of a data set or service (table 3).

Table 3. Aspect level

Text	Sentiment
Omicron is dangerous and cause death but being vaccinated can avoid the seriousness of illness	Neutral

3.2. Approaches for COVID Sentiment Classification

The emergence of large data sets has demanded the creation of effective analytics tools (Ianni et al., 2020). In Figure 1, there are three types of sentiment categorization techniques that were used during COVID-19. They are machine learning, lexicon-based, and hybrid methods.

Figure 1. Approaches of sentiment analysis

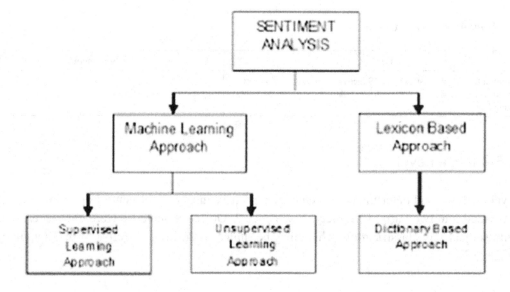

3.3. Machine Learning Approaches

For COVID, the machine learning-based techniques utilise well-known ML algorithms for sentiment categorization. Additionally, they fall under the categories of supervised and unsupervised learning techniques.

3.4. Supervised Learning

Documents for supervised learning already have labels on them (Xiang et al., 2021). The class of a document is predicted using pre-defined training data. The supervised model may be divided into four categories based on Figure 1. They are decision tree (DT), random forest (RF), naive bayes (NB), support vector machine (SVM), and regression (Ogunmola et al., 2021).

Decision Tree: A decision support tool that uses a tree-like structure to contain conditional statements is known as a "decision tree." High stability and accuracy will be categorised based on their lowest cross-validation error. The whole train dataset's basic decision rules are used to train the model to predict the class values (Adamu & Syaheerah, 2021; Rustam et al., 2021; Xiang et al., 2021).

Random Forest: The Decision Tree Family Member Random Forest selects random cases as well as random characteristics (Adamu & Syaheerah, 2021; Rustam et al., 2021; Xiang et al., 2021).

Naive Bayes: Based on the Bayes Theorem, naive Bayes is one of the supervised machine learning algorithms (Adamu & Syaheerah, 2021; Samuel et al., 2020). It is often referred to as independence Bayes or naive Bayes. It has been highly recommended for categorization due to its speed and simplicity. From Equation (1), probability (p) is defined as:

$$P (A/B) = P (A/B) * P (B) / P (A) \tag{1}$$

Support Vector Machine: Support Vector Machine (SVM) is a statistical learning-based machine learning technique that finds the hyperplane (Rustam et al., 2021) by translating feature space into high-dimensional data. It's described as having an input format and an output format. Either positive or negative output is produced. The SVM classifier is quite costly, and its execution speed will be slower (Adamu & Syaheerah, 2021; Rustam et al., 2021; Xiang et al., 2021).

Regression: It is a statistical technique that uses one or more independent variables to describe the connection between the dependent (target) and independent (predictor) variables.

3.5. Unsupervised Learning

Unsupervised learning is independent of any training subject or domain. It prevents the challenge of gathering and delivering labelled training data (Sharma et al., 2021). The data is not labelled in unsupervised learning. This approach has been employed in COVID-related sentiment classification. K-means clustering has also been used for sentiment identification (Flint et al., 2022).

3.6. Lexicon-Based Approach

An algorithm with a rapid classification speed to determine if the polarity is "positive, negative, or neutral" is known as a lexicon-based approach (Devi & Sharma, 2022). Lexicons are only a group of words that may be used in dictionary-based and corpus-based approaches (Aishwarya et al., 2019). During COVID-19, sentimental analysis was carried out using both dictionary-based and corpus-based methods (Devi & Nayyar, 2021).

The dictionary technique uses an existing vocabulary, whereas corpus-based analysis considers the likelihood that an emotion term would appear with a positive or negative group of words (Monica Priya & Sathiaseelan, 2017).

4. SENTIMENT ANALYSIS PROCESS

Opinion mining, a natural language processing (NLP) technology, is utilised for sentiment analysis to determine if data is favourable, negative, or neutral. Since the synonyms are similar, it is sometimes known as review mining and opinion mining, and sometimes it varies a little depending on the severity of the issue (Arslan et al., 2021). Throughout the COVID-19 epidemic, people experienced a range of emotions, and they communicated those sentiments via various "social media platforms." The public mass media platforms are a countless "source of data and information" for understanding how society felt about the COVID devastation and how they reacted to it. The phases of sentiment analysis are clearly illustrated in Figure 2.

Figure 2. Systematic steps of sentiment analysis

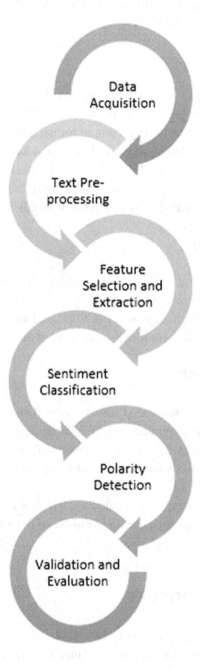

4.1. Data Acquisition During COVID-19 Investigation

According to studies, 90% of individuals use Twitter as an electronic database, with the other 10% using online media such as Reddit, Yelp, health grades, WeChat accounts, etc. With about 81.47 million registered users, Twitter is regarded as the most popular social networking platform (Adamu & Syaheerah, 2021). People communicate "tweets"—messages—about public and international events. An estimated 500 million tweets are posted every day, for a total of 200 billion every year (Chitalapudi et al., 2021). The tweets are categorised according to their subjects, which include politics, personal opinions, and national economic concerns, notably the COVID-19 pandemic (Baker et al., 2021).

4.2. Text Pre-Processing

The pre-processing step must be effective for better analysis results. This procedure deals with text data preparation and cleansing. Tokenization, which divides the text into smaller units for easier access to each word; stop word removal, which eliminates similar words that don't give relevant data; and other processing like stemming and lemmatization may also be included (Pinaki Mohanty et al., 2022).

4.3. Feature Selection and Extraction

In this stage, certain data are chosen and extracted from the original data set by merging them into features to decrease the amount of data. There are several methods for feature extraction, including "Bag-of-Words, Negation Handling, N-gram, Term Frequency-Inverse Document Frequency (TF-IDF), Term Document Matrix (TDM), and Bag of Words (BOW)" (Nirmal Varghese Babu, 2021).

4.4. Sentiment Classification

Machine learning classifiers should be used in the sentiment analysis to offer a thorough analysis. The best classification techniques for the CORONO Virus challenge are "Support Vector Machine (SVM), Naive Bayes (NB), Decision Tree (DT), and Random Forest (RF)" (Naseem et al., 2021).

4.5. Polarity Detection

As a general rule, it's important to detect whether a sentence is subjective or objective while doing sentimental analysis. From Figure 3, if the supplied line is assigned as objective, no more significant tasks are required; however, if the given line is assigned as subjective, its polarity, such as positive, negative, or neutral, must be known (Hamzah et al., 2020).

Figure 3. Sentence classification

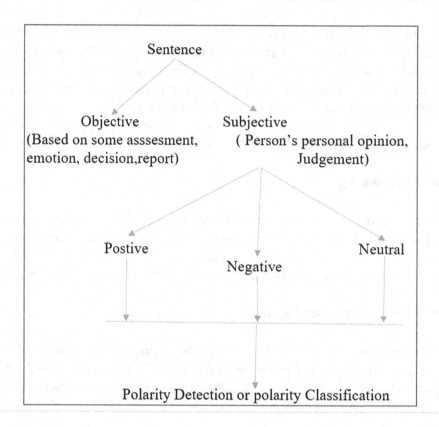

4.6. Validation and Assessment

In order to choose the optimum method for sentiment analysis for the sort of research topic being studied, machine learning techniques are finally implemented by Python, Rapid Miner, etc. Using the Python APIs Scraper and Tweepy, we can extract the data from the tweets on Twitter and filter it to solve our problems for sentiment analysis (Baker et al., 2021; Singh et al., 2021).

5. SENTIMENT ANALYSIS APPLICATIONS IN COVID-19

People's actions and outlooks have been significantly affected by COVID, which has drawn the attention of researchers in the field of sentimental categorization. During COVID-19, a variety of issues fell under the sentimental classification.

5.1. Analysis of Public Opinion and Mental Health Issues in Lock Down

During the spread of COVID-19, several lives were lost. It is essential to implement measures that tend to reduce mobility and lead to less human-to-human contact in order to inhibit the transmission of coronaviruses. The only action that has been taken by practically all of the nations on the globe is "lockdown," which involves shutting down public transportation and airspace. These consequences have therefore led to depression, loneliness, anxiety, and other psychological problems, particularly for students. People's lives have been impacted, and this has led to several psychological problems, including depression. It is required to implement measures that tend to prevent the mobility of people in order to inhibit the spread of the coronavirus. People use social media platforms like Twitter to share their feelings and emotions during this period, which helps academics comprehend the mental condition of the populace (Das & Dutta, 2021; Agarwal et al., 2021; Ajantha Devi & Nayyar, 2021). Using data from Twitter, a " analysis of people's actions and sentiments during COVID-19" was conducted. The number of tweets during the COVID scenario is higher in youth, according to the analysis of tweets based on the age of social media users (Xiang et al., 2021; Hung et al., 2020).

5.2. Attitudes About Vaccination in the COVID Situation

Researchers analysed conception movements to identify people's attitudes toward the COVID vaccine. The use of intolerance and unfair behaviour towards others has increased under COVID. The researchers attempt to explain differences in people's perceptions of prejudice before and after (Müller & Salathé, 2020; Nguyen et al., 2020).

5.3. Reviews of Restaurants

During COVID-19, numerous restaurants received bad evaluations for their contributions at the time of the Corona virus epidemic. Analyzing consumer feedback is crucial for enhancing product quality. To obtain high-quality cuisine and sustain high quality, the researchers studied both consumer attitudes and hotel management (Luo and Xu, 2021).

5.4. Reopening Opinions at COVID-19

COVID has either directly or indirectly affected the lives of billions of people. The economic crisis, uncertainty, and worry brought on by COVID-19 have all contributed to complications in reopening following the COVID situation (Samuel et al., 2020). Long-term lockdown is not a solution; rather, it poses a threat to any nation's economy. Both public sector workers and students have been impacted by COVID-19. Therefore, the researchers attempted to analyse public opinion about the decision to reopen following the COVID-19 disasters (Rahman et al., 2020). The most common uses of sentiment analysis are in business, politics, finance, healthcare, and education. Sentiment analysis can provide users running for various positions with real benefits. It enables campaign managers to monitor voter sentiment toward various subjects and how it relates to the candidate's remarks and deeds. The financial markets are yet another crucial area for sentiment research, and each publicly traded corporation is the subject of countless news stories, articles, blogs, and tweets. It is questionable whether creating new educational policies for pupils would be fulfilling in the field of education. Social media platforms provide a useful forum for patients to express their wants and concerns in the healthcare industry by providing information on diseases, outbreaks, and patient mood and attitude. In order to determine a patient's health insurance coverage and his treatment needs, sentiment analysis of patient data from social media is quite helpful (Birjali & Kasri, 2021).

5.5. Challenges Related to Sentiment Analysis

The requirement for enhanced compositional sentiment modelling is one of several unanswered research topics in sentiment analysis. The sentiment analysis system faces significant challenges from noisy data, including spelling errors, missing punctuation, and slang. This suggests that the sentiment of the entire sentence, including the sentiment shifters, the sentiment-bearing words, and the sentence structure, may be more accurately measured at the sentence level. Each product is referred to by a number of different names, both inside and across papers. The detection of interrogative phrases in a significant paper, spam reviews, and other issues (Gulati et al., 2022) When analysing noisy text with misspellings, missing punctuation, and slang, the sentiment analysis system has serious difficulties. Due to these problems, it delivers practical solutions to these problems, and moreover, sentiment analysis will expand quickly.

6. FUTURE IMPACTS OF COVID-19

Future impacts of the COVID investigation and suggestions for future implications are listed:

- It is critical to implement real-time "monitoring and visualization."
- Take into account home data and social and economic considerations.
- Look at a large amount of data and investigate online mediums and datasets.
- More focused themes may be examined to aid policymakers, the administration, and local communities in moments of disaster.
- It is important to perform sentiments for several age groups.
- To improve the accuracy of future predictions, use deep learning algorithms.

Comparing Techniques of Sentiment Analysis and Applications for the Period of COVID-19 (Table 4).

Table 4. Sentiment analysis techniques and applications during COVID-19

Authors and year of Published	Data Set	Techniques	Applications	Future ways
Adamu & Syaheerah, (2021)	Twitter	Naïve Bayes, Support Vector, Machine, Decision tree, Random Forest	Sentiment mining on corona virus impact	Large Data, Consider multiple language
Abd Rahim & Mohd Rafie, (2020)	Social Media	Support Vector Machine	Sentiment Analysis on Vaccination	Need improvements in Pre-processing Techniques
Rustam, et al., (2021)	Twitter	SVC,RF, XGBoost, DT, TextBlob, BOW, TF-IDF	Identification of sentiments in trending Covid-19 news	Focus on Deep Learning method on smaller set of datasets.
Flint et al., (2022)	Social Media	Clustering algorithm-K-means Algorithm, Regression.	COVID-19 Pandemic and lockdown related issues.	Understanding "Cross Sectional analysis of covid-19" on adults feelings and behaviour.
Das & Dutta, (2021)	Twitter	Line Chart Scatter Plot Diagram	Public sentiment during lockdown	Concentrate on English and examine negative emotion
Hung et al., (2020)	Twitter	LDA, VADER	Identification of sentiments in Leading topics	Real time Posting Exact population is not represented.
Nguyen et al., (2020)	Twitter	SVM	Changes in racial sentiment	Observe and evaluate racial viewers
Luo and Xu (2021)	Yelp	Random Forest, LSTM	Online Restaurant review	Need better reviewer a location of restaurant
Raheja, & Asthana (2021)	Twitter	Subjectivity, Polarity, Sentence Classification	Analysis of sentiment classification in Covid situation	--------

7. CONCLUSION

In this study, the fundamental idea behind sentiment analysis, along with its procedures, levels, and methodologies, as well as the issues and challenges connected to the coronavirus, were discussed. According to the findings of this study, sentimental analysis at COVID-19 is still an emerging field with a wide range of fascinating topics that make use of cutting-edge machine learning and deep learning techniques. Several studies have shown that the Naive Bayes and SVM machine learning algorithms are two of the most common choices for conducting sentiment analysis during COVID. As a consequence of this, many people believe that Twitter will be the social media medium that will be used the most for any future health care research issue.

REFERENCES

Abd Rahim, N., & Mohd Rafie, S. (2020). Sentiment Analysis of Social Media Data in Vaccination. *IJETER*, *2020*, 5259–5264.

Abdul Mohaimin Rahat, A., & Kahir, A. K. M. (2019). *Comparison of Naïve Bayes and SVM based on Sentiment Analysis using Review Dataset*. IEEE.

Adamu, H., & Syaheerah, L. (2021). Rohail Hassan,AssuntaDi Vaio and Ahmad Sufril Azllan Mohamed,Framing twitter public sentiment on Nigerian government COVID-19 palliatives distribution using machine learning. *Nural Hashimah Ahamed Hassain Malim, 13*(6).

Agarwal, A., Agarwal, B., Harjule, P., & Agarwal, A. (2021). Mental health analysis of students in major cities of India during COVID-19. In *Algorithms for Intelligent Systems* (pp. 51–67). Springer Singapore.

Aishwarya, R., Ashwatha, C., Deepthi, A., & Raja, B. (2019). A Novel Adaptable Approach for sentiment Analysis. *IJSCSEIT*, 254–263.

Ajantha Devi, V., & Nayyar, A. (2021). Evaluation of geotagging twitter data using sentiment analysis during COVID-19. In *Lecture Notes in Networks and Systems* (pp. 601–608). Springer Singapore.

Arslan, F., Singh, B., Sharma, D. K., Regin, R., Steffi, R., & Rajest, S. S. (2021). Optimization technique approach to resolve food sustainability problems. *2021 International Conference on Computational Intelligence and Knowledge Economy (ICCIKE)*. IEEE. 10.1109/ICCIKE51210.2021.9410735

Baker, O., Liu, J., Gosai, M., & Sitoula, S. (2021). Twitter sentiment analysis using machine learning algorithms for COVID-19 outbreak in New Zealand. *2021 IEEE 11th International Conference on System Engineering and Technology (ICSET)*. IEEE.

Baker, O., Liu, J., Gosai, M., & Sitoula, S. (2021). Twitter sentiment analysis using machine learning algorithms for COVID-19 outbreak in New Zealand. *2021 IEEE 11th International Conference on System Engineering and Technology (ICSET)*. IEEE.

Birjali, M., Kasri, M., & Beni-Hssane, A. (2021). A comprehensive survey on sentiment analysis: Approaches, Challenges, and Trends. *Knowledge-Based Systems, 226*, 1–26. doi:10.1016/j.knosys.2021.107134

Chitalapudi, N., Battineni, G., & Amenta, F. (2021). Sentimental Analysis of COVID -19 Tweets Using Deep Learning Models. *Infectious Disease Reports, 13*(2), 329–339. doi:10.3390/idr13020032 PMID:33916139

Cirillo, S., Polese, G., Salerno, D., Simone, B., & Solimando, G. (2023). Towards Flexible Voice Assistants: Evaluating Privacy and Security Needs in IoT-enabled Smart Homes. *FMDB Transactions on Sustainable Computer Letters, 1*(1), 25–32.

COVID-19 pandemic in India. (2020). Wikipedia. https://en.Wikipedia.org/wiki/COVID-19 .

Das, S., & Dutta, A. (2021). Characterizing public emotions and sentiments in COVID-19 environment: A case study of India. *Journal of Human Behavior in the Social Environment, 31*(1–4), 154–167. doi: 10.1080/10911359.2020.1781015

Deepak Kumar Jain, P., Boyapati, J., & Venkatesh, M. (2022). An Intelligent Cognitive-Inspired Computing with Big Data Analytics Framework for Sentiment Analysis and Classification, " Information Processing and Management. *Information Processing & Management*, 1–4.

Devi, A., & Nayyar, A. (2021). *Evaluation of Geotagging Twitter Data Using Sentiment Analysis During COVID-19*. Springer.

Devi, V., & Sharma, A. (2022). Sentiment analysis approaches, types, challenges, and applications: An exploratory analysis. *2022 Seventh International Conference on Parallel, Distributed and Grid Computing (PDGC)*. IEEE. 10.1109/PDGC56933.2022.10053180

Flint, S. W., Piotrkowicz, A., & Watts, K. (2022). Use of Artificial Intelligence to understand adults' thoughts and behaviours relating to COVID-19. *Perspectives in Public Health, 142*(3), 167–174. doi:10.1177/1757913920979332 PMID:33472547

Gulati, K., Saravana Kumar, S., Sarath Kumar Boddu, R., Sarvakar, K., Kumar Sharma, D., & Nomani, M. Z. M. (2022). Comparative analysis of machine learning-based classification models using sentiment classification of tweets related to COVID-19 pandemic. *Materials Today: Proceedings, 51*, 38–41. doi:10.1016/j.matpr.2021.04.364

HamzahF.BintiC.LauH.NazriD. V.LigotG.Cheng Lianf TanM. K. B. M. (2020). Corono Tracker: Worldwide COVID-19 outbreak data analysis and prediction. Bull World Health Organ, 1–32.

Hung, M., Lauren, E., Hon, E. S., Birmingham, W. C., Xu, J., Su, S., Hon, S. D., Park, J., Dang, P., & Lipsky, M. S. (2020). Social network analysis of COVID-19 sentiments: Application of artificial intelligence. *Journal of Medical Internet Research, 22*(8), e22590. doi:10.2196/22590 PMID:32750001

Ianni, M., Masciari, E., Mazzeo, G. M., Mezzanzanica, M., & Zaniolo, C. (2020). Fast and effective Big Data exploration by clustering. *Future Generation Computer Systems, 2020*, 84–94. doi:10.1016/j.future.2019.07.077

Imran, A. S., Daudpota, S. M., Kastrati, Z., & Batra, R. (2020). Cross-cultural polarity and emotion detection using sentiment analysis and deep learning on COVID-19 related tweets. *IEEE Access : Practical Innovations, Open Solutions, 8*, 181074–181090. doi:10.1109/ACCESS.2020.3027350 PMID:34812358

Jeba, J. A., Bose, S. R., & Boina, R. (2023). Exploring Hybrid Multi-View Multimodal for Natural Language Emotion Recognition Using Multi-Source Information Learning Model. *FMDB Transactions on Sustainable Computer Letters, 1*(1), 12–24.

Jeganathan, J., Vashist, S., Nirmala, G., & Deep, R. (2023). A Cross Sectional Study on Anxiety and Depression Among Patients with Alcohol Withdrawal Syndrome. *FMDB Transactions on Sustainable Health Science Letters, 1*(1), 31–40.

Luo, Y. & Xu, X. (2021). Comparative Study of Deep learning models for anlyzing online restaurant reviews in the era of the COVID-19 pandemic. *INT.F. Hosp. Manag., 94*. https://doi.org/. doi:10.1016/j.iijhm.2020.102849

Monica Priya, C., & Sathiaseelan, J. G. (2017). An Explorative Study on Sentimental Analysis. *WCCCT*, 140–142.

MüllerM.SalathéM. (2020). Addressing machine learning concept drift reveals declining vaccine sentiment during the COVID-19 pandemic. In arXiv [cs.SI]. https://arxiv.org/abs/2012.02197

Naseem, U., Razzak, I., Khushi, M., Eklund, P. W., & Kim, J. (2021). *COVIDSenti:A Large-Scale Benchmark Twitter Data Set for COVID-19 Sentiment Analysis*. IEEE.

Nguyen, T. T., Criss, S., Dwivedi, P., Huang, D., Keralis, J., Hsu, E., Phan, L., Nguyen, L. H., Yardi, I., Glymour, M. M., Allen, A. M., Chae, D. H., Gee, G. C., & Nguyen, Q. C. (2020). Exploring U.s. shifts in anti-Asian sentiment with the emergence of COVID-19. *International Journal of Environmental Research and Public Health*, *17*(19), 7032. doi:10.3390/ijerph17197032 PMID:32993005

Nirmal Varghese Babu, E. (2021). Sentiment Analysis in Social Media Data for Depression Detection Using Artificial Intelligence:A Review. *SN Computer Science*, 1–20. PMID:34816124

Nirmala, G., Premavathy, R., Chandar, R., & Jeganathan, J. (2023). An Explanatory Case Report on Biopsychosocial Issues and the Impact of Innovative Nurse-Led Therapy in Children with Hematological Cancer. *FMDB Transactions on Sustainable Health Science Letters*, *1*(1), 1–10.

Ogunmola, G. A., Singh, B., Sharma, D. K., Regin, R., Rajest, S. S., & Singh, N. (2021). Involvement of distance measure in assessing and resolving efficiency environmental obstacles. *2021 International Conference on Computational Intelligence and Knowledge Economy (ICCIKE)*. IEEE. 10.1109/ICCIKE51210.2021.9410765

Pandit, P. (2023). On the Context of Diabetes: A Brief Discussion on the Novel Ethical Issues of Non-communicable Diseases. *FMDB Transactions on Sustainable Health Science Letters*, *1*(1), 11–20.

Pinaki Mohanty, R., Kumar, R., & Sharma, V. (2022). *Pradeep kumar singh, "Multimedia Tools and Applications*. Springer.

Pradha, S., Halgamuge, M. N., & Tran Quoc Vinh, N. (2019). Effective Text Data Preprocessing Technique for Sentiment Analysis in Social Media Data. *2019 11th International Conference on Knowledge and Systems Engineering (KSE)*. IEEE.

Priscila, S. S., Rajest, S. S., Tadiboina, S. N., Regin, R., & András, S. (2023). Analysis of Machine Learning and Deep Learning Methods for Superstore Sales Prediction. *FMDB Transactions on Sustainable Computer Letters*, *1*(1), 1–11.

Raheja, S., & Asthana, A. (2021). Sentimental analysis of twitter comments on covid-19. *2021 11th International Conference on Cloud Computing, Data Science & Engineering (Confluence)*. IEEE.

Rahman, M. M., Ali, G. G. M. N., Li, X. J., Paul, K. C., & Chong, P. H. J. (2020). Twitter and census data analytics to explore socioeconomic factors for post-COVID-19 reopening sentiment. SSRN *Electronic Journal*. doi:10.2139/ssrn.3639551

Rajkumar, S., Vishal, S., & Shirsat Sachin, N. (2019). Sentiment Analysis on Product Reviews Using Machine Learning Techniques. Advances In Intelligent Systems and Computing. Springer.

Rustam, F., Khalid, M., Aslam, W., Rupapara, V., Mehmood, A., & Choi, G. S. (2021). A performance comparison of supervised machine learning models for Covid-19 tweets sentiment analysis. *PLoS One*, *16*(2), e0245909. doi:10.1371/journal.pone.0245909 PMID:33630869

Samuel, J., Ali, G. G., Rahman, E., & Esawi, Y. (2020). Covid -19 public sentiment insights and machine learning for tweets classification. *Information (Basel)*, *2020*, 1–22.

Samuel, J., Md Mokhlesur Rahman, G. G., Md Nawaz Ali, Y., Samuel, A., Pelaez, P. H., Chong, J., & Yakubov, M. (2020). *Feeeling Positive about Reopening? New Normal Scenarios from COVID-19 US Reopen Sentiment Analytics*. IEEE Acccess.

Sathya, A., & Mythili, M. (2022). An Investigation of Machine Learning Algorithms in sentiment Analysis. *Advances and Applications in Mathematical Sciences*, 4575–4584.

Saxena, D., & Chaudhary, S. (2023). Predicting Brain Diseases from FMRI-Functional Magnetic Resonance Imaging with Machine Learning Techniques for Early Diagnosis and Treatment. *FMDB Transactions on Sustainable Computer Letters*, *1*(1), 33–48.

Sharma, D. K., Jalil, N. A., Regin, R., Rajest, S. S., Tummala, R. K., & Thangadurai. (2021). Predicting network congestion with machine learning. 2021 *2nd International Conference on Smart Electronics and Communication (ICOSEC)*. IEEE.

Singh, M., Kumar Jakhar, A., & Pandey, S. (2021). Sentiment Analysis on the impact of coronavirus in social life using the BERT model. *Social Network Analysis and Mining*, *11*(1), 8–11. doi:10.100713278-021-00737-z PMID:33758630

Suganthi, M., & Sathiaseelan, J. G. R. (2023). Image Denoising and Feature Extraction Techniques Applied to X-Ray Seed Images for Purity Analysis. *FMDB Transactions on Sustainable Health Science Letters*, *1*(1), 41–53.

Vashishtha, E., & Dhawan, G. (2023). Bridging Generation Gap on Analysis of Mentor-Mentee Relationship in Healthcare Setting. *FMDB Transactions on Sustainable Health Science Letters*, *1*(1), 21–30.

Vinoth Kumar, V., Karthick Raghunath, K., Muthukumaran, V., Joseph, R. B., Bechi Akshay, I., & Uday, K. (2022). Aspect based sentiment analysis and smart classification in uncertain feedback pool. *International Journal of System Assurance Engineering and Management*, 252–262.

Vishal, A., & Kharde, S. (2016). Sentiment Analysis of Twitter Data: A Survey of Techniques. *International Journal of Computer Applications*, *139*(11), 1–10.

Xiang, X., Lu, X., Halavanau, A., Xue, J., Sun, Y., Lai, P. H. L., & Wu, Z. (2021). Modern senicide in the face of a pandemic: An examination of public discourse and sentiment about older adults and COVID-19 using machine learning. *The Journals of Gerontology. Series B, Psychological Sciences and Social Sciences*, *76*(4), e190–e200. doi:10.1093/geronb/gbaa128 PMID:32785620

Zhou, Z., Fang, A., & Liu, Q. (2019). transformer network based on position and self-attention mechanism for aspect-level sentiment classification. *IEEE Access : Practical Innovations, Open Solutions*, *7*, 127754–127764. doi:10.1109/ACCESS.2019.2938854

Chapter 15
An Analysis of Directing Protocols for Subaquatic Wireless Sensor Systems

M. Vedhapriya
SRM Institute of Science and Technology, India

J. Dhilipan
SRM Institute of Science and Technology, India

ABSTRACT

A submerged sensor network comprises of numeral different sensors and independent submerged vehicles sent to facilitate submerged, associate, and divide data between themselves to complete detecting and observing capacities. The submerged sensor networks have a wide scope of utilizations like contamination observing, catastrophic anticipations, facilitated route, under ocean investigations, an advanced military capacity, mine investigation, and so on. Submerged sensor networks present extraordinary tests to the current advances utilized in earthly sensor organization since submerged climate varies from earthbound radio climate regarding energy expenses and channel engendering peculiarities. Audile remote correspondence is utilized instead of wireless recurrence and optical sign in submerged sensor organization. A portion of the issues where submerged sensor network contrast from earthly are restricted for data transfer capacity, battery power, and disappointment of sensor hubs due to snarling and consumption.

1. INTRODUCTION

Remote sensor networks have acquired prevalence in later years because of ongoing progressions in Microcomputer Electro Mechanical Systems (MEMS) (Akyildiz & Su, 2002); (Yick, et al., 2008), remote interchanges, and Digital hardware (Jain, et al., 2022). The hubs are outfitted with information handling and imparting parts like at least one sensor, a radio, a processor, a memory, a power source, and an actuator (Buddhi, et al., 2022a). These type of sensor hubs detects, measure, gather information from the climate, and communicate the gathered information (Figure 1).

DOI: 10.4018/979-8-3693-1301-5.ch015

Figure 1. Wireless sensor network

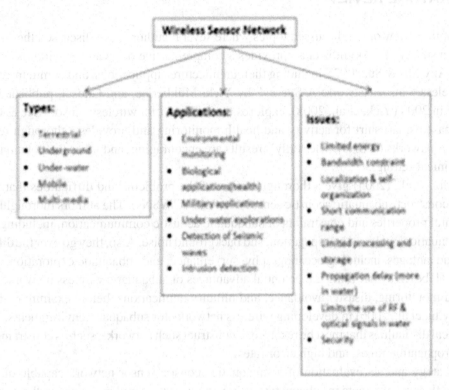

The sensor-based hubs are conveyed in an ad hoc way or pre-arranged way (Ead, & Abbassy, 2018). In an ad hoc way, the sensor hubs are sent haphazardly into the field, and the organization is then left not attended to accomplish checking (Buddhi, et al., 2022a). In an ad hoc way, the organization's support, for example, overseeing the network and recognizing disappointments, becomes troublesome (Derindere Köseoğlu, et al., 2022). For instance, a wearable Smart Vest measures circulatory strain, pulse, internal heat level, and so forth to screen patients proficiently and voltaic skin reaction (GSR), which estimates the ceaseless varieties in the electrical attributes of skin that has to be created (Dhanush, et al., 2022). They can be a better option for a specific WSN application if the sensor nodes' tasks are set in stone for the duration of the program and when there are enough nodes to justify the expense of developing an ASIC (Ead & Abbassy, 2021). Networks of specialized sensors dispersed worldwide that track and record environmental and physical factors and communicate the acquired data to a centralized location are known as wireless sensor networks (WSNs) (Gehlot, et al., 2022; Sharma, et al., 2022).

However, given their greater versatility and easier usage, microcontrollers are currently the preferred option in WSN technology (Joseph, et al., 2022; Santoso, 2021). Although "convenient programmability over several orders of energy consumption and data processing requirements is a worthy research goal," this is not necessarily the best option (Joseph, 2022; Santoso, 2019). Additionally, it is an appealing design and research option to divide processing jobs between some low-level, fixed functionality built into a very energy-efficient ASIC and high-level, flexible, rarely used processing on a microcontroller (Kazmi, et al., 2021; Sharma, et al., 2021).

2. LITERATURE REVIEW

The literature review of the discussed topics where several authors have discussed the "wireless sensor networks a survey" by Akyildiz et al. provides a comprehensive overview of wireless sensor networks (WSNs) (Akyildiz & Su, 2002), including their architecture, applications, and communication protocols and "Wireless Sensor Network: A Survey" by Yick, Mukherjee, and Ghosal, published in Computer Networks in 2008 (Yick, et al., 2008), explores the creation of a wireless sensor (Lee & Chung, 2009). network-based smart shirt for activity and health monitoring and provides a thorough review of wireless sensor networks (WSNs). The study's results are encouraging, and it has the potential to be used in several clinical settings.

Akyildiz, et al., (2005) give a thorough review of the problems and difficulties that need to be resolved to construct subaquatic acoustic sensor networks (UWSNs). The authors thoroughly examine the fundamental properties and constraints of subaquatic acoustic communication, including the impact of signal attenuation, multi-path propagation, and background noise. Also, they go over the different UWSN uses and advantages, including oceanography, surveillance, and subaquatic exploration.

Cui et al. begin by outlining the potential advantages of subaquatic wireless networks, such as environmental monitoring, disaster avoidance, and military applications, before examining the special difficulties (Cui, et al., 2006) in developing wireless networks for subaquatic environments. They describe the technical difficulties that must be resolved to construct such networks, such as constrained bandwidth, lengthy propagation times, and high error rates.

The strategy and act evaluation of a subaquatic acoustic sensor network capable of detecting and measuring the size of targets in subaquatic environments are covered in the paper "Understand acoustic sensor networks: Target size detection and Performance Analysis" by Liang and Cheng (2009). The report thoroughly examines the UASN and illustrates the difficulties in creating such networks. The paper discusses the various architectures and protocols suggested for UASN deployment while giving an outline of the current state of UASN research.

Peach & Yarali, (2013) deliver an improved understanding of subaquatic sensor network architecture, basic characteristics, and applications, and examines the propagation limitations of acoustic communication.

Manvi & Manjula, (2011) give the difficulties and problems with the application of subsurface acoustic radar networks (UASNs). The study covers various UASN-related topics, including their architecture, communication protocols, localization strategies, and energy usage.

According to the author Ranjan & Ranjan, (2013) Subaquatic/wireless networks are a type of wireless network that enables communication between subaquatic devices. UWCNs are used in various types of claims, such as - oceanographic data collection, offshore oil and gas exploration, environmental monitoring, and subaquatic investigation.

The paper "VBF: Vector-based Forwarding Protocol for Underwater Sensor Networks" proposes a new routing protocol for subaquatic sensor networks (Xie, et al., 2006). The Vector-Based Forwarding (VBF) protocol is designed to address communication challenges in the subaquatic environment, such as low bandwidth, high latency, and unreliable links. The authors first provide an overview of the characteristics of subaquatic sensor networks and the challenges they present. They then introduce the VBF protocol, which is based on a vector-based approach that uses the direction of the next hop to determine the forwarding path. The authors also describe VBF's mechanisms to handle packet forwarding, routing loops, and packet loss. Additionally, Xie et al. (2006a) proposed a vector-based forwarding (VBF) protocol for subaquatic sensor networks with significant consideration in topical years for their possible bids in several subaquatic monitoring and surveillance scenarios. "A survey on routing techniques in underwater wireless sensor networks," published in the Journal of Network and Computer Applications in 2011 by Ayaz, Muhammad, et al., provides a comprehensive review of various directing methods used in subaquatic wireless sensor networks (UWSNs).

Yan, et al., (2008) propose a new direction-finding protocol for subaquatic sensor networks (UWSNs) called Depth-based Routing (DBR). The authors argue that existing routing protocols for UWSNs are unsuitable for large-scale networks and do not consider the deepness of nodes in the directing course, which is a critical factor in UWSNs.

Ayaz, (2011) provides a detailed analysis of the existing routing protocols for UWSNs, classified into three categories: geographic-based, hierarchical, and location-free. They discuss each protocol's advantages, disadvantages, and suitability for different UWSN scenarios. "A survey on routing techniques in underwater wireless sensor networks" provides a comprehensive review of the state-of-the-art routing techniques in subaquatic wireless sensor networks (UWSNs). The article highlights the unique challenges associated with UWSNs, such as the high attenuation of radio signals and the limited bandwidth for data transmission.

Manjeshwar, & Agarwal, (2001) propose a new routing protocol called TEEN ('Threshold-sensitive Energy Efficient sensor Network protocol') for wireless sensor networks (WSNs). The authors argue that existing routing protocols for WSNs do not consider sensor nodes' inadequate energy and computational sources, leading to inefficient energy consumption and network lifetime. TEEN aims to address these issues by introducing threshold-sensitive mechanisms that allow nodes to selectively participate in data transmission and processing based on their energy levels and relevance to the task.

Lindsey & Raghavendra, (2002) cover recent advancements in UWSN routing techniques, such as energy-efficient, secure, and hybrid routing protocols. The authors discuss the limitations of existing routing protocols and provide insights into the future research directions for UWSN routing. The article examines the unique challenges UWSNs face and explores how different routing techniques can address these challenges. "PEGASIS: Power-Efficient Gathering in Sensor Information Systems" by Lindsey and Raghavendra presents a protocol for data gathering in wireless sensor networks (WSNs) to prolong network time by reducing energy consumption. The authors propose a chain-based topology, where nodes form a chain that routes data to the descending node. The protocol combines two techniques: chain-based routing and collaborative communication.

Domingo & Prior, (2007) provide a detailed description of the DBR protocol and compares its performance with that of existing protocols through simulation results. The replication outcomes show that DBR outpaces the prevailing protocols regarding package delivery ratio and liveliness effectiveness. The authors also conduct a sensitivity analysis of various parameters used in the DBR protocol to understand their impact on the performance of the protocol.

Ayaz, (2009) focuses on the target size detection and performance analysis of subacquatic acoustic sensor networks.

Chen, et al., (2010) present a sending protocol designed for subaquatic wireless sensor networks (UWSNs). The authors identify the unique challenges UWSNs pose, such as high attenuation and multi-path interference, and propose a hop-by-hop lively addressing-based directing protocol that aims to improve energy efficiency and lessen the figure of collisions in the network.

The authors claim that their protocol reduces energy consumption and surges network lifetime compared to other prevailing protocols. "DCR: Depth-Controlled routing protocol for underwater sensor networks" by Coutinho et al. (2013) presents a routing protocol for subaquatic sensor networks that consider the depth of the nodes in the network. The evaluation of the proposed protocol using simulations and comparing it with other routing protocols for subaquatic sensor networks shows that DCR outperforms the other protocols in terms of packet delivery ratio and energy consumption.

3. SORTS OF SENSOR NETWORKS

Based on the environment of usage, remote sensor organizations can be categorized as (Yick, et al., 2008); (Lee & Chung, 2009). Terrestrial Wireless Sensor Networks, where a terrestrial WSN comprises numerous sensor hubs dispersed in an intended area in an ad hoc or planned manner. Sensor hubs in terrestrial WSNs can essentially send data to the origin station (Kumar, et al., 2022). Backup power is constrained in earthbound WSNs, although sensor hubs can recharge using solar energy. Wireless sensor networks delivered subaquatic: Submerged subaquatic sensor grids (Mohamed Mesbah, 2016). Forwarding a data packet onto the subsequent intermediate relay node in any routing protocol that is currently in use can be used because the routing module is independent of other components (Pattana-Anake, & Joseph, 2022). In the case of topological changes, it presumes that the routing protocol offers new routes (Pachauri, et al., 2021b). Admission control is based on the maximum/minimum bandwidth required; this module distributes bandwidth to flows. Once the bandwidth has been reserved, a soft state mechanism must periodically update the reservation (Sadek, et al., 2021). The receipt of data packets often updates made reservations. In Packet scheduling, the packet scheduling module manages packets that must be forwarded to other nodes. An ongoing session might need to be diverted during a path break because of host mobility. The reserve must be reinstated through the flow restoration method as promptly and effectively as possible. These technologies' most important development is the hardware's miniaturization. The power consumption of the fundamental parts of a sensor node has decreased due to smaller feature sizes in chips to the point where the building of WSNs is now feasible. This is especially important for microcontrollers and memory chips, but radio modems in charge of wireless communication have improved greatly in terms of energy efficiency.

3.1 Subsurface Sensor Grids (Yick, et al., 2008; Akyildiz, et al., 2005)

Sensor hubs are utilized to perform cooperative observing assignments over a given region in the submerged circumstances, and Submerged sensor organizations can be utilized for different applications like helped route, oceanographic information assortment, location of contamination level, seaward action assessment, calamity counteraction, and strategic perception and anticipate regular unsettling influences in the sea. The capacity of these organizations to screen, explore, and track submerged events has expanded considerably in building UWSN. While point-to-point communication is the main method used by ad hoc networks, broadcast communication is the main method used by wireless sensor networks. Unlike ad hoc networks, wireless sensor networks are constrained by the sensors' power, energy, and processing capacity.

4. GENERAL CONSTRUCTION OF SUBAQUATIC SENSOR NETWORK

Figure 2 displays a simple submerged sensor organization's design. It involves several groups of submerged aquatics (UW - LAN). Separately sensor hub connects to the group's sink hub (Gateway). The sink hubs transport the data that the sensor hubs have gathered to the surface station. In contrast to ground-based radar network nodes, subaquatic sensor network nodes are non-static. In its place, they move due to various undersea activities and environmental conditions with water currents. Energy conservation is a significant issue that is disturbing subaquatic radar networks (Pachauri, et al., 2021a). Most offered energy-efficient algorithms become ineffective for subaquatic sensor networks due to nodes' mobility. However, these current ground-based routing protocols cannot function effectively in subaquatic environments due to mobility and fast changes in network architecture.

Figure 2. Architecture of subaquatic sensor network

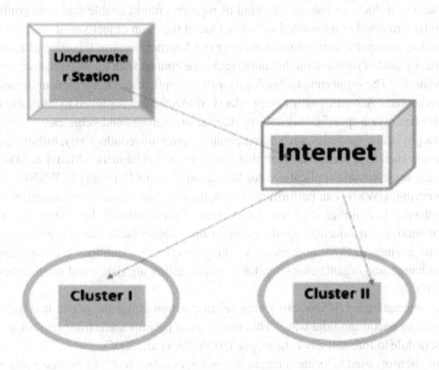

The idyllic packet size depended on the protocols and their properties, the ordered load, and the bit-error rate. Using the best packet size selection would significantly progress the act of multi-hop subaquatic networks in terms of throughput efficacy, expectancy, source utilization, and vigor consumption. Using the suggested strategies, energy consumption is balanced in a subaquatic setting. This study makes several significant contributions, including highlighting the differences between deep and shallow oceans and presenting the influence of temperature on noise, mistakes, and procedures owing to environmental fluctuation. Classification of routing methods and comparison of them in terms of limited expectancy, load balancing, energy consumption, multi-path, topographical information, communiqué overhead, and period of complexity are also encompassed.

5. APPLICATIONS

Applications and difficulties of technologies for subaquatic acoustic communication Research centers have focused heavily on creating subaquatic acoustic communication in recent years due to its priceless benefit to military and commercial uses. Applications for subaquatic acoustic networks may include employing switch centers or gateways to transfer data between nodes inside the specific network's coverage area and outside of it. Sending and receiving information among these nodes is one of the most crucial uses of subaquatic communication networks (UANs), which were developed to make undersea communication easier.

One of the main objectives of scientists at research centers is to enable subaquatic Internet communications because it does not require any kind of rope and might enable real-time contact with the intended subaquatic manned or unmanned vehicles. One of the main objectives of scientists at research centers is to enable subaquatic communications over the Internet because this type of communication does not require any kind of rope and might enable real-time contact with the intended subaquatic human or unmanned vehicles. The supporting technology for these applications is wireless underwater acoustic networking. Underwater Acoustic Sensor Networks (UW-ASNs) are deployed to carry out cooperative monitoring activities over a specific area and include various sensors and vehicles.

The different physical boundaries, such as temperature, pressure, conductivity, turbidity, and specific toxins, may be screened by a sensor network that was delivered subaquatic (Manvi & Manjula, 2011). The following are some notable applications for Subaquatic Sensor Networks (UWSN).

Natural observing: UWSNs can perform synthetic, natural, and atomic contamination reviews. It is additionally conceivable to utilize it to give the element of the synthetic slurry (which is a deferral of unsolvable elements) of anti-infection agents, estrogen-like chemicals, and insect sprays. It can likewise be utilized for observing sea flows and winds, working on climate conditions estimate, distinguishing environmental change, and organic checking, for example, following fishes and microorganisms (Akyildiz, et al., 2005).

Calamity counteractions: UWSNs can gauge seismic action along the ocean bottom from distant areas and foresee an oncoming tidal wave. This observation permits waterfront regions to be told and cautioned on schedule to forestall any catastrophe (Akyildiz, et al., 2005).

Helped route: Sensors used to locate subaquatic wrecks, treacherous rocks in deep water, and hazards on the seafloor (Akyildiz, et al., 2005); (Manvi & Manjula, 2011).

Below ocean investigations: subaquatic sensor organizations can be applied to recognizing inundated emollient pitches or repositories and help search for esteemed reserves (Akyildiz, et al., 2005); (Manvi & Manjula, 2011).

Excavation surveillance: A synchronized procedure of several subaquatic sound vehicles equipped with optical and acoustic sensors which can be cast-off to quickly assess the climate and identify objects like mine (Manvi & Manjula, 2011).

Sea inspecting networks: To perform a quick, comfortable, flexible inspection of the waterfront marine climate, a grid of sensors and submerged related vehicles are used (Manvi & Manjula, 2011).

According to its supporters, wireless sensor networks will make many current application areas easier, asserting that brand-new ones will be created. This assertion depends on several variables, but we'll focus on a few of the potential application cases. In addition to the requirement for inexpensive, easily networkable, and potentially long-lasting sensor nodes, an essential and fundamental component for creating practical applications

6. CONVENTIONAL SLANT OF SUBAQUATIC AND SENSOR DISPOSITION

The conventional methodology is to send submerged sensors, recording information during observing meetings and afterward taking the gadgets out to recover the information from the gadget. This slant has specific weaknesses, as referenced underneath

- Needs online framework reconfiguration: There is no connection between the inland station and the observation device, and it would be unreasonable to change the framework once a certain event takes place.
- Difficult to determine the device's status (sensor hub): On the coastal station, determining whether the device had malfunctioned or was still functional was implausible.
- Capacity restriction: The sensors have a limited capacity limit, allowing them to store a limited amount of data while being checked.

7. DESIGN PROBLEMS WITH SUBAQUATIC NETWORKS

The RF signal can only travel a short distance in water due to severe attenuation and the impact of ingestion in submerged environments. Radio waves in the 30-300 HZ range can travel great distances while submerged, but only at low repetition rates. High transmission power and a large receiving wire are necessary to transmit this recurrence range (Akyildiz, et al., 2005; Liang & Cheng, 2009). Furthermore, as view correspondence is necessary for optical sign transmission, exceptionally high accuracy in laser beam directing is required (Ranjan & Ranjan, 2013). The following is a list of some of the key issues with correspondence media:

- The transfer speed in the submerged sensor is restricted because data transmission of the submerged audio channel depends basically on communication/ transmission misfortune which, increments together reach and recurrence (Akyildiz, et al., 2005).
- The mobile-operated control is restricted in submerged sensors and can never be recharged because sun-powered energy can never be cast-off in submerged (Akyildiz, et al., 2005).
- The engendering suspension in submerged is significantly higher than in radio recurrence earthly channel.
- Most of the sensors might move with the current; in this manner, deciding the sensor's area develops one of the difficulties (Yan, et al., 2008).
- Submerged sensor devices are expensive owing to the mandatory ongoing and unreasonable upkeep (Yan, et al., 2008).

8. FUNDAMENTALS OF ACOUSTIC PROPAGATION

Spread in submerged represents a significant test for innovations that are, as of now, utilized in earthly sensor networks. The proliferation speediness of acoustic surfs is five significant degrees gentler than transistor surfs, introducing a more noteworthy test that should be overwhelmed with calculations, conventions, and hub situations (Peach & Yarali, 2013; Ranjan & Ranjan, 2013). Submerged spread is affected by a few variables: Route misfortune, Multi-path engendering, Highly engendering deferral, and Doppler impacts. Submerged acoustic connections are ordered into various classes relying on their reach extremely long, elongated, intermediate, short, and extremely short (Akyildiz, et al., 2005). Performance evaluation of underwater wireless acoustic sensor networks with submissively mobile sensor nodes that move under the impact of powerful oceanic forces, node mobility, and acoustic signal. Passive node mobility is given due to the performance-related study and produces insightful results when a mobility model that simulates realistic maritime circumstances is used. Only recently have some fundamental advancements in supporting technologies made the construction of such wireless sensor networks feasible.

9. STEERING IN THE SUBSURFACE SENSOR NETWORK

Due to sea flows, limited power, and a considerable prorogation delay in auditory correspondence, steering in a submerged sensor network is challenging, given the changing geography of the hubs. Consequently, during the layout of a directing convention for a sensor network, we must account for elements like extended spread latency, low correspondence transmission capacity, dynamic geography, and energy productivity. Utilizing switch centers or gateways to transfer data between nodes inside the coverage area of the specific network and even outside of it. Sending and receiving information among these nodes is one of the most crucial uses of underwater communication networks (UANs), which were developed to make undersea communication easier. One of the main objectives of scientists in research centers is to enable underwater Internet communication because it does not require any kind of rope and might enable real-time contact with the desired underwater manned or unmanned vehicles.

The field of underwater wireless sensor networks has attracted much attention lately due to its major advancements in ocean surveillance, marine monitoring, and application deployment for subaquatic target detection. However, The literature hasn't gathered the state-of-the-art to find the most current developments fueled by subaquatic sensor technologies. Therefore, this study provides the most recent analysis of the available data by analyzing studies from the last five years on numerous characteristics that support network activities and applications in UWSN environments.

Depending on what kind of purpose it serves, subaquatic communication can be wireless, or it can need a wire or cable. The most effective way will depend on the specifics of the setting and the level of communication that needs to be established. Both of these methods have advantages and disadvantages. When communication must occur at depths where wire communication would be impractical or impossible, wireless communication is preferable.

Due to their high bit error rates, long propagation times, and limited bandwidths, subaquatic acoustic communication networks are also susceptible to malicious attacks. The acoustic communication channels need more complex security measures because they are specially made and different from the communication networks used on land. Underwater communication systems struggle with energy conservation regularly. Due to the enormous cost of redeploying subsea equipment, the main goal in building them is to keep them under for as long as feasible. For the technology to operate for a longer time subaquatic, it is essential to conserve energy, which must be considered when designing protocols.

Using acoustic and optical sensors, UANs are also utilized in combat, mostly to find concealed mines. The accuracy of vector hydrophones, reverberation analysis, the effectiveness of scanning sonar to find subaquatic objects, backscattering measurement, and other developments in subaquatic communication are still being worked on.

Commercial parametric sonar is typically employed in applications involving imaging of the ocean floor and the identification of submerged objects, such as hidden mines, but it is also used in applications analyzing ocean floor scattering. Hydrophones and sonar are the most frequent equipment needed for subaquatic sound communication. We list some main obstacles that modern subaquatic communications networks must overcome below. Although subaquatic acoustic communication networks have a wide range of industrial and academic uses, one significant drawback is the high cost of acoustic modems utilized in combat, mostly to use acoustic and optical sensors to find concealed mines (Srisook, et al., 2022). There is still room for improvement in subaquatic communication.

9.1 The Vector-Based Forwarding (VBF) (Xie, et al., 2006; Ayaz, 2011)

Vector grounded sending / VBF area created on steering convention, which is hearty, versatile, and energy proficient. In this convention, parcel sending from basis to objective is conveyed in tedious and interleaved ways, making VBF powerful against bundle misfortune and hub disappointment. In VBF, every parcel contains three elements the place of source (S), the objective (O), and the forwarded (FW). The VBF source hub registers a vector from oneself to the objective that determines the sending way. The hubs inside the directing line are qualified to advance parcels, while the hubs that live external the directing line are ineligible to forward parcels. VBF utilizes variation calculation to change sending strategy.

In the event that it lies in the steering pipe, the hub holds the bundle for a period span T variation given beneath TA (adaptive) $= \sqrt{\alpha} * TD + (r-d)$ Where TD is a delay which is a predefined greatest postponement, v(o) is the proliferation speediness of aural sign in the aquatic and d be the remoteness among this hub and next / hand-off hub, r is broadcast array. Sensor nodes might not have universal ID with high overhead and numerous sensors. The flexibility of these WSNs, which makes them capable of supporting a wide range of very different real-world applications, makes them both a formidable research and technical challenge. As a result, neither a single set of technical specifications nor a single design approach can fully capture the design space for all networks related to wireless. For instance, in many applications, individual network nodes must rely on onboard batteries because they are difficult to connect to a cable power source. Therefore, the energy efficiency of any recommended remedy in such a case is crucial.

9.2 Protocol for Depth-Based Directing (DBD) (Yan, et al., 2008; Ayaz, 2011))

Profundity origin directing purposes for the multilink submerged sensing grid design, where several sink hubs are normally arranged at the aquatic surface. The DBD functions as follows: when a hub gets an information bundle, it initially recovers the profundity dp of parcel past bounce. The hub then, at that point, contrasts its profundity dc and the profundity gotten from the parcel, for example, dp. If dc < dp, for example, the hub is nearer to the aquatic outward, and then it views itself as a competent hub towards advanced information bundle; the parcel is disposed of because the bundle came from and is nearer to the hub, which is nearer to the surface. In DBD, numerous adjoining hubs of a sending hub can advance parcels to the following jump. In the DBD convention, there might be an impact and energy utilization. If all the hubs program the parcel and diminish the impact, furthermore, energy utilization, the quantity of sending hubs ought to be controlled. In this manner, to save energy, excess bundles should be smothered. DBD utilizes the possibility of a need line Q1 to lessen the number of sending hubs and bundle history cradle Q2 to guarantee that hubs advance a similar parcel just a single time in a certain time stretch (Santoso, 2014).

9.3 Distributed Subaquatic Clustering Plot (DUCS) (Ayaz, 2011; Domingo, & Prior, 2007)

For earthly sensor organizations to work on the adaptability, longevity, and energy effectiveness of the organization, numerous different leveled or group-based directing conventions, TEEN "((T)Threshold touchy (E)Energy (E)Efficient sensor (N)Network convention)" (Manjeshwar, & Agarwal, 2001) and PEGASIS "(Power(P) Efficient(E) Gathering (GA) in Sensor(S) Information(I) Systems(S)) " (Lindsey & Raghavendra, (2002), have been proposed. A GPS-free guiding standard is DUCS. DUCS is a flexible self-assembling convention where the arrangement of clusters is completed with the aid of transmitted calculation. In DUCS, activity is divided into two rounds: the group formation or bunch creation process, during which the group leader is chosen, and the network activity stage, during which information is transferred. A hub initially sets its likelihood of becoming a group by utilizing the following recipe:

Where C(i) addresses the hub's backup and C(Max) addresses the most extreme backup limit, CHP is the little consistent part used to set the starting likelihood rate of group heads to restrict the number of bunch head declarations (UmaMaheswaran, et al., 2022).

9.4 Dynamic Addressing Based Hop by Hop Steering Protocol (H2-Touch) (Ayaz, 2011; Chen, et al., 2010)

Another difficulty in submerged sensor networks that needs to be resolved is the requirement for full layered area data of hubs by steering conventions like the 'VBF' (Xie, et al., 2006) and the Local of the Methods for Subaquatic Wireless and Radar Grids / Networks (Ayaz, 2009). Regarding multilink engineering, H2-DAB is vigorous, adaptable, and vigor efficient. H2 -Spot was created to address the hub versatility issue brought on by water flows. Issue the H2 -Touch uses dynamic locations to give sensor hubs new agreeable addresses at distinct depth stretches to resolve hub portability.

9.5 Multi-Path Steering Protocol With Low Propagation Delay (MPR) (Coutinho, et al., 2013)

In this convention information parcel at the source, the hub, is isolated into a few time allotments given the transmission capacity, and two bounce transmissions are utilized for communicating the information parcel to transfer hubs which communicate the information to the objective. Before sending information, hand-off hubs look at transmission planning to distinguish impact. The two benefits of multi-path: bundle drip rate is diminished because the heap is circulated across numerous ways, and high organization heartiness is accomplished. In the MPR convention, multi-way transmission is utilized by source, hand-off, and objective hub. The MPR convention comprises three stages: (1) Proliferation defers assortment stage, (2) Intermediate hub choice stage, (3) Relay hub choice stage

9.6 Depth-Controlled Steering/Routing Etiquette (DCR)

A topographical steering convention with a grid/network geography controller is the profundity control directing convention (Singh, et al., 2022a). The construction of sensor hubs to expand the network and conveyance rate can be considered for the first time under this geographic directing convention. When a hub has information to send using the eager sending method, it chooses the following neighbor as the succeeding bounce closest to the target and then sends the bundle to them. This convention provides combined computations to arrange hubs that can never reach the goals through multi-hop messages and computes novel profundity for totality (Singh, et al., 2022b). The components of a wireless sensor network must first be established and made accessible before construction can begin. These nodes must be small, inexpensive, or energy-efficient and have the appropriate sensors, the necessary computation and memory resources, and adequate communication facilities. They must also be equipped with the necessary resources for computation and memory (Singh, et al., 2022c).

10. CONCLUSION

The discussion of applications, difficulties, and problems in submerged sensor organizations was dealt with in this study. Regarding submerged channel features, steering in UWSN is a key problem, which is why scientists are considering it seriously. Cost reductions due to smaller chips and increased energy efficiency are required to make the deployment of redundant nodes feasible. Each directing convention's strategy is contingent on the application's goals, needs, and rationality, both of which depend on the organization's available resources. In this way, we looked at some newly proposed directing conventions for submerged sensor organization and reasoned that each convention we looked at has both merits and drawbacks. In light of the steering problems and challenges for submerged sensor organization and the shortcomings of recently presented conventions, some new calculations might be suggested, providing a professional steering convention for UWSN to address future challenges. So, advancing steering methods appropriate for submerged environments is seen as a development of a study zone that will considerably increase the stability and productivity of these organizations.

REFERENCES

Akyildiz, I. F., Pompili, D., & Melodia, T. (2005). Subacquatic acoustic sensor networks: Research challenges. *Ad Hoc Networks*, *3*(3), 257–279. doi:10.1016/j.adhoc.2005.01.004

Akyildiz, I. F., & Su, W. (2002). Yogesh Sankarasubramaniam, and Erdal Cayirci. *Computer Networks*, *38*(4), 393–422. doi:10.1016/S1389-1286(01)00302-4

Ayaz, M. (2009). *Hop-by-Hop Dynamic Addressing Based (H2 DAB) Routing Protocol for Subacquatic Wireless Sensor Networks*. IEEE.

Ayaz, M., Baig, I., Abdullah, A., & Faye, I. (2011). A survey on routing techniques in subacquatic wireless sensor networks. *Journal of Network and Computer Applications, 34*(6), 1908–1927. doi:10.1016/j.jnca.2011.06.009

Buddhi, D., Prabhu, Hamad, A. A., Sarojwal, A., Alanya-Beltran, J., & Chakravarthi, M. K. (2022a). Power System Monitoring, Control and protection using IoT and cyber security. *2022 International Conference on Innovative Computing, Intelligent Communication and Smart Electrical Systems (ICSES).* IEEE. 10.1109/ICSES55317.2022.9914167

Buddhi, D., & Varghese, L. J., Neeraja, Hamid, S. S., Ramya.D, & Chakravarthi, M. K. (2022b). Harmonic Distortion reduction in Power System to improve Reliability and power quality. *2022 International Conference on Innovative Computing, Intelligent Communication and Smart Electrical Systems (ICSES).* IEEE. 10.1109/ICSES55317.2022.9914129

Chen, Y.-S., Juang, T.-Y., Lin, Y.-W., & Tsai, I.-C. (2010). A low propagation delay multi-path routing protocol for subacquatic sensor networks. *Journal of Internet Technology, 11*(2), 153–165.

Coutinho, R. W. L., Vieira, L. F. M., & Loureiro, A. A. F. (2013). DCR: Depth-Controlled Routing protocol for underwater sensor networks. *2013 IEEE Symposium on Computers and Communications (ISCC).* IEEE. 10.1109/ISCC.2013.6754988

Cui, J.-H., Kong, J., Gerla, M., & Zhou, S. (2006). The challenges of building mobile subacquatic wireless networks for aquatic applications. *Network (Bristol, England), 20*(3), 12–18.

Derindere Köseoğlu, S., Ead, W. M., & Abbassy, M. M. (2022). Basics of Financial Data Analytics. In *Financial Data Analytics* (pp. 23–57). Springer International Publishing. doi:10.1007/978-3-030-83799-0_2

Dhanush, S., Mohanraj, S. C., Sruthi, V. S., Cloudin, S., & Joseph, F. J. (2022). CODEDJ-Private Permissioned Blockchain Based Digital Wallet with Enhanced Security. In *IEEE International Conference on Bio-Neuro Informatics Models and Algorithms.* IEEE.

Domingo, M. C., & Prior, R. (2007). A distributed clustering scheme for subacquatic wireless sensor networks. in personal, indoor and mobile radio communications. In *Proceedings of the IEEE 18th International Symposium on PIMRC.*

Ead, W., & Abbassy, M. (2018). Intelligent systems of machine learning approaches for developing E-services portals. *EAI Endorsed Transactions on Energy Web, 167292*, 167292. Advance online publication. doi:10.4108/eai.2-12-2020.167292

Ead, W. M., & Abbassy, M. M. (2021). IoT based on plant diseases detection and classification. *2021 7th International Conference on Advanced Computing and Communication Systems (ICACCS).* IEEE.

Gehlot, A., Rajat Mohan, L., Gupta, A., Anandaram, H., Alanya-Beltran, J., & Kalyan Chakravarthi, M. (2022). Smart online oxygen supply management though internet of things (IoT). *2022 International Conference on Innovative Computing, Intelligent Communication and Smart Electrical Systems (ICSES).* IEEE. 10.1109/ICSES55317.2022.9914246

Jain, B., Sirdeshpande, S., Gowtham, M. S., Josephson, P. J., Chakravarthi, M. K., & Pant, B. (2022). Exploratory data analysis based on micro grids generation for control communication and monitoring via wireless sensor network. *2022 2nd International Conference on Advance Computing and Innovative Technologies in Engineering (ICACITE).* IEEE.

Joseph, A. J. J., Joseph, F. J. J., Stanislaus, O., & Das, D. (2022). Classification methodologies in healthcare. In Evolving Predictive Analytics in Healthcare: New AI techniques for real-time interventions (pp. 55–73). doi:10.1049/PBHE043E_ch4

Joseph, F. J. (2022). IoT Based Aquarium Water Quality Monitoring and Predictive Analytics Using Parameter Optimized Stack LSTM. In *2022 International Conference on Information Technology (InCIT).* IEEE. 10.1109/InCIT56086.2022.10067725

Kazmi, S. A., Gupta, A. K., Uddin, N., & Chauhan, Y. K. (2021). The imperative role of solar power assistance for embedded based climatic parameters measurement systems. In Applied Soft Computing and Embedded System Applications in Solar Energy (pp. 187–214). CRC Press. doi:10.1201/9781003121237-10

Kumar, S., Kumar, N. M. G., Geetha, B. T., Sangeetha, M., Chakravarthi, M. K., & Tripathi, V. (2022). Cluster, cloud, grid computing via network communication using control communication and monitoring of smart grid. *2022 2nd International Conference on Advance Computing and Innovative Technologies in Engineering (ICACITE).* IEEE.

Lee, Y.-D., & Chung, W.-Y. (2009). Wireless sensor network based wearable smart shirt for ubiquitous health and activity monitoring. *Sensors and Actuators. B, Chemical, 140*(2), 390–395. doi:10.1016/j.snb.2009.04.040

Liang, Q., & Cheng, X. (2009). Subacquatic acoustic sensor networks: Target size detection and performance analysis. *Ad Hoc Networks, 7*(4), 803–808. doi:10.1016/j.adhoc.2008.07.008

Lindsey, S., & Raghavendra, C. (2002). PEGASIS: Power- Efficient Gathering in Sensor Information Systems. *IEEE Aerospace Conference Proceedings,* (pp. 1125–1130). IEEE. 10.1109/AERO.2002.1035242

Manjeshwar, A., & Agarwal, D. P. (2001). *TEEN: a routing protocol for enhanced efficiency in wireless sensor networks.*

Manvi, S. S., & Manjula, B. (2011). Issues in subacquatic acoustic sensor networks. *International Journal on Computer and Electrical Engineering, 3*(1), 101–111.

Mohamed, & Mesbah, S. (2016). Effective e-government and citizens adoption in Egypt. *International Journal of Computer Applications, 133*(7), 7–13. doi:10.5120/ijca2016907886

Pachauri, R., Gupta, A. K., Mishra, R. G., & Chauhan, Y. (2021a). *Various Power Management Schemes For Efficient Wind Energy Conversion System.*

Pachauri, R. K., Pardhe, M. K., Kazmi, S. A., & Gupta, A. K. (2021b). Improved SDK-based Shade Dispersion Methodology to Achieve Higher GMPP of PV Systems under Shading Scenarios. In *2021 IEEE Madras Section Conference (MASCON)* (pp. 1–6). IEEE. 10.1109/MASCON51689.2021.9563589

Pattana-Anake, V., & Joseph, F. J. J. (2022). Hyper parameter optimization of stack LSTM based regression for PM 2.5 data in Bangkok. *2022 7th International Conference on Business and Industrial Research (ICBIR)*. IEEE.

Peach, C., & Yarali, A. (2013). An overview of subacquatic sensor. *Networks*.

Ranjan, A., & Ranjan, A. (2013). Subacquatic Wireless Communication Network. *Advance in Electronic and Electric Engineering, 3*(1), 41–46.

Sadek, R. A., Abd-alazeem, D. M., & Abbassy, M. M. (2021). A new energy-efficient multi-hop routing protocol for heterogeneous wireless sensor networks. *International Journal of Advanced Computer Science and Applications, 12*(11). doi:10.14569/IJACSA.2021.0121154

Santoso, L. W. (2014). Analysis of the Impact of Information Technology Investments - A Survey of Indonesian Universities. *ARPN JEAS, 9*(12).

Santoso, L. W. (2019). Cloud technology: Opportunities for cybercriminals and security challenges. *2019 Twelfth International Conference on Ubi-Media Computing (Ubi-Media)*. IEEE.

Santoso, L. W. (2021). Adaptive educational resources framework for ELearning using rule-based system. In *Information and Communication Technology for Intelligent Systems* (pp. 385–396). Springer Singapore. doi:10.1007/978-981-15-7078-0_36

Sharma, A. K., Pachauri, R. K., Choudhury, S., Mahela, O. P., Khan, B., & Gupta, A. K. (2022). Improved power maxima point of photovoltaic system using umbrella optimizing technique under PSCs: An experimental study. *IET Renewable Power Generation, 16*(10), 2059–2075. doi:10.1049/rpg2.12486

Sharma, D. K., Singh, B., Anam, M., Villalba-Condori, K. O., Gupta, A. K., & Ali, G. K. (2021). *Slotting learning rate in deep neural networks to build stronger models. 2021 2nd International Conference on Smart Electronics and Communication (ICOSEC)*. IEEE.

Singh, D., Keerthi Nayani, A. S., Sundar Rajan, M., Yadav, R., Alanya-Beltran, J., & Chakravarthi, M. K. (2022a). Implementation of virual instrumentation for signal acquisition and processing. *2022 International Conference on Innovative Computing, Intelligent Communication and Smart Electrical Systems (ICSES)*. IEEE. 10.1109/ICSES55317.2022.9914143

Singh, R., Mishra, P. A., Prakash, A., Tongkachok, K., Upadhyaya, M., & Kalyan Chakravarthi, M. (2022b). Smart device for effective communication in the healthcare system. *2022 International Conference on Innovative Computing, Intelligent Communication and Smart Electrical Systems (ICSES)*. IEEE. 10.1109/ICSES55317.2022.9914093

Singh, T., Rastogi, P., Pandey, U. K., Geetha, A., Tiwari, M., & Chakravarthi, M. K. (2022c). Systematic healthcare smart systems with the integration of the sensor using cloud computing techniques. *2022 2nd International Conference on Advance Computing and Innovative Technologies in Engineering (ICACITE)*. IEEE.

Srisook, N., Tuntoolavest, O., Danphitsanuparn, P., Pattana-Anake, V., & Joseph, F. J. (2022). Convolutional Neural Network Based Nutrient Deficiency Classification in Leaves of Elaeis guineensis Jacq. *International Journal of Computer Information Systems and Industrial Management Applications, 14,* 19–27.

Uma Maheswaran. S. K., Nassa, V. K., Singh, B. P., Pandey, U. K., Satyala, H., & Chakravarthi, M. K. (2022). An inventory system utilizing neural network in the prediction of machine learning techniques. *2022 2nd International Conference on Advance Computing and Innovative Technologies in Engineering (ICACITE).* IEEE.

Xie, P., Cui, J.-H., & Lao, L. (2006). *Networking technologies, services, and protocols; performance of computer and communication networks; mobile and wireless communications systems.* Springer.

Yan, H., Shi, Z. J., & Cui, J.-H. (2008). DBR: depth-based routing for subacquatic sensor networks. In *Proceedings of the 7th international IFIP-TC6 networking conference on adhoc and sensor networks, wireless networks, next generation internet.* Singapore: Springer-Verlag.

Yick, J., Mukherjee, B., & Ghosal, D. (2008). Wireless sensor network survey. *Computer Networks, 52*(12), 2292–2330. doi:10.1016/j.comnet.2008.04.002

Chapter 16

A Study on Anti-Inflammatory Analgesic Effect of Focus Religiosa Compared to Standard Drugs in Wister Rats

Sakhare Pritam M.
Krishna Institute of Medical Sciences, India

S. A. Jadhav
Krishna Vishwa Vidyapeeth, India

ABSTRACT

Inflammation is caused by tissue damage, which is caused by pathogenic causes such tissue injury, infection, or cardiac infarction. Inflammation can be caused by either infectious or noninfectious triggers. Inflammation is characterized by redness, heat, swelling, pain, and loss of tissue function, which results from local vascular, immune, and inflammatory cell responses to any infection or injury. When a tissue is damaged, our bodies send out a series of chemical signals to trigger reactions that promote tissue repair. All of these cues stimulate circulating leukocytes to chemotactically migrate to the site of injury. As a result of being activated, leukocytes release cytokines, which set off other inflammatory processes in the body. Inflammatory disorders can be treated with a wide variety of medications nowadays. Nonsteroidal anti-inflammatory medicines (NSAIDs) and steroidal anti-inflammatory drugs (NSAIDs) are two examples that have proven effective. However, due to the potential for major side effects, their usage is limited.

1. INTRODUCTION

Chronic inflammation may be insidious in onset or may follow acute inflammation (Veeraiah, et al., 2022). It is of longer duration and is related to the proliferation of blood vessels, fibrosis and tissue destruction, along with the presence of lymphocytes and macrophages (Bennet and Brown, 2003). Basically,

DOI: 10.4018/979-8-3693-1301-5.ch016

the ideal treatment for any pain is to cure the cause: hence, before the treatment planning, we should go for the diagnosis (Dey, et al., 1995). Sometimes, only treating the underlying cause does not give immediate relief from the pain (Fan, et al., 2014). In addition to this, certain disorders, such as trauma, post-operative pain, cancer, and others, can cause excruciating pain and necessitate the use of analgesics that work quickly and efficiently (Paramasivan & Venkatesh, 2016). Strong analgesics, such as opioid medication, are essential for relieving the excruciating pain caused by cancer metastases (Ambika, et al., 2019). Inflammation is characterized by redness, heat, swelling, pain, and loss of tissue function, all of which come from local vascular, immunological, and inflammatory cell responses to any infection or injury. Inflammation can occur in response to any type of injury or infection (Gulecha, et al., 2011). Opioid analgesics have been utilized for a long time as a therapy option for both acute and chronic pain due to the effectiveness of these medications (Vashishtha, et al., 2020). Frequent use of drugs belonging to this class is being discouraged as a result of concerns over their acceptability and safety (Gupta, 2009). In addition, reports linking them to drug misuse and dependence have led to a general decrease in acceptance of these behaviors among many people (Laurence and Bacharach, 1964). Because opioids are known to cause addiction, extensive research has been done to find molecules that do not have the same adverse effects (Lowensten, 2005).

The aggressive function of inflammation is now well understood, along with its significance in the healing and restoration process (Kaur, et al., 2011). Inflammation is now understood to include the whole process, from the onset of a reaction, through the emergence of the classic indications listed above, through the final stages of healing and return to the normal look and function of the affected organ or tissue (Makhija, et al., 2010). However, in other cases, the underlying cause cannot be identified, and chronic inflammation develops, which may endure for years or even a lifetime (Mittal, et al., 2019). Conditions including rheumatoid arthritis, osteoarthritis, psoriasis, inflammatory bowel illness, etc., fall under this category (Sharma, et al., 2016).

Inflammation research necessitates interdisciplinary efforts (Saxena, 2022). The study of the immune system is often required to comprehend the occurrences associated with the initiation and maintenance of inflammatory diseases (Sreelekshmi, et al., 2007). In order to determine a person's susceptibility to inflammatory diseases, scientists now consider the molecular biology and genetics underpinning cellular responses to be of equal importance (Vogel, et al., 2002). However, pharmacological research is crucial for pinpointing the causes of persistent and sometimes fatal inflammation and creating effective novel therapeutics. Studies of immunological and cellular responses, as well as the pharmacological process that underlies medication discovery, are thus crucial to the study of inflammation (Turner, 1965).

1.1. Aim of the Study

To evaluate the anti-inflammatory & analgesic activity of Ficus Religiosa bark & leaf extract in Wistar Rats.

1.2. Objectives

- To prepare a methanolic extract of leaves and stem bark of Ficus Religiosa.
- To evaluate the analgesic activity of two different doses of the above extract.
- To evaluate the anti-inflammatory activity of the above extracts in two different doses by using carrageenan-induced paw oedema.

2. REVIEW OF LITERATURE

Etiology of inflammation: Infectious agents, such as bacteria, viruses, and their toxins, fungi, and parasites, are possible causes of inflammation. Immune system components, including cell-mediated and antigen-antibody interactions. Physical factors, such as temperature extremes, radiation, and impact. Organic and inorganic toxins and other chemical agents 5. Foreign bodies and other inert materials.

Types of inflammation: On the basis of duration and mode of onset, the inflammatory reaction can be classified as:

Acute inflammation: It comes on quickly and lasts for only a brief time (a few minutes to several hours). Inflammation symptoms coexist with constitutional symptoms. Exudation of fluid, plasma, and leukocyte emigration make up the microscopic image (Harsh and Mohan, 2010).

3. TERMINATION OF ACUTE INFLAMMATION

Subsequent changes in the damaged area vary with the nature and duration of the injurious stimulus, the type of tissue involved and the degree of destruction of tissue. Any of the following may occur:

- Resolution.
- Healing by scar formation with or without regeneration of lost parenchymal cells.
- Suppuration.
- An acute course may get converted to a chronic one.

3.1. Sub-Acute Inflammation

One to six weeks of this can be detected in tubular structures like the appendix or fallopian tube (or more). Acute inflammatory vascular exudative alterations and persistent inflammatory, proliferative changes are hallmarks of this condition (Paramasivan, 2016).

3.2. Mechanism of Action of Anti-Inflammatory Drugs

They act as anti-inflammatory by inhibiting COX enzyme and hence by blocking the synthesis of PGs that lead to inflammation. Aspirin irreversibly inhibits COX by acetylating one of its serine residues, while other NSAIDs are competitive and reversible inhibitors.

3.3 Beneficial Clinical Effects

- Analgesia.
- Antipyresis.
- Anti-inflammatory (high dose of aspirin).
- Anti-thrombotic (Low dose of aspirin).
- Closure of ductus arteriosus.

3.4. Phenomenon of Pain

The following considerations should be incorporated into any theory of pain: A persistent ache can linger long after an injury has healed, even if no damage or illness was ever-present. Severe tissue damage often occurs painlessly. Negative feelings (such as worry, fear, or sadness) are inseparable from the experience of pain and have the power to alter both the intensity of the pain and the victim's reaction to it. Both the spinal cord and the brain play a significant role in the processing of afferent nociceptive and other signals. In addition to being a sensory experience, pain also elicits emotional (affective) responses. Modalities of Pain and the Physiological Basis for Distinct Pain States: Recognizing that not all pain is the same and that several factors influence the patient's pain report and, by extension, the analgesic's efficacy is essential to any discussion of the action of analgesic drugs. As a heuristic, it might be helpful to see pain in terms of the following various sequences of events.

3.5. Acute Nociception

Small high-threshold sensory afferents (A and C fibres) are activated acutely, sending brief information into the spinal cord, which subsequently activates neurons that extend counter laterally to the thalamus and, ultimately, the somatosensory cortex. The medial thalamus and the limbic system's anterior cingulate cortex are both targets of a spinofugal projection that runs parallel to itself.

3.6. Sensory vs. Affective Dimensions

High-intensity peripheral stimuli provide data that triggers certain pathways, which in turn activates higher-order systems proportional to the unpleasantness of the stimulus. This is indicative of the sensory-distinctive nature of pain (such as the ability to accurately estimate and characterize the pain state). There is a clear separation between pain as a unique sensation served by discrete neurophysiological systems and pain as suffering, which can be triggered by painful stimuli and elicit profound emotional responses (the original sensation plus the reactions evoked by the sensation; the affective, motivational dimension). Therefore, powerful segmental analgesia can be achieved with intrathecal injection of opioids without compromising motor or sensory function or creating major subjective effects.

3.7. Classification of Pain

There might be a difference between *rapid pain* and *slow pain*. Following the first *bright,* acute, localized sensation (fast pain), the body experiences a more prolonged and widespread version of the same unpleasant sensation (slow pain). It appears that the A pain fibers are responsible for quick pain while the C pain fibers are responsible for slower pain. Inflammatory and neuropathic pain are two types of chronic pain that fall within the pathologic category. Acute pain often has a quick start and recedes during the healing process. Since it performs a necessary protective function, acute pain might be thought of as *good pain.*

Dependent on the degree of discomfort, the associated worry may be mild, moderate, or severe.

- When the nervous system is injured, the result is a type of pain called neuropathic pain.

- Slow-conducting type C fibers play a crucial role in the transmission of chronic pain (but to a lesser extent by fast-conducting A-delta fibers).

Pain is experienced differently by each individual, making it hard to establish objective measures. At the same time, pain assessment measures are crucial for providing an objective measure of suffering. The visual analogue scale, numerical pain intensity scales, pain thermometer, facial expression scale, and descriptor pain scale are all examples of verified pain measures.

3.8. Anatomy

Leaves of the Ficus Religiosa The leaves and young branches are glossy, smooth, slightly leathery, widely oval in form, and abruptly constricted at the tip into a long tail. The base is rounded or heart-shaped. There is a strong central nerve in the leaf, which should be taken into account. In addition, the leaf has 5–9 lateral pairs that come together at the leaf's edge to form a curvy line. Most of the leaves are pendulous or trailing. They typically drop their leaves in the springtime (March and April) and occasionally in the fall (in some regions).

3.9. Foodstuffs

People commonly refer to them as figs. The months of May and June are prime times for harvesting these figs, but the fruit is available all year round in some regions. Because birds and bats enjoy eating Peepal fruit so much, the seeds often escape digestion and wind up in random places, like the gutter or the wall of a home, where they might begin to grow.

Bark is flat or slightly curved, and its thickness ranges from 5 to 8 millimeters. Its exterior surface is grey or ash with thin or membranous flakes and is typically coated with crustose lichen brown or ash colored. Flowers - They are concealed among the figs. Figs often emerge at an oblique angle between the leaf stalk and the branch. When unripe, their skin is smooth and green; when ripe, it's purple. Near the fig's apex opening are a scattering of male flowers.

Under the microscope, the F. religiosa bark can be seen to be composed of two distinct layers: the outside, thick periderm and the inner, secondary phloem. Both the phellem and the phelloderm are sub-layers of the Periderm. The Phellem zone is 360 millimeters thick and has a very irregular and undulating cross-section. Phellem cells are arranged in tangential membrane layers, and the older membrane layers exfoliate in a similar fashion. Phelloderm is a large, separate zone. Lignification is the process through which phelloderm cells become sclereids. Ficus religiosa has been utilized in traditional medicine for a wide variety of diseases due to its therapeutic capabilities. Traditional medicine makes use of the plant's bark, leaves, fruits, and other components to cure a wide range of illnesses. The bark can be used to cure gonorrhea and ulcers, while the leaves can be applied topically to treat skin conditions.

4. MATERIALS AND METHODS

This dissertation's protocol was reviewed and approved by both the Institutional Ethical Committee (IEC) and the Institutional Animal Ethical Committee before any research was conducted (IAEC). The methodology used in this dissertation has been approved by the International Academic Ethics Committee. Once the study was approved, it was conducted according to CPCSEA guidelines (Committee for the Purpose of Control and Supervision on Experiments on Animals).

4.1. Materials

Before beginning the research, the protocol for this dissertation was initially presented to both the Institutional Ethical Committee (IEC) and the Institutional Animal Ethical Committee. This fact should be brought to your attention (IAEC). The IAEC awarded its official stamp of approval to the methodology used in the dissertation. Following receipt of approval, the investigation was carried out in accordance with the guidelines established by the CPCSEA (Committee for the Purpose of Control and Supervision on Experiments on Animals).

4.2. Experimental Animals

During the course of this investigation, adult, disease-free Wistar rats of both sexes and weighing between 120 and 200 grammes were obtained from the Central animal house under the Department of Pharmacology at the Krishna Institute of Medical Sciences in Karad. These rats were maintained in conditions that were optimal with regard to their housing, temperature, ventilation, and feeding. In the course of the inquiry, which lasted for a whole calendar year, a total of seventy-two Wistar rats were utilized.

Rats were acclimated to a 12:12 hour light-dark cycle for ten days previous to the day of the experiment. They were fed regular pellet rat food and given access to water at all times. The animals were transported to the Post Graduate research laboratory of the department an hour before the experiment began, and they were housed in a quiet, dimly lit area to get used to the conditions there.

We had to create 12 distinct categories for the animals. These classifications were consistent across the two models used in this research to assess the analgesic and anti-inflammatory effects of the study's medications.

Both the Carrageenan-induced rat paw edoema model and the guinea pig nasal polyp model may be used to assess the acute anti-inflammatory effects of various medications. And the Tail-Flick Pain Rating Scale for Assessing Analgesic Effectiveness of Experimental Drugs.

There were six animals in each group. A single usage was made of each animal. Temperatures ranged from 27 to 37 degrees Celsius, and all measurements were taken between 10 a.m. and 5 p.m. Animals used in experiments were treated humanely and in accordance with the regulations set out by the Indian National Science Academy and the Committee for the Purpose of Control and Supervision of Experiments on Animals (CPCSEA) (INSA).

4.3. Equipment

- Syringes - 1ml syringes with 27G needle.
- An oral feeding tube for the administration of drugs.
- Mercury Plethysmograph for measuring paw oedema fitted with an air-tight column of tubing and 2ml syringe at one end.
- Digital weighing machine.
- Analgesiometer.
- Stopwatch to record the reaction time.

- Rat restrainer.
- So xhlet apparatus is for the preparation of extracts.

4.4. Drugs and Chemicals

- Ibuprofen, obtained from Krishna Hospital Pharmacy.
- Carrageenan: obtained from Hi Media lab, Mumbai. It is a mixture of polysaccharides composed of sulphated galactose units and is derived from Irish Sea moss. This was administered intradermally as a suspension in 1% warm normal saline, in the volume of 0.05 ml, in the hind paw of the rat to induce acute inflammation.
- In the KIMS Pharmacology Laboratory, an extract of the leaves of the Ficus Religiosa tree was made using methanol. We chose to test two different dosages of leaf extract: 100 milligrams per kilogram (MEL100) and 200 milligrams per kilogram (MEL200) (MEL200)
- In the KIMS Pharmacology Laboratory, an extract of the stem bark of the Ficus Religiosa tree was prepared using methanol. We have decided to test stem bark extract at two different levels, namely 125 mg/kg (MES125) and 250 mg/kg (MES250)
- Normal Saline as controlled. (NS)

5. METHODS

5.1. Inclusion Criteria

- Healthy Wistar Rats of either sex weighing 120-200gm.
- Wistar Rats, which are not used previously for any study.

5.2. Exclusion Criteria

- Previously used and injured rats will not be included.
- Female pregnant Wistar rats will be excluded from the study.

Groups were divided as follows, and drugs were administered orally.

Following groups are used to evaluate the analgesic activity of leaves and stem bark extract of ficus religiosa:

Group1: 0.9 percent NS,10ml/kg, P.O
Group2: IBU, 40 mg/kg, P.O
Group 3: MEL, 100mg/kg, P.O
Group4: MEL, 200mg/kg, P.O
Group5: MES, 125mg/kg, P.O
Group 6: MES, 250mg/kg, P.O

Following groups are used to evaluate the anti-inflammatory activity of leaves and stem bark extract of ficus religiosa:

Group1: 0.9% NS,10ml/kg P.O
Group2: IBU, 40mg/kg, P.O.
Group 3: MEL,100mg/kg, P.O
Group 4: MEL,200mg/kg, P.O
Group 5: MES,125mg/kg, P.O
Group 6: MES, 250 mg/kg, P.O

6. ALL DRUGS WERE ADMINISTERED ORALLY

6.1. Plants Materials and Preparation of Plant Extract

Before starting the study, we have done the authentication of leaves and stem bark of Ficus Religiosa by the botanist.

6.2. Drugs

Leaves and stem bark of plant Ficus Religiosa were collected, and its authentication was done by a botanist.1)Leaves of Ficus religiosa were collected and washed with fresh water to remove adhered dirt and foreign particles. Then, they were shade dried. Methanolic extract of powder from dried leaves was obtained by soxhlet apparatus.2) Stem bark of ficus religiosa was collected, shade dried and powdered. Then, the methanolic extract of this powder was obtained by using the soxhlet apparatus.

7. DISCUSSION

Our ancestors used to divide inflammation into five distinct categories based on visual observation. These categories were: redness (rubor), swelling (tumour), heat (calor; only applicable to the extremities of the body), pain (dolour), and loss of function (function-latest). Celsus, who lived in ancient Rome between the years 30 and 38 B.C., identified the first four symptoms; Galen, who lived between 130 and 200 A.D., identified the fifth symptom. 140 The body's natural reaction to any form of damage to the microcirculation and the tissues directly around it is inflammation. This definition has only been formulated relatively lately.

The conventional concept of inflammation may explain the observed alterations in appearance. When blood vessels dilate, more blood flows to the skin's surface, creating a flushed appearance and a sense of heat (because of the additional number of erythrocytes passing through the area). Several factors contribute to edoema: cell infiltration into the injured region, fluid leakage from the dilated blood arteries into the surrounding tissues, and, in prolonged inflammatory reactions, connective tissue deposition. Pain, on the other hand, results from the stretching of swollen sensory nerves and the direct actions of mediators, both of which may be traced back to the original injury or the inflammatory response. When a joint loses its mobility, it loses function. When healthy cells are replaced by scar tissue, the joint loses function and can't move.

Until the late 19th century, inflammation was thought to be a normal element of the healing process. Metchnikoff and others in the nineteenth century established inflammation's role in the body's natural defences and recuperative processes.

Inflammation is now understood to be a more nuanced immune response to tissue injury and infection (albeit not every infection always results in inflammation). Acute inflammation, such as that caused by S. aureus of the skin, to chronic inflammation, which can cause remodelling of the artery wall in the case of atherosclerosis, or the bronchial wall in the case of asthma and chronic bronchitis, or the debilitating joint destruction associated with rheumatoid arthritis, is another example of the diversity of inflammation.

Major immune system cells, including basophils and neutrophils, are essential to this process. Immune cells such as T cells, mast cells, etc. Certain types of leukocytes may be seen in the inflammatory lesions. This ensures that the right amount of leukocytes is recruited throughout the inflammatory process. Extracellular regulators and mediators like cytokines, prostaglandins, leukotrienes, growth factors, complements, and peptides govern these comprehensive processes.

The discovery of several of these mediators over the last 20 years has expanded our knowledge of the control of the course of inflammation while also teaching us something about the intricacy of this phenomenon.

Major immune system cells, including basophils and neutrophils, play a role in this process. Various types of cells, such as T cells, mast cells, etc. Certain types of leukocytes can be detected in the inflammatory lesions. That implies inflammation is controlled such that the right number of leukocytes are recruited. Extracellular regulators and mediators such as cytokines, prostaglandins, leukotrienes, growth factors, complement, and peptides govern these whole processes. Our present knowledge of the biochemical mechanisms at play in inflammatory diseases is reflected in the design of many medications used to treat these ailments. Non-steroidal anti-inflammatory medicines (NSAIDs) such as aspirin are commonly used to treat the pain associated with rheumatoid arthritis, while corticosteroids and other disease-modifying anti-rheumatic therapies are often used to alleviate additional symptoms. Chemical compounds that regulate pain transmission are released into the extracellular tissue whenever there is tissue injury. For the activation of pain, the chemical substances responsible are histamine, substance P, bradykinin, leukotrienes and prostaglandins. These mediators can cause other reactions like vasodilatation, vasoconstriction or alteration in the permeability of capillary at the site of injury. Aspirin and morphine, among others, have seen increased consumption in the last several decades. Almost 30% of individuals might see a 50% reduction in pain from these medications. Further, they have quite negative side effects. Opiates have been demonstrated in a number of studies to result in physical dependence, addiction, and tolerance, whereas NSAIDs are more likely to result in gastrointestinal issues. Traditional herbal remedies have traditionally been the first line of defense against illness. They are therapeutic because of the complex chemical substances found in them. Ficus is an example of such a tree species. It's no secret that many of the species in this genus have useful qualities that may be put to good use for humanity.

8. RESULTS

Methanolic extract of Ficus religiosa stem bark has also been used. We chose two dosages, one at 125mg/ kg and the other at 250mg/kg. When compared with the placebo and the gold standard medicine ibuprofen, we found that both dosages had anti-inflammatory effects. Compared to both the control and ibuprofen, MES250's anti-inflammatory effects were most noticeable within the first hour. Extracts from both the leaves and the stem bark were tested for their anti-inflammatory and analgesic effects, and the results were compared.

The results of our study and the conclusions derived thereof are summarized as follows:

In carrageenan-induced paw oedema model by plethysmograph:

- However, MES250 has shown better anti-inflammatory than MEL100.

For anti-inflammatory activity, we have done carrageenan-induced paw edema in rat models and tail flick methods for analgesic activity.

For pre-clinical evaluation of the anti-inflammatory and analgesic activity of methanolic extract of leaves, have selected two different doses of 100mg/kg (MEL100) and 200 mg/kg (MEL200) which were given orally.

To evaluate the anti-inflammatory and analgesic activity of methanolic extract of stem bark, two different doses (125mg/kg (MES125) and 250mg/kg (MES2S0)) were selected and given orally.

The above two activities were compared with ibuprofen (10ml/kg) as a standard drug.

From the results of our study, it is evident that amongst all the extracts, MES250 has shown a strong anti-inflammatory activity when compared with the control and the standard drug ibuprofen.

9. CONCLUSION

These days, non-steroidal anti-inflammatory medicines, more often known as NSAIDs, are widely used as analgesics and can be prescribed for any type of pain, whether it be acute or chronic. The nonsteroidal anti-inflammatory medicines (NSAIDs) are the pharmacological class that is used the most frequently because they reduce inflammation and pain. In addition to this, corticosteroids unquestionably play a part in the process of relieving both pain and inflammation. However, because of the potentially harmful effects of using them for an extended period of time, this is not an option. Opioids are yet another category of medication that is utilized in the management of painful conditions. However, they are also experiencing dose-related adverse effects such as drowsiness and respiratory depression, amongst other things. Since the beginning of time, numerous plants used for medical purposes have been widely known in India. The medicinal benefits of several plants, including herbal remedies, are discussed in our ancient Vedas. The Ficus religiosa tree is believed to be the oldest living plant with a documented planting date. Leaf juice has been used for the treatment of asthma, cough, sexual difficulties, diarrhea, haematuria, earache, and toothache, as well as countless other conditions, according to reports that it has numerous medicinal benefits in traditional medicine. Additionally, the bark of this plant is widely utilized in the treatment of pain and inflammation in traditional medical practices. despite the fact that there are relatively few research available on their ability to reduce inflammation and alleviate pain. As a result, we have decided to use the methanolic extract of Ficus religiosa leaves and stem bark for the purpose of assessing the anti-inflammatory and analgesic effects in respective rat models.

9.1. Limitations of the Study

The efficacy of leaves and stem bark extracts of ficus religiosa as an anti-inflammatory and analgesic agent can be further evaluated using other related models in different species.

REFERENCES

Ambika, S., Gopinath, S., Saravanan, K., Sivakumar, K., Sukantha, T. A., & Paramasivan, P. (2019). Preparation and characterization of nanocopper ferrite and its green catalytic activity in alcohol oxidation reaction. *Journal of Superconductivity and Novel Magnetism*, *32*(4), 903–910. doi:10.100710948-018-4715-7

Bennet, P. N., & Brown, M. J. (2003). *Pain and analgesics: Clinical Pharmacology* (9th ed.). Churchill Livingstone.

Dey, N. C., Sinha, D., & Dey, P. K. (1995). Text book of Pathology. Calcutta: New Central Book Agency (Pvt) Limited.

Fan, S. H., Ali, N. A., & Basri, D. F. (2014). Evaluation of analgesic activity of the methanol extract from the galls of Quercus infectoria (Olivier) in rats. *Evidence-Based Complementary and Alternative Medicine*, 2014. PMID:25254062

Gulecha, V., Sivakumar, T., Upaganlawar, A., Mahajan, M., & Upasani, C. (2011). Screening of Ficus Religiosa leaves fraction for analgesic and anti-inflammatory activities. *Indian Journal of Pharmacology*, *43*(6), 662. PMID:22144770

Gupta, S. K. (2009). *Drug screening methods (Pre-clinical evaluation of new drugs)* (2nd ed.). JAYPEE Brothers Medical Publishers Limited.

Harsh and Mohan. (2010). Text book of Pathology (6 ed). New Delhi: JAYPEE Brothers Medical Publishers Private Limited.

Kaur, A., Rana, A. C., Tiwari, V., Sharma, R., & Kumar, S. (2011). Review on ethanomedicinal and pharmacological properties of Ficus religiosa. *Journal of Applied Pharmaceutical Science*, *1*(8), 6–11.

Laurence, D. R., & Bacharach, A. L. (1964). *Evaluation of Drug Activities: Pharmacometrics* (Vol. 2). Academic Press Inc.

Lowensten, D. H. (2005). Pain: Pathophysiology and management.In : Fields HL,Martin JB edts Harrisons principles of internal medicine. Mc Graw Hills Companies.

Makhija, I. K., Sharma, I. P., & Khamar, D. (2010). Phytochemistry and pharmacological properties of Ficus religiosa: An overview. *Annals of Biological Research*, *1*(4), 171–180.

Mittal, Srishty & Thapar, Lakhvinder. (2019). *Vitamin D Levels Between The Tuberculosis Infected And Non – Infected Subjects In 16-25 Years Of Age.*

Paramasivan, P., & Venkatesh, P. (2016). Controllable synthesis of CuFe2O4 nanostructures through simple hydrothermal method in the presence of thioglycolic acid. *Physica E, Low-Dimensional Systems and Nanostructures, 84*, 258–262. doi:10.1016/j.physe.2016.05.037

Paramasivan, P., & Venkatesh, P. (2016). A novel approach: Hydrothermal method of fine stabilized superparamagnetics of cobalt ferrite (CoFe2O4) nanoparticles. *Journal of Superconductivity and Novel Magnetism, 29*(11), 2805–2811. doi:10.100710948-016-3586-z

Saxena, D. (2022). *A Non-Contact Based System to Measure SPO2 and Systolic/Diastolic Blood Pressure Using Rgb-Nir Camera (Order No. 29331388).* ProQuest Dissertations & Theses A&I; ProQuest Dissertations & Theses Global. (2697398440).

Sharma, D., Dangi, C. B., & Kaur, M. A. (2016). Review on pharmacological activities and therapeutic potentials of Ficus religiosa (Pipal). *Indian Journal of Applied Research, 6*(1), 623–626.

Sreelekshmi, R., Latha, P.G., Arafat, M.M., S Shyamal,V. J. Shine, G. I., & Anuja. (2007). Anti-inflammatory, analgesic and anti-lipid peroxidation studies on stem bark of ficus. *Religiosa Linn, 6*(5).

Turner, R. A. (1965). *Screening Methods in Pharmacology.* Academic Press Inc.

Vashishtha, E., Sherman, L., Sajjad, T., & Mehmood, N. (2020). Use of anti-viral therapy in treatment of Covid 19. *Journal of Advanced Medical and Dental Sciences Research, 8*(11), 273–276.

Veeraiah, V., Pankajam, A., Vashishtha, E., Dhabliya, D., Karthikeyan, P., & Chandan, R. R. (2022). Efficient COVID-19 identification using deep learning for IoT. *2022 5th International Conference on Contemporary Computing and Informatics (IC3I).* IEEE.

Vogel, H. G., Vogel, W. H., Schölkens, B. A., Sandow, J., Müller, G., & Vogel, W. F. (2002). Analgesic, anti-inflammatory, and anti-pyretic activity1. In *Drug Discovery and Evaluation* (pp. 670–773). Springer Berlin Heidelberg. doi:10.1007/3-540-29837-1_9

Chapter 17
Comparing Bishop Score and Transvaginal Ultrasonographic Cervical Factors to Predict Labor Induction

Bahulekar Ashitosh
Krishna Institute of Medical Sciences, India

R. P. Patange
Krishna Institute of Medical Sciences, India

ABSTRACT

The excitement of being a mother and holding your child in your arms is also accompanied by increased stress levels, worry, and unpredictability of giving birth. Every labour develops individually, posing a unique set of obstacles for the mother to overcome, the partner to be amazed at, and the obstetrician to reflect on. Predicting when the labour pains will start after induction, how they will be associated with gradual cervical dilatation, and how they will end in a vaginal delivery is one of the issues that the pregnant lady, her family, and the attending obstetrician most frequently think about. Transvaginal ultrasonography is increasingly employed in obstetrics, particularly in the second and third trimesters when it is used to estimate the length of the cervical canal. Transvaginal ultrasound measurements of cervical length and the condition of the internal os of the cervix during the second trimester help define an inadequate cervix and aid in the choice to do a cervical encirclage.

1. INTRODUCTION

The process of giving birth is accompanied with feelings of anxiety, stress, anticipation, and uncertainty; nonetheless, motherhood is a joyful experience overall, and the delight of meeting one's new baby comes hand in hand with these feelings (Bahn, 1998). Every woman's labor progresses in her own individual manner, with each stage presenting a new set of challenges for the lady to face, as well as questions and

DOI: 10.4018/979-8-3693-1301-5.ch017

concerns for the woman's relatives and the obstetrician to ponder (Bartha et al., 2005). One of the most difficult questions for an expecting mother, her family, and the treating physician to answer is when labor pains will begin following an induction of labor, how they will correlate with cervical dilation, and whether or not a vaginal birth will occur as a result. Predicting when labor pains will begin after induction is one of the most difficult things to do (Chandra et al., 2001).

1.1. Anatomy and Physiology of The Cervix

There are several transformations that occur in the cervix throughout pregnancy and birth. Labor is the process through which the fetus is delivered to the outside world after spending its whole life within the uterus (Elghorori, et al., 2006).

1.2. Anatomy

The cervix is a tube that is hollow and stretches into the vagina to produce fornices. This process takes place throughout pregnancy (Rozenberg et al., 2005). It measures between two and three centimeters in length (12) and has two sets of minute openings on either end. These openings, known as the internal and external ora, are connected by the endocervical canal (Suganthi & Sathiaseelan, 2023). It is composed of two pieces, one that is located above the vaginal opening and one that is located below it (both of which are technically the portio vaginalis). The peritoneum encircles the supravaginal region and surrounds it from behind. Women who have had several children have a longitudinal slit rather than the circular external os that nulliparous women have. When speaking of the uterus, the term "flexion" refers to the angle produced between the long axis of the corpus and the cervix, whereas the term "version" refers to the angle formed by the uterus's junction with the upper vagina. Both terms are used interchangeably. The lining of the endocervix is made up of columnar epithelium, while the lining of the ectocervix is made up of stratified squamous epithelium (Cirillo et al., 2023). The lower uterine segment at term develops from the isthmus, which is the area between the anatomical internal os and the histological internal os. Because of this, the lower uterine segment at term has a special relevance in obstetrics (Chandra, 2001).

In the cervix, the smooth muscles, fibroblasts, and blood vessels are embedded in an extracellular matrix made up of collagen (type I (70%) and type III (30%)), elastin, and proteoglycans. The tensile strength of collagen is best preserved in fibers longer than 20 meters in length (Pandit 2023). The structure of collagen is a triple helix (Anand et al., 2023). It may form fibers, bundles, and fibrils by cross-linking. The human cervix contains the tiny molecular-weight proteoglycan decorin, which plays a role in the formation of collagen (Vashishtha & Dhawan, 2023). During pregnancy, cervical cells create a substance called decorin. There is a disorder of the collagen fibers as the decorin to collagen ratio rises, since this leads to a scattering of the collagen fibrils (Vashishtha et al., 2020). Collagenases break down collagen to gradually weaken the collagen matrix and permit cervical dilatation during a medical abortion (Verhoeven et al., 2012).

Bands of elastin, 20-30 m in thickness, run parallel to the collagen fibers. They are incredibly elastic, and under mechanical stress, the cervix may dilate to double its normal size.

Along its length, the cervix varies in the proportion of connective tissue to smooth muscle. Connective tissue makes up a larger percentage of the distal section than smooth muscle does in the upper cervical region near the myometrium.

The cervix is made up of smooth muscle cells and fibroblasts. The cervix becomes hyperplastic, or thickened, due to the proliferation of smooth muscle cells and fibroblasts in early pregnancy. Normal cell death (apoptosis) happens later in pregnancy. Further cell growth is inhibited by decorin, and it also aids in the dispersion of collagen fibers. The cervix becomes more distensible because water is drawn in as a result of the collagen's disarray.

1.3. Mechanisms of Cervical Ripening

Cervical ripening is influenced by a variety of variables, including decorin, hyaluronic acid, cytokines, proteases, and hormones. The cervix's water content and collagen structure are both improved by these variables. Decorin causes collagen to disperse throughout the body (Nirmala et al., 2023).

The extracellular matrix may also be broken down by enzymes. Matrix metalloproteinases (MMPs) 1 and 8, as well as collagenases and elastases, cleave collagen helices during cervix remodeling (Jeganathan et al., 2023).

When applied to the cervix, hyaluronic acid causes the cervix to swell and ripen because it raises the water content of the cervix and promotes the manufacture of proteolytic enzymes by cervical fibroblasts. It has also been shown to accelerate neutrophilic chemotaxis and induce neovascularization in the cervix in late pregnancy (Jeba et al., 2023).

Progesterone and oestrogen receptors may be found in the cervix. In the short term, both oestrogen and progesterone receptors are being suppressed. Production of collagenase in the human cervix during pregnancy is triggered by oestrogen and its precursors. There is evidence that progesterone may reduce interleukin-8 production in the cervix.

1.4. Pre-Induction Cervical Assessment

Certain prelabor cervical features are related to the pace at which labor progresses. Inducement to commencement of labor time, active phase of labor time, and delivery mode may all be predicted using different scoring systems.

The success or failure of an elective induction of labor may be predicted using a scoring system that Bishop published in 1964.

Previous descriptions of ripeness are reflected in the Bishop score. The extent of the cervical effacement is measured in terms of the cervical canal. Full effacement occurs when the cervix is the same thickness as the lower uterine segment next to it. A percentage of effacement was formerly part of the Bishop score, but the more objective assessment of cervical length is now part of the modified Bishop score.

The standard method of measuring cervical dilatation is by sweeping the inspecting finger from one side of the cervical opening to the other. When the cervix's diameter reaches 10 centimeters, it is considered completely dilated since the presenting section of the fetus may normally pass through it (Munshi et al., 2022).

The cervical os and the location of the fetal head determine whether the cervix is posterior, mid, or anterior.

Cervical consistency may be classified as either soft, firm, or intermediate. The position of the ischial spines provides data about the level or station of the exhibiting fetal part in the delivery canal. Station zero is reached when the lowest component of the exhibiting fetal part is now at the height of the spines. The superior and inferior halves of the pelvis may be thought of as separate fifths, thanks to the ischial

spines. One centimetre above or below the spines is one fifth of a whole. Therefore, the designation is -5, -4, -3, - 2, and -1, as the presenting foetal component descends from the inlet towards the ischial spines. As the presenting foetal portion makes its way down from the spines, it will pass through stations +1, +2, +3, +4, and +5 on the way to delivery. At the introitus, the fetus's head should be visible, which occurs at station
+5.

1.5. Induction of Labor

Labor induction is the induction of contractions in the uterus prior to the commencement of labour by natural means. Induction refers to the process of bringing on labour through artificial means before the time that it would have occurred naturally. This necessitates two events: first, the maturation of the cervix, and second, the contractions of the uterus. A cervical dilation of 3–4 cm or larger in the presence of uterine contractions is typically recognised as an appropriate threshold for diagnosing active labour. This is because it might be difficult to accurately recognise true labour at early stages of cervical dilatation. Inducing labour can be accomplished through a variety of methods, including as the administration of prostaglandins (PgE1 and PgE2), oxytocin, mifepristone, or even with the use of mechanical instruments (hygroscopic dilators, a cervical ripening balloon catheter, an amniotomy, membrane sweeping, etc.). Inducing labour before term may be necessary for a number of different reasons, including a protracted pregnancy, hypertensive illnesses of pregnancy, foetal development limitation, oligohydramnios, gestational diabetes mellitus, premature rupture of membranes, and decreased foetal movements.

Predicting whether or not an induction of labour will be successful is traditionally done by calculating the Bishop score from a per-vaginal examination of the cervix. Yet studies have shown that this evaluation has poor prognostic value for the result of induction, particularly in women with a low Bishop score, since it is subjective, not repeatable, and cannot determine the condition of the internal os and membranes when the external cervical os is closed.

The use of transvaginal ultrasonography is expanding in the field of obstetrics, particularly in the second and third trimesters for measuring the length of the cervical canal. In the second trimester, a transvaginal ultrasonographic evaluation of cervical length and the state of the internal os of the cervix is used to define an inadequate cervix and aid in the decision to perform a cervical encirclage if one is indicated. Measuring the cervical length transvaginally has mostly been used to detect cervical abnormalities in women who are at risk for premature delivery. Some research has looked at how other cervical characteristics, such as cervical angle and funnelling of the internal os, may be used to foretell how a labour would go. Since the Bishop score does not take into account the supravaginal section of the cervix or the state of the internal os in a non-laboring cervix, transvaginal ultrasonography is a useful tool.

The goal of this research was to see whether transvaginal ultrasonography, which provides an objective measure of the cervical length, might improve upon the clinical evaluation given by the Bishop score in predicting the success of induction. In such a case, the transvaginal ultrasonographic assessment of cervical length may be utilised as a trustworthy instrument in addition to the Bishop score, adding even another level of information to the study of successfully inducing labour.

The Bishop score, which is obtained from a pervaginal examination of the cervix, has traditionally been used to predict whether or not an induction of labour will be effective. However, research has indicated that induction has poor predictive value, especially for women with low Bishop scores. The internal os and membranes cannot be evaluated during the closed external cervical os due to the subjective nature of the evaluation, its lack of reproducibility, and its inability to do so. The goal of this research was to see if an objective measurement of the cervical length using transvaginal ultrasonography may improve clinical evaluation using the Bishop score for predicting induction success. Transvaginal cervical length evaluation has been frequently used to detect cervical abnormalities in pregnant women at high risk. If this is the case, then both the Bishop score and the transvaginal ultrasonographic assessment of cervical length can be utilised as trustworthy techniques, providing further depth to studies on the efficacy of inducing labour. Clinical examination and electrical impedance measurements across the cervix using an 8-mm tetrapolar pencil probe have been utilised to examine their correlations in determining cervical favorability (O'Connell et al., 2003). To a statistically significant degree, the cervix's favourable characteristics were linked to its resistance.

Nulliparae undergoing prostraglandin induction of labour had their serum nitrite and nitrate levels measured, and the results showed that women who gave birth within 15 hours of induction had considerably lower levels of both nitrite and nitrate than those who gave birth later (Facchinetti et al. 1998).

2. REVIEW OF LITERATURE

Around 2-3 cm in length, the cervix extends into the vagina to produce the fornices. It is cylindrical in shape, with small holes at either end (the internal and external ora, joined by the endocervical canal). The portio vaginalis consists of two sections: the supravaginal and the infravaginal. At the back, the peritoneum wraps around the supravaginal area. Nulliparous women have a circular external os, while multiparous women have a transverse slit. Version refers to the angle formed by the uterus's junction with the upper vagina, while flexion describes the angle formed by the long axis of the uterine corpus and the cervix. Cervical tissue includes smooth muscle, fibroblasts, and blood vessels embedded in an extracellular matrix made up of collagen (type I (70%) and type III (30%)), elastin, and proteoglycans. For collagen to retain its tensile strength, the fibres must be at least 20 metres long. Collagen has a three-helix structure. It's possible to form fibres, bundles, and fibrils by cross-linking the strands. Decorin, a tiny molecular-weight proteoglycan found in the human cervix, has a role in the formation of collagen. During pregnancy, cells in the cervix create a substance called decorin. A higher decorin-to-collagen ratio leads to collagen fibril dispersal and fibre disarray. Collagenases break down collagen, gradually weakening the collagen matrix, which permits cervical dilatation during an abortion.

To better anticipate the result of elective induction of labour, Bishop established a scoring system in 1964 for evaluating the cervix prior to induction.

When describing ripeness, the Bishop score matches the prior description. The degree of cervical effacement is measured in terms of the cervical canal's reduced length. Complete, or one hundred percent, effacement occurs when the cervix thins to the same thickness as the surrounding lower uterine segment. Effacement was originally measured as a percentage in the Bishop score, but this was later changed to a more objective cervical length measurement in the modified Bishop score (Table 1).

Table 1. Bishop score

Parameters	Bishop Score			
	0	One	Two	Three
Cervical dilatation	Closed	1 to 2 centimetres	3 to 4 centimetres	5 centimetres
Effacement	0-30%	40 to 50%	60 to 70 percent	More than 80 percent
Consistency	Stable	Average	Lenient	
Position	Position-Posterior	Position-Mid	Anterior	

Bishop score is 4 or less: unfavourable cervix; cervical ripening prior to induction of labor is needed.

Table 2. Modified bishop score

Parameters	Modified Bishop Score						
	0		One		Two		Three
Cervical dilatation	Closed		1 to centimetres	2	3 to centimetres	4	5 centimetres
Cervical length	More than centimetres	3	2 to centimetres	3	1 to 2centimetres		More than centimetres	1
Consistency	Stable		Average		Lenient		
Position	Position-Posterior		Position-Mid		Anterior		

The Bishop score was adjusted in a different way by Friedman, (1967) (Table 2). The latent phase of the first stage of labour was negatively associated with the preinduction cervical score, while the active phase was not evaluated in the evaluation of 408 multiparas undergoing labour induction. The latent period was not uniformly affected by the variables used to calculate the Bishop score. They advocated for cervical dilatation to be given twice the weight of head position compared to consistency, station, and effacement. It was proven for the whole system that the chance of a successful induction rose with higher scores. It's worth noting that these authors advocated for the addition of "modifiers" to the scoring system in question in an effort to improve the predictive power of the system.

3. MATERIALS AND METHODS

Duration of study- November 2019 to November 2021

3.1. Inclusion Criteria

Singleton pregnancies, nulliparous patients, vertex-presented live birth at 37–42 weeks gestation, pre-induction NST pattern of comfort, Patients who are willing to participate in the trial and who have no medical reasons to avoid a vaginal birth

3.2. Exclusion Criteria

Less than 37 weeks of gestation, foetal malpresentations, multifetal gestation, non-reassuring FHR tracing, congenital anomalies of the foetus, history of uterine surgery, history of antepartum haemorrhage, cephalo- pelvic disproportion, and any other condition that would rule out the possibility of a vaginal delivery are all examples of conditions that would rule out the possibility of a vaginal delivery.

4. RESULTS

Table 3. Indications for induction of labor in the subjects

Indication	Number	(%)
Prolonged pregnancy	19	(23%)
Hypertensive disorders of pregnancy	20	(22.4%)
Hypertensive disorder with fetal growth restriction	1	(1.1%)
Gestational diabetes mellitus	5	(5.6%)
Oligohydramnios	16	(18%)
Prelabor rupture of membranes	16	(18.0%)
Fetal growth restriction	9	(10.11%)
Decreased fetal movements	3	(3.4%)
Total	89	(100%)

Indicators for inducing labour are listed above in a table 3. About a quarter of the women (n = 19) had their pregnancies induced because they were expected to be full-term for longer than 41 weeks. Pregnancy- related hypertensive conditions accounted for 20% of all inductions (n = 20). Only one out of every 1,200 subjects (1.1%) was induced due to high blood pressure and foetal growth restriction. The incidence of induced delivery due to GDM was 5.6% (n = 5). Ultrasound and clinical examination revealed oligohydramnios in 18% (n = 16), thus initiating labour. Prelabor rupture of membranes was induced in 18% (n = 6) of births. 9.11% (n = 9) of inductions were for foetal growth restriction, while 3.41% (n = 3) were for reduced foetal movements.

Table 4. Outcome of induction against cervical length measured on TVUS

Cervical length on TVUS (cm)	No. of inductions	No. of successful inductions	No. of failed induction
<1	00		
1- 2	31(34.8%)	30	01
2.1- 3	40(44.9%)	28	12
3.1- 4	18(20.2%)	04	14
Total	89(100%)	62(100%)	27(100%)

By chi square/fishers exact test, p value =0.0001, highly significant

According to the data shown in table 4, none of the participants who had a CL of one centimetre were induced. Induction was successful for 96 percent (n = 30) of the 31 patients whose CL measured between 1 and 2 centimetres, while induction was unsuccessful for 4 percent (n = 1) of the subjects. Induction was successful for seventy percent (n = 28) of the forty participants whose CL measured between two and three centimetres, while it was unsuccessful for thirty percent (n = 12) of the subjects. In the group of 18 participants whose CL measured between 3.1 and 4.0 cm, only 23 percent (n = 4) experienced a successful induction, while 77 percent (n = 14) experienced an unsuccessful induction.

5. DISCUSSION

Successful induction of labour was defined in our research as cervical dilatation up to 4 cm after a maximum of 2 instillations of PgE2 gel, in accordance with institutional standards. Other criteria, such as evaluation of initiation to birth interval, manner of delivery, etc., have been utilised in studies around the globe. However, subsequent stops of cervical dilatation, insufficient uterine contractions, uterine inertia, etc. may all play a role in the active phase of labour lasting for an unusually long time. There is no correlation between the Bishop score and the success of induction if a caesarean section is necessary due to foetal conditions such as nonreactive CTG trace, meconium-stained liquor, abruptio placenta, non-descent of the foetal head, deep transverse arrest, midcavity, or outlet cephalopelvic disproportion. Multiple induction strategies have been used in previous research, which may function as a confounding variable.

Results of induction of labour may be predicted accurately by both the TVUS measurement of the cervical canal and the Bishop Score. The cervix has historically been assessed using the Bishop score both before induction and again after inducement, as well as during childbirth. The Bishop score is helpful because it allows you to evaluate the foetal head's descent, consistency, and cervix position all in one simple measurement. The relative positions of the woman's head and shoulders, as well as the confirmation of synclitism, are additional criteria to be evaluated during labour that help with decision-making about the labouring woman. Only a vaginal examination can provide these details. This is one of the benefits of using Bishop scores.

An extended induction-to-active phase interval, the need for several applications of PgE2 gel, and a greater failure rate were all associated with a Bishop score in the 1-3 range. Inducing labour in patients with a Bishop score between 4-6 was often effective after a single application of PgE2 gel, although in a few instances, further applications were necessary. People who scored 7 or above on the Bishop scale were successfully inducted.

Although TVUS measurement of cervical length is objective and highly reproducible, using an ultrasound to check progress during induction of labour might be inconvenient. Moreover, a Bishop score of 4 and a cervical length of 2.45 cm are revealed to be the optimum cutoff values for predicting induction success and failure, respectively. With a Bishop score of 4 or above, inducing labour is likely to succeed, whereas a score of less than 4 increases the likelihood of induction failure and increases the time from induction to the active phase. The varying cutoffs found across research are further discussed below.

When the cervical length is long, induction is less likely to be successful, and vice versa when the cervical length is short. However, the probability of induction success rises with the Bishop score and decreases with the Bishop score. This demonstrates the positive correlation between cervical size and the time it takes to go from inducing labour to the active phase of labour, as well as the negative correlation between cervical length and the success rate of inducing labour.

Comparing the two variables' receiver operating characteristic (ROC) curves revealed that the area under the curve for cervical length as assessed by TVUS was greater than that for the Bishop Score. Therefore, the results indicate that TVUS-measured cervical length is a more accurate predictor of induction of labour success than Bishop score.

The funnelling of the internal os and the existence of a bag of membranes are shown to be statistically significant in predicting the induction outcome. The existence of funnelling may be detected with a sensitivity of 70.96 percent and a specificity of 22.3 percent. When the external os of the cervix is closed, the funnelling of the internal os shortens the cervix, which is an advantageous result. The creation of a bag of membranes is facilitated by the internal os funnelling.

Results: NPV = 88%; NPV = 53.84%. Sensitivity = 56 percent, specificity = 14.8 percent, positive predictive value = 89.74 percent, and negative predictive value = 46.4 percent for the membrane bag.

TVS cervical measures, including cervical length and posterior cervical angle, are better objective criteria than Bishop score for predicting the success of induction, according to research.

Our results, in which cervical length was shown to be more predictive than Bishop score, are consistent with these findings.

The 2016 study by Nikbhakt, Hemadi, (2016) looked at 148 cases and found that in primiparous women, transvaginal cervical length is more accurate than the Bishop score. The research determined that a Bshop score of 4 and a cervical length of 20 mm were appropriate cutoffs.

In a study that involved 200 women and was conducted in 2016, Rizwana et al. (2016) found that a cervical length of 3 centimetres and a cervical angle of more than 100 were statistically significant factors for preinduction cervical length, funnelling, and posterior cervical angle. The ROC curves of 122 patients were analysed for a study, however the researchers were unable to determine an adequate threshold for continuous variables that relate to sonographic cervical measures. As a result, the regression model conducted its analysis with these variables taking the form of continuous variables. The Bishop Score, the position of the cervical cervix, and the age of the mother were all independent predictors of vaginal birth. In their research, transvaginal ultrasonography did not perform as well as digital cervical examination in predicting whether or not an induction of labour would be successful.

Only the Bishop Score and the number of previous children were found to be independent predictors of vaginal delivery in induced labour, according to Gonen et al. (1998)'s prospective evaluation of 86 research subjects. A recent randomised study that compared the use of transvaginal sonographic assessment and the Bishop Score to guide preinduction cervical ripening with prostaglandins found that transvaginal ultrasonography resulted in a reduction in the amount of prostaglandins used without affecting the rate at which labour could be induced successfully. An evaluation of the favorability of the cervix using the Bishop score is recommended by the RCOG (2001) guidelines for inducing labour. These guidelines were published in 2001.

6. CONCLUSION

Although both the Bishop score and the cervical length as assessed by TVUS are trustworthy indications of how an induction of labour will progress, the latter provides a more accurate picture of how things will turn out than the former does. It has been suggested that the cervical length determined by transvaginal ultrasound (TVUS), as an alternative to the Bishop score, could be used to induce labour in settings that have access to the technology required for TVUS as well as staff who have been properly educated to utilise it. A Bishop score of 4 and a cervical length of 2.45 cm are both good cutoff parameters for predicting whether or not an induction would be successful. Inducing labour has a greater chance of being effective if specific circumstances are satisfied, such as the presence of a bag of membranes and the funnelling of the internal os. Inducing labour also has a higher success rate in women who have already given birth.

REFERENCES

Anand, P. P., Kanike, U. K., Paramasivan, P., Rajest, S. S., Regin, R., & Priscila, S. S. (2023). Embracing Industry 5.0: Pioneering Next-Generation Technology for a Flourishing Human Experience and Societal Advancement. *FMDB Transactions on Sustainable Social Sciences Letters*, *1*(1), 43–55.

Bahn, S. (1998). Maternal and neonatal outcome following prolonged labor induction. *Obstetrics and Gynecology*, *92*(3), 403–407. PMID:9721779

Bartha, J. L., Romero-Carmona, R., Martínez-Del-Fresno, P., & Comino-Delgado, R. (2005). Bishop score and transvaginal ultrasound for preinduction cervical assessment: a randomized clinical trial: Bishop score and TVS for preinduction cervical assessment. *Ultrasound in Obstetrics & Gynecology*, *25*(2), 155–159. doi:10.1002/uog.1813 PMID:15660437

Chandra, S. (2001). Transvaginal ultrasound and digital examination in predicting successful labor induction. *Obstetrics and Gynecology*, *98*(1), 2–6. PMID:11430948

Chandra, S., Crane, J. M. G., Hutchens, D., & Young, D. C. (2001). Transvaginal ultrasound and digital examination in predicting successful labor induction. *Obstetrics and Gynecology*, *98*(1), 2–6. PMID:11430948

Cirillo, S., Polese, G., Salerno, D., Simone, B., & Solimando, G. (2023). Towards Flexible Voice Assistants: Evaluating Privacy and Security Needs in IoT-enabled Smart Homes. *FMDB Transactions on Sustainable Computer Letters*, *1*(1), 25–32.

Elghorori, M. R. M., Hassan, I., Dartey, W., & Abdel-Aziz, E. (2006). A way to lend objectivity to Bishop score. Journal of Obstetrics and Gynaecology. *Journal of Obstetrics & Gynaecology*, *26*(4), 311–316. doi:10.1080/01443610600594922

Facchinetti, F., Gandolfi, A., Longo, M., & Volpe, A. (1998). Serum nitrites predict the response to prostaglandin-induced delivery at term. *Journal of the Society for Gynecologic Investigation*, *5*(3), 140–143. doi:10.1016/S1071-5576(97)00117-2 PMID:9614643

Friedman, E. A. (1967). *Pre labor status evaluation 2nd Weighted score*. 29.

Gonen, R., Degani, S., & Ron, A. (1998). Prediction of successful induction of labor: Comparison of transvaginal ultrasonography and the Bishop score. *European Journal of Ultrasound*, *7*(3), 183–187. doi:10.1016/S0929-8266(98)00042-1 PMID:9700213

Jeba, J. A., Bose, S. R., & Boina, R. (2023). Exploring Hybrid Multi-View Multimodal for Natural Language Emotion Recognition Using Multi-Source Information Learning Model. *FMDB Transactions on Sustainable Computer Letters, 1*(1), 12–24.

Jeganathan, J., Vashist, S., Nirmala, G., & Deep, R. (2023). A Cross Sectional Study on Anxiety and Depression Among Patients with Alcohol Withdrawal Syndrome. *FMDB Transactions on Sustainable Health Science Letters, 1*(1), 31–40.

Munshi, M., Zilani, M. N. H., Islam, M. A., Biswas, P., Das, A., Afroz, F., & Hasan, M. N. (2022). Novel compounds from endophytic fungi of Ceriops decandra inhibit breast cancer cell growth through estrogen receptor alpha in in-silico study. *Informatics in Medicine Unlocked, 32*(101046), 101046. doi:10.1016/j.imu.2022.101046

Nikbhakt, R., Hemadi, M., (2016). Transvaginal cervical length and bishop score value in predicting successful labor induction with an emphasis on the parity. *Int J pharmaceut res allied sciences, 5*(2), 114-118.

Nirmala, G., Premavathy, R., Chandar, R., & Jeganathan, J. (2023). An Explanatory Case Report on Biopsychosocial Issues and the Impact of Innovative Nurse-Led Therapy in Children with Hematological Cancer. *FMDB Transactions on Sustainable Health Science Letters, 1*(1), 1–10.

O'Connell, M. P., Tidy, J., Wisher, S. J., Avis, N. J., Brown, B. H., & Lindow, S. W. (2000). An in vivo comparative study of the pregnant and nonpregnant cervix using electrical impedance measurements. *BJOG, 107*(8), 1040–1041. doi:10.1111/j.1471-0528.2000.tb10410.x PMID:10955439

Pandit, P. (2023). On the Context of Diabetes: A Brief Discussion on the Novel Ethical Issues of Non-communicable Diseases. *FMDB Transactions on Sustainable Health Science Letters, 1*(1), 11–20.

RCOG. (2001). Induction of labour. In Evidence based Clinical Guideline Number 9. London.

Rizwana, H., Aquisha, B., & Shruti, G. (2016). Study of transvaginal sonographic assessment of cervix in predicting the success of labor induction in nulliparous women. *JK Science, 18*(1), 6–11.

Rozenberg, P., Chevret, S., Chastang, C., & Ville, Y. (2005). Comparison of digital and ultrasonographic examination of the cervix in predicting time interval from induction to delivery in women with a low Bishop score. *BJOG, 112*(2), 192–196. doi:10.1111/j.1471-0528.2004.00549.x PMID:15663583

Suganthi, M., & Sathiaseelan, J. G. R. (2023). Image Denoising and Feature Extraction Techniques Applied to X-Ray Seed Images for Purity Analysis. *FMDB Transactions on Sustainable Health Science Letters, 1*(1), 41–53.

Vashishtha, E., & Dhawan, G. (2023). Bridging Generation Gap on Analysis of Mentor-Mentee Relationship in Healthcare Setting. *FMDB Transactions on Sustainable Health Science Letters, 1*(1), 21–30.

Vashishtha, E., Sherman, L., Sajjad, T., & Mehmood, N. (2020). Use of anti-viral therapy in treatment of Covid 19. *Journal of Advanced Medical and Dental Sciences Research, 8*(11), 273–276.

Verhoeven, C. J. M., Rückert, M. E. P. F., Opmeer, B. C., Pajkrt, E., & Mol, B. W. J. (2012). Ultrasonographic fetal head position to predict mode of delivery: a systematic review and bivariate meta-analysis: Fetal head position in prediction of mode of delivery. *Ultrasound in Obstetrics & Gynecology, 40*(1), 9–13. doi:10.1002/uog.10102 PMID:21953834

Chapter 18
Macrolide's Anti–Inflammatory Effects on Acute and Subacute Inflammation (Azithromycin, Clarithromycin, and Roxithromycin)

Vandana M. Thorat
Krishna Institute of Medical Sciences, India

Mahesh Manohar Bharambe
Krishna Vishwa Vidyapeeth, India

ABSTRACT

The key characteristics of acute inflammation are the exudation of fluid and plasma proteins and the emigration of leukocytes, mostly neutrophils, and it often begins within minutes or hours in response to infection and tissue damage and lasts for many hours. After the harmful agents have been removed, the acute inflammatory response fades, but if the response fails to eradicate the stimuli, the reaction might develop into a prolonged phase referred to as chronic inflammation. Since there is no safe, effective anti-inflammatory drug, scientists continue to study inflammation. Azithromycin, Clarithromycin, and Roxithromycin were tested for anti-inflammatory properties in Wistar rats with acute and sub-acute inflammation. Karad's largest animal house supplied 200–300g Wistar rats. Before the studies, the animals were used to the 24-hour cycle of light and dark for ten days. There was generally enough water and rat pellets. The IAC authorised this study (Institutional Animal Ethics Committee).

DOI: 10.4018/979-8-3693-1301-5.ch018

1. INTRODUCTION

Despite the availability of safer and more potent anti-inflammatory agents, research into inflammation remains a hot topic. Inflammation is a multifaceted and ever-changing state characterised by a cascade of molecular and cellular responses aimed at eliminating harmful invaders and repairing or replacing compromised tissue. Patients often seek medical care for relief from pain and inflammation (Chensue & Ward, 1990). Inflammation is a complicated response in tissues which consists mostly of reactions of blood vessels and leukocytes, and which serves primarily as a defensive response (Fernandes, et al., 2017).

Inflammation is a factor that is shared by a number of conditions, including bronchial asthma, chronic obstructive pulmonary disease, chronic sinusitis, bronchiolitis, cystic fibrosis, uveitis, autoimmune illnesses, rheumatoid arthritis, and ankylosing spondylitis (Gosavi, et al., 2015). The implicated inflammatory processes are to blame for the hypersensitive reactions, which can be lethal at times and are triggered by things like insect stings, toxins, and drugs (Vashishtha, 2019). These ailments are all extremely debilitating and restricting in some way. The plasma proteins, the circulating leukocytes (white blood cells), and the tissue phagocytes that are formed from the circulating cells are the basic types of defences that the body possesses (Scaglione and Rossoni, 1998). This is achieved by the concerted efforts of the vascular system, the leukocytes, and the plasma proteins (Munshi, et al., 2019). Inflammatory reactions at the cellular and vascular levels are triggered by soluble components obtained from plasma proteins that are activated or created in response to an inflammatory stimulus. These proteins are activated when an inflammatory stimulus is present (Ratzinger, et al., 2014).

Acute inflammation is characterised by several key features, the most important of which are the discharge of fluid and plasma proteins as well as the emigration of leukocytes, most of which are neutrophils (Munshi, et al., 2022). This type of inflammation typically begins within minutes or hours as a response to tissue injury or infection and can continue for many hours. However, if the response does not eradicate the stimulus, the response may evolve into a prolonged phase known as chronic inflammation, which continues long after the acute phase has ended. This phase of the response is known to endure for a very long time (Winter, et al., 1962). Chronic inflammation is characterised by an inflammatory response that lasts for an extended period of time and includes the proliferation of blood vessels, the presence of lymphocytes and macrophages, the formation of fibrosis, and the destruction of healthy tissue. Chronic inflammation is associated with more tissue damage and a longer duration of inflammation. Chronic inflammation is characterised by an inflammatory response that lasts for an extended period of time (Vashishtha & Sherman, 2018). Innate immunity, which includes acute inflammation, and adaptive immunity, which also includes chronic inflammation, are in the forefront when it comes to the methods that the host uses to defend itself (Mahdi, et al., 2006).

When the trigger is removed, inflammation stops. Short half-lives of leukocytes in tissues facilitate the breakdown and dissipation of mediators, bringing relief to the inflammatory response. Anti-inflammatory systems are activated to help regulate the host's reaction and limit any potential harm (Munshi, et al., 2018). As soon as the inflammatory response has eliminated the harmful stimuli, the tissue healing process may begin. During the healing process, damaged tissue is replaced by newly regenerated, healthy cells, and any remaining flaws are filled up by connective tissue (scarring) (Shinkai, et al., 2008).

Some conditions may actually be worse off with some inflammation. Necrotic tissues' innate abilities and the systems meant to remove alien invaders may cause damage to healthy tissues. Injuries and illnesses may be brought on by inflammation if it is either redirected towards self-tissues (as in autoimmune disorders) or not properly managed. Idiopathic pulmonary fibrosis, type 2 diabetes, and cancer are only a few examples of the many illnesses that have been linked to inflammation. The healing process is intrinsically linked to the inflammatory response (Md, et al., 2014). Defects caused by injury are repaired by either the growth of new fibrous tissue or the proliferation of new native parenchymal cells, or both (Grégoire et al., 2018).

It has long been acknowledged that current approaches to treating inflammation are controversial and inadequate. Various inflammatory disorders are now treated with a wide variety of medications, including nonsteroidal anti-inflammatory drugs (NSAIDs), steroidal anti-inflammatory drugs (SAIDs), and disease-modifying anti-rheumatic drugs (DMARDs). While up to this point, the findings have been promising, and there is a risk of major side effects, including fatal ones, which has led to a restriction of the medications' usage (Stellari, et al., 2014). There are a number of medications that have shown promise in the treatment of inflammatory illnesses like gout and rheumatoid arthritis, including penicillamine, allopurinol, etc (Iwamoto, et al., 2011).

Several adrenergic agonists, calcium channel blockers, and calcium have been shown to have anti-inflammatory effects in small-scale experimental trials. In addition to nonsteroidal anti-inflammatory medicines (NSAIDs), sulfonamides such as sulfamethiazole and statins have been shown to have anti-inflammatory efficacy in animal models. Anti-inflammatory medications like these are not without side effects; therefore, scientists are always looking for new and improved options (Ianaro, et al., 2000).

Macrolides, a class of antibiotics, have been used clinically for a long time to treat infections brought on by Gram-positive bacteria like Haemophilus influenzae and Gram-negative bacteria including Legionella pneumophila, Chlamydia, and Mycobacteria.

Antibiotics of the macrolide class have advantages over other classes, including once-daily dosing, improved absorption, and favourable tolerance (Stricker, et al., 2010). Macrolides are unique in that they not only have antibacterial action but may also alter several components of the immune response. Macrolides seem to have an impact on many steps in the inflammatory process, including neutrophil migration, pro-inflammatory cytokine synthesis, and the phagocytic oxidative burst (Green, 1972). It has been hypothesised that the interaction between leukocytes and macrolides is crucial, albeit the precise mechanism of these actions is unclear. Leukocytes have the capacity to accumulate macrolides, leading to intracellular concentrations greater than those achieved in the extracellular fluid. This capacity to alter phagocyte activity is crucial for the antibacterial *defence* and the inflammatory response to infections. The anti-inflammatory effects of macrolides have been attributed, at least in part, to their antioxidant properties, according to some research (Nakamura, et al., 2019).

There has been much conjecture concerning the anti-inflammatory effects of macrolide antibiotics, despite the fact that their effectiveness has been evaluated in a number of studies using animal models (Vashishtha, 2020). However, the processes that cause these effects remain unknown. The anti-inflammatory effects of macrolides have paved the way for their investigational use in bronchial asthma and other inflammatory and infectious disorders affecting the airways. Although macrolides may have anti-inflammatory properties, a 2005 Cochrane review concluded that the evidence for their use in chronic asthma was insufficient and that further research was needed to confirm this. The current study aimed to evaluate the anti-inflammatory activity of Macrolides in acute and sub-acute models of inflammation in Wistar rats because there is a dearth of published literature regarding animal studies done to evaluate the anti-inflammatory activity of macrolide antibiotics (Veeraiah, et al., 2022).

1.1. Aim

The goal of this research was to evaluate the effectiveness of the macrolide antibiotics (Azithromycin, Clarithromycin, and Roxithromycin) against acute and subacute inflammation in Wistar rat models.

1.2. Objectives

- For the purpose of conducting research on the anti-inflammatory properties of azithromycin, clarithromycin, and roxithromycin using Wistar rats as a model of acute and sub-acute inflammation.
- In a Wistar rat model of acute and subacute inflammation, the purpose of this study was to examine the anti-inflammatory effects of azithromycin, clarithromycin, and roxithromycin and to compare these antibiotics to the gold standard drug, which is aspirin.
- Purpose: The purpose of this study was to examine the efficacy of Azithromycin, Clarithromycin, and Roxithromycin in reducing inflammation.

2. MATERIAL AND METHOD

2.1. Experimental Animals

Male and female Wistar rats weighing between 200 and 300 g were collected from the Krishna Institute of Medical Sciences major animal house in Karad. Before doing any tests on the animals, we let them adjust to the light-dark cycle for ten days (Munshi, et al., 2021). They were fed the regular rat pellet diet and given access to water at all times. IAEC has given its clearance to the current investigation (Institutional Animal Ethics Committee). All procedures were conducted in accordance with CPCSEA (Committee for the Purpose of Control and Supervision of Experiments on Animals) regulations.

2.2. Drugs

Pure powder forms of azithromycin, clarithromycin, and roxithromycin were purchased from Century Pharmaceuticals Ltd. in Vadodara. The Central Pharmacy of KIMS in Karad was the source of the injection ketamine (10 ml vial of 50 mg/ml) (Troikaa Pharmaceuticals Ltd.), aspirin (Reckitt Benckiser India Ltd.), carrageenan, and gum acacia powder.

- Clarithromycin, Roxithromycin and Azithromycin: A pure powder form of one hundred milligrammes of each drug being tested was mixed into ten millilitres of a solution containing one percent gum acacia. Because none of the medications were particularly soluble in sterile water, gum acacia was employed in the role of a suspending agent.
- Aspirin: The standard solution of aspirin was prepared by dissolving 325 mg of the dispersible tablet in 5 ml of sterile water.
- Carrageenan was prepared as suspension with 1% in 0.9% normal saline, 113.

2.3. Groups

The animals were separated into the aforementioned five categories. In both the acute and sub-acute models of inflammation, there were a total of six mice in each group. Total Wistar rats utilised for the study = 60.

2.4. Model for Acute Inflammation

Using a carrageenan-induced rat paw oedema model and a mercury plethysmograph, the anti-inflammatory properties of the compounds were studied (Vashishtha, et al., 2020). To ensure the animals were always dipped for subsequent measurements, a red ink mark was placed on one paw at the position of the lateral malleolus. An oral gavage feeding needle was used to provide the drugs to the various groups one hour before the emphysema induction. In order to cause the paw oedema, 0.05 ml of freshly made 1% suspension of carrageenan in normal saline was injected intradermally into the plantar area of one of the rats' hind paws. As shown in Figure 1, the amount of paw oedema was measured in millilitres (ml) using a mercury plethysmograph at 0 (immediately after carrageenan injection) and 1, 2, 3, 4, and 5 hours after the injection. By comparing the pre-and post-oedema readings, the true oedema volume could be determined. If you can prevent or slow the increase in mean paw oedema relative to a control group, you have demonstrated anti-inflammatory action. For both the control and experimental groups, the percentage of oedema inhibition was determined using the following method:

Figure 1. Plethysmographic measurement of the rat paw oedema volume in the acute inflammation study

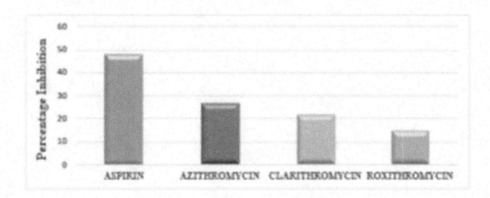

3. MODEL FOR SUB-ACUTE INFLAMMATION

3.1. Method for Foreign Body-Induced Granuloma

On the first day of the trial, oral gavage feeding needles gave all medications to groups. Ketamine (50 mg/kg, i.e.) anaesthetised the rats. Following the removal of excess hair from above the axillae, two 10 mg cotton pellets (sterilised by autoclaving at 120°C) were implanted subcutaneously via tiny incisions made in both axillae (Figures 2 and 3). After anaesthesia, animals were maintained in clean cages and sutured. Treatment began on pellet implantation day one and was repeated daily for ten days. The rats used to remove the cotton pellets were euthanised on day eleven due to ketamine overdoses (Figures 4 and 5). After removing any extra tissue and drying the cotton pellets in a hot air oven overnight at 60 °C, their dry weight was removed. The pellet weight differential before and after insertion determined the net granuloma. For each research group, the mean dry weight of granuloma was estimated to be mg/100 g rat body weight. Reducing the average dry weight of granulomas relative to a control group is indicative of their anti-inflammatory efficacy. The formula used to determine the percentage of inhibition of the mean dry weight of granulomas for both the control and test groups is as follows:

Figure 2. Sterilized cotton pellets used as a foreign body

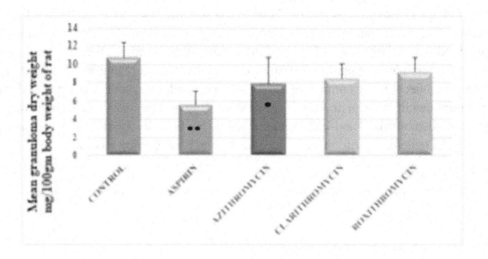

Figure 3. Implantation of cotton pellet as a foreign body in the sub-acute inflammatory study (indicated by arrow)

Figure 4. Dissection of cotton pellet covered with granulation tissue on the 11th day (indicated by arrow)

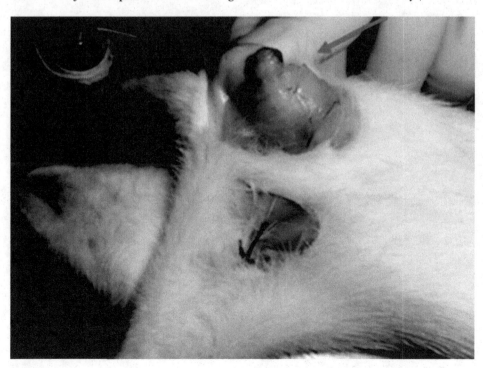

Figure 5. Cotton pellets covered with granulation tissue

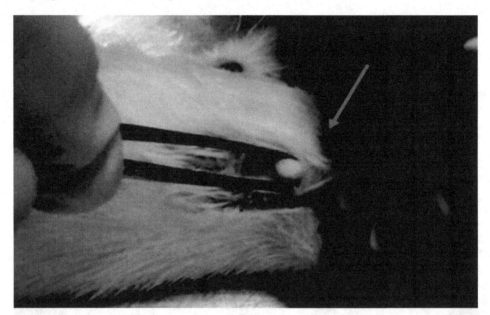

3. STATISTICAL ANALYSIS

A one-way ANOVA was performed on the data (mean SD). Dunnett's multiple comparison tests were then run as a post-hoc analysis. Contrast between aspirin and macrolides. GraphPad Instate version 3.06 was used for all statistical procedures, and p 0.05 was statistically significant (Table 1).

3.1. Result

Table 1. ANOVA

Time after carrageenan injection	Paw edema volume in ml (Mean ± SD)				ANOVA	
	Aspirin (200mg/kg)	Azithromycin (20mg/kg)	Clarithromycin (20mg/kg)	Roxithromycin (20mg/kg)	F value	p value
1 hr	0.291±0.102	0.375±0.136	0.375±0.136	0.375±0.136	0.6250	0.6072
2 hr	0.250±0.273	0.583±0.129 *	0.791±0.102 **	0.625±0.136 **	10.230	0.0003
3 hr	0.083±0.129	0.416±0.129 **	0.5±0.158 **	0.791±0.102 **	29.646	< 0.0001
4 hr	0.041±0.102	0.291±0.102 *	0.25±0.223	0.625±0.136 **	15.620	< 0.0001
5 hr	0.041±0.102	0.166±0.129	0.125±0.136	0.50±0.00 **	21.212	< 0.0001

3.2. Dunnett's Multiple Comparison Test

Table 2. The effects of Azithromycin, Clarithromycin, and Roxithromycin treatments on Carrageenan-induced paw emphysema was compared to aspirin

1 h - Aspirin Vs Azithromycin $p > 0.05$,	Aspirin Vs Clarithromycin $p > 0.05$,	Aspirin Vs Roxithromycin $p > 0.05$.
2 h - Aspirin Vs Azithromycin $p < 0.05$,	Aspirin Vs Clarithromycin $p < 0.01$,	Aspirin Vs Roxithromycin $p < 0.01$
3 h - Aspirin Vs Azithromycin $p < 0.01$,	Aspirin Vs Clarithromycin $p < 0.01$,	Aspirin Vs Roxithromycin $p < 0.01$
4 h - Aspirin Vs Azithromycin $p < 0.05$,	Aspirin Vs Clarithromycin $p > 0.05$,	Aspirin Vs Roxithromycin $p < 0.01$
5 h - Aspirin Vs Azithromycin $p > 0.05$,	Aspirin Vs Clarithromycin $p > 0.05$,	Aspirin Vs Roxithromycin $p < 0.01$

In a model of a disease that changes over time, data show that different doses of azithromycin, clarithromycin, and roxithromycin reduced inflammation much more than the control group (table 2). Azithromycin, clarithromycin, and roxithromycin were tested for their anti-inflammatory effects and compared to aspirin. Azithromycin and aspirin were found to have equivalent anti-inflammatory effects after 5 hours ($p > 0.05$); however, after 2 hours, 3 hours, and 4 hours, azithromycin was found to be less effective than aspirin. Azi's anti-inflammatory properties formed the basis for these observations.

The anti-inflammatory impact of clarithromycin was about equivalent to that of aspirin when the medication was administered every 4 to 5 hours ($p > 0.05$), but it was much less than that of aspirin when given every 2 and 3 hours. At 2-hour, 3-hour, 4 hours, and 5-hour intervals, it was discovered that the anti-inflammatory impact of roxithromycin was not as effective as that of aspirin.

Table 3. Drug treatments

S. No	Drug Treatment	Mean granuloma dry weight mg/100 g body weight (Mean ± SD)	Percentage inhibition (%)
1.	Aspirin (200mg/kg)	5.60±1.435	48.42
2.	Azithromycin (20mg/kg)	7.96 ± 2.885	26.71
3.	Claritiiromycin (20mg/kg)	8.50 ± 1.637*	21.74
4.	Roxithromycin (20mg/kg)	9.25= 1.527 *	14.7

ANOVA: F = 3.872, p = 0.0247.

Dunnett's multiple comparison Test:

Aspirin Vs Azithromycin p > 0.05
Aspirin Vs Clarithromycin p < 0.05
Aspirin Vs Roxithromycin p < 0.01

Table 3 shows the difference in granuloma dry weight between aspirin and the three different antibiotics (azithromycin, clarithromycin, and roxithromycin).

Figure 6. Effect of various treatments on mean granuloma dry weight

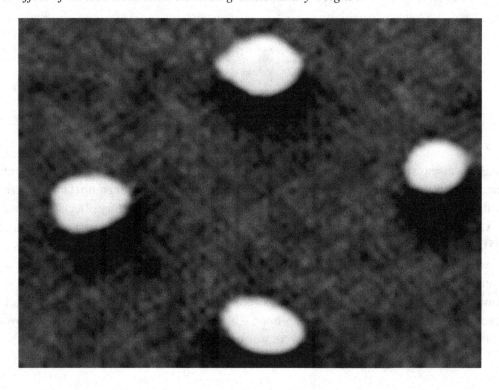

Figure 7. Percentage inhibition of granulometry weight

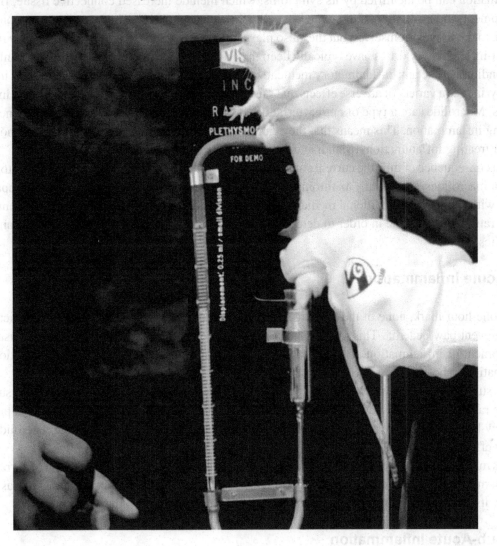

The mean granuloma dry weight was 8.50 ±1.638 and 9.25±1.528 in the clarithromycin and roxithromycin (20 mg/kg) treated groups, respectively, and the percentage inhibition was 21.73% and 14.8% ($p > 0.05$). (Tables 2, Figures 6 and 7). Then, granulomas in the azithromycin group were weighed on average to see how they stacked up against those in the aspirin group. The group given azithromycin had a similar mean granuloma dry weight to the group given aspirin ($p > 0.05$). It demonstrates that the anti-inflammatory efficacy of azithromycin and aspirin in a subacute form of inflammation was equivalent.

4. DISCUSSION

A significant component of the body's defence mechanism is known as the inflammatory response. Vasodilation, an increase in vascular permeability, and leukocyte migration to damaged tissues are the three key vascular components that are responsible for mediating the acute inflammatory response. Chronic inflammation can be identified by its symptoms, which include increased connective tissue, fibroblast development, and infiltration of mononuclear cells (Stricker et al.,2010). These mediators not only cause damage to the tissues themselves, but they also play a role in the development of inflammatory illnesses.

Anti-inflammatory drugs have typically been the go-to treatment for the vast majority of inflammatory conditions. The anti-inflammatory medications that are currently available, despite their increased efficacy, induce a variety of adverse effects that raise considerable concerns when they are used in clinical settings. Macrolides are a type of antibacterial drugs, but it appears that they can also be beneficial in lowering inflammation. This means that they can be added to the list of alternatives that are now available for treating inflammation. (Mahdi and colleagues, 2006)

As a consequence of this, the current study was carried out to investigate the anti-inflammatory properties of macrolides, specifically azithromycin, clarithromycin, and roxithromycin, and to compare their effects with those of the traditional medicine aspirin in acute and sub-acute models of inflammation in Wistar rats. This was done in order to determine whether or not macrolides possess anti-inflammatory properties.

4.1. Acute Inflammation

At the one-hour mark, none of the investigational medicines had shown a statistically significant ability to prevent paw oedema. This may be the result of one or both of the following causes: insufficient development of inflammation at 1 hour, a delayed beginning of the effect of study medications, or a combination of both of these mechanisms.

The study (Winter et al., 1962) found that three to five hours after injecting a phlogistic substance into the rat's hind paw, the paw oedema reaches a peak, and the same quantity of edoema is preserved for a few hours. In other words, one hour after carrageenan administration, the three macrolides were equally effective as aspirin.

This may explain why not enough inflammation was induced 1 hour after the injection of carrageenan. At the same time that inflammation was becoming worse (around the second hour), medicine was starting to show its effects in the form of edoema suppression (which lasted until the fifth hour).

4.2. Sub-Acute Inflammation

At least three reaction phases are present in the foreign body-induced granuloma model. There are three distinct stages, which are called transudative, exudative, and proliferative, respectively. Increases in the granuloma's dry weight indicate entry into the proliferative phase. In this model of inflammation at a subacute stage, we determined the average weight of the granuloma when it was dry. The reduction in mean dry granuloma weight was taken into consideration as evidence of anti-inflammatory activity.

While aspirin showed a greater percentage reduction in granuloma dry weight by inhibiting its growth (48.43%), only azithromycin (20 mg/kg) was shown to significantly reduce granuloma dry weight when compared to the control group (p 0.05). Its anti-inflammatory impact was also equivalent to that of aspirin (200 mg/kg) (p > 0.05).

So, it was shown that the effects of azithromycin, clarithromycin, and roxithromycin on inflammation were much stronger in the acute model than in the subacute model. The current findings support previous research that found macrolide antibiotics to be anti-inflammatory in a variety of animal models of inflammation (Ianaro et al., 20005; Gosavi et al., (2015)6; and Scaglione et al., (1998).

Macrolides' anti-inflammatory efficacy is a side effect of their anti-infective properties; nevertheless, additional research is required in both acute and chronic inflammation models. As a corollary to this kind of pre-clinical research, studies in humans are also necessary to bolster the findings and verify the effectiveness of long-term usage of macrolides as prospective anti-inflammatory medicines in normal clinical procedures.

In our study, we found that the activity of roxithromycin was lower than that of azithromycin and clarithromycin, which is in contrast to the findings of earlier studies, which found that roxithromycin had a superior anti-inflammatory potential to azithromycin and clarithromycin. Our findings for the acute model of inflammation are consistent with the aforementioned research findings. According to Gosavi et al. (2015)6, a granuloma model created with cotton pellets had no significant anti-inflammatory effects. On the other hand, we discovered that azithromycin was efficient in reducing the average dry weight of the granulomas.

5. OBSERVATION AND RESULTS

In the current investigation, therapeutically equivalent doses of the macrolides Azithromycin, Clarithromycin, and Roxithromycin were administered to Wistar rats in order to investigate the possibility that these antibiotics possess anti-inflammatory properties. The acute and sub-acute models of inflammation were used to test the effectiveness of these antibiotics.

5.1. Acute Inflammation (Carrageenan Induced Paw Edema Method)

Actions of the Principal Mediators of Inflammation: Amphetamines (especially histamine) have a vasodilatory and permeability-increasing effect on blood vessels.

Different kinds of arachidonic acid metabolites (prostaglandins and leukotrienes) are involved in vascular responses, leukocyte chemotaxis, and other inflammatory reactions; lipoxins block these effects.

Key cytokines in acute inflammation include tumour necrosis factor (TNF), interleukin-1 (IL-1), and chemokines. Cytokines are proteins produced by a wide variety of cells and typically work at short range to mediate various effects, most notably leukocyte recruitment and movement.

Proteins in the complement system are essential for leukocyte chemotaxis, opsonisation, phagocytosis of microorganisms and other particles, and cell death after activation by bacteria or antibodies.

The rise in mean paw edema was considered as a measure of inflammation and hence the potential to control this rise in edema as compared to the control group implied anti-inflammatory activity. The mean paw edema volumes measured using plethysmograph in 'ml' as mercury displacement for the control group at 1hr, 2hr, 3hr, 4hr and 5hr intervals were 0.416 ± 0.204, 0.958 ± 0.245, 1.208 ± 0.245, 1.083 ± 0.129 and 0.916 ± 0.129 respectively (Table-1, Graph-1). The corresponding mean paw edema volumes in the aspirin-treated group (200mg/kg) at 1hr, 2hr, 3hr, 4hr, and 5hr intervals were 0.291 ± 0.102, 0.250 ± 0.273, 0.083 ± 0.129, 0.041 ± 0.102 and 0.041 ± 0.102 respectively (Table-1, Graph-1) with the calculated percentage inhibitions of 30.95%, 73.95%, 93.33%, 96.29% and 95.65% respectively (Table-2, Graph-2). Statistically significant inhibition of paw edema volume was shown by the aspirin-treated group ($p < 0.01$) when compared to control at 2hr, 3hr, 4hr, and 5hr intervals (Table-1, Graph-1).

The paw edema volumes in ml in Azithromycin treated group (20mg/kg) at 1hr, 2hr, 3hr, 4hr, and 5hr intervals were 0.375 ± 0.136, 0.583 ± 0.129, 0.416 ± 0.129, 0.291 ± 0.102 and 0.166 ± 0.129 respectively

(Table-1, Graph-1), with the calculated percentage inhibitions of 11.90%, 39.58%, 65.83%, 73.14% and 82.60% respectively (Table-2, Graph-2). Azithromycin treatment group showed statistically significant inhibition of paw edema volume (p < 0.01) when compared to control at 2hr, 3hr, 4hr, and 5hr intervals.

Clarithromycin treated group (20mg/kg) showed statistically significant inhibition (p < 0.01) of paw edema at 3hr, 4hr and 5hr intervals, with mean paw edema volumes of 0.5 ± 0.158, 0.25 ± 0.223, 0.125 ± 0.136 respectively, with the calculated percentage inhibition of 58.33%, 76.85% and 86.95% respectively when compared to the control group.

In the group given 20 milligrammes of roxithromycin per kilogramme of body weight, the computed percentages of inhibition were 35.41 percent, 33.33 percent, 41.66 percent, and 45.65 percent, respectively, for paw edoema volumes in millilitres at 2-, 3-, 4-, and 5-hour intervals, respectively. Comparisons between the treatment group and the control group showed that the amount of paw edoema was reduced by Roxithromycin (p 0.05) at 2hr and (p 0.01) at 3hr, 4hr, and 5hr intervals.

In the acute model of inflammation, the data shown above show that the antibiotics Azithromycin, Clarithromycin, and Roxithromycin, when administered at a dose of 20 mg/kg, had anti-inflammatory effects in comparison to the control group. It was discovered that the anti-inflammatory effect of azithromycin was comparable to that of aspirin after comparing the anti-inflammatory effects of azithromycin, clarithromycin, and roxithromycin to those of aspirin. Roxithromycin's anti-inflammatory effect was found to be distinct from that of aspirin (p > 0.05) at 5hr but inferior to aspirin at 2hr, 3hr, and 4hr. At 4 and 5 hours, clarithromycin's anti-inflammatory efficacy was equivalent to that of aspirin (p > 0.05), whereas at 2 and 3 hours, it was inferior. A comparison of Roxithromycin and aspirin for anti-inflammatory effects at 2-, 3-, 4-, and 5-hour intervals revealed that aspirin was more effective.

At 1 hour, we can see that none of the treatments significantly reduced paw edoema. This might be because the inflammation isn't progressing fast enough after 1 hour, the research medicines aren't taking effect quickly enough, or both.

6. CONCLUSION

From the findings of the present experimental study says that we conclude that Anti-inflammatory effects of azithromycin, clarithromycin, and roxithromycin at therapeutic levels are substantial when compared to the control and moderate when compared to aspirin in an animal study of acute inflammation. The results of this research support the idea that Macrolides, both as monotherapy and in combination with conventional drugs, may be useful in treating a variety of inflammatory conditions related to acute infections. We caution against using macrolides for chronic inflammatory disorders because their overuse might cause resistant strains of bacteria to emerge; nonetheless, they can be useful in treating acute infections that arise from such illnesses. Accordingly, we propose that macrolides, which have properties that are anti-infective, immunomodulatory, and additionally anti-inflammatory, may be more appropriate for patients who have disease conditions in which there is an infection associated with inflammation. Some examples of these conditions include chronic obstructive pulmonary disease (COPD), asthma, chronic sinusitis, bronchiolitis, bronchiectasis, cystic fibrosis, and osteomyelitis.

REFERENCES

Chensue, S. W., & Ward, P. A. (1990). Inflammation. In I. Damjanov & J. Linder (Eds.), *Anderson's Pathology* (10th ed., pp. 387–413s). Mosby Year Book.

Fernandes, P., Martens, E., & Pereira, D. (2017). Nature nurtures the design of new semi- synthetic macrolide antibiotics. *The Journal of Antibiotics, 70*(5), 527–533. doi:10.1038/ja.2016.137 PMID:27899792

Gosavi, P.A., Jaju, J.B., Ubale, V.M., Pawar, G.R., Dharmadhikari, S.C. (2015). *Study of evaluation of anti-inflammatory activity of macrolide antibiotics in rats: an experimental study.*

Green, K. L. (1972). The anti-inflammatory effect of catecholamines in the peritoneal cavity and hind paw of the mouse. *British Journal of Pharmacology, 45*(2), 322–332. doi:10.1111/j.1476-5381.1972.tb08086.x PMID:5048650

Grégoire, M., Uhel, F., Lesouhaitier, M., Gacouin, A., Guirriec, M., Mourcin, F., Dumontet, E., Chalin, A., Samson, M., Berthelot, L.-L., Tissot, A., Kerjouan, M., Jouneau, S., Le Tulzo, Y., Tarte, K., Zmijewski, J. W., & Tadié, J.-M. (2018). Impaired efferocytosis and neutrophil extracellular trap clearance by macrophages in ARDS. *The European Respiratory Journal, 52*(2), 1702590. doi:10.1183/13993003.02590-2017 PMID:29946009

Ianaro, A., Ialenti, A., Maffia, P., Sautebin, L., Rombolà, L., & Carnuccio, R. (2000). Anti-inflammatory activity of macrolide antibiotics. *The Journal of Pharmacology and Experimental Therapeutics, 292*(1), 156–163. PMID:10604943

Iwamoto, S., Kumamoto, T., Azuma, E., Hirayama, M., Ito, M., Amano, K., Ido, M., & Komada, Y. (2011). The effect of azithromycin on the maturation and function of murine bone marrow-derived dendritic cells. *Clinical and Experimental Immunology, 166*(3), 385–392. doi:10.1111/j.1365-2249.2011.04480.x PMID:22059997

M, A., K, T., Munshi, Y, J., M, R., & M, S. (2019). Assessment of heavy metal contents in commercial feedstuffs and broiler (Gallus domesticus) meat and its impact on Swiss albino mice as an animal model. *Agricultural Science Digest - A Research Journal, (of).* doi:10.18805/ag.D-4898

Mahdi, J. G., Mahdi, A. J., & Bowen, I. D. (2006). The historical analysis of aspirin discovery, its relation to the willow tree and antiproliferative and anticancer potential. *Cell Proliferation, 39*(2), 147–155. doi:10.1111/j.1365-2184.2006.00377.x PMID:16542349

Md, N., Hasan, M., Munshi, M. H., Rahman, S. M. N., & Alam, A. (2014). Evaluation of antihyperglycemic activity of Lasia spinosa leaf extracts in Swiss albino mice. *World Journal of Pharmacy and Pharmaceutical Sciences, 3*(10), 118–124.

Munshi, M., Sohrab, M. H., Begum, M. N., Rony, S. R., Karim, M. A., Afroz, F., & Hasan, M. N. (2021). Evaluation of bioactivity and phytochemical screening of endophytic fungi isolated from Ceriops decandra (Griff.) W. Theob, a mangrove plant in Bangladesh. *Clinical Phytoscience, 7*(1), 81. Advance online publication. doi:10.118640816-021-00315-y

Munshi, M., Tumu, K. N., Hasan, M. N., & Amin, M. Z. (2018). Biochemical effects of commercial feedstuffs on the fry of climbing perch (Anabas testudineus) and its impact on Swiss albino mice as an animal model. *Toxicology Reports, 5*, 521–530. doi:10.1016/j.toxrep.2018.04.004 PMID:29707493

Munshi, M., Zilani, M. N. H., Islam, M. A., Biswas, P., Das, A., Afroz, F., & Hasan, M. N. (2022). Novel compounds from endophytic fungi of Ceriops decandra inhibit breast cancer cell growth through estrogen receptor alpha in in-silico study. *Informatics in Medicine Unlocked*, 32(101046), 101046. doi:10.1016/j.imu.2022.101046

Nakamura, S., Ikeda-Dantsuji, Y., Jin, L., Higashi, Y., Abe, M., Inukai, T., Nagi, M., Urai, M., & Miyazaki, Y. (2019). Macrolides inhibit capsule formation of highly virulent Cryptococcus gattii and promote innate immune susceptibility. *Antimicrobial Agents and Chemotherapy*, 63(6), e02364–e18. doi:10.1128/AAC.02364-18 PMID:30936099

Ratzinger, F., Haslacher, H., Poeppl, W., Hoermann, G., Kovarik, J. J., Jutz, S., Steinberger, P., Burgmann, H., Pickl, W. F., & Schmetterer, K. G. (2014). Azithromycin suppresses CD4+ T-cell activation by direct modulation of mTOR activity. *Scientific Reports*, 4(1), 1–0. doi:10.1038rep07438 PMID:25500904

Scaglione, F., & Rossoni, G. (1998). Comparative anti-inflammatory effects of roxithromycin, azithromycin and clarithromycin. *The Journal of Antimicrobial Chemotherapy*, 41(suppl_2), 47–50. doi:10.1093/jac/41.suppl_2.47 PMID:9579712

Shinkai, M., Henke, M. O., & Rubin, B. K. (2008). Macrolide antibiotics as immunomodulatory medications: Proposed mechanisms of action. *Pharmacology & Therapeutics*, 117(3), 393–405. doi:10.1016/j.pharmthera.2007.11.001 PMID:18289694

Stellari, F. F., Sala, A., Donofrio, G., Ruscitti, F., Caruso, P., Topini, T. M., Francis, K. P., Li, X., Carnini, C., Civelli, M., & Villetti, G. (2014). Azithromycin inhibits nuclear factor-κB activation during lung inflammation: An in vivo imaging study. *Pharmacology Research & Perspectives*, 2(5), e00058. doi:10.1002/prp2.58 PMID:25505605

Stricker, T. P., Kumar, V., Abbas, A. K., Fausto, N., & Ster, J. C. (2010). *Robbins and Cotran pathologic basis of disease.*

Vashishtha, E. (2019). Effects of Maternal Smoking on Fetus and Child Development: A literature review. *International Research Journal of Natural and Applied Sciences*, 6(1), 92–107.

Vashishtha, E. (2020). Reducing Patient wait time in outpatient settings: A lean six sigma approach. *International Journal of Research in Medical and Basic Sciences*, 6(1), 15–35.

Vashishtha, E., & Sherman, L. (2018). Socioeconomic Status and Childhood Obesity. *International Journal of Physical and Social Sciences*, 8(11), 184–194.

Vashishtha, E., Sherman, L., Sajjad, T., & Mehmood, N. (2020). Use of anti-viral therapy in treatment of Covid 19. *Journal of Advanced Medical and Dental Sciences Research*, 8(11), 273–276.

Veeraiah, V., Pankajam, A., Vashishtha, E., Dhabliya, D., Karthikeyan, P., & Chandan, R. R. (2022). Efficient COVID-19 identification using deep learning for IoT. *2022 5th International Conference on Contemporary Computing and Informatics (IC3I)*. IEEE.

Winter, C. A., Risley, E. A., & Nuss, G. W. (1962). Carrageenin-induced edema in hind paw of the rat as an assay for anti-inflammatory drugs. *Proceedings of the Society for Experimental Biology and Medicine*, 111(3), 544–547. doi:10.3181/00379727-111-27849 PMID:14001233

Chapter 19
Impact of Digitalization on Youth and Its Relevance Regarding Demonetization

Manisha Raj
Karnavati University, India

ABSTRACT

This study focuses on the positive and negative effects of digitalization on youth and how demonetization has led to digitalization over a period of five years. The study focuses on or revolves around three major objectives: they are to study the level of digitalization among youth in Indian economy, to study the impact of demonetization on youth in India, and to study the relationship between digitalization and demonetization. There is a large amount of secondary data that is available, and which is analyzed in this chapter and primary study has also been conducted with 150 respondents. The behavior, emotions, and motivation of youth in general and in relation to digital technologies, especially the meaning attached to mobile phones, the Internet, and computer-based games should also be given attention to reach this target group. The probable outcomes of the research of the study would reflect the level of digitalization in the economy and how demonetizations affected digitalization and what are the impact digitalization.

1. INTRODUCTION

The digitalization of youth signifies their full involvement in the consumption, production, and sharing of digital content using various interconnected or interfaced digital devices. The announcement of demonetization led to a huge cash shortage for the months that followed, which created significant disturbance throughout the economy. Demonetization has made people adopt digital wallets and debit and credit cards as a mode of payment. Such digital payments have in a large way replaced cash payments, at least in urban areas. The path toward digitization in India started with various e-commerce start-ups like Jabong, SnapDeal, Flipkart, etc. These e-businesses have helped to initiate the process of attracting customers to online channels in the country. Most of these e-businesses carry on a huge part of their businesses through cash transactions, but what they did do was and continues to do is make people fa-

DOI: 10.4018/979-8-3693-1301-5.ch019

miliarise themselves with different modes of production like digital wallets, leading to the convenience of cashless transactions and online channels (Al-Naif & Al Shraah, 2018).

2. LITERATURE REVIEW

Luke (2008) revolves around understanding and determining the factors affecting changing consumer behaviour and also examining the same behaviour and its impact on digital marketing. The findings of the research paper are as follows: Many of the consumers of the present time have permission to use digital media, but lack awareness about its optimum utilization. Respondents feel that customers take very little time to purchase, and the majority of the respondents feel that all-time purchases are possible online. They also state that the use of smartphones has increased because they are easy to carry, due to which shopping behaviour has also grown. Youth (2019) revolves around the focus on the necessary conditions for social inclusion, including young people's capacities like the "human capital" (or competencies) required by young people now a day in order to access and negotiate for digital technologies (Al-maaitah, et al., 2021a).

The paper finds out that digitalization in youth work is not just a response to the digitalization of society and the changes and challenges this brings but is also an opportunity to apply new and better ways to achieve social inclusion. Al Shraah et al. (2022) reviewed the literature to analyse the pattern of modes of payment for transactions and also to investigate the effect of demonetizations on the use of different modes of payment or instruments for payment (Al-maaitah, et al., 2021b). The paper finally concludes that while the usage of cards for transactions as a percentage of total transactions has increased, mobile transactions and the share of point-of-sale transactions (PoS) have registered a decrease after demonetizations. Abu-Rumman (2021) explained around the digital finance providers and in Bangalore street sellers, conducted immediately after the announcement of demonetization. The outcomes of the paper are that poorer people, affected by a shortage of cash from the very immediate effect of the government's announcement of demonetization, have better and more direct knowledge than everyone else in Indian society, and information poverty comes with major factors that aggravate the unbanked street sellers facing demonetization.

Al Shraah et al. (2013) informed about the effects of demonetization on the digitalization of the economy, and the paper also gave suggestions to improve the structure of digitalization in India. The outcome given by the research paper is that the digital revolution has a transformational impact in terms of the formalisation of the economy, especially the BHIM app and other digital instruments used by the government to make the system transparent and vigilant. Abu-Rumman and Qawasmeh (2021) revolve around demonetization in the context of the present state of the Indian economy, and this paper also focuses its attention on the impact of demonetization on the informal economy of India.

This Chapter talks about the various initiatives taken by the government to develop the country and ensure the efficient working of the economy, including curbing corruption, boosting the customer base of banking systems, reducing unemployment with "Make in India," improving entrepreneurial skills among youths with "MUDRA," and various other programmes. Kathial (2018) reviewed the relationship between digitalization and demonetization. The main outcome of the paper is that demonetization has promoted and pushed millions of people into the country's digital economy. New bank accounts are being opened, e-payment services are seeing increased rates of growth, cash-on-delivery in e-commerce has crashed, and digitally-focused sectors like the online grocery business have witnessed a boom in the economy.

3. RESEARCH METHODOLOGY

Research is defined as the careful consideration of a study regarding a particular concern or problem using scientific methods. Research involves inductive and deductive methods. Thus, in this study, a careful inquiry has been done, using various techniques of research, including trend analysis, chi-square, and the T test, to analyse the impact of digitalization on youth and the impact of demonetization on youth. Lastly, this paper also tries to find the impact of demonetization on digitalization. For this purpose, secondary data inference and primary data analysis have been done. For secondary research, various research papers have been analyzed, and their main ideas have been put forward. For the primary research, which plays its role in the third section of this paper, a sample of 150 people has been taken through a structured questionnaire. Both qualitative and quantitative approaches have been applied for this study, and the analysis of the collected data has been done using statistical tools such as the chi-square and T tests.

4. DATA ANALYSIS

4.1. Objective One

To study the level of digitalization among youth in the Indian economy: To satisfy the objective, I have run a chi-square test to check the association between how much time a youth spends on his or her mobile phone and whether more usage of mobile phones has led to lower grades in their studies.

*Table 1. Time spent on mobile phones by youth * lower grades by usage of mobile phones cross tabulation count*

Time Spent on Mobile Phones by Youth		Lower Grades by Usage of Mobile Phones			Total
		No	Yes	Maybe	
	2 to 4 hours	2	5	7	14
	4 to 6 hours	11	21	11	43
	6 to 8 hours	8	47	7	62
	8 to 10 hours	2	11	7	20
	10 and more	2	5	4	11
Total		25	89	36	150

Table 1 shows that there are 14 people who think that youth use mobile phones for 2 to 4 hours. It also reflects that there are 43 people who think that youth use mobile phones for 4 to 6 hours. It also reflects that there are 62 people who think that youth use mobile phones for 6 to 8 hours a day. It also reflects that there are 20 people who think that youth use mobile phones for 8 to 10 hours a day. It also reflects that there are 11 people who think that youth use mobile phones for 10 hours or more. Table 1 also asserts that the number of people who say that more phone usage does not affect the grades of youth or that more mobile phone usage does not lead to lower grades is 25. Table 1 also asserts that the number of people who say that more phone usage affects the grades of youth or that more mobile phone usage leads to lower grades is 89. Table 1 also asserts that the number of people who are not certain that more usage of phones affects the grades of youth or who are confused that more usage of mobile phones leads to lower grades is 36. And the total number of people who have answered the questionnaire is 150.

Table 2. Chi-square tests

	Value	df	Asymp. Sig. (2-sided)
Pearson Chi-Square	18.414a	8	.018
Likelihood Ratio	18.193	8	.020
Linear-by-Linear Association	.020	1	.888
N of Valid Cases	150		
a. 6 cells (40.0%) have expected count less than 5. The minimum expected count is 1.83.			

H0: The usage of mobile phones does not affect the grades of the youth. H1: The usage of mobile phones does affect the grades of the youth (table 2). The chi-square test shows that the Pearson chi-square value is 18.414 and the p value of the likely hood ratio is taken as the assumption of expected count is broken, so the significance value is 0.020, which is less than 0.05 level of significance. The degree of freedom is 8. As a result, our result is statistically significant, and as the p value is less than our chosen level of significance, i.e., 0.05, this means that we reject the null hypothesis and accept the alternative hypothesis, which shows that there is an association between the usage of mobile phones by youth and grades. This shows that with more usage of mobile phones, there has been a decline or downfall in the grades of the youth in their studies. To satisfy the objective, I have run a chi-square test to check the association between how much time a youth spends on his or her mobile phone and whether the usage of mobile phones has made youth more likely to get involved in wrong practices.

*Table 3. Time spent on mobile phones by youth * phone usage made youth more prone to be involved in wrong practices cross tabulation count*

Time Spent on Mobile Phones by Youth		Phone Usage Made Youth More Prone to Be Involved in Wrong Practices			Total
		Disagree	Yes	Neutral	
	2 to 4 hours	5	4	5	14
	4 to 6 hours	5	27	11	43
	6 to 8 hours	1	49	12	62
	8 to 10 hours	2	7	11	20
	10 and more	1	7	3	11
Total		14	94	42	150

This table 3 shows that there are 14 people who think that youth use mobile phones for 2 to 4 hours. It also reflects that there are 43 people who think that youth use mobile phones for 4 to 6 hours. It also reflects that there are 62 people who think that youth use mobile phones for 6 to 8 hours a day. It also reflects that there are 20 people who think that youth use mobile phones for 8 to 10 hours a day. It also reflects that there are 11 people who think that youth use mobile phones for 10 hours or more. The table 3 also asserts that the number of people who say that more phone usage does not make youth more prone to being involved in wrong practises is 14; The table 3 also asserts that the number of people who say that more phone usage does make youth more prone to being involved in wrong practises is 94. The table 3 also asserts that the number of people who are neutral about the idea that more phone usage makes youth more prone to being involved in wrong practises is 42. And the total number of people who have answered the questionnaire is 150.

Table 4. Chi-square tests

	Value	df	Asymp. Sig. (2-sided)
Pearson Chi-Square	29.595a	8	.000
Likelihood Ratio	27.231	8	.001
Linear-by-Linear Association	2.873	1	.090
N of Valid Cases	150		
a. 6 cells (40.0%) have expected count less than 5. The minimum expected count is 1.03.			

H0: the usage of mobile phone does not make youth prone to wrong practices.

H1: the usage of mobile phone does make youth prone to wrong practices.

The chi-square test shows that the Pearson chi-square value is 29.595, and the p value of the likely hood ratio is taken as the assumption of expected count is broken, so the significance value is 0.001, which is less than the 0.05 level of significance (table 4). The degree of freedom is 8. As a result, our result is statistically significant, and as the p value is less than our chosen level of significance, i.e., 0.05, this means that we reject the null hypothesis and accept the alternative hypothesis, which shows that there is an association between the usage of mobile phones by youth and their involvement in wrong practices. This shows that with more usage of mobile phones, youth are more prone to involvement in wrong practices. To satisfy the objective We have run chi-square tests to check the association between how much time a youth spends on his or her mobile phone and how more usage of mobile phones has led youth to disrespect their parents.

*Table 5. Time spent on mobile phones by youth * has more usage of mobile phones has led youth to disrespect their parents cross tabulation count*

Time Spent On Mobile Phones By Youth	Has More Usage Of Mobile Phones Has Led Youth To Disrespect Their Parents			Total
	No	Yes	Maybe	
2 to 4 hours	6	4	4	14
4 to 6 hours	11	19	13	43
6 to 8 hours	13	43	6	62
8 to 10 hours	5	8	7	20
10 and more	3	6	2	11
Total	38	80	32	150

This table 5 shows that there are 14 people who think that youth use mobile phones for 2 to 4 hours. It also reflects that there are 43 people who think that youth use mobile phones for 4 to 6 hours. It also reflects that there are 62 people who think that youth use mobile phones for 6 to 8 hours a day. It also reflects that there are 20 people who think that youth use mobile phones for 8 to 10 hours a day. It also reflects that there are 11 people who think that youth use mobile phones for 10 hours or more. The table 5 also asserts that the number of people who say that more phone usage does not lead youth to disrespect their parents is 38. The table 5 also asserts that the number of people who say that more phone usage does lead youth to disrespect their parents is 80. The table 5 also asserts that the number of people who are not certain that more phone usage leads youth to disrespect their parents is 32. And the total number of people who have answered the questionnaire is 150.

Table 6. Chi-square tests

	Value	df	Asymp. Sig. (2-sided)
Pearson Chi-Square	15.810a	8	.045
Likelihood Ratio	16.238	8	.039
Linear-by-Linear Association	.010	1	.922
N of Valid Cases	150		
a. 5 cells (33.3%) have expected count less than 5. The minimum expected count is 2.35.			

H0: the usage of mobile phone does not make youth to disrespect their parents.

H1: the usage of mobile phone does make youth to disrespect their parents.

The chi-square test shows that the Pearson chi-square value is 15.810 and the p value of the likely hood ratio is taken, as the assumption of expected count is broken, so the significance value is 0.039, which is less than the 0.05 level of significance (Table 6). The degree of freedom is 8. As a result, our result is statistically significant, and as the p value is less than our chosen level of significance, i.e., 0.05, this means that we reject the null hypothesis and accept the alternative hypothesis, which shows that there is an association between the usage of mobile phones by youth and youth disrespecting their parents. This shows that with more mobile phone usage, youth have disrespected their parents more. All these three chi-square tests show that the use of phones has a negative effect on youth. The first chi-square test shows that with the increased usage of mobile phones, there has been a negative impact on the studies of the youth, leading to lower grades. This shows that there is a direct relationship between mobile phone usage and the lower grades. The second chi-square test shows that the increased usage of mobile phones has made the youth more prone to getting involved in wrong practices, showing a deterioration in the ethics of the youth with the usage of mobile phones. The third chi-square demonstrates that increased mobile phone usage has caused youth to disrespect their parents and degrade their values.

4.2. Objective Two

To study the impact of demonetizations on youth in India and according to you which mode of payments has witnessed the highest increase in its usage by youths? (Table 7).

Table 7. Mode of payments

Mode of Payments	Increase in Usage in Mode of Payments	No of Respondents
E-wallets (Paytm, PayUMoney etc.)	73.9	119
Debit cards	12	18
Credit cards	5.3	8
Net Banking	2	3
Others	1.4	2
Total		140

Figure 1. Mode of payments

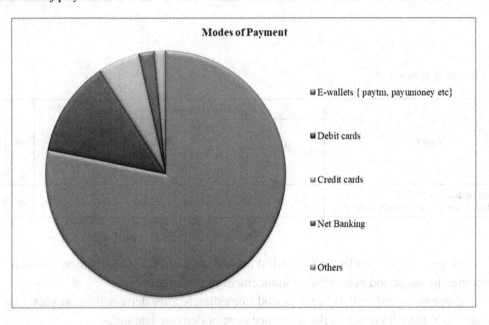

The above pie chart shows (Figure 1) that out of 150 respondents, 119 believe that e-wallets are the mode of payment that has witnessed the highest increase among the youth. This means that there has been a drastic shift from a cash-based economy to a digital-based economy among the youth after demonetization. Only 18 (12%) of 150 respondents believe that the debit card has seen the greatest increase in youth usage.Then only 8 (5.3%) respondents believe that credit cards as a mode of payment have witnessed the highest usage by youth. Then Only 3 (2%) respondents believe that it is net banking that has witnessed the highest increase in its usage by the youth as a mode of payment after the announcement of demonetization. The above study shows that demonetization has made youth use more digital wallets, or e-wallets, for making payments and has given rise to online transactions among youth. The impact of demonetization on youth is very effective.

4.3. Objective Three

To study the relationship between digitalization and demonetization: to study the relationship between digitalization and demonetization. A T-test has been conducted to study the impact of demonetization on digitalization by comparing the usage of digital wallets before the announcement of demonetization in 2015 and immediately after the announcement of demonetization in 2017 (Table 8).

Table 8. T test 1-paired samples statistics

		Mean	N	Std. Deviation	Std. Error Mean
	Before Demonetization Year 2015	1.7000	150	1.14546	.09353
	Immediately After Demonetization Year 2017	4.0733	150	1.85406	.15138

Table 9. Paired samples test

Pair 1	Paired Differences					t	df	Sig. (2-tailed)
	Mean	Std. Deviation	Std. Error Mean	95% Confidence Interval of the Difference				
				Lower	Upper			
(BeforeDemonetizationYear2015) – (ImmediatelyAfterDemonetizationYear2017)	-2.37333	2.27194	.18550	-2.73989	-2.00678	-12.794	149	.000

H0: The usage of digital wallets in the period immediately after demonetization shows no increase when compared to the period before the announcement of demonetization.

H1: The usage of digital wallets in the period immediately after demonetization shows an increase when compared to the period before the announcement of demonetization.

According to Table 9, there has been an increase in the mean value from the period before the announcement of demonetization to the period immediately after the announcement of demonetization. The value of the mean shows that the average usage of the digital wallets before the announcement of demonetization was 1.7000, and the value of the mean showing the average usage of the digital wallets immediately after the announcement of demonetization was 4.0733. These values reflect that there has been a tremendous increase in the usage of digital wallets immediately after the announcement of demonetization when compared to the usage of digital wallets in the period before the announcement of demonetization. This also reflects that there has been a tremendous shift from the use of cash to the use of digital wallets since the announcement of demonetization. There was a shortage of cash prevalent during that period, which was highly replaced by the use of digital wallets after demonetization. This massive shift resulted in an increase in the average mean value in the period immediately after the announcement of demonetization.

This increase in the mean value of the usage of digital wallets from the period before demonetization to the period immediately after the announcement of demonetization has been validated by a T test conducted. By using the T test conducted here, we can conclude that there has been an increase in the usage of digital wallets in the period immediately after the announcement of demonetization. The significance value of the 2-tailed test is.000 at degree of freedom 149, which is less than the value of the 0.005 significance level. As a result, we reject the null hypothesis and accept the alternative hypothesis that reflects that there has been an increase in the usage of digital wallets when compared from the period before the announcement of demonetization to the usage of digital wallets in the period immediately after the announcement of demonetization. This massive increase in the usage of digital wallets was a result of the prevalent shortage of cash during that time. to study the relationship between digitalization and demonetization. A T-test has been conducted to study the impact of demonetization on digitalization by comparing the usage of digital wallets immediately after the announcement of demonetization in 2017 and 3 years after the announcement of demonetization in 2019 (Table 10).

4.4. T Test Two

Table 10. Paired samples statistics

		Mean	N	Std. Deviation	Std. Error Mean
Pair 1	Immediately After Demonetization Year 2017	4.0733	150	1.85406	.15138
	After 3 Years Of Demonetization Year 2019	2.8267	150	1.23564	.10089

Table 11. Paired samples test

Pair 1	Paired Differences					t	df	Sig. (2-tailed)
	Mean	Std. Deviation	Std. Error Mean	95% Confidence Interval of the Difference				
				Lower	Upper			
(Immediately After Demonetization Year 2017) - (After 3 Years Of Demonetization Year 2019)	1.24667	2.00983	.16410	.92240	1.57093	7.597	149	.000

H0: The usage of digital wallets in the period 3 years after demonetization shows no decrease when compared to the usage of digital wallets in the period immediately after demonetization.

H1: The usage of digital wallets in the period 3 years after demonetization shows a decrease when compared from the usage of digital wallet in the period immediately after demonetization.

According to the table 11, there has been a decrease in the mean value from the period immediately after the announcement of demonetization to the period after 3 years of the announcement of demonetization. The value of the mean shows that the average usage of the digital wallets immediately after the announcement of demonetization is 4.0733, and the value of the mean showing the average usage of the digital wallets after 3 years of the announcement of demonetization is 2.8267. These values reflect that there has been a tremendous decrease in the usage of digital wallets 3 years after the announcement of demonetization when compared to the usage of digital wallets in the period immediately after the announcement of demonetization. This also reflects the fact that there has been a tremendous fall in the usage of digital wallets in the three years since the announcement of demonetization. There was a massive fall in the users of the digital wallets after 3 years of demonetization.

The main reasons behind the fall in the users of the digital wallets are the lack of financial literacy, the lack of technical know-how, and the unwillingness to replace the digital wallet as a medium of payment instead of cash. With the increase in the flow of cash, the users of the digital wallet have seen a downfall after a few years of demonetization. This massive fall has resulted in a decrease in the average mean value in the period of 3 years after the announcement of demonetization. This decrease in the mean value of the usage of digital wallets from the period immediately after the announcement of demonetization to the period 3 years after the announcement of demonetization has been validated by a T test conducted.

By using the T test conducted here, we can conclude that there has been a decrease in the usage of digital wallets in the period of 3 years after the announcement of demonetization. The significance value of the 2-tailed test is.000, which is less than the value of the 0.005 significance level. As a result, we reject the null hypothesis and accept the alternative hypothesis that reflects that there has been decrease in the usage of digital wallets when compared to the period immediately after the announcement of demonetization to the usage of digital wallets in the period 3 years after the announcement of demonetization. This massive fall in the usage of digital wallets is a result of the lack of financial literacy, the lack of technical know-how, and the unwillingness to replace digital wallets as a medium of payment instead of cash.

A trend analysis through a bar graph has been done to show the number of frequent users (very often and often users) of digital wallets at different periods of time.

Figure 2. Frequent users (very often and often users) of digital wallets at different periods

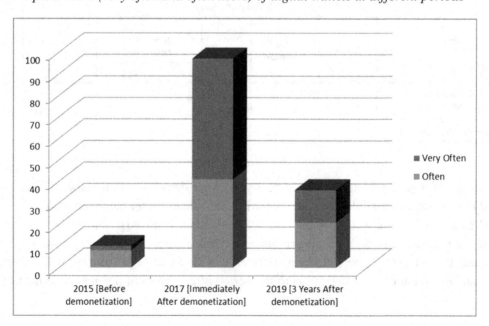

The above Figure 2 shows the frequent users of digital wallets, including the very often and the often users of digital wallets. The above graph displays the usage of digital wallets over different periods of time. Three different time periods have been displayed. 1st period reflecting the frequent users of the digital wallets before the announcement of demonetization in 2015. The second period reflects the frequent users of the digital wallets immediately after the announcement of demonetization in 2017. The third period reflects the frequent users of digital wallets after three years of demonetization.

The above bar graph shows that there are 10 frequent users out of 150 respondents to my questionnaire who frequently used digital wallets before the announcement of demonetization. Then, out of which 8 used digital wallets often and 2 respondents to my questionnaire used them very often before the announcement of demonetization, Then the second period, which displays the period immediately after the announcement of demonetization, shows that 97 respondents out of 150 respondents to my questionnaire work frequently using digital wallets immediately after the announcement of demonetization, out of which 41 were often users and 56 were very often users, showing that there has been a tremendous increase in the number of people using digital wallets immediately after the announcement of demonetization. This was due to the shortage of cash prevalent in the economy.

This graph shows a tremendous shift from 10 to 97 frequent users of digital wallets immediately after the announcement of demonetization in 2017. Then the third period, which displays the period i.e., 3 years after the announcement of demonetization in 2019, has witnessed a fall in the frequent users of the digital wallets after 3 years of demonetization, reflecting that with the flow of cash back into the economy and a lack of technical know-how and financial literacy, there has been a tremendous decline in the frequent users of the digital wallets, which is witnessed after 3 years of demonetization. 36 out of 150 respondents to my questionnaire were frequent users of digital wallets after 3 years of demonetization; out of them, 21 were often users of digital wallets, and 15 were very often users of digital wallets. The fall from 97 respondents to 36 respondents reflects that with the passage of time and the inability of people to maintain the digital usage of e-wallets, there has been a decline or tremendous fall in the usage of digital wallets after 3 years of demonetization. showing that after 3 years of demonetization, the economy came to a little higher position than where it started.

5. CONCLUSION

This research paper is conducted to focus on the positive and negative effects of digitalization on youth and how demonetization has led to digitalization. The data analysis that has been conducted consists of a T test, a Chi-square, and an analysis of pie charts and bar graphs, which have led to the conclusion that with more usage of mobile phones, there has been a negative impact on the youth, and as a result, digitalization leads to a more negative impact than a positive impact on the youth. From the T test, we can conclude that the impact of demonetization on digitalization has been tremendous, leading to an increase in the use of digital wallets immediately after the announcement of demonetization, but after 3 years, the economy has witnessed a downfall in the usage of digital wallets, reaching a slightly higher position than where it started. The analysis of the pie chart shows that with the increase in demonetization, E-wallets have been frequently used as a mode of payment by the youth, so with demonetization, there has been a shift in preference among the youth in the mode of payment from cash to digital wallets.

REFERENCES

Abu-Rumman, A. (2021). Effective Knowledge Sharing: A Guide to the Key Enablers and Inhibitors. In D. Tessier (Ed.), *Handbook of Research on Organizational Culture Strategies for Effective Knowledge Management and Performance* (pp. 133–156). IGI Global. doi:10.4018/978-1-7998-7422-5.ch008

Abu-Rumman, A. and Qawasmeh, R. (2021). Assessing international students' satisfaction of a Jordanian university using the service quality model. *Journal of Applied Research in Higher Education.* doi:10.1108/JARHE-05-2021-0166

Al-maaitah, D. A., Tha'er Majali, M. A., & Almaaitah, T. A. (2021a). The role of leadership styles on staffs job satisfaction in public organizations. *Journal of Contemporary Issues in Business and Government, 27*(1), 772–783.

Al-maaitah, T. A., Tha'er Majali, M. A., & Almaaitah, D. A. (2021b). The Impact of COVID-19 on the Electronic Commerce Users Behavior. *Journal of Contemporary Issues in Business and Government, 27*(1), 772–783.

Al-Naif, K. L., & Al Shraah, A. E. M. (Eds.). (2018). Working capital management and profitability: Evidence from Jordanian mining and extraction industry sector. IUG Journal of Economics and Business, 2(1), 42–60.

Al Shraah, A., Abu-Rumman, A., Alqhaiwi, L. A., & AlSha'ar, H. (2022). The impact of sourcing strategies and logistics capabilities on organizational performance during the COVID-19 pandemic: Evidence from Jordanian pharmaceutical industries. *Uncertain Supply Chain Management, 10*(3), 1077–1090. doi:10.5267/j.uscm.2022.2.004

Al Shraah, A., Irtaimeh, H. J., & Rumman, M. A. (2013). The Strategic Human Resource Management Practices in Implying Total Quality Management (TQM): An Empirical Study on Jordanian Banking Sector. *International Journal of Management, 4*(5), 179–190.

Kathial, K. (2018). Impact of demonetization on digital transactions in India. *Asian Journal of Management, 9*(1), 281. doi:10.5958/2321-5763.2018.00042.2

Luke, A. (2008) Digital Innovation In Schooling: Policy Efficacy, Youth Cultures And Pedagogical Change. *Discussion Paper for Nordic Digital Learning Resources Study Meetings.* OECD.

Youth, D. (2019). *Mobile Phones And Text Messaging: Assessing The Profound Impact Of A Technological Afterthought.* NIH.

Chapter 20
Neonatal Iron Status and Body Composition as Influenced by Mother's Anaemia

Danesh B. Potdar
Krishna Institute of Medical Sciences, India

C. D. Aundhakar
Krishna Institute of Medical Sciences, India

ABSTRACT

Iron is a micronutrient which is crucial for growth of fetus during pregnancy, and maternal iron is the major source of fetal iron. As the demand of iron increases during pregnancy, it becomes difficult to ensure sufficient maternal iron stores. Literature suggests that maternal iron deficiency anaemia might influence the iron reserves of newborns and also affect growth and development of fetus and newborns after birth. The aim of this chapter is to examine the association between maternal anaemia and newborn anthropometric parameters, namely haemoglobin and iron reserves after birth. This 18-month research was a cross-sectional analysis of data from a large hospital. Blood samples were taken from both the mother and the newborn to analyse haemoglobin and serum ferritin levels during the initial stage of labour. The mean age of enrolled pregnant women was 25.81 ± 4.67 years and most of them belonged to 21-30 years of age (72.32%).

1. INTRODUCTION

Fetal iron is mostly derived from maternal iron, as iron is a vitamin that is crucial for the growth of the foetus throughout pregnancy. Keeping up with the increased iron needs of a pregnant woman is no easy feat. According to the available literature, a mother's iron deficiency anaemia may impair her newborn's iron stores, as well as the fetus's and newborn's growth and development after delivery (Baker & Greer, 2010). This was cross-sectional research carried out over the course of 18 months at a major teaching hospital. There was a total of 112 pregnant women enrolled in the study, all of whom had been diag-

DOI: 10.4018/979-8-3693-1301-5.ch020

nosed with iron deficiency anaemia and were stratified according to the severity of their anaemia as determined by WHO criteria. The World Health Organization classifies pregnant women as anaemic if their haemoglobin is 11 g/dL or below at any moment throughout their pregnancies. The infants of the women who participated in the study were also included to examine the relationship between their iron status at birth and other anthropometric variables (Gupta, et al., 2013). The widespread belief that an inadequate amount of iron is present during pregnancy and in neonates, which stunts their development, is based on this fact (Camaschella, 2019).

Because it affects around one-third of the world's population, anaemia is one of the most serious health disorders that may be found anywhere in the world. This blood illness affects a significant number of young children (42 percent of those 5 years old or younger) as well as pregnant women (40 percent of the world's total). According to the fourth iteration of the Indian National Family Health Survey (NFHS-4), conducted in 2015–2016, anaemia affects 53% of Indian women between the ages of 15 and 49. (Garzon et al., 2020). The percentage of women who are anaemic differs according to whether or not they are pregnant or breastfeeding: anaemia affects 58% of women who are breastfeeding, 50% of women who are pregnant, and 52% of women who are neither pregnant nor breastfeeding. There could be other factors at play, but research suggests that iron deficiency is responsible for more than half of all episodes of anaemia (Parks et al., 2019).

Overall, 75% of all cases of anaemia in pregnant women are caused by a lack of iron, whether they live in a rich country or a poor one. Physiological changes during pregnancy raise the average daily iron need by 4.4 mg, which is often not enough to fulfil the maternal demand imposed by pregnancy and leads to the development of IDA in pregnant women (Tandon et al., 2018). The World Health Organization classifies pregnant women as anaemic if their haemoglobin is 11 g/dL or below at any moment throughout their pregnancies. However, iron levels and needs change during pregnancy. Negative prenatal and postnatal effects for mother and child might result from IDA going undiagnosed and untreated. Pallor, shortness of breath, palpitations, hair loss, headache, vertigo, leg cramps, cold intolerance, disorientation, and irritability are all possible symptoms of IDA in pregnant women. Perinatal infections, preeclampsia, heart failure, hemorrhagic complications, and even mortality is all more likely to occur in pregnant women with IDA. If IDA continues after giving birth, a woman may have fatigue, lowered work capacity, impaired attention, decreased breast milk supply, and an increased risk of postpartum depression. Recent meta-analyses have linked maternal anaemia to a 20% increase in maternal mortality and an 18% increase in perinatal mortality in South Asian countries like India (Terefe et al., 2015).

Iron is one of the most vital elements for foetal development since its need is so high throughout development, and foetal growth and development in the uterus are critical for a child's general development and well-being. Iron is essential for the fast proliferation of cells and for normal brain development throughout embryonic development. It's vital for a kid's brain and body to grow and develop, as well as for the formation of new red blood cells (RBC), muscle cells, and myoglobin. Thus, low birth weight and height, as well as neonatal anaemia, correspond with an inadequate amount of iron in the foetus and newborn. If a newborn's iron levels are low, doctors need to treat him or her right away so that he or she doesn't suffer from high blood pressure, impaired cognitive development, and a weakened immune system as an adult.

2. MATERNAL ANAEMIA AND NEWBORN IRON AND HAEMOGLOBIN STORES

The saturation of the foetal transferrin-binding transferrin receptor on the fetal-facing (basal) layer of the syncytiotrophoblast, which is responsible for iron transport, sends a signal to the placenta about the amount of iron that the foetus requires. In response to an increase in foetal iron demand or maternal iron insufficiency, TfR mRNA quantities and placental TfR expression both rise. This results in increased iron transport to the apical (maternal-facing) surface, which in turn leads to increased placental iron absorption. After the mother's iron reserves have been depleted, the placenta responds to foetal signals by transporting additional iron from the mother to the foetus. This process continues until the end of the pregnancy. It is possible for the entire maternal unit to develop an iron deficiency; however, even if the TfR gene in the placenta is activated, not enough iron will be delivered to the developing foetus to allow normal iron levels to be restored. When the foetal SF level declines, the haemoglobin level also drops, and eventually there are signs of ID when the baby is delivered.

If ID is so common among pregnant women, how iron is absorbed throughout pregnancy may shed light on why fewer babies are born severely anaemic. Newborns have increased ferritin levels because iron is actively transferred from the mother to the foetus through the placenta. In the event of iron insufficiency, the placenta is better equipped to compete with the erythroid marrow of the pregnant woman for circulating transferrin iron, ensuring a sufficient supply of iron for the developing child.

Researchers have demonstrated that when comparing the ferritin levels in the serum of the mother and the foetus, the fetus's ferritin level is almost always found to be higher than the mother's ferritin level. These findings demonstrate that the foetus may be protected from iron insufficiency by the efficacy of the active iron transport system that runs across the placenta. This protection may occur regardless of the iron status of the mother during pregnancy. There is evidence of iron deficiency in foetal erythropoiesis in maternal anaemia. This evidence includes elevated levels of serum erythropoietin in the umbilical cords of babies born to anaemic mothers compared to healthy controls and a negative correlation between maternal haemoglobin and cord serum erythropoietin in these infants.

As a result, the placental active iron transport mechanism does not completely protect the foetus from the iron shortage that is present in the mother. According to a number of studies, infants who are delivered to mothers who do not have adequate iron storage tend to have lower cord blood ferritin levels and are at an increased risk of having an iron deficiency. The need of iron prophylaxis during pregnancy has been demonstrated even further by the discovery that infants who were born to mothers who were given iron treatment had higher cord blood ferritin concentrations than infants who were born to moms who were given a placebo treatment.

3. AIM OF STUDY

To examine the association between maternal anaemia and newborn anthropometric parameters, namely haemoglobin and iron reserves after birth.

3.1. Diagnosing Iron Deficiency Anaemia in Pregnant Women

The diagnosis of IDA to some extent is difficult during pregnancy due to the physiological changes in women which may impact the serum levels of biochemical markers for predicting iron status.

3.2. Iron Deficiency Anaemia

Higher needs, decreased intake, increased loss, and/or impaired absorption can all contribute to a negative iron balance, which over time can lead to iron insufficiency. As the highest amount of body's iron is consumed for haemoglobin synthesis to produce 200 billion erythrocytes daily, IDA (decreased haemoglobin and ferritin) is commonly regarded as a subset of iron deficiency.

Figure 1. Stages of iron reduction with increasing severity of iron deficiency

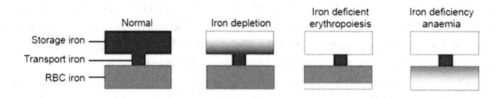

The iron reduction can be summarized through three stages of increasing severity (Figure 1).

3.3. Anaemia and Maternal Mortality and Morbidity

Women who are pregnant and have IDA have a significantly increased risk of perinatal mortality and morbidity. There is a wide variation of maternal mortality rates across various developing countries, with India having the lowest rate at 27 deaths per one million live births and Pakistan having the highest at 194 deaths.

3.4. Supplementation in Pregnant Women and Lactating Mothers

Following the first trimester of pregnancy, all pregnant women should take 100 iron pills daily (300 mg of ferrous sulphate with 100 mg of elemental iron and 500 g of folic acid). To reduce the incidence of neural tube defects in the developing infant, it is suggested that all women of childbearing age take 400 g of folic acid tablets throughout the preconception period and during the first trimester of pregnancy. Additionally, even if the woman is not anaemic in the postpartum period, she should be given a prophylactic regimen (1 tablet daily for 100 days).

3.5. Maternal Iron Deficiency Anaemia and Effect on Newborn, Infant, and Child Health

Iron must be given by the mother in order for there to be growth and development in the foetus. Iron is actively transmitted across the placenta. According to the studies that have been conducted, the placenta is responsible for delivering around 270 milligrammes (mg) of iron to the developing foetus. In order to meet the requirements of the foetus during the third trimester, an average of 5.6 milligrammes of iron per day is carried across the placenta from either the mother's diet or her endogenous sources. As a consequence, close to 80 percentage of a full-term infant's total foetal iron is deposited during the third trimester of pregnancy.

3.6. Complications of Iron Deficiency Anaemia During Pregnancy

Anaemia is an extremely serious global concern as it is highly associated with both maternal and fetal morbidity. Effects of IDA on mother are fatigue, pallor, poor exercise tolerance, tachycardia, and suboptimal work capacity. Furthermore, exhausted blood reserves during delivery may increase the requirement of blood transfusion, placental abruption, heart failure, preeclampsia, and maternal death. Iron deficiency in mothers also influences iron concentration in umbilical cord blood. IDA may increase oxidative stress. However, microcytic erythrocytes have a shorter survival time partly because of oxidative damage to the erythrocyte membrane (Table 1).

Table 1. Complications associated with iron deficiency anaemia in pregnancy

Antepartum Complications	Intrapartum Complications
Preterm delivery risk	Prolonged labor
Membranes' premature rupture	Increased rates of operative delivery and induced labor
Pre-eclampsia	Fetal distress
Intrauterine death	Abruption
Intercurrent infection	
Antepartum haemorrhage	
Congestive heart failure	
Postpartum Complications	**Fetal Outcome**
Postpartum haemorrhage	Low birth weight
Purperal sepsis	Prematurity
Lactation failure	Infections
Pulmonary thromboembolism	Neonatal anaemia
Subinvolution of uterus	Abnormal cognitive development
Postpartum depression	

3.7. Anaemia and Maternal Mortality and Morbidity

There is an increased danger of perinatal death and morbidity for babies born to mothers with IDA. Maternal mortality rates vary widely across developing nations, from 27 in India to 194 in Pakistan per 1,00,000 live births. There were 70 fatalities among mothers with haemoglobin levels of 10 g/dL for every 10,000 live births in Indonesia, compared to 19.7 deaths among nonanaemic women. Puerperial maternal mortality has been linked to weakened resistance to complications brought on by massive blood loss, elevated infection risk, and exhaustion.

3.8. Supplementation in Pregnant Women and Lactating Mothers

After the first trimester of pregnancy, the National Nutrition and Anaemia Control Program (NNACP) advises that all pregnant women take 100 iron pills (300 mg of ferrous sulphate including 100 mg of elemental iron and 500 g of folic acid).

3.9. Maternal Iron Deficiency Anaemia/Effect on Newborn, Infant, and Child Health

Fetal growth and development rely on iron supplied by the mother, which is actively transferred across the placenta. According to the available research, the placenta provides the growing foetus with about 270 milligrammes (mg) of iron. An average of 5.6 mg/day of iron is transported across the placenta from maternal dietary or endogenous sources to fulfil foetal needs in the third trimester. Thus, almost 80% of a full-term infant's foetal iron is deposited throughout the third trimester.

4. MATERIAL AND METHODS

4.1. Study Design

Research based on observations, employing a cross-sectional methodology, with a study period of one year and six months Tertiary care hospital, which served as the location for the research. Ethical considerations the research was carried out in accordance with the generally acknowledged norms of clinical practise, and the institution's ethics committee gave its blessing to the methodology of the study before it was carried out. Before allowing any pregnant women to participate in the trial, we first secured their signed permission after fully informing them about the procedure.

Study participants: a. Sample Size Calculation

$$N = SDI^2 + SD2^2 \times 13 \div (M1 - M2)^2$$
$$= \frac{(0.8 \times 0.8 + 0.5 \times 0.5) \times 13}{(10.5 - 7.3)(10.5 - 7.3)}$$
$$= \frac{(0.64 + 0.25) \times 13}{3.2 \times 3.2} = \frac{0.89 \times 13}{10.24} = 112$$

Inclusion Criteria: Infants of both sexes whose moms have iron deficiency anaemia, as defined by WHO, Type of Transportation Used (normal or caesarean section both)

Exclusion Criteria: Bleeding before delivery; Anaemia so severe it necessitates a transfusion;

- Persistent medical problems related to pregnancy
- Newborns admitted to a NICU
- newborn infants with obvious birth defects or genetic disorders

Maternal Sample: Pre-delivery sample: Haemoglobin analysis requires 3 ml of venous blood in an EDTA bulb, but serum ferritin levels only require 2 ml of venous blood in a plain bulb.

Baby Sample: Cord blood sample: Haemoglobin levels may be determined from a sample of 3 millilitres of cord blood obtained from the umbilical vein in an EDTA bulb, and serum ferritin levels can be determined from a sample of 2 millilitres of cord blood collected in a plain bulb.

Study Outcomes: The main outcome of this study was inferred from cord blood haemoglobin and ferritin levels and their correlation to the levels of maternal haemoglobin and ferritin levels. The impact of maternal anaemia on fetal haemoglobin stores and ferritin levels and how it ultimately impacts anthropometric characteristics of newborns was evaluated.

5. RESULTS AND OBSERVATIONS

The study enrolled a total of 112 pregnant women who were diagnosed with IDA (Table 2).

Table 2. Distribution of age among enrolled pregnant women

Age	Frequency	Percentage
Less than 20 years	7	6.25%
21 to 30	81	72.32%
31 to 40	24	21.43%
Total	112	100%
Mean, years	25.81 ± 4.67	

Seventy-two percent of the pregnant women enrolled with IDA were between the ages of 21 and 30, followed by 21.43 percent (n=24) who were between the ages of 31 and 40, and 6.25 percent (n=7) who were younger than 20. Overall, the enrolled women had a mean age of 25.81 +/- 4.67 years (Table 3).

Table 3. Parity status of enrolled pregnant women

Age	Frequency	Percentage
Primigravida	54	48.2%
Multigravida	58	51.80%
Total	112	100%

In the present study, 48.2% (n=54) women were primigravida and rest of the 51.8% (n=58) women were multigravida (Table 4).

Table 4. Maternal haemoglobin and serum ferritin levels during first stage of labor

Parameters	Frequency	Percentage
Mother haemoglobin/Severity of Anaemia		
Mild 10 to 10.9 g/dL	39	34.82%
Moderate 7 to 9.9g/dL	60	53.57%
Severe i.e. less than 7 g/dL)	13	116%
Mean Haemoglobin, g/dL	8.92 ± 1.46	
Mean Serum Ferritin, µg/L	12.63 ± 1.36	

At 8.92 1.46 g/dL, the mean haemoglobin level of labouring pregnant women was high. Of the total number of women surveyed (112) 11.6% (n=13), 53.57% (n=60), and 34.82% (n=39) had haemoglobin values between 7 and 9.9 g/dL (classified as severe), 7 to 9.9 g/dL (classified as moderate), and 10 to 10.9 g/dL (classified as mild). During labour, pregnant women's serum ferritin levels were, on average, 12.63 1.36 g/L (Table 5).

Table 5. Maternal haemoglobin and serum ferritin levels among different age groups

	Women Age Group			p-value
	≤20 years	21-30 years	31-40 years	
Mothers Haemoglobin, g/dL	8.41 ± 1.26	9.12 ± 1.33	8.51 ± 2.09	0.144
Mothers Ferritin, µg/L	12.17 ± 0.93	12.81 ±1.27	12.15 ±1.66	0.072

There was not a significant age link seen between maternal haemoglobin levels and trimester (p = 0.144). Additionally, there was not a link found between the levels of maternal blood ferritin and the gestational age of the baby (p = 0.072).

6. RESULTS

Most of the pregnant women enrolled were between the ages of 21 and 30, making up 72.32 percent of the total population. The average age of the pregnant women enrolled was 25.81 4.67 years. Overall, moderate-to-severe anaemia affected 65.17 percent of females. Anaemic pregnant women had mean haemoglobin values of 8.92 1.46 g/dL and mean serum ferritin levels of 12.63 1.36 g/L. Mean concentrations of haemoglobin in cord blood were 15.24 1.04 g/dL, while serum ferritin concentrations were 27.79 4.37 g/L. Haemoglobin levels 14 g/dL were seen in only 15.18 percent of infants delivered to mothers with iron deficient anaemia. The average cranial circumference of all newborns was 32.21 1.51 cm, the average total body length was 43.59 1.35 cm, and the average body weight was 2.37 0.29 kg. Moderate and severe levels of maternal haemoglobin were positively correlated with neonatal anthropometric variables (p0.001).

6.1. The Limitations of the Present Study Include

In order to evaluate iron deficiency anaemia, we have solely taken haemoglobin and serum ferritin levels into consideration. Even while erythrocyte protoporphyrin, total iron binding capacity (TIBC), serum iron, red blood cell indices, and transferrin saturation were all assessed, it is feasible that additional measurements could have showed a more relevant link.

During the labour process, the mother's haemoglobin levels were checked. Fetal outcomes may have been more accurately evaluated if the mother's iron status had been monitored from the beginning of pregnancy.

Infants born prematurely who needed hospitalisation to a neonatal intensive care unit (NICU) were also not included because their mothers had anaemia.

7. DISCUSSION

Iron deficiency is the leading underlying cause of low haemoglobin concentration, which in turn impairs the delivery of oxygen to the uterus, placenta, and foetus. An high haemoglobin level, on the other hand, is not indicative of healthy iron status but rather of the potential for pregnancy-related problems due to inadequate plasma volume expansion. Serum ferritin has long been accepted as a reliable marker of total body iron storage. Newborns born to moms with IDA have considerably lower ferritin levels, suggesting they have less reserves of iron. In addition, the haemoglobin concentration of infants born to women with IDA is much lower, which may account for the fact that less recycled heme iron is being added to the iron pool. The majority of anaemic females, 72.32 percent, were in the 21-30 age range. Kaur et al. (2015), who completed the current study, found that anaemic pregnant women had a mean age of 25.8 3.8 years. In a similar vein, El-Farrash et al (2012) found that the average age of anaemic pregnant women was 25.2 3.3 years, which was not significantly different from the age of the control group (p=0.12).

7.1. Severity of Iron Deficiency Anaemia

Table 6. Prevalence of mild, moderate, and severe anaemia among pregnant women

Studies	Mild anaemia	Moderate anaemia	Severe anaemia
Present study	34.8	53.57%	11.6%
Behal et al., (2018)	41.39%	52.56%	6.04%
Yi et al. (2013)	92.75%	6.66%	0.58%
Bora et al. (2014)	21.6%	70.1%	8.3%
Al-Hilli (2010)	70%	22%	8%
Kaur et al. (2015)	10%	78%	12%

Of the women surveyed for this study, 53.57% had moderate anaemia, 34.82% had mild anaemia, and 11.6% had severe anaemia. The frequency of mild and severe anaemia among pregnant women has varied widely between research (table 6).

7.2. Mean Maternal Haemoglobin and Ferritin Levels

Table 7. Mean maternal haemoglobin levels

Study	Mean haemoglobin (mean ± SD)
Present study	8.92 ± 1.46 g/dL
Agrawal et al. (2016)	9.9 ± 1.3 g/dL
Bora et al. (2014)	8.83 ± 1.24 g/dL
Behal et al., (2018)	9.43 ± 1.26 g/dL
Shukla et al. (2019)	10.39 ± 0.52 g/dL
Kaur et al. (2015)	7.8 ± 1.14 g/dL

All of the women in this research had a mean haemoglobin level of 8.92 1.46 g/dL, which is indicative of mild to severe anaemia. Table 7 compares the mean haemoglobin concentrations of the current research to those of other investigations. In this study, researchers observed that the average maternal serum ferritin level was 12.63 1.36 g/L. Both mothers and their babies in this research had blood ferritin levels below 30 g/L, indicating declining iron reserves. This finding is consistent with the hypothesis that iron reserves are low in anaemic pregnant women, with subsequent effects on the iron stores of their newborns.

This study found that the levels of haemoglobin and serum ferritin in cord blood were significantly affected by the presence of maternal anaemia. In addition, it was shown that a baby's head size, body length, and body weight were significantly related to the severity of the mother's iron deficiency anaemia. Using correlations between maternal haemoglobin and serum ferritin levels and cord blood haemoglobin and serum ferritin levels, the current research aimed to investigate the impact of maternal anaemia on newborn iron reserves. Newborn anthropometric parameters (including length, head circumference, and birth weight) were also measured and compared to determine the impact of maternal anaemia.

The study comprised a total of 112 pregnant women who met the criteria for IDA established by the WHO and who delivered their babies at term. They were categorised as having either mild (Hb: 10-10.9 g/dL), moderate (Hb: 7-9.9 g/dL), or severe (Hb: 7 g/dL) anaemia based on their prenatal haemoglobin levels. This study also included the newborn children of the mothers who participated in order to determine whether or not there was an association between neonatal iron status and anthropometric characteristics.

On the basis of the amount of haemoglobin found in their cord blood, newborns were categorised as either anaemic (Hb: less than 14 g/dL) or non-anaemic (Hb: more than 14 g/dL). For each newborn that was included in the study, the anthropometric data that were evaluated included body length, head circumference, and body weight (a body weight of less than 2.5 kg is deemed underweight according to the WHO). All of the data were analysed using analysis of variance (one-way ANOVA), and for the correlation analysis, Pearson's correlation coefficient was used with a threshold of significance of 5%.

The average age of all of the women who participated in the study was 25.81 4.67 years, and 72.32 percent (81/112) of the pregnant women who had IDA were in the age range of 21-30. During the first stage of labour, the mean levels of haemoglobin and serum ferritin in anaemic women were 8.92 1.46 g/dL and 12.63 1.36 g/L, respectively. During this time, anaemic women also had lower than normal iron levels. The mean levels of haemoglobin in cord blood were 15.24 g/dL, and the mean levels of serum ferritin were 27.79 g/L. Only 15.18 percent (17/112) of children born to an IDA mother had an anaemic haemoglobin level (Hb: less than 14 g/dL).

There was a significant and positive association between the levels of haemoglobin and ferritin in the cord blood of neonates and the levels of haemoglobin and ferritin in the mother (p0.001 when considering both), which suggests that there is a correlation between the levels of haemoglobin and ferritin in the cord blood of neonates and the levels of haemoglobin and ferritin in the mother. It was found that maternal haemoglobin levels (moderate and severe anaemia) have a favourable link with the anthropometric characteristics of neonates (p less than 0.001 for all three).

In conclusion, one may draw the conclusion from the findings of the current study that maternal IDA (particularly severe anaemia) has a considerable impact on the levels of neonatal haemoglobin and cord blood ferritin in newborns of women who suffer from iron deficiency anaemia. The anthropometric characteristics of babies, such as body weight, body length, and head circumference, are also altered, particularly in the case of severely anaemic and moderately anaemic moms.

8. CONCLUSION

The results of this study reveal that maternal iron deficiency anaemia has a significant influence on the levels of haemoglobin and serum ferritin in infants. It was discovered that there is a significant connection between the levels of haemoglobin in the mother, particularly in moderately and severely anaemic mothers, and the levels of haemoglobin and serum ferritin in the infant. The levels of the iron-storing proteins haemoglobin and ferritin in the cord blood of infants whose mothers suffered from iron deficiency anaemia were significantly lower than normal. In addition, the findings of this study demonstrated that the levels of haemoglobin and serum ferritin in mothers who were moderately or severely anaemic were substantially connected with the anthropometric characteristics of their infants, including body weight, length, and head size. For this reason, maintaining a haemoglobin level of 11 g/dL or higher throughout pregnancy and continuing to do so even after delivery while breastfeeding is essential for the development of a healthy foetus and baby.

REFERENCES

Agrawal, V., Jain, V., & Sahu, P. (2016). Cord blood iron status in maternal iron deficiency anaemia. *National Journal of Integrated Research in Medicine, 7*(3), 21–24.

Al-Hilli, N. M. (2010). The effect of maternal anaemia on cord blood haemoglobin and newborn birth weight. *Karbala J Med., 2*(8-9), 13–19.

Baker, R. D., & Greer, F. R. (2010). Diagnosis and prevention of iron deficiency and iron-deficiency anemia in infants and young children (0-3 years of age). *Pediatrics, 126*(5), 1040–1050. doi:10.1542/peds.2010-2576 PMID:20923825

Behal, M., Vinayak, R., & Sharma, A. (2018). Maternal anaemia and its effects on neonatal anthropometric parameters in patients attending a tertiary care institute of Solan, Himachal Pradesh, India. *International Journal of Reproduction, Contraception, Obstetrics and Gynecology*, 7(2), 553. doi:10.18203/2320-1770.ijrcog20180171

Bora, R., Sable, C., Wolfson, J., Boro, K., & Rao, R. (2014). Prevalence of anemia in pregnant women and its effect on neonatal outcomes in Northeast India. *The Journal of Maternal-Fetal & Neonatal Medicine*, 27(9), 887–891. doi:10.3109/14767058.2013.845161 PMID:24041147

Camaschella, C. (2019). Iron deficiency. *Blood*, 133(1), 30–39. doi:10.1182/blood-2018-05-815944 PMID:30401704

El-Farrash, R. A., Ismail, E. A. R., & Nada, A. S. (2012). Cord blood iron profile and breast milk micronutrients in maternal iron deficiency anemia. *Pediatric Blood & Cancer*, 58(2), 233–238. doi:10.1002/pbc.23184 PMID:21548016

Garzon, S., Cacciato, P. M., Certelli, C., Salvaggio, C., Magliarditi, M., & Rizzo, G. (2020). Iron deficiency anemia in pregnancy: Novel approaches for an old problem. *Oman Medical Journal*, 35(5), e166. doi:10.5001/omj.2020.108 PMID:32953141

Gupta, A., Kumar, R., Mohan, A., & Rahi, S. (2013). *Guidelines for Control of Iron Deficiency Anaemia*. Ministry of Health and Family Welfare, Government of India.

Kaur, M., Chauhan, A., Manzar, M. D., & Rajput, M. M. (2015). Maternal anaemia and neonatal outcome: A prospective study on urban pregnant women. *Journal of Clinical and Diagnostic Research : JCDR*, 9(12), QC04. doi:10.7860/JCDR/2015/14924.6985 PMID:26816949

Parks, S., Hoffman, M., Goudar, S., Patel, A., Saleem, S., Ali, S. A., Goldenberg, R. L., Hibberd, P. L., Moore, J., Wallace, D., McClure, E. M., & Derman, R. J. (2019). Maternal anaemia and maternal, fetal, and neonatal outcomes in a prospective cohort study in India and Pakistan. *BJOG*, 126(6), 737–743. doi:10.1111/1471-0528.15585 PMID:30554474

Shukla, A. K., Srivastava, S., & Verma, G. (2019). Effect of maternal anemia on the status of iron stores in infants: A cohort study. *Journal of Family & Community Medicine*, 26(2), 118. doi:10.4103/jfcm.JFCM_115_18 PMID:31143084

Tandon, R., Jain, A., & Malhotra, P. (2018). Management of iron deficiency anemia in pregnancy in India. *Indian Journal of Hematology & Blood Transfusion : An Official Journal of Indian Society of Hematology and Blood Transfusion*, 34(2), 204–215. doi:10.100712288-018-0949-6 PMID:29622861

Terefe, B., Birhanu, A., Nigussie, P., & Tsegaye, A. (2015). Effect of maternal iron deficiency anemia on the iron store of newborns in ethiopia. *Anemia*, 808204, 1–6. doi:10.1155/2015/808204 PMID:25734012

Yi, S., Han, Y., & Ohrr, H. (2013). Anemia before pregnancy and risk of preterm birth, low birth weight and small-for-gestational-age birth in Korean women. *European Journal of Clinical Nutrition*, 67(4), 337–342. doi:10.1038/ejcn.2013.12 PMID:23403878

Chapter 21
Risk Factors for Non-Communicable Diseases in Maharashtra Urban Slums

Aparna V. S. (4f6acc7b-355b-477f-8a54-2c7f8428691f
Krishna Institute of Medical Sciences, India

Supriya S. Patil
Krishna Institute of Medical Sciences, India

ABSTRACT

The prevalence of "non-communicable diseases (NCDs)" including diabetes and heart disease is on the rise, both worldwide and in India. Because HIV affects people of both sexes everywhere, it poses a significant problem for all health care systems right now. Unplanned rapid urbanization, globalization of unhealthy lifestyles, and ageing population are the reasons for the development of these diseases. Physical inactivity and diets that are unhealthy result in increased blood glucose, raised blood pressure, obesity, and elevated blood lipids. All these metabolic risk factors can lead to cardiovascular disease, one of the leading non-communicable diseases (NCD) which cause premature deaths. Tobacco and alcohol use, lack of exercise, poor diet, and high blood pressure are some of the most important causes of NCDs. The high prevalence of NCDs in India is mostly attributable to the prevalence of overweight and obesity as well as excessive blood glucose and abnormal serum cholesterol. If such risks are adequately addressed, premature mortality in India from NCDs might be decreased.

1. INTRODUCTION

Those who don't get enough exercise raise their chance of dying by 20% to 30%. Recent studies suggest that inactivity contributes to the deaths of around 1.6 million individuals worldwide every year (Agarwal, et al., 2018). Non-communicable diseases (NCDs) such as diabetes mellitus, cardiovascular disease, and stroke have emerged as significant public health concerns in India because of the toll they take on the country's economy and society (Anand, et al., 2007). Those who do not engage in appropriate physical

DOI: 10.4018/979-8-3693-1301-5.ch021

activity raise their chance of dying by 20% to 30%. Statistics show that inactivity kills around 1.6 million individuals worldwide every year (Kumar, et al., 2018).

To conduct NCD risk factor surveillance, the STEPs approach has been developed by World Health Organization (WHO) to help member countries to monitor these risk factors and introduce appropriate interventions for reducing them (Li, et al., 2017). In response to the growing need to know non-communicable disease trends across countries as a part of the global surveillance strategy, the WHO STEPS approach has been introduced. WHO STEPS (2022) approach includes three standardised steps, i.e., assessment of behavioural, anthropometric and biochemical risk factors for analysing NCD risk factors. For monitoring within-country trends for NCDs and for making between-country comparisons, STEPS information by using the same standardised questions and protocols can be used by all countries (Alleyne, et al., 2013).

Urban poor among the urban population is in a disadvantageous position as they are at greater risk of developing NCDs because of the adopted urban lifestyle due to urbanisation; at the same time, the situation is much worsened by their lack of knowledge and information about health and poor socio-economic status (Radhika, et al., 2007). Urban poor have less access to healthcare mainly due to the same reasons. Very fewer studies have assessed comprehensively the risk factors of NCD using the STEPS approach, including all three steps – behavioural, anthropometric and biochemical risk factors among the Indian population, particularly in urban slums (Thankappan, et al., 2010). The majority of studies were carried out, including behavioural and anthropometric risk factors, excluding biochemical risk factors. So, our study was planned to be carried out including all three WHO STEPS – behavioural risk factors, anthropometric risk factors and biochemical risk factors in urban slums (Sivanantham, et al., 2021).

2. REVIEW OF LITERATURE

It was previously believed that the prevalence of many NCDs was a disease of the wealthy because of its correlation to rising incomes. However, recent years have shown an increase in the incidence of these conditions in the world's poorest nations, despite the fact that this was not the case in the past. The prevalence of noncommunicable diseases has led to an increase in mortality rates in low- and middle-income countries. In the industrialised world, noncommunicable diseases connected to cardiovascular disease were generally considered to be the ailment of wealthy people.

In 2013, WHO produced a worldwide action plan for the prevention and control of noncommunicable diseases for the period 2013-2020. The plan consists of nine worldwide targets, all of which are focused on having the largest impact possible on the prevention and management of noncommunicable diseases (NCDs). According to the Agenda 2030 for Sustainable Development put forth by the United Nations, the most significant problem facing the world today is that of non-communicable diseases. The goal of the agenda is to cut the number of early deaths caused by NCDs by one-third by the year 2030 through increased efforts in prevention and treatment. WHO is playing a critical leadership role in the coordination and promotion of the worldwide battle against noncommunicable diseases (NCDs). In 2014, the World Health Organization (WHO) established the Global coordination mechanism for the Prevention and Control of non-communicable diseases, also known as the GCM/NCD (United Nations, 2021).

In 2013, WHO produced a worldwide action plan for the prevention and control of noncommunicable diseases for the period 2013-2020. The plan consists of nine worldwide targets, all of which are focused on having the largest impact possible on the prevention and management of noncommunicable diseases (NCDs). According to the Agenda 2030 for Sustainable Development put forth by the United Nations, the most significant problem facing the world today is that of non-communicable diseases. The goal of the agenda is to cut the number of early deaths caused by NCDs by one-third by the year 2030 through increased efforts in prevention and treatment. WHO is playing a critical leadership role in the coordination and promotion of the worldwide battle against noncommunicable diseases (NCDs). In 2014, the World Health Organization (WHO) established the Global coordination mechanism for the Prevention and Control of non-communicable diseases, also known as the GCM/NCD. This mechanism assists Member States, United Nations organisations, and other partners in participating in cross-sectoral collaboration for the purpose of preventing and controlling non-communicable illnesses. The World Health Organization's (WHO) Department for the 'Prevention of NCDs' has as its primary objective the reduction of significant risk factors for NCDs, the most important of which are the harmful use of alcohol, poor diet, and lack of physical exercise (Table 1).

Table 1. Core, expanded and optional items of the WHO STEPS approach

Core, Expanded and Optional Items		
Core Items	**Expanded Items**	**Optional Items**
Step 1 Behavioural Risk Factors	A person's age, gender, level of education, and Using tobacco products, consuming alcohol, and The consumption of fruit and vegetables, the consumption of salt, and the the history of which involves physical activities - raised blood pressure, - Diabetes - raised total cholesterol - cardiovascular illnesses, advise on lifestyle choices, and screening for cervical cancer	1. Information on a broader range of demographic factors, including greatest level of education, ethnicity, marital status, employment status, and income of the household. 2. Leaving smoking, being exposed to secondhand smoke in the surroundings 3. Alcohol use disorders 4. Awareness of the health risks associated with consuming excessive amounts of salt 5. Control of salt intake 6. Sedentary behaviour	Cancer of the cervix Concerning mental illness and suicide Policy on tobacco use Oral health Sexual health Mistreatment and harming of others
Step 2 Physical Risk Factors	Blood pressure, as well as The subject's height and weight, Measurement around the waist	Hip circumference Heartrate	Statistical analysis of one's level of physical activity
Step 3 Biochemical Risk Factors	Blood sugar during fasting Cholesterol in its entirety salt and creatinine levels in the urine	HDL-cholesterol Fasting triglycerides	

The high death rate caused by NCDs is a growing issue for society and national governments throughout the world. The prevalence of chronic non-communicable illnesses among adults in both developed and developing countries is rising rapidly. In 2016, NCDs such as cardiovascular disease, cancer, and chronic respiratory illness were responsible for 41 million of the 57 million fatalities that occurred in the globe that year.

Chronic illnesses, often known as non-communicable diseases (NCDs), are characterised by a gradual or non-existent improvement over time.

16 Diseases or health problems that have persisted for more than three months are considered chronic.

3. HISTORICAL ASPECTS OF NON-COMMUNICABLE DISEASES

Chronic illnesses have been around since ancient times. The English physician Thomas Sydenham (1624–89) established a distinction between chronic and acute diseases. God is said to be the inventor of acute ailments, whereas human beings are the source of chronic diseases. In his book Chronic Sickness in the 20th Century: A History, George Weisz defines chronic illness as a relatively recent phenomenon for which modern science and society must provide workable remedies (Oommen, et al., 2016).

Research conducted in the early part of the twentieth century indicated that the United States had a narrower age distribution than Europe. Insurance firms have seen a decline in mortality rates as a result of lengthened lifespans. They were the first to realise the potential financial and health benefits of scheduling routine checkups on a regular basis in the hopes that early detection of disease would increase life expectancy and save costs. Because of this, epidemiologists and public health specialists in the United States have begun paying more attention to the chronic illness movement in an effort to improve the medical system. After World War II, the United States established the National Health Survey, and the Committee on Chronic Diseases (CCD) persisted in making chronic illness prevention and treatment a priority. Hospitals that treat people with chronic conditions have begun intensive rehabilitation programmes for individuals who have suffered from polio, stroke, or the after-effects of accidents or war wounds.

The definition of chronic illness changed over the course of many decades. Diseases including cancer, heart disease, rheumatism, joint diseases, and dementia were all recognised as chronic conditions for quite some time before the discovery of insulin.

Thus, American medical and public health involvement with chronic disease contributed to the concept of 'screening' and 'rehabilitation' to the world. Physical therapy departments were integrated into the hospital for their treatment. Earlier, chronic disease patients were treated in hospitals, but later Thomas McKeown studied the impact of treating the chronically ill in the hospital. Not only the fact that many elderly people with chronic diseases are blocking beds, but they can have a better outcome medically, psychologically and socially if they are treated outside of the hospital.

3.1. Magnitude of Problems Worldwide

In 2016, there were 57 million deaths around the globe. Some 41 million of these deaths were attributable to non-communicable illnesses, including cardiovascular disease, cancer, and chronic obstructive pulmonary disease. Almost 28 million people lost their lives to non-communicable diseases, and most of them lived in low- and middle-income nations. Since the year 2000, when there were 31,000,000 NCD deaths globally, the figure has risen in every area. In 2016, heart disease (responsible for 17.9 million deaths, or 44%), cancer (responsible for 9 million deaths, or 16%), respiratory disease (responsible for 3.8 million deaths, or 9%) due to asthma and COPD, and diabetes (responsible for 1.1 million deaths, or 1% of NCD deaths) were the leading causes of death from NCDs (1.6 million or 4 per cent of NCD deaths). The worldwide mortality rate from NCDs was 539 per 100,000 people in 2016 when adjusted for age. A person with a life expectancy of 70 has a 23% risk of dying between the ages of 30 and 70 from the four main NCDs (27% in men and 20% in women), meaning that a person with a life expectancy of 30 has a 1 in 4 chance of death from these illnesses well before the stage of 70.

3.2. Magnitude of Problems in Developed Countries

At the turn of the twentieth century, the United Kingdom and France, along with the United States, witnessed a significant drop in the prevalence of infectious diseases. It has been noted that individuals are living longer because to the advancements that have been made in medical facilities. Chronic illness was a secondary topic of discussion in health policy discussions taking place in both the United Kingdom and France. Chronic diseases have emerged as one of the most significant challenges facing humanity in the twenty-first century. By the year 2010, chronic diseases accounted for seven of the top ten leading causes of death in the United States. Furthermore, these disorders impacted fifty percent of all adults in the country and were the primary driver of medical costs.

More individuals are surviving to longer ages, increasing the prevalence of chronic illnesses, while life expectancy is rising in most nations. Mortality rates in low- and middle-income nations have historically followed different patterns than those in high-income ones.

3.3. Epidemiological Transition in India

There has been an epidemiologic shift from infectious to chronic illnesses, which is killing individuals in low- and middle-income nations at socially and economically active ages. This is according to the World Health Organization. The shift from contagious to chronic non-communicable illnesses throughout time is largely explained by Omran's idea (NCDs). The ratio of DALYs attributable to CMNNDs (Communicable, Maternal, Neonatal, and Nutritional Diseases) to DALYs attributable to NCDs and injuries is the epidemiological transition ratio.

While India is in the middle of this rapid transformation, it is crucial to study the progression to a certain stage of epidemiological transition. Disease patterns in India have seen dramatic structural changes over the course of the last three decades. Between the early 1970s and the mid-1990s, the prevalence of NCDs in rural India rose from 35.7 to 54.9%, whereas the prevalence of communicable illnesses fell from 47% to 22.1. There is a double burden of communicable illnesses and non-communicable diseases in India, and the death rate is low, but the morbidity rate is high. Overall, the trajectory of 'health transition' is seen in the exponential increase in morbidity rates in recent decades and a concurrent drop in fatality rates.

3.4. Magnitude of Problems in Maharashtra

The life expectancy of males and females in urban Maharashtra was only 59 years in 1981; however, it has increased to 66.4 years for males and 69.8 years for females in 2005-06, and it is expected to rise further to 70.9 years and 74.7 years, respectively, in 2021 and 2025. In 1981, the life expectancy of males and females in urban Maharashtra was only 59 years. Since 1990, non-communicable diseases have been responsible for the majority of fatalities that occur in metropolitan areas of Maharashtra.

Historically, many NCDs were called diseases of the rich and have been directly linked to economic growth, but now the burden of NCDs has increased in developing countries. Also, the burden of NCDs has doubled the mortality in low and middle-income countries. NCDs due to cardiovascular diseases (CVDs) were mainly regarded as diseases of the rich in developed countries.

In 2013, WHO produced a worldwide action plan for the prevention and control of noncommunicable diseases for the period 2013-2020. The plan consists of nine worldwide targets, all of which are focused on having the largest impact possible on the prevention and management of noncommunicable diseases (NCDs). 28 According to the Agenda 2030 for Sustainable Development put forth by the United Nations, the most significant problem facing the world today is that of non-communicable diseases. The World Health Organization (WHO) is playing a key leadership role in the global fight against noncommunicable diseases (NCDs). The goal for the agenda in the coordination and promotion of the global fight against NCDs is to reduce the number of premature deaths caused by NCDs by one-third through prevention and treatment by the year 2030.

In 2014, the World Health Organization (WHO) established the Global coordination mechanism for the Prevention and Control of non-communicable diseases, also known as the GCM/NCD. This mechanism assists Member States, United Nations organisations, and other partners in participating in cross-sectoral collaboration for the purpose of preventing and controlling non-communicable illnesses. The reduction of major risk factors for noncommunicable diseases (NCDs) is the primary focus of the WHO's Department for "The Prevention of NCDs." These major risk factors include smoking, hazardous use of alcohol, bad food, and lack of physical activity.

3.5. Magnitude of Problems Among Urban Poor

In the last two decades, cardiovascular fatalities have risen sharply in poor and middle-income nations while falling steadily in high-income nations. Lifestyle changes and the adoption of hazardous behaviours were thought to increase the urban poor's vulnerability to NCDs as a result of globalisation. When comparing rural and urban areas in developing nations, urban areas have higher rates of NCD risk factors like hypertension. The rise in obesity and non-communicable diseases (NCDs) among the urban population is only one example of how modern living habits—such as poor nutrition and lack of exercise—have contributed to this so-called disease of urbanisation. If current trends continue, by 2050, 70% of the world's population will reside in metropolitan regions, even though only half of the world's population already resides there.

Negative effects of population change include the emergence of slum and squatter communities in metropolitan areas. UN-HABITAT estimates that almost 433 million people, or 38 percent of the total population of low and medium-income nations, live in urban slums across Asia. The term slum community refers to a broad category of low-income settlements characterised by poor housing and few public services.

4. STEPS NCD RISK FACTOR SURVEILLANCE RATIONALE

The following are the goals of the surveillance of the most frequent risk factors for NCDs and NCDs themselves:

- Gather comparable data both internationally and domestically in each country.
- Create standardised measuring tools in order to facilitate comparisons throughout time and between nations.
- Stop the spread of noncommunicable diseases before they become epidemics Assist health services in planning and determining public health priorities
- Predict the future caseloads of noncommunicable diseases.

- Control and assess the impact of actions on the entire population

The WHO-ICMR (2009) six-site survey and studies carried out between April 2003 and March 2005 in six Indian states (Haryana, Tamil Nadu, Assam, Maharashtra, Kerala, and Delhi) are two examples of surveys that were carried out in India utilising the STEPS technique. The STEPS Instrument includes three distinct levels or steps of risk factor evaluation, which are as follows: Step 1 (a questionnaire), Step 2 (physical assessments), and Step 3 (an interview) (biochemical measures). Each step includes both core and expanded items. Core items are those that countries are strongly encouraged to include in the instrument adapted for their survey.

Expanded items are those that countries may choose to include in order to gather more information on a particular subject. Countries are strongly encouraged to include core items. Tobacco use, dangerous alcohol drinking, a poor diet (low fruit and vegetable consumption), a high salt intake, and insufficient physical activity are the most modifiable behavioural risk factors. The most important biological risk factors are being overweight or obese, having high blood pressure, having high blood glucose levels, and having an abnormal lipid profile, which includes having high cholesterol. The STEPS NCD risk factor surveillance programme does, as a result, take into account these eight important behavioural and biological risk factors.

4.1. Studies Conducted Using Who Steps Approach

In 2013, a survey titled "Prevalence of Non-communicable Risk Factors by STEPS Approach" was carried out in the Republic of Moldova, which is located in south-eastern Europe. The goals of the survey were as follows: 1) to determine the prevalence of behavioural risk factors for NCDs in the population aged 18–69 years; and 2) to determine the prevalence of genetic risk factors for NCDs in the population aged 18–69 years. 2) to determine the prevalence of biological risk factors for noncommunicable diseases (NCDs), such as hypertension, hypercholesterolemia, and hyperglycemia, in the population aged 18–69 years; 3) to determine whether there is a significant difference in the prevalence of risk factors between the sexes, areas of residence, and age groups.

5. MATERIALS AND METHODS

Study design: Observational cross-sectional study Study area: Urban slum area, which is the field practice area of the Department of Community Medicine, KIMS Karad.

Study subjects: Adult population in the age group 18 years and above. Sample size: Sample size was estimated using the formula $n=4pq/L^2$ Sample size calculation: According to the previous study conducted by Srivastav et al. (2017). 61 in Uttar Pradesh, the Prevalence of smoking in the study was 12.5%. Here, P= Expected prevalence of smoking Q=100-p =87.5, L=precision level 5 n = 4x12.5x87.5/25 n =175

Prevalence of total cholesterol in the study - 10.6%, P=Expected prevalence of Total cholesterol, Q=100-p =89.4, L= precision level 5 n = 4x 10.6 x 89.4 / 25 n=152

The sample size was rounded off to 200 for this study.

For the study, a sample size of 200 participants was included in STEP 1 and STEP 2 and a total of 153 participants were included in STEP 3.

5.1. Sampling Technique

The KIMS, Karad campus was located around two kilometres away from the study area, which consisted of two adopted urban slums. These were the areas that the Department of Community Medicine used as their field practise areas. Approximately 450 families can be found in each slum. One household from every other one in the neighbourhood was chosen, and an adult who was at least 18 years old and lived in that household was approached and asked about participating in the study. One person from each family was chosen at random using a straightforward lottery system from the pool of volunteers who were willing to participate.

Inclusion criteria: Adults in the age group of >18 years.

Exclusion criteria:

- Critically ill patients (on dialysis, bedridden patients)
- Pregnant and lactating women.

5.2. Demographics and Sampling

There were a total of 4807 respondents who were chosen at random to take part in the poll. All of them ranged in age from 18 to 69, and the group included members of both sexes as well as people who lived in each of the districts and the Gagauz-Yeri territorial administrative unit. Assuming a 95 percent confidence interval (CI) (Z=1.96), a 5 percent acceptable margin of error, a complex sampling design effect coefficient of 1.5, and equal representation of sexes in each age group, we used the prevalence of overweight and obesity that was found during the prior survey on the health status of the population (P=50 percent). This was done under the assumption that there was also a 95 percent confidence interval (Z=1.96). Following the completion of the calculations, the number of individuals comprising the sample was found to be 4608. This number was then increased by twenty percent, bringing the total number of individuals comprising the sample to 5760. This was done in order to take into account the possibility of non-response or errors in recording.

6. DISCUSSION OF RESULTS

The current research used a sample size of 200 adults in an urban slum region, the field practice area selected by the Department of Community Medicine. This method of estimating the incidence of risk factors for NCDs was developed by the WHO and is called the Standardized Template for Epidemiologic Studies. Two hundred people took part in WHO STEP 1 and 2, while 153 people took part in WHO STEP 3.

Age and gender-wise distribution of the study participants: In our study, among the 200 study participants, the majority were females 122 (61%), in comparison to males 78 (39%). However, there was no statistically significant difference in the gender-wise distribution.

According to the findings of the United States National Health and Nutrition Examination Survey, a bigger number of smokeless tobacco users had elevated BMIs, with about 70 percent of smokeless tobacco users having a BMI that was higher than 26.1 (i.e. considered overweight or obese). The results of our study showed that 46.2 percent of smokeless tobacco users were also overweight or obese. These new findings contradict those findings.

In a study on smoking conducted among the urban slum population, a study from Mumbai showed the overall prevalence of smoking as very high when compared to our study, with 66.7% using a smoke form of tobacco. The difference in the smoking habit can be due to the male and female proportion included in the study; 60% were males in this study, while in our study, 60% were females.

6.1. Excess Salt Intake

In the study done among the urban slum population by Oli et al. (2013) by the WHO STEPS approach, about 14% of the respondents were taking high salt-containing food, while in our study, 48.5% were using extra salt in their diet. In the study by Thulaseedharan et al. (2021), consumption of <5 grams of salt was 29%, females had less salt intake than males (18% vs 49%), a higher proportion of elders consumed <5 grams of salt per day (37% in 50-70 years vs 25% in 18-35), salt intake was low among (14% in obese vs 34% among those with BMI<25), daily intake of salt was relatively low among those who were not on the treatment of diabetes or hypertension. In our study, excess salt in diet was used more by females than males (54.6% vs 45.4%), excess salt was used by younger age 51.5% among the 18-45 age group and 48.5% among the 18-45 age group, excess salt was used among 46.3% overweight/obese, 57.1% diabetic participants were using excess salt and 59.3% hypertensive participants were using excess salt (p=0.01).

Among the anthropometric risk factors, the prevalence of hypertension- 40.5%, BMI >24.9 kg/m2 – 47.5%, and abdominal obesity – based on raised waist circumference and waist–hip ratio was 44.5% and 46%, respectively. Mean waist – hip ratio was found to be higher among females - 0.91 ± 0.75. Newer hypertensive participants detected by our study were 21.5%. Among the participants with a past history of hypertension, 39.5% were found to have their blood pressure not under control.

In our study, the prevalence of biochemical risk factors for raised total cholesterol was 33.3%, raised triglycerides – 28.8% and raised LDL cholesterol – 26.8%. Among the study population, high HDL levels which are considered a protective factor for cardiovascular diseases, were observed among 77.8% study population. The mean HDL levels of the study population were high - 46.24 ± 8.62 mg/dl. Newer diabetics detected from our study was 5.9%.

7. CONCLUSION

Non-communicable disease risk factors were shown to be very prevalent among the urban slum community in our research location, as measured by the WHO STEPS technique. It was revealed that the study population had a higher incidence of health behaviours, such as smokeless tobacco use (59.5%), with the majority of users being females. Among the 12.4% of the participants with a past history of diabetics, the majority i.e, 63.2% participants had higher fasting sugar levels observed, indicating that their blood sugar levels are not under control. In this study area, it was found that the people who have been detected to be hypertensive and diabetic were not adhering to proper treatment. Knowledge and proper awareness regarding non-communicable diseases, their risk factors, consequences of chronic diseases and how NCDs can act as silent killers are deficient among the urban poor. Proper surveillance of NCD risk factors is very important in the modern world where change of lifestyle is happening fast.

Proper health education regarding the risk factors of NCD, need for surveillance of NCD risk factors, adherence to proper treatment need to be given to the urban population in this study area.

REFERENCES

Agarwal, D., Ahmad, S., Singh, J. V., Shukla, M., Kori, B., & Garg, A. (2018). Prevalence of Risk Factors of Non-Communicable Diseases in a Rural Population of Eastern Uttar Pradesh. *International Journal of Medical and Dental Sciences.*, *7*(2), 1667–1675. doi:10.18311/ijmds/2018/20122

Alleyne, G., Binagwaho, A., Haines, A., Jahan, S., Nugent, R., Rojhani, A., & Stuckler, D. (2013). Lancet NCD Action Group. Embedding non-communicable diseases in the post-2015 development agenda. *Lancet*, *381*(9866), 566–574. doi:10.1016/S0140-6736(12)61806-6 PMID:23410606

Anand, K., Shah, B., Yadav, K., Singh, R., Mathur, P., Paul, E., & Kapoor, S. K. (2007). Are the urban poor vulnerable to non-communicable diseases? A survey of risk factors for non-communicable diseases in urban slums of Faridabad. *The National Medical Journal of India*, *20*(3), 115–120. PMID:17867614

Kumar, A., Choudhury, R., & Yadav, S. (2018). A study of non-communicable diseases risk factors among the tribal population of Lefunga block, Tripura: Cross sectional study. *International Journal of Community Medicine and Public Health*, *5*(10), 4478–4484. doi:10.18203/2394-6040.ijcmph20183996

Li, G., Wang, H., Wang, K., Wang, W., Dong, F., Qian, Y., & Shan, G. (2017). The association between smoking and blood pressure in men: A cross-sectional study. *BMC Public Health*, *17*(1), 797. doi:10.118612889-017-4802-x PMID:29017534

National Institute of Medical Statistics. (2009). *IDSP Non-Communicable Disease Risk Factors Survey, Phase-I States of India, 2007-08*. WHO. https://www.who.int/ncds/surveillance/steps/2007_STEPS_Report_India_7States.pdf

Oli, N., Vaidya, A., & Thapa, G. (2013). Behavioural risk factors of non-communicable diseases among Nepalese urban poor: A descriptive study from a slum area of Kathmandu. *Epidemiology Research International*, 2013.

Oommen, A. M., Abraham, V. J., George, K., & Jose, V. J. (2016). Prevalence of risk factors for non-communicable diseases in rural & urban Tamil Nadu. *The Indian Journal of Medical Research*, *144*(3), 460. doi:10.4103/0971-5916.198668 PMID:28139545

Radhika, G., Sathya, R. M., Sudha, V., Ganesan, A., & Mohan, V. (2007). Dietary salt intake and hypertension in an urban south Indian population— [CURES - 53]. *The Journal of the Association of Physicians of India*, *55*, 405–411. PMID:17879493

Sivanantham, P., Sahoo, J., Lakshminarayanan, S., Bobby, Z., & Kar, S. S. (2021). Profile of risk factors for Non-Communicable Diseases (NCDs) in a highly urbanised district of India: Findings from Puducherry district-wide STEPS Survey, 2019–20. *PLoS One*, *16*(1), e0245254. doi:10.1371/journal.pone.0245254 PMID:33434194

Srivastav, S., Mahajan, H., Goel, S., & Mukherjee, S. (2017). Prevalence of risk factors of non- communicable diseases in a rural population of district Gautam-Budh Nagar, Uttar Pradesh, using the World Health Organization STEPS approach. *Journal of Family Medicine and Primary Care*, *6*(3), 491–497. doi:10.4103/2249-4863.222027 PMID:29416995

Thankappan, K. R., Shah, B., Mathur, P., Sarma, P. S., Srinivas, G., & Mini, G. K. (2010). Risk factor profile for chronic non-communicable diseases: Results of a community-based study in Kerala, India. *The Indian Journal of Medical Research*, *131*(1), 53. PMID:20167974

Thulaseedharan, J. V., Sarma, P. S., Thankappan, K. R., Soman, B., Varma, R. P., & Srinivasan, K. (2021). Consumption of fruits, vegetables and salt in the context of control of type 2 diabetes and hypertension in Kerala, India. *Journal of Family Medicine and Primary Care*, *10*(7), 2646. doi:10.4103/jfmpc.jfmpc_2469_20 PMID:34568150

United Nations. (2021). *Non-Communicable Diseases Deemed Development Challenge of 'Epidemic Proportions' in Political Declaration Adopted During Landmark General Assembly Summit*. UN. https://www.un.org/press/en/2011/ ga11138.doc.htm (accessed on 4 May 2021).

Chapter 22
Serum Procalcitonin, Ischemia Modified Albumin Biomarkers in Tertiary Hospital Sepsis Patients

A. V. Sontakke
Krishna Institute of Medical Sciences, India

S. R. Patil
Krishna Vishwa Vidyapeeth, India

ABSTRACT

Sepsis is described as a medical emergency situation due to the body's systemic immunological response to an infection that can lead to end-stage organ dysfunction and even death. Sepsis is one of the major causes of morbidity and mortality in critically morbid patients; however, there is a significant advancement in the understanding of the pathophysiology of this clinical syndrome, hemodynamic monitoring tools, and resuscitation measures. Due to the body's systemic immune reaction to an infection, which may result in end-stage organ malfunction and even death, sepsis is referred to as a medical emergency. It is one of the top ten leading causes of death globally. The epidemiological burden of sepsis is difficult to ascertain globally. Despite tremendous progress in the understanding of the pathogenesis of this clinical illness, hemodynamic monitoring systems, and resuscitation techniques, sepsis continues to be one of the leading causes of morbidity and mortality in critically ill patients.

1. INTRODUCTION

The Germ theory of disease in the 1800 century recognizes that sepsis is a debilitating and dangerous condition. Sepsis caused due to infection stimulates the host's defense to an extent where the host's own tissues are damaged (Cetinkaya, et al., 2014). Once the infectious agent invades the host's body, macrophages get activated and phagocytize them (Chuang, et al., 2006). This causes the secretion of pro-inflammatory cytokines activating the innate immunity of the body and recruitment of white blood cells (WBC / neutrophils) to the inflammatory site (Rad, et al., 2020). After phagocytosis, the neutrophils

DOI: 10.4018/979-8-3693-1301-5.ch022

& macrophages kill bacteria through a combination of several methods like enzymatic degradation or respiratory burst producing free radicals and killing the bacteria by lipid peroxidation process, cross-link formation and DNA damage (Hu, et al., 2018). These mechanisms eradicate bacteria efficiently (Elewa, et al., 2015).

The inflammatory reaction could, however, be heightened, and bacteria could escape. Sepsis usually results from an overactive inflammatory response, but it can also be brought on by a serious bacterial infection that triggers a powerful inflammatory response and results in collateral damage (Kumar and Anand, 2016). In patients with severe sepsis, the main factor contributing to morbidity and mortality is the onset of widespread tissue hypoperfusion and oxidative damage. Cells and tissues are severely damaged by oxidative stress as a result of widespread reactive oxygen species (ROS) generation and tissue hypoperfusion and hypoxia (Boina, 2022). Ischemia and oxidative damage brought on by sepsis are thought to play a significant part in the pathophysiology of organ dysfunction and to be the first stage in the progression of multiple organ failure and mortality (Yin, et al., 2017).

An intelligent clinical response may benefit from prompt recognition of the aforementioned development (Pandya, et al., 2022). The oxidative alteration of cellular macromolecules, promotion of cell death by apoptosis, and structural damage to tissues are all consequences of the sepsis' hyper oxidative state, which comes from an imbalance between D oxidants and antioxidants. Additionally, as a result of the counter-regulatory mechanisms activated by the onset of sepsis, inflammatory macromolecules such cytokines, chemokines, and vasoactive peptides are released (Vashishtha & Dhawan, 2023). These biomolecules have an immediate impact on metabolism in terms of cells, tissues, and organs. Mitochondrial dysfunction and oxygen utilization inhibition are two such effects that have been linked to sepsis. Therefore, it is crucial to analyze and interpret not just one test but a series of tests in order to understand and clarify the pathophysiologic mechanisms underlying sepsis (Jeganathan, et al., 2023).

Early classification and identification of patients who are more likely to die present severe clinical challenges for healthcare professionals, as prompt selection of the most effective therapeutic strategy and location for care are both essential in healthcare settings (Koksal, et al., 2007). In order to comprehend and clarify the pathophysiological mechanisms that take place in sepsis patients, it is crucial to analyze and interpret the findings of a variety of tests rather than just one. Numerous biomarkers have also been suggested concurrently. Procalcitonin is the most well-investigated biomarker in patients with sepsis or septic shock (PCT). Although PCT is correlated with organ failure and sepsis severity, specific outcomes can be predicted through dynamic changes in PCT levels during sepsis.

2. REVIEW OF LITERATURE

The relevance of lactate in sepsis patients as a biomarker of risk is of particular interest. As a sign of altered tissue perfusion, lactate has frequently been utilized as a marker. Greater lactate concentrations are associated with higher mortality rates, whereas hospital-associated lactate clearance is a marker for lower mortality rates. It is obvious that metabolic acidosis results in sepsis as a side effect of lactate buildup. Severe lactate buildup or decreased lactate clearance may be the causes of elevated serum lactate levels in sepsis. Given that the clearance of lactate is dependent on the hepatic and renal processes, this suggests that an increased serum lactate level is a sign of organ malfunction (Vijayan, et al., 2017).

The liver creates C-reactive protein (CRP), an acute phase reactant. Normal plasma concentrations of CRP are below ten mg/l, but they can rise significantly in response to trauma, inflammation, or other stimuli that cause tissue damage. Another strong stimulation is a bacterial illness, which raises CRP levels quickly and within hours (Jekarl, et al., 2019). The diagnosis of infection and the monitoring of the clinical course can both benefit from changes in plasma CRP levels, with a decline indicating the clearance of the illness (Khater, et al., 2016). The cyclic pentameter structure of CRP is composed of five identical subunits. The whole protein has a diameter of 102 nm (1 ngström = 10-10 m) and a molecular weight of 118000 daltons. Interleukin-6 (IL-6) is primarily responsible for inducing CRP synthesis in hepatocytes, but IL-1 and IL-6 can work together to boost it (interleukin-1). The acute phase reactant that has been investigated the most so far is CRP.

3. INFLAMMATION AND ISCHEMIA

An overly procoagulant condition may also be a symptom of severe sepsis. As a result, there may be ischemic cell injury, which will amplify the harm from the unneeded inflammation. By changing leukocyte trafficking, producing apoptotic microparticles, and escalating cellular hypoxia, an ischemic and inflammatory microvasculature, in turn, further perturbs the host response. Numerous cellular metabolic and ultrastructural alterations are caused by protracted ischemia. Adenosine 5'-triphosphate (ATP), phosphocreatine, and other energy-rich phosphates cannot be synthesized again as a result of the deficits in cellular oxidative phosphorylation brought on by ischemia. Calcium, sodium, and water are thus more likely to enter the cell due to altered membrane ATP-dependent ionic pump activity. Ischemia induces the development of some pro-inflammatory gene products and bioactive substances within the endothelium, such as constitutive nitric oxide synthase and thrombomodulin, as well as others that are protective, such as leukocyte adhesion molecules and cytokines (e.g., prostacyclin, nitric oxide) (Rad, et al., 2022). As a result, tissue is more susceptible to further damage upon reperfusion when ischemia is present. Additionally, adenine nucleotide catabolism during ischemia causes the intracellular buildup of hypoxanthine, which is later changed into harmful reactive oxygen species (ROS) with the restoration of molecular oxygen (Rohit, et al., 2019).

In this chaotic process, mitochondrial malfunction, an acquired intrinsic defect in cellular respiration known as cytopathic hypoxia, also plays a significant role in reducing cellular oxygen consumption.

3.1. Reactive Oxygen Species and Mitochondrial Energy Generation

To produce energy from oxygen, mitochondria use enzymes housed in their inner membrane, which has a vast surface area but is impermeable. The electron transport chain consists of five chemical complexes that work together to generate an electron flow that ultimately results in ATP (Prashanth and Anand, 2015). Mitochondrial membrane potential is generated when electrons are exchanged for protons (Suganthi & Sathiaseelan, 2023). Byproducts of this process include reactive oxygen species (ROS), which are produced when molecular oxygen fails to undergo a complete four-electron reduction to water (Fig. 1). Damage to mitochondrial proteins, membranes, and mtDNA from ROS generation is a real concern (mitochondrial DNA). Cytochrome c (Cyt c) is released into the cytosol after mitochondrial oxidative damage, and this triggers the cell death process known as apoptosis. The inner membrane's permeability has been increased, allowing tiny molecules to pass through. Multiple cellular processes are modulated by cell signalling pathways, in which mitochondrial ROS play a key role (fig.2).

Figure 1. Schematic of mitochondrial electron transport chain electron sources (indicated by a red star). H+, proton flux; CoQ, coenzyme Q10 (ubiquinone); Cyt c, cytochrome c
(Galley, 2011)

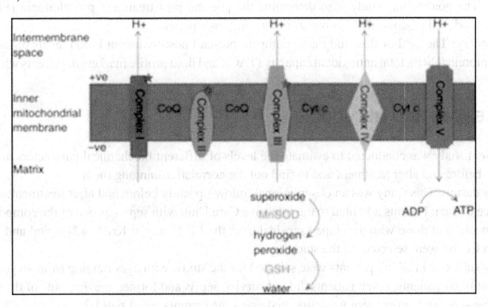

Figure 2. Overview of mitochondrial ROS production and its consequences
(Galley, 2011)

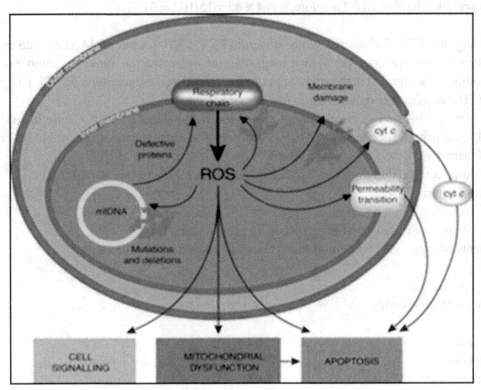

4. OBJECTIVES OF THE STUDY

Primary: The goal of this study is to determine the pre-and post-treatment procalcitonin (PCT) and ischemia-modified albumin (IMA) concentrations in sepsis patients.

Secondary: The goal of this study is to compare pre-and post-treatment blood levels of lactate, C-reactive protein (CRP), total antioxidant capacity (TAC), and lipid profile markers in patients with sepsis.

5. MATERIALS AND METHODS

The present study was conducted to estimate the levels of different biochemical parameters in patients of sepsis before and after treatment and to find out the correlations among them.

Study design: This study was an observational follow-up study before and after treatment.

Source of data: Patients admitted to the Intensive Care Unit, with sepsis as one of the components in the diagnosis, and those who developed sepsis during the I.C.U stay at Krishna Hospital and Medical Research Centre were selected for the study.

Study subjects: In all, 67 patients were selected for the study, with ages ranging from 46 years to 75 years. Out of 67 patients, seven patients did not survive sepsis and formed the dropouts of the study.

Sample size: The sample size was estimated using the formula n = 4 p q/ L2
Where,

- n = sample size
- p = percentage of normal values after treatment = 85% q = 100 - p = 15%
- L = precision level = 10% Therefore, n = 4 x 85 x 15/102 = 51

Assuming that 85% of abnormal values of serum PCT, CRP, Lactate, IMA, TAC and parameters of Lipid Profile would revert to the normal range after the treatment, the minimum number of cases of sepsis required to be enrolled in the study as per inclusion and exclusion criteria was 51 ± 6 (10% drop out) = 57. The number was rounded off to 60.

Study setting: This study was carried out in Krishna Hospital and Medical Centre in collaboration with the Department of Biochemistry, Krishna Institute of Medical Sciences Deemed to be University, Karad, Maharashtra.

Study duration: The study was conducted from December 2019 to October 2021.
Inclusion criteria:

- All patients with sepsis are between 46 to 75 years of age.
- Patients who provided written informed consent to participate in the study.

Exclusion criteria:
Patients with pre-existing:

- Renal disease
- Heart disease
- Liver disease

- HIV
- Cancer
- COVID-19

Ethics: Approval from the Institutional Ethics Committee of KIMSDU, Karad, was taken.

6. METHODOLOGY

Written informed consent was obtained from all the participants after explaining the need for the study. A detailed medical history was elicited for all participants enrolled in the study, and a proforma was used to collect the baseline data. The purposive sampling method - based on the physician's provisional diagnosis at the time of admission, was used for selecting the study subjects. Patients who were suspected of having a bacterial infection and having SOFA (Sequential Organ Failure Assessment) score of 2 or more points from the baseline were diagnosed with sepsis by the physician.

6.1. Sample Collection

Blood samples were collected on two occasions: firstly, on the admission of the patient to I.C.U. and secondly, when the patient was in the recovery phase from sepsis. 5ml of blood was drawn from the peripheral vein of patients under all aseptic precautions and was collected in plain vacutainers. Arterial blood for ABG analysis was taken from the radial artery using a heparinized 2cc BD syringe, and the sample was processed immediately so as to prevent the clotting of blood. For other parameters, venous blood was allowed to stand for 30 minutes, and serum was separated by centrifugation at 3000 rpm for 10 minutes. The serum obtained was used for the following tests:

- Serum Procalcitonin (PCT) by fluorescence immunoassay on Finecare FIA system.
- Serum C - reactive protein (CRP) by quantitative turbidimetric immunoassay on EM 360 auto analyzer.
- Serum Lactate levels by arterial blood gas (ABG) analysis.
- Serum Ischemia Modified Albumin (IMA) by albumin cobalt binding (ACB) method on the spectrophotometer.
- Serum Total Antioxidant Activity (TAC) by Ferric reducing antioxidant power (FRAP) method.
- Total Cholesterol by CHOD-PAP method on EM360 auto analyzer.
- Serum Triglycerides (TG) by GPO method on EM360 auto analyser
- Serum High Density Lipoproteins (HDL) by CHOD-CHER method on EM360 auto analyser.
- Serum Low-Density Lipoproteins (LDL) by calculation using Friedewald Levy Fredrickson equation.
- Serum Very Low-Density Lipoproteins (VLDL) by calculation using formula VLDL=TG/5.

7. SERUM PROCALCITONIN

Method: PCT was measured by a rapid quantitative test based on fluorescence immunoassay technology.

Kit: Finecare PCT kit

7.1. Principle

The Finecare PCT Rapid Quantitative test makes use of a sandwich immunodetection technique. When a blood sample is placed in the cartridge's specimen well, the PCT antibodies on the sample pad bind to PCT antigens in the sample, creating immune complexes that may be identified by the fluorescence-labeled detector. The PCT antibodies halt the movement of the detector antibody-PCT complexes as they travel towards the nitrocellulose matrix of the test strip via capillary action. Detector antibodies glow at a rate proportionate to the amount of PCT captured.

7.2. Procedure

Step 1 – Preparation: Before testing, 'Use' is activated in the setting and saved. It is made sure that the lot number of the test cartridge matches the ID chip as well as the detection buffer. ID chip is inserted into the Finecare TM FIA system.

Step 2 – Sampling: 75 μl of whole blood or 50 μl serum or plasma is transferred with a transfer pipette and added into the detection buffer tube.

Step 3 – Mixing: The lid of the detection buffer tube is closed, and the sample mixture is mixed thoroughly by shaking it about ten times.

Step 4 – Loading: 75 μl of sample mixture is pipetted and added to the sample well of the test cartridge.

Step 5 – Testing: Finecare TM FIA system has two test modes: standard test mode and quick test mode. To process the test in standard mode, the test cartridge is inserted into the Test Cartridge holder of the Finecare TM FIA system right after adding the sample mixture to the sample well. Testing is started by pressing the test on the screen. For quick mode, the timer is set, and the countdown starts right after adding the sample well and is left for 15 minutes at room temperature. Then the test cartridge is inserted into the test cartridge holder of the Finecare TM FIA system, and the test is started. Finecare TM FIA system starts scanning the sample-loaded test cartridge immediately.

Reference range: 0 - 0.5 ng/ml

Linearity: Serial concentrations of PCT controls at 0.5 ng/ml, 2.0 ng/ml, 5.0 ng/ml, 10.0 ng/ml, 50.0 ng/ml, 100.0 ng/ml were tested three times, showing a correlation coefficient (R) of ≥ 0.990.

8. SERUM C: REACTIVE PROTEIN

Method: C - reactive protein was measured by quantitative turbidimetric immunoassay.

Kit: CRP ERBA Mannheim Kit

Principle: Agglutination occurs when the samples containing CRP are mixed with latex particles coated with specific anti-human CRP. This leads to a change in absorbance, the amount of which is dependent on the CRP content of the patient's sample and can be measured by comparison from a calibrator of known CRP concentration at 546 nm (530 – 550).

Reagent composition:

- R1 – Diluent: Tris buffer 20 mmol/L, pH 8.2
- R2 – Latex: Latex particles coated with goalIgG anti-human CRP, pH 7.3 with preservative.
- CRP-CAL: Calibrator

Normal range: up to 6 mg/L or 0.6 mg/dl

9. SERUM LACTATE

Method: Direct method - Arterial Blood Gas (ABG) analysis.

Equipment: The test was conducted on an ABG analysis machine – ABL800 FLEX in the ICU of Krishna Hospital, Karad.

Principle: The lactate electrode (E7077) in the ABL800 FLEX ABG apparatus uses a platinum anode and a silver cathode. The electrode is protected by a multilayer membrane and an electrolyte solution-filled electrode jacket. The membrane has three distinct layers: an outside membrane layer that is lactate-permeable, an enzyme-containing middle layer, and an inner membrane layer that is H2O2-permeable.

An ammeter is used to measure the current through the chain after applying a polarization voltage of 675 mV to the electrode chain, causing lactate molecules to travel across the outer membrane of the multilayer membrane. The enzyme lactate oxidase, which gets arrested between the inner and outer membrane layers, causes the conversion of lactate by the following reaction: Lactate + $O_2 \rightarrow$ pyruvate + H_2O_2

The outer membrane layer and oxidation of H_2O_2 at the platinum anode provide O_2 for this reaction. The enzyme reaction leads to the production of H_2O_2, which is transported to the platinum anode through the inner membrane. $H_2O_2 \rightarrow 2H+ + O_2 + 2e-$

An electrical current is produced by the oxidation of H_2O_2 by applying a potential to the electrode chain, and its amount is proportional to the amount of H_2O_2, which in turn is directly related to the amount of lactate.

Reference range: 0.4 – 0.8 mmol/l

10. SERUM ISCHEMIA MODIFIED ALBUMIN

The albumin cobalt binding (ACB) assay was utilised to determine IMA. The fundamental idea is that the N-terminal region of human serum albumin has the inherent capacity to combine with certain metals, such as cobalt and nickel, amongst others. Ischemia causes alterations in the N-terminal part of albumin, which leads to a decrease of the protein's ability to bind cobalt and other metals. These changes can take place as a result of acetylation or the depletion of one or more amino acids. Ischemia Modified Albumin is the name given to this particular altered form of albumin (IMA). In this particular analysis, cobalt serves the function of an indicator. In order to determine the amount of free cobalt in a sample of serum, a known quantity of cobalt is first added to the sample, and then the concentration of the coloured complex that is produced after reacting with dithiothreitol (DTT) is measured using a spectrophotometer.

Limitations

- The nutritional status of the patients could not be assessed before the measurement of the lipid profile.

- Due to the COVID-19 pandemic during my study, I had to exclude many study participants who contracted COVID-19 infection.

11. DISCUSSION

The purpose of this study was to measure and compare the levels of inflammation, ischemia, tissue hypoperfusion and oxidative stress in patients of sepsis before and after treatment. The study was carried out on patients with sepsis admitted to the intensive care unit of Krishna Hospital and Research Centre, Karad. This was an observational follow-up study, before and after treatment, in which the pathophysiological changes occurring in sepsis were measured using levels of serum procalcitonin, CRP, IMA, lactate, TAC, cholesterol, HDL, LDL, VLDL and triglycerides. The baseline (before treatment) levels of all these parameters were disturbed in patients of sepsis, which improved after treatment and were within or near the normal range, indicating that in sepsis, along with inflammation, there is the instigation of multiple pathological processes and on obliteration, of the causative factor, they revert back to normal analogous to inflammation.

Excessively increased incidence of sepsis is observed in elderly patients, age being an autonomous predictor of mortality. Compared to younger patients of sepsis, aged nonsurvivors of sepsis expire earlier during hospitalization, and aged survivors usually require skilled nursing or rehabilitative care after hospitalization. In the present study, the mean age of patients with sepsis was 59.8 years, with a range of 46 - 75 years. Lee et al. (2015) and Singer et al. (2014) studied patients with a similar mean age of 62.7 ± 16.2 years and 64 ± 19 years, respectively.

High levels of PCT indicate flared-up inflammatory processes going on in the patients of sepsis in response to infection, which start subsiding on appropriate treatment, and the values reduce as patients start recovering. In sepsis, systemic infection and severe inflammation, the serum PCT levels usually upsurge distinctly, reaching values of tens to hundreds to thousands-fold of normal levels. Similar mean values of PCT before treatment (44.05 ± 31.6 ng/ml) were seen, but it was done in premature babies of 7–28 days of age. Such similarity in values of PCT in adults and premature babies might be because of the fact that the PCT values obtained were from the premature babies who were in late stages of sepsis where the disease process might have been more advanced and profound, whereas in the present study, the adult patients were enrolled and before treatment, PCT values were obtained at the time of admission when the disease process might have just set in or was in the early stage. The above study enrolled 21 healthy controls for comparing the results, and the difference was found to be highly significant (p<0.001), whereas, in our study, the comparison was made between the before-treatment and after-treatment values (1.705 ± 1.99 ng/ml) for which the difference was also significantly high (p=0.000).

In a study by Isik et al. (2020) the values of PCT in patients with highly probable sepsis were 5.85 ± 1.39 ng/ml and 9.3 ± 9.9 ng/ml, respectively. The probable reason for this might be the study population selected for these studies: newborn infants, whereas, in our study adult population was enrolled. In the study, the PCT values of both groups were compared with that of patients not having sepsis, and it was observed that the difference was significantly high (p=0.001.

The present observational follow-up study was carried out in patients of sepsis admitted to the ICU of Krishna Hospital and Research Centre, Karad, to study the utility of serum procalcitonin, ischemia-modified albumin and other biomarkers in patients of sepsis admitted in a tertiary care hospital, before and after treatment. A total of 60 patients (35 males and 25 females) with an age range between 46 to

75 years were enrolled in the study, using a purposive sampling method, and multiple parameters were measured in them before and after treatment. The patients who did not survive sepsis were excluded from the study and were the dropouts of the study.

The research was carried out at the Krishna Hospital and Research Centre in Karad, Maharashtra, in collaboration with the Department of Biochemistry at the Karad Institute of Medical Science and Research (KIMSDU).

The absorbance units were used to express the values of the IMA (ABSU). The present study discovered that the IMA in patients who were admitted had a range of values, ranging from 1.1028 to 2.1575 ABSU, with a mean value of 1.45 0.27 ABSU.

Concerning lipids, the current investigation found that individuals with sepsis who had not yet received treatment exhibited symptoms of dyslipidemia. The reference range that was considered for total cholesterol was 140 – 200 mg/dl, and the range that was considered for HDL was 30 – 80 mg/dl, the range that was considered for LDL was 80 –130 mg/dl, the range that was considered for VLDL was 8 – 40 mg/dl, and the range that was considered for triglycerides was 35 –135 mg/dl.

All other lipid parameters were either lower than the reference range or were within the reference range, with the exception of triglycerides, which had a value that was high before treatment (199.93 26.57 mg/dl). Triglycerides were the only lipid parameter that had a value that was higher than the reference range. Before therapy, the patients' total cholesterol, HDL cholesterol, LDL cholesterol, and very low density lipoprotein (VLDL) levels had respective mean values of 112.98 17.80 mg/dl, 21.63 5.34 mg/dl, 51.50 15.64 mg/dl, and 39.85 5.35 mg/dl. Following the administration of the medication, values for all of the parameters showed a statistically significant (p = 0.000) improvement.

12. CONCLUSION

From the results of our study, it is proved that in sepsis, there is a concomitant existence of inflammation, ischemia, tissue hypoxia, oxidative stress and dysregulation of lipid metabolism. Since PCT is an established sensitive marker of inflammation and its upsurge in sepsis has been witnessed in several studies, therefore elevation in the levels of other parameters along with PCT before treatment and their improving trend after the treatment indicates that these changes occur solely due to sepsis in response to an infection and not due to any other cause. Moreover, a positive correlation of PCT with IMA, lactate and TAC shows that the ischemic processes, tissue hypoxia and oxidative stress start occurring simultaneously along with inflammation as a response to infection. This gives us a picture of a cascade of reactions that start taking place simultaneously in the body after the invasion of a foreign agent and implies that inflammation is not the only culprit causing damage in sepsis.

Also, studies have been done to find out the importance of IMA in cardiac ischemia, intestinal ischemia and cerebral stroke, and therefore there is a scope of identifying IMA as an early marker of ischemia as it starts rising as soon as ischemic processes start in the body and its levels are detectable much before actual damage is caused to the organ or organ system. Therefore, the levels of IMA may be helpful in monitoring and stratifying the patients according to the severity, followed by timely appropriate measures, thereby preventing serious complications. Thus, it can be seen that there have been very few of these studies have been done in this aspect, particularly in India, and therefore, this study will be helpful in understanding the importance of selected biomarkers in sepsis and would add to our knowledge about the same. It must be highlighted, moreover, that this study has been conducted solely in a rural area, and despite limited resources, it could be completed with the maximum form of accuracy and without hurdles.

REFERENCES

Boina, R. (2022). Assessing the Increasing Rate of Parkinson's Disease in the US and its Prevention Techniques. *International Journal of Biotechnology Research and Development, 3*(1), 1–18.

Cetinkaya, A., Erden, A., Avci, D., Karagoz, H., Karahan, S., Basak, M., Bulut, K., Gencer, V., & Mutlu, H. (2014). Is hypertriglyceridemia a prognostic factor in sepsis? *Therapeutics and Clinical Risk Management, 10*, 147. PMID:24600230

Chuang, C. C., Shiesh, S. C., Chi, Ch., Tu, Y. F., Hor, L. I., Shieh, C. C., & Chen, M. F. (2006). Serum total antioxidant capacity reflects severity of illness in patients with severe sepsis. *Critical Care, 10*(1), 36. doi:10.1186/cc4826 PMID:16507162

Elewa, A., Anber, N., & Zaki, M.E., El, Deek, A.B. (2015). Evaluation of Soluble E-Selectin and Total Antioxidant Capacity as Prognostic Biomarkers of Sepsis in Children. *International Journal of Current Microbiology and Applied Sciences, 4*(11), 665–673.

Galley, H. F. (2011). Oxidative stress and mitochondrial dysfunction in sepsis. *British Journal of Anaesthesia, 107*(1), 57–64. doi:10.1093/bja/aer093 PMID:21596843

Hu, C., Zhou, Y., Liu, C., & Kang, Y. (2018). Pentraxin-3, procalcitonin and lactate as prognostic markers in patients with sepsis and septic shock. *Oncotarget, 9*(4), 5125–5136. doi:10.18632/oncotarget.23701 PMID:29435167

Isik, D. U., Kavurt, A. S., Aydemir, O., Baş, A. Y., & Demirel, N. (2020). Serum ischemia-modified albumin levels in neonatal sepsis and septic shock. *TürkKadınSağlığıveNeonatoloji Dergisi., 2*(1), 7–12.

Jeganathan, J., Vashist, S., Nirmala, G., & Deep, R. (2023). A Cross Sectional Study on Anxiety and Depression Among Patients with Alcohol Withdrawal Syndrome. *FMDB Transactions on Sustainable Health Science Letters, 1*(1), 31–40.

Jekarl, D. W., Lee, S., Kim, M., Kim, Y., Woo, S. H., & Lee, W. J. (2019). Procalcitonin as a prognostic marker for sepsis based on Sepsis-3. *Journal of Clinical Laboratory Analysis, 33*(9), e22996. doi:10.1002/jcla.22996 PMID:31420921

Khater, W. S., Salah-Eldeen, N. N., Khater, M. S., & Saleh, A. N. (2016). Role of suPAR and lactic acid in diagnosing sepsis and predicting mortality in elderly patients. *European Journal of Microbiology & Immunology, 6*(3), 178–185. doi:10.1556/1886.2016.00011 PMID:27766166

Koksal, N., Harmanci, R., Çetinkaya, M., & Hacimustafaoglu, M. (2007). Role of procalcitonin and CRP in diagnosis and follow-up of neonatal sepsis. *The Turkish Journal of Pediatrics, 49*(1), 21. PMID:17479640

Kumar, P.A., & Anand, U. (2016). Multiple biomarkers to assess the pathophysiological state in critically Ill patients with sepsis. *Indian Journal of Clinical Biochemistry, 31*(3), 310-4.

Lee, S. H., Lee, J. M., Kim, C. Y., Park, M. S., Park, B. H., Jung, W. J., & Chung, K. S. (2015). Prognostic implications of serum lipid metabolism over time during sepsis. *Intensive Care Medicine Experimental*, *3*(S1), A226. doi:10.1186/2197-425X-3-S1-A226 PMID:26351639

Pandya, S., Gadekallu, T. R., Reddy, P. K., Wang, W., & Alazab, M. (2022). InfusedHeart: A novel knowledge-infused learning framework for diagnosis of cardiovascular events. *IEEE Transactions on Computational Social Systems*, 1–10. doi:10.1109/TCSS.2022.3151643

Prashanth, A. K., & Anand, U. (2015). Clinical significance of ischemia modified albumin in critically ill patients with sepsis. *Indian Journal of Clinical Biochemistry*, *30*(2), 194–197. doi:10.100712291-014-0434-4 PMID:25883428

Rad, D., Dixon, D., & Rad, G. (2020). Digital outing confidence as a mediator in the digital behavior regulation and internet content awareness relationship. Brain. *Broad Research in Artificial Intelligence and Neuroscience*, *11*(1), 84–95. doi:10.18662/brain/11.1/16

Rad, D., Egerau, A., Roman, A., Dughi, T., Balas, E., Maier, R., & Rad, G. (2022). A preliminary investigation of the technology acceptance model (TAM) in early childhood education and care. Brain. *Broad Research in Artificial Intelligence and Neuroscience*, *13*(1), 518–533. doi:10.18662/brain/13.1/297

Rohit, Y. V., Raghu, K., & Shabnum, M. (2019). Study of ischemia-modified albumin as a biomarker in critically ill patients with sepsis. *Saudi Critical Care Journal.*, *3*(3), 104. doi:10.4103ccj.sccj_16_19

Singer, A. J., Taylor, M., Domingo, A., Ghazipura, S., Khorasonchi, A., Thode, H. C. Jr, & Shapiro, N. I. (2014). Diagnostic characteristics of a clinical screening tool in combination with measuring bedside lactate level in emergency department patients with suspected sepsis. *Academic Emergency Medicine*, *21*(8), 853–857. doi:10.1111/acem.12444 PMID:25155163

Suganthi, M., & Sathiaseelan, J. G. R. (2023). Image Denoising and Feature Extraction Techniques Applied to X-Ray Seed Images for Purity Analysis. *FMDB Transactions on Sustainable Health Science Letters*, *1*(1), 41–53.

Vashishtha, E., & Dhawan, G. (2023). Bridging Generation Gap on Analysis of Mentor-Mentee Relationship in Healthcare Setting. *FMDB Transactions on Sustainable Health Science Letters*, *1*(1), 21–30.

Vijayan, A. L., Ravindran, S., Saikant, R., Lakshmi, S., & Kartik, R. (2017). Procalcitonin: A promising diagnostic marker for sepsis and antibiotic therapy. *Journal of Intensive Care*, *5*(1), 1–7. doi:10.118640560-017-0246-8 PMID:28794881

Yin, M., Liu, X., Chen, X., Li, C., Qin, W., Han, H., Guo, H., Yang, H., Cao, D., Du, Z., Wu, D., & Wang, H. (2017). Ischemia-modified albumin is a predictor of short-term mortality in patients with severe sepsis. *Journal of Critical Care*, *37*, 7–12. doi:10.1016/j.jcrc.2016.08.005 PMID:27610585

Compilation of References

Balasubramanian, P., Diwan, R., & Nadar, A. (2019). Analysis of Facial Emotion Recognition. In *3rd International Conference on Trends in Electronics and Informatics (ICOEI)* (pp. 945–949). IEEE.

Abalkheel, A. (2022). Amalgamating Bloom's taxonomy and artificial intelligence to face the challenges of online EFL learning amid post-COVID-19 in Saudi Arabia. *International Journal of English Language and Literature Studies*, *11*(1), 16–30. doi:10.18488/5019.v11i1.4409

Abbassy, M., & Ead, W. M. (2020). Intelligent Greenhouse Management System. 2020 6th *International Conference on Advanced Computing and Communication Systems (ICACCS)*. IEEE.

Abbassy, Mohamed M., & Abo-Alnadr, A. (2019). Rule-based emotion AI in Arabic customer review. International Journal of Advanced Computer Science and Applications : IJACSA, 10(9). doi:10.14569/ijacsa.2019.010093

Abbassy, Mohamed M., & Ead, W. M. (2020). Intelligent Greenhouse Management System. 2020 6th International Conference on Advanced Computing and Communication Systems (ICACCS). IEEE.

Abbassy, M. M., & Mohamed, A. A. (2016). Mobile Expert System to Detect Liver Disease Kind. *International Journal of Computer Applications*, *14*(5), 320–324.

Abd Rahim, N., & Mohd Rafie, S. (2020). Sentiment Analysis of Social Media Data in Vaccination. *IJETER*, *2020*, 5259–5264.

Abdelgawad, H., Tolba, M., Elakkiya, R., & Ali, S. (2020). Real-time traffic monitoring and control system based on computer vision and machine learning. *IEEE Access : Practical Innovations, Open Solutions*, 8, 58555–58568. IEEE.

Abdul Mohaimin Rahat, A., & Kahir, A. K. M. (2019). *Comparison of Naïve Bayes and SVM based on Sentiment Analysis using Review Dataset*. IEEE.

Abu-Rumman, A. and Qawasmeh, R. (2021). Assessing international students' satisfaction of a Jordanian university using the service quality model. *Journal of Applied Research in Higher Education*. doi:10.1108/JARHE-05-2021-0166

Abu-Rumman, A. (2021). Effective Knowledge Sharing: A Guide to the Key Enablers and Inhibitors. In D. Tessier (Ed.), *Handbook of Research on Organizational Culture Strategies for Effective Knowledge Management and Performance* (pp. 133–156). IGI Global. doi:10.4018/978-1-7998-7422-5.ch008

Accorsi, R., Cholette, S., Manzini, R., & Tufano, A. (2018). A hierarchical data architecture for sustaina-ble food supply chain management and planning. *Journal of Cleaner Production*, *203*, 1039–1054. doi:10.1016/j.jclepro.2018.08.275

Acquaah, G. (2007). *Principles of Plant Genetics and Breeding* (1st ed.). Blackwell Publishing.

Adams, C., Pente, P., Lemermeyer, G., & Rockwell, G. (2023). Ethical principles for artificial intelligence in K-12 education. *Computers and Education: Artificial Intelligence, 100131*.

Adamu, H., & Syaheerah, L. (2021). Rohail Hassan,AssuntaDi Vaio and Ahmad Sufril Azllan Mohamed,Framing twitter public sentiment on Nigerian government COVID-19 palliatives distribution using machine learning. *Nural Hashimah Ahamed Hassain Malim, 13*(6).

Afsharian, S. P., Alizadeh, A., & Chehrehpak, M. (2016). Effects of applying radio frequency identification in supply chain management: An empirical study of manufacturing enterprises. *International Journal of Business Information Systems, 23*(1), 97. doi:10.1504/IJBIS.2016.078026

Agarwal, R., Hariharan, S., Nagabhushana Rao, M., & Agarwal, A. (2021). Weed identification using K-means clustering with color spaces features in multi-spectral images taken by UAV. *2021 IEEE International Geoscience and Remote Sensing Symposium IGARSS*. IEEE.

Agarwal, A., Agarwal, B., Harjule, P., & Agarwal, A. (2021). Mental health analysis of students in major cities of India during COVID-19. In *Algorithms for Intelligent Systems* (pp. 51–67). Springer Singapore.

Agarwal, D., Ahmad, S., Singh, J. V., Shukla, M., Kori, B., & Garg, A. (2018). Prevalence of Risk Factors of Non-Communicable Diseases in a Rural Population of Eastern Uttar Pradesh. *International Journal of Medical and Dental Sciences., 7*(2), 1667–1675. doi:10.18311/ijmds/2018/20122

Agarwal, R. (2014). Edge detection in images using modified bit-planes Sobel operator. In *Advances in Intelligent Systems and Computing* (pp. 203–210). Springer India.

Aggarwal, C. C., Ashish, N., & Sheth, A. (2013). The internet of things: A survey from the data-centric perspective. In *Managing and Mining Sensor Data* (pp. 383–428). Springer US. doi:10.1007/978-1-4614-6309-2_12

Aggarwal, K., Mijwil, M. M., Al-Mistarehi, A.-H., Alomari, S., Gök, M., Zein Alaabdin, A. M., & Abdulrhman, S. H. (2022). *Has the Future Started?* The Current Growth of Artificial Intelligence, Machine Learning, and Deep Learning., doi:10.52866/ijcsm.2022.01.01.013

Agrawal, V., Jain, V., & Sahu, P. (2016). Cord blood iron status in maternal iron deficiency anaemia. *National Journal of Integrated Research in Medicine, 7*(3), 21–24.

Ahmed, A., Jalal, A., & Kim, K. (2021). Multi-objects Detection and Segmentation for Scene Understanding Based on Texton Forest and Kernel Sliding Perceptron. *Journal of Electrical Engineering & Technology, 16*(2), 1143–1150. doi:10.100742835-020-00650-z

Aho, A.-M. (2015). Product Data Analytics Service Model for Manufacturing Company. *Lecture Notes in Business Information Processing, 224*, 282–296. doi:10.1007/978-3-319-21009-4_22

Ahsan, M. M., Luna, S. A., & Siddique, Z. (2022). Machine-learning-based disease diagnosis: A comprehensive review. *Healthcare (Basel), 10*(3), 541. doi:10.3390/healthcare10030541 PMID:35327018

Aishwarya, R., Ashwatha, C., Deepthi, A., & Raja, B. (2019). A Novel Adaptable Approach for sentiment Analysis. *IJSCSEIT*, 254–263.

Ajantha Devi, V., & Nayyar, A. (2021). Evaluation of geotagging twitter data using sentiment analysis during COVID-19. In *Lecture Notes in Networks and Systems* (pp. 601–608). Springer Singapore.

Akgun, S., & Greenhow, C. (2021). Artificial intelligence in education: Addressing ethical challenges in K-12 settings. *AI and Ethics*, 1–10. PMID:34790956

Akyildiz, I. F., Pompili, D., & Melodia, T. (2005). Subacquatic acoustic sensor networks: Research challenges. *Ad Hoc Networks, 3*(3), 257–279. doi:10.1016/j.adhoc.2005.01.004

Akyildiz, I. F., & Su, W. (2002). Yogesh Sankarasubramaniam, and Erdal Cayirci. *Computer Networks, 38*(4), 393–422. doi:10.1016/S1389-1286(01)00302-4

Al Shraah, A., Abu-Rumman, A., Alqhaiwi, L. A., & AlSha'ar, H. (2022). The impact of sourcing strategies and logistics capabilities on organizational performance during the COVID-19 pandemic: Evidence from Jordanian pharmaceutical industries. *Uncertain Supply Chain Management, 10*(3), 1077–1090. doi:10.5267/j.uscm.2022.2.004

Al Shraah, A., Irtaimeh, H. J., & Rumman, M. A. (2013). The Strategic Human Resource Management Practices in Implying Total Quality Management (TQM): An Empirical Study on Jordanian Banking Sector. *International Journal of Management, 4*(5), 179–190.

Alajmi, M., & Khan, S. (2013). *Mobile Community Networks Information Investigation for Additional Significance.*

Alam, A. (2021, December). Should robots replace teachers? Mobilisation of AI and learning analytics in education. In *2021 International Conference on Advances in Computing, Communication, and Control (ICAC3)* (pp. 1-12). IEEE. 10.1109/ICAC353642.2021.9697300

Alayli, S. (2023). Unravelling the Drivers of Online Purchasing Intention: The E-Commerce Scenario in Lebanon. *FMDB Transactions on Sustainable Social Sciences Letters, 1*(1), 56–67.

Alharbi, A. R., Qureshi, A. H., & Fatani, M. (2020). Design and development of a pressure sensing system for pilot masks. *International Journal of Applied Engineering Research: IJAER, 15*(20), 420–428.

Al-Hilli, N. M. (2010). The effect of maternal anaemia on cord blood haemoglobin and newborn birth weight. *Karbala J Med., 2*(8-9), 13–19.

Alleyne, G., Binagwaho, A., Haines, A., Jahan, S., Nugent, R., Rojhani, A., & Stuckler, D. (2013). Lancet NCD Action Group. Embedding non-communicable diseases in the post-2015 development agenda. *Lancet, 381*(9866), 566–574. doi:10.1016/S0140-6736(12)61806-6 PMID:23410606

Al-maaitah, D. A., Tha'er Majali, M. A., & Almaaitah, T. A. (2021a). The role of leadership styles on staffs job satisfaction in public organizations. *Journal of Contemporary Issues in Business and Government, 27*(1), 772–783.

Al-maaitah, T. A., Tha'er Majali, M. A., & Almaaitah, D. A. (2021b). The Impact of COVID-19 on the Electronic Commerce Users Behavior. *Journal of Contemporary Issues in Business and Government, 27*(1), 772–783.

Al-Naif, K. L., & Al Shraah, A. E. M. (Eds.). (2018). Working capital management and profitability: Evidence from Jordanian mining and extraction industry sector. IUG Journal of Economics and Business, 2(1), 42–60.

Ambika, S., Gopinath, S., Saravanan, K., Sivakumar, K., Sukantha, T. A., & Paramasivan, P. (2019). Preparation and characterization of nanocopper ferrite and its green catalytic activity in alcohol oxidation reaction. *Journal of Superconductivity and Novel Magnetism, 32*(4), 903–910. doi:10.100710948-018-4715-7

Anand, K., Shah, B., Yadav, K., Singh, R., Mathur, P., Paul, E., & Kapoor, S. K. (2007). Are the urban poor vulnerable to non-communicable diseases? A survey of risk factors for non-communicable diseases in urban slums of Faridabad. *The National Medical Journal of India, 20*(3), 115–120. PMID:17867614

Anand, P. P., Kanike, U. K., Paramasivan, P., Rajest, S. S., Regin, R., & Priscila, S. S. (2023). Embracing Industry 5.0: Pioneering Next-Generation Technology for a Flourishing Human Experience and Societal Advancement. *FMDB Transactions on Sustainable Social Sciences Letters, 1*(1), 43–55.

Anonymous. (2000). *Plant Protection Manual for Selected Vegetables: French beans, Brassicas, and Tomatoes.* GTZ/ICIPE CD-ROM.

Arslan, F., Singh, B., Sharma, D. K., Regin, R., Steffi, R., & Rajest, S., S. (2021). Optimization technique approach to resolving food sustainability problems. *2021 International Conference on Computational Intelligence and Knowledge Economy (ICCIKE)*. IEEE.

Arslan, F., Singh, B., Sharma, D. K., Regin, R., Steffi, R., & Suman Rajest, S. (2021). Optimization technique approach to resolve food sustainability problems. *2021 International Conference on Computational Intelligence and Knowledge Economy (ICCIKE)*. IEEE. 10.1109/ICCIKE51210.2021.9410735

Aryal, A., Liao, Y., Nattuthurai, P., & Li, B. (2018). The emerging big data analytics and IoT in supply chain management: A systematic review. *Supply Chain Management*, 25(2), 141–156. doi:10.1108/SCM-03-2018-0149

Assi, L., Carter, K., Deaver, E., Anay, R., & Ziehl, P. (2018). Sustainable concrete: Building a greener future. *Journal of Cleaner Production*, 198, 1641–1651. doi:10.1016/j.jclepro.2018.07.123

Atmatzidou, S., & Demetriadis, S. (2016). Advancing students' computational thinking skills through educational robotics: A study on age and gender relevant differences. *Robotics and Autonomous Systems*, 75, 661–670. doi:10.1016/j.robot.2015.10.008

Attaran, M. (2020). Digital technology enablers and their implications for supply chain management. *Supply Chain Forum an International Journal*, 21(3), 158–172. doi:10.1080/16258312.2020.1751568

Averre, W. C. (2000). *Black Rot of Cabbage and Related Crops. Vegetable Disease Information Note 16 (VDIN 0016)*. North Carolina Extension Service Publisher, North Carolina State University at Raleigh.

Ayaz, M. (2009). *Hop-by-Hop Dynamic Addressing Based (H2 DAB) Routing Protocol for Subacquatic Wireless Sensor Networks*. IEEE.

Ayaz, M., Baig, I., Abdullah, A., & Faye, I. (2011). A survey on routing techniques in subacquatic wireless sensor networks. *Journal of Network and Computer Applications*, 34(6), 1908–1927. doi:10.1016/j.jnca.2011.06.009

Bahmani, B., Moseley, B., Vattani, A., Kumar, R., & Vassilvitskii, S. (2012). Scalable k-means++. *Proceedings of the VLDB Endowment International Conference on Very Large Data Bases*, 5(7), 622–633. doi:10.14778/2180912.2180915

Bahn, S. (1998). Maternal and neonatal outcome following prolonged labor induction. *Obstetrics and Gynecology*, 92(3), 403–407. PMID:9721779

Bai, G., Meng, Y., & Liu, L. (2019). A new path tracking method based on visual feedback and iterative learning control. *IEEE Access : Practical Innovations, Open Solutions*, 7, 161064–161073.

Baker, O., Liu, J., Gosai, M., & Sitoula, S. (2021). Twitter sentiment analysis using machine learning algorithms for COVID-19 outbreak in New Zealand. *2021 IEEE 11th International Conference on System Engineering and Technology (ICSET)*. IEEE.

Baker, R. D., & Greer, F. R. (2010). Diagnosis and prevention of iron deficiency and iron-deficiency anemia in infants and young children (0-3 years of age). *Pediatrics*, 126(5), 1040–1050. doi:10.1542/peds.2010-2576 PMID:20923825

Bansal, V., Pandey, S., Shukla, S. K., Singh, D., Rathod, S. A., & Gonzáles, J. L. A. (2022). A frame work of security attacks, issues classifications and configuration strategy for IoT networks for the successful implementation. *2022 5th International Conference on Contemporary Computing and Informatics (IC3I)*. IEEE.

Banu, A., Naidu, S. M., Vinjamuri, S. N., Dattu, G., Sridevi, M., & Chakravarthi, N. R. (2022). Experimentally investigating the influence of static mixers on the performance of a solar water heater. *Materials Today: Proceedings*, 62(4), 2370–2375. doi:10.1016/j.matpr.2022.04.851

Barbara, D. J., Roberts, A., & Xu, X.-M. (2008). Virulence characteristics of apple scab (*Venturia inaequalis*) isolates from monoculture and mixed orchards. *Plant Pathology*, *57*(3), 552–561. doi:10.1111/j.1365-3059.2007.01781.x

Baron, R. J. (1981). Mechanisms of human facial recognition. *International Journal of Man-Machine Studies*, *15*(2), 137–178. doi:10.1016/S0020-7373(81)80001-6

Bartha, J. L., Romero-Carmona, R., Martínez-Del-Fresno, P., & Comino-Delgado, R. (2005). Bishop score and transvaginal ultrasound for preinduction cervical assessment: a randomized clinical trial: Bishop score and TVS for preinduction cervical assessment. *Ultrasound in Obstetrics & Gynecology*, *25*(2), 155–159. doi:10.1002/uog.1813 PMID:15660437

Bavassano, G., Ferrari, C., & Tei, A. (2020). Blockchain: How shipping industry is dealing with the ultimate technological leap. *Research in Transportation Business & Management*, *34*(100428), 100428. doi:10.1016/j.rtbm.2020.100428

Behal, M., Vinayak, R., & Sharma, A. (2018). Maternal anaemia and its effects on neonatal anthropometric parameters in patients attending a tertiary care institute of Solan, Himachal Pradesh, India. *International Journal of Reproduction, Contraception, Obstetrics and Gynecology*, *7*(2), 553. doi:10.18203/2320-1770.ijrcog20180171

Belis, M., & Guiasu, S. (1968). – A quantitative-qualitative measure of information in Cybernetics System, IEEE Trans. Inform. *Theory, IT*, *14*, 593–594.

Below, J. L., Skinner, C. H., Fearrington, J. Y., & Sorrell, C. A. (2010). Gender differences in early literacy: Analysis of kindergarten through fifth-grade dynamic indicators of basic early literacy skills probes. *School Psychology Review*, *39*(2), 240–257. doi:10.1080/02796015.2010.12087776

Benloucif, A., Nguyen, A., & Sentouh, C. (2019). Cooperative trajectory planning for haptic shared control between driver and automation. *IEEE Transactions on Intelligent Transportation Systems*, *20*(3), 9846–9857.

Bennet, P. N., & Brown, M. J. (2003). *Pain and analgesics: Clinical Pharmacology* (9th ed.). Churchill Livingstone.

Berente, N., Gu, B., Recker, J., & Santhanam, R. (n.d.). *Managing AI Managing Artificial Intelligence*. MIS Quarterly, *1*. doi:10.25300/MISQ/2021/16274

Berrie, A. M., & Xu, X.-M. (2003). Managing apple scab (*Venturia inaequalis*) and powdery mildew (*Podosphaera leucotricha*) using Adem (TM). *International Journal of Pest Management*, *49*(3), 243–249. doi:10.1080/0967087031000101089

Bhandari, A., Prasad, P. W. C., Alsadoon, A., & Maag, A. (2021). Object detection and recognition: Using deep learning to assist the visually impaired. *Disability and Rehabilitation. Assistive Technology*, *16*(3), 280–288. doi:10.1080/17483107.2019.1673834 PMID:31694420

Bhbosale, S., Pujari, V., & Multani, Z. (n.d.). National Seminar on "Trends in Geography, Commerce, IT And Sustainable Development" Advantages And Disadvantages Of Artificial Intelligence. *AI Journal*. www.aiirjournal.com

Bhoumik, S., Chatterjee, S., Sarkar, A., Kumar, A., & John Joseph, F. J. (2020). Covid 19 prediction from X ray images using fully connected convolutional neural network. *CSBio '20: Proceedings of the Eleventh International Conference on Computational Systems-Biology and Bioinformatics*. New York, NY, USA: ACM. 10.1145/3429210.3429233

Bila, J. (2008). Status of Bacterial Black rot of Brassicas in Southern Region of Mozambique: Survey, Detection and Identification of the Causal Agent *Xanthomonas campestris* pv. *campestris*. [M.Sc. thesis, University of Copenhagen, Denmark].

Bila, J., Mortensen, C. N., Andresen, M., Vicente, J. G., & Wulff, E. G. (2013). – *Xanthomonas campestris* pv. *campestris* Race 1 is the main causal agent of black rot of Brassicas in Southern Mozambique. *African Journal of Biotechnology*, *12*(26), 602–610.

Birjali, M., Kasri, M., & Beni-Hssane, A. (2021). A comprehensive survey on sentiment analysis: Approaches, Challenges, and Trends. *Knowledge-Based Systems*, *226*, 1–26. doi:10.1016/j.knosys.2021.107134

Boina, R. (2022). Assessing the Increasing Rate of Parkinson's Disease in the US and its Prevention Techniques. *International Journal of Biotechnology Research and Development*, *3*(1), 1–18.

Bonnin, G., & Jannach, D. (2014). Automated generation of music playlists: Survey and experiments. *ACM Computing Surveys*, *47*(2), 1–35. doi:10.1145/2652481

Bora, R., Sable, C., Wolfson, J., Boro, K., & Rao, R. (2014). Prevalence of anemia in pregnant women and its effect on neonatal outcomes in Northeast India. *The Journal of Maternal-Fetal & Neonatal Medicine*, *27*(9), 887–891. doi:10.31 09/14767058.2013.845161 PMID:24041147

Borenstein, J., & Howard, A. (2020). Emerging challenges in AI and the need for AI ethics education. *AI and Ethics*, *1*(1), 61–65. doi:10.1007/s43681-020-00002-7

Bostrom, N., &Yudkowsky, E. (2018). The Ethics of Artificial Intelligence. *Artificial Intelligence Safety and Security*, 57–69. doi:10.1201/9781351251389-4

Breazeal, C., Dautenhahn, K., & Kanda, T. (2016). Social Robotics. *Springer Handbooks*, 1935–1972. doi:10.1007/978-3-319-32552-1_72/COVER

Briganti, G., & le Moine, O. (2020). Artificial Intelligence in Medicine: Today and Tomorrow. *Frontiers in Medicine*, *7*, 27. doi:10.3389/fmed.2020.00027 PMID:32118012

Bruno, J., Veuas, S. J., Wayne, L. J., Romero, R. N., & Baumgartner, P. (2020). *USA department of Internal Medicine and Gerontology (Professor J.-L Albarede)* (Vol. 87131). World Health Organisation Collaborative Center to Promote the Safety of Aged Individuals.

Brynjolfsson, E., & Mcafee, A. (n.d.). *Artificial Intelligence, For Real*.

Buchanan, B. G. (2005). A (Very) Brief History of Artificial Intelligence. *AI Magazine*, *26*(4), 53–53. doi:10.1609/AIMAG.V26I4.1848

Buckingham, D. (2013). *Beyond technology: Children's learning in the age of digital culture*. John Wiley & Sons.

Buddhi, D., & Varghese, L. J., Neeraja, Hamid, S. S., Ramya.D, & Chakravarthi, M. K. (2022b). Harmonic Distortion reduction in Power System to improve Reliability and power quality. *2022 International Conference on Innovative Computing, Intelligent Communication and Smart Electrical Systems (ICSES)*. IEEE. 10.1109/ICSES55317.2022.9914129

Buddhi, D., Prabhu, Hamad, A. A., Sarojwal, A., Alanya-Beltran, J., & Chakravarthi, M. K. (2022a). Power System Monitoring, Control and protection using IoT and cyber security. *2022 International Conference on Innovative Computing, Intelligent Communication and Smart Electrical Systems (ICSES)*. IEEE. 10.1109/ICSES55317.2022.9914167

Bundy, A. (2016). Preparing for the future of Artificial Intelligence. *AI & SOCIETY 2016, 32*(2), 285–287. doi:10.1007/s00146-016-0685-0

Buragadda, S., Rani, K. S., Vasantha, S. V., & Chakravarthi, M. K. (2022). HCUGAN: Hybrid Cyclic UNET GAN for Generating Augmented Synthetic Images of Chest X-Ray Images for Multi Classification of Lung Diseases. *International Journal of Engineering Trends and Technology*, *70*(2), 229–238. doi:10.14445/22315381/IJETT-V70I2P227

Burchill R T. (1975). The value of eradicant treatment in the control of apple scab and apple powdery mildew. *OILB/SROP*, 249–258.

Burchill, R. T., & Cook, R. T. A. (1971). The interaction of urea and micro-organisms in suppressing the development of perithecia of Venturia inaequalis (Cke.) Wint. In Ecology of Leaf Surface Micro Organisms, (pp. 471–483). London: Academic Press.

Burchill, R. T. 1966. Air-dispersal of fungal spores with particular reference to apple scab [*Venturia inaequalis* (Cooke) Winter]. In *The Eighteenth Symposium of the Colston Research Society*, (pp. 135–141). Butterworths Scientific Publications.

Burchill, R. T., & Cook, M. E. (1975). Control of scab and powdery mildew of apple with a reduced number of sprays. *Plant Pathology*, *24*(4), 194–198. doi:10.1111/j.1365-3059.1975.tb01893.x

Burchill, R. T., & Hutton, K. E. (1965). The suppression of ascospore production to facilitate the control of apple scab (*Venturia inaequalis* (Cke.) Wint.). *Annals of Applied Biology*, *56*(2), 285–292. doi:10.1111/j.1744-7348.1965.tb01237.x

Burchill, R. T., & Swait, A A J. (1977). Eradication of perithecial stage of apple scab with surfactants. *Annals of Applied Biology*, *87*(2), 229–231. doi:10.1111/j.1744-7348.1977.tb01879.x

Burke, R., Felfernig, A., & Göker, M. H. (2011). Recommender Systems: An Overview. *AI Magazine*, *32*(3), 13–18. doi:10.1609/aimag.v32i3.2361

Butt D J, Swait A A J, Robinson J D. 1990. Evaluation of fungicides against apple powdery mildew and scab. *Tests of Agrochemicals and Cultivars*, supplement of *Annals of Applied Biology* 116, pp. 34–35.

Butt, D. J., Jeger, M. J., Swait, A A J., & Soutter, R. D. (1981). The 1981 apple scab epidemic. *Grower*, *96*, 4–5.

Camaschella, C. (2019). Iron deficiency. *Blood*, *133*(1), 30–39. doi:10.1182/blood-2018-05-815944 PMID:30401704

Castellucci, H. I. (2018). A review of the methodology and applications of anthropometry in ergonomics and product design. *Ergonomics*, *61*(12), 1696–1720. doi:10.1080/00140139.2018.1502817 PMID:30022717

Celetti, M., & Kristen, C. (2002). *Black Rot of Crucifer Crops*. Ministry of Agriculture, Food and Rural Affairs.

Çelik, T., Özkaramanlı, H., & Demirel, H. (2007). Fire and smoke detection without sensors: Image processing based approach. In *2007 15th European Signal Processing Conference* (pp. 1794-1798). IEEE.

Celton, J.-M., Christoffels, A., Sargent, D. J., Xu, X.-M., & Rees, D. J. G. (2010). Genome-wide SNP identification by high-throughput sequencing and selective mapping allows sequence assembly positioning using a framework genetic linkage map. *BMC Biology*, *8*(1), 155. doi:10.1186/1741-7007-8-155 PMID:21192788

Cetinkaya, A., Erden, A., Avci, D., Karagoz, H., Karahan, S., Basak, M., Bulut, K., Gencer, V., & Mutlu, H. (2014). Is hypertriglyceridemia a prognostic factor in sepsis? *Therapeutics and Clinical Risk Management*, *10*, 147. PMID:24600230

Chakrabarti, P., Bhuyan, B., Chaudhuri, A., & Bhunia, C. T. (2008). A novel approach towards realizing optimum data transfer and Automatic Variable Key(AVK). *International Journal of Computer Science and Network Security*, *8*(5), 241–250.

Chakravarthi, K., & Venkatesan, N. (2015). Design and Implementation of Adaptive Model-Based Gain Scheduled Controller for a Real-Time Non-Linear System in LabVIEW. *Research Journal of Applied Sciences, Engineering and Technology*, *10*(2), 188–196.

Chakravarthi, M. K., & Venkatesan, N. (2015). Design and Implementation of LabVIEW Based Optimally Tuned PI Controller for A Real Time Non Linear Process. *Asian Journal of Scientific Research*, *8*(1), 95–106. doi:10.3923/ajsr.2015.95.106

Chakravarthi, M. K., & Venkatesan, N. (2016). Implementation of a Multi user Secured Remote Data Logger for Real Time Hybrid System. *Indian Journal of Science and Technology*, *9*(35).

Chakravarthi, M. K., & Venkatesan, N. (2018). Adaptive type-2 fuzzy controller for nonlinear delay dominant MIMO systems: An experimental paradigm in LabVIEW. *International Journal of Advanced Intelligence Paradigms, 10*(4), 354–373. doi:10.1504/IJAIP.2018.092033

Chakravarthi, M., Vinay, P. K., & Venkatesan, N. (2015). Design and Simulation of Internal Model Controller for a Real Time Nonlinear Process. *Indian Journal of Science and Technology, 8*(19), 1–6. doi:10.17485/ijst/2017/v10i19/91682

Chandra, S. (2001). Transvaginal ultrasound and digital examination in predicting successful labor induction. *Obstetrics and Gynecology, 98*(1), 2–6. PMID:11430948

Chandy, T.W. & Mcliod, J. B. (1960). On a functional equation. *Proc. Edinburgh Maths, 43,* 7-8.

Chang, B. (2019). Reflection in learning. *Online Learning : the Official Journal of the Online Learning Consortium, 23*(1), 95–110. doi:10.24059/olj.v23i1.1447

Chassignol, M., Khoroshavin, A., Klimova, A., & Bilyatdinova, A. (2018). Artificial Intelligence trends in education: A narrative overview. *Procedia Computer Science, 136,* 16–24. doi:10.1016/j.procs.2018.08.233

Chen, M. S., & Tsai, Y. L. (2007). The Research of Usability in Elder Care Centers' Bathroom. In 會議名稱: *The International Conference on Kansei Engineering and Emotion Research.*

Chensue, S. W., & Ward, P. A. (1990). Inflammation. In I. Damjanov & J. Linder (Eds.), *Anderson's Pathology* (10th ed., pp. 387–413s). Mosby Year Book.

Chen, T. H., Wu, P. H., & Chiou, Y. C. (2004). An early fire-detection method based on image processing. In *2004 International Conference on Image Processing, 2004. ICIP'04.* (Vol. 3, pp. 1707-1710). IEEE. 10.1109/ICIP.2004.1421401

Chen, X., Xie, H., & Hwang, G. J. (2020). A multi-perspective study on artificial intelligence in education: Grants, conferences, journals, software tools, institutions, and researchers. *Computers and Education: Artificial Intelligence, 1,* 100005. doi:10.1016/j.caeai.2020.100005

Chen, Y.-S., Juang, T.-Y., Lin, Y.-W., & Tsai, I.-C. (2010). A low propagation delay multi-path routing protocol for subacquatic sensor networks. *Journal of Internet Technology, 11*(2), 153–165.

Chen, Z., Zhang, J., & Tao, D. (2021). Recursive context routing for object detection. *International Journal of Computer Vision, 129*(1), 142–160. doi:10.100711263-020-01370-7

Chhaya, K., Khanzode, A., & Sarode, R. D. (n.d.-a). *Advantages And Disadvantages Of Artificial Intelligence And Machine Learning: A Literature Review.* IAEME. http://www.iaeme.com/IJLIS/index.asp30http://www.iaeme.com/IJLIS/issues.asp?JType=IJLIS&VType=9&IType=1JournalImpactFactor

Chhaya, K., Khanzode, A., & Sarode, R. D. (n.d.-b). *Advantages And Disadvantages Of Artificial Intelligence And Machine Learning: A Literature Review.* IAEME. http://www.iaeme.com/IJLIS/index.asp30http://www.iaeme.com/IJLIS/issues.asp?JType=IJLIS&VType=9&IType=1JournalImpactFactor

Chiang, C. Y., Barnes, C., Angelov, P., & Jiang, R. (2020). Deep Learning-Based Automated Forest Health Diagnosis From Aerial Images. *IEEE Access : Practical Innovations, Open Solutions, 8,* 144064–144076. doi:10.1109/ACCESS.2020.3012417

Chino, D. Y., Avalhais, L. P., Rodrigues, J. F., & Traina, A. J. (2015). Bowfire: detection of fire in still images by integrating pixel color and texture analysis. In *2015 28th SIBGRAPI conference on graphics, patterns and images* (pp. 95-102). IEEE. 10.1109/SIBGRAPI.2015.19

Chitalapudi, N., Battineni, G., & Amenta, F. (2021). Sentimental Analysis of COVID -19 Tweets Using Deep Learning Models. *Infectious Disease Reports*, *13*(2), 329–339. doi:10.3390/idr13020032 PMID:33916139

Chitra, S., Kumaratharan, N., & Ramesh, S. (2018). Enhanced brain image retrieval using carrier frequency offset compensated orthogonal frequency division multiplexing for telemedicine applications. *International Journal of Imaging Systems and Technology*, *28*(3), 186–195. doi:10.1002/ima.22269

Choi, M. (2016). A concept analysis of digital citizenship for democratic citizenship education in the internet age. *Theory and Research in Social Education*, *44*(4), 565–607. doi:10.1080/00933104.2016.1210549

Chopra, P., Junath, N., Singh, S. K., Khan, S., Sugumar, R., & Bhowmick, M. (2022). Cyclic GAN model to classify breast cancer data for pathological healthcare task. *BioMed Research International*, *6336700*, 1–12. doi:10.1155/2022/6336700 PMID:35909482

Christauskas, C., Miseviciene, R., Driscoll, A., Daugelaite, J., Sleator, R. D., Heupel, T., & Schmitz, S. (2016). Overview of business innovations and research opportunities in blockchain and introduction to the special issue. *International Journal of Production Economics*, *2*(1).

Chuang, C. C., Shiesh, S. C., Chi, Ch., Tu, Y. F., Hor, L. I., Shieh, C. C., & Chen, M. F. (2006). Serum total antioxidant capacity reflects severity of illness in patients with severe sepsis. *Critical Care*, *10*(1), 36. doi:10.1186/cc4826 PMID:16507162

Chumbley, E. M., Stolfi, A., & McEachen, J. C. (2017). Risk factors for cervical pain in F-15C pilots. *Aerospace Medicine and Human Performance*, *88*(11), 1000–1007. doi:10.3357/AMHP.4848.2017 PMID:29046175

Chung, J., Gulcehre, C., Cho, K., & Bengio, Y. (2014). Empirical evaluation of gated recurrent neural networks on sequence modeling. In arXiv [cs.NE]. https://arxiv.org/abs/1412.3555

Chu, S. K. W., Reynolds, R. B., Tavares, N. J., Notari, M., & Lee, C. W. Y. (2021). *21st century skills development through inquiry-based learning from theory to practice*. Springer International Publishing.

Cirillo, S., Polese, G., Salerno, D., Simone, B., & Solimando, G. (2023). Towards Flexible Voice Assistants: Evaluating Privacy and Security Needs in IoT-enabled Smart Homes. *FMDB Transactions on Sustainable Computer Letters*, *1*(1), 25–32.

Cook, R. T. A. (1974). Pustules on wood as sources of inoculum in apple scab and their response to chemical treatments. *Annals of Applied Biology*, *77*(1), 1–9. doi:10.1111/j.1744-7348.1974.tb01381.x

Coronado Mondragon, A. E., Coronado Mondragon, C. E., & Coronado, E. S. (2021). Managing the food supply chain in the age of digitalisation: A conceptual approach in the fisheries sector. *Production Planning and Control*, *32*(3), 242–255. doi:10.1080/09537287.2020.1733123

Coşkun, M., Yildirim, Ö., Uçar, A., & Demir, Y. (2017). An overview of popular deep learning methods. *European Journal of Technique*, *7*(2), 165–176. doi:10.23884/ejt.2017.7.2.11

Coslor, C. C., Sundin, G. W., & Wise, J. C. (2019). The efficacy of trunk injections of emamectin benzoate and phosphorous acid for control of obliquebanded leafroller and apple scab on semi-dwarf apple. *Crop Protection (Guildford, Surrey)*, *118*, 44–49. doi:10.1016/j.cropro.2018.12.012

Coutinho, R. W. L., Vieira, L. F. M., & Loureiro, A. A. F. (2013). DCR: Depth-Controlled Routing protocol for underwater sensor networks. *2013 IEEE Symposium on Computers and Communications (ISCC)*. IEEE. 10.1109/ISCC.2013.6754988

COVID-19 pandemic in India . (2020). Wikipedia. https://en.Wikipedia.org/wiki/COVID-19 .

Critchlow, A. J. (1985). *Introduction to robotics*. MacMillan Press Ltd.

Crosse, J. E., Garrett, C. M. E., & Burchill, R. T. (1968). Changes in the microbial population of apple leaves associated with the inhibition of the perfect stage of *Venturia inequalis* after urea treatment. *Annals of Applied Biology, 61*(2), 203–216. doi:10.1111/j.1744-7348.1968.tb04526.x

Cui, L., Gao, M., Dai, J., & Mou, J. (2021). Improving supply chain collaboration through operational excel-lence approaches: an IoT perspective. *Industrial Management and Data Systems*. Emerald Group Publishing Ltd.

Cui, Z., Ke, R., Pu, Z., & Wang, Y. (2018). Deep bidirectional and unidirectional LSTM recurrent neural network for network-wide traffic speed prediction. In arXiv [cs.LG]. https://arxiv.org/abs/1801.02143

Cui, F. (2020). Deploy and integrate smart sensors with IoT devices detecting fire disasters in huge forest environments. *Computer Communications, 150*, 818–827. doi:10.1016/j.comcom.2019.11.051

Cui, J.-H., Kong, J., Gerla, M., & Zhou, S. (2006). The challenges of building mobile subacquatic wireless networks for aquatic applications. *Network (Bristol, England), 20*(3), 12–18.

Da Silva Coqueiro, R., Barbosa, A. R., & Borgatto, A. F. (2009). Anthropometric measurements in the elderly of Havana, Cuba: Age and sex differences. *Nutrition (Burbank, Los Angeles County, Calif.), 25*(1), 33–39. doi:10.1016/j.nut.2008.07.007 PMID:18834720

Das, S., & Dutta, A. (2021). Characterizing public emotions and sentiments in COVID-19 environment: A case study of India. *Journal of Human Behavior in the Social Environment, 31*(1–4), 154–167. doi:10.1080/10911359.2020.1781015

Dawal, S. Z. M., Ismail, Z., Yusuf, K., Abdul-Rashid, S. H., Shalahim, N. S. M., Abdullah, N. S., & Kamil, N. S. M. (2015). Determination of the significant anthropometry dimensions for user-friendly designs of domestic furniture and appliances-Experience from a study in Malaysia. *Measurement, 59*, 205–215. doi:10.1016/j.measurement.2014.09.030

De Vass, T., Shee, H., & Miah, S. J. (2018). The effect of "Internet of Things" on supply chain integration and performance: An organisational capability perspective. *AJIS. Australasian Journal of Information Systems, 22*. doi:10.3127/ajis.v22i0.1734

De Vass, T., Shee, H., & Miah, S. J. (2021). Iot in supply chain management: A narrative on retail sector sustainability. *International Journal of Logistics, 24*(6), 605–624. doi:10.1080/13675567.2020.1787970

Deepa, B., Gayathiridevi, K., Chakravarthi, M., Shajahan, A., & Sree, S. (2022). Slow evaporation technique to grow 3 - Amino benzene sulfonic acid single crystal for Non-Linear optical (NLO) transmission. *Materials Today: Proceedings, 62*(4), 2119–2123. doi:10.1016/j.matpr.2022.03.045

Deepak Kumar Jain, P., Boyapati, J., & Venkatesh, M. (2022). An Intelligent Cognitive-Inspired Computing with Big Data Analytics Framework for Sentiment Analysis and Classification," Information Processing and Management. *Information Processing & Management*, 1–4.

Density-based algorithm for clustering data - MATLAB . (2021). Mathworks. https://www.mathworks.com/help/radar/ref/clusterdbscan-system-object.html

Derindere Köseoğlu, S., Ead, W. M., & Abbassy, M. M. (2022). Basics of Financial Data Analytics. In *Financial Data Analytics* (pp. 23–57). Springer International Publishing. doi:10.1007/978-3-030-83799-0_2

Devi, A., & Nayyar, A. (2021). *Evaluation of Geotagging Twitter Data Using Sentiment Analysis During COVID-19*. Springer.

Devi, R. D., Sreevalli, P., & Prathyusha, M. (2020). *Prediction of Diseases using Random Forest classification algorithm.* Zeichen Journal.

Devi, V., & Sharma, A. (2022). Sentiment analysis approaches, types, challenges, and applications: An exploratory analysis. *2022 Seventh International Conference on Parallel, Distributed and Grid Computing (PDGC).* IEEE. 10.1109/PDGC56933.2022.10053180

Dey, N. C., Sinha, D., & Dey, P. K. (1995). Text book of Pathology. Calcutta: New Central Book Agency (Pvt) Limited.

Dhanush, S., Mohanraj, S. C., Sruthi, V. S., Cloudin, S., & Joseph, F. J. (2022). CODEDJ-Private Permissioned Blockchain Based Digital Wallet with Enhanced Security. In *IEEE International Conference on Bio-Neuro Informatics Models and Algorithms.* IEEE.

Dietterich, T. G. (1997). Machine-Learning Research. *AI Magazine, 18*(4), 97–97. doi:10.1609/AIMAG.V18I4.1324

Domingo, M. C., & Prior, R. (2007). A distributed clustering scheme for subacquatic wireless sensor networks. in personal, indoor and mobile radio communications. In *Proceedings of the IEEE 18th International Symposium on PIMRC.*

Doss, R., Gupta, S., Chakravarthi, M. K., Channi, H. K., Koti, A. V., & Singh, P. (2022). Understand the application of efficient green cloud computing through the micro smart grid in order to power internet data centers. 2022 2nd International Conference on Advance Computing and Innovative Technologies in Engineering (ICACITE).

Dwivedi, P. P., & Sharma, D. K. (2021). Lower and Upper Bounds for 'Useful' Renyi Information Rate. Advances in Computing and Data Sciences. ICACDS 2021. Communications in Computer and Information Science (Vol. 1441). Springer. doi:10.1007/978-3-030-88244-0_26

Ead, W. M., & Abbassy, M. M. (2021). IoT based on plant diseases detection and classification. *2021 7th International Conference on Advanced Computing and Communication Systems (ICACCS).* IEEE.

Ead, W. M., & Abbassy, M. M. (2022). A general cyber hygiene approach for financial analytical environment. In *Financial Data Analytics* (pp. 369–384). Springer International Publishing. doi:10.1007/978-3-030-83799-0_13

Ead, W., Emad, & Abbassy, M. M. (2021). A general framework information loss of utility-based anonymization in data publishing. *Turkish Journal of Computer and Mathematics Education, 12*(5), 1450–1456. doi:10.17762/turcomat.v12i5.2102

Ead, W., & Abbassy, M. (2018). Intelligent systems of machine learning approaches for developing E-services portals. *EAI Endorsed Transactions on Energy Web, 167292,* 167292. Advance online publication. doi:10.4108/eai.2-12-2020.167292

Ekman, P., & Friesen, W. (1978). *A technique for the measurement of facial movement.* Consulting Psychologists Press.

Elewa, A., Anber, N., & Zaki, M.E., El, Deek, A.B. (2015). Evaluation of Soluble E-Selectin and Total Antioxidant Capacity as Prognostic Biomarkers of Sepsis in Children. *International Journal of Current Microbiology and Applied Sciences, 4*(11), 665–673.

El-Farrash, R. A., Ismail, E. A. R., & Nada, A. S. (2012). Cord blood iron profile and breast milk micronutrients in maternal iron deficiency anemia. *Pediatric Blood & Cancer, 58*(2), 233–238. doi:10.1002/pbc.23184 PMID:21548016

Elghorori, M. R. M., Hassan, I., Dartey, W., & Abdel-Aziz, E. (2006). A way to lend objectivity to Bishop score. Journal of Obstetrics and Gynaecology. *Journal of Obstetrics & Gynaecology, 26*(4), 311–316. doi:10.1080/01443610600594922

Elkin, M., Sullivan, A., & Bers, M. U. (2018). Books, butterflies, and 'bots: Integrating engineering and robotics into early childhood curricula. *Early engineering learning,* 225-248.

Emil, S., & Cress, C. (2014). Faculty perspectives on programme curricular assessment: Individual and institutional characteristics that influence participation engagement. *Assessment & Evaluation in Higher Education*, *39*(5), 531–552. doi:10.1080/02602938.2013.855998

Erickson, R. (2020). *Technology challenges for smart Military Bases*. Aximgeo. https://www.aximgeo.com/blog/technology-challenges-for-smart-military-bases

Etzioni, A., & Etzioni, O. (2017). Incorporating Ethics into Artificial Intelligence. *The Journal of Ethics*, *21*(4), 403–418. doi:10.100710892-017-9252-2

Evolving artificial intelligence . (n.d.). eLibrary. https://www.elibrary.ru/item.asp?id=5780219

Fabela, O., Patil, S., Chintamani, S., & Dennis, B. H. (2017). *Estimation of effective thermal conductivity of porous media utilizing inverse heat transfer analysis on cylindrical configuration* (Vol. 8). Heat Transfer and Thermal Engineering. doi:10.1115/IMECE2017-71559

Facchinetti, F., Gandolfi, A., Longo, M., & Volpe, A. (1998). Serum nitrites predict the response to prostaglandin-induced delivery at term. *Journal of the Society for Gynecologic Investigation*, *5*(3), 140–143. doi:10.1016/S1071-5576(97)00117-2 PMID:9614643

Fan, J., & Pan, J. (2020). *Contemporary Experimental Design, Multivariate Analysis and Data Mining*. Springer International Publishing. doi:10.1007/978-3-030-46161-4

Fan, S. H., Ali, N. A., & Basri, D. F. (2014). Evaluation of analgesic activity of the methanol extract from the galls of Quercus infectoria (Olivier) in rats. *Evidence-Based Complementary and Alternative Medicine*, 2014. PMID:25254062

Fan, Y., Zhang, L., Lin, T., & Xu, B. (2018). Pressure sensing system for pilot masks based on MEMS pressure sensor and LabVIEW. *Measurement*, *129*, 159–166.

Fazil, M., Khan, S., Albahlal, B. M., Alotaibi, R. M., Siddiqui, T., & Shah, M. A. (2023). Attentional Multi-Channel Convolution With Bidirectional LSTM Cell Toward Hate Speech Prediction. *IEEE Access : Practical Innovations, Open Solutions*, *11*, 16801–16811. doi:10.1109/ACCESS.2023.3246388

Felix, E. A., & Lee, S. P. (2017). Integrated approach to software defect prediction. *IEEE Access : Practical Innovations, Open Solutions*, *5*, 21524–21547. doi:10.1109/ACCESS.2017.2759180

Feng, H., Wang, X., Duan, Y., Zhang, J., & Zhang, X. (2020). Applying blockchain technology to improve agri-food traceability: A review of development methods, benefits and challenges. *Journal of Cleaner Production*, *260*(121031), 121031. doi:10.1016/j.jclepro.2020.121031

Fernandes, P., Martens, E., & Pereira, D. (2017). Nature nurtures the design of new semi- synthetic macrolide antibiotics. *The Journal of Antibiotics*, *70*(5), 527–533. doi:10.1038/ja.2016.137 PMID:27899792

Fernie, G. (1994). Technology to assist elderly people's safe mobility. *Experimental Aging Research*, *20*(3), 219–228. doi:10.1080/03610739408253968 PMID:7957484

Flint, S. W., Piotrkowicz, A., & Watts, K. (2022). Use of Artificial Intelligence to understand adults' thoughts and behaviours relating to COVID-19. *Perspectives in Public Health*, *142*(3), 167–174. doi:10.1177/1757913920979332 PMID:33472547

Forsyth, D. & Ponce, J. (2003). *Computer vision : a modern approach.*

Fosch-Villaronga, E., Van der Hof, S., Lutz, C., & Tamò-Larrieux, A. (2021). Toy story or children story? Putting children and their rights at the forefront of the artificial intelligence revolution. *AI & Society*, 1–20. PMID:34642550

Friedman, E. A. (1967). *Pre labor status evaluation 2nd Weighted score.* 29.

Galley, H. F. (2011). Oxidative stress and mitochondrial dysfunction in sepsis. *British Journal of Anaesthesia, 107*(1), 57–64. doi:10.1093/bja/aer093 PMID:21596843

Gao, L.-Q., Berrie, A., Yang, J.-R., & Xu, X.-M. (2009). Within- and between-orchard variability in the sensitivity of *Venturia inaequalis* to myclobutanil, a DMI fungicide, in the UK. *Pest Management Science, 65*(11), 1241–1249. doi:10.1002/ps.1816 PMID:19606427

Gao, Y., Zhang, L., Zhao, X., & Lu, H. (2018). Traffic monitoring based on machine learning algorithms: A review. *IEEE Access : Practical Innovations, Open Solutions, 7*, 18362–18377.

Garcia, E., Jimenez, M. A., de Santos, P. G., & Armada, M. (2007). The evolution of robotics research. *IEEE Robotics & Automation Magazine, 14*(1), 90–103. doi:10.1109/MRA.2007.339608

Garg, A., Ghosh, A., & Chakrabarti, P. (2017). Gain and bandwidth modification of microstrip patch antenna using DGS. In *Proc. International Conference on Innovations in Control, Communication and Information Systems (ICICCI-2017).* India.

Garzon, S., Cacciato, P. M., Certelli, C., Salvaggio, C., Magliarditi, M., & Rizzo, G. (2020). Iron deficiency anemia in pregnancy: Novel approaches for an old problem. *Oman Medical Journal, 35*(5), e166. doi:10.5001/omj.2020.108 PMID:32953141

Gayakwad, M., Patil, S., Joshi, R., Gonge, S., & Pande, S. D. (2022). Credibility Evaluation of User-Generated Content Using Novel Multinomial Classification Technique. *International Journal on Recent and Innovation Trends in Computing and Communication, 10*(2s), 151–157. doi:10.17762/ijritcc.v10i2s.5922

Gehlot, A., Rajat Mohan, L., Gupta, A., Anandaram, H., Alanya-Beltran, J., & Kalyan Chakravarthi, M. (2022). Smart online oxygen supply management though internet of things (IoT). *2022 International Conference on Innovative Computing, Intelligent Communication and Smart Electrical Systems (ICSES).* IEEE. 10.1109/ICSES55317.2022.9914246

George, J., Abraham, A., & Ndakukamo, E. (2023). Futuristic applications of voice user interference on child language development. *Future Technology, 2*(3), 5–11. doi:10.55670/fpll.futech.2.3.2

Ghazalibiglar, H. (2014). *Biocontrol of Black rot of Brassicas.* Lincoln University.

Gillio, S., Parasco, A., Forester, K., Bellahsene, T., Berman, K., Fernandez, C., & Tourso, A. (2019). *Technology and its Impact on the Individual.*

Glenn, D. E. A. (2022). *Social Emotional Learning: Teachers' Perceptions and Understandings regarding the Five Social Emotional Learning Competencies* [Doctoral dissertation, College of Saint Elizabeth].

Goldsmith, J., & Burton, E. (2017). Why Teaching Ethics to AI Practitioners Is Important. *Proceedings of the AAAI Conference on Artificial Intelligence, 31*(1), 110–114. doi:10.1609/aaai.v31i1.11139

Gomoll, A., Hmelo-Silver, C. E., & Šabanović, S. (2022). Co-constructing professional vision: Teacher and researcher learning in co-design. *Cognition and Instruction, 40*(1), 7–26. doi:10.1080/07370008.2021.2010210

Gonen, R., Degani, S., & Ron, A. (1998). Prediction of successful induction of labor: Comparison of transvaginal ultrasonography and the Bishop score. *European Journal of Ultrasound, 7*(3), 183–187. doi:10.1016/S0929-8266(98)00042-1 PMID:9700213

Gosavi, P.A., Jaju, J.B., Ubale, V.M., Pawar, G.R., Dharmadhikari, S.C. (2015). *Study of evaluation of anti-inflammatory activity of macrolide antibiotics in rats: an experimental study.*

Gowtham, S., Ch, T., Kumar, N. S. M. P., Devi, M., Chakravarthi, S., Kumar, R., & Kumar, K. (2022). A Survey on Additively Manufactured Nanocomposite Biomaterial for Orthopaedic Applications. *Journal of Nanomaterials, 2022*, 2022. doi:10.1155/2022/8998451

Grachev, S., Skobelev, P., Mayorov, I., & Simonova, E. (2020). Adaptive clustering through multi-agent technology: Development and perspectives. *Mathematics, 8*(10), 1664. doi:10.3390/math8101664

Green, K. L. (1972). The anti-inflammatory effect of catecholamines in the peritoneal cavity and hind paw of the mouse. *British Journal of Pharmacology, 45*(2), 322–332. doi:10.1111/j.1476-5381.1972.tb08086.x PMID:5048650

Greff, K., Srivastava, R. K., Koutnik, J., Steunebrink, B. R., & Schmidhuber, J. (2017). LSTM: A search space odyssey. *IEEE Transactions on Neural Networks and Learning Systems, 28*(10), 2222–2232. doi:10.1109/TNNLS.2016.2582924 PMID:27411231

Grégoire, M., Uhel, F., Lesouhaitier, M., Gacouin, A., Guirriec, M., Mourcin, F., Dumontet, E., Chalin, A., Samson, M., Berthelot, L.-L., Tissot, A., Kerjouan, M., Jouneau, S., Le Tulzo, Y., Tarte, K., Zmijewski, J. W., & Tadié, J.-M. (2018). Impaired efferocytosis and neutrophil extracellular trap clearance by macrophages in ARDS. *The European Respiratory Journal, 52*(2), 1702590. doi:10.1183/13993003.02590-2017 PMID:29946009

Greiner, C., Jovy-Klein, F., & Peisl, T. (2021). AI as co-workers: An explorative research on technology acceptance based on the revised Bloom taxonomy. In *Proceedings of the Future Technologies Conference (FTC) 2020, Volume 1* (pp. 27-35). Springer International Publishing.

Grimus, M. (2020). Emerging technologies: Impacting learning, pedagogy and curriculum development. *Emerging technologies and pedagogies in the curriculum*, 127-151.

Gudavalli, N., & Vagvala, P. (2018). *Impact of Built-Environment on Fear of Falling (FOF) in Elderly. Humanizing work and work Environment (HWWE 2016)*. English.

Guidetti, A. (2023). *Artificial Intelligence as General Purpose Technology: An Empirical and Applied Analysis of Its Perception.*

Gulati, K., Saravana Kumar, S., Sarath Kumar Boddu, R., Sarvakar, K., Kumar Sharma, D., & Nomani, M. Z. M. (2022). Comparative analysis of machine learning-based classification models using sentiment classification of tweets related to COVID-19 pandemic. *Materials Today: Proceedings, 51*, 38–41. doi:10.1016/j.matpr.2021.04.364

Gulecha, V., Sivakumar, T., Upaganlawar, A., Mahajan, M., & Upasani, C. (2011). Screening of Ficus Religiosa leaves fraction for analgesic and anti-inflammatory activities. *Indian Journal of Pharmacology, 43*(6), 662. PMID:22144770

Gunturu, V., Bansal, V., Sathe, M., Kumar, A., Gehlot, A., & Pant, B. (2023). Wireless communications implementation using blockchain as well as distributed type of IoT. *2023 International Conference on Artificial Intelligence and Smart Communication (AISC)*. IEEE. 10.1109/AISC56616.2023.10085249

Gunzi, A. (2017). Vehicle Detection and Tracking using Computer Vision. *Chatbots Life*. https://chatbotslife.com/vehicle-detection-and-tracking-using-computer-vision-baea4df65906

Gupta, A., Kumar, R., Mohan, A., & Rahi, S. (2013). *Guidelines for Control of Iron Deficiency Anaemia*. Ministry of Health and Family Welfare, Government of India.

Gupta, S. K. (2009). *Drug screening methods (Pre-clinical evaluation of new drugs)* (2nd ed.). JAYPEE Brothers Medical Publishers Limited.

Gupta, S., Gill, J. K., & Bal, S. B. (2017). A comparative study on reasons of home accidents amongst elederly of rural and urban households of Ludhiana district. *Advance Research Journal of Social Science*, 8(2), 316–322. doi:10.15740/HAS/ARJSS/8.2/316-322

Hamet, P., & Tremblay, J. (2017). Artificial intelligence in medicine. *Metabolism: Clinical and Experimental*, 69, S36–S40. doi:10.1016/j.metabol.2017.01.011 PMID:28126242

Hamsagayathri, P., & Vigneshwaran, S. (2021). Symptoms based disease prediction using machine learning techniques. *2021 Third International Conference on Intelligent Communication Technologies and Virtual Mobile Networks (ICICV)*. IEEE. 10.1109/ICICV50876.2021.9388603

HamzahF.BintiC.LauH.NazriD. V.LigotG.Cheng Lianf TanM. K. B. M. (2020). Corono Tracker: Worldwide COVID-19 outbreak data analysis and prediction. Bull World Health Organ, 1–32.

Han, K., Cao, J.-H., Chen, S.-H., & Liu, W.-W. (2013). A software reliability prediction method based on software development process. *2013 International Conference on Quality, Reliability, Risk, Maintenance, and Safety Engineering (QR2MSE)*. IEEE.

Harden, R. M. (2001). AMEE Guide No. 21: Curriculum mapping: a tool for transparent and authentic teaching and learning. *Medical Teacher*, 23(2), 123–137. doi:10.1080/01421590120036547 PMID:11371288

Harsh and Mohan. (2010). Text book of Pathology (6 ed). New Delhi: JAYPEE Brothers Medical Publishers Private Limited.

Hasiholan, B. P., Susilowati, I. H., & Satrya, C. (2019). *The conformity of anthropometric measurements of bathroom and bedroom designs for.*

Hassan, M. M., Ahamad, T., & Das, S. (2022). An ensemble learning approach for chronic kidney disease prediction using different machine learning algorithms with correlation based feature selection. *2022 25th International Conference on Computer and Information Technology (ICCIT)*. IEEE.

Hennig, C., Meila, M., Murtagh, F., & Rocci, R. (Eds.). (2015). *Handbook of cluster analysis*. CRC press. doi:10.1201/b19706

He, X., Yan, S., Hu, Y., Niyogi, P., & Zhang, H. J. (2005). Face recognition using Laplacianfaces. *IEEE Transactions on Pattern Analysis and Machine Intelligence*, 27(3), 328–340. doi:10.1109/TPAMI.2005.55 PMID:15747789

Holzinger, A., Langs, G., Denk, H., Zatloukal, K., & Müller, H. (2019). Causability and explainability of artificial intelligence in medicine. *Wiley Interdisciplinary Reviews. Data Mining and Knowledge Discovery*, 9(4), e1312. doi:10.1002/widm.1312 PMID:32089788

Huang, C., Zhang, Z., Mao, B., & Yao, X. (2022). An Overview of Artificial Intelligence Ethics. *IEEE Transactions on Artificial Intelligence*. doi:10.1109/TAI.2022.3194503

Huang, H. H. C. 1997 – Biological control of soil-borne diseases in Canada, In: *International Symposium on Clean Agriculture*, Sapporo, OECD.

Huang, Y. J., Zhu, W. H., Wang, Y. X., Chen, W., & Chen, X. (2019). A motion planning and tracking framework for autonomous vehicles based on artificial potential field-elaborated. *IEEE Transactions on Industrial Electronics*, 66(7), 5581–5591. doi:10.1109/TIE.2019.2898599

Hu, C., Zhou, Y., Liu, C., & Kang, Y. (2018). Pentraxin-3, procalcitonin and lactate as prognostic markers in patients with sepsis and septic shock. *Oncotarget*, 9(4), 5125–5136. doi:10.18632/oncotarget.23701 PMID:29435167

Hu, H., Li, Z., Yan, J., Wang, X., Xiao, H., Duan, J., & Zheng, L. (2007). Anthropometric measurement of the Chinese elderly living in the Beijing area. *International Journal of Industrial Ergonomics*, *37*(4), 303–311. doi:10.1016/j.ergon.2006.11.006

Hung, B. T., & Chakrabarti, P. (2022). Parking lot occupancy detection using hybrid deep learning CNN-LSTM approach. In *Algorithms for Intelligent Systems* (pp. 501–509). Springer Nature Singapore.

Hung, M., Lauren, E., Hon, E. S., Birmingham, W. C., Xu, J., Su, S., Hon, S. D., Park, J., Dang, P., & Lipsky, M. S. (2020). Social network analysis of COVID-19 sentiments: Application of artificial intelligence. *Journal of Medical Internet Research*, *22*(8), e22590. doi:10.2196/22590 PMID:32750001

Hunter, J. E., Abawi, G. S., & Becker, R. F. (1975). – Observation on the source and spread of *Xanthomonas campestris* in epidemic of black rot in New York. *The Plant Disease Reporter*, *59*, 384–387.

Hunter, L. D. (1975). Phloridzin and apple scab. *Phytochemistry*, *14*(7), 1519–1522. doi:10.1016/0031-9422(75)85343-X

Hurtado-Romero, A., Del Toro-Barbosa, M., Gradilla-Hernández, M. S., Garcia-Amezquita, L. E., & García-Cayuela, T. (2021). Probiotic properties, prebiotic fermentability, and GABA-producing capacity of microorganisms isolated from Mexican milk Kefir grains: A clustering evaluation for functional dairy food applications. *Foods*, *10*(10), 2275. doi:10.3390/foods10102275 PMID:34681324

Hutton, K. E., & Burchill, R. T. (1965). The effect of some fungicides and herbicides on ascospore production of *Venturia inaequalis* (Cke.) Wint. *Annals of Applied Biology*, *56*(2), 279–284. doi:10.1111/j.1744-7348.1965.tb01236.x

Hu, Y., Zhan, J., Zhou, G., Chen, A., Cai, W., Guo, K., Hu, Y., & Li, L. (2022). Fast forest fire smoke detection using MVMNet. *Knowledge-Based Systems*, *241*, 108219. doi:10.1016/j.knosys.2022.108219

Ianaro, A., Ialenti, A., Maffia, P., Sautebin, L., Rombolà, L., & Carnuccio, R. (2000). Anti-inflammatory activity of macrolide antibiotics. *The Journal of Pharmacology and Experimental Therapeutics*, *292*(1), 156–163. PMID:10604943

Ianni, M., Masciari, E., Mazzeo, G. M., Mezzanzanica, M., & Zaniolo, C. (2020). Fast and effective Big Data exploration by clustering. *Future Generation Computer Systems*, *2020*, 84–94. doi:10.1016/j.future.2019.07.077

Iivari, N., Sharma, S., & Ventä-Olkkonen, L. (2020). Digital transformation of everyday life–How COVID-19 pandemic transformed the basic education of the young generation and why information management research should care? *International Journal of Information Management*, *55*, 102183. doi:10.1016/j.ijinfomgt.2020.102183 PMID:32836640

Imran, A. S., Daudpota, S. M., Kastrati, Z., & Batra, R. (2020). Cross-cultural polarity and emotion detection using sentiment analysis and deep learning on COVID-19 related tweets. *IEEE Access : Practical Innovations, Open Solutions*, *8*, 181074–181090. doi:10.1109/ACCESS.2020.3027350 PMID:34812358

Indrakumari, R., Poongodi, T., & Jena, S. (2020). Heart Disease Prediction using Exploratory Data Analysis. In *International Conference on Smart Sustainable Intelligent Computing and Applications*. Elsevier. 10.1016/j.procs.2020.06.017

Isik, D. U., Kavurt, A. S., Aydemir, O., Baş, A. Y., & Demirel, N. (2020). Serum ischemia-modified albumin levels in neonatal sepsis and septic shock. *TürkKadınSağlığıveNeonatoloji Dergisi.*, *2*(1), 7–12.

Ivankova, G. V., Mochalina, E. P., & Goncharova, N. L. (2020). Internet of Things (IoT) in logistics. *IOP Conference Series. Materials Science and Engineering*, *940*(1), 012033. doi:10.1088/1757-899X/940/1/012033

Ivanovsky, L., Khryashchev, V., Lebedev, A., & Kosterin, I. (2017). Facial expression recognition algorithm based on deep convolutional neural network". In *21st Conference of Open Innovations Association*.

Iwamoto, S., Kumamoto, T., Azuma, E., Hirayama, M., Ito, M., Amano, K., Ido, M., & Komada, Y. (2011). The effect of azithromycin on the maturation and function of murine bone marrow-derived dendritic cells. *Clinical and Experimental Immunology*, *166*(3), 385–392. doi:10.1111/j.1365-2249.2011.04480.x PMID:22059997

Jain, A. K., Misra, T., Tyagi, N., Suresh Kumar, M. V., & Pant, B. (2022). A Comparative Study on Cyber security Technology in Big data Cloud Computing Environment. *2022 5th International Conference on Contemporary Computing and Informatics (IC3I)*. IEEE.

Jain, A. K., Misra, T., Tyagi, N., Suresh Kumar, M. V., & Pant, B. (2022a). A Comparative Study on Cyber security Technology in Big data Cloud Computing Environment. *2022 5th International Conference on Contemporary Computing and Informatics (IC3I)*. IEEE.

Jain, A. K., Ross, D. S., & Babu, M. K. Dharamvir, Uike, D., & Gangodkar, D. (2022b). Cloud computing applications for protecting the information of healthcare department using smart internet of things appliance. *2022 5th International Conference on Contemporary Computing and Informatics (IC3I)*. IEEE.

Jain, A. K., Ross, D. S., Babu, M. K., Dharamvir, U. D., & Gangodkar, D. (2022). Cloud computing applications for protecting the information of healthcare department using smart internet of things appliance. *2022 5th International Conference on Contemporary Computing and Informatics (IC3I)*. IEEE.

Jain, B., Sirdeshpande, S., Gowtham, M. S., Josephson, P. J., Chakravarthi, M. K., & Pant, B. (2022). Exploratory data analysis based on micro grids generation for control communication and monitoring via wireless sensor network. *2022 2nd International Conference on Advance Computing and Innovative Technologies in Engineering (ICACITE)*. IEEE.

Jain, R., Chakravarthi, M. K., Kumar, P. K., Hemakesavulu, O., Ramirez-Asis, E., Pelaez-Diaz, G., & Mahaveerakannan, R. (2022). Internet of Things-based smart vehicles design of bio-inspired algorithms using artificial intelligence charging system. *Nonlinear Engineering*, *11*(1), 582–589. doi:10.1515/nleng-2022-0242

Jain, V., Al Ayub Ahmed, A., Chaudhary, V., Saxena, D., Subramanian, M., & Mohiddin, M. K. (2023). Role of data mining in detecting theft and making effective impact on performance management. In *Smart Innovation, Systems and Technologies* (pp. 425–433). Springer Nature Singapore.

Jaiswal, A., & Raju, S. (2020). Facial Emotion Detection Using Deep Learning". In *2020 International Conference for Emerging Technology (INCET)* (pp. 1–5).

James, G. M., & Sujatha, S. (2021). Categorising Apple Fruit Diseases Employing Hybrid Neural Clustering Classifier. *Materials Today: Proceedings*. doi:10.1016/j.matpr.2020.12.139

Jayalakshmi, J., & Ramesh, S. (2020). Compact fractal wearable antenna for wireless body area communications. *Telecommunications and Radio Engineering*, *79*(1), 71–80. doi:10.1615/TelecomRadEng.v79.i1.70

Jayanthi, R., & Florence, L. (2019). Software defect prediction techniques using metrics based on neural network classifiers. *Cluster Computing*, *22*(1), 77–88. doi:10.100710586-018-1730-1

Jeba, J. A., Bose, S. R., & Boina, R. (2023). Exploring Hybrid Multi-View Multimodal for Natural Language Emotion Recognition Using Multi-Source Information Learning Model. *FMDB Transactions on Sustainable Computer Letters*, *1*(1), 12–24.

Jeganathan, J., Vashist, S., Nirmala, G., & Deep, R. (2023). A Cross Sectional Study on Anxiety and Depression Among Patients with Alcohol Withdrawal Syndrome. *FMDB Transactions on Sustainable Health Science Letters*, *1*(1), 31–40.

Jeger, M. J., Swait, A. A. J., & Butt, D. J. (1982). Overwintering of *Venturia inaequalis*, the causal agent of apple scab, on different cultivars. *Annals of Applied Biology, 100*, 91–98.

Jeger, M. J. (1981). Disease measurement in a study of apple scab epidemics. *Annals of Applied Biology, 99*(1), 43–51. doi:10.1111/j.1744-7348.1981.tb05128.x

Jeger, M. J. (1984). Relating disease progress to cumulative numbers of trapped spores - apple powdery mildew and scab epidemics in sprayed and unsprayed orchard plots. *Plant Pathology, 33*(4), 517–523. doi:10.1111/j.1365-3059.1984. tb02876.x

Jeger, M. J., & Butt, D. J. (1983). Overwintering of *Venturia inaequalis* the causal agent of apple scab in relation to weather. *Annals of Applied Biology, 103*(2), 201–218. doi:10.1111/j.1744-7348.1983.tb02757.x

Jeger, M. J., & Butt, D. J. (1984). Management of orchard diseases in the United Kingdom. *Plant Protection Bulletin, 32*, 61–66.

Jekarl, D. W., Lee, S., Kim, M., Kim, Y., Woo, S. H., & Lee, W. J. (2019). Procalcitonin as a prognostic marker for sepsis based on Sepsis-3. *Journal of Clinical Laboratory Analysis, 33*(9), e22996. doi:10.1002/jcla.22996 PMID:31420921

Jiang, F., Jiang, Y., Zhi, H., Dong, Y., Li, H., Ma, S., Wang, Y., Dong, Q., Shen, H., & Wang, Y. (2017). Artificial intelligence in healthcare: Past, present and future. *Stroke and Vascular Neurology, 2*(4), 230–243. doi:10.1136vn-2017-000101 PMID:29507784

Jiang, H., Meng, X., Ma, J., Sun, X., Wang, Y., Hu, T., & Wang, S. (2021). Control effect of fungicide pyraclostrobin alternately applied with Bordeaux mixture against apple Glomerella leaf spot and its residue after preharvest application in China. *Crop Protection (Guildford, Surrey), 142*, 105489. doi:10.1016/j.cropro.2020.105489

Joachims, T. (1998). Text categorization with Support Vector Machines: Learning with many relevant features. [Berlin, Heidelberg: Springer Berlin Heidelberg.]. *Machine Learning, ECML-98*, 137–142.

Joe, F., Ravi, T., & Justus, J. (2011). Classification of correlated subspaces using HoVer representation of Census Data. *2011 International Conference on Emerging Trends in Electrical and Computer Technology*. IEEE.

Jolly, A., & Jindal, N. (2016). Birla sekaran, Dinesh," Transparent Proxy Cache server using Raspberry Pi. *Indian Journal of Science and Technology, 9*(44).

Jonassen, D. H. (2000). Toward a design theory of problem solving. *Educational Technology Research and Development, 48*(4), 63–85. doi:10.1007/BF02300500

Jones, K. S. (1994). Natural Language Processing: A Historical Review. Current Issues in Computational Linguistics: In Honour of Don Walker, 3–16. doi:10.1007/978-0-585-35958-8_1

Jordan, M. I., & Mitchell, T. M. (2015). Machine learning: Trends, perspectives, and prospects. *Science, 349*(6245), 255–260. doi:10.1126cience.aaa8415 PMID:26185243

Joseph, A. J. J., Joseph, F. J. J., Stanislaus, O., & Das, D. (2022). Classification methodologies in healthcare. In Evolving Predictive Analytics in Healthcare: New AI techniques for real-time interventions (pp. 55–73). doi:10.1049/PBHE043E_ch4

Joseph, F. J. J. (2019). Twitter based outcome predictions of 2019 Indian general elections using decision tree. *2019 4th International Conference on Information Technology (InCIT)*. IEEE.

Joseph, F. J. (2022). IoT Based Aquarium Water Quality Monitoring and Predictive Analytics Using Parameter Optimized Stack LSTM. In *2022 International Conference on Information Technology (InCIT)*. IEEE. 10.1109/InCIT56086.2022.10067725

Joseph, F. J. J. (2020). Effect of supervised learning methodologies in offline handwritten Thai character recognition. *International Journal of Information Technology : an Official Journal of Bharati Vidyapeeth's Institute of Computer Applications and Management, 12*(1), 57–64. doi:10.100741870-019-00366-y

Joseph, F. J. J., & Auwatanamongkol, S. (2016). A crowding multi-objective genetic algorithm for image parsing. *Neural Computing & Applications, 27*(8), 2217–2227. doi:10.100700521-015-2000-2

Józefowicz, R., Zaremba, W., & Sutskever, I. (2015). An Empirical Exploration of Recurrent Network Architectures. *International Conference on Machine Learning*, (pp. 2342–2350). IEEE.

Kakani, V., Nguyen, V. H., Kumar, B. P., Kim, H., & Pasupuleti, V. R. (2020). A critical review on computer vision and artificial intelligence in food industry. *Journal of Agriculture and Food Research, 2*, 100033. doi:10.1016/j.jafr.2020.100033

Kalyanakrishnan, S., Panicker, R. A., Natarajan, S., & Rao, S. (2018). Opportunities and Challenges for Artificial Intelligence in India. *AIES 2018 - Proceedings of the 2018 AAAI/ACM Conference on AI, Ethics, and Society*, 164–170. 10.1145/3278721.3278738

Kamran, M., Khan, H. U., Nisar, W., Farooq, M., & Rehman, S.-U. (2020). Blockchain and Internet of Things: A bibliometric study. *Computers & Electrical Engineering, 81*(106525), 106525. doi:10.1016/j.compeleceng.2019.106525

Kanade, T., Cohn, J., & Tian, Y. (2000). Comprehensive database for facial expression analysis". In *Proceedings Fourth IEEE International Conference on Automatic Face and Gesture Recognition*. 10.1109/AFGR.2000.840611

Kanjalkar, J., Kanjalkar, P., Aole, K., Ansari, A., Abak, H., & Tiwari, A. (2023a). Analysis of Machine Learning Algorithms for COVID Detection Using Deep Learning. *7th International Conference on Data Management, Analytics and Innovation*. Springer. 10.1007/978-981-99-1414-2_31

Kanjalkar, J., Kanjalkar, P., Deshmukh, T., Deshmukh, J., Dhamal, P., & Bhalerao, A. (2022). A novel system for AYUSH healthcare services using classification and regression. *International Journal on Recent and Innovation Trends in Computing and Communication, 10*(1s), 232–240. doi:10.17762/ijritcc.v10i1s.5830

Kanjalkar, P., Chinchole, P., Chitre, A., Kanjalkar, J., & Sharma, P. (2023b). Economical solution to automatic evaluation of an OMR sheet using image processing. In *Data Management, Analytics and Innovation* (pp. 665–683). Springer Nature Singapore. doi:10.1007/978-981-99-1414-2_48

Kant, K. (2021). *Housing for Elderly and Differently-Abled*. Notion Press.

Karpathy, A., Johnson, J., & Fei-Fei, L. (2015). Visualizing and understanding recurrent networks. In arXiv [cs.LG]. https://arxiv.org/abs/1506.02078

Kathial, K. (2018). Impact of demonetization on digital transactions in India. *Asian Journal of Management, 9*(1), 281. doi:10.5958/2321-5763.2018.00042.2

Kaur, A., Rana, A. C., Tiwari, V., Sharma, R., & Kumar, S. (2011). Review on ethanomedicinal and pharmacological properties of Ficus religiosa. *Journal of Applied Pharmaceutical Science, 1*(8), 6–11.

Kaur, M., Chauhan, A., Manzar, M. D., & Rajput, M. M. (2015). Maternal anaemia and neonatal outcome: A prospective study on urban pregnant women. *Journal of Clinical and Diagnostic Research : JCDR, 9*(12), QC04. doi:10.7860/JCDR/2015/14924.6985 PMID:26816949

Kayalvizhi, K., & Ramesh, S. (2020). Design and Analysis of Reactive Load Dipole Antenna using Genetic Algorithm Optimization. *Applied Computational Electromagnetics Society Journal, 35*(3), 279–287.

Kazmi, S. A., Gupta, A. K., Uddin, N., & Chauhan, Y. K. (2021). The imperative role of solar power assistance for embedded based climatic parameters measurement systems. In Applied Soft Computing and Embedded System Applications in Solar Energy (pp. 187–214). CRC Press. doi:10.1201/9781003121237-10

Kendall, D. G. (1964). – Functional equations in information theory. *Zeitschrift für Wahrscheinlichkeitstheorie und Verwandte Gebiete, 2*(3), 225–229. doi:10.1007/BF00533380

Kesidou, S., & Roseman, J. E. (2002). How well do middle school science programs measure up? Findings from Project 2061's curriculum review. *Journal of Research in Science Teaching, 39*(6), 522–549. doi:10.1002/tea.10035

Kewalramani, S., Kidman, G., & Palaiologou, I. (2021). Using Artificial Intelligence (AI)-interfaced robotic toys in early childhood settings: A case for children's inquiry literacy. *European Early Childhood Education Research Journal, 29*(5), 652–668. doi:10.1080/1350293X.2021.1968458

Khalifa, I., Abd Al-glil, H., & M. Abbassy, M. (2013). Mobile Hospitalization. *International Journal of Computer Applications, 80*(13), 18–23. doi:10.5120/13921-1822

Khalifa, I., Abd Al-glil, H., & M. Abbassy, M. (2014). Mobile Hospitalization for Kidney Transplantation. *International Journal of Computer Applications, 92*(6), 25–29. doi:10.5120/16014-5027

Khan, S. (2016). How Data Mining Can Help Curb City Crime. [IJCTA]. *International Journal of Control Theory and Applications, 9*(23), 483–488.

Khan, S. (2021a). Study Factors for Student Performance Applying Data Mining Regression Model Approach. *International Journal of Computer Science Network Security, 21*(2), 188–192.

Khan, S. (2021b). Data visualization to explore the countries dataset for pattern creation. [IJOE]. *International Journal of Online and Biomedical Engineering, 17*(13), 4–19. doi:10.3991/ijoe.v17i13.20167

Khater, W. S., Salah-Eldeen, N. N., Khater, M. S., & Saleh, A. N. (2016). Role of suPAR and lactic acid in diagnosing sepsis and predicting mortality in elderly patients. *European Journal of Microbiology & Immunology, 6*(3), 178–185. doi:10.1556/1886.2016.00011 PMID:27766166

Khinchin, A. I. (1957). *Mathematical Foundations of Information Theory*. Dover Publications.

Kim, B., & Lee, J. (2019). A video-based fire detection using deep learning models. *Applied Sciences (Basel, Switzerland), 9*(14), 2862. doi:10.3390/app9142862

Kim, S. W., Lee, J. G., Kim, J. W., Kim, S. W., & Lee, J. H. (2019). Breathing Monitoring System for High-Altitude Fighter Pilots. In *Proceedings of the 2019 International Conference on Information and Communication Technology Convergence (ICTC)* (pp. 951–954). Jeju Island, Korea (South).

Kivunja, C. (2014). Do You Want Your Students to Be Job-Ready with 21st Century Skills? Change Pedagogies: A Pedagogical Paradigm Shift from Vygotskyian Social Constructivism to Critical Thinking, Problem Solving and Siemens' Digital Connectivism. *International Journal of Higher Education, 3*(3), 81–91. doi:10.5430/ijhe.v3n3p81

Koksal, N., Harmanci, R., Çetinkaya, M., & Hacimustafaoglu, M. (2007). Role of procalcitonin and CRP in diagnosis and follow-up of neonatal sepsis. *The Turkish Journal of Pediatrics, 49*(1), 21. PMID:17479640

Kosarkar, N., Basuri, P., Karamore, P., Gawali, P., Badole, P., & Jumle, P. (2022). Disease Prediction using Machine Learning. *2022 10th International Conference on Emerging Trends in Engineering and Technology - Signal and Information Processing (ICETET-SIP-22)*. IEEE.

Kose, S. A. T. O. S. H. I. (2001). Design guidelines of dwellings for the ageing society: Japanese approach toward universal design. In *Proceedings of the CIB World Building Congress* (pp. 179-188). Springer.

Krishnan, S., & Geetha. (2019). Prediction of heart disease using machine learning algorithms. *2019 1st International Conference on Innovations in Information and Communication Technology (ICIICT)*. IEEE.

Kulkarni, J. B., Sheela, M., & Chetty, R. (2019). Depth Analysis of Single View Image Objects based on Object Detection and Focus Measure. *International Journal of Advanced Trends in Computer Science and Engineering*, *5*(8), 2608–2612. doi:10.30534/ijatcse/2019/112852019

Kulkarni, S., Gadkari, R., & Nagarkar, A. (2020). Risk factors for fear of falling in older adults in India. *Journal of Public Health (Berlin)*, *28*(2), 123–129. doi:10.100710389-019-01061-9

Kumar Jain, A. (2022a). Hybrid Cloud Computing: A Perspective. *International Journal of Engineering Research & Technology (Ahmedabad)*, *11*(10), 1–06.

Kumar Jain, A. (2022b). Multi-Cloud Computing & Why do we need to Embrace it. *International Journal of Engineering Research & Technology (Ahmedabad)*, *11*(09), 1–06.

Kumar Jain, A. (2022c). Overview of Serverless Architecture. *International Journal of Engineering Research & Technology (Ahmedabad)*, *11*(09), 1–06.

Kumar Patale, V., & Chakravarthi, M. K. (2014). RF Harvesting Circuitry for Ambient Backscatter Technology ". *International Journal of Applied Engineering Research: IJAER*, *9*(19), 5769–5778.

Kumar, K. S., Yadav, D., Joshi, S. K., Chakravarthi, M. K., Jain, A. K., & Tripathi, V. (2022). Blockchain technology with applications to distributed control and cooperative robotics. *2022 5th International Conference on Contemporary Computing and Informatics (IC3I)*.

Kumar, K. S., Yadav, D., Joshi, S. K., Chakravarthi, M. K., Jain, A. K., & Tripathi, V. (2022). Blockchain technology with applications to distributed control and cooperative robotics. *2022 5th International Conference on Contemporary Computing and Informatics (IC3I)*. IEEE.

Kumar, N., Kharkwal, N., Kohli, R., & Choudhary, S. (2016). Ethical aspects and future of artificial intelligence. *2016 1st International Conference on Innovation and Challenges in Cyber Security*, 111–114. 10.1109/ICICCS.2016.7542339

Kumar, P., Hati, A. S., Padmanaban, S., Leonowicz, Z., & Chakrabarti, P. (2020). Amalgamation of transfer learning and deep convolutional neural network for multiple fault detection in SCIM. *2020 IEEE International Conference on Environment and Electrical Engineering and 2020 IEEE Industrial and Commercial Power Systems Europe (EEEIC / I&CPS Europe)*. IEEE.

Kumar, P.A., & Anand, U. (2016). Multiple biomarkers to assess the pathophysiological state in critically Ill patients with sepsis. *Indian Journal of Clinical Biochemistry*, *31*(3), 310-4.

Kumar, S., Kumar, N. M. G., Geetha, B. T., Sangeetha, M., Chakravarthi, M. K., & Tripathi, V. (2022). Cluster, cloud, grid computing via network communication using control communication and monitoring of smart grid. *2022 2nd International Conference on Advance Computing and Innovative Technologies in Engineering (ICACITE)*. IEEE.

Kumar, A., Choudhury, R., & Yadav, S. (2018). A study of non-communicable diseases risk factors among the tribal population of Lefunga block, Tripura: Cross sectional study. *International Journal of Community Medicine and Public Health*, *5*(10), 4478–4484. doi:10.18203/2394-6040.ijcmph20183996

Kumar, R., Kapoor, N., & Singh, P. K. (2018). Development of a LabVIEW-Based Data Acquisition System using NI USB-6363 for Real-Time Signal Processing Applications. *Iranian Journal of Electrical and Computer Engineering*, *8*(2), 894–902. doi:10.11591/ijece.v8i2.pp894-902

Larose, D. T., & Larose, C. D. (2014). *Discovering knowledge in data: an introduction to data mining* (Vol. 4). John Wiley & Sons. doi:10.1002/9781118874059

Laurence, D. R., & Bacharach, A. L. (1964). *Evaluation of Drug Activities: Pharmacometrics* (Vol. 2). Academic Press Inc.

Leca, A., Rouby, F., Saudreau, M., & Lacointe, A. (2020). Apple leaf wettability variability as a function of genotype and apple scab susceptibility. *Scientia Horticulturae*, *260*, 108890. doi:10.1016/j.scienta.2019.108890

Lee, S. H., Lee, J. M., Kim, C. Y., Park, M. S., Park, B. H., Jung, W. J., & Chung, K. S. (2015). Prognostic implications of serum lipid metabolism over time during sepsis. *Intensive Care Medicine Experimental*, *3*(S1), A226. doi:10.1186/2197-425X-3-S1-A226 PMID:26351639

Lee, S., Oh, E., & Hong, G. R. S. (2018). Comparison of factors associated with fear of falling between older adults with and without a fall history. *International Journal of Environmental Research and Public Health*, *15*(5), 982. doi:10.3390/ijerph15050982 PMID:29757960

Lee, Y.-D., & Chung, W.-Y. (2009). Wireless sensor network based wearable smart shirt for ubiquitous health and activity monitoring. *Sensors and Actuators. B, Chemical*, *140*(2), 390–395. doi:10.1016/j.snb.2009.04.040

Lee, Y., & Shim, J. (2019). False positive decremented research for fire and smoke detection in surveillance camera using spatial and temporal features based on deep learning. *Electronics (Basel)*, *8*(10), 1167. doi:10.3390/electronics8101167

Li, J., & Oussalah, M. (2010). Automatic Face Emotion Recognition System. In *IEEE 9th International Conference on Cybernetic Intelligent Systems* (pp. 1–6). ieEE.

Liang, Q., & Cheng, X. (2009). Subacquatic acoustic sensor networks: Target size detection and performance analysis. *Ad Hoc Networks*, *7*(4), 803–808. doi:10.1016/j.adhoc.2008.07.008

Li, B. H., Yang, J. R., Li, B. D., & Xu, X. M. (2007). Incidence-density relationship of pear scab (*Venturia nashicola*) on fruits and leaves. *Plant Pathology*, *56*(1), 120–127. doi:10.1111/j.1365-3059.2006.01496.x

Li, B.-H., & Xu, X.-M. (2002). Infection and development of apple scab (*Venturia inaequalis*) on old leaves. *Journal of Phytopathology*, *150*(11-12), 687–691. doi:10.1046/j.1439-0434.2002.00824.x

Li, F., Fisher, K. J., Harmer, P., McAuley, E., & Wilson, N. L. (2003). Fear of falling in elderly persons: Association with falls, functional ability, and quality of life. *The Journals of Gerontology. Series B, Psychological Sciences and Social Sciences*, *58*(5), P283–P290. doi:10.1093/geronb/58.5.P283 PMID:14507935

Li, G., Wang, H., Wang, K., Wang, W., Dong, F., Qian, Y., & Shan, G. (2017). The association between smoking and blood pressure in men: A cross-sectional study. *BMC Public Health*, *17*(1), 797. doi:10.118612889-017-4802-x PMID:29017534

Li, H., Sun, J., Xu, Z., & Chen, L. (2017). Multimodal 2D+3D Facial Expression Recognition With Deep Fusion Convolutional Neural Network. *IEEE Transactions on Multimedia*, *19*(12), 2816–2831. doi:10.1109/TMM.2017.2713408

Lindsey, S., & Raghavendra, C. (2002). PEGASIS: Power- Efficient Gathering in Sensor Information Systems. *IEEE Aerospace Conference Proceedings*, (pp. 1125–1130). IEEE. 10.1109/AERO.2002.1035242

Lin, J., Wang, J., & Shao, L. (2019). Traffic monitoring with computer vision and machine learning. *Transportation Research Part C, Emerging Technologies*, *89*, 205–227.

Liu, F., Wang, Q., & Yan, X. (2019). An integrated radar and vehicle-to-vehicle communication system for longitudinal and lateral vehicle following. *IEEE Transactions on Intelligent Transportation Systems*, *21*(2), 707–717.

Liu, W., & Gao, Z. (2014). Study on IOT based architecture of logistics service supply chain. *International Journal of Grid and Distributed Computing*, *7*(1), 169–178. doi:10.14257/ijgdc.2014.7.1.15

Li, W., Zhang, Y., & Wong, K.-K. (2020). Traffic monitoring with intelligent video analysis: A survey. *Journal of Ambient Intelligence and Humanized Computing*, *11*(4), 1271–1284.

Li, Z., & Dajun, L. (2014). Design of a Data Acquisition System Using NI USB-6363 and LabVIEW for Structural Health Monitoring. *Journal of Sensors*, 1–8. doi:10.1155/2014/589249

Lo, C. T., & Wang, K. M. (2001). – Inoculum sources of black rot of wasabi, caused by *Phoma wasabiae*. *Plant Pathology Bulletin*, *10*, 88–92.

Lohit Ujjainiya, M., Chakravarthi, K., & Soni, A. (2014). Development and Implementation of Gesture Controlled Automatic Audio System. *International Journal of Computer Applications*, *106*(13), 25–28.

Lohith Ujjaniya, M. K. (2015). Raspberry - Pi based cost effective vehicle collision avoidance system using image processing. *Journal of Engineering and Applied Sciences (Asian Research Publishing Network)*, *10*(7), 3001–3005.

Long, D., & Magerko, B. (2020, April). What is AI literacy? Competencies and design considerations. In *Proceedings of the 2020 CHI conference on human factors in computing systems* (pp. 1-16). ACM. 10.1145/3313831.3376727

Lorenzen-Ewing, T.B. (2015). *Exploring physical and social environmental barriers and facilitators that affect older adults' fear of falling: A sample funding proposal.*

Lowensten, D. H. (2005). Pain: Pathophysiology and management. In : Fields HL, Martin JB edts Harrisons principles of internal medicine. Mc Graw Hills Companies.

Luckin, R., Holmes, W., Griffiths, M., & Forcier, L. B. (2016). *Intelligence unleashed: An argument for AI in education.*

Lu, D., & Teng, Q. (2012). A application of cloud computing and IOT in logistics. *Journal of Software Engineering and Applications*, *05*(12), 204–207. doi:10.4236/jsea.2012.512B039

Luke, A. (2008) Digital Innovation In Schooling: Policy Efficacy, Youth Cultures And Pedagogical Change. *Discussion Paper for Nordic Digital Learning Resources Study Meetings*. OECD.

Luna, L. C., Mariaono, R. L. R., & Souto-Mairo, M. A. (2002). – Production of a biocontrol agent for crucifers' black rot disease. *Brazilian Journal of Chemical Engineering*, *19*(2), 133–140. doi:10.1590/S0104-66322002000200007

Luo, Y. & Xu, X. (2021). Comparative Study of Deep learning models for anlyzing online restaurant reviews in the era of the COVID-19 pandemic. *INT.F. Hosp. Manag.*, *94*. https://doi.org/. doi:10.1016/j.iijhm.2020.102849

Lv, C., Hu, X., Sangiovanni-Vincentelli, A., Marina, C., Li, Y., & Cao, D. (2019). Driving-style-based co-design optimization of an automotive active suspension. *IEEE Transactions on Industrial Electronics*, *65*(4), 2965–2975. doi:10.1109/TIE.2018.2850031

Lv, C., Wang, H., Cao, D., Zhao, Y., Auger, J. D., Sullman, M., Matthias, R., Skrypchuk, L., & Mouzakitis, A. (2018). Characterization of driver neuromuscular dynamics for human-automation collaboration. *IEEE/ASME Transactions on Mechatronics*, *23*(4), 1814–1824. doi:10.1109/TMECH.2018.2812643

M, A., K, T., Munshi, Y, J., M, R., & M, S. (2019). Assessment of heavy metal contents in commercial feedstuffs and broiler (Gallus domesticus) meat and its impact on Swiss albino mice as an animal model. *Agricultural Science Digest - A Research Journal, (of)*. doi:10.18805/ag.D-4898

Machardy, W. E., & Jeger, M. J. (1982). An approach to integrate control measures for use in apple scab management programs. *Phytopathology*, *72*, 264–264.

MacHardy, W. E., & Jeger, M. J. (1983). Integrating control measures for the management of primary apple scab, *Venturia inaequalis* (Cke.) Wint. *Protection Ecology*, *5*, 103–125.

Maedche, A., Legner, C., Benlian, A., Berger, B., Gimpel, H., Hess, T., Hinz, O., Morana, S., & Söllner, M. (2019). AI-based digital assistants: Opportunities, threats, and research perspectives. *Business & Information Systems Engineering*, *61*(4), 535–544. doi:10.100712599-019-00600-8

Mahdi, J. G., Mahdi, A. J., & Bowen, I. D. (2006). The historical analysis of aspirin discovery, its relation to the willow tree and antiproliferative and anticancer potential. *Cell Proliferation*, *39*(2), 147–155. doi:10.1111/j.1365-2184.2006.00377.x PMID:16542349

Mahesha, C. R., Suprabha, R., Kumar, N. M., Kosanam, K., Anandaram, H., Ramana Murty Naidu, S. C. V., & Govindarajan, V. (2022). Effect of friction stir welding on the mechanical and microstructural behaviour of AA7075 aluminium alloy. *Advances in Materials Science and Engineering*, *2022*, 1–8. doi:10.1155/2022/2788479

Makhija, I. K., Sharma, I. P., & Khamar, D. (2010). Phytochemistry and pharmacological properties of Ficus religiosa: An overview. *Annals of Biological Research*, *1*(4), 171–180.

Maki, B. E., Holliday, P. J., & Topper, A. K. (1991). Fear of falling and postural performance in the elderly. *Journal of Gerontology*, *46*(4), M123–M131. doi:10.1093/geronj/46.4.M123 PMID:2071833

MalikS.BibiN.KhanS.SultanaR.RaufS. A. (2017). Mr Doc: A doctor appointment application system. Retrieved from https://arxiv.org/abs/1701.08786

Manavalan, E., & Jayakrishna, K. (2019). A review of Internet of Things (IoT) embedded sustainable supply chain for industry 4.0 requirements. *Computers & Industrial Engineering*, *127*, 925–953. doi:10.1016/j.cie.2018.11.030

Manjeshwar, A., & Agarwal, D. P. (2001). *TEEN: a routing protocol for enhanced efficiency in wireless sensor networks.*

Manvi, S. S., & Manjula, B. (2011). Issues in subacquatic acoustic sensor networks. *International Journal on Computer and Electrical Engineering*, *3*(1), 101–111.

María, J. J. L., Polo, O. C. C., & Elhadary, T. (2023). An Analysis of the Morality and Social Responsibility of Non-Profit Organizations. *FMDB Transactions on Sustainable Technoprise Letters*, *1*(1), 28–35.

Martínez-López, F. J., & Casillas, J. (2013). Artificial intelligence-based systems applied in industrial marketing: An historical overview, current and future insights. *Industrial Marketing Management*, *42*(4), 489–495. doi:10.1016/j.indmarman.2013.03.001

Massomo, S.M.S., Mabagala, R.B., Swai, I.S., Hockenhull, J., & Mortensen, C.N. 2003 – Evaluation of varietal resistance in cabbage against the black rot pathogen *Xanthomonas campestris* pv.*campestris* in Tanzania. *Crop Protection* *23*(4), 315–325. 29

Mccarthy, J. (2004). *What Is Artificial Intelligence?* Stanford. http://www-formal.stanford.edu/jmc/

McDermott, D. (1976). Artificial intelligence meets natural stupidity. *ACM SIGART Bulletin*, *57*(57), 4–9. doi:10.1145/1045339.1045340

Md Yunus, M., Ang, W. S., & Hashim, H. (2021). Factors affecting teaching English as a Second Language (TESL) postgraduate students' behavioural intention for online learning during the COVID-19 pandemic. *Sustainability (Basel)*, *13*(6), 3524. doi:10.3390u13063524

Md, N., Hasan, M., Munshi, M. H., Rahman, S. M. N., & Alam, A. (2014). Evaluation of antihyperglycemic activity of Lasia spinosa leaf extracts in Swiss albino mice. *World Journal of Pharmacy and Pharmaceutical Sciences, 3*(10), 118–124.

Miah, S. (2021). IoT in Supply Chain Manage-ment: Opportunities and Challenges for Businesses in Early Industry 4.0 Context. Operations and Supply Chain Management. *International Journal (Toronto, Ont.), 14*(2), 148–161.

Mijwil, M. M., Aggarwal, K., Mutar, D. S., Mansour, N., Singh, R., & Singh, S. (2022). The Position of Artificial Intelligence in the Future of Education: An Overview. *Asian Journal of Applied Sciences, 10*(2), 2321–0893. doi:10.24203/ajas.v10i2.6956

Miller, S. A. (2002). *Disease management for conventional and tomato growers.* New York State Vegetable Conference and Berry Growers Meeting Proceedings. New York.

Miller, S. A., & Lewis, I. M. L. (2005). *Hot water treatment of vegetable seeds to eradicate bacterial plant pathogens in organic production systems. Plant Pathology Extension Fact Sheet HYG-3086- 05.* The Ohio State University.

Miller, S. A., Sahin, F., & Rowe, C. R. (1996). *Black rot of crucifers. Extension fact sheet HYG-3125-96.* The Ohio State University.

Mills, W. D., & La Plante, A. (1954). Diseases and insects in the orchard. *Cornell University Extension Bulletin,* 711.

Ming, C. K., & Thiry, J. Y. T. (2017). Independent Bathing for Older Adults: The Conceptualization of the iMagic-BOX Portable Walk-In Bathtub. In *International Conference on Cross-Cultural Design* (pp. 161-170). Springer, Cham. 10.1007/978-3-319-57931-3_13

Minsky, M. (1961). Steps Toward Artificial Intelligence. *Proceedings of the IRE, 49*(1), 8–30. doi:10.1109/JRPROC.1961.287775

Mirza, I., Mahapatra, A., Rego, D., & Mascarenhas, K. (2019). Human Heart Disease Prediction Using Data Mining Techniques. In *2019 IEEE International Conference on Advances in Computing, Communication and Control (ICAC3).* IEEE.

Mishkoff, H. C. (1986). *Understanding artificial intelligence.* Howard W. Sams and Co., Inc.

Mittal, Srishty & Thapar, Lakhvinder. (2019). *Vitamin D Levels Between The Tuberculosis Infected And Non – Infected Subjects In 16-25 Years Of Age.*

Mohamed, & Mesbah, S. (2016). Effective e-government and citizens adoption in Egypt. *International Journal of Computer Applications, 133*(7), 7–13. doi:10.5120/ijca2016907886

Monica Priya, C., & Sathiaseelan, J. G. (2017). An Explorative Study on Sentimental Analysis. *WCCCT,* 140–142.

Monte-Sano, C., De La Paz, S., & Felton, M. (2014). Implementing a disciplinary-literacy curriculum for US history: Learning from expert middle school teachers in diverse classrooms. *Journal of Curriculum Studies, 46*(4), 540–575. doi:10.1080/00220272.2014.904444

Moore M H. (1932). Some fundamental considerations regarding successful control of apple scab. *The Fruit Grower.*

Moura, M. M., de Oliveira, L. E. S., Sanquetta, C. R., Bastos, A., Mohan, M., & Corte, A. P. D. (2021). Towards Amazon Forest Restoration: Automatic Detection of Species from UAV Imagery. *Remote Sensing (Basel), 13*(13), 2627. doi:10.3390/rs13132627

MüllerM.SalathéM. (2020). Addressing machine learning concept drift reveals declining vaccine sentiment during the COVID-19 pandemic. In arXiv [cs.SI]. https://arxiv.org/abs/2012.02197

Munshi, M., Sohrab, M. H., Begum, M. N., Rony, S. R., Karim, M. A., Afroz, F., & Hasan, M. N. (2021). Evaluation of bioactivity and phytochemical screening of endophytic fungi isolated from Ceriops decandra (Griff.) W. Theob, a mangrove plant in Bangladesh. *Clinical Phytoscience*, 7(1), 81. Advance online publication. doi:10.118640816-021-00315-y

Munshi, M., Tumu, K. N., Hasan, M. N., & Amin, M. Z. (2018). Biochemical effects of commercial feedstuffs on the fry of climbing perch (Anabas testudineus) and its impact on Swiss albino mice as an animal model. *Toxicology Reports*, 5, 521–530. doi:10.1016/j.toxrep.2018.04.004 PMID:29707493

Munshi, M., Zilani, M. N. H., Islam, M. A., Biswas, P., Das, A., Afroz, F., & Hasan, M. N. (2022). Novel compounds from endophytic fungi of Ceriops decandra inhibit breast cancer cell growth through estrogen receptor alpha in in-silico study. *Informatics in Medicine Unlocked*, 32(101046), 101046. doi:10.1016/j.imu.2022.101046

Musliner, D. J., Hendler, J. A., Agrawala, A. K., Durfee, E. H., Strosnider, J. K., & Paul, C. J. (1995). The Challenges of Real-Time Al. *Computer*, 28(1), 58–66. doi:10.1109/2.362628

Nakamura, S., Ikeda-Dantsuji, Y., Jin, L., Higashi, Y., Abe, M., Inukai, T., Nagi, M., Urai, M., & Miyazaki, Y. (2019). Macrolides inhibit capsule formation of highly virulent Cryptococcus gattii and promote innate immune susceptibility. *Antimicrobial Agents and Chemotherapy*, 63(6), e02364–e18. doi:10.1128/AAC.02364-18 PMID:30936099

Nanda, N., & Prakash, V. (2023). Dumisani Lickson Namakhwa, Sandeep Dwarkanath Pande, Sk Hasane Ahammad, "A DenseNet CNN-based liver lesion prediction and classification for future medical diagnosis. *Scientific African*, 20.

Naseem, U., Razzak, I., Khushi, M., Eklund, P. W., & Kim, J. (2021). *COVIDSenti:A Large-Scale Benchmark Twitter Data Set for COVID-19 Sentiment Analysis*. IEEE.

National Institute of Medical Statistics. (2009). *IDSP Non-Communicable Disease Risk Factors Survey, Phase- I States of India, 2007-08*. WHO. https://www.who.int/ncds/surveillance/steps/2007_STEPS_Report_India_7States.pdf

Ng, D. T. K., Luo, W., Chan, H. M. Y., & Chu, S. K. W. (2022). Using digital story writing as a pedagogy to develop AI literacy among primary students. *Computers and Education: Artificial Intelligence*, 3, 100054. doi:10.1016/j.caeai.2022.100054

Nguyen, T. T., Criss, S., Dwivedi, P., Huang, D., Keralis, J., Hsu, E., Phan, L., Nguyen, L. H., Yardi, I., Glymour, M. M., Allen, A. M., Chae, D. H., Gee, G. C., & Nguyen, Q. C. (2020). Exploring U.s. shifts in anti-Asian sentiment with the emergence of COVID-19. *International Journal of Environmental Research and Public Health*, 17(19), 7032. doi:10.3390/ijerph17197032 PMID:32993005

Nikbhakt, R., Hemadi, M., (2016). Transvaginal cervical length and bishop score value in predicting successful labor induction with an emphasis on the parity. *Int J pharmaceut res allied sciences*, 5(2), 114-118.

Nirmal Varghese Babu, E. (2021). Sentiment Analysis in Social Media Data for Depression Detection Using Artificial Intelligence:A Review. *SN Computer Science*, 1–20. PMID:34816124

Nirmala, G., Premavathy, R., Chandar, R., & Jeganathan, J. (2023). An Explanatory Case Report on Biopsychosocial Issues and the Impact of Innovative Nurse-Led Therapy in Children with Hematological Cancer. *FMDB Transactions on Sustainable Health Science Letters*, 1(1), 1–10.

Niss, M., & Højgaard, T. (2019). Mathematical competencies revisited. *Educational Studies in Mathematics*, 102(1), 9–28. doi:10.100710649-019-09903-9

O'Connell, M. P., Tidy, J., Wisher, S. J., Avis, N. J., Brown, B. H., & Lindow, S. W. (2000). An in vivo comparative study of the pregnant and nonpregnant cervix using electrical impedance measurements. *BJOG*, 107(8), 1040–1041. doi:10.1111/j.1471-0528.2000.tb10410.x PMID:10955439

Oak, R., Du, M., Yan, D., Takawale, H., & Amit, I. (2019). Malware detection on highly imbalanced data through sequence modeling. *Proceedings of the 12th ACM Workshop on Artificial Intelligence and Security*. New York, NY, USA: ACM. 10.1145/3338501.3357374

Ogunmola, G. A., Singh, B., Sharma, D. K., Regin, R., Rajest, S. S., & Singh, N. (2021). Involvement of distance measure in assessing and resolving efficiency environmental obstacles. *2021 International Conference on Computational Intelligence and Knowledge Economy (ICCIKE)*. IEEE. 10.1109/ICCIKE51210.2021.9410765

Oli, N., Vaidya, A., & Thapa, G. (2013). Behavioural risk factors of non-communicable diseases among Nepalese urban poor: A descriptive study from a slum area of Kathmandu. *Epidemiology Research International*, 2013.

Ombuna, G. J., Nyangeri, B. J., & Maobe, S. N. (2019). – Control of black rot disease in cabbage by integration of mulching, pruning and hot water treatment of seeds. *Plant Pathology & Quarantine Journal of Fungal Biology*, 9(1), 23–29. doi:10.5943/ppq/9/1/3

Ong, J. N. D., Zhang, H., Lee, V. Y. A., Phua, C., Sim, K., Liu, Y., & Zhang, X. (2012). The Accurate Falling Detection System For The Elderly (AFDE). *APEC Youth Scientist Journal*, 4, 83–93.

Onsando, J. M. (1992). Black rot of Crucifers. In H. S. Chaube, U. S. Singh, A. N. Mukhopadyay, & J. Kumar (Eds.), *Plant Diseases of International Importance. Diseases of Vegetables and Oil Seed Crops* (pp. 243–252). Prentice Hall.

Oommen, A. M., Abraham, V. J., George, K., & Jose, V. J. (2016). Prevalence of risk factors for non-communicable diseases in rural & urban Tamil Nadu. *The Indian Journal of Medical Research*, 144(3), 460. doi:10.4103/0971-5916.198668 PMID:28139545

Otipa, M., Kamau, R., & Gekone, M. (2013). Pest management decision guide: green and yellow list. Black rot disease-Plantwise. East African pest management innovation lab. The Ohio State University, College of food, Agriculture and Environmental Sciences.

Pachauri, R., Gupta, A. K., Mishra, R. G., & Chauhan, Y. (2021a). *Various Power Management Schemes For Efficient Wind Energy Conversion System*.

Pachauri, R. K., Pardhe, M. K., Kazmi, S. A., & Gupta, A. K. (2021b). Improved SDK-based Shade Dispersion Methodology to Achieve Higher GMPP of PV Systems under Shading Scenarios. In *2021 IEEE Madras Section Conference (MASCON)* (pp. 1–6). IEEE. 10.1109/MASCON51689.2021.9563589

Pande, S. D., & Chetty, M. S. R. (2021). Fast medicinal leaf retrieval using CapsNet. In *Advances in Intelligent Systems and Computing* (pp. 149–155). Springer Singapore.

Pande, S., & Chetty, M. S. R. (2018). Analysis of Capsule Network (Capsnet) Architectures and Applications. *Journal of Advanced Research in Dynamical and Control Systems*, 10(10), 2765–2771.

Pande, S., & Chetty, M. S. R. (2019). Bezier Curve Based Medicinal Leaf Classification using Capsule Network. *International Journal of Advanced Trends in Computer Science and Engineering*, 8(6), 2735–2742. doi:10.30534/ijatcse/2019/09862019

Pandit, P. (2023). On the Context of Diabetes: A Brief Discussion on the Novel Ethical Issues of Non-communicable Diseases. *FMDB Transactions on Sustainable Health Science Letters*, 1(1), 11–20.

Pandya, S., Gadekallu, T. R., Reddy, P. K., Wang, W., & Alazab, M. (2022). InfusedHeart: A novel knowledge-infused learning framework for diagnosis of cardiovascular events. *IEEE Transactions on Computational Social Systems*, 1–10. doi:10.1109/TCSS.2022.3151643

Pan, H., Badawi, D., & Cetin, A. E. (2020). Computationally efficient wildfire detection method using a deep convolutional network pruned via Fourier analysis. *Sensors (Basel)*, *20*(10), 2891. doi:10.339020102891 PMID:32443739

Paramasivan, P., & Venkatesh, P. (2016). A novel approach: Hydrothermal method of fine stabilized superparamagnetics of cobalt ferrite (CoFe2O4) nanoparticles. *Journal of Superconductivity and Novel Magnetism*, *29*(11), 2805–2811. doi:10.100710948-016-3586-z

Paramasivan, P., & Venkatesh, P. (2016). Controllable synthesis of CuFe2O4 nanostructures through simple hydrothermal method in the presence of thioglycolic acid. *Physica E, Low-Dimensional Systems and Nanostructures*, *84*, 258–262. doi:10.1016/j.physe.2016.05.037

Parks, S., Hoffman, M., Goudar, S., Patel, A., Saleem, S., Ali, S. A., Goldenberg, R. L., Hibberd, P. L., Moore, J., Wallace, D., McClure, E. M., & Derman, R. J. (2019). Maternal anaemia and maternal, fetal, and neonatal outcomes in a prospective cohort study in India and Pakistan. *BJOG*, *126*(6), 737–743. doi:10.1111/1471-0528.15585 PMID:30554474

Patidar, H., Chakrabarti, P., & Ghosh, A. (2017). Parallel Computing Aspects in Improved Edge Cover based Graph Coloring Algorithm. *Indian Journal of Science and Technology*, *10*(25), 1–9. doi:10.17485/ijst/2017/v10i25/115117

Patil, S., Chintamani, S., Grisham, J., Kumar, R., & Dennis, B. H. (2015). Inverse determination of temperature distribution in partially cooled heat generating cylinder. *Volume 8B: Heat Transfer and Thermal Engineering*.

Patil, S., Chintamani, S., Dennis, B. H., & Kumar, R. (2021). Real time prediction of internal temperature of heat generating bodies using neural network. *Thermal Science and Engineering Progress*, *23*(100910), 100910. doi:10.1016/j.tsep.2021.100910

Pattana-Anake, V., & Joseph, F. J. J. (2022). Hyper parameter optimization of stack LSTM based regression for PM 2.5 data in Bangkok. *2022 7th International Conference on Business and Industrial Research (ICBIR)*. IEEE.

Pattana-anake, V., Danphitsanuparn, P., & John Joseph, F. J. (2021). BettaNet: A deep learning architecture for classification of wild Siamese Betta species. *IOP Conference Series. Materials Science and Engineering*, *1055*(1), 012104. doi:10.1088/1757-899X/1055/1/012104

Peach, C., & Yarali, A. (2013). An overview of subacquatic sensor. *Networks*.

Pedro, F., Subosa, M., Rivas, A., & Valverde, P. (2019). *Artificial intelligence in education: Challenges and opportunities for sustainable development*.

Pinaki Mohanty, R., Kumar, R., & Sharma, V. (2022). *Pradeep kumar singh, "Multimedia Tools and Applications*. Springer.

Ponn, T., Kröger, T., & Diermeyer, F. (2020). Identification and explanation of challenging conditions for camera-based object detection of automated vehicles. *Sensors (Basel)*, *20*(13), 3699. doi:10.339020133699 PMID:32630350

Pradha, S., Halgamuge, M. N., & Tran Quoc Vinh, N. (2019). Effective Text Data Preprocessing Technique for Sentiment Analysis in Social Media Data. *2019 11th International Conference on Knowledge and Systems Engineering (KSE)*. IEEE.

Prasad, A., Gupta, D., & Chakrabarti, P. (2013). *Monitoring Users in Cloud Computing : Evaluating the Centralized Approach*. In 2nd International Conference on Advanced Computing, Networking and Security (ADCONS), India.

Prasad, A., & Chakrabarti, P. (2014). Extending Access Management to maintain audit logs in cloud computing. *International Journal of Advanced Computer Science and Applications*, *5*(3). doi:10.14569/IJACSA.2014.050320

Prashanth, A. K., & Anand, U. (2015). Clinical significance of ischemia modified albumin in critically ill patients with sepsis. *Indian Journal of Clinical Biochemistry*, *30*(2), 194–197. doi:10.100712291-014-0434-4 PMID:25883428

Preece, T. F. (1961). Scabbed wood on Bramley's seedling apple. *Plant Pathology*, *10*, 39–40.

Prince, H., Hati, A. S., Chakrabarti, P., Abawajy, J. H., & Keong, N. W. (2021). Development of energy efficient drive for ventilation system using recurrent neural network. *Neural Computing & Applications*, *33*(14), 8659–8668. doi:10.100700521-020-05615-x

Priscila, S. S., Rajest, S. S., Tadiboina, S. N., Regin, R., & András, S. (2023). Analysis of Machine Learning and Deep Learning Methods for Superstore Sales Prediction. *FMDB Transactions on Sustainable Computer Letters*, *1*(1), 1–11.

Priyanka, P., Brajesh, K., & Shashank, M. (2022). Comparison of various deep convolutional neural network models to discriminate apple leaf diseases using transfer learning. *Journal of Plant Diseases and Protection*, *129*(6), 1461–1473. doi:10.100741348-022-00660-1

Provost, F. (n.d.). *On Applied Research in Machine Learning*.

Rabiner, L., & Juang, B. H. (1993). *Fundamentals of speech recognition*. Prentice-Hall, Inc.

Rad, D., Dixon, D., & Rad, G. (2020). Digital outing confidence as a mediator in the digital behavior regulation and internet content awareness relationship. Brain. *Broad Research in Artificial Intelligence and Neuroscience*, *11*(1), 84–95. doi:10.18662/brain/11.1/16

Rad, D., Egerau, A., Roman, A., Dughi, T., Balas, E., Maier, R., & Rad, G. (2022). A preliminary investigation of the technology acceptance model (TAM) in early childhood education and care. Brain. *Broad Research in Artificial Intelligence and Neuroscience*, *13*(1), 518–533. doi:10.18662/brain/13.1/297

Radhika, G., Sathya, R. M., Sudha, V., Ganesan, A., & Mohan, V. (2007). Dietary salt intake and hypertension in an urban south Indian population— [CURES - 53]. *The Journal of the Association of Physicians of India*, *55*, 405–411. PMID:17879493

Raheja, S., & Asthana, A. (2021). Sentimental analysis of twitter comments on covid-19. *2021 11th International Conference on Cloud Computing, Data Science & Engineering (Confluence)*. IEEE.

Rahman, M. M., Ali, G. G. M. N., Li, X. J., Paul, K. C., & Chong, P. H. J. (2020). Twitter and census data analytics to explore socioeconomic factors for post-COVID-19 reopening sentiment. SSRN *Electronic Journal*. doi:10.2139/ssrn.3639551

Raja, M. S., Anurag, M., Reddy, C. P., & Sirisala, N. R. (2021). Machine learning based heart disease prediction system. *2021 International Conference on Computer Communication and Informatics (ICCCI)*. IEEE. 10.1109/ICCCI50826.2021.9402653

Rajesh, K. M., & Naveenkumar, M. (2016). A Robust Method for Face Recognition and Face Emotion Detection System using Support Vector Machines". In *2016 International Conference on Electrical, Electronics, Communication, Computer and Optimization Techniques (ICEECCOT)* (pp. 1–5). 10.1109/ICEECCOT.2016.7955175

Rajeyyagari, S., Hung, B. T., & Chakrabarti, P. (2022). Applications of artificial intelligence in biomedical image processing. *2022 Second International Conference on Artificial Intelligence and Smart Energy (ICAIS)*. IEEE. 10.1109/ICAIS53314.2022.9742773

Rajkumar, S., Vishal, S., & Shirsat Sachin, N. (2019). Sentiment Analysis on Product Reviews Using Machine Learning Techniques. Advances In Intelligent Systems and Computing. Springer.

Rallapalli, V., Menghani, D., Gallani, H., & Aasija, G. (2022). *Online Doctor Appointment System*. Vivekanand Education Society.

Ramesh, S., & Rao, T. R. (2015). High gain dielectric loaded exponentially tapered slot antenna array based on substrate integrated waveguide for V-band wireless communications. [International Journal of Electronics and Communications]. *AEÜ. International Journal of Electronics and Communications*, *69*(1), 48–55. doi:10.1016/j.aeue.2014.07.014

Ramírez-Correa, P. E., Arenas-Gaitán, J., & Rondán-Cataluña, F. J. (2015). Gender and acceptance of e-learning: A multi-group analysis based on a structural equation model among college students in Chile and Spain. *PLoS One*, *10*(10), e0140460. doi:10.1371/journal.pone.0140460 PMID:26465895

Ranjan, A., & Ranjan, A. (2013). Subacquatic Wireless Communication Network. *Advance in Electronic and Electric Engineering*, *3*(1), 41–46.

Rashi, A., & Madamala, R. (2022). Minimum relevant features to obtain AI explainable system for predicting breast cancer in WDBC. [IJHS]. *International Journal of Health Sciences*, 1312–1326. doi:10.53730/ijhs.v6nS9.12538

Ratzinger, F., Haslacher, H., Poeppl, W., Hoermann, G., Kovarik, J. J., Jutz, S., Steinberger, P., Burgmann, H., Pickl, W. F., & Schmetterer, K. G. (2014). Azithromycin suppresses CD4+ T-cell activation by direct modulation of mTOR activity. *Scientific Reports*, *4*(1), 1–0. doi:10.1038rep07438 PMID:25500904

RCOG. (2001). Induction of labour. In Evidence based Clinical Guideline Number 9. London.

Reddy, G. P., Kumar, Y. V. P., & Chakravarthi, M. K. (2022a). Communication technologies for interoperable smart microgrids in urban energy community: A broad review of the state of the art, challenges, and research perspectives. *Sensors (Basel)*, *22*(15), 5881. doi:10.339022155881 PMID:35957438

Reddy, P., Gogulamudi, Y., & Maddikera Kalyan Chakravarthi, A. (2022b). Refined Network Topology for Improved Reliability and Enhanced Dijkstra Algorithm for Optimal Path Selection during Link Failures in Cluster Microgrids. *Sustainability*, *14*(16).

Rejeb, A., Simske, S., Rejeb, K., Treiblmaier, H., & Zailani, S. (2020). Internet of Things research in supply chain management and logistics: A bibliometric analysis. *Internet of Things*, *12*(100318), 100318. doi:10.1016/j.iot.2020.100318

Ren, Y., Zheng, L., & Khajepour, A. (2019). Integrated model predictive and torque vectoring control for path tracking of 4-wheel driven vehicles. *Journal of Mechanical Science and Technology*, *33*(3), 1063–1072.

Riedl, M. O. (2019). Human-centered artificial intelligence and machine learning. *Human Behavior and Emerging Technologies*, *1*(1), 33–36. doi:10.1002/hbe2.117

Rizwana, H., Aquisha, B., & Shruti, G. (2016). Study of transvaginal sonographic assessment of cervix in predicting the success of labor induction in nulliparous women. *JK Science*, *18*(1), 6–11.

Robinson, H., MacDonald, B., & Broadbent, E. (2014). The role of healthcare robots for older people at home: A review. *International Journal of Social Robotics*, *6*(4), 575–591. doi:10.100712369-014-0242-2

Rogge, S. A., & Meyhofer, R. (2021). Leaf age is important for assessment of resistance in chrysanthemum against Frankliniella occidentalis. *Journal of Plant Diseases and Protection*, *128*(2), 511–516. doi:10.100741348-020-00402-1

Rohit, Y. V., Raghu, K., & Shabnum, M. (2019). Study of ischemia-modified albumin as a biomarker in critically ill patients with sepsis. *Saudi Critical Care Journal.*, *3*(3), 104. doi:10.4103ccj.sccj_16_19

Roll, I., McNamara, D., Sosnovsky, S., Luckin, R., & Dimitrova, V. (2021). *Artificial intelligence in education.* Springer International Publishing.

Rosen, M. A., DiazGranados, D., Dietz, A. S., Benishek, L. E., Thompson, D., Pronovost, P. J., & Weaver, S. J. (2018). Teamwork in healthcare: Key discoveries enabling safer, high-quality care. *The American Psychologist*, *73*(4), 433–450. doi:10.1037/amp0000298 PMID:29792459

Ross, R. G., & Burchill, R. T. (1968). Experiments using sterilized apple-leaf discs to study the mode of action of urea in suppressing perithecia of *Venturia inaequalis* (Cke.) Wint. *Annals of Applied Biology*, *62*(2), 289–296. doi:10.1111/j.1744-7348.1968.tb02824.x

Rouhiainen, L. (2018). *Artificial Intelligence: 101 things you must know today about our future.* Lasse Rouhiainen.

Rozenberg, P., Chevret, S., Chastang, C., & Ville, Y. (2005). Comparison of digital and ultrasonographic examination of the cervix in predicting time interval from induction to delivery in women with a low Bishop score. *BJOG*, *112*(2), 192–196. doi:10.1111/j.1471-0528.2004.00549.x PMID:15663583

Rs, D. (2018). #023 CNN object detection. *Master Data Science.* https://datahacker.rs/deep-learning-object-detection/

Rustam, F., Khalid, M., Aslam, W., Rupapara, V., Mehmood, A., & Choi, G. S. (2021). A performance comparison of supervised machine learning models for Covid-19 tweets sentiment analysis. *PLoS One*, *16*(2), e0245909. doi:10.1371/journal.pone.0245909 PMID:33630869

Ryan, R. P., Vorhölter, F. J., Potnis, N., Jones, J. B., Van Sluys, M.-A., Bogdanove, A. J., & Dow, J. M. (2011). – Pathogenomics of Xanthomonas: Understanding bacterium-plant interactions. *Nature Reviews. Microbiology*, *9*(5), 344–355. doi:10.1038/nrmicro2558 PMID:21478901

Ryu, D., & Baik, J. (2016). Effective multi-objective naïve Bayes learning for cross-project defect prediction. *Applied Soft Computing*, *49*, 1062–1077. doi:10.1016/j.asoc.2016.04.009

Rzayeva, Z., & Alasgarov, E. (2019). Facial Emotion Recognition using Convolutional Neural Networks". In 2019 IEEE 13th International Conference on Application of Information and Communication Technologies (AICT) (pp. 1–5).

Sadek, R. A., Abd-alazeem, D. M., & Abbassy, M. M. (2021). A new energy-efficient multi-hop routing protocol for heterogeneous wireless sensor networks. *International Journal of Advanced Computer Science and Applications*, *12*(11). doi:10.14569/IJACSA.2021.0121154

Said, F. B., & Tripathi, S. (2023). Epistemology of Digital Journalism Shift in South Global Nations: A Bibliometric Analysis. *FMDB Transactions on Sustainable Technoprise Letters*, *1*(1), 47–60.

Sakhnini, J., Karimipour, H., Dehghantanha, A., Parizi, R. M., & Srivastava, G. (2021). Security aspects of Internet of Things aided smart grids: A bibliometric survey. *Internet of Things*, *14*(100111), 100111. doi:10.1016/j.iot.2019.100111

Samuel, J., Md Mokhlesur Rahman, G. G., Md Nawaz Ali, Y., Samuel, A., Pelaez, P. H., Chong, J., & Yakubov, M. (2020). *Feeeling Positive about Reopening? New Normal Scenarios from COVID-19 US Reopen Sentiment Analytics.* IEEE Acccess.

Samuel, J., Ali, G. G., Rahman, E., & Esawi, Y. (2020). Covid -19 public sentiment insights and machine learning for tweets classification. *Information (Basel)*, *2020*, 1–22.

Sandeep, S. R., Ahamad, S., Saxena, D., Srivastava, K., Jaiswal, S., & Bora, A. (2022). To understand the relationship between Machine learning and Artificial intelligence in large and diversified business organisations. *Materials Today: Proceedings*, *56*, 2082–2086. doi:10.1016/j.matpr.2021.11.409

Santoso, L. W. (2014). Analysis of the Impact of Information Technology Investments - A Survey of Indonesian Universities. *ARPN JEAS, 9*(12).

Santoso, L. W. (2019). Cloud technology: Opportunities for cybercriminals and security challenges. *2019 Twelfth International Conference on Ubi-Media Computing (Ubi-Media).* IEEE.

Santoso, L. W. (2021). Adaptive educational resources framework for ELearning using rule-based system. In *Information and Communication Technology for Intelligent Systems* (pp. 385–396). Springer Singapore. doi:10.1007/978-981-15-7078-0_36

Sanusi, I. T., Olaleye, S. A., Agbo, F. J., & Chiu, T. K. (2022). The role of learners' competencies in artificial intelligence education. *Computers and Education: Artificial Intelligence, 3,* 100098. doi:10.1016/j.caeai.2022.100098

Sathya, A., & Mythili, M. (2022). An Investigation of Machine Learning Algorithms in sentiment Analysis. *Advances and Applications in Mathematical Sciences,* 4575–4584.

Saxena, D. (2022). *A Non-Contact Based System to Measure SPO2 and Systolic/Diastolic Blood Pressure Using Rgb-Nir Camera (Order No. 29331388).* ProQuest Dissertations & Theses A&I; ProQuest Dissertations & Theses Global. (2697398440).

Saxena, D., & Chaudhary, S. (2023). Predicting Brain Diseases from FMRI-Functional Magnetic Resonance Imaging with Machine Learning Techniques for Early Diagnosis and Treatment. *FMDB Transactions on Sustainable Computer Letters, 1*(1), 33–48.

Sayonara, MP, Mariano, RLR, & Sami, JM, Gil Silva, Elizabeth AAM. (1999). – Antagonism of yeasts to Xanthomonas campestris pv. campestris on cabbage phylloplane in field. *Journal of Microbiology (Seoul, Korea), 30*(3), 375–379.

Scaglione, F., & Rossoni, G. (1998). Comparative anti-inflammatory effects of roxithromycin, azithromycin and clarithromycin. *The Journal of Antimicrobial Chemotherapy, 41*(suppl_2), 47–50. doi:10.1093/jac/41.suppl_2.47 PMID:9579712

Seebold, K., Bachi, P., & Beale, J. (2008). Black rot of crucifers. UK Cooperative Extension Service. University of Kentucky-College of Agriculture.

Sepasgozar, S. S., & Pierre, S. (2022). Network traffic prediction model considering road traffic parameters using artificial intelligence methods in VANET. *IEEE Access : Practical Innovations, Open Solutions, 10,* 8227–8242. doi:10.1109/ACCESS.2022.3144112

Shabbir, J., & Anwer, T. (2018). *Artificial Intelligence and its Role in Near Future.* https://doi.org/ doi:10.48550/arxiv.1804.01396

Shah, K., Laxkar, P., & Chakrabarti, P. (2020). A hypothesis on ideal Artificial Intelligence and associated wrong implications. *Advances in Intelligent Systems and Computing, 989,* 283–294. doi:10.1007/978-981-13-8618-3_30

Shan, C., Chen, B., Hu, C., Xue, J., & Li, N. (2014). *Software defect prediction model based on LLE and SVM. 2014 Communications Security Conference (CSC 2014).* Institution of Engineering and Technology.

Shannon, C.E. (1948). A mathematical theory of communication. *Bell System Technical Journal 27,* 379–423(Part I) 623–656(Part II).

Sharma, D. K., Jalil, N. A., Regin, R., Rajest, S. S., Tummala, R. K., & Thangadurai. (2021). Predicting network congestion with machine learning. 2021 2nd International Conference on Smart Electronics and Communication (ICOSEC). IEEE.

Sharma, D. K., Jalil, N. A., Regin, R., Rajest, S. S., Tummala, R. K., & Thangadurai. (2021a). Predicting network congestion with machine learning. *2021 2nd International Conference on Smart Electronics and Communication (ICOSEC).* IEEE.

Sharma, D. K., Singh, B., Anam, M., Villalba-Condori, K. O., Gupta, A. K., & Ali, G. K. (2021). *Slotting learning rate in deep neural networks to build stronger models. 2021 2nd International Conference on Smart Electronics and Communication (ICOSEC).* IEEE.

Sharma, D. K., Singh, B., Raja, M., Regin, R., & Rajest, S. S. (2021b). An Efficient Python Approach for Simulation of Poisson Distribution. *2021 7th International Conference on Advanced Computing and Communication Systems (ICACCS).* IEEE.

Sharma, D. K., Singh, B., Regin, R., Steffi, R., & Chakravarthi, M. K. (2021c). Efficient Classification for Neural Machines Interpretations based on Mathematical models. *2021 7th International Conference on Advanced Computing and Communication Systems (ICACCS).* IEEE.

Sharma, A. K., Pachauri, R. K., Choudhury, S., Mahela, O. P., Khan, B., & Gupta, A. K. (2022). Improved power maxima point of photovoltaic system using umbrella optimizing technique under PSCs: An experimental study. *IET Renewable Power Generation, 16*(10), 2059–2075. doi:10.1049/rpg2.12486

Sharma, A. K., Panwar, A., Chakrabarti, P., & Vishwakarma, S. (2015). Categorization of ICMR using feature extraction strategy and MIR with ensemble learning. *Procedia Computer Science, 57*, 686–694. doi:10.1016/j.procs.2015.07.448

Sharma, D., Dangi, C. B., & Kaur, M. A. (2016). Review on pharmacological activities and therapeutic potentials of Ficus religiosa (Pipal). *Indian Journal of Applied Research, 6*(1), 623–626.

Sharma, K., Singh, B., Herman, E., Regine, R., Rajest, S. S., & Mishra, V. P. (2021). Maximum information measure policies in reinforcement learning with deep energy-based model. *2021 International Conference on Computational Intelligence and Knowledge Economy (ICCIKE).* IEEE. 10.1109/ICCIKE51210.2021.9410756

Sharma, S. N., & Singh, A. M. (2012). Development of a Flight Test Data Acquisition and Analysis System using LabVIEW. *International Journal of Computer Applications, 41*(8), 1–6. doi:10.5120/6321-8599

Shavarani, S. M., Golabi, M., & Izbirak, G. (2021). A capacitated biobjective location problem with uniformly distributed demands in the UAV-supported delivery operation. *International Transactions in Operational Research: A Journal of The International Federation of Operational Research Societies, 28*(6), 3220–3243. doi:10.1111/itor.12735

Shinkai, M., Henke, M. O., & Rubin, B. K. (2008). Macrolide antibiotics as immunomodulatory medications: Proposed mechanisms of action. *Pharmacology & Therapeutics, 117*(3), 393–405. doi:10.1016/j.pharmthera.2007.11.001 PMID:18289694

Shirkhorshidi, A. S., Aghabozorgi, S., Wah, T. Y., & Herawan, T. (2014). Big data clustering: A review. In *Computational Science and Its Applications – ICCSA 2014* (pp. 707–720). Springer International Publishing. doi:10.1007/978-3-319-09156-3_49

Shriram, K., Chakravarthi, M. K., Kumar, Y. V., Kumar, V. B., Pradeep, D. J., & Reddy, C. P. (2022). Acute Decisive Fuzzy Haptic Surface Response System for Tactile Sensitivity. In *2022 International Conference on Decision Aid Sciences and Applications (DASA)* (pp. 438–442). IEEE. 10.1109/DASA54658.2022.9765045

Shukla, A. K., Srivastava, S., & Verma, G. (2019). Effect of maternal anemia on the status of iron stores in infants: A cohort study. *Journal of Family & Community Medicine, 26*(2), 118. doi:10.4103/jfcm.JFCM_115_18 PMID:31143084

Shyam, R. S. (2017). -(a)). Role of m-Banking for Indian Rural Consumers, its Adaptation Strategies, and Challenges: Consumer Behavior Analysis [J]. *International Journal of Information Engineering and Electronic Business, 6*, 35–42.

Siau, K., & Wang, W. (1 C.E.). Artificial Intelligence (AI) Ethics: Ethics of AI and Ethical AI. *Database Management, 31*(2), 74–87. doi:10.4018/JDM.2020040105

Sibbel, A. (2009). Pathways towards sustainability through higher education. *International Journal of Sustainability in Higher Education, 10*(1), 68–82. doi:10.1108/14676370910925262

Sihare, S. (2022). FUTURE DIGITAL MARKETING REVOLUTIONIZING E-COMMERCE. *Towards Excellence, 14*(1).

Sihare, S. R. (2017). -(b)). Role of m-Banking for Indian rural consumers, its adaptation strategies, and challenges: Consumer behavior analysis. *International Journal of Information Engineering and Electronic Business, 9*(6), 35. doi:10.5815/ijieeb.2017.06.05

Sihare, S. R. (2018). Roles of E–content for E–business: Analysis. *International Journal of Information Engineering and Electronic Business, 12*(1), 24. doi:10.5815/ijieeb.2018.01.04

Silva, D., & Hui, S. C. (2003). Real-time Facial Feature Extraction and Emotion Recognition. *Fourth International Conference on Information, Communications and Signal Processing, 2003 and the Fourth Pacific Rim Conference on Multimedia.*

Singer, A. J., Taylor, M., Domingo, A., Ghazipura, S., Khorasonchi, A., Thode, H. C. Jr, & Shapiro, N. I. (2014). Diagnostic characteristics of a clinical screening tool in combination with measuring bedside lactate level in emergency department patients with suspected sepsis. *Academic Emergency Medicine, 21*(8), 853–857. doi:10.1111/acem.12444 PMID:25155163

Singh, A., & Chakrabarti, P. (2013). Ant based resource discovery and mobility aware trust management for Mobile Grid systems. *2013 3rd IEEE International Advance Computing Conference (IACC).* IEEE.

Singh, T., Rastogi, P., Pandey, U. K., Geetha, A., Tiwari, M., & Chakravarthi, M. K. (2022c). Systematic healthcare smart systems with the integration of the sensor using cloud computing techniques. *2022 2nd International Conference on Advance Computing and Innovative Technologies in Engineering (ICACITE).* IEEE.

Singh, A. K., & Bansal, R. C. (2015). LabVIEW-Based Data Acquisition and Control System Using NI USB-6363 for the Identification of Amplitude Modulation in FM Radio Broadcasts. *Measurement Science Review, 15*(5), 242–248. doi:10.1515/msr-2015-0034

Singh, D., Keerthi Nayani, A. S., Sundar Rajan, M., Yadav, R., Alanya-Beltran, J., & Chakravarthi, M. K. (2022). Implementation of virual instrumentation for signal acquisition and processing. *2022 International Conference on Innovative Computing, Intelligent Communication and Smart Electrical Systems (ICSES).* IEEE. 10.1109/ICSES55317.2022.9914143

Singh, M., Kumar Jakhar, A., & Pandey, S. (2021). Sentiment Analysis on the impact of coronavirus in social life using the BERT model. *Social Network Analysis and Mining, 11*(1), 8–11. doi:10.100713278-021-00737-z PMID:33758630

Singh, R., Mishra, P. A., Prakash, A., Tongkachok, K., Upadhyaya, M., & Kalyan Chakravarthi, M. (2022). Smart device for effective communication in the healthcare system. *2022 International Conference on Innovative Computing, Intelligent Communication and Smart Electrical Systems (ICSES).* IEEE. 10.1109/ICSES55317.2022.9914093

Sinha, A. K., Shankar Hati, A., Benbouzid, M., & Chakrabarti, P. (2021). ANN-based Pattern Recognition for Induction Motor Broken Rotor Bar Monitoring under Supply Frequency Regulation. *Machines, 9.*

Siva Ramkumar, M., Priya, R., Rajakumari, R. F., Valsalan, P., Chakravarthi, M., Charlyn Pushpa Latha, G., & Rajan, K. (2022). Review and Evaluation of Power Devices and Semiconductor Materials Based on Si, SiC, and Ga-N. *Journal of Nanomaterials, 2022,* 2022. doi:10.1155/2022/8648284

Sivanantham, P., Sahoo, J., Lakshminarayanan, S., Bobby, Z., & Kar, S. S. (2021). Profile of risk factors for Non-Communicable Diseases (NCDs) in a highly urbanised district of India: Findings from Puducherry district-wide STEPS Survey, 2019–20. *PLoS One, 16*(1), e0245254. doi:10.1371/journal.pone.0245254 PMID:33434194

Smart, D. C., & Holly, W. L. (2013). *Managing Black Rot of Cabbage and other Crucifer Crops in Organic Farming Systems*. Cornell University.

Soleymani, M., Asghari-Esfeden, S., Fu, Y., & Pantic, M. (2016). Analysis of EEG Signals and Facial Expressions for Continuous Emotion Detection. *IEEE Transactions on Affective Computing, 7*(1), 17–28. doi:10.1109/TAFFC.2015.2436926

Soni, D., Gagrani, M., Rathore, A., & Chakravarthi, M. K. (2014). Study of Different Controller's Performance for a Real Time Non-Linear System. *International Journal of Advancements in Electronics and Electrical Engineering, 3*(3), 10–14.

Sonnad, S., Sathe, M., Basha, D. K., Bansal, V., Singh, R., & Singh, D. P. (2022). The integration of connectivity and system integrity approaches using Internet of Things (IoT) for enhancing network security. *2022 5th International Conference on Contemporary Computing and Informatics (IC3I)*. IEEE.

Sreelekshmi, R., Latha, P.G., Arafat, M.M., S Shyamal, V. J. Shine, G. I., & Anuja. (2007). Anti-inflammatory, analgesic and anti-lipid peroxidation studies on stem bark of ficus. *Religiosa Linn, 6*(5).

Srinivas, K., Velmurugan, P. R., & Andiyappillai, N. (2023). Digital Human Resources and Management Support Improve Human Resources Effectiveness. *FMDB Transactions on Sustainable Management Letters, 1*(1), 32–45.

Srisook, N., Tuntoolavest, O., Danphitsanuparn, P., Pattana-Anake, V., & Joseph, F. J. (2022). Convolutional Neural Network Based Nutrient Deficiency Classification in Leaves of Elaeis guineensis Jacq. *International Journal of Computer Information Systems and Industrial Management Applications, 14*, 19–27.

Srivastav, S., Mahajan, H., Goel, S., & Mukherjee, S. (2017). Prevalence of risk factors of non- communicable diseases in a rural population of district Gautam-Budh Nagar, Uttar Pradesh, using the World Health Organization STEPS approach. *Journal of Family Medicine and Primary Care, 6*(3), 491–497. doi:10.4103/2249-4863.222027 PMID:29416995

Stead, W. W. (2018). Clinical Implications and Challenges of Artificial Intelligence and Deep Learning. *Journal of the American Medical Association, 320*(11), 1107–1108. doi:10.1001/jama.2018.11029 PMID:30178025

Stellari, F. F., Sala, A., Donofrio, G., Ruscitti, F., Caruso, P., Topini, T. M., Francis, K. P., Li, X., Carnini, C., Civelli, M., & Villetti, G. (2014). Azithromycin inhibits nuclear factor-κB activation during lung inflammation: An in vivo imaging study. *Pharmacology Research & Perspectives, 2*(5), e00058. doi:10.1002/prp2.58 PMID:25505605

Stenhagen, M., Ekström, H., Nordell, E., & Elmståhl, S. (2013). Falls in the general elderly population: A 3-and 6-year prospective study of risk factors using data from the longitudinal population study 'Good ageing in Skane'. *BMC Geriatrics, 13*(1), 1–11. doi:10.1186/1471-2318-13-81 PMID:23919320

Stern, L., & Roseman, J. E. (2004). Can middle-school science textbooks help students learn important ideas? Findings from Project 2061's curriculum evaluation study: Life science. *Journal of Research in Science Teaching, 41*(6), 538–568. doi:10.1002/tea.20019

Stricker, T. P., Kumar, V., Abbas, A. K., Fausto, N., & Ster, J. C. (2010). *Robbins and Cotran pathologic basis of disease*.

Su, J., & Yang, W. (2022). *Artificial intelligence in early childhood education: A scoping review*. Computers and Education: Artificial Intelligence, 100049.

Su, J., Zhong, Y., & Ng, D. T. K. (2022). A meta-review of literature on educational approaches for teaching AI at the K-12 levels in the Asia-Pacific region. *Computers and Education: Artificial Intelligence, 100065.*

Suganthi, M., & Sathiaseelan, J. G. R. (2023). Image Denoising and Feature Extraction Techniques Applied to X-Ray Seed Images for Purity Analysis. *FMDB Transactions on Sustainable Health Science Letters, 1*(1), 41–53.

Sun, P., Boukerche, A., & Tao, Y. (2020). SSGRU: A novel hybrid stacked GRU-based traffic volume prediction approach in a road network. *Computer Communications*, *160*, 502–511. doi:10.1016/j.comcom.2020.06.028

Surve, J., Umrao, D., Madhavi, M., Rajeswari, T. S., Bangare, S. L., & Chakravarthi, M. K. (2022). Machine learning applications for protecting the information of health care department using smart internet of things appliances -A REVIEW. *2022 2nd International Conference on Advance Computing and Innovative Technologies in Engineering (ICACITE)*. IEEE.

Sussman, R., & Gifford, R. (2012). Please turn off the lights: The effectiveness of visual prompts. *Applied Ergonomics*, *43*(3), 596–603. doi:10.1016/j.apergo.2011.09.008 PMID:21963251

Suthar, V., Bansal, V., Reddy, C. S., Gonzáles, J. L. A., Singh, D., & Singh, D. P. (2022). Machine Learning Adoption in Blockchain-Based Smart Applications. *2022 5th International Conference on Contemporary Computing and Informatics (IC3I)*. IEEE.

Sutton, B., Sutton, R. S., & Barto, A. G. (1998). *Reinforcement learning: An introduction*.

Suwa, M., Sugie, N., & Fujimora, K. (1978). A Preliminary Note on Pattern Recognition of Human Emotional Expression. In *Proc. Int'l Joint Conf. Pattern Recognition* (pp. 408–410). IEEE.

Swait A A J, Butt D J. 1990. Fungicides as antisporulants against apple powdery mildew and scab. *Tests of Agrochemicals and Cultivars*, supplement of *Annals of Applied Biology, 116*, pp. 36–37.

Taherkhani, N., & Pierre, S. (2015). 'Improving dynamic and distributed congestion control in vehicular ad hoc networks. *Ad Hoc Networks*, *33*, 112–125. doi:10.1016/j.adhoc.2015.04.008

Tambaip, B., Hadi, A. F. F., & Tjilen, A. P. (2023). Optimizing Public Service Performance: Unleashing the Potential of Compassion as an Indicator of Public Service Motivation. *FMDB Transactions on Sustainable Management Letters*, *1*(2), 46–55.

Tandon, R., Jain, A., & Malhotra, P. (2018). Management of iron deficiency anemia in pregnancy in India. *Indian Journal of Hematology & Blood Transfusion : An Official Journal of Indian Society of Hematology and Blood Transfusion*, *34*(2), 204–215. doi:10.100712288-018-0949-6 PMID:29622861

Tang, T., & Chen, B. (2021). F-Measure Optimization of Forest Flame Salient Object Detection Based on Boundary Perception. In *Artificial Intelligence in China* (pp. 436–442). Springer. doi:10.1007/978-981-15-8599-9_50

Taylor, J. D., Conway, J., Roberts, S. J., & Vicente, J. G. (2002). – Sources and origin of resistance to Xanthomonas campestris pv. campestris in Brassica genomes. *Phytopathology*, *92*(1), 105–111. doi:10.1094/PHYTO.2002.92.1.105 PMID:18944146

Teixeira, D. K. D. S., Andrade, L. M., Santos, J. L. P., & Caires, E. S. (2019). Falls among the elderly: Environmental limitations and functional losses. *Revista Brasileira de Geriatria e Gerontologia*, *22*(3), 22. doi:10.1590/1981-22562019022.180229

Teng, Z., Kim, J. H., & Kang, D. J. (2010). Fire detection based on hidden Markov models. *International Journal of Control, Automation, and Systems*, *8*(4), 822–830. doi:10.100712555-010-0414-2

Terefe, B., Birhanu, A., Nigussie, P., & Tsegaye, A. (2015). Effect of maternal iron deficiency anemia on the iron store of newborns in ethiopia. *Anemia*, *808204*, 1–6. doi:10.1155/2015/808204 PMID:25734012

Thankappan, K. R., Shah, B., Mathur, P., Sarma, P. S., Srinivas, G., & Mini, G. K. (2010). Risk factor profile for chronic non-communicable diseases: Results of a community-based study in Kerala, India. *The Indian Journal of Medical Research*, *131*(1), 53. PMID:20167974

The writing process in a multimedia environment. (2003). Horizon. http://horizon.unc.edu/projects/monograph/CD/Language_Music/Simard.html

Thulaseedharan, J. V., Sarma, P. S., Thankappan, K. R., Soman, B., Varma, R. P., & Srinivasan, K. (2021). Consumption of fruits, vegetables and salt in the context of control of type 2 diabetes and hypertension in Kerala, India. *Journal of Family Medicine and Primary Care, 10*(7), 2646. doi:10.4103/jfmpc.jfmpc_2469_20 PMID:34568150

Tidjon, L. N., & Khomh, F. (2022). The different faces of ai ethics across the world: a principle-implementation gap analysis. arXiv preprint arXiv:2206.03225.

Tiwari, M., Chakrabarti, P., & Chakrabarti, T. (2018). Novel work of diagnosis in liver cancer using Tree classifier on liver cancer dataset (BUPA liver disorder). *Communications in Computer and Information Science, 837*, 155–160. doi:10.1007/978-981-13-1936-5_18

Tiwari, M., Chakrabarti, P., & Chakrabarti, T. (2018). Performance analysis and error evaluation towards the liver cancer diagnosis using lazy classifiers for ILPD. *Communications in Computer and Information Science, 837*, 161–168. doi:10.1007/978-981-13-1936-5_19

Tong, W., Hussain, A., Bo, W. X., & Maharjan, S. (2019). Artificial intelligence for vehicle-to-everything: A survey. *IEEE Access : Practical Innovations, Open Solutions, 7*, 10823–10843. doi:10.1109/ACCESS.2019.2891073

Töreyin, B. U., Dedeoğlu, Y., Güdükbay, U., & Cetin, A. E. (2006). Computer vision-based method for real-time fire and flame detection. *Pattern Recognition Letters, 27*(1), 49–58. doi:10.1016/j.patrec.2005.06.015

Tripathi, S., & Al-Shahri, M. (2023). Problems and Prospects on the Evolution of Advertising and Public Relations Industries in Oman. *FMDB Transactions on Sustainable Management Letters, 1*(1), 1–11.

Tsang, Y. P., Choy, K. L., Wu, C. H., Ho, G. T. S., Lam, H. Y., & Koo, P. S. (2017). An IoT-based cargo monitoring system for enhancing operational effectiveness under a cold chain environment. *International Journal of Engineering Business Management, 9*, 184797901774906. doi:10.1177/1847979017749063

Tu, M. (2018). An exploratory study of Internet of Things (IoT) adoption intention in logistics and supply chain management: A mixed research approach. *International Journal of Logistics Management, 29*(1), 131–151. doi:10.1108/IJLM-11-2016-0274

Tu, M., Lim, M. K., & Yang, M. (2018). IoT-based production supply chian management and logistics system - Part 2: IoT-based cyber-physical system: a framework and evaluation. *Industrial Management & Data Systems, 118*, 96–125. doi:10.1108/IMDS-11-2016-0504

Turner, R. A. (1965). *Screening Methods in Pharmacology.* Academic Press Inc.

Tverberg, H. (1958). – A new derivation of the information function. *Mathematica Scandinavica, 6*, 297–298. doi:10.7146/math.scand.a-10555

Uday Kiran Ruttala, M. S., & Balamurugan, M. K. (2015). NFC based Smart Campus Payment System". NFC Based Smart Campus Payment System. *Indian Journal of Science and Technology, 8*, 1–5.

Uddin, M. Z., Khaksar, W., & Torresen, J. (2017). Facial Expression Recognition Using Salient Features and Convolutional Neural Network. *IEEE Access : Practical Innovations, Open Solutions, 5*, 26146–26161. doi:10.1109/ACCESS.2017.2777003

Uike, D., Agarwalla, S., Bansal, V., Chakravarthi, M. K., Singh, R., & Singh, P. (2022). Investigating the role of block chain to secure identity in IoT for industrial automation. *2022 11th International Conference on System Modeling & Advancement in Research Trends (SMART).* IEEE.

Uma Maheswaran. S. K., Nassa, V. K., Singh, B. P., Pandey, U. K., Satyala, H., & Chakravarthi, M. K. (2022). An inventory system utilizing neural network in the prediction of machine learning techniques. *2022 2nd International Conference on Advance Computing and Innovative Technologies in Engineering (ICACITE)*. IEEE.

United Nations. (2021). *Non-Communicable Diseases Deemed Development Challenge of 'Epidemic Proportions' in Political Declaration Adopted During Landmark General Assembly Summit*. UN. https://www.un.org/press/en/2011/ga11138.doc.htm (accessed on 4 May 2021).

Vanitha, M., Ramesh, S., & Chitra, S. (2019). Wearable antennas for remote health care monitoring system using 5g wireless technologies. *Telecommunications and Radio Engineering*, 78(14), 1275–1285. doi:10.1615/TelecomRadEng.v78.i14.50

Vashishtha, E. (2019). Effects of Maternal Smoking on Fetus and Child Development: A literature review. *International Research Journal of Natural and Applied Sciences*, 6(1), 92–107.

Vashishtha, E. (2020). Reducing Patient wait time in outpatient settings: A lean six sigma approach. *International Journal of Research in Medical and Basic Sciences*, 6(1), 15–35.

Vashishtha, E., & Dhawan, G. (2023). Bridging Generation Gap on Analysis of Mentor-Mentee Relationship in Healthcare Setting. *FMDB Transactions on Sustainable Health Science Letters*, 1(1), 21–30.

Vashishtha, E., & Sherman, L. (2018). Socioeconomic Status and Childhood Obesity. *International Journal of Physical and Social Sciences*, 8(11), 184–194.

Vashishtha, E., Sherman, L., Sajjad, T., & Mehmood, N. (2020). Use of anti-viral therapy in treatment of Covid 19. *Journal of Advanced Medical and Dental Sciences Research*, 8(11), 273–276.

Veeraiah, V., Pankajam, A., Vashishtha, E., Dhabliya, D., Karthikeyan, P., & Chandan, R. R. (2022). Efficient COVID-19 identification using deep learning for IoT. *2022 5th International Conference on Contemporary Computing and Informatics (IC3I)*. IEEE.

Venkateswaran, P. S., & Viktor, P. (2023). A Study on Brand Equity of Fast-Moving Consumer Goods with Reference to Madurai, Tamil Nadu. *FMDB Transactions on Sustainable Technoprise Letters*, 1(1), 13–27.

Verhoeven, C. J. M., Rückert, M. E. P. F., Opmeer, B. C., Pajkrt, E., & Mol, B. W. J. (2012). Ultrasonographic fetal head position to predict mode of delivery: a systematic review and bivariate meta-analysis: Fetal head position in prediction of mode of delivery. *Ultrasound in Obstetrics & Gynecology*, 40(1), 9–13. doi:10.1002/uog.10102 PMID:21953834

Verma, K., Srivastava, P., & Chakrabarti, P. (2018). Exploring structure oriented feature tag weighting algorithm for web documents identification. *Communications in Computer and Information Science*, 837, 169–180. doi:10.1007/978-981-13-1936-5_20

Vijayalakshmi, S., Saini, A., Srinivasan, A., & Singh, N. (2021). Disease prediction over big data from healthcare institution". In *2021 IEEE International Conference on Advance Computing and Innovative Technologies in Engineering (ICACITE)*. IEEE. 10.1109/ICACITE51222.2021.9404567

Vijayan, A. L., Ravindran, S., Saikant, R., Lakshmi, S., & Kartik, R. (2017). Procalcitonin: A promising diagnostic marker for sepsis and antibiotic therapy. *Journal of Intensive Care*, 5(1), 1–7. doi:10.118640560-017-0246-8 PMID:28794881

Vinoth Kumar, V., Karthick Raghunath, K., Muthukumaran, V., Joseph, R. B., Bechi Akshay, I., & Uday, K. (2022). Aspect based sentiment analysis and smart classification in uncertain feedback pool. *International Journal of System Assurance Engineering and Management*, 252–262.

Vishal, A., & Kharde, S. (2016). Sentiment Analysis of Twitter Data: A Survey of Techniques. *International Journal of Computer Applications*, *139*(11), 1–10.

Vishwanathraddi, A., & Chakravarthi, M. (2017). Arduino-based wireless mobot. *Asian Journal of Pharmaceutical and Clinical Research*, *10*(13), 61–65. doi:10.22159/ajpcr.2017.v10s1.19562

Viswakarma, S., Chakrabarti, P., Bhatnagar, D., & Sharma, A. K. (2014). *Phrase Term Static Index Pruning Based on the Term Cohesiveness*. In International Conference on Computational Intelligence and Communication Networks (CICN), India.

Vogel, H. G., Vogel, W. H., Schölkens, B. A., Sandow, J., Müller, G., & Vogel, W. F. (2002). Analgesic, anti-inflammatory, and anti-pyretic activity1. In *Drug Discovery and Evaluation* (pp. 670–773). Springer Berlin Heidelberg. doi:10.1007/3-540-29837-1_9

Volkovich, Z., Toledano-Kitai, D., & Weber, G.-W. (2013). Self-learning K-means clustering: a global optimization approach. Journal of Global Optimization : An International Journal Dealing with Theoretical and Computational Aspects of Seeking Global Optima and Their Applications in Science. *Journal of Global Optimization*, *56*(2), 219–232. doi:10.100710898-012-9854-y

Wang, D., Wu, J., & Lin, Q. (2017). A novel method for designing and optimizing the layout of facilities in bathroom for the elderly in home-based rehabilitation. *Disability and Rehabilitation. Assistive Technology*, *13*(4), 333–341. doi:10.1080/17483107.2017.1319426 PMID:28453365

Wang, H., Liu, B., & Ping, X. (2019). Path tracking control for autonomous vehicles based on a kinematic model. *IEEE Transactions on Intelligent Transportation Systems*, *20*(5), 1929–1938.

Wang, P., Gao, S., Li, L., Cheng, S., & Zhao, L. (2019). Automatic steering control strategy for unmanned vehicles based on robust backstepping sliding mode control theory. *IEEE Access : Practical Innovations, Open Solutions*, *7*, 64984–64992. doi:10.1109/ACCESS.2019.2917507

Wang, T., & Cheng, E. C. K. (2021). An investigation of barriers to Hong Kong K-12 schools incorporating artificial intelligence in education. *Computers and Education: Artificial Intelligence*, *2*, 100031. doi:10.1016/j.caeai.2021.100031

Wang, T., Zhang, Z., Jing, X., & Zhang, L. (2016). Multiple kernel ensemble learning for software defect prediction. *Automated Software Engineering*, *23*(4), 569–590. doi:10.100710515-015-0179-1

Wang, X., Huang, T., & Chakrabarti, P. (2022). Adaptive RBF neural network control for nonlinear system. In *Complex Systems: Spanning Control and Computational Cybernetics: Foundations* (pp. 435–455). Springer International Publishing. doi:10.1007/978-3-030-99776-2_22

Ward, S. (2012). What to measure? Review of measurements in anthropometric studies of elderly populations. In *Proceedings of the 48th Annual Human Factors and Ergonomics Society of Australia Conference* (pp. 11-14). Springer.

Welch, L., Lewitter, F., Schwartz, R., Brooksbank, C., Radivojac, P., Gaeta, B., & Schneider, M. V. (2014). Bioinformatics curriculum guidelines: Toward a definition of core competencies. *PLoS Computational Biology*, *10*(3), e1003496. doi:10.1371/journal.pcbi.1003496 PMID:24603430

Wikipedia contributors. (2023). *Automatic clustering algorithms*. Wikipedia. https://en.wikipedia.org/w/index.php?title=Automatic_clustering_algorithms&oldid=1136139398

Williamson, B., & Eynon, R. (2020). Historical threads, missing links, and future directions in AI in education. *Learning, Media and Technology*, *45*(3), 223–235. doi:10.1080/17439884.2020.1798995

Williams, R., Park, H. W., Oh, L., & Breazeal, C. (2019, July). Popbots: Designing an artificial intelligence curriculum for early childhood education. *Proceedings of the AAAI Conference on Artificial Intelligence, 33*(01), 9729–9736. doi:10.1609/aaai.v33i01.33019729

Winter, C. A., Risley, E. A., & Nuss, G. W. (1962). Carrageenin-induced edema in hind paw of the rat as an assay for anti-inflammatory drugs. *Proceedings of the Society for Experimental Biology and Medicine, 111*(3), 544–547. doi:10.3181/00379727-111-27849 PMID:14001233

Witkowski, K. (2017). Internet of things, big data, industry 4.0 – innovative solutions in logistics and supply chains management. *Procedia Engineering, 182*, 763–769. doi:10.1016/j.proeng.2017.03.197

Wrzesien, M., Treder, W., Klamkowski, K., & Rudnicki, W. R. (2018). Prediction of the apple scab using machine learning and simple weather stations. *Computers and Electronics in Agriculture.* doi:10.1016/j.compag.2018.09.026

Wu, B., Liang, A., Zhang, H., Zhu, T., Zou, Z., Yang, D., & Su, J. (2021). Application of conventional UAV-based high-throughput object detection to the early diagnosis of pine wilt disease by deep learning. *Forest Ecology and Management, 486*, 118986. doi:10.1016/j.foreco.2021.118986

Wuest, T., Weimer, D., Irgens, C., & Thoben, K. D. (2016). *Machine learning in manufacturing: advantages, challenges, and applications.* Taylor & Francis. doi:10.1080/21693277.2016.1192517

Wu, S., Guo, C., & Yang, J. (2020). Using PCA and one-stage detectors for real-time forest fire detection. *Journal of Engineering (Stevenage, England), 2020*(13), 383–387. doi:10.1049/joe.2019.1145

Wu, X., Kumar, V., Ross Quinlan, J., Ghosh, J., Yang, Q., Motoda, H., & Steinberg, D. (2008). Top 10 algorithms in data mining. *Knowledge and Information Systems, 14*(1), 1–37. doi:10.100710115-007-0114-2

Wu, Y., Tan, H., Qin, L., Ran, B., & Jiang, Z. (2018). A hybrid deep learning based traffic flow prediction method and its understanding. *Transportation Research Part C, Emerging Technologies, 90*, 166–180. doi:10.1016/j.trc.2018.03.001

Xia, L. (2015). Facial Expression Recognition Based on SVM. In *7th International Conference on Intelligent Computation Technology and Automation.* IEEE.

Xiangming, X. (2013). Research on apple scab (Venturia inaequalis) at East Malling Research. *Aspects of Applied Biology*, 119.

Xiang, X., Lu, X., Halavanau, A., Xue, J., Sun, Y., Lai, P. H. L., & Wu, Z. (2021). Modern senicide in the face of a pandemic: An examination of public discourse and sentiment about older adults and COVID-19 using machine learning. *The Journals of Gerontology. Series B, Psychological Sciences and Social Sciences, 76*(4), e190–e200. doi:10.1093/geronb/gbaa128 PMID:32785620

Xiaoxi, M., Weisi, L., Dongyan, H., Minghui, D., & Li, H. (2017). Facial Emotion Recognition. In *IEEE 2nd International Conference on Signal and Image Processing* (pp. 77–81). IEEE.

Xie, P., Cui, J.-H., & Lao, L. (2006). *Networking technologies, services, and protocols; performance of computer and communication networks; mobile and wireless communications systems.* Springer.

Xu, F., Uszkoreit, H., Du, Y., Fan, W., Zhao, D., & Zhu, J. (2019). Explainable AI: A Brief Survey on History, Research Areas, Approaches and Challenges. Lecture Notes in Computer Science (Including Subseries Lecture Notes in Artificial Intelligence and Lecture Notes in Bioinformatics), 11839 LNAI, 563–574. https://doi.org/doi:10.1007/978-3-030-32236-6_51/COVER

Xu, Z., Xuan, J., Liu, J., & Cui, X. (2016). MICHAC: Defect prediction via feature selection based on maximal information coefficient with hierarchical agglomerative clustering. *2016 IEEE 23rd International Conference on Software Analysis, Evolution, and Reengineering (SANER).* IEEE.

Xu, S., Zhu, J., Jiang, J., & Shui, P. (2020). Sea-surface floating small target detection by multifeature detector based on isolation forest. *IEEE Journal of Selected Topics in Applied Earth Observations and Remote Sensing, 14*, 704–715. doi:10.1109/JSTARS.2020.3033063

Xu, X.-M., & Butt, D. J. (1996). AdemTM a PC-based multiple disease warning system for use in the cultivation of apples. *Acta Horticulturae*, (416), 293–296. doi:10.17660/ActaHortic.1996.416.37

Xu, X.-M., Butt, D. J., & van Santen, G. (1995). A dynamic model simulating infection of apple leaves by *Venturia inaequalis. Plant Pathology, 44*(5), 865–876. doi:10.1111/j.1365-3059.1995.tb02746.x

Xu, X.-M., Gao, L.-Q., & Yang, J.-R. (2010). Are insensitivities of *Venturia inaequalis* to myclobutanil and fenbuconazole correlated? *Crop Protection (Guildford, Surrey), 29*(2), 183–189. doi:10.1016/j.cropro.2009.07.002

Xu, X.-M., Harvey, N., Roberts, A. L., & Barbara, D. J. (2013). Population variation of apple scab (*Venturia inaequalis*) within mixed orchards in the UK. *European Journal of Plant Pathology, 135*(1), 97–104. doi:10.100710658-012-0068-4

Xu, X.-M., Roberts, T., Barbara, D., Harvey, N. G., Gao, L.-Q., & Sargent, D. J. (2009). A genetic linkage map of *Venturia inaequalis*, the causal agent of apple scab. *BMC Research Notes, 2*(1), 163–163. doi:10.1186/1756-0500-2-163 PMID:19689797

Xu, X.-M., & Robinson, J. (2005). Modelling the effects of wetness duration and fruit maturity on infection of apple fruits of Cox's Orange Pippin and two clones of Gala by *Venturia inaequalis. Plant Pathology, 54*(3), 347–356. doi:10.1111/j.1365-3059.2005.01177.x

Xu, X.-M., Yang, J.-R., Thakur, V., Roberts, A. L., & Barbara, D. J. (2008). Population variation of apple scab (*Venturia inaequalis*) isolates from Asia and Europe. *Plant Disease, 92*(2), 247–252. doi:10.1094/PDIS-92-2-0247 PMID:30769384

Yaganteeswarudu, A. (2020). Multi Diasese Prediction Model by using Machine Learning and Flask API". In *IEEE, 2020 5th International Conference on Communication and Electronics Systems (ICCES).* IEEE.

Yamak, P. T., Yujian, L., & Gadosey, P. K. (2019). A comparison between ARIMA, LSTM, and GRU for time series forecasting. *Proceedings of the 2019 2nd International Conference on Algorithms, Computing and Artificial Intelligence.* IEEE.

Yan, H., Shi, Z. J., & Cui, J.-H. (2008). DBR: depth-based routing for subacquatic sensor networks. In *Proceedings of the 7th international IFIP-TC6 networking conference on adhoc and sensor networks, wireless networks, next generation internet.* Singapore: Springer-Verlag.

Yang, H.-F., Dillon, T. S., & Chen, Y.-P. P. (2017). Optimized structure of the traffic flow forecasting model with a deep learning approach. *IEEE Transactions on Neural Networks and Learning Systems, 28*(10), 2371–2381. doi:10.1109/TNNLS.2016.2574840 PMID:27448371

Yang, W. (2022). Artificial Intelligence education for young children: Why, what, and how in curriculum design and implementation. *Computers and Education: Artificial Intelligence, 3*, 100061. doi:10.1016/j.caeai.2022.100061

Yick, J., Mukherjee, B., & Ghosal, D. (2008). Wireless sensor network survey. *Computer Networks, 52*(12), 2292–2330. doi:10.1016/j.comnet.2008.04.002

Yin, M., Liu, X., Chen, X., Li, C., Qin, W., Han, H., Guo, H., Yang, H., Cao, D., Du, Z., Wu, D., & Wang, H. (2017). Ischemia-modified albumin is a predictor of short-term mortality in patients with severe sepsis. *Journal of Critical Care*, *37*, 7–12. doi:10.1016/j.jcrc.2016.08.005 PMID:27610585

Yi, S., Han, Y., & Ohrr, H. (2013). Anemia before pregnancy and risk of preterm birth, low birth weight and small-for-gestational-age birth in Korean women. *European Journal of Clinical Nutrition*, *67*(4), 337–342. doi:10.1038/ejcn.2013.12 PMID:23403878

Youth, D. (2019). *Mobile Phones And Text Messaging: Assessing The Profound Impact Of A Technological Afterthought*. NIH.

Zannah, A. I., Rachakonda, S., Abubakar, A. M., Devkota, S., & Nneka, E. C. (2023). Control for Hydrogen Recovery in Pressuring Swing Adsorption System Modeling. *FMDB Transactions on Sustainable Energy Sequence*, *1*(1), 1–10.

Zan, X., Zhang, X., Xing, Z., Liu, W., Zhang, X., Su, W., & Li, S. (2020). Automatic Detection of Maize Tassels from UAV Images by Combining Random Forest Classifier and VGG16. *Remote Sensing (Basel)*, *12*(18), 3049. doi:10.3390/rs12183049

Zawacki-Richter, O., Marín, V. I., Bond, M., & Gouverneur, F. (2019). Systematic review of research on artificial intelligence applications in higher education–where are the educators? *International Journal of Educational Technology in Higher Education*, *16*(1), 1–27. doi:10.118641239-019-0171-0

Zhang, C., & Lu, Y. (2021). Study on artificial intelligence: The state of the art and future prospects. *Journal of Industrial Information Integration*, *23*, 100224. doi:10.1016/j.jii.2021.100224

Zhang, H., Lee, I., Ali, S., DiPaola, D., Cheng, Y., & Breazeal, C. (2022). Integrating ethics and career futures with technical learning to promote AI literacy for middle school students: An exploratory study. *International Journal of Artificial Intelligence in Education*, 1–35. PMID:35573722

Zhang, H., Zhao, M., Liu, L., Zhong, H., Liang, Z., Yang, Y., & Wang, Y. (2020). Deep multimodel cascade method based on CNN and random forest for pharmaceutical particle detection. *IEEE Transactions on Instrumentation and Measurement*, *69*(9), 7028–7042. doi:10.1109/TIM.2020.2973843

Zhang, J., Li, M., Feng, Y., & Yang, C. (2020). Robotic grasp detection based on image processing and random forest. *Multimedia Tools and Applications*, *79*(3), 2427–2446. doi:10.100711042-019-08302-9

Zhang, L., Yang, Y., Wu, J., Zhang, X., & Zhang, Z. (2021). Hybrid control strategy for Jiaolong HOV based on QPSO-MPC and ASMC. *International Journal of Advanced Robotic Systems*, *18*(4), 17298814211030085.

Zhang, Y., Tang, Z., & Ji, X. (2020). Object detection in video surveillance: A survey and a new benchmark. *Computer Vision and Image Understanding*, *182*, 27–52.

Zhou, Z., Fang, A., & Liu, Q. (2019). transformer network based on position and self-attention mechanism for aspect-level sentiment classification. *IEEE Access : Practical Innovations, Open Solutions*, *7*, 127754–127764. doi:10.1109/ACCESS.2019.2938854

About the Contributors

S. Suman Rajest is currently working as Dean of Research and Development (R&D) & International Student Affairs (ISA) at Dhaanish Ahmed College of Engineering, Chennai, Tamil Nadu, India. He is an Editor in Chief of the International Journal of Human Computing Studies and The International Journal of Social Sciences World, He is the Chief Executive Editor of the International Journal of Advanced Engineering Research and Science, International Journal of Advanced Engineering, Management and Science, The International Journal of Health and Medicines, The International Journal of Management Economy and Accounting Fields and The International Journal of Technology Information and Computer and also he is an Editorial Board Member in International Journal of Management in Education, Scopus, Inderscience, EAI Endorsed Transactions on e-Learning, and Bulletin of the Karaganda university Pedagogy series. He is also a Book Series Editor in IGI Global Publisher, Springer, etc. All of his writing, including his research, involves elements of creative nonfiction in the Human Computing learning system. He is also interested in creative writing and digital media, Learning, AI, student health learning, etc. He has published 155 papers in peer-reviewed international journals. He has authored and co-authored several scientific book publications in journals and conferences and is a frequent reviewer of international journals and international conferences and also, he is also a reviewer in Inderscience, EAI Journals, IGI Global, Science Publications, etc....

Bhopendra Singh is an Associate Professor in Engineering & Architecture Department, Amity University Dubai, UAE, from October 2011 to date, respectively. He is a competent & versatile professional with 25 years of experience in Strategic Planning, Academic Operations, Teaching & Mentoring. He is currently serving as a Head of Industry Relations-Engineering and senior faculty at Amity University in Dubai. He is an individual with a proactive attitude, thinking out of the box and generating new design solutions and ideas. His research parts are actively involved in accreditation like IET, WASAC, DQA Award, and HCERF Visits. Signed several MOU with industries like Cisco, Emircom, Tele logic, Siemens, Dewa R&D. Coordinating with other reputed institutions like IIT Indore for research and student's internship. Organizing industry visit industry Guest lectures for engineering students. Organizing training for engineering students. Arranging internship for engineering students since July 2018. Coordinator of Board of Studies (2011 to 2014). Member of IQAC (2012-2014). Developed and installed lab for engineering programs (2011-2012). Member of sports committee from (2011-2015). He teaches as per academic curriculum to students, recognizing and nurturing each student's creative potential. Teach students using a systematic instructional methodology comprising lecture plans (following the credit allotted to each subject), discussion groups, seminars, case studies, field assignments, and independent and/or group projects. Recently, he has been the technique program committee, the technique reviews, and the track chair for international conferences published by Springer-ASIC/LNAI Series. He is serving as the editor in chief of the editorial board of international journals, and he authored/edited different books by Springer, Wiley, CRC Press, and filed many Patents. Finally, he is a member of ISTE, IET, IEEE, Etc…

Ahmed J. Obaid is a Asst. Professor at the Department of Computer Science, Faculty of Computer Science and Mathematics, University of Kufa, Iraq. Dr. Ahmed holds a Bachelor in Computer Science, degree in – Information Systems from College of Computers, University of Anbar, Iraq (2001-2005), and a Master Degree (M. TECH) of Computer Science Engineering (CSE) from School of Information Technology, Jawaharlal Nehru Technological University, Hyderabad, India (2010-2013), and a Doctor of Philosophy (PhD) in Web Mining from College of Information Technology, University of University of Babylon, Iraq (2013-2017). He is a Certified Web Mining Consultant with over 14 years of experience in working as Faculty Member in University of Kufa, Iraq. He has taught courses in Web Designing, Web Scripting, JavaScript, VB.Net, MATLAB Toolbox's, and other courses on PHP, CMC, and DHTML from more than 10 international organizations and institutes from USA, and India. Dr. Ahmed is a member of Statistical and Information Consultation Center (SICC), University of Kufa, Iraq.

R. Regin is currently working as an Assistant Professor in the Department of Computer Science and Engineering at the SRM Institute of Science and Technology, Chennai, Tamil Nadu, India. He has a specialization in the branch of information and communication. He holds experience of 10+ years in teaching faculty and research. He has also published papers in 55 reputed international journals, 40 international conferences, and 15 national conferences. He is a member of professional bodies like IE and IETE. He is also a Book Series Editor for IGI Global Publisher, Springer, etc. He is the Editor-in-Chief of the International Journal of Technology Information and Computers, Growing Scholar USA, and a member of the Journal Ilmiah Teunuleh's Editorial Advisory Board. He does research work in the fields of VANET, WSN, MANET, Cloud Computing, Network Security, and Information Security. He is a reviewer for many reputed journals like Springer, Inderscience, etc

Karthikeyan Chinnusamy, Sr Principal with more than 25 years of experience in IT, Product Dev, R&D and Education fields. Fellow IETE, Fellow IE, Sr Member IEEE, Sr Member ACM, Project management Institute (PMI), Reviewer, Editorial Board Member of R&D Journals. Board Member & Program Director SF DAMA. SME in Data Governance, GDPR, HIPAA Compliance, Data Management, Data Architecture, Master Data, Data Quality, AI/ML, Analytics and reporting in Payment processing, Customer, Finance, CRM and License domains. Mentor in SFDC Mig, Data.com, ERP, Architecture, R&D, Embedded systems, VLSI,Adv Information processing. I am also reviewer for IEEE Silicon Valley Sr Member Elevation and Speaker, Volunteer for SFBay ACM. Reviewer of Journals in Springer Nature.

***

Hesham Mohammed Ali Abdullah is Assistant Professor (Ph.D. in Computer Science)-Jouf University- KSA . He obtained his Ph.D degree in Computer Science from Bharathiar University, Coimbatore, India in 2018, He completed his Master of Computer Applications (MCA) degree in 2013 from Bharathiar University; he has obtained his BSc Degree in July 2006 from The National University, Yemen, His research interests include Cognitive Radio Ad Hoc Network, Wireless Communication, network security, big data,IoT, Machine learning, and Data Visualization. He has publication around 12 papers in national and international journals

Mahesh Bharambe is with the Department of Pharmacology, Krishna Vishwa Vidyapeeth (Formerly known as KIMSDU), Karad, Maharashtra, India.

Prasad Chinchole is an AI/ML enthusiast and data scientist.

Archit Chitre is a Fullstack Developer.

Chandra Shekar D.V. holds a Doctorate degree in the area of computer science and Engineering, Having 23 years of Experience in Teaching and Research, Published various papers in image processing, data mining and bio medical engineering, Done research minor and major project for AICTE funding agency, Edited and published book chapters in the area of Machine learning, Deep learning and AI in Scopus edited volumes like, Springer, CRC, IGI and other publishing organization.

J. Dhilipan, Professor & Head, Department of MCA, SRMIST, Ramapuram. He completed M.Sc, MBA, MPhil and completed his Doctorate in 2014. His area of interest is Cloud Computing, E Commerce & Data Analysis. He published 30 research articles in reputed journal and conference proceedings.

A. V. Senthil Kumar is working as a Director & Professor in the Department of Research and PG in Computer Applications, Hindusthan College of Arts and Science, Coimbatore since 05/03/2010. He has to his credit 11 Book Chapters, 265 papers in International and National Journals, 25 papers in International Conferences, 5 papers in National Conferences, and edited Nine books (IGI Global, USA). He is an Editor-in-Chief for various journals. Key Member for India, Machine Intelligence Research Lab (MIR Labs). He is an Editorial Board Member and Reviewer for various International Journals. He is also a Committee member for various International Conferences. He is a Life member of International Association of Engineers (IAENG), Systems Society of India (SSI), member of The Indian Science Congress Association, member of Internet Society (ISOC), International Association of Computer Science and Information Technology (IACSIT), Indian Association for Research in Computing Science (IARCS), and committee member for various International Conferences

Rupesh Kumar Sinha has more than 27 years of experience in Management Education and, Software industry and at present, he is an Associate Professor in the area of Decision Sciences at CMS Business School, JAIN (Deemed-to-be, University) Bangalore. He is also a PhD guide. He has filed 4 patents in his name and got 22 publications in reputed International journals. He teachers Statistics, Operations research, Python, Tableau, Spreadsheet Modeling, Supply Chain Analytics, Data analytics etc. He is a NASSCOM Licensed Master Trainer and Microsoft Certified Professional in Visual Basic, Windows Architecture. He has designed various courses in Analytics, Operations Management, Supply Chain Management at the level of MBA in the Business School and individual courses like Advanced Excel, Cognos, Tableau, Watson Analytics, SPSS etc. Before joining Business School, he worked with Krupanidhi School of Management and was Professor in the area of Analytics. He worked with various B Schools such as IFIM for Business School, Bangalore for 10 years as HOD of Operations and IT. He has also worked as visiting faculty at Symbiosis, Bangalore. He had given training on analytics at various

B-Schools and Engineering colleges on visual analytics. He also headed a project to do computerization of 13 Lacs BPL family data. His area of research is SCM, Analytics and Contemporary issues.

R. Patange is with the Department of Obstetrics and Gynaecology, Krishna Vishwa Vidyapeeth, Krishna Institute of Medical Sciences, Karad, Maharashtra, India.

Chhavi S. is a college student doing bachelor's in computer science. She seeks opportunities to develop her skills, is actively involved in extracurricular activities, and is committed to personal and professional growth.

Sneha S. is a product design student currently pursuing her passion for UX Design in India.

Subiksha S. is a college student currently studying computer science. She likes to read and continuously expand her understanding of various subjects.

Ravishankar S. Ulle is defined by perseverance, hard work, kindness, and empathy. After two years in corporate had a career transition in research and academia since 2011. Ph.D. in Total Quality Management with nearly 12 years of industry, academic, and research experience having core competencies in research, teaching, administration, student mentoring, publications, design, and execution of academic courseware. Has experience and skills in developing various activities to accommodate different learning styles and optimize students' intellectual capacity which builds confidence in them, thus molding them as responsible citizens. His research contribution serves as a basis for academic writing for publication in various reputed peer-reviewed journals. Participated in various workshops, faculty developmental activities, and academic conferences for the diversity of knowledge development.

Priyanka Sharma is born in Jaipur, Rajasthan, India, in 1991. She Received her B.Tech. degree from Rajasthan Technical University, Kota, Rajasthan India, in 2012 in Information Technology and M.Tech. degree from Rajasthan Technical University, Kota, Rajasthan India, in 2016 in Computer Science. She is working as an Assistant Professor in the department of Computer Science & Engineering, Swami Keshvanand Institute of Technology, Management & Gramothan, Jaipur, Rajasthan, India. She has guided various M.Tech. research scholars. She is member of IEEE, ACM and various professional societies. She has published more than 15 research papers in national and international journals/conferences, book chapters. Also, she has taken part in forums hosted by Infosys, TCS, Oracle, and IBM. His area of interest is investigating the advancements in machine learning and deep learning applications. She has received accolades on a number of times in a variety of fields, including Designation as an Active Reviewer by some well-known journals. She was also given recognition by Infosys, India, for her remarkable performance in the Campus Link Program.

Shyam R. Sihare completed his Ph.D. at Raksha Shakti University in Ahmedabad, India. He holds a Master's degree in Computer Science from Nagpur University, Nagpur, India, which he obtained in 2003. Additionally, he attained an M. Phil. in Computer Science from Madurai Kamraj University, Madurai, India. In 2011 and 2018, he successfully cleared the Professor Eligibility Test GSLET (Gujarat) and MS-SET (Maharashtra) in India, respectively. Furthermore, he completed his MCA from IGNOU in New Delhi, India, in 2011. Currently, Dr. Sihare serves as an Assistant Professor in Computer Science and Application at Dr. APJ Abdul Kalam Govt. College in Silvassa, Dadra & Nagar Haveli (UT), India. His research interests encompass a wide range of areas including Quantum Computing, Quantum Algorithms, Quantum Cryptography, and Classical Computer Algorithms.

Abhishek Wankhade is a student at Vishwakarma Institute of Technology in Computer Engineering Department.

Index

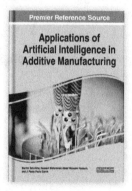

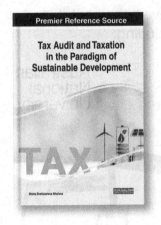

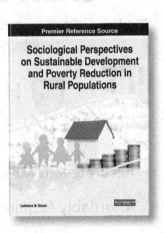

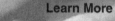

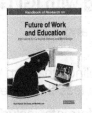

Printed in the United States
by Baker & Taylor Publisher Services